CASES IN PORTFOLIO MANAGEMENT

CASES IN PORTFOLIO MANAGEMENT

Robert F. Vandell
Late of the Darden Graduate School of Business Administration
University of Virginia

With the assistance of
Mark T. Finn
President
Delta Financial, Inc.

1988

Homewood, Illinois 60430

To my children,
Chip, Trudy, and Warren.

Acquisitions editor: *Gary L. Nelson*
Project editor: *Susan Trentacosti*
Production manager: *Stephen K. Emry*
Cover designer: *Maureen McCutcheon*
Compositor: *Weimer Typesetting Co., Inc.*
Typeface: *10/12 Times Roman*
Printer: *The Maple-Vail Book Manufacturing Group*

ISBN 0-256-06231-5

Library of Congress Catalog Card No. 87–83235

Printed in the United States of America

3 4 5 6 7 8 9 0 MP 5 4 3 2 1 0 9 8

CASES IN PORTFOLIO MANAGEMENT

Robert F. Vandell
Late of the Darden Graduate School of Business Administration
University of Virginia

With the assistance of
Mark T. Finn
President
Delta Financial, Inc.

1988

Homewood, Illinois 60430

To my children,
Chip, Trudy, and Warren.

Acquisitions editor: *Gary L. Nelson*
Project editor: *Susan Trentacosti*
Production manager: *Stephen K. Emry*
Cover designer: *Maureen McCutcheon*
Compositor: *Weimer Typesetting Co., Inc.*
Typeface: *10/12 Times Roman*
Printer: *The Maple-Vail Book Manufacturing Group*

ISBN 0-256-06231-5

Library of Congress Catalog Card No. 87–83235

Printed in the United States of America

1 2 3 4 5 6 7 8 9 0 MP 5 4 3 2 1 0 9 8

Introduction

Portfolio Management involves a top-down look at the process of managing portfolios and at the strategic and tactical decisions that determine the ongoing character of a portfolio. Item selection, which is based on detailed security analysis and the choices relating to adding or deleting individual securities to or from a portfolio, lies beyond the underlying portfolio organizational structure and the methodology designed to facilitate good implementation and is not the focal point of this book.

The cases are written from the viewpoint of either a client or a manager of funds with a product being marketed to certain potential clients. In some cases the clients are individuals with limited resources to invest. At the other extreme, sponsors are the large pension funds that hire numerous managers to help them achieve their objectives. Clients have unique objectives, circumstances (e.g., wealth, tax exposure), needs, tastes, and beliefs that shape the way they think about their investment requirements. They may or may not be knowledgeable, understanding, perceptive, or systematic (unemotional) in how they reach the major decisions that profoundly affect their own or their organization's welfare. They may or may not understand the limits of their skills or the dangers they expose themselves to when they are less than all-wise "economic men." Their choices are bewildering in number, and the array of potential combinations is staggering. Thousands of portfolio alternatives are available for even a small IRA investment, and there are sharp constraints on the time an individual can or should devote to the choice. Somehow individuals must boil down this complexity to levels they can deal with constructively within the time they have available. How can this all best be done?

The fund manager has a portfolio product (or family of products)—born of his or her knowledge, experience, and skills—that must be marketed to certain types of potential clients. The product does not have hard, stable features that make manufacture routine; it must be reshaped continuously as characteristics of the ingredients change yet directed toward some enduring concept of what it should be. Production methods must change with technology and with circumstances. The future performance characteristics of the product—even a well-conceived and well-designed one—are uncertain, and the past performance record may or may not be useful in describing what it will do next or even what the boundaries of performance uncertainty are. The fund manager also faces a bewildering array of ever-changing alternatives for potential use in his or her portfolio. These alternatives must be distilled to workable levels that facilitate the analysis necessary for intelligent choice and action. Each product faces an often large array of competitive products with somewhat similar but fuzzy general characteristics. The product must be packaged and sold in ways that not only appeal to potential clients but also differentiate it from other products targeted toward the same buyers. The organization must provide as many as possible of the resources necessary to achieve the desired ends, and the resources must be organized purposefully and efficiently to provide the wherewithal for achievement. The issue is, how can all these activities be done successfully?

Why Cases?

This book is designed to provide perspective—through the background descriptions and the factors bearing on the focal issues—on the "how" questions of portfolio management. Cases are used because no single all-encompassing solution exists to any of the problems encountered. Certain principles may guide us toward answers we consider better, but today's principles may be contradicted, amplified, or supplemented as we learn more. In any case, we must adapt principles to the realities of circumstances, and the reasoning process that bridges the gap is often demanding. Cases help students acquire the knowledge, understanding, skill, and wisdom necessary for successful decision making in changing circumstances.

Knowledge is rote learning. We acquire facts, opinions, or theories from many sources, including formal education. We do not remember all we learn. Some information is discarded as better information becomes available. Much is just forgotten. The context that limits its meaning may become distorted. Humans are not like computer memory banks that remember all they have been fed (so long as they don't malfunction!). For humans, motivation to master facilitates knowledge retention. Educators use a final exam as one motivation for knowledge retention. If information is relevant to our lives, we are more strongly motivated to remember it. Case experiences let us apply such information to people's situations. A good memory and the ability to access needed information expeditiously are assets—but they are not sufficient for success.

Understanding implies more than knowledge. A formula may be memorized, but understanding a formula suggests that it makes sense to the learner and that the learner has acquired some awareness of how and when the formula can be applied to achieve some desired end and when it cannot be. Understanding facilitates the organization of data and experiences, so that they form sensible patterns or lead to useful generalizations. At the same time, it encourages differentiation: we recognize that the formula is incomplete in a certain situation because of circumstances, or timing, or people. Learning is internalized in the sense that it influences future behavior beyond the context in which the knowledge was acquired. Cases provide the opportunity to apply knowledge in contexts that test it, so they help students grow in awareness.

Skill requires knowledge and understanding—the more the better. A physical analogy may be helpful. It is one thing to read a book on how to play tennis to gain knowledge and understanding. It is quite another to win on the tennis courts. The latter requires skill in using knowledge and understanding to one's advantage. Skill in both physical and mental activities requires practice at employing understanding efficiently and effectively under a variety of circumstances. As new experiences occur, a feedback mechanism refines and enhances understanding and tends to increase its practical value. The preparation and discussion of cases should add to students' experience base and prepare them for a business world where skill is valued.

A lot of people have a level of mastery—say, of chess—evidencing skill. Some are better than others—evidencing more understanding and skill. Some world chess masters progress long after others reach a plateau. Apparently, at some point, experience alone does not lead to growth; something else takes its place. The term I use is wisdom. Wisdom involves some native talents like intelligence and aptitude, but it also involves perception, foresight, and determination. The product is superior behavior. Decisions and their implementation work out to better advantage more frequently. Wisdom depends on knowledge, understanding, and skill, but it comes sooner and more completely to some. If wisdom can be taught, I don't know how. It can be provided through exposure to experience under the guidance of wise mentors acting like chess coaches. Case experiences are one means of providing this opportunity for growth in wisdom.

There are two products of learning: generalization and differentiation. Theories are examples of generalizations. Differentiation, in contrast, distinguishes between things based on their context. Which theory is applicable in these circumstances? What are the practical limits of this theory in the forms I have learned it?

The ability to generalize creatively is highly valued in the academic world. Our texts tend to reflect what we regard as the best of these generalizations. Generalizations are helpful to businesspeople too, but dealing with complex business situations often creates a more valuable skill. Decisions must fit circumstances as they evolve, and successful implementation of decisions may be more critical than the original decision itself. Who does what when—a set of implementation decisions—is abetted by differentiation skills.

Generalization provides a useful framework for facilitating differentiation and for improving the generalizations themselves. Cases, it is true, are not the most efficient means of teaching generalizations currently perceived to be the most useful. The learning generalizations, however, are often decoupled from experience in using them. Cases do provide the means of testing generalizations in the practical world where they may or may not fit.

Those who find the case method anathema usually center their arguments on the inefficiencies of using cases to teach theory and principles, which are described as enduring. No doubt they are right, although having watched theory flip-flop many times in my career and having experienced the practical limits of the applied uses of many theories, my perception of their enduring value is more constrained than some people's. The cases used here frequently involve currently prevailing investment theories, but the practitioners using the theories are often doing so in a purposeful way that flies in the face of the theory's underlying premise: they are trying to locate and exploit inefficiencies in an "efficient" market.

Are Markets Inefficient?

If markets are efficient, why bother to study active management practices? The simple answer is, that's where the career opportunities are today and will be tomorrow.

A businessperson thinks about problems differently from an academic. Academics seek unqualified truths through deductive logic and tests of statistical validity, but they have not found many truths so far. A person in business is more interested in the economic value of information that is based on observed and analyzed patterns: he or she asks, "Am I going to be better off using information on established tendencies or rejecting it?" Such people will use hypotheses born of opportunities that are well short of the point at which an academic would find them unqualified truths. Moreover, the ways portfolio managers use information are very different from the ways academics seek to test it. The business issue is, does it work?

Wearing my academic hat, I can say that pricing anomolies—opportunities to make money—do not last long or occur that frequently. After all, if a $20 bill were left on a street corner for all to see, it would quickly be picked up. The "opportunity" would disappear. Putting my business hat on, however, I argue that we don't yet know how to define value opportunities unambiguously. With the advent and testing of arbitrage pricing theory (APT), we learned that more than one factor influences prices. Unfortunately, the tests could not determine how many factors there were, what each factor was, or whether the influence was stable or unstable over time. We have no means of determining even crudely what the price of any risky security should be in theory. Worse, we cannot deduce answers logically. We only hypothesize and then test the validity of our hypotheses empirically. The theories of more astute businesspeople may fair well in this testing. In fact, practitioners were already using APT methods to economic advantage in applied tests before the concept hit the academic literature, as certain cases in this volume will illustrate.

Portfolio management is a loser's game, so the argument runs. The capital markets are a zero-sum activity; each transaction has a potential winner and loser, and the size of the gains or losses is the same over any adversary's specified period. One can win only by being better than one's adversaries with greater consistency. Because the players are all well-informed, generally quite smart people, winning with sufficient consistency is hard. Worse, transactions cost money. Information gathering and processing costs money. Managers charge fees for their services to cover these costs and others related to servicing the clients and to make a profit. Total costs erode performance and raise the required average for winning net of costs. Concentrated portfolios of active managers are more risky than efficient-market alternatives, because risk adjustment further reduces the probability of being a net winner. Indexing against a broad market portfolio proxy, with lower transactions and service costs, is a more efficient way of participating in the markets for risky assets than is portfolio management. Moreover, the published evidence tends to confirm this hypotheses. In short, the markets are too efficient for successful active management.

These arguments are widely known and hard to refute. Nevertheless, more clients every year, including large pension sponsors, opt to place more funds with active managers than with passive managers.[1] True, the amounts indexed have grown rapidly over the last 15 years, but the amounts invested with active managers who opened for business in the last 15 years have grown collectively more rapidly. Rightly or wrongly, people and organizations with the money to invest believe they can do better with active investments.

Indexing is size-efficient. A relatively small number of managers dominate the market. Operations are largely machine-driven, and a small cadre of people can handle the sales, reporting, operations, and execution support systems in each firm. In contrast, beyond some point, active management tends to become size-inefficient. There are thousands of active-management firms; they employ more people to handle jobs that require more skill, and they generally offer higher rewards for performance than do the indexers. These firms are where the opportunity lies and where the rewards for success run high. An entire industry is thriving providing active managers with the information and software technology necessary to operate. Pension plans and other big investors hire these managers and often employ their own staffs to assist with the management tasks. Consultants and their staffs also serve these clients. All told, there are probably about 1,000 people associated with active management for each person employed in handling passive portfolios.

The academic appraisal of performance is based on models that we now know are seriously misspecified and incomplete. The models' criteria do not relate to the needs of clients as clients define them or to the manager's objective in serving the clients attracted to his or her approach. Many larger clients and most managers are completely familiar with theoretical constructs of evaluation models, as are the consultants who advise them, yet they choose to appraise performance differently. (Use of the capital asset pricing model, for example, has waned to the point that I rarely see it in performance appraisal today.) Perhaps we should discover why.

Fortunately for active managers, the academic literature is now sprinkled with reports of persistent inefficiencies in the marketplace (small stocks and low price/earnings ratio investment strategies are two examples) that reflect common, long-standing practitioner beliefs. I am certain that if we, as businesspeople do, spend time searching systematically and sensibly for inefficiencies, we will find them.

The cases here do not answer the basic issue, are the capital markets efficient or not? The cases do exemplify investors and managers who seem to be doing a good job. They are not representative of the universe, but if I were entering the marketplace for investors, these are the sort of practitioners I would study.

---

[1]The author was, along with about 180 business academics, associated with a consulting firm. Several years ago at the height of belief and evidence in efficient markets, we were offered a choice between several active managers and a passive indexer for investing the equity component of our pension plan. Not one person chose the passive indexer! Do we practice what we preach?

To the Student: The Challenges of the Case Method

For the novice, the case method is a frustrating learning experience at first. You are asked to put yourself in the shoes of a businessperson with a problem to solve and to work your way through to a solution that is better than alternative ones and will work well when implemented. Yet you don't have the knowledge, experience, or judgment of the real executive in the situation, and the problems are often tough ones. You will flounder and procrastinate with case preparation. The more you push yourself to be purposeful and decisive, the more you will gain from the experience. Mistakes are expected. They help you grow in ability.

The problems are not neat and confined like a typical math problem. Some data may be helpful, other data are less material. Data may be estimates or opinions of arguable value—not concrete facts. Some data you would like to have may be missing, often for good reason—namely, they would be too costly to acquire in a timely manner. Even the facts may change with changing times and circumstances.

Solution does not depend on any formula you have just mastered. You will have to decide which method of analysis is most likely to get you the kind of information you want. Through inexperience, you may select the saw to pound the nail in the wall. The formulas and other tools of analysis in your tool kit may be inadequate. You will have to create some new ones or adapt some you have learned elsewhere.

Some of the information available is soft, i.e., not quantified. You will have to learn how to adapt your findings to fit the facts that you cannot crunch in your analysis.

No common solution is clearly the best; there are only better ones and poorer ones. The criteria for deciding which is "the best" are ambiguous and value-based. Moreover, even the seemingly best solution may not work well as the future unfolds.

Finally, you will be working under more time pressures than the real-life executive has and with less human assistance and other resources at your command. You will have to be quite selective in what you choose to do. Your analysis may have to be cruder than your training makes you comfortable with. Remember, in real life "ball park estimates" are often sufficient to move your thinking in the right direction.

The classroom discussion may seem disorderly. It does not have the logical learning flow of a good lecture. However, despite its disorder, the session will cover an unusual amount of information. If you are involved, you will absorb, evaluate, order, and retain a surprising quantity of knowledge.

At first your classroom experience will also be frustrating. Your preparatory work will look meager compared with the achievement of the entire class operating under the guidance of a skilled instructor. Although this makes sense, many students feel humbled.

Participating in class by both talking and listening (evaluating), while important, is also uncomfortable. It is no fun, for example, to see your favored ideas "shot down in flames" by a classmate who sees the problem differently.

Students like to know how they are doing, but assessing relative performance in the hectic give and take of a case-method classroom is difficult. Students may feel that they do not know what they need to know or comprehend what they have already learned and mastered. No text clearly lays out the learning requirements.

You will, however, become more aware of what you must do well to succeed in business. More importantly, your ability to attack problems purposefully and to make good decisions will grow. Development of skills appears to be the main reason the case method has such value in later life, yet skill improvement is hard to recognize.

These and other frustrations are endemic to any participatory learning process that challenges you to stretch your capabilities. They have no cure. Your anxieties will abate, however, as your confidence grows about your ability to deal effectively in messy problem-solving situations.

The case method has a big payoff. Skills and worldly wisdom are valued by businesspeople when they recruit. Case-method students, in turn, seem better prepared than others to handle themselves successfully on their first job and to progress up to the organization ladder.

To the Student: How to Gain from a Case Method Experience

The simple answer is through commitment. The more you can put yourself in the shoes of the decision maker in the case situation and do your best to solve the problem at hand, the more you will gain from the experience—irrespective of the initial quality of your efforts. The more you listen and evaluate what your peers have to say, the more you participate in class by laying out your ideas for others to evaluate and by defending these ideas when you think they are useful, the greater your opportunity for growth in understanding. In brief, success comes if you become involved in the process and participate in it fully, no matter how uncomfortable you may feel.

The value of your work will increase with discipline. There are certain identifiable subtasks involved in reaching better answers to complex issues.

Analysis starts with a clear definition of the real problem to be solved. A businessperson in a case may define the problem in terms of its symptoms, not its causes. Misspecifying the real problem is unlikely to lead to an appropriate solution.

With a clear statement of task, the next step is to determine the major alternative ways in which the problem can be resolved. The case may state the alternatives, but the businessperson may not recognize some of them. In brief, this step contains an element of creative thinking.

The next step is to identify the questions that will have to be answered in order to judge which alternative is likely to prove better. This task may be facilitated by thinking ahead to the kind of information you would want to resolve the central issue. The information needs imply the questions you are seeking to answer.

Once you know where you analysis is going and what kinds of data you will need, the next step is to decide how to obtain this information efficiently and with enough accuracy for the purposes at hand. Some information may already be available in the case; here the task is to assemble and evaluate it. In other cases, you may have to process the available data into a useful form. You must select the appropriate tool of analysis (methodology, formula, etc.) to do so.

A plan of attack should now be shaping up. Analysis consumes time, and time is constrained for you and for businesspeople. A set of priorities must evolve. The perceived importance of the analysis that is needed to resolve the the central issue shapes these priorities (but sometimes information gained from one analysis is prerequisite to another, and this alters desired sequencing). More important questions should be attacked first. A crude schedule of how much time you will spend on each task is helpful at this juncture. You will rarely stick to the time plan, but it helps to know the kinds of adjustments you will have to make later as the analysis progresses.

Your analysis prepares you for the most important part of the process: reaching decisions. Sometimes trade-offs can be made systematically using established techniques of integration analysis. Sometimes your synthesis will be more subjective. It is important that you push yourself to make a decision and spell out your reasons: "Mr. X should do Y because . . . despite . . . "

Decisions must be implemented; thus, the last step is to lay out a plan of implementation: who, what, when, and how to achieve what end. If conditions change, how should the implemention be modified? A fair decision well implemented usually succeeds more than a better decision implemented less well.

In class you will find new ideas and approaches to solving the problem. Some will be better, some poorer than your own. These new ideas are the fuel that feeds your growth. Your task is to assess their usefulness. Good preparation facilitates these assessments.

The broader the participation from the class, the wider the array of new ideas to learn from. Almost everyone will see something different in the case facts that influences their analyses and judgments. Frequent participation by you helps.

A good case class will expose you to more ideas than you can properly assess. A postclass synthesis is thus helpful. Two types of analysis are especially productive. How could I improve my plan of attack on this type of problem in the future? What have I learned that might be useful in resolving different types of problems? Occasionally you may only half understand some technique of analysis that seemed particularly insightful and productive. Try to complete your understanding of it. These "debriefing" experiences can be the most important contributors to your growth.

Experience is the best teacher, some say. It can be. It is certainly the predominant way we learn and grow—particularly in the business world. The case method provides you with the opportunity and discipline to improve your skills in learning from experience.

An Outline of the Book

Each instructor using this book will have different objectives and be working with students with different levels of experience. Instructors design the course to meet those specific needs. As a consequence, their learning sequence may be quite different from the one now set forth.

A topical outline never does justice to a case book. Each case involves a myriad of factors beyond those represented by the topics. A person developing a case course weaves together a number of factors to provide reinforcement, contrasting or different approaches to similar problems, coverage of a diversity of problems, and building blocks that carry forward learning achievements to later applications.

The first two cases here illustrate the kinds of problems clients face in designing an investment program for themselves. One client is a new widow with limited capital to meet her life needs. The other is a sizable pension plan that has reformulated its investment strategy and has reached a critical and touchy implementation decision. The importance of the client's interest recurs in most of the cases that follow, and these two contrasting cases lay a foundation for later understanding.

Two cases on performance measurement follow. Both are written from the viewpoint of a fund manager worrying about specific aspects of a funds performance and what might be done about it. Performance evaluation also remains important in many cases that follow.

The next three cases concern managers who are trying to use some aspect of modern portfolio theory in their active management work. These cases help in the process of relating theory to practice.

Several cases cover practitioners' efforts to develop strategies to exploit anomolies uncovered by research and analysis developed internally or purchased externally. These cases also involve theory-derived investment strategies.

Asset-mix determination is often regarded as the most important strategic decision made by a client because it involves the income/risk trade-off at its most fundamental level. An asset-mix strategy sets the target allocation of available funds to major asset classes. The first two cases on asset-mix approach the issue from the viewpoint of pension fund sponsors, who have, or seem about to reach, extreme solutions to the asset-mix question. The next two cases illustrate more conventional approaches to resolving the asset-mix issue and the problems the solutions pose for the clients who must use them. Market timing and hedged portfolio strategy are then presented as alternative ways of resolving the asset-mix problem.

Equity management provides the widest swing in portfolio results. A series of six cases illustrates the problems and opportunities involved in managing equity portfolios to achieve some desired end. Each manager in the case defines the task differently and approaches the evaluation problem differently.

Pension funds and many individuals employ several fund managers to invest their equity funds. How can these funds be deployed to best achieve the client's objectives? Several cases take up this issue next.

Fixed-income and equities are not the only vehicles in which clients invest their capital. Two cases take up more specialized investment approaches that use security types not normally considered in conventional approaches.

A look back at the asset allocation decision in light of actuarial considerations closes the book.

This book tries to provide a relatively comprehensive exposure to the kinds of problems that most worry clients and fund managers. The cases are both challenging and important. The book is structured to provide a logical learning progression.

Bon appétit!

Acknowledgments

All but two of the cases in *Cases in Portfolio Management* were written by faculty members of the Colgate Darden Graduate School of Business Administration, University of Virginia. The Darden Sponsors hold the copyrights to all these cases, and they are reproduced here with their permission. Two cases were written at the Harvard Graduate School of Business Administration, and their copyrights are held by the President and Fellows of Harvard University. These cases are used with their permission. I appreciate all this cooperation.

The field research for a number of cases appearing in this book was funded by the Sponsors of the Darden School through the Case Research Program. The school and Dean John W. Rosenblum have extended to me all the support I have sought for this and other research activities, and this support has been of great value to my growth in understanding of practical portfolio management. I have also benefited from a leave of absence in order to serve as chief investment officer for the Virginia Supplemental Retirement System, where I gained first-hand experience in designing and running a multibillion-dollar pension portfolio. My many friends on the firing lines of the investment business have shared generously of their time, experience, and insights in ways I found invaluable. Mark Finn, president of Delta Financial Inc., was particularly helpful in advising me on several case manuscripts.

All the cases in this book are based on real-world problems and were written in the field with the cooperation of business firms or individual investors. I am indebted to each person and each organization that made these cases possible. Michael Berry, a Darden colleague, wrote one of the cases in the book. A number of individuals helped me, as research assistants or students, with the writing of several others.

If the cases seem well written (as well as challenging), then much of the credit belongs to the editorial support staff at Darden, ably led by Bette Collins. My several secretaries over the years all deserve a bouquet of flowers for translating my handwritten scrawl into finished manuscripts. Kay Russo, Cindy Fraser, and Betty Jean Blincoe, and merit particular mention.

The cases have all been taught in the Darden MBA program, and about half of them have been used in practitioner courses run by our Executive Programs activity. Several have been taught at other graduate and undergraduate schools with considerable success. Many of these students and other instructors have provided me with valuable feedback that has helped me to improve the quality of the cases.

I have drawn heavily on academic research and on discussion with my academic colleagues to help me understand my subject area. The number and caliber of the investment and finance faculty members has grown enormously in the last 20 years, as has the quantity and quality of their theoretical and empirical research. Business executives, who in growing numbers attempt to follow and to use this research toward practical ends, also have contributed (largely unpublished) research that has further enriched my understanding. The chasm that grew between academic research and business understanding is increasingly being bridged. I hope that this book also helps bring together the interests of academics with the problems of practitioners.

Robert F. Vandell

Contents in Brief

Contents

Part I

The Client's Point of View

Margaret Wheeler

On June 14, 1982, Henry Wheeler died from injuries sustained in an automobile accident. His will, which was subsequently entered into probate, left virtually all of his estate to his wife Margaret, then 53 years old. In mid-August, Henry Wheeler, Jr., met with his mother to discuss how the proceeds of the estate should be employed.

When he arrived at his mother's early Friday evening, he thought his task would be easy, but by mid-afternoon Saturday, the problem had become much more complex. Both his mother's needs and the income that would be available to meet those needs had many permutations. Uncertainties over inflation and taxes, and his mother's long life expectancy, further complicated the problem.

Aside from the knowledge gained from an investment course he had taken the previous spring while an MBA student at a leading graduate school, Henry Jr. had little experience with investments; he also had little time to spare. His new marketing job was demanding, and he was anxious to establish a fast-start track record with his employer. After the birth of his first son in July (he had married in June 1981), Henry Jr. also needed more time for his wife, his new house (which required considerable landscaping), and the new baby. Yet he felt a deep sense of obligation to his mother and knew she would require financial planning and investment advice.

The Wheeler family had been a close one, and the suddenness of the father's death had proved a deep shock to all, but especially to Margaret. In late August she was still grief-stricken and found it difficult to concentrate on family business

---

This case was prepared by a Professor of the Colgate Darden Graduate School of Business Administration, University of Virginia.

matters. Margaret had always left financial planning and investments to her husband and was bewildered at the prospect of having to manage these affairs herself. Although she had kept a separate checking account (which she had difficulty balancing) designed to cover household needs, she had little financial experience that might prove helpful. Margaret had concentrated on being a homemaker and on assisting in certain local charitable activities. She had no skills that might be readily marketable at a premium, and her B.A. in history earned from a state university more than 30 years previously did not seem to prepare her for the life she now faced. The recession in progress in 1982 did not improve her prospects of finding a job.

Henry Sr. had been a successful executive and had recently been named treasurer of the moderate-sized firm where he had worked since graduation from college. His salary had just reached the six-figure level. The Wheeler family had always lived comfortably, but not extravagantly, in an attractive suburb near his city of employment. He had accumulated a modest investment portfolio of $100,000. Besides Henry Jr., two other children, a daughter Gertrude (20), and a son William (18), survived him. Gertrude was a rising senior (English major) at the local state university, and shortly after graduating, she planned to marry a law student now in his first year. William was about to enter Brown University as a drama major.

The Estate

The family home, purchased seven years before at a cost of $230,000, had a market value of approximately $350,000, and an 8 percent mortgage of $140,000 outstanding, which required annual interest and principal payments of approximately $14,200. The spacious house had five bedrooms, living, dining, and family rooms, and a kitchen, situated on two acres of land, with a lawn and gardens to tend. The house was fully furnished and no major repairs were anticipated. Property taxes would be $4,600 in 1982. The house had been jointly owned.

Henry Sr.'s firm provided life insurance benefits of $100,000 for Margaret, and Henry had independently taken out a life insurance policy of $60,000 with her as beneficiary. Benefits, which were not taxable, could either be taken as a lump sum or as a lifetime annuity equal to 7.57 percent per year of the principal value under both policies.

Henry Sr. also had accumulated pension fund benefits that amounted to a shade less than $300,000. Benefits could either be paid over 10 years ($40,800/year) or over Margaret's lifetime ($24,750/year). These benefits would be taxable as income in the year received. A lump-sum payment to the estate, which would create a sizable income tax liability in 1982, was not a practical alternative.

Henry Sr.'s small savings account would be consumed by funeral and legal expenses. Margaret's savings would be largely depleted for living expenses by the time that material income was received from the estate.

The details of Henry Sr.'s stock portfolio are reported in Exhibit 1. (For all practical purposes, market value was essentially the same as the cost basis for capital gains purposes.) These stocks had been selected for their capital gains potential, not their current income expectations, for tax reasons.

Margaret owned a relatively new car. Henry Sr.'s 1979 Buick would pass to Margaret, but the two younger children had spoken for it. Aside from household furnishings, these assets constituted the entirety of Henry Wheeler's estate. No material estate taxes were anticipated.

Margaret had recently inherited $50,000 from her mother, and these funds were invested in a tax-exempt money market mutual fund, currently yielding 11.6 percent. Margaret also had jewelry of modest value (about $20,000), which she did not wish to sell. No further inheritance was expected. Margaret had a life insurance policy of $5,000 that was fully paid up with a cash surrender value of $3,640. She could receive social security survivor benefits at age 62 or age 65, depending on which was more advisable. Those figures would be $282 or $750 per month (in 1982), respectively, and might be adjusted upward with inflation in the future.

Margaret's Needs

With his mother's help and with data from the family checkbooks, Henry Jr. had put together the following estimate of normal expenses for his mother (assuming no change in lifestyle) for the next 12 months:

Mortgage	$14,200
Property taxes	4,600
Electricity	1,900
Fuel	2,100
Other utilities	1,200
Food and household	10,200
Maintenance	1,500
Clothing	800
Medical and Blue Cross	1,500
Automobile (excluding depreciation)	1,600
Vacation	1,600
Other	2,000
Total	$43,200

These expenses did not include federal or state income taxes. Margaret would need to have a gross income of over $60,000 to meet her requirements after taxes. Charitable contributions, which had been made at the rate of $4,500 in 1981, were also excluded, but Henry Jr. assumed his mother would want to continue some of these contributions, if feasible.

Henry Jr. also had to consider the educational needs of his brother and sister ($12,000 and $6,000 per year, respectively, net of summer savings). Neither would qualify for financial aid. While it might be feasible to borrow these funds in part and have the children assume some of the repayment responsibility, Margaret did not want to see this happen.

Henry Jr. decided he should allow $8,000 every three years for automobile replacement and major home renovation. He also considered it desirable to set up a reserve of about $10,000 to cover major medical needs or other contingencies.

Beyond current needs, Henry Jr. worried about inflation. He estimated that it had run at 7.4 percent per year or more in the 1970s and had been at double digit levels in the early 1980s. While inflation was now abating, future rates were highly uncertain and could have a significant effect on his mother's future needs.

Margaret had a life expectancy of slightly over 25 years, and some prospect of living considerably longer: both her parents had lived to be in their mid-80s. She did not smoke or drink, except occasionally, and she was in excellent health.

Margaret's Alternatives

As Henry Jr. saw it, his mother had several alternatives: (1) attempt to live off the income and the capital of the estate, (2) go to work to supplement her income, (3) remarry, (4) cut down on expenses, or (5) some combination of these. How the estate was invested might also affect her circumstances.

Margaret had always been taught that it was important not to spend capital. She also wanted her children to benefit from her husband's achievements when she died. Because certain of the estate assets could be paid as annuities, the distinction between capital and income was somewhat fuzzy. Henry Jr. decided that his and his siblings' vested interest in inheritance of a residual estate could not be an important factor in his deliberations.

It might be feasible for Margaret to get a job as a retail clerk for about $8,000 per year. On the other hand, if she spent $2,000 at a nearby secretarial school, she might upgrade her skills to have an entry-level wage expectation of $12,000 per year, and her intelligence could prove to be more of an asset financially if she worked as a secretary.

Because his mother was quite attractive and personable, remarriage might be a real possibility, Henry Jr. thought. However, the unmarried-female-to-male ratio was rising steadily at her age level, and Henry Jr. was afraid that some of the males her age might be interested in younger women. In any case, his mother was clearly not ready to have this issued raised.

Because the house accounted for most of Margaret's expenses, Henry Jr. considered ways to reduce this portion of her budget. Margaret did not want to make any changes now, at least not until Gertrude was married. She was very fond of her home and grounds, both of which reflected her taste and her energy. Nevertheless, the house was now clearly more than she needed.

One alternative was to rent a two-bedroom apartment in a nearby community. Rents for the kind of apartment she would want would run $800 to $950 per month plus all utilities. However, Margaret did not like this idea because she enjoyed gardening and she wanted to have space for her children and grandchild to stay when they visited her.

Another alternative was to buy a more modest home. Attractive three-bedroom homes could be purchased for $140,000 to $160,000 within a vicinity close enough so that church, club, and other associations could be maintained. Mortgages on houses now carried interest rates of 14 percent plus 3 points, Henry Jr. had learned. Property taxes would be approximately the same percentage of market value. Utilities for a new house might cost 75 percent of their current level.

Henry Jr. did not believe that discretionary expenditures could be reduced by more than 15 percent without the pinch becoming noticeable. They might even increase, because certain activities that his father had previously handled (e.g., lawn care, routine household maintenance) might now require an outside service.

All three children were willing to share in Margaret's financial support when this became feasible for them, but that might take a while. Although Margaret would resist this idea, it was a potential cushion in the event of unforeseen developments.

Investment Alternatives

Henry Jr. recognized the need to make two decisions in the next several weeks, both of which could have profound long-term implications. First, he had to decide, with his mother's help, whether the pension benefits should be paid over a 10-year term or over Margaret's life. Second, he had to advise his mother as to whether she should accept a lump-sum payment of the insurance proceeds or the lifetime-annuity alternative made available by the insurance companies.

Any net cash proceeds, either from the sale of the house or from the life insurance properties, would have to be invested. Although both his father's and mother's marketable investments had been employed in a way that made sense while Henry Sr. was alive and receiving a high income, they might make much less sense, given Margaret's unfolding circumstances. When Henry Jr. had broached this subject with his mother, he found some resistance to making too many changes. In Margaret's eyes, Henry Sr. had financial savvy for making good long-term investments (whereas Henry Jr. did not, by implication), and she found it hard to grasp that her changed circumstances might alter what had heretofore been sensible.

Henry Jr. decided to think first in terms of basic security types. He recalled some information he had learned in his investment course on the long-term rates of return and return volatility for Treasury bills, corporate bonds, common stocks, and the like. (These data are summarized in Exhibit 2.) He was uncertain, however, how he should interpret this information in light of prevailing market conditions.

Treasury bills, he knew, had a high level of principal safety. However, the income recently had fluctuated significantly. Returns were now 9.8 percent, but the year before, new issues of 90-day Treasury bills were as high as 15.4 percent.

Fixed-income securities promised a stable interest income but had more uncertainty as to principal market value. At the outset of the month, quality long-term industrial bonds had been priced to yield 15.1 percent. A bond rally was in progress, however, and yields had already fallen almost 100 basis points in August 1982.

The Standard & Poor's 500 Index was currently priced to provide a dividend yield of 6.2 percent. Dividend safety was less than for income from quality bonds. As businesses prospered, however, dividend income might tend to rise significantly.

Henry Jr. had seen one service estimating a long-term total rate of return of 19.04 percent, including capital appreciation, for the Standard & Poor's 500 Index, as of the beginning of August 1982. Stock market prices had since fallen. Capital appreciation was very uncertain in the short run, he realized. On the other hand, he sensed that the stock market might be nearer a bottom than a top at the moment and, given the prospects of lower inflation and a recovery economy, might rally in the future, as the bond market had already.

Besides settling these basic issues of asset deployment, Henry Jr. had to consider the specifics of security selection: what kinds of fixed-income or equity securities should be purchased for his mother's account? Stocks, for example, ranged from high-yielding securities with low appreciation prospects, such as utilities, to more promising growth companies offering little or no dividend yield. Should he, for example, consider mutual funds as a means of increasing the diversity of investments, and if so, how should they be selected? He had also to consider the tax consequences of his investment plan. Would tax-free municipals, either short- or long-term bonds such as his mother held through a municipal fund, be better than taxable securities?

Henry Jr. also had to worry about the ongoing management of the portfolio once it was set up. He could, on the one hand, try to establish the portfolio on a sound, permanent basis—one that would require little continuous attention on his part. Alternatively, he could locate someone to manage the account for his mother, following guidelines he and Margaret would establish. The local bank's trust department, which had a reputation for being very conservative, would manage the assets for a fee of about .3 percent of the principal value of the assets managed. A local investment management firm, whose performance record was excellent, would also be willing to manage the portfolio for a fee of 1 percent of asset value. Or Henry Jr. could select several mutual funds with different investment objectives and compose a portfolio that would be easier for him to monitor.

To help him with these deliberations, Henry Jr. had brought with him copies of Value Line Investment Services, Lipper Mutual Fund Service, and Security Research Twelve-Year Cycle Service—all borrowed from the business library of his firm. One way of following his mother's portfolio was to have his mother subscribe to one or more services such as these.

Henry Jr. also had to worry about timing. If his hunch about the stock market was right, his father's equity portfolio might perform very well over the next 6 to 12 months.

Income Taxes

Clearly, the investment decisions he was about to make would have a significant effect on taxes. To gain some perspective, Henry Jr. had looked at the 1983 tax schedule for a single person (see Exhibit 3). For simplicity, he decided to assume that his mother's state income taxes would amount to about 12 percent of federal taxes in 1983. The tax law could change considerably in the future, he was aware. He also checked the tax rates of 1979 (see Exhibit 4), before the Reagan administration's tax reductions. Would these higher tax rates be reinstituted with a change in administration, he wondered? Already considerable concern had been evident in Congress about the impending size of the federal deficit. Increasing taxes might be an easier way of reducing the deficit than further cutting expenditures.

* * * * *

Given the time available, Henry Jr. believed that he had most of the information that would be helpful and was unlikely to learn much more that would be useful for his planning. The question before him was where to begin the process of putting together, with his mother, a plan that would best meet her needs.

EXHIBIT 1
Henry Wheeler's Stock Portfolio

Company	*Number of Shares*	*Aug. 2, 1982, Market Price*	*Aug. 2, 1982, Market Value*	*Most Recent Quarter Dividend per Share*	*Expected Annual Dividend Income*
Anheuser Busch	100	$54.500	$ 5,450	$.37	$ 148
Apple Computer, Inc.	300	14.000	4,200	—	—
Capital Cities Communication	100	77.000	7,700	.05	20
Digital Equipment Company	100	67.375	6,738	—	—
Federal Express Corporation	100	46.675	4,668	—	—
Helmerich & Payne	400	16.375	6,550	.07	112
Hewlett Packard	200	42.875	8,575	.06	48
Holiday Inns	200	27.375	5,475	.20	160
IBM	100	66.750	6,675	.86	344
Johnson & Johnson	200	41.750	8,350	.25	200
McDonald's Corporation	100	74.375	7,438	.30	120
Motorola Inc.	100	67.750	6,775	.40	160
Piedmont Aviation	200	26.625	5,325	.07	56
Public Service Company of New Mexico	200	26.750	5,350	.70	560
Schlumberger	200	37.250	7,450	.24	192
Wang Laboratories B	200	28.125	5,625	.04	32
Total			$102,364		$2,152

EXHIBIT 2
Total Annual Returns of Various Security Classes (*1926–1981*)

Series	Geometric Mean	Arithmetic Mean	Standard Deviation	Distribution
Common stocks	9.1%	11.4%	21.9%	
Small stocks	12.1	18.1	37.3	
Long-term corporate bonds	3.6	3.7	5.6	
Long-term government bonds	3.0	3.1	5.7	
U.S. Treasury bills	3.0	3.1	3.1	
Inflation	3.0	3.1	5.1	

−90x   0x   +90x

Source: R. G. Ibbotson and R. A. Sinquefield, *Stocks, Bonds, Bills and Inflation: The Past and the Future* (Charlottesville, Va.: The Financial Analysts Research Foundation, 1942).

EXHIBIT 3
Excerpts from 1983 Tax Table—Single Individuals

Taxable Income					
Over	***But Not Over***	***Pay***	**+**	***Tax Rate***	***On Excess Over***
$34,100	$41,500	$ 7,953		40%	$34,100
41,500	55,300	10,913		45	41,500
55,300	—	17,123		50	55,300

EXHIBIT 4
Excerpts from 1979 Tax Table—Single Individuals

Taxable Income					
Over	***But Not Over***	***Tax***			***Of the Amount Over***
$ 41,500	$ 55,300	$13,392	+	55%	$ 41,500
55,300	81,800	20,982	+	63	55,300
81,800	108,300	37,677	+	68	81,800
108,300	—	55,697	+	70	108,300

Magnolia Pension Portfolio and Non-Index Indexing

The war was over and an unstable peace reigned. The Finance and Investment Committees had finally reached a compromise on the potentially critical last chink of the only divisive element that remained in reaching a new set of policies for the firm's pension portfolio, the indexing issue. The issue, simply stated, was: How much of the fund's equity pension portfolio would be indexed? And, although less controversial, How? Now it was up to Wilburn Ravenol, newly named Chief Investment Officer, to decide how to implement the resulting compromise in ways that the two camps could agree upon.

The fund had grown to a current market value of about $4 billion as of June 30, 1984 (two weeks before the policy was finalized). This sum was projected to double over the next four to five years. The market value of the equity component was almost $2.5 billion and it might grow somewhat more rapidly than the total portfolio. Since implementation of the new policy would take at least several years—perhaps four—plans were based on a portfolio size of $8 billion.

Policy Background

Magnolia's basic portfolio strategy was hammered out at a three-day retreat. Briefly it could be summarized as follows:

Asset Mix	*Policy*	*Range*
Equities	60%	± 10%
Fixed income	30	± 10
Money market funds (cash)	0	+ 10
Real estate	10	± 5
Total	100%	

Only the real estate represented a significant change from the present portfolio position (+5 percent). Cash as a practical matter could not be held to zero and would probably average at least 3 percent if the portfolio was kept as fully utilized as possible.

Money market funds would continue to be managed in-house. Cash up to 3 percent of the portfolio was to be managed for its liquidity. About 25 percent of the liquid funds would be kept in selected high-quality "overnight" securities. The balance of this portfolio would be invested in high-quality securities with maturities of less than 90 days, usually with "ladder-spaced" maturities, again for liquidity reasons.

Any excess cash funds could be invested for a combination of liquidity/interest-rate goals with maturities up to two years. This policy allowed the manager some discretion in selecting securities and maturities, although this part of the portfolio was rarely more than 20 percent invested in maturities longer than one year. Guidelines in place fully detailed the "explicits" of each element.

There was no sense of urgency in implementing the real estate policy target. The new policy was considered to be a four-year goal. Most important of all, Mr. Ravenol had received authority to hire a full-time real estate person to oversee and help implement the policy and to form a Real Estate Committee of local experts (investors, not developers, preferably with national experience) to help shape details of the policy and plan its implementation. Neither the Investment Committee nor the Finance Committee (Trustees), as a group, had felt comfortable about the real estate managers hired or about the concepts that had governed their actions to date.

All the fixed income had been managed by a local banker who had a set way of investing money and would not do it any other way. The portfolio was primarily invested in long-term (high-quality) securities usually with maturities of about 20 years on average. These securities were highly volatile and by 1980 had a market value slightly less than 70 percent of their cost (because interest rates had risen rapidly—reflecting rising inflation) despite new inflows and trading roll-over. The favorable (deflationary) conditions beginning in late 1981 had helped restore much of the lost book value. Performance, unfortunately, was reported to the Board of Directors and beneficiaries in terms of total returns (interest plus appreciation or, here, depreciation) of value, and so, to say the least, this banker's credibility was below zero by 1980. There were many other less risky ways of running a fixed-income portfolio profitably these days, so that his strategy at best looked "old-fashioned" in a "modern" world. Yet this was the firm's primary bank of account, and top management had been reluctant to disrupt this arrangement. The new Chief Investment Officer, as part of his requirements for accepting his position, insisted that he have the freedom to manage the portfolio to meet its special objectives without impairment. In the future, the fixed income was to be managed largely externally by other managers. The old bank could compete for its share but was unlikely to win any "support."

The "core" half of new fixed-income strategy was to achieve a specific objective: matching or modestly beating the reference objective, the "Shearson-Lehman" Index (representative portfolio similar to the government/corporate composite market) with three or so managers following diverse strategies. The balance was to be managed more imaginatively or aggressively, using a diverse mix of five or so managers, capable of adding value to performance relative to "the" index over most four-year periods individually and, more assuredly, collectively. Mr. Ravenol was left to shape details of the strategy and to find these "superior" fixed-income managers.

The equity strategy had two components: active and passive. The key issue was: how much of each? All involved knew the fund was going to grow to the point, and may have reached the point already, where it could not all be managed actively and well. The fund equity portfolio had been performing poorly now for three years (relative to the S&P 500 Index), and in the last six months the shortfall was too sizable not to be startling to all. Some attributed the failure to poor portfolio construction: too much invested in variations of the same style; not enough invested in a diversity of other good proven styles with countercyclical impacts; too much money with very large managers collectively managing multi-billions in assets by the same "style," where size tended to become an impediment to performance; too little with managers with more flexibility and freedom available to gain good performance. Others supported the theme of the indexers that active management, collectively, was a "loser's" game—and that indexing with its low turnover and management costs was the surest way of gaining near market performance. Not losing much, even at the expense of possibly not winning, seemed a comfort when dealing with the Board of Directors and reporting to participants. Magnolia, after all, had an unusually high commitment to equities relative to most other large pension funds. That was market risk enough! The battle of regaining the support of the Directors seemed particularly important.

All agreed that the active portfolio had to be based on different concepts. The strategy that flowed from these discussions, abetted and focused by a consultant and Mr. Ravenol, took a three-tiered shape:

Tier	*Percent of Active*	*Number of Managers*
Core managers	50	5
Support managers	40	8
Development managers	10	10
Total	100%	23

The number of managers was the ultimate constraining force. The increase of actual active managers from five to nine over the last five years had already created a strain on the current "overseers" process. The Finance Committee still believed in the value of face-to-face experience with all managers, periodically, to help them feel comfortable with the level of fiduciary responsibility they bore. A satisfactory plan for preserving this relationship was a necessary precursor to any increase in number of managers, and one had been found. The plan also freed time from the monthly Investment and Finance Committee meetings to implement the number of changes in this "new" plan with due deliberation yet with due speed. The members of the Investment and Finance Committees all held responsible full-time positions in the firm or elsewhere, and service was "voluntary" and unrecompensed, except for the satisfaction of the achievements of service.

The core portfolio was to consist of five managers, each of whom would employ a different "style" with different opportunities and exposure. The styles were premised as follows (briefly): fundamental long-term growth, earnings momentum (current rate of earnings change), fundamental value (low price/earnings), dividend yield, and "top-down" group rotation. Each of these managers would have a long performance history, would probably manage funds well in excess of $1 billion but not "too much" more (perhaps $4 billion). Eight of the existing nine equity managers fit the core concept but the weeding down process would leave only four as likely survivors (if that many). Two managers were to be terminated in the near-term future. As a group, the core was expected to achieve a 50 basis-point excess return over five years relative to the S&P 500 Index and after "costs." An approximate 20 percent market value commitment to each core manager, rebalanced periodically from cash inflows, seemed a good first-order planning goal.

Five of the support managers would manage funds in the same approximate styles as the core managers and would be "candidates-in-waiting" for promotion to the core group. The remaining three would manage by other styles that were probably infeasible on a scale of $1 billion, given current market liquidity conditions. Each manager was expected to have at least eight years of proven performance, at least five of which were "stand alone"—as a team operating independently of a larger organization's "umbrella." All would currently be managing portfolios with perhaps two thirds the number of portfolio "items" as the core managers; i.e., they would be more concentrated with larger stock and industry bets. All were currently managing between $300 million and $1 billion, with a lesser amount preferred. All were expected to have "sensible" caps to the amount of new-client dollars solicited before "closing the doors"—dollar limits that would sustain their ability to manage money the "same way" (unlike the existing core manager types, who currently kept their doors "open for new business," perhaps to the growing detriment of current clients). Secondary managers as a group were expected to average 2 percent per year more than the S&P 500 Index after costs over five years; sampling of some possibilities made this goal seem achievable.

The development fund managers would be experimental. Each would manage by different styles with no preconditions as to what those styles had to be. Some might be "promotable," but this would not be "structured." Others might never be capable of handling the amounts secondary managers might have to carry on the fund's behalf. All the managers were expected to have proven track records, enough of which was "independent" to the point that the support structure for their methodology was "in place" and operating smoothly. Each might be very small—perhaps only $50 million under current management—and certainly not "too large." Here, the Chief Investment Officer and the consultant expected to be among the first of other large clients who had "discovered" them. Each would manage more concentrated portfolios, capable of making larger bets, within a specialized spectrum of the market. A consultant, specializing in these types of managers, was to be retained to help identify and select, and then monitor certain elements of the performance of these managers over time. Mr. Ravenol was hopeful that this group could collectively provide "excess" returns that were superior to those of the support managers' over five years' time.

The changes were to be scheduled to be implemented slowly in a phased plan over three to four years. All believed that considerable attention to doing the improvement well would be as important as having a good plan. Exhibit 1 applies Magnolia's asset-mix policy to a possible $8 million portfolio.

Of the current equity portfolio, approximately 25 percent had been allocated to two well-known S&P 500 Indexers. As a group, these indexers were expected to come within 20 basis points per year of the index over five years' time after costs.

Mr. Ravenol's Reaction to the Policy Changes

Mr. Ravenol was happy in general with the policy decisions reached to date. He would have preferred more flexibility (say ± 20 percent) in the range of freedom given for the equity portfolio because he believed the asset-mix status could be favorably adapted to intermediate-performance prospects. The consultant, who had been so helpful in selling and conceiving parts of the plan to the Investment and Finance Committees, was adamantly against the concept of "market timing," unfortunately. In his experience, market timing was more often done poorly than well. It was more important to Mr. Ravenol to maintain the goodwill of the consultant and to assure himself that the committees would respect his real value to them and to him, than it was to win each and every point of disagreement. He knew, for example, that asset-mix actuals for equity would average higher than the target simply because the market climate over time was generally more favorable for equities than other major alternatives. He also hoped that some favorable experience with market-timing managers might pave the way for reconsideration later.

The real estate flexibility was all Mr. Ravenol considered feasible currently, given the mixed and largely misunderstood performance of the current real estate portfolio in the disinflationary period of the 1980s. He knew, however, in some periods he would want the freedom to increase the size of these funds substantially. Real estate, for example, had been one of the better means of protecting real values and achieving the fundamental goal of the portfolio during the ravaging inflationary period that grew out of the Vietnam economic policy that promoted "guns and butter" when in truth we could not support both concurrently without high economic risks.[1]

This firm's portfolio, like most others, had not realized the value of real estate as a protective investment until it was almost too late in the 1970s to benefit from participating in some of the conditional protective rewards, and the actions themselves had set this portfolio up for later disappointments during the disinflationary period that followed. Real estate would not benefit in "all weather." This was true for every other investment vehicle also. So Mr. Ravenol remained happy with both the current real estate policy and for the slow plans for implementing it for the time being, for their immediate outlook for this investment was not encouraging.

The Committees

Under the ERISA laws, the Board of Directors of Magnolia were held responsible, as Fiduciaries, for the performance of the portfolio. (A brief summary of the fiduciary responsibilities or the original ERISA Act is provided in Appendix A.) Of importance to these people, ERISA specifically voided any protective provisions in pension plans or in trust agreements that relieved any individual from personal liabilities for losses resulting from their acts or from failure to act appropriately. As a matter of common practice, the Board of Directors delegated its responsibilities to Trustees, who in this case were the Finance Committee, to fulfill their responsibilities and to review and report to them on performance every six months. The report was received and reviewed twice a year (often for no more than 15 minutes) and the Board accepted the "performance as according to plan, given market conditions." The Directors received and approved a report each year from the actuary and the Finance Committee recommended the proposed annual dollar funding level and time schedule for payments to the fund by the corporation. Finally, the Board approved the appointment of the membership of the Finance Committee (along with other senior-level committees), as a block.

---

[1]For Mr. Ravenol, the inflation, although not the severity of the inflationary risks that followed, were an anticipatable danger. He also recognized that solving the inflation problems at hand then created the risk of such future dangers as impaired world competitive position for the dollar—because of government actions and of the response of some managers to these conditions (it had been too easy for some firms to raise prices to keep real earnings "high enough" in the short run without recognizing the opportunities this gave to some international competitors operating in different economic and social climates). In Ravenol's mind Volcker had been right in his policies of guarding against early rebirth of inflation while at the same time achieving the desirable international competitive end of reducing the trading value of the dollar to more realistic levels. Ravenol believed the economy and the markets had not fully responded to the current deflationary environment because of the interference from the conflicting economic goals of full employment, growth opportunities, satisfactory trading opportunities, and the responsibilities of social benefits and other national priorities, as well as stable prices. He did not think real estate was a particularly favorable immediate investment alternative at this time so there was no urgency to building up the base. However, real estate was an inflexible investment vehicle for moving large amounts of capital in and out of a commitment rapidly. And people would not necessarily feel comfortable with the timing of such a move, given results.

The Finance Committee was composed of the five most senior finance people. They met once a month for a full day extending occasionally into the evening, if necessary. Their general responsibilities were to approve all corporate policies relating to the finance activity; to verify compliance with these policies; to review performance relative to goals; to approve budgets, including the capital budgets (or to recommend actions, as appropriate, to the Directors); to allocate capital (and/or receive back) funds to each division and other major activities; and to accomplish a potpourri of other necessary actions, including major implementing decisions. Their responsibilities to the Pension activity were similar except that they also had to approve each funding decision to managers, each new management contract (upon advice of the corporate legal department), and to acknowledge the receipt of any updates on their responsibilities, the limits and freedoms of their policy actions, any relevant legal interpretations (all from the legal department with any changes highlighted), and a compliance report or recommendation (from the legal department). In practice, they usually met for two hours each month with the Chief Investment Officer (and those members of the Investment Committee who were available) to perform reviews and other necessary business. The second hour was generally devoted to hearing a report from a manager, reviewing his performance in more detail, and the like. This was, to many members, the most enjoyable part of the day and, if feasible, often extended informally into a cocktail party. The Committee could and occasionally did call for a more detailed evaluation of any fund manager whose performance appeared out of line.

The Investment Committee was composed of two insiders with investment experience (one had served as a Trustee to the Endowment portfolio of a nearby college, the other ran a large portfolio for his family) and three non-affiliated outsiders (one ran a large counseling business managing portfolios for individuals, another was an experienced trust officer in a nearby bank with substantial independent investment experience, and the third ran equity portfolios for large pension clients). The experience of this group was unusual for a corporation to have available, and valuable to Mr. Ravenol. (The members of the Finance Committee and all but one Director had little investment experience beyond managing their own—often limited—wealth.)

Mr. Ravenol had considerable experience running other pension funds for smaller corporations and saw his current position as fulfilling his career objective at the age of 40. His small staff had typically been corporate people, assigned to this department from the corporation for about three years. As a condition of his employment, Mr. Ravenol had insisted that his staff be career specialists in the future and that their salaries be adapted to market conditions necessary to make a career more attractive for individuals with about five years of useful experience.

He had yet to develop a reward system based on performance contributions to make the job more valuable to them. He had already hired two key equity staff. He had one inexperienced bond assistant to replace, the ability to hire a real estate resource, and three support/administrative staff available. Staffing was still at a minimum level to do the work and to control it, and more PCs and programming skills were urgently required. All these and the remaining problems seemed solvable, however.

Resolution of the Indexing Policy

If left to their own minds, the Investment Committee, who were a little more aware of the opportunities to find "good" outside managers and to improve the structure of the portfolio,[2] were concerned lest the commitment already made of 25 percent to indexing was too high, and would have preferred a lower level.

The Finance Committee had been scared by the recent and five-year underperformance of the portfolio. They also had the difficult task of explaining the performance to the Directors and supervising the preparation of the annual report to plan participants. Fortunately, the cost-to-payroll ratio had been declining because of generally favorable market conditions since 1979. The Directors, and hence the Finance Committee, tended to regard this measure as the prime test of success despite the narrow purpose set forth by the ERISA laws. The Finance Committee's problem was compounded by the wide variety of strategies that were feasible to protect the interest of beneficiaries fully against the most foreseeable risks in most markets while in a few markets (like that of the 1970s) almost no strategy will protect the purchasing power of pensions to beneficiaries—although current commitments remained safe. A second set of criteria to guide decisions was often necessary. The Committee was also heavily influenced by an indexer who made it sound extremely difficult for any active managers to beat the market over the long run and in many short-run periods as well. He had some convincing looking data to support that case. The data did not square well with the data they had from SEI (a major provider of investment evaluation, consulting, and software services to the financial community) and other sources for the same period. Investment Committee members were suspicious, while the Finance Committee members were convinced. The latter seemed collectively to prefer a solution of 70 to 80 percent indexing.

With the help of the consultant, a compromise was worked out. The proposal was to index 30 percent immediately and increase this proportion to 50 percent at

---

[2]Some of the recent underperformance was due, in their minds, to the biases of the two previous investment managers. Both had strongly favored one style of equity management and overcommitted the portfolio to this style before and after the Investment Committee was formed in mid-1981 and despite their counsel against it. Except for a burst in performance from September 1982 to March 1983, this style had seriously underperformed the market in its various forms since late 1978. The burst was quickly eroded in the months that followed.

The second reason was more immediate. There are simply some markets when the large majority of managers could not match the common standard of performance, the S&P 500 Index. The "nifty-fifty" market from 1969 to later 1973 was the longest and most dramatic example. This had been true again since June of 1983, and seriously so. In other periods, most managers outperformed the market and on balance did so over almost all postwar periods of 12 years or longer (the period surrounded by the nifty-fifty market being the major exception). Most manager studies were done with this period weighted disproportionally to normal and were overweighted with bank trust department pools and some mutual funds (e.g., balanced firms) for whom criteria were inappropriate. Risk adjustment, as practiced, often biased the results further.

the end of four years, when the policy would be reconsidered. There was an important qualifier to this recommendation. Within four years half of these funds were to be invested in non-S&P-500 type equity indexing. The opportunities for what later became known as "Non-Index Indexing" were:

1. Other broad-based equity indices.
2. Special-purpose indexing, i.e., diversified portfolios designed to mirror certain sub-universes within the market. A "Yield-Tilt" fund, biased toward higher-yield stocks, was cited as an example of a fund that produced favorable results over six years for non-taxed clients.
3. Market timing, by moving between broad-based indices representing different types of asset classes. Several managers offered services of this kind, moving, for example, between S&P 500 Indexing and money market funds and reportedly were doing well. Both present indexers offered this type of service to their clients for an added fee.
4. Broadly diversified equity portfolios following highly disciplined styles of stock selection. Several interesting sounding examples were cited.

The "retreat," where policy was to be proposed by the Investment Committee, discussed, and approved, it was hoped unanimously, by the Finance Committee, fell apart when the Investment Committee proposed its (compromise) positions on indexing. Tempers of one or two members on each side flared as discussion progressed and arguments became heated, emotional, and sometimes overly personal. The majority of the Finance Committee saw it as a sensible interim solution subject to reconsideration later. As this position became apparent, the Finance Committee approved it unanimously if in some cases reluctantly, but with particular emphasis on the fact that it would be reviewed in four years.

Portfolio Goals

Magnolia's portfolio objectives were stated more for public and legal consumption than for practical guidance purposes.

The existing goals were drawn up before Mr. Ravenol arrived and he had mixed feelings about their practical value. In his view the following general factors (all relevant to Magnolia) should be more important in setting goals and evaluating performance relative to goals.

1. Pension funds sponsors ideally could take a long-term perspective. It was often 20 years or more before the accumulated value of $1 invested was typically paid out in benefits. Fund inflows to pension funds generally exceeded payments, although this could change rapidly in the near-term future.[3] Cash income from investments still tended to cover payment needs in most firms. As a consequence,

---

[3]Pension funds have been an important source of new capital to the capital markets and one must wonder about the potential economic consequences if pensions become a user not supplier of new capital.

there is little need for portfolio liquidity, and investments could still be made based on their long-term merits. Only tactical decisions, like market timing, might require ready cash.

2. Practical considerations intervene in the ideal. Sponsors had to first assess the recent performance and prospects of asset-class and management-style commitments. In volatile markets this was at best not easy to do and, as often as not, masked the long-term implications of results and caused overreactions. The second practical consideration involved "scorekeepers."

3. Of these, the actuary was currently the most important. The actuary determined funding costs, and Directors, Trustees, and key top management were more often concerned with rising cost-to-payroll ratios than with actual performance. That's where portfolio risk hit home hardest. The actuary's method tended to smooth out market variability. Actuarial goals (required rates of return) were conservative in the context of long-term goals. The goals appeared easy to achieve in almost all markets using a wide variety of asset-mix strategies. The simplest general rule of thumb was: if one meets the actuarial goal on average over five years, risks will normally be minimal. Excess performance usually was accumulated as a cushion before costs began falling relatively. The opening cushion frequently would carry a firm through the difficult years. More often than not it was the risks of focusing on the nominal performance that caused problems. In the 1970s, an actuary often reported "You have met your actuarial goal, but your funding costs are higher." (These costs generally rose faster because of high rates of inflation until very recently, when costs began dropping rapidly again.)

4. An actuary assumed some inflation in his cost estimates. When actual inflation rates exceeded this assumption, costs would tend to increase unless there was offsetting overperformance. In periods like the 1970s and 1940s, inflation tended to exceed the actuarial rates, creating serious problems. Worse, inflation rates tend to be negatively correlated with portfolio performance. (Almost any sensible *ex ante* asset-mix strategy would have produced negative real returns in both the 1940s and 1970s.) Pension benefit plans often had to be revised upward in recognition of the fact that true pension benefits could only be measured in terms of their purchasing power. The only true test of performance was to assess whether or not real portfolio returns averaged between 2 percent and 3 percent (depending) over four to five years. In the short term, this goal was an impossible task to achieve in some economic states. Over 20 years, it tended to be easy. The new Financial Accounting Standards Board (FASB) rules might ultimately complicate these problems because of their possible annual "reporting" effects.

5. In practice, horizons might be even shorter. Pension management, for all its importance, was not usually a normal career path. Corporate managers either performed the task part time or hoped to be promoted out from the job in relatively short order. How they "looked" to others this year might be more important than meeting the more meaningful longer-term objectives. In reports, the complexity of the market dynamics had often to be simplified. "How well did we do" often meant for equity performance: Did the composite beat the S&P 500 Index? As a long-term goal it was very reasonable to achieve this on average. In the short run, it was more misleading than helpful as a comparative reference. Whenever there was a period of protracted underperformance, as there had been recently, money started flooding into indexers because "it is better to be safe than sorry—FOR ME." There were many good, constructive reasons to index but this was not one.

6. Consultants might worsen the situation. Too much emphasis could be on recent performance, not enough on long-term performance. In the short run, a good portfolio should have its share of winners and losers. Attention was focused on the big losers. How serious is it? What, if anything, should we do about it? The important questions of Why? or Is this normal for this manager? rarely were explored and the data available were usually poor for these purposes. A higher rate of manager turnover resulted. If manager turnover exceeded 10 percent per year over five years it was usually due to misinformation, not good judgment. The fund managers themselves were not stupid. Many increased their turnover (shortened their investmment horizon) and increased their diversification in response. This risk-averse strategy adoption might be necessary for them even though it proved costly to the sponsor over the longer term.

Magnolia's goals were:

A. *Composite Portfolio*. The total portfolio performances should (using a total rate-of-return measure):

   1. Exceed actuarial requirements (currently 7 percent per year based on a 4 percent per year inflation rate assumption) by 1 percent per year over most five-year periods.

B. *Equity Portfolio*. The total equity performance should (same criteria):

   1. Exceed the Standard & Poor's 500 Index total return by 1 percent per year or more over most five-year periods.

   2. Exceed the inflation rate (CPI) by 7 percent or more per year over most five-year periods.

   3. Exceed actuarial requirements by 5 percent per year or more over most five-year periods.

   4. Minimize downside exposure (i.e., poor relative performance) in possible protracted, relatively severe, down periods for the market (i.e., as measured by the S&P 500 Index).

C. *Fixed-Income Portfolio* (including cash investments). The total fixed-income portfolio performance should:

   1. Exceed the Shearson-Lehman Composite (a broad measure of bond market performance) by 50 basis points per year over most five-year periods.

   2. Exceed the inflation rate (CPI) by 1 percent per year or more over most five-year periods.

D. *Real Estate*. The total real estate portfolio performance should:

   1. Exceed an appropriate index (now the Russell Index) by 1 percent per year or more over most five-year periods.

2. Exceed the inflation rate (CPI) by 6 percent or more over most five-year periods.

Mr. Ravenol did not believe these goals, as stated, allowed for the circumstances where all goals were collectively easy or virtually impossible to achieve prospectively. They seemed in various ways inconsistent with one another. They were never mentioned by anyone during policy formulation and the only reference considered was: match or beat the index chosen for each security class. A four- to five-year planning and measurement horizon still seemed to be in force although he was not sure it might not be as unrealistically short as one year in some Finance Committee members' mindset. The bottom-line goals remained: to reduce the cost without too much portfolio risk of not doing so. Prudence and beneficiary safety seemed taken for granted. His analysis of individual managers was based upon his beliefs about what were important factors for them to consider during decision making. As inflation risks seemed low at the moment, his emphasis was on nominal returns. He preferred to watch inflation closely, and to focus on it sharply when the risks of higher intermediate inflation rates appeared more dangerous. He would worry about resetting goals later.

Progress toward Implementing the Strategy

A little more than two years later in early October 1986, Mr. Ravenol was very pleased with the early accomplishments in implementing the policy. Overall, the strategies even partly implemented seemed to be working well. Because of very favorable fixed-income and equity markets, and to a lesser extent because each asset class was outperforming its target index over the period, the portfolio had grown rapidly in total market value and had reached the $7.7 billion level at the end of September 1986. Growth had caused some implementation problems.

Mr. Ravenol was particularly pleased with the composite performance of the equity portfolio over the last two years. The market climate had not been favorable for many managers, and the median performance of all equity managers was well below the S&P 500 Index and only about 30 percent of reported managers had superior performance.[4] This was achieved despite the fact that one core, three specialty, and five development managers had serious underperformance. In two

---

[4]Whenever the Dow Jones Industrials either beat or about matched the S&P 500 Index, this type of performance was normal. It was also true whenever the value-weighted S&P 500 Index beat the equal-weighted index for the same 500 stocks. Over longer periods and in the larger majority of market years, the reverse was true and managers tended to outperform these indices. On a composite basis, the portfolio was systematically underweighted in the largest capitalization securities, often seriously so. The last time Mr. Ravenol checked, only Philip Morris among the largest 25 capitalization stocks (generally about 30 percent of the S&P 500 weight) had a commitment from the composite portfolio approximately equal to its weight in the S&P 500 Index. This was only because three of the five core managers, and several other managers, found the security sufficiently attractive (for different fundamental reasons) to make significant overcommitments to this stock. Whenever an important group within the S&P 500, as in the nifty-fifty market, had significant overperformance relative to the general market, manager underperformance, sometimes very substantial, was likely.

cases the problem related to style disfavor and these sorts of problems had to be accepted as normal—that's why style diversification was so important. The rest related to performance of smaller-capitalization stocks. The NASDAQ Industrial Index, the most representative of this group, had seriously underperformed the S&P 500 since June 1983 except for brief spurts, and some parts of this market were dead weights for the previous five months. Protracted good and bad runs for this group were not uncommon although over longer periods performance was usually quite superior. Some sectors of this market looked "dirt cheap" compared to normal historic value characteristics.

Five of the nine initial managers had been retained, four as core managers and one as a specialty manager, and one was later added to fill out the core plan. Only one of the original core managers was still being watched closely and might still be changed. Funds allocated among these managers had been rebalanced (by removing money most frequently to equal the interim target amounts—it was difficult to remove too much money from them during the early implementation phases). The core group had received top time priority.

Five new specialty managers were hired within the first year to bring the total to six, two shy of the target. Giving good back-up to the core group was considered the most important objective and had been accomplished first. The committees felt comfortable with these additions. Most of the back-up specialty managers had performed well compared to the core group in the interim and had very attractive historic performance. Several had closed the doors to new business when they reached their target size and this too was pleasing. Any core-manager change necessary now seemed feasible from the back-up group without the need for additional search. The list would be completed within 12 months, and the styles and a smallish list of six potential managers had been identified tentatively.

The 10 development managers had been funded about a year ago. However, two had already been "promoted" to be specialty managers. A list of six candidates for the two open slots had been invited to present their case at a recent Investment Committee, and two had been recommended to and approved by the Finance Committee, subject to the usual need to iron out contract terms.

Except for the two specialty manager vacancies, the task of completing the active equity strategy was completed and the portfolio was back at a maintenance level.

The fixed-income strategy had been thrashed out at the conceptual level. The core strategy had been refined, managers interviewed, recommended, and funded with one exception (where contract discussion had been more protracted). The core strategy was designed to add value to the broad and widely representative Shearson-Lehman Index. Three types of managers were to be hired: one specializing in shorter-maturity investments, with maturities less than three years; another specializing in intermediate-term securities with similar duration characteristics to the reference index; the last emphasized longer-term maturities. All did some shifting of portfolio characteristics such as duration, sector, and security selection within their specialty range. The three types of managers would be funded to achieve a common composite characteristic of a duration similar to the reference index and were rebalanced periodically toward this end. A duration match using managers with superior performance records and prospects, yet one that allowed good participation in whatever part of the time-sector phase of the market was performing best and that allowed suitable diversification, seemed to be the decision process most likely to achieve the desired core objective over time.

Eight managers had been interviewed for the three slots by the Investment Committee and five had been recommended to the Finance Committee and approved by them. Two intermediate- and longer-term managers had been hired, because all had very attractive (similar) track records, yet were achieving their ends by different means. A little added diversity seemed desirable. Each of these managers was to be allocated about half of the funds scheduled for their time-sector.

The specialty fixed-income managers' plan was still at the conceptual level. Each was to be an aggressive manager specializing in making money by some distinctive style. (A high-yield junk-bond manager might be one example.) Detailed planning would not begin for several months, with an eye toward finishing the task by the following June. The existing fixed-income manager was still performing satisfactorily managing the remaining funds in his hands.

Real estate policies had been hammered out by the Real Estate Committee and approved by the Finance Committee. Existing managers were rebalanced to form a highly diversified core designed to beat an agreed-upon index target modestly over time. The plan for the more specialized managers was being organized for implementation at that time. No sense of urgency had yet been imparted to this task, given the unfolding market circumstances.

As noted, the two S&P 500 indexers had been hired and were performing as expected. When the portfolio grew in size rapidly over the time and the implementation of the equity plan was still progressing, the residual amounts were allocated to these indexers and the amount being indexed had approached 50 percent. Until recently S&P 500 indexing had been the only form of indexing undertaken. (The non-index funding and remaining unresolved problems will be discussed later.)

The only unexpected problem had arisen in the spring of 1986. Several members of the Finance Committee became very concerned that the equity market had risen too much and might be vulnerable to a relapse. The Investment Committee was less concerned because long-term fixed-income total returns had been 24 percent per year—4 percent more than the S&P 500 Index—since the disinflationary markets began in earnest in October 1981. Market adjustments seemed more attributable to downward discount rate adjustments, which generally favored longer duration equities. Nevertheless, it seemed better to find a way to maintain the peace and get on with the critical task. The staff investigated S&P 500 portfolio insurance (hedging) as the most interesting alternative available and, ultimately, the two S&P 500 indexers were employed to insure their part of the portfolio so that the S&P 500 would earn no worse than 0 percent per year over two years. To the Investment Committee the proposal was a relatively inexpensive experiment to test the potential benefits of a new investment tool, which seemed to have uncertain costs and value implication for the future.

These changes were not achieved without strains. In a new equity manager search, for example, the staff typically had interviewed five potential managers in their offices, based on recommendations and data provided by the consultant. Three were selected and interviewed by the Investment Committee and only one was recommended and approved by the Finance Committee. (From time to time, one or more of the Finance Committee would meet with the interview sessions conducted by the Investment Committee.) Even so, time was at a premium. Fortunately, the quality of the staff had improved and been expanded to help achieve the temporary and continuing ability to meet the expanded workload needs. The Investment Committee had met 18 times per year, often for full days (not counting the retreat and special-purpose meetings), and were anxious to return soon to a less demanding monthly schedule, given their other responsibilities. The Finance Committee, too, had given considerably more time to pension activities, and a review retreat would be continued. Two more full days were being devoted to hands-on meetings with all active equity managers with both committees participating. Further time would have to be found for other similar management reviews for other major fund commitment areas. Fortunately, all concerned were feeling considerable pride in their achievements to date and implementation planning was about 6 to 12 months ahead of schedule. All were relieved that work pace could now slow.

The staff faced and solved many other operational problems. The performance and verification analysis had to be revamped and adapted to many new forms of investments. An incentive pay system had been worked out and approved. Performance review material was improved to expedite monthly and quarterly reviews in ways that also improved understanding of market forces. Programs to use new computer equipment were worked out. A new and superior control over transactions and market impact costs was developed and was working well. And so on.

Instrumental to this whole process was a willingness of the Finance Committee to delegate more responsibility to the Investment Committee, and, in turn, the Investment Committee to rely more heavily on staff analysis (with the help of a key, respected consultant) for support. The committees found this dependency justified by Mr. Ravenol and his superior staff. Relationships showed more respect and cordiality than in the past, although both committees were careful that they understood the implications of decisions-in-process through careful questioning.

The Remaining Key Problem: Non-Index Indexing

Only three non-index managers had been hired. In the first category, the staff had proposed and received approval to seek out an equal-weighted S&P 500 Index fund, using an imaginative rebalancing scheme to control transaction costs and to add value-over-time relative to the raw index. The Finance Committee also approved two managers with structured, highly diversified strategies for tilting the portfolio. One tilt was toward yield, the other toward long-term fundamental growth. Other factors were controlled to reduce other risks. A yield manager for this type of fund with eight years of real performance plus additional back-test support had been found and funded. The record showed superior total return performance over time with very attractive defensive properties. The growth manager hiring was based on attractive-looking back-test information only. Altogether only 10 percent of indexing funds had been allocated to these activities as yet. Several similar possibilities were under study by the staff, and about half of available funds for non-indexing would be put to these types of purposes (in Mr. Ravenol's mind).

The two remaining possible areas of investment envisioned were timing between indices and structured, highly diversified, but managed portfolios. Mr. Ravenol feared they might prove controversial and open some old sores. All clearly involved some form of very active management, and were not "passive" in most senses of the word. Yet as he and his staff began investigating practical alternatives, he found them surprisingly attractive. If anything, he became even more enthusiastic about this form of non-index indexing and wanted his first presentation to be a powerful one.

The indexing issue was not wholly dead. Good performance had abated concern, but a really poor set of market conditions for managers generally, as had happened in the last quarter, might offset the progress made to date. When fixed income had come up, the Finance Committee wondered if one of the new forms of indexing against fixed-income indices such as the Shearson-Lehman benchmark might prove attractive. This interest died when they saw the five bond managers' records when approving the implementation of the core. Finally, the Finance Com-

EXHIBIT 1
Magnolia's Asset-Mix Targets Applied to $8 Billion Portfolio (*$ millions*)

Asset Mix	Target Percent	Dollar Commitment of $8 Billion	Number of Managers	Dollar per Manager
Cash Securities	0%		1	
Fixed-Income	30	$2,400		
Core	15	1,200	3*	$400
Specialty	15	1,200	5	240
Equity	60	4,800		
Indexing	30	2,400		
S&P 500	15	1,200	2	600
Non-S&P 500	15	1,200	?	?
Active	30	2,400		
Core	15	1,200	5	240
Specialty Mgrs.	12	960	8	120
Development Fund	3	240	10	24
Real Estate†	10	800		
Core	5	400	5	80
Specialty	5	400	1	400

*Subsequently changed to five, four of which would share the per-manager allocation equally, one of which would receive the full amount. Collectively, they would receive the planned balance that was developed. Better strategy to some extent emerged later. Because "cash" was considered a part of this total, actuals would never reach targets.

† Allocations reflect strategy later developed, as described in the case.

mittee seemed to be more skeptical and questioning than usual in approving the three non-index indexers approved to date.

Mr. Ravenol had asked his key staff to prepare a written summary report (based on a diverse group of three managers), both illustrative of the kinds of opportunities available and somewhat better than typical. The report for the Investment Committee would be brief and would omit much of the support work that had been done by his staff. The three managers would also be available at the meeting scheduled next week to present their case. He was hopeful the Committee might recommend all three to the Finance Committee at this meeting, although the procedure (no alternatives to consider) was unusual. He planned to study the report and revise it as necessary that night. He believed that packaging the report might be crucial and he planned to spend considerable time and thought on how best to present the case.

The report draft is shown in its entirety in Appendix B.

Appendix A

SUMMARY OF FIDUCIARY RESPONSIBILITY*

ERISA mandates "fiduciary responsibility" for any pension plan trustee, for investment managers of pension assets, and for any other persons who may have responsibility and authority in the management of a plan or in controlling, allocating, and disposing of the plan's assets. Fiduciaries, so defined, must discharge their duties solely in the interests of the participants in given plans. They are made liable for asset losses resulting from violation of the "prudent man" rule, which requires them "to discharge their duties with the care, skill, prudence, and diligence which a prudent man acting in a like capacity would use under conditions prevailing at the time." More specially, a fiduciary is prohibited from such transactions as dealing with the plan for his or her own account or selling anything to, buying anything from, receiving a gift from, or lending money from plan assets to, a "party-in-interest" under a plan (i.e., the plan-sponsoring employer, plan participants, the unions involved, or persons providing services to the plan) or investing more than 10 percent of plan assets in the employer's securities or real property.

The act requires diversification of the investments of the plan, geographically, by industry and by type of vehicle, so that the risk of loss be minimized, except when selling off fund assets in order to diversify would itself result in substantial loss and would clearly not be prudent at the time.

ERISA empowers participants and beneficiaries—or their unions, or the U.S. Department of Labor acting on their behalf—to sue fiduciaries for "fiduciary irre-

---

*Source: *The Financial Reality of Pension Funding under ERISA*, written by Jack L. Treynor, Patrick J. Regan, and William W. Priest, Jr. (Homewood, Ill.: Dow Jones-Irwin, 1976), p. 100.

sponsibility" on such charges as pursuing inappropriate investment policies or making imprudent investment decisions, or persuading professional investment managers, placed in charge of some part of plan assets, to do either. A fiduciary may also be held liable for losses caused by other fiduciaries if the fiduciary concealed their acts or was negligent in not seriously trying to stop their breach of responsibility.

Appendix B

DRAFT OF STAFF REPORT ON THREE MANAGER CANDIDATES

Introduction

This report focuses on three managers who qualify for consideration as non-index indexers. All three approach the problem differently. All three might be in the outer ranges of what many individuals consider passive. The combined performance of all three tends to be better than any one alone.

Here, we summarize the strategy of each manager separately and give the full names, addresses, telephone numbers, and contact person as a general reference at the end of the report.

All three include appropriate transactions costs in their simulation analysis. All three experience lower-than-estimated actual transactions costs. Entry (except for Index-Plus) and exit transactions costs are not included, nor is the management fee, which tends to be at the low end of the active equity manager range. Security lending income sometimes reduces the management fee. Active manager performance is generally reported and available in the same format. Actual composite performance is substituted in the last two examples for the period available. Simulation information seems realistic in light of actual performance in all cases.

The Managers

Wells Fargo's Market-Timing Strategy

Wells Fargo's management began gathering data that might be used for active and passive portfolio management in the early 1970s. They were an early entry into S&P indexing, and have gained a large market share. They tended also to be early entrants, if not always originators, of other equity and debt indices which have since gained popularity. Only one serious competitor, Mellon, has since emerged and that group is staffed by key Wells Fargo people who helped shape and implement many of these strategies, including the one reviewed here. Wells has the longest test and actual performance record available. No visible difference between Wells' and Mellon's (briefer) actual record existed.

In the early 1970s Wells Fargo began estimating the total rate-of-return data for individual securities, using a variable-growth dividend discount model similar to later applications by other firms. The derivative products remain important. A yield-tilt (tax) index portfolio was introduced in the late 1970s and is still actively used by non-taxed clients and by us. More relevant, market-timing applications were developed, tested, and introduced from these inputs.

Individual stock estimates of long-term total return expectations could be combined with reasonable reliability into a composite estimate of the S&P 500's, using individual securities' weights as appropriate. Comparisons between the long-term returns of stocks could be compared with yields on long-term fixed-income securities or short-term money market funds. The spreads between the return estimates for equities and fixed-income securities varied widely. The spread information was then used as a bond manager might use it: when the spreads become unusually wide, more funds should be given to the riskier security; when the spread narrowed, more were moved to the safer security. The two-asset timing strategies were implemented first, marketed successfully, and provided very satisfactory actual results. A three-asset mix strategy was also being tested, and that strategy was implemented several years ago. The three asset classes are Wells' S&P 500 Index Fund, its long-term Government Bond-Index Fund, and its own Money Market Fund.

In this strategy, return estimates were put into a Markowitz-type optimization model (that considered variance and covariance inputs derived from history). Most of the time, the "safer" security was easy to recognize. However, in the late 1970s and early 1980s long-term quality fixed-income securities became more volatile than large-cap equities. So also did all covariance characteristics alter significantly at this time. Wells' risk inputs recognized but responded slowly to the more recent changes. Return inputs tend to be more sensitive to current market changes and tend to be the primary driving force of the strategy anyway.

The three-asset strategy tends to win by not losing as much in bad equity markets and its performance is "okay" in up markets. Over several years of ups and downs it tends to outperform the S&P 500. We collected monthly performance data from 1973 forward through June 1986. We valued both its intermediate-term performance and its defensive properties most heavily. If the fund doesn't always "win" in the short term, we would much prefer to win in bad markets than in good ones. The three-asset performance results have some interesting inflation-hedge characteristics too. The three-asset strategy performed almost as well as real estate assets over protracted periods during the most difficult inflationary years of the 1970s, with lower risks in disinflationary periods that followed. We were primarily focusing on the strategy's values as a pure substitute for S&P indexing, however.

Others may be more interested in the market-timing strategy properties. Here a more appropriate benchmark for testing performance would be some steady-state asset-mix policy. Performance for the timing strategy will look better and be more consistent than even a more aggressive asset mix like 70 percent equities, 20 percent bonds, and 10 percent cash equivalents (rebalanced monthly). The defensive properties alone will appeal to many. And for many purposes, it is a cheaper, better, and lower-risk (opportunity costs) than hedging (insurance against adverse market performance using futures) for other than very short-term occasional "insurance" use.

Brignoli's Efficient Market Strategy

For academics, the Brignoli strategy is an interesting and relatively pure test of the weak-form efficient market theory, yet one undertaken by someone with a knowledge of market behavior and with creativity. The strategy is premised on the theory that stock volatility is good and portfolio volatility is bad. "Excess profits" are made by capitalizing upon the "random walk" characteristics of stock behavior by means of efficient trading rules.

The only inputs to the model are the historic volatility and paired covariance measures of individual stocks. The only judgment required was how these variables should be measured, an ordinary testing problem.

A large universe is screened to select about 700 stocks with sufficient market liquidity (since efficient trading is required). This group is then reduced by perhaps 50 to eliminate those firms that might be considered imprudent (much the same way pure indexers will eliminate a few stocks that might be considered imprudent). The less volatile stocks are eliminated in shrinking the universe down to a more manageable group of about 300. This group is then optimized using classic Markowitz methodology to produce low composite variability but high individual variability. In this process there is a clear trade-off between the number of securities included (the larger this number, the better for the trading strategy) and risk minimization (the more concentrated a few become, the better). This balance is struck by a limit on the amount committed to any one security, a constraint that is severe enough to assure a universe of at least 100 securities. A minimal constraint, as well, prevents overly small commitments to a large sample of securities with unimportant effects. Both constraints, in different forms, are common parts of any optimization models used (sparingly) by practitioners today. The model tests well. *Ex ante* betas tend to be near 1, but with much higher residual error, for example. *Ex post* results are heavily influenced by the strategy.

Optimization occurs periodically (currently every six months). The trade-off between the value of reoptimizing and the added cost of rebalancing is still under study and, if anything, will be done less frequently. Once the portfolio is rebalanced, it is governed by trading rules based on random walk beliefs. Whenever a security exceeds target weight by *X* percent it is trimmed back to its target weight. Similarly, cash flows and sales receipts are used to fill stocks more than *X* percent below the target weight. ("*X*" has been determined after extensive testing and may be confidential.) Otherwise cash is kept as fully invested as practical. Trading must, of course, be done very efficiently (transaction and market impact considered) yet often quickly, in less than "block"-sized trades. To the extent skill and experience play a role in performance, it is at the trading desk. Excess profits come from trading.

The optimal portfolio has persistent biases. It is more nearly equal-weighted than value-weighted. The portfolio, left on its own, tracks the equal-weighted S&P

500 better and produces some consistent excess returns over time against this measure. (As a general reference, the equal-weighted index tended to perform very well, on balance, from 1974 into early 1983 relative to the normal index. Thereafter it has performed consistently poorly and at times seriously so.) Excess returns are benefited or harmed by the performance spread between these indices. Equal weighting and the selection process create a persistent small-firm effect. There is strong bias away from certain low volatility groups (like utilities) and toward others with higher volatility.

Despite these biases, we have looked on Brignoli results as a pure S&P 500 Index substitute. It may not be the best way for others to view the potential of the account. Brignoli went live in 1983 and our data is based on actuals thereafter. Their simulation begins in 1974.

Index-Plus Fundamental Factors Strategy

Index-Plus is designed around the following basic fundamental premises:

1. Low price-earnings ratio stocks tend to outperform high price-earnings stocks.
2. Stocks with higher earnings momentum tend to outperform stocks with lower earnings momentum.
3. Stocks with favorable earnings surprises tend to outperform stocks with unfavorable earnings surprises.
4. Low-capitalization stocks tend to outperform high-capitalization stocks.
5. A combination of these factors works better than any single factor separately.

While Glenn Kent was overseeing the (now) Honeywell Inc. pension portfolio, he discovered a unique data base and strategy testing system at Abel-Noser, then a small New York broker. Abel-Noser had begun collecting a data base, including consensus analyst estimates of earnings and dividends, quarterly and yearly, from mid-1973 forward. The data base, brought up to date and still being improved, allowed the measuring of forward price-earnings ratios, earnings surprise, forward yield, etc., much the same way practicing security analysts tend to do in their work. Other factors commonly used by analysts, such as earnings momentum, price to book value, relative p/e (current p/e minus historic average p/e), etc., were calculated and stored for over 1,000 firms and replenished as firms merged or otherwise vanished. Stocks were then ranked by selected criteria from best to worst and the ranking normalized at the outset of each quarterly period. For all factors in a time period and for all time periods, one could determine the relative ranking for each company against a universe of 1,000 stocks. The data base remains unique in a sea of competitors supplying historic information on securities. The normalized rank data then fed a simulation model.

The simulation is extremely good by practitioner standards and more flexible and more realistic than any academic model I have seen. The primary judgment input calls for specifying weights for specific factors to determine a composite rank for each. The composite rank in turn is determined by the weighted individual normalized factor rank for each security in each time period. The composite company ranks are ordered from best to worst at the outset of each quarter of the simulation. One may also eliminate any stock from further considerations using personalized constraints to avoid selecting, say, securities with inadequate liquidity or undesirable financial risk. The simulation draws on the composite rankings of the "working" universe to undertake its test.

The simulation proper is sales-driven. New securities are only purchased to replace securities sold. The number of securities in the portfolio remains constant over time and must be prespecified along with the initial dollar size of the portfolio. Purchases are always equal-weighted. Both the size of the working universe and the equal-weighting system usually cause a small-firm effect on the portfolio relative to the S&P 500 Index. The sales criteria, based on the composite company ranks, and perhaps some new exclusion rules applied only to stocks held, are no doubt the most important judgment ingredients. Purchases are always made from the top of the composite list ranking from stocks not already owned. "Trimming" and "filling" rules are usually added. Prespecified transaction costs are levied, including the initial portfolio, and composite transaction costs are monitored. Dividends are automatically reinvested at the end of the quarter. The model holds cash to a minimum while achieving its initial equal-weighting objectives very closely. And so on.

The model then spins out performance by quarters, comparing portfolio returns against the S&P 500 Index as it goes. The performance of the universe net of exclusions can also be monitored. The model can print out reams of detail, including the detailed performance of each security in each and every quarter and why it was purchased or held, why it was sold, if at all, and what its performance was.

The process is experimental trial-and-error testing and combinations are enormous. Models, of course, act automatically. In practice, decisions can be made daily from live (rapidly updated) data bases. Most users employ modest judgment in implementing the system, or simply use it as a strategy screening device for new buys and old portfolios.

At the time Glenn Kent learned about the system, little testing had yet been undertaken and run and printout times were much slower than is true today. After considerable testing and encouraging results, a 200-stock portfolio using temporary ranking weights was initiated in late 1980 and full-quarterly-data actual results are available from then on. After further studies the portfolio was abruptly cut to 100 securities, its present size, at the outset of 1982. Experimentation continued and the current decision rules and methods were adopted at the beginning of 1983. Both changeovers, unlike the initial startup, caused underperformance for about nine months for reasons now understood. The actual data used in this study goes live from 1983 forward. The specific decision rules, weights, etc., are confidential, but reflect the first of the factors spelled out at the outset of this part of this section. The raft of academic and business testing of these ideas that is now available make this strategy more understandable.

The Abel-Noser data base has been used to test and design a variety of other strategies, both active and passive, by others (reportedly with success). Kent has left Honeywell to form Kent Associates, and is now marketing this product along with another (similar to our development fund) to pension clients.

Data here runs from July 1973 to June 1986.

Analysis

In the following section, we will compare the performance of each of the three managers against the S&P 500 bogey (using Ibbotson and Sinquefield inputs through 1985, extended through reliable public sources thereafter) and a composite equal-weighted strategy (rebalanced quarterly) consisting of the three managers using quarterly inputs from 1974 (the period where all managers have common history). In particular, 1973 was an extremely difficult year for active managers, and where feasible we will add earlier comparisons for two managers. All data is after transactions costs except the S&P's data. The composite index does not charge for rebalancing but these costs would be minor.

Table 1 reports the annual compound rate of return for all strategies for the 12½ years. All these managers and the composite provide very attractive excess return for the common period. Differences are not material.

Returns on all strategies are excellent relative to the S&P 500. The three strategies except Wells all had more variability than the S&P. The variability of the composite results is surprisingly low. The addition of one year makes a big comparison difference for Wells Fargo and the S&P in particular. The Timing strategy had exceptionally fine relative performance during the final throes of the "nifty-fifty" market. Index-Plus also did well for six months. Both were uncommon events!

[Charts 1 through 4][1] show the annual compound growth of each strategy and the S&P 500 Index for 12.5 years. The accumulated wealth-index differential

TABLE 1
Annual Compound Total Rate of Return *(four strategies; Jan. 1974 to June 1986)*

	Annual Compound Total Returns					
	12.5 Years			*Full Period*		
Fund	*Fund*	*Index*	*Difference*	*Fund*	*S&P 500*	*Difference*
Index-Plus	19.35%	13.08%	6.27%	18.35%	12.12%	6.23%
Brignoli	20.24	13.08	7.16			
Wells Fargo Timing Strategy	19.58	13.08	6.50	18.30	10.65	7.65
Composite Equal-Weighted Index	19.91	13.08	6.83			

Note: Index-Plus = 13 years; Wells Fargo Timing = 13.5 years. Index-Plus uniquely deducts a 2 percent transaction cost for initial funding.

[1]Charts referred to in the original document have been omitted for space reasons.

quickly becomes large and continues to widen over the period. [Charts 5 through 8] show the relative growth of each strategy compared with the S&P 500 Index (strategy wealth minus S&P wealth). These later charts rise when performance is better than the S&P 500 Index. Down periods provide a quick overview of the magnitude and duration of difficult times for a strategy.

Table 2 shows quarterly return data for the period in the context of arithmetic statistics. These are the only non-overlapping data available for meaningful analysis. Quarterly standard deviations do not provide a useful time-adjusted basis for projecting annual (underestimated) or four-year (overestimated) standard deviations.

[Charts 9A to 12A] show the annual moving total rates of return for each strategy and the S&P 500 Index for the period December 31, 1974, to June 30, 1986. The accompanying [Charts 9B to 12B] record the return differentials for these data. All three strategies record one-year periods of underperformance, which is to be expected from any good manager. The Wells Fargo timing strategy generally has its best performance in weak S&P 500 Index markets. The magnitude of differences can be very sizable. Strong defensive characteristics in bad equity markets are very desirable for a large multi-managed equity portfolio. Index-Plus and Brignoli also experience relatively short periods of underperformance. These problem periods seem less related to general market conditions than to difficult periods unique to their strategy. By overlaying these charts, one can see it is relatively uncommon for two managers to experience underperformance concurrently. Often, at least one is having strong offsetting performance. Diversification would seem likely to add downside stability in most markets, and would seem to further stabi-

TABLE 2

Quarterly Analysis (Arithmetic) *(four strategies and the S&P 500 Index; Jan. 1974 to June 1986)*

	Index-Plus	*Brignoli*	*Wells Fargo Timing Strategy*	*Composite Index*	*S&P 500 Index*
12.5 Years					
Average	4.96%	5.15%	4.47%	4.96%	3.51%
Std. deviation	9.51	9.50	6.53	8.16	8.79
Coefficient of variation	1.92x	1.84x	1.37x	1.64x	2.50x
13 Years					
Average	4.77%		4.67%		3.29%
Std. deviation	9.82		6.43		8.79
Coefficient of variation	2.67x		1.37x		2.60x
13.5 Years					
Average			4.48%		2.95%
Std. deviation			6.38		8.80
Coefficient of variation			1.42x		2.98x

Note: Arithmetic statistics can be misleading. Skewing and kurtosis runs generally higher with all the attendant, meaningful problems intact.

lize performance. Indeed it does. As the composite data show, there were only three (scattered) years of underperformance (from the 47 observations) in the sample period; all three were extremely strong years for the S&P 500. Collective performance in down markets was exceptionally strong generally. The statistical odds (law of permutation) of this consistent performance happening by chance are infinitesimal. Limited 1973 experience suggests that it would have continued in every bad management year, and the composite index showed particularly strong performance in the 1970s when inflation was running at its worst. As shown best in [Chart 12A] the general stability of performance in the face of very volatile market conditions is just short of amazing.

The annual arithmetic statistics for all one-year periods (modestly overlapping) reinforce these conclusions, as shown in Table 3.

[Charts 13A and B to 16A and B] are designed the same way as the previous set except that they record annual compound rates of return over four-year periods—all those that occur between December 31, 1977, to June 30, 1986 (35 in all). The Wells Fargo market timing strategy has the most serious negative returns over four-year periods. These are clustered in years when the market is doing well relative to surrounding periods. Index-Plus has barely perceptible negative performance (0.1 percent per year) in one strong market period, when poor equal-weighted performance from one of its three criteria converged with unusual adverse start-up costs for the portfolio to go live (seemingly a random change from a relatively

TABLE 3
Annual Total Rates of Return *(four strategies and the S&P 500 Index; Dec. 30, 1974, to June 30, 1986, modestly overlapping data)*

	Index-Plus	*Brignoli*	*Wells Fargo Timing Strategy*	*Combined Strategy*	*S&P 500 Index*
Annual					
Average	21.18%	22.43%	20.51%	21.38%	15.24%
Std. deviation	18.25	18.67	15.42	16.40	17.92
Coefficient of variation	0.86x	0.83x	0.75x	0.77x	1.18x
Differences (Fund less S&P 500) Annual Data					
Average	5.94%	7.20%	5.27%	6.14%	
Std. deviation	6.41	5.43	9.90	4.23	
Coefficient of variation	1.08x	0.75x	1.88x	0.69x	

Full Period	***13 Years***			***13.5 Years***		
	Index-Plus	*S&P 500*	*Diff.*	*Wells Fargo Timing Strategy*	*S&P 500 Index*	*Diff.*
Average	19.44%	13.52%	5.92%	19.16%	12.43%	6.73%
Std. deviation	19.93	19.57	6.42	15.52	19.94	11.01
Coefficient of variation	1.03x	1.45x	1.09x	0.81x	1.60x	1.64x

neutral draw). Brignoli had unusually stable results around a high mean. Only the Wells Fargo timing strategy shows larger volatility than the market index but around a higher mean. Skewing and kurtosis (surprising to some) still distort the data; downside risk tends to be overstated in standard deviation calculations, for example. The composite portfolio can absorb the added volatility of the index fund. Of the four strategies, Index-Plus tends to show the least annual volatility. Brignoli is more consistent in its margin of victory over the S&P 500 Index. 1973 would have added to the Wells Fargo Index's luster. Index-Plus had a good relative last half for 1973 although it tarnished its average return slightly. The good relative performance of the composite index through the years of high inflation would have also helped. Managers should probably value this sort of performance highly, given how their actuaries view results.

Table 4 records the seriously overlapping results for the four-year periods. It confirms conclusions reached already.

Table 5 reports the performance of these strategies in protracted bull and bear markets, with reference to the S&P 500 Index. The strong downside protection of the Wells Fargo timing strategy and its effect on the composite strategy are clearly in evidence. Neither of the other strategies tend to work poorly in down markets either, an added plus for the composite index.

The Wells Fargo timing strategy has its problems in protracted bull markets but was not as harmful overall as most people might anticipate. The other strategies tend to have very good market performance in bull markets. The composite port-

TABLE 4
Four-Year Annual Compound Total Return *(four strategies and the S&P 500 Index; Dec. 31, 1977, to June 30, 1986, overlapping data)*

	Index-Plus	*Brignoli*	*Wells Fargo Timing Strategy*	*Composite Index*	*S&P 500 Index*
Comparable 12.5 Years (overlapping) Data					
Average	18.77%	20.38%	18.78%	19.42%	13.15%
Std. deviation	4.43	4.90	7.53	4.83	5.51
Std. average	0.24x	0.24x	0.40x	0.25x	0.42x
Differences					
Average	5.63%	7.23%	5.63%	6.27%	
Std. deviation	3.45	1.71	4.55	1.41	
Std. dev./avg.	0.61x	0.24x	0.81x	0.22x	

Full Data	***13 Years***			***13.5 Years***		
	Index-Plus	*S&P 500*	*Diff.*	*Wells Fargo Timing Strategy*	*S&P 500*	*Diff.*
Average	18.42%	12.56%	5.86%	18.19%	11.97%	6.22%
Std. deviation	4.60	5.98	2.80	7.35	6.28	4.67
Std. dev./avg.	0.25x	0.47x	0.48x	0.40x	0.52x	0.75x

TABLE 5
Three Fund Managers and Two Indices: Comparative Performance in Up and Down Markets *(Jan. 1, 1974, to June 30, 1986)*

	Quarters	*Index-Plus*	*Brignolí*	*Wells Fargo & Asset Mix*	*Comp. Index*	*S&P 500 Index*
Up						
10/74 to 12/76	9	41.79%	42.09%	26.33%*	36.69%	31.71%
1/78 to 3/81	13	25.12	25.00	19.47	23.36	17.59
4/82 to 6/83	5	40.32*	52.49	51.28	48.03	45.65
7/84 to 6/86	8	39.29	34.98	38.70	37.73	33.45
Average		34.61	35.26	29.70	33.32	28.49
Down						
1/74 to 9/74	2	−28.77%	−34.81%	−2.21%	−22.46%	−41.11%
1/77 to 12/77	4	0.01	3.64	−7.03	−1.17	−7.18
4/81 to 3/82	4	−6.24	−10.50	11.23	−2.06	−12.93
7/83 to 6/84	4	−6.84*	5.86	−5.60*	−2.29	−4.60
Average		−9.87	−8.65	−1.08	−6.37	−16.07

*Failed to beat the S&P 500 Index.

folio achieves the best of both worlds. It does very well in down markets yet it still looks good in up markets. One wins more by not losing as much in bad markets but these gains are magnified when one can also win in up markets. Its composite performance over time is relatively strong. Because of the equity-only managers' styles, of Index-Plus and Brignoli, these strategies will probably perform most well (and do) when the small-firm effect is working at its best. The small funds' performance over the last three-plus years when active managers on average lost ground to the S&P 500 (and more surprising, to the Dow Industrial) overall was poor. This was the worst run for the small managers' group since the "nifty-fifty" market. One need only look at the four-year record (since early 1983) of the NASDAQ Industrial Index, considered by many small-cap managers to be the best reflection of a reasonable target, for them to see this.

When good return potential and bottomside risk protection are important to managers, a combination of "non-index" indexers appears to be worthy of a good close look. All three managers look attractive and in composite their performance looks even better.

Manager References

Brignoli, Curley & Roberts Associates
15 West 39th St.
New York, N.Y. 10018
212/869-4233
Contact Person: Duane G. Roberts

Index-Plus
Abel/Noser Corp.
90 Broad Street
New York, N.Y. 10004
212/344-2610

Wells Fargo Investment Advisors
50 California Street
MAC 0119-112
San Francisco, Calif. 94163
415/434-6000

Part II

Performance Evaluation

Performance Management Company

MEMORANDUM

TO: Martin Beck, President
FROM: William Hines, Research Department
SUBJECT: An Analysis of Polaris Fund's Performance, 1962–1971

At your request, I have performed some analyses of the performance of Polaris Fund over the period from just after its inception to the middle of 1971. The data I have used include quarterly per-share net asset value, dividends, and capital gains distributions for Polaris Fund, quarterly prices for the Standard & Poor's 500 Stock Index and quarterly dividends on this index, and the yield on three-month Treasury bills; I have also had access to the June 1971 portfolio of Polaris Fund and have used it as additional evidence in trying to explain the reasons for the fund's performance. As I indicate later in the report, additional evidence would have been useful in performing these analyses, but I believe I have sufficient data to reach useful conclusions in which I can have confidence.

I have divided my analysis into three separate sections, aimed at answering three questions: (1) On the basis of a reasonable standard of performance, has Polaris Fund's performance over the entire period studied been superior, neutral, or inferior; (2) Is there a discernible difference in the fund's performance before

---

This material has been adapted with revision from a memorandum prepared for a firm which remains anonymous. The name of the fund and of the persons involved have been disguised. Reproduced with permission.

and after its portfolio manager changed; and (3) To the extent that there is such a difference, is it possible to suggest any reasons for it? I consider each of these questions in turn in the next three sections.

I. Polaris Fund's Overall Performance: 1962:1–1971:2

To measure Polaris Fund's performance during this period, I have relied on measurement techniques recommended by the Bank Administration Institute (BAI) in its 1968 report on the measurement of pension fund performance. These techniques have come into increasing use in the investments industry and are, in my view, valid when applied to mutual funds as well as to pension funds.

The foundation of the BAI procedures is to compare the return (capital gains plus dividends) of the fund to the return of an unmanaged, "yardstick" portfolio of equal risk; or, if the fund's risk level has been varied, to a yardstick portfolio whose risk level is constant and equal to the average level for the fund. Two different measures of risk are suggested, and the yardstick portfolio corresponding to each provides the basis for a measure of a different dimension of the fund's and its manager's performance:

1. Market-related risk or market volatility: to the extent that the fund outperforms a yardstick with equal market volatility, the portfolio manager has been able to (*a*) change his market exposure so as to increase it in rising markets and decrease it in falling markets, or (*b*) pick "winners" that outperform the market; that is, he has produced superior market timing or item selection.
2. Total risk or total dispersion of return: total risk or dispersion contains both market volatility (No. 1) and uncertainty of return, which could have been diversified away but which the portfolio manager presumably took on in an effort to achieve better market timing or item selection; thus, it is possible for a portfolio manager to achieve superior market timing/item selection but to have managed such an undiversified portfolio that, when performance is measured against a total-risk yardstick, it is inferior.

The yardstick portfolio, regardless of which risk measure is used, is constructed from the same constituents: the return (including dividends) on the S&P 500 Index (or a similar broad market index) and a "riskless" asset such as Treasury bills. To create a yardstick portfolio whose risk level is less than the S&P Index, the investment is divided between the S&P and Treasury bills; for a yardstick with risk level greater than the S&P, funds are assumed borrowed at the Treasury bill rate (i.e., a negative investment in Treasury bills) and the investment in the S&P Index is thereby leveraged. The BAI argues that such a strategy—leveraging or deleveraging an investment in the S&P Index to provide the appropriate risk level—could, to a close approximation, have been followed by an investor and, therefore, provides an appropriate unmanaged yardstick against which to judge the efficacy of the portfolio manager's decisions.

I have applied the BAI procedures to Polaris Fund's quarterly return over the period of first-quarter 1962 to second-quarter 1971, constructing yardstick portfolios with risk levels equal to Polaris Fund's market volatility and its total risk (dispersion of return). As indicated in Table 1, Polaris Fund's market volatility for this period was 1.18 as compared with 1.0 (by definition) for the S&P Index. Because Polaris Fund's market volatility exceeded the S&P's, the yardstick portfolio is based on borrowing and leveraged investment in the S&P Index; specifically, such a yardstick portfolio is based on a strategy of borrowing 18 percent and investing 118 percent in the S&P Index.

The actual quarterly returns for this yardstick portfolio are shown in column 5 of Table 2. As an example of how these returns have been computed, consider the fourth quarter of 1962, during which the S&P Index returned 13.1 percent and Treasury bills, .73 percent on a quarterly basis. For this quarter the return on the yardstick portfolio with risk level equal to Polaris Fund's market-related risk (volatility) was

$$1.18 \times 13.1\% + (-.18) \times .73\% = 15.3\%$$

as shown in column 5. Also shown in Table 2, column 7, is the amount by which Polaris Fund's return (column 2) exceeded or fell short of this yardstick portfolio's return in each quarter. Again for 1962:4, Polaris Fund's return (6.9 percent) was 8.4 percent below the yardstick portfolio's.

As indicated earlier, the amount by which Polaris Fund's return exceeds the yardstick portfolio with equal market volatility is a measure of the fund manager's item selection. This difference ("excess return") is shown quarterly in column 7,

TABLE 1
Summary Performance Data for Polaris Fund and for S&P 500 Index

	Polaris Fund	*S&P 500*
Average quarterly return		
(Capital gains and dividends)	5.7%	2.0%
Volatility: All markets	1.18	1.0
Up markets	.31	1.0
Down markets	1.49	1.0
Standard deviation of quarterly return	12.9	7.3
Polaris Fund quarterly average return in excess of S&P Index— Treasury bills strategy with same *market volatility* (See Table 2 for details):		
Entire period	3.6	—
1962:1–1968:3	5.8	—
1968:4–1971:2	−2.3	—
Polaris Fund average quarterly return in excess of S&P Index—Treasury bills strategy with same *standard deviation* (See Table 2):		
Entire period	3.1	—
1962:1–1968:3	4.9	—
1968:4–1971:2	−2.3	—
Fund diversification: squared correlation between fund return and S&P 500 Index	.46	—

TABLE 2

Detailed Quarterly Performance Data for Polaris Fund and S&P 500 Index *(representative quarters, 1962–1971)*

(1) *Year and Quarter*	*(2)* *Polaris Fund Return*	*(3)* *S&P Return*	*(4)* *T-bills Return*	*(5)* *Return of S&P with Same Mkt. Volatility*	*(6)* *Return of S&P with Same Std. Deviation*	*(7)* *Excess Return (2) − (5)*	*(8)* *Excess Return (2) − (6)*
1962:1	8.4%	−2.1%	.63%	−2.6%	−4.1%	11.0%	12.5%
2	−25.6	−20.5	.68	−24.3	−35.9	−1.3	10.3
3	1.1	3.7	.68	4.2	5.9	−3.1	−4.8
4	6.9	13.1	.73	15.3	22.1	−8.4	−15.2
1963:1	12.0	6.4	.73	7.4	10.5	4.6	1.5
2	14.5	5.0	.73	5.8	8.1	8.7	6.4
3	18.9	4.2	.78	4.8	6.7	14.1	12.2
4	10.0	5.4	.83	6.2	8.7	3.8	1.3
1964:1	9.5	6.1	.90	7.0	9.9	2.5	−.4
2	3.8	4.2	.90	4.8	6.6	−1.0	−2.8
3	2.9	3.8	.88	4.3	5.9	−1.4	−3.0
4	5.3	1.4	.88	1.5	1.8	3.8	3.5
1965:1	22.6	2.4	.98	2.7	3.4	20.0	19.2
2	−9.8	−1.6	1.00	−2.1	−3.5	−7.7	−6.3
3	28.7	7.7	.98	8.9	12.6	19.8	16.1
4	31.0	3.5	1.00	4.0	5.3	27.1	25.7
1966:1	20.0	−2.7	1.05	−3.4	−5.4	23.4	25.4
2	0.9	−4.2	1.20	−5.2	−8.1	6.1	9.0
3	−13.7	−8.8	1.18	−10.6	−16.1	−3.1	2.4
4	4.3	5.9	1.30	6.7	9.3	−2.4	−4.9
1967:1	29.6	13.2	1.33	15.3	21.8	14.3	7.8
2	18.1	1.3	1.15	1.3	1.4	16.8	16.7
3	16.4	7.5	1.35	8.6	12.0	7.8	4.4
4	3.7	.5	1.13	.4	.0	3.3	3.7

(1)	(2)	(3)	(4)	(5)	(6)	(7)	(8)
1968:1	−6.5	−5.7	1.28	−7.0	−10.8	.5	4.3
2	6.9	11.2	1.28	13.0	18.4	−6.1	−11.5
3	10.3	3.9	1.45	4.3	5.7	6.0	4.6
4	0.4	1.9	1.33	2.0	2.3	−1.6	−1.9
1969:1	−8.2	−1.5	1.40	−2.0	−3.6	−6.2	−4.6
2	−5.7	−3.0	1.58	−3.8	−6.3	−1.9	.6
3	1.4	−3.9	1.55	−4.9	−7.9	6.3	9.3
4	11.2	−.3	1.78	−.7	−1.8	11.9	13.0
1970:1	−12.6	−1.8	1.93	−2.5	−4.5	−10.1	−8.1
2	−22.7	−18.0	1.75	−21.5	−32.4	−1.2	9.7
3	9.2	16.9	1.78	19.6	27.9	−10.4	−18.7
4	0.5	10.4	1.60	12.0	16.8	−11.5	−16.3
1971:1	11.7	9.7	1.30	11.2	15.8	.5	−4.1
2	0.4	.2	.85	.1	−.3	.2	.7
Averages	5.7	2.0	1.15	2.1	2.6	3.6	3.1

Column Explanations:

(1) Year and quarter to which returns correspond.
(2) Quarterly return for Polaris Fund (capital gains plus dividends).
(3) Quarterly return for S&P 500 Index (capital gains plus dividends).
(4) Return, reduced to quarterly rate, of a 3-month Treasury bill bought at beginning of period.
(5) Quarterly return on an investment strategy combining borrowing at Treasury bill rate and investment in S&P Index to produce a "fund" with *market volatility* equal to Polaris Fund's.
(6) Quarterly return on an investment strategy combining borrowing at Treasury bill rate and investment in S&P Index to produce a "fund" with *standard deviation* of return equal to Polaris Fund's.
(7) Quarterly return of Polaris Fund in excess of S&P-Treasury bills strategy with same *market volatility*.
(8) Quarterly return of Polaris Fund in excess of S&P-Treasury bills strategy with same *standard deviation*.

Table 2, and can be averaged to provide an average measure of item-selection performance. As shown in Table 1 and at the bottom of column 7, on the second sheet of Table 2, the average excess return over the entire period measured against this yardstick portfolio is +3.6 percent per quarter, indicating a noticeably superior market timing/item selection capability for the fund during 1962–1971.

The second yardstick portfolio, based on total dispersion of return, can be constructed in a similar manner. I have measured dispersion by the standard deviation[1] of return and have tabulated these risk measures in Table 1. As indicated there, the fund's risk on this measure also exceeded the S&P's, in this case being 12.9/7.3 = 1.73 times as risky. Consequently, the yardstick portfolio based on this risk measure would involve borrowing 73 percent and investing 173 percent in the S&P.

The returns of the yardstick portfolio based on total (standard deviation) risk are shown in column 6, Table 2, and the excess returns of Polaris Fund against this yardstick are shown in column 8 of the same table. Averaged over the entire period, this excess return is +3.1 percent per quarter (see bottom of column 8, Table 2, and the last section of Table 1), indicating that, by this more stringent standard, Polaris Fund's performance was also better than an unmanaged strategy.

A comparison of Polaris Fund's performance on these two yardsticks indicates that the fund's attempts at market timing and item selection during this entire period were more than sufficiently successful to offset the additional level of risk that resulted from the fund's limited diversification. (The limited degree of diversification in the fund is reflected by the fact that its squared correlation with the market is .46, as compared with a value of 1.00 for a fund with complete diversification; this level is relatively low for a mutual fund.) When the fund's performance is charged for this added level of risk, its risk-adjusted performance declines, but only from 3.6 percent to 3.1 percent better than an unmanaged strategy on a quarterly basis. As can be seen from the overall record of Polaris Fund, giving up perfect diversification to exploit market timing and item selection can be an effective strategy if the fund's market timing/item selection capabilities are sufficient to compensate fundholders for the added risk to which such a strategy exposes them.

II. A Comparison of Performance by the Two Fund Managers

We can examine the effect of the change in portfolio managers by comparing the fund's performance during the tenure of each portfolio manager. To do this I have computed the fund's average excess return against both yardstick portfolios for the two periods, 1962:1–1968:3 and 1968:4–1971:2, reflecting the change of management in later 1968.

---

[1]The BAI study suggests the average absolute error as an alternative to the standard deviation. I have chosen the latter measure because it has some conceptually useful properties and because it is somewhat easier to compute. It is unlikely that the results of the analysis are noticeably influenced by the choice between these two measures.

The results of these comparisons are shown in Table 1. Against the unmanaged yardstick portfolio with equal market volatility, Polaris Fund had a substantial positive excess return of 5.8 percent per quarter in the 1962–1968 period, but a negative excess return of 2.3 percent per quarter in the 1968–1971 period. Compared with the unmanaged portfolio with equal total risk, the results are much the same: the fund markedly outperformed the yardstick (+4.9 percent per quarter) in the earlier period but substantially underperformed the yardstick (−2.3 percent) in the later period.

The evidence on this issue is quite compelling. The fund's market timing/item selection, which was somewhat superior over the entire period, was in fact noticeably superior in the earlier period but became inferior in the later period. In the same manner, the fund's total performance degenerated markedly from the earlier to the later period. On the basis of either risk measure, the first portfolio manager appears to have turned in superior performance, while the second manager has an inferior performance record.

Although all these conclusions are subject to statistical error, the magnitude of the shift—particularly in the total performance measure—is so sizable that the results are most unlikely to have been distorted by this type of error; indeed, in the case of the total performance measure, the odds are about 50 to 1 that the performance during the earlier period was superior to the performance in the later period. The change in fund manager appears to have made a marked difference.

III. Reasons for the Decline in Performance

In view of the apparent deterioration in the Polaris Fund's performance, it is worthwhile to explore the causes for this shift. The data I have readily available are not very well suited to answering this question, but they are sufficient to allow me to conduct several studies bearing on this issue. I hasten to add, however, that I feel on somewhat less firm ground in exploring this issue than with the two previous questions.

Since the second period was dominated by adverse markets, I first examined the way the portfolio manager appeared to adjust the fund's market volatility in bull and bear markets. Ideally, one would like the portfolio manager to increase the fund's market exposure (volatility) in up markets and decrease it in down markets. Failure to adjust the fund's market exposure appropriately would be evidence of ineffective market timing and would contribute to its poor performance.

To examine shifts in the fund's volatility, I used regression analysis techniques to estimate volatility in up and down markets. The results, tabulated in Table 1, show a decided shift in volatility between up and down markets, but the shift is completely perverse: volatility is much greater (1.49) in down markets than in up markets (.31). As before, these estimates are subject to statistical error, particularly the estimate of down-market volatility, since there are relatively few quarters of down markets. However, the magnitude of the difference is so great that one can be reasonably sure that down-market volatility exceeds up-market volatility; the odds favoring this conclusion are about 32 to 1.

I have also analyzed some different evidence bearing on the shift of market volatility. Based on the holdings in Polaris Fund's portfolio as of June 1971, I obtained estimates of the market volatility (taken from a report prepared by a large brokerage firm) of each security in the portfolio.[2] I then computed an estimate of the portfolio's market volatility as of that date by weighting each security's volatility by the market value of its holding. The resulting estimate of volatility for the portfolio, 1.34, is somewhat above the overall average, 1.18, despite the fact that the S&P Index declined moderately during the second quarter of 1971. To a degree this evidence supports the findings discussed just above.

Taken together, these pieces of evidence suggest that the management of Polaris Fund's market volatility has been rather unsuccessful. By itself this evidence is equally adverse for both fund managers, but the fund manager during the later period displayed markedly less effective item selection, and this failure, taken together with his poor management of volatility, could explain the deterioration of performance. In any case, it seems apparent that the fund's overall performance in the past could have been—and presumably in the future could be—enhanced by more effective adjustment of market volatility or exposure in the face of changing market conditions.

Finally, I have examined the pattern of excess returns (Table 2, columns 7 and 8) during the tenure of the second fund manager. Although the evidence is unclear, there is some indication that the largest negative excess returns come just after market turns; this is particularly striking in 1970, during which the manager turned in his worst performance by this measure. To the extent that the worst performance comes just after market turns, this evidence is compatible with the conclusion that the fund manager has followed a strategy that has caused him to ride a trend too long and that he has not been sufficiently flexible in his portfolio decisions.

---

[2]In fact, my coverage was only about 90 percent of the portfolio's market value, but the omitted securities should have little effect on the analysis.

T. Rowe Price New Horizons Fund, Inc.

In early July 1977, Tom Barry, executive vice-president and director, as well as active portfolio manager, for the T. Rowe Price New Horizons Fund, Inc., was concerned again about two recurring issues. The New Horizons Fund had, in his mind, continued to achieve its objectives in a superior way, yet this achievement had not been translated into clearly superior market performance. First, although the Fund appeared to be positioned, or nearly positioned, for attractive long-term capital appreciation, performance had been hurt by market factors beyond his control. Second, the Fund's potential, given its performance, was difficult to market so as to attract new investments in the Fund.

The New Horizons Fund had been initiated on June 3, 1960, by T. Rowe Price Associates, Inc. The investment objective of the Fund was long-term growth of capital to be achieved by investing primarily in common stocks of small growth companies with the potential to become major companies in the future. New Horizons was a no-load fund—that is, no "sales" commissions were charged to new investors. As investment adviser, T. Rowe Price Associates, Inc., received an annual fee of ½ of 1 percent for the first $500 million of average daily new assets and ⁴⁄₁₀ of 1 percent of assets in excess of this amount. In return, Price Associates provided investment supervisory and administrative services. Specifically, the Associates obtained and evaluated information relating to the economy, industries, businesses, security markets, and securities; formulated a program for the manager

---

This case was prepared by a Professor of the Colgate Darden Graduate School of Business Administration of the University of Virginia as a basis for class discussion rather than to illustrate effective or ineffective handling of an administrative situation.

of the Fund's assets; recommended securities to be purchased or sold by the Fund; provided the services of the Fund executives and administrators; paid all sales and promotional expenses; and provided administrative support services and facilities. Other costs were borne by the Fund.

T. Rowe Price Associates also managed private funds for individual clients, pension funds, and other types of portfolios in addition to other mutual funds with different objectives. In certain of the client accounts, the portfolio managers might invest a small fraction of the equity funds—say 5 percent—in the New Horizons Fund (with no duplicatory fees).

The underlying philosophy of T. Rowe Price Associates was spelled out in the Fund's prospectus (dated May 1, 1977):

> T. Rowe Price Associates pioneered the Growth Stock Theory of Investing more than 40 years ago, and it continues today as the basis for the Fund's investment approach. Management of the Fund believes that inflation represents a more serious long-term problem for investors than stock market fluctuations and recessionary periods, and that one of the best ways to offset inflation is through ownership of shares of companies whose earnings are growing at above-average rates.
>
> The Growth Stock Theory is based on the belief that when earnings of a company grow faster than inflation and faster than the economy in general over the long term, eventually the stock market should recognize this overall success with a higher valuation of the stock and over the long term the company should be able to raise its dividend.

The prospectus described the investment program of the Fund as follows:

> The Fund invests primarily in a diversified group of small, emerging growth companies. . . . To qualify for investment by the Fund, a company should be expected to demonstrate over the long term at least a 15 percent rate of earnings growth compounded annually. Allowing for those companies which may not meet a 15 percent rate every year, management believes that a 12 percent compound rate is a reasonable expectation for the earnings growth of the overall portfolio. Current income is not a factor in the selection of stocks for investment by the Fund. . . .
>
> Generally, the Fund does not trade in securities for short-term profits but, when circumstances warrant, securities may be sold without regard to the length of time held. The Fund's portfolio turnover rates in the years 1976, 1975, and 1974 were 19.7 percent, 25.8 percent, and 12.9 percent, respectively.

Although certain additional types of investments the Fund could make were also spelled out, most investments by the Fund were in small growth companies. Management defined its concept of a small growth company as follows:

> a . . . company . . . which has demonstrated, or is expected to achieve, long-term growth of earnings, reaching a new high level per share during each succeeding major business cycle. Capable management operating in fertile areas is one of the most important characteristics of a growth company. Such a company should employ sound financial and accounting policies and also demonstrate various features such as effective research, successful product development and marketing, efficient service and pricing flexibility. Management of the Fund seeks to avoid investing in

companies where operating results may be adversely affected by excessive competition, severe governmental regulation, or unsatisfactory labor conditions.

The New Horizons portfolio was unlike those of a venture capital firm. Most of the companies, while small, had an established track record at the time of initial investment. On the other hand, most firms were too small to be considered by typical fund managers, and a good many of the stocks in the portfolio were not likely to be familiar to experienced professionals. For example, about the time the T. Rowe Price Growth Fund took an active interest in an established, more sizable company, the New Horizons Fund would be in the process of reducing its portfolio position in that company.

The New Horizons Fund tended to have a large number of investments. As shown in Exhibit 1, its portfolio as of December 31, 1976, was composed of 85 different stocks (exclusive of stocks being accumulated). These securities were representative of a large diversity of businesses, but not in a way that was necessarily reflective of such yardsticks as the Standard & Poor's 500 Index.

The portfolio contained a number of relatively small positions representing cost positions of well under a million dollars. If experience proved favorable, a position would be increased at a later date. Most of the larger commitments involved firms with longer established track records.

Management was geared to finding over 100 securities in which it might hold a position. Toward this end, it followed the early development of about 300 very small firms. Of these, perhaps 50 might reach the point at which an extensive analysis would be made. About 15 new investments might actually be made in a given year. Firms in the portfolio were, of course, actively followed as well.

Management did not rely on conventional sources of information to identify promising new firms. Rather, they relied on a variety of ways to generate these ideas internally.

The prospectus was quite careful to note:

> Investors should realize that the very nature of investing in small companies involves greater risk than is customarily associated with more established companies. Small companies often have limited product lines, markets or financial resources, or they may be dependent upon one-man management. The securities of small companies may have limited marketability and may be subject to more abrupt or erratic market movement than larger companies or the market averages in general.
>
> While over the long term the Fund has significantly out-performed the Standard & Poor's 500 Stock Index, the Fund's performance during periods of general stock market decline has generally been significantly worse than that of the S&P. Accordingly, the Fund believes that its shares are suitable for investment only by persons who can invest without concern for current income and who are in a financial position to assume above-average investment risk in search of above-average, long-term reward.

Twice in the past when the portfolio had appeared temporarily overvalued, management had closed down taking in new account money.

Mutual funds were required to report results to their shareholders in certain specified ways. An example of a New Horizons report is shown in Exhibit 2. The dark area in the report shows the growth in asset value per share, assuming dividends and capital gains were paid out. The lighter area shows the change in capital values, assuming capital gains distributions were reinvested (without tax) in the fund. This result might be comparable to the performance of a stock index. New Horizons' results were reported after management, transactions, and service costs, whereas an index does not reflect these costs. Over this same period, the Standard & Poor's Index had risen from 56.23 to 100.48, or by 78 percent. The New Horizons gain was larger, as shown in Exhibit 2. Today it is more common to look at results on a total-return basis; that is, to assume reinvestment of all dividend and capital gains income. On this basis, the New Horizons performance showed a gain from $10,000 on June 3, 1960, to $31,374 on March 31, 1977, or a rate of 7.53 percent per year. The total rate of return for the Standard & Poor's 500 Stock Index for the same period was 7.1 percent per year.

Shareholders often looked to shorter-term performance such as shown in Exhibit 3 (taken from the Fund's quarterly report for the first quarter of 1977). The comparatively high volatility of the Fund is evident in this exhibit.

Short-term price movements of the portfolio appeared to afford a very poor indicator of performance toward the long-term objectives of the Fund. Management had consequently devised another basis for measurement. This measure had been explained to stockholders by Mr. Barry at the annual meeting (April 26, 1977) as follows (the exhibit numbers have been changed to refer to case exhibits):

> We are proud of the record of New Horizons portfolio companies, and Exhibit 4 shows the return on invested capital, pretax margin, and annual earnings growth over the last five years. In each case, results are substantially greater than comparable statistics for the average U.S. company. These figures are evidence of excellent management and fertile fields in which New Horizons' companies are operating.
>
> Exhibit 5 shows the Fund's accomplishment versus its goal of 12 percent annual earnings growth for portfolio companies. The growth in net asset value per share of the Fund has not paralleled the earnings growth of its portfolio companies because of portfolio transactions and wildly fluctuating price/earnings ratios. In the past, earnings growth was calculated using the year-end portfolio, which is a valid method, but it minimizes the effect of disappointing earnings of companies which were eliminated throughout the year. We have initiated another method of calculating this figure which averages the earnings growth of January 1 and December 31 portfolios in any given year to weigh equally both the eliminated companies and new holdings. Since inception in 1960, earnings growth of New Horizons' portfolio companies has exceeded the goal.
>
> Earnings growth of portfolio companies is displayed in another way in Exhibit 6, which also shows earnings increases or decreases for S&P 500 companies. In every year except 1973, the change in earnings for the Fund's portfolio has been better than the S&P 500. The degree to which the Fund's companies' earnings exceeded the S&P 500 depends on the time in an economic cycle. For example, in 1976, there was little relative earnings advantage, because industrial companies had a strong

recovery from the 1975 recession, while New Horizons' companies' earnings were growing from a successful 1975.

Management anticipates that 1977 will be an excellent year for the Fund's portfolio companies. In Exhibit 7 the average compound growth in earnings per share (and a one standard-deviation range) were computed from 1961 to 1976 for the New Horizons portfolio and for the Standard & Poor's Index. Not only was the earnings-per-share growth of the New Horizons Fund substantially higher, but it was also much more stable.

The greater earnings-per-share growth stability of the New Horizons companies was not translated into market performance. As shown in Exhibit 8, the capital appreciation of the Fund, while more sizable, was considerably less stable than for the Standard & Poor's 500 Index. Exhibit 9 shows the reason clearly: the price/earnings volatility of the firms in the New Horizons portfolio was high relative to the Standard & Poor's Index. This relative price/earnings ratio had reached its lowest recorded point in early 1977. The relative price/earnings ratios of the New Horizons companies had halved relative to the Standard & Poor's Index and had hurt performance in the short run. Mr. Barry hoped that this phenomenon was temporary and that recovery would commence shortly. Absolute price/earnings ratios for New Horizons' companies are shown in the same exhibit.

The erratic, and recently poor, performance of the New Horizons Fund was not atypical of small growth-company funds. Exhibit 10 contains information from the Wiesenburger Investment Companies Service, considered by management to have the set of objectives most comparable to the New Horizons Fund.

Exhibit 11 shows the quarterly results of the Standard & Poor's Index and of the Fund from near its inception (July 1, 1960) through the first quarter of 1977 (all dividends assumed reinvested). Alphas and betas were computed (logarithmically) based on the equation:

$$\ln [1+(R_p-R_F)] = \alpha + \beta \ln [1+(R_m-R_F)]$$

Standard deviations were also computed. On a risk-adjusted basis, performance was less encouraging than anticipated, as can be seen from the low alpha and the high standard deviation disparity.

Despite the short-term volatility, the strong fundamental character of the New Horizons portfolio had achieved superior long-term performance. Therefore, these modern methods of measuring portfolio performance seemed misleading to Mr. Barry.

Mr. Barry had read several studies that indicated that the foregoing equation was "misspecified" or incorrect; alpha (α) was higher in reality than measured by the model, and beta (β) was lower in *ex post* security market lines. If the model was incorrect, New Horizons' performance was not being measured properly. The formula appeared to significantly overstate return-performance "expectations" for portfolios with high betas such as his fund had.

As Mr. Barry reviewed these data, several thoughts went through his head. Was it right to focus on fundamental performance alone, when market performance was out of phase for protracted periods? He hoped that short-term volatility was not a significant risk consideration for the type of shareholders investing in the New Horizons Fund, but felt that the poor market results for the last five years (see Exhibit 3) must certainly be discouraging for some stockholders and potential investors.

At the end of 1971 the performance record had been outstanding by any comparison, but the potential was low (at least in retrospect). By 1977 the reverse was true; the Fund appeared to be ideally positioned to take advantage of any renewed investor interest in the type of small growth firms sought out by New Horizons' management. The strong fundamental performance of this group suggested the high probability of an upward price/earnings ratio evaluation at some point. Yet it was hard to attract new funds in the face of the record. The dichotomy between performance and potential presented a difficult challenge. Given regulations that sharply restricted speculating about future performance, how should the Fund be marketed to investors, many of whom would not be highly sophisticated?

Finally, Mr. Barry was pondering whether he could or should attempt to minimize the market risks of the portfolio. Diversification into different types of stocks would only dilute the strong fundamental performance and the hope for superior long-term results. Market timing (that is, shifting from stocks into liquid assets when the market outlook for small growth companies was discouraging) seemed more useful than diversification. A market-timing strategy would be difficult to implement, of course, although proper action would be clear in retrospect. Was this a proper course for a special-purpose fund, or was timing the responsibility of shareholders? Did long-term performance override short-term risk if that performance appeared likely to be very attractive? How important was market volatility to New Horizons' shareholders? What were the risks of being out of the short-growth market in part if that market continued to surge? Looking at Exhibit 9, what should the liquid-asset strategy have been, say, in mid-1967, in mid-1971, at the end of 1973, or in mid-1975? How should such a strategy be undertaken? These questions did not seem to be easy to answer.

EXHIBIT 1
Portfolio of Investment in Securities (*December 31, 1976*)

Number of Shares	*Common Stocks—93.3%*	*Average Cost*	*Value*
Building & Real Estate—6.8%			
70,000	FLEETWOOD ENTERPRISES, INC. Nationwide mobile home builder	$ 749,634	$ 1,347,500
425,000	LOWE'S COMPANIES, INC. Building supply and appliance chain	4,715,152	12,750,000
37,000	NATIONWIDE HOMES, INCORPORATED A leading manufacturer of modular homes in the U.S.	551,517	494,875
263,000	RYAN HOMES, INC. A leading home builder, primarily in the Midwest	4,724,463	5,227,125
244,200	THE RYLAND GROUP, INC. Homebuilders operating largely in mid-Atlantic and southeastern states	4,028,162	4,212,450
		$ 14,768,928	$ 24,031,950
Chemicals, Specialty—3.6%			
169,000	BETZ LABORATORIES, INC. A leader in the field of water treatment chemicals and service	$ 5,959,460	$ 4,647,500
255,200	LOCTITE CORPORATION Develops and markets new adhesive processes	3,667,425	4,880,700
27,800	*RAYCHEM CORPORATION Produces irradiated heat shrinkage products and non-melting wire insulation	3,250,522	3,169,200
		$ 12,877,407	$ 12,697,400
Commercial Distribution—7.7%			
18,550	GENUINE PARTS COMPANY Wholesale distributor of auto parts	$ 597,667	$ 695,625
352,400	W. W. GRAINGER, INC. Manufactures and distributes electric motors and related equipment	9,006,259	10,572,000
120,000	KAR PRODUCTS, INC. Distributor of expendable items for the repair and maintenance of automotive and industrial equipment	1,777,524	2,040,000
165,000	LAWSON PRODUCTS, INC. Distributor of expendable items for the repair and maintenance of automotive and industrial equipment	3,467,062	2,145,000
203,000	NATIONAL CHEMSEARCH CORPORATION Manufacturer of maintenance and specialty chemicals	1,378,803	4,643,625
200,000	SNAP-ON TOOLS CORPORATION Produces hand tools for mechanics	6,353,480	6,750,000

EXHIBIT 1 *(continued)*

Number of Shares	Common Stocks	Average Cost	Value
101,100	WAXMAN INDUSTRIES, INC. Marketer of plumbing, electrical, and floor protective products for the do-it-yourself customer	636,038	278,025
		$ 23,216,833	$ 27,124,275
Communications—4.5%			
255,700	*AMERICAN TELEVISION AND COMMUNICATIONS CORPORATION One of the leading systems operators in the CATV field	$ 7,378,859	$ 5,241,850
21,000	*CALIFORNIA MICROWAVE, INC. Communications equipment manufacturer	249,062	399,000
43,000	COMMUNICATIONS INDUSTRIES, INC. Manufactures communications equipment and provides mobile communications services	738,250	720,250
44,000	*COMTECH LABORATORIES INC. Satellite communications equipment	606,937	605,000
250,600	*COX CABLE COMMUNICATIONS, INC. One of the largest cable television companies	4,705,949	4,354,175
296,500	*FARINON ELECTRIC Producer of microwave communications equipment	5,394,685	3,632,125
45,000	PLANTRONICS, INC. Produces headsets and data switching equipment largely for telephone companies	800,637	1,102,500
		$ 19,874,379	$ 16,054,900
Consumer & Business Services—8.2%			
242,000	ALEXANDER & ALEXANDER SERVICES INC. International insurance brokerage and actuarial services	$ 7,588,612	$ 9,226,250
66,400	FLIGHT SAFETY INTERNATIONAL, INC. Pilot training with primary emphasis on corporate pilots making the transition to jets	500,274	813,400
164,500	GENERAL BINDING CORPORATION Equipment for binding and laminating printed materials	2,737,250	1,891,750
75,000	JOHN H. HARLAND COMPANY A major manufacturer and distributor of bank checks	1,799,546	1,396,875
147,900	FRED S. JAMES & CO., INC. A leading insurance broker in the U.S. and abroad	4,340,170	3,013,463
184,000	SERVICEMASTER INDUSTRIES INC. Commercial and residential cleaning service	4,241,603	6,118,000

EXHIBIT 1 *(continued)*

Number of Shares	Common Stocks	Average Cost	Value
197,000	*TYMSHARE, INC. A leading independent remote access computer services company	4,173,400	3,841,500
250,000	UNITED STATES LEASING INTERNATIONAL, INC. Largest independent lessor of capital equipment in North America	3,025,948	2,718,750
		$ 28,406,803	$ 29,019,988
Cosmetics & Toiletries—1.1%			
199,100	MARY KAY COSMETICS, INC. Markets cosmetics through party plan selling in the home	$ 4,115,486	$ 4,056,662
Electronics & Instrumentation—9.4%			
139,700	AUTOMATIC SWITCH COMPANY Major designer and manufacturer of solenoid valves and electrically operated switches	$ 6,609,114	$ 5,518,150
125,900	*DATA GENERAL CORPORATION Manufacturer of minicomputers	2,842,255	5,712,713
38,000	*ESL INCORPORATED Strategic and tactical reconnaissance systems	746,250	779,000
32,000	*FINNIGAN CORPORATION A specialized instrument manufacturer of gas chromatograph/mass spectrometers	765,813	336,000
135,250	*INTEL CORPORATION Designs, manufactures and markets sophisticated electronic circuits used in computers	5,582,492	7,979,750
167,000	MOLEX INCORPORATED Connectors and terminals for electrical products	4,224,152	3,173,000
40,000	*ORION RESEARCH INCORPORATED Manufacturer of analytical inert, primarily specific, ion electrodes	240,000	170,000
100,000	SCOPE INCORPORATED Applied technology company with strong capabilities in pattern recognition	2,299,450	1,250,000
267,500	*TERADYNE, INC. Produces automatic test equipment for the electronics industry	4,514,193	3,811,875
52,500	WATERS ASSOCIATES, INC. Leading manufacturer of liquid chromatography systems	1,536,846	1,640,625
120,000	WATKINS-JOHNSON COMPANY Manufacturer of defense electronic systems and components	2,737,391	2,865,000
		$ 32,097,956	$ 33,236,113

EXHIBIT 1 ***(continued)***

Number of Shares	Common Stocks	Average Cost	Value
Energy—Equipment & Services—6.2%			
135,000	BAKER INTERNATIONAL CORPORATION A major supplier of field tools and services	$ 5,346,223	$ 6,075,000
180,800	CAMERON IRON WORKS, INC. Leading supplier of pressure control equipment to the oil and gas industry	6,465,745	5,876,000
140,000	HELMERICH & PAYNE, INC. Petroleum producer and contract driller	5,045,250	6,282,500
125,000	ROWAN COMPANIES, INC. A leading contract drilling company	4,020,758	3,562,500
		$ 20,877,976	$ 21,796,000
Entertainment & Leisure—1.0%			
135,850	OSHMAN'S SPORTING GOODS, INC. Large chain of retail sporting goods stores	$ 2,900,589	$ 1,719,112
135,000	*VICTORIA STATION INCORPORATED Restaurant chain featuring a nostalgic railroad motif and specializing in prime rib	$ 3,029,125	$ 1,890,000
		$ 5,929,714	$ 3,609,112
Food & Beverage—4.8%			
134,500	PIONEER HI-BRED INTERNATIONAL, INC. A leading producer of hybrid seed corn	$ 2,466,724	$ 3,228,000
387,600	TROPICANA PRODUCTS, INC. Largest producer of non-concentrated orange juice	6,632,086	12,015,600
90,000	*VALMONT INDUSTRIES, INC. Largest producer of center pivot irrigation equipment in the U.S.	2,240,813	1,755,000
		$ 11,339,623	$ 16,998,600
Health Care—4.5%			
90,000	*ALZA CORPORATION Research and development of therapeutic systems	$ 1,906,285	$ 1,192,500
123,000	*COBE LABORATORIES, INC. Hemodialysis products	2,212,875	2,859,750
22,500	*DATASCOPE CORP. Manufactures electronic medical equipment and related disposable products	333,750	455,625
153,000	EXTRACORPOREAL MEDICAL SPECIALTIES, INC. Produces medical equipment, specializing in the manufacture of artificial kidney coils	2,678,050	1,912,500
50,000	IVAC CORPORATION Produces electronic medical instruments	652,500	1,143,750
135,000	NEW ENGLAND NUCLEAR CORPORATION A leading producer of radioactive chemicals and pharmaceuticals	5,552,487	3,948,750

EXHIBIT 1 *(continued)*

Number of Shares	Common Stocks	Average Cost	Value
53,500	PURITAN-BENNETT CORPORATION Specialty medical products for inhalation therapy	2,361,237	1,083,375
125,500	SIGMA-ALDRICH CORPORATION Biochemical and organic products for medical research	3,411,147	2,604,125
40,500	*VALLEYLAB, INC. Produces electrosurgical equipment	279,598	546,750
		$ 19,387,929	$ 15,747,125
Insurance—3.9%			
265,100	AMERICAN INTERNATIONAL REINSURANCE COMPANY, INC. Large international insurance organization	$ 13,025,813	$ 8,350,650
277,000	COLONIAL LIFE & ACCIDENT INSURANCE COMPANY A leading specialty accident insurance company	7,477,309	2,700,750
157,200	MERCURY GENERAL CORPORATION Specialty auto insurer based in California	6,091,750	2,672,400
		$ 26,594,872	$ 13,723,800
Retailing—13.8%			
67,500	BROOKS FASHION STORES, INC. Chain of specialty stores merchandising medium-priced young women's apparel	$ 497,275	$ 683,437
270,000	ECKERD DRUGS, INC. Large discount drug chain in the southeast	2,639,888	4,353,750
187,600	HICKORY FARMS OF OHIO, INC. National chain of specialty food stores	2,552,037	1,641,500
150,000	THE LIMITED STORES, INC. Chain of specialty stores merchandising higher-priced young women's apparel	1,099,000	3,525,000
147,500	LONGS DRUG STORES, INC. California-based chain of discount drug centers	1,084,378	4,996,563
200,000	*MERVYN'S West coast apparel chain	6,982,000	6,400,000
128,000	PAYLESS CASHWAYS, INC. A do-it-yourself building supplies chain located in Southwestern U.S.A.	2,373,055	3,904,000
100,000	PAY 'N PAK STORES, INC. Retailers of do-it-yourself building supplies	1,348,488	1,350,000
127,000	PETRIE STORES CORPORATION Chain of specialty stores merchandising lower-priced young women's apparel	6,528,709	9,588,500
538,500	WAL-MART STORES, INC. Chain of discount and variety stores in rural midwestern communities	2,701,558	8,346,750
268,125	*H. J. WILSON CO., INC. Catalog retailer primarily in southern states	4,784,825	4,088,906
		$ 32,591,213	$ 48,878,406

EXHIBIT 1 ***(continued)***

Number of Shares	Common Stocks	Average Cost	Value
Transportation Services—4.9%			
425,900	BANDAG, INCORPORATED The leading independent producer of tire retreads, supplies, and equipment	$ 10,706,635	$ 7,612,963
326,736	LEASEWAY TRANSPORTATION CORP. Provides full-maintenance leasing and contract trucking services	4,838,997	9,883,764
		$ 15,545,632	$ 17,496,727
Miscellaneous: Consumer—2.5%			
152,200	A. T. CROSS COMPANY Quality pens and pencils	$ 5,361,863	$ 6,088,000
182,375	THE HARTZ MOUNTAIN CORPORATION A leading manufacturer of pet supplies	2,269,100	2,370,875
38,000	TAYLOR RENTAL CORPORATION Rental centers and wholesaler of hardware supplies	555,620	361,000
		$ 8,186,583	$ 8,819,875
Miscellaneous: Technology—5.9%			
82,500	*IONICS, INCORPORATED World's leading producer of brackish water treatment plants	$ 2,429,929	$ 1,258,125
384,600	MILLIPORE CORPORATION Tools and techniques for precision filtration of laboratory and industrial process fluids	4,506,913	8,653,500
240,700	SAMUEL MOORE AND COMPANY Engineered tubular and wire products for industry	4,141,195	2,437,088
118,000	PALL CORPORATION Manufacturer of ultra-fine fiber filters	1,852,746	3,628,500
48,000	*QUANTOR CORPORATION A leading manufacturer of computer output microfilm equipment	224,438	252,000
166,500	TENNANT COMPANY Manufacturer of industrial and commercial floor maintenance equipment	4,216,764	4,495,500
		$ 17,371,985	$ 20,724,713
Undisclosed Stocks Being Acquired—4.5%		$ 15,244,276	$ 15,845,112
Total Common Stocks—93.3%		$308,427,595	$329,860,758
U.S. Government Obligations, Federal Agencies, & Corporate Notes—5.8%			
U.S. Government Obligations—3.5%			
$12,610,000	U.S. Treasury Bills, 4.60% to 5.23%, 2/10/77 to 5/19/77	$ 12,354,226	$ 12,354,226

EXHIBIT 1 *(concluded)*

Number of Shares	Common Stocks		Average Cost	Value
Federal Agencies—1.7%				
$3,000,000	Farm Credit Banks, 5% to 5.10%, 2/23/77 to 3/15/77		$ 2,949,500	$ 2,949,500
$3,000,000	Federal National Mortgage Association, 4.80% to 5%, 3/21/77 to 5/19/77		2,936,545	2,936,545
			$ 5,886,045	$ 5,886,045
Corporate Notes—0.6%				
$970,000	Amoco Credit Corporation, 5¼%, 1/4/77		$ 956,986	$ 956,986
$844,000	Ford Motor Credit Company, 4½%, 1/3/77		844,000	844,000
$500,000	Texas Utilities Company, 4.55%, 1/18/77		498,230	498,230
			$ 2,299,216	$ 2,299,216
Total U.S. Government Obligations, Federal Agencies, & Corporate Notes—5.8%			$ 20,539,487	$ 20,539,487
Total Investments		99.1%	$328,967,082†	$350,400,245
Other Assets Less Liabilities		0.9%	$ 3,188,550	$ 3,188,550
Net Assets		100%	$332,155,632	$353,588,795

*Non-Income Producing
†The total aggregate cost for federal tax purposes: $329,360,274.

EXHIBIT 2

Illustration of an Assumed Investment of $10,000 *(with capital gain distributions accepted in additional shares)*

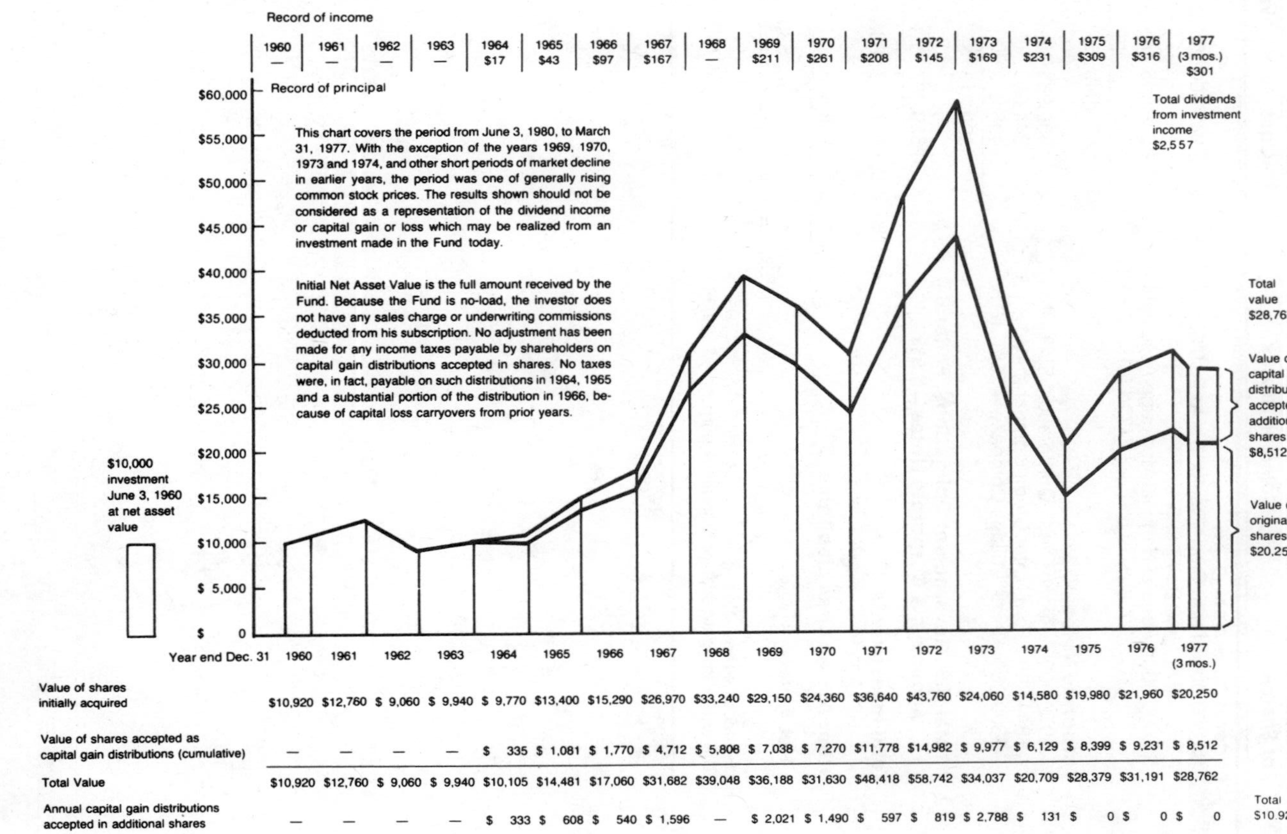

Year end Dec. 31	1960	1961	1962	1963	1964	1965	1966	1967	1968	1969	1970	1971	1972	1973	1974	1975	1976	1977 (3 mos.)	
Value of shares initially acquired	$10,920	$12,760	$ 9,060	$ 9,940	$ 9,770	$13,400	$15,290	$26,970	$33,240	$29,150	$24,360	$36,640	$43,760	$24,060	$14,580	$19,980	$21,960	$20,250	
Value of shares accepted as capital gain distributions (cumulative)	—	—	—	—	$ 335	$ 1,081	$ 1,770	$ 4,712	$ 5,808	$ 7,038	$ 7,270	$11,778	$14,982	$ 9,977	$ 6,129	$ 8,399	$ 9,231	$ 8,512	
Total Value	$10,920	$12,760	$ 9,060	$ 9,940	$10,105	$14,481	$17,060	$31,682	$39,048	$36,188	$31,630	$48,418	$58,742	$34,037	$20,709	$28,379	$31,191	$28,762	
Annual capital gain distributions accepted in additional shares	—	—	—	—	$ 333	$ 608	$ 540	$ 1,596	—	$ 2,021	$ 1,490	$ 597	$ 819	$ 2,788	$ 131	$ 0	$ 0	$ 0	Total $10,923

EXHIBIT 2 *(concluded)*

Results:

With all distributions taken in cash:

Initial investment, June 3, 1960	$10,000
Total value, March 31, 1977	20,250
Dividends from investment income	1,957
Distributions from capital gains	9,020

With capital gain distributions accepted in additional shares and income dividends taken in cash:

Initial investment, June 3, 1960	$10,000
Value of initial investment	20,250
Value of capital gains (cost—$10,923)	8,512
Total value, March 31, 1977	28,762
Dividends from investment income	2,557

With all dividends and distributions accepted in additional shares:

Initial investment, June 3, 1960	$10,000
Value of initial investment	20,250
Value of capital gains (cost—$11,165)	8,665
Value of dividends from investment income (cost—$2,051)	2,459
Total value, March 31, 1977	31,374

EXHIBIT 3
Investment Accomplishment

Changes in Net Asset Value per Share

For the three months ended March 31, 1977, from $7.32 to $6.75 or − 7.8%

For the twelve months ended March 31, 1977, from $7.57 to $6.75 or −10.8

Annual Changes—Principal Value

Year End	*Rowe Price New Horizons Fund*	*Standard & Poor's 500 Stocks*	*Year End*	*Rowe Price New Horizons Fund*	*Standard & Poor's 500 Stocks*
1960*	+ 9.2%	+ 3.3%	1969	− 7.3%	−11.4%
1961	+16.8	+23.1	1970	−12.6	+ 0.1
1962	−29.0	−11.8	1971	+53.1	+10.8
1963	+ 9.7	+18.9	1972	+21.3	+15.6
1964	+ 1.7	+13.0	1973	−42.1	−17.4
1965	+43.2	+ 9.1	1974	−39.2	−29.7
1966	+17.8	−13.1	1975	+37.0	+31.5
1967	+85.7	+20.1	1976	+ 9.9	+19.1
1968	+23.3	+ 7.7			

*From inception 6/3/60 to 12/31/60.

Summary

	1 Year, Ended 3/31/77	**5 Years, Ended 3/31/77**	**10 Years, Ended 3/31/77**	**From Inception 6/3/60 to 3/31/77**
Rowe Price New Horizons Fund	−10.8%	−50.1%	+32.1%	+187.6%
Standard & Poor's 500 Stocks	− 4.2	− 8.2	+ 9.1	+ 75.0

The performance of the Fund for various periods is compared with the performance of the Standard & Poor's 500 Stocks, which is a group of unmanaged securities, widely regarded by investors as representative of the performance of the stock market in general. The Fund results assume the acceptance of all capital gain distributions in additional shares on the dates of reinvestment, but does not assume the reinvestment of income dividends. The accomplishments should be considered in the light of the New Horizons Fund's investment policy and objectives, the characteristics and quality of its portfolio securities, and the periods selected.

EXHIBIT 4
Composite Portfolio Results

	1972	*1973*	*1974*	*1975*	*1976 Estimated*
Return on invested capital	17.4%	17.8%	17.8%	17.6%	19.1%
Pretax profit margin	14.7	14.6	14.0	14.0	15.2
Growth in earnings per share	26.8	24.1	15.3	14.8	28.8

Each of the above three sets of figures is calculated by averaging the weighted results of the beginning and the end of the year portfolio companies.

EXHIBIT 5
New Horizons Fund Accomplishment versus Goal
(index value initialized at 100)

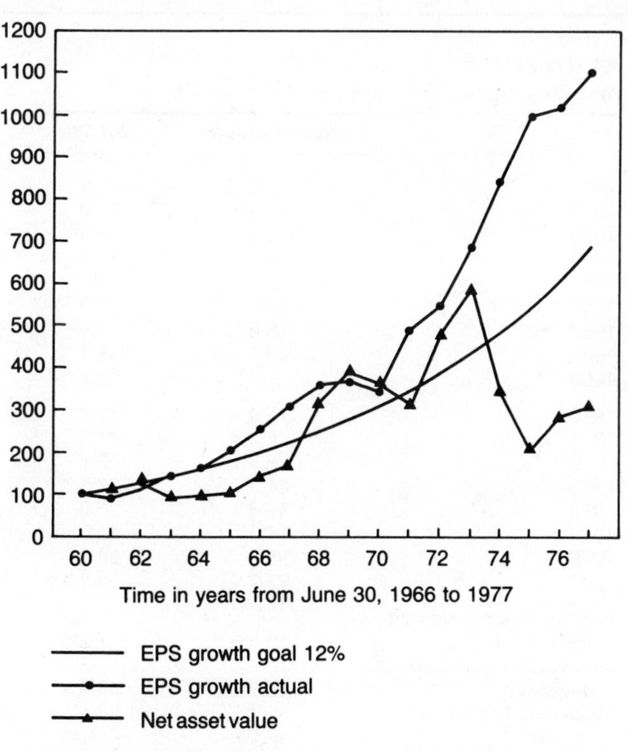

EXHIBIT 6
Earnings Growth: New Horizons versus Standard & Poor's 500 Stock Index (*percentage change over prior year*)

We believe that, in the long run, stocks of companies with superior earnings performance will eventually reflect this growth in superior market performance. In the following table, earnings growth for the Fund is calculated by averaging the weighted earnings growth of the beginning and end-of-year portfolio companies.

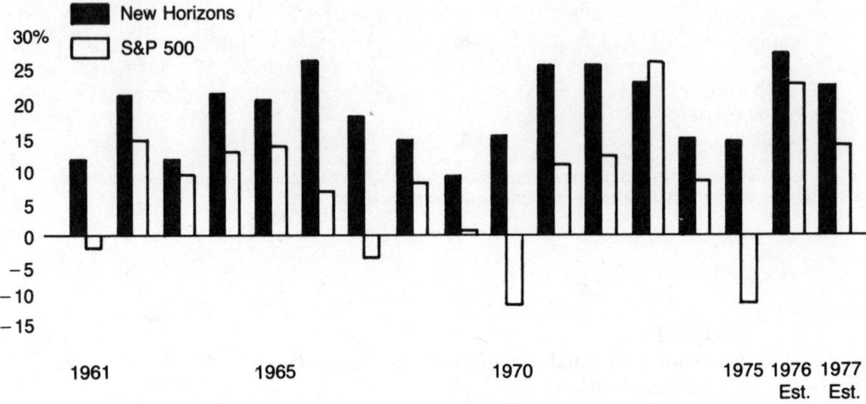

EXHIBIT 7
Weighted Average Earnings per Share Growth

	New Horizons	*S&P 500*
1961	12.0	− 2.4
1962	21.9	15.0
1963	12.0	9.5
1964	22.4	13.2
1965	20.9	14.1
1966	27.3	6.9
1967	18.6	− 4.0
1968	14.7	8.1
1969	9.2	0.3
1970	15.4	−11.2
1971	26.9	11.1
1972	26.8	12.6
1973	24.1	27.1
1974	15.3	8.9
1975	14.8	−10.5
1976	28.8	24.5
1977	23.2	14.2 est.
Average compound rate, 1961–1976	19.3%	7.2%
Mean plus 1 standard deviation	25.7%	18.9%
Mean less 1 standard deviation	13.2%	− 3.4%

EXHIBIT 8
Ratio of New Horizons Fund to Standard & Poor's 500

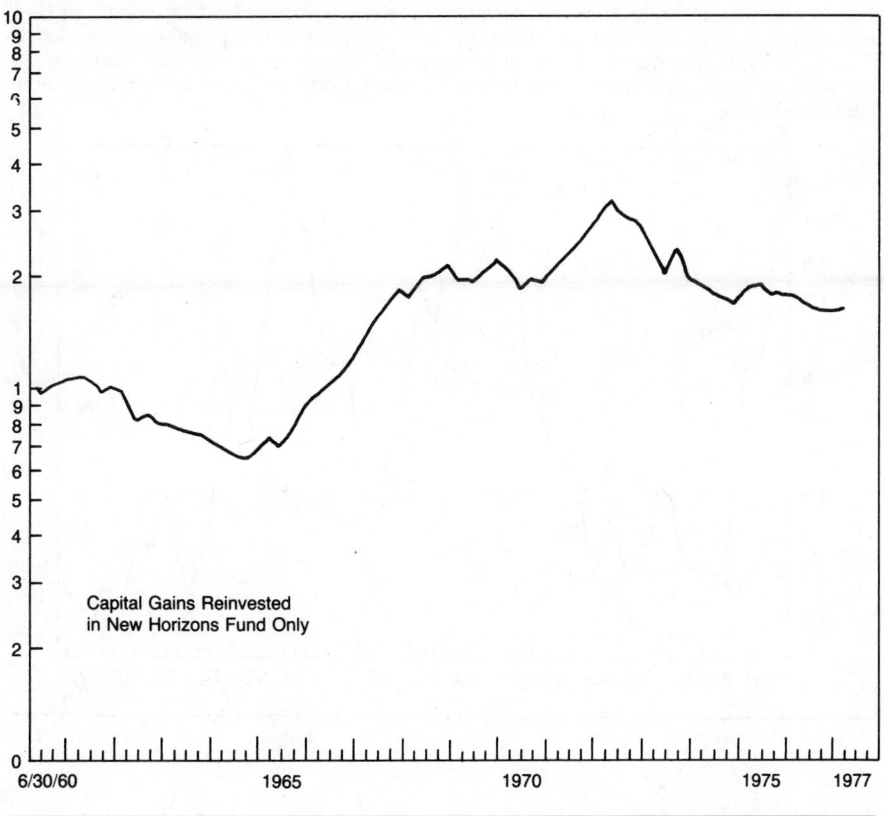

EXHIBIT 9A
New Horizons Fund P/E versus Standard & Poor's 500 P/E

This chart is intended to show the history of the average price/earnings ratios of New Horizons portfolio companies as compared with the price/earnings ratio of Standard & Poor's 500 Index. The market prices of the stocks are as of each quarter-end. Earnings are earnings per share estimated by the Fund's Investment Adviser for 12 months ahead from each quarter-end.

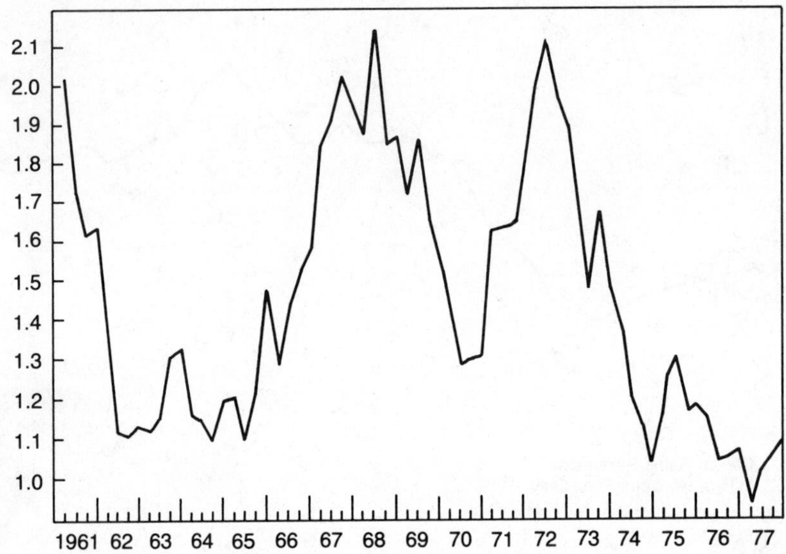

EXHIBIT 9B
New Horizons Fund Price/Earnings Ratio

This chart is intended to show the history of the average price/earnings ratios of portfolio companies as computed quarterly. The market prices of the stocks are as of each quarter-end. Earnings are earnings per share estimated by Fund's Investment Adviser for 12 months ahead from each quarter-end.

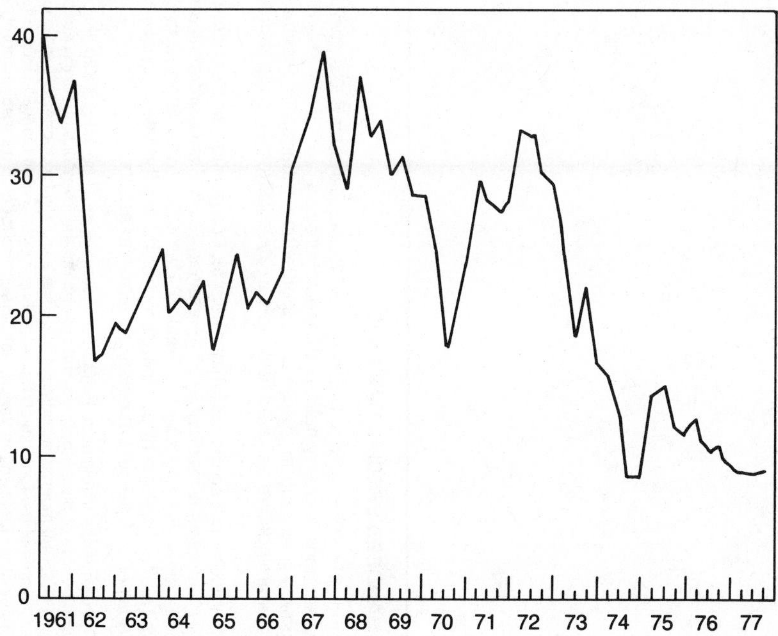

EXHIBIT 10
Competitive Funds

VANCE, SANDERS SPECIAL FUND, INC.

Vance, Sanders Special Fund began operations on November 12, 1968, and is managed by Vance, Sanders & Co., which is also the fund's principal underwriter. The fund may engage in short-term transactions and may hold restricted securities.

"Above-average" capital appreciation is the fund's investment goal, and in pursuit of this objective it stands to assume above-average risk. Investments will be made in companies of varying size whose earnings are believed to be in a relatively strong growth trend or whose shares are believed to be undervalued.

At the end of 1976, the fund had 96.1 percent of its assets in common stocks, of which the major proportion was concentrated in five industry groups: financial services (14.1% of assets), electronics (11.1%), drugs & medical (9.5%), retailing (8.3%), and aircraft & aerospace (7.8%). The five largest individual investments were Ogilvy & Mather International (5.1% of assets), Frank B. Hall & Co. (5%), Globe Life & Accident Insurance (4.5%), Compugraphic Corp. (4.4%), and Payless Cashways (3.9%). The rate of portfolio turnover during the latest fiscal year was 22 percent of average assets. Unrealized depreciation was less than one quarter of 1 percent of calendar year-end assets.

Special Services: The voluntary accumulation plan also serves for dividend reinvestment. Periodic investments must be at least $20. Income dividends are invested at net asset value. Accumulation plan payments may be made by way of pre-authorized checks against the investor's checking account. A 30-day, one-time reinstatement privilege is available for redeeming shareholders. A level payment monthly withdrawal plan is available without charge to accounts worth at least $5,000 at the offering price; variable payments may also be arranged. Shares of the fund which have a net asset value of at least $1,000 and which have been held for at least 30 days may be exchanged at net asset value for those of any other funds in the Vance, Sanders group for a $5 transaction charge. A Keogh Plan, prototype corporate pension and profit-sharing plans, Individual Retirement Accounts, and 403(b) investment accounts are available.

Statistical History

	At Year-Ends								Annual Data				
						Percent of Assets in						Offering Price ($)	
Year	Total Net Assets ($)	Number of Share-holders	Net Asset Value per Share ($)	Offer-ing Price ($)	Yield (%)	Cash & Equiv-alent	Bonds & Pre-ferreds	Com-mon Stocks	Income Div-idends ($)	Capital Gains Distribu-tion ($)	Expense Ratio (%)	High	Low
1976	47,139,249	18,023	7.92	8.66	0.7	4	—	96	0.06	—	0.95	8.66	6.50
1975	40,620,916	19,227	5.91	6.46	1.7	6	—	94	0.11	—	1.04	7.51	4.66
1974	29,903,807	18,810	4.17	4.56	2.9	29	—	71	0.13	—	0.91	7.65	4.46
1973	44,894,168	18,906	6.19	6.77	1.7	14	—	86	0.12	0.31	0.84	11.06	6.47
1972	70,373,975	21,535	9.97	10.90	0.3	3	3	94	0.04	1.31	0.86	13.27	10.21
1971	66,985,602	21,978	10.32	11.50	0.4	9	3*	88	0.05	—	0.55	11.50	8.13
1970	42,715,875	20,100	7.53	8.23	1.0	15	—	85	0.08	—	0.55	8.75	5.29
1969	35,741,182	17,200	7.80	8.53	1.6	9	—	91	0.14	—	0.58	10.08	7.69
1968	19,817,619	5,600	9.08	9.92	—	19	—	81	—	—	—	9.15	9.08

Note: Initially offered 11/11/68 at $10.00 per share.

*Includes a substantial proportion in convertible issues.

Directors: M. Dozier Gardner, V.P.; Landon T. Clay, Pres.; Boardman Bump; William F. Morton; Jack L. Treynor.

Investment Adviser: Vance, Sanders & Co., Inc. Compensation to the Adviser is ½ of 1 percent annually, paid quarterly, of average net assets up to the first $150 million and on a gradually diminishing scale thereafter.

Custodian and Transfer Agent: New England Merchants National Bank, Boston, MA 02108.

Distributor: Vance, Sanders & Co., Inc., One Beacon St., Boston, MA 02108.

Sales Charge: Maximum is 8½ percent of offering price; minimum is 1¾ percent at $1 million. Reduced charges begin at $12,500 and are applicable to subsequent and combined purchases of the fund and any of the other currently offered funds in the Vance, Sanders group on a permanent basis.

Dividends: Income dividends are paid semi-annually, in January and July. Capital gains, if any, will be paid in July.

Shareholder Reports: Issued quarterly. Fiscal year ends June 30. The 1976 prospectus was effective in August.

Qualified for Sale: In all states and D.C.

Address: One Beacon St., Boston, MA 02108.

Telephone: (617) 723-8000.

EXHIBIT 10 ***(continued)***

An assumed investment of $10,000 in this fund, with capital gains accepted in shares, is illustrated below.

Vance, Sanders Special Fund, Inc.

Cost of investment November 12, 1968 $10,000

(Initial Net Asset Value $9,150)

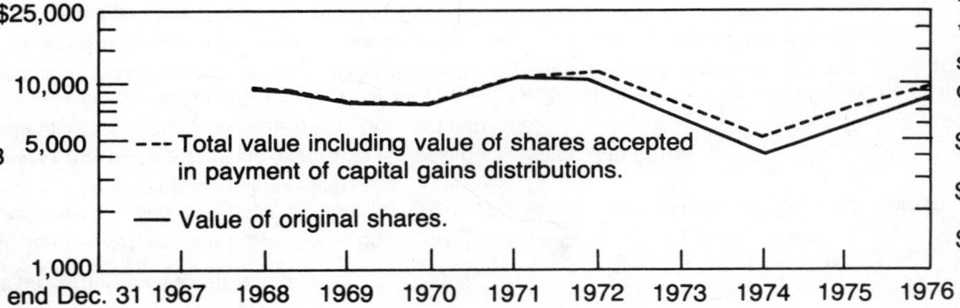

$25,000
10,000
5,000
1,000

--- Total value including value of shares accepted in payment of capital gains distributions.

— Value of original shares.

Year end Dec. 31 1967 1968 1969 1970 1971 1972 1973 1974 1975 1976

December 31, 1976

***(Including $1,428 value of shares accepted as capital gains distributions)**

$9,348 total value of investment*

$7,920 value of original shares

$806 total income dividends

Value of shares initially acquired through investment of $10,000	$9,080	$7,800	$7,530	$10,520	$9,970	$6,190	$4,170	$5,910	$7,920
Value of shares accepted as capital gains distribution (cumulative)	—	—	—	—	1,272	1,116	752	1,065	1,428
Total value	9,080	7,800	7,530	10,520	11,242	7,306	4,922	6,975	9,348
Dividends paid from investment income	—	140	80	50	42	140	153	130	71

Dollar amounts of capital gains distributions accepted in shares were:

1968	$ —	1973	$ 350
1969	—	1974	350
1970	—	1975	—
1971	—	1976	—
1972	1,310	Total	$1,660

Results taking all dividends and distributions in STOCK.

Initial investment at offering price, Nov. 12, 1968	$10,000
Total dividends from income reinvested	847
Total amount invested	10,847
Total value, Dec. 31, 1976	10,417*

*Includes value of shares received in payment of $1,722 capital gains.

Results taking all dividends and distributions in CASH.

Initial investment at offering price, Nov. 12, 1968	$10,000
Total value, Dec. 31, 1976	7,920
Distributions from capital gains	1,620
Dividends from investment income	730

EXPLORER FUND, INC.

Founded in December 1967, Explorer Fund is one of 14 funds comprising the $2 billion Vanguard Group of Investment Companies. A subsidiary, jointly owned by the funds in the group, provides at cost most administrative services, including corporate management, administrative, financial and legal services, including the review and evaluation of advisory and distribution services.

The fund was designed primarily for business executives and managers, professional people, and other investors with substantial resources. Its approach to investing is cited as "aggressive and venturesome" with maximum long-term capital growth as its objective. Effective February 9, 1977, the sale of fund shares was put on a no-load basis.

At the close of 1976, the fund had 89.3 percent of its assets in common stocks in five industry groups: medical technology (37.7% of assets), electronic & data processing (25.5%), basic industry (15%), communications (6.8%), and consumer services (4.2%). The five largest individual investments were Cox Cable (6.8% of assets), Millipore Corp. (6%), Datascope Corp. (5.9%), Gilford Instruments Laboratories (5.8%), and Tennant Co. (4.5%). The rate of portfolio turnover during the latest fiscal year was 11 percent of average assets. Unrealized depreciation was 15.9 percent of calendar year-end assets.

Special Services: An open account arrangement serves for accumulation and provides for automatic dividend reinvestment. Minimum initial investment is $500; subsequent purchases must be $50 or more. Accumulation payments may be made by way of pre-authorized checks drawn against the investor's checking account. Shares of the fund may be exchanged for those of other funds in the group at no charge. Keogh Plans (which may be split-funded); prototype corporate profit-sharing, thrift and pension plans; and Individual Retirement Accounts are also available. An unusual redemption value program issued by the Harleysville Mutual Insurance Co. is available in certain states.

Directors: John C. Bogle, Chmn. and Pres.; Richard F. Corroon; Robert W. Doran; Paul B. Firstenberg; Barbara B. Hauptfuhrer; James T. Hill, Jr.; John T. Jackson; John Jeppson, III; Charles D. Root, Jr.; James O. Welch, Jr.

Investment Adviser: Wellington Management Company. Compensation to the Adviser is at an annual rate of 0.445 percent on the first $250 million of average net assets, scaling down in successive steps to 0.10 percent on assets over $700 million. This base fee may be increased or decreased up to 0.075 percent depending on the fund's performance relative to that of the Standard & Poor's 500 Stock Index.

Expense Ratio: 1.17 percent.

Distributor: None; shares are sold directly by the fund.

Sales Charge: None; shares are offered at net asset value (effective 2-9-77).

Dividends: Income dividends and capital gains, if any, are paid after the close of the fiscal year.

Shareholders Reports: Issued quarterly. Fiscal year ends October 31. The 1977 prospectus was effective in February.

Qualified for Sale: In all states and D.C.

Number of Shareholders: 862.

Address: P.O. Box 1100, Valley Forge, Pa. 19482.

Telephone: (215) 293-1100.

EXHIBIT 10 *(continued)*

Statistical History

	At Year-Ends				*Annual Data*	
Year	***Total Net Assets ($ million)***	***Net Asset Value per Share ($)***	***Offering Price ($)†***	***Yield (%)***	***Income Dividends ($)***	***Capital Gains Distributions ($)***
1976	9.0	17.81	19.46	0.6	0.12	—
1975	9.9	15.35	16.78	0.6	0.10	—
1974	9.1	12.58	13.75	1.8	0.25	—
1973	15.9	19.74	21.57	1.3	0.28	—
1972	27.6	27.12	29.64	—	—	—
1971	29.9	22.40	23.83	0.8	0.185	—
1970	29.3	18.12	19.28	2.4	0.46	—
1969	46.4	24.99	26.59	1.3	0.35	—
1968	58.0	28.69	30.52	1.6	0.48	—
1967	16.6	24.99	26.59	—	—	—

†Sale of shares on no-load basis effective 2/9/77.

NICHOLAS FUND, INC.

Nicholas Fund was organized as the Nicholas Strong Fund in July 1968 and in August of the same year acquired the assets of Bradley Investment Club, a private investment partnership. Initial public offering of its shares was on July 14, 1969. The present name was adopted in 1974. The fund's investment policy stresses capital appreciation as an objective, with income a secondary consideration. Investments for the most part will be in common stocks.

At the close of 1976, the fund had 89.9 percent of its assets in common stocks, the low such position for the year and down from a high of 94.3 percent at the end of March. About 57 percent of assets was concentrated in four industry groups: retail trade (19.9% of assets), industrial products & services (15.2%), foods & food services (12.3%), and consumer products & services (9.8%). The five largest individual common stock investments were Waste Management (7.2% of assets), Gelco Corp. (6.5%), Flight Safety International (6%), Sambo's Restaurants (4.9%), and Pic 'n Save Corp. (4.8%). The rate of portfolio turnover during the latest fiscal year was 26.8 percent of average assets. Unrealized appreciation was 15.2 percent of year-end assets.

Special Services: A voluntary accumulation plan requires an initial investment of $500; subsequent investments may be $100 or more. Automatic dividend reinvestment is available; fractional shares resulting from reinvestment may be paid in cash, at the option of the fund. An Individual Retirement Account Plan and Keogh Plan are available.

Statistical History

	At Year-Ends								Annual Data				
					Percent of Assets in							Offering Price ($)	
Year	Total Net Assets ($)	Number of Share-holders	Net Asset Value per Share ($)	Yield (%)	Cash & Equiv-alent	Bonds & Pre-ferreds	Com-mon Stocks	Income Div-idends ($)	Capital Gains Distribu-tion ($)	Expense Ratio (%)		High	Low
1976	34,256,757	10,700	14.55	0.4	10	—	90	0.059	—	1.01		14.55	11.95
1975	37,832,765	13,600	11.91	0.8	6	—	94	0.101	—	1.08		13.51	8.17
1974	25,515,484	14,600	8.13	0.6	19	—	81	0.047	—	0.91		12.74	7.27
1973	43,583,283	16,345	12.27	—	6	—	94	—	—	0.85		26.16	11.69
1972	103,709,640	16,500	25.96	—	10	—	90	—	0.44	1.06		27.37	20.37
1971	50,029,061	8,400	20.61	—	7	—	93	—	—	1.01		20.61	11.02
1970	6,388,902	3,000	11.11	—	3	2	95	—	—	0.92		15.13	7.37
1969	3,262,530	1,400	14.70	—	9	4	87	—	—	NM		16.35*	11.06*

NM. Not meaningful.

*From July 14, 1969, to end of year.

Directors: Albert O. Nicholas, Pres. & Treas.; Ted D. Kellner; David E. Leichtfuss; Melvin L. Schultz.

Investment Adviser: Nicholas Company, Inc. Compensation to the Adviser is .60 percent annually of the average monthly net assets up to $50 million, and ½ of 1 percent on assets over $50 million.

Custodian, Transfer and Dividend Disbursing Agent: First Wisconsin Trust Company, Milwaukee, WI.

Distributor: None; shares are sold directly by the fund.

Sales Charge: None. Minimum purchase is $500; subsequent purchase must be at least $100. There is a 1 percent redemption fee for shares held six months or less.

Dividends: Income dividends and capital gains, if any, are paid annually within two months after the close of the fund's fiscal year.

Shareholder Reports: Issued quarterly. Fiscal year ends March 31. The 1976 prospectus was effective in July.

Qualified for Sale: In all states and D.C., except AL, ID, IA, KS, KY, ME, NH, ND, OK, and VT.

Address: 312 East Wisconsin Ave., Milwaukee, WI 53202.

Telephone: (414) 272-6133.

EXHIBIT 10 ***(continued)***

An assumed investment of $10,000 in this fund, with capital gains accepted in shares, is illustrated below.

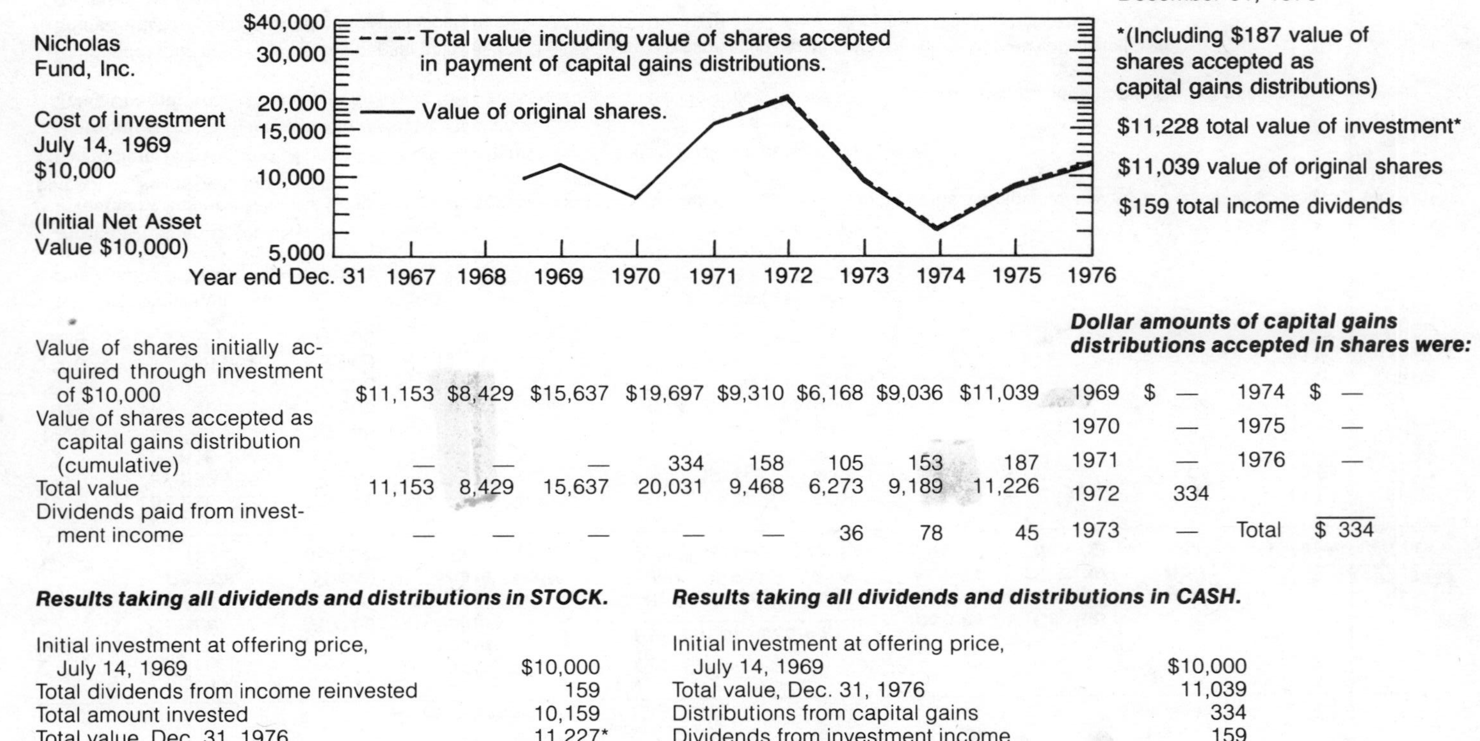

Value of shares initially acquired through investment of $10,000	$11,153	$8,429	$15,637	$19,697	$9,310	$6,168	$9,036	$11,039
Value of shares accepted as capital gains distribution (cumulative)	—	—	—	334	158	105	153	187
Total value	11,153	8,429	15,637	20,031	9,468	6,273	9,189	11,226
Dividends paid from investment income	—	—	—	—	—	36	78	45

Dollar amounts of capital gains distributions accepted in shares were:

1969	$ —	1974	$ —
1970	—	1975	—
1971	—	1976	—
1972	334		
1973	—	Total	$ 334

Results taking all dividends and distributions in STOCK.

Initial investment at offering price, July 14, 1969	$10,000
Total dividends from income reinvested	159
Total amount invested	10,159
Total value, Dec. 31, 1976	11,227*

*Includes value of shares received in payment of $334 capital gains.

Results taking all dividends and distributions in CASH.

Initial investment at offering price, July 14, 1969	$10,000
Total value, Dec. 31, 1976	11,039
Distributions from capital gains	334
Dividends from investment income	159

PUTNAM VOYAGER FUND, INC.

Organized in June 1968, Putnam Voyager Fund is subtitled a "speculative" mutual fund seeking capital appreciation. Accordingly, management has stated that potential for capital growth will be the sole criterion in the selection of portfolio securities and current income will not be a consideration. Portfolio will consist primarily of common stocks, although convertible bonds and preferreds and warrants may also be held if, in management's judgment, this would further the investment objective. The fund has borrowing power which it intends to use to create capital leverage from time to time. At fiscal midyear, January 31, 1977, no bank loans were outstanding.

At that time, the fund held 93.8 percent of its assets in common stocks, of which the major proportion was concentrated in five industry groups: energy related (13.9% of assets), retail (11.6%), financial (9.7%), insurance (8.6%), and conglomerates (6.6%). The five largest individual holdings were Imperial Corp. of America (5.6% of assets), Helmerich & Payne (4.7%), First Charter Financial (4.1%), Occidental Petroleum (4%), and Teledyne (3.8%). The rate of portfolio turnover during the latest fiscal year was 98.4 percent of average assets. Unrealized appreciation was 9.7 percent of 1977 fiscal midyear-end assets.

Statistical History

	At Year-Ends								*Annual Data*				
						Percent of Assets in						*Offering Price ($)*	
Year	*Total Net Assets ($)*	*Number of Share-holders*	*Net Asset Value per Share ($)*	*Offer-ing Price ($)*	*Yield (%)*	*Cash & Equiv-alent*	*Bonds & Pre-ferreds*	*Com-mon Stocks*	*Income Div-idends ($)*	*Capital Gains Distribu-tion ($)*	*Expense Ratio (%)*	*High*	*Low*
1976	55,910,542	10,109	12.44	13.60	—	4	1	95	—	0.53	1.89	14.02	11.21
1975	39,053,046	10,371	10.13	11.07	—	12	—	88	—	—	2.12	12.64	7.40
1974	25,059,263	10,582	7.16	7.83	3.1	7	—	93	0.245	—	1.27	10.21	6.04
1973	35,392,339	11,150	9.93	10.85	0.7	29	—	71	0.072	—	1.22	13.49	9.91
1972	49,286,516	11,817	12.01	13.13	—	3	—	97	—	—	1.62	13.15	9.22
1971	33,102,339	12,994	8.52	9.31	—	1	—	99	—	—	2.01	9.33	6.79
1970	25,917,855	14,102	6.37	6.96	—	3	—	97	—	—	1.01	9.30	5.65
1969	31,932,776	13,660	8.40	9.18	—	12	—	88	—	—	NM	11.88	8.84

Note: Initially offered April 1, 1969 at $11.23 per share.
NM: Not meaningful; not a full year.

EXHIBIT 10 ***(continued)***

An assumed investment of $10,000 in this fund, with capital gains accepted in shares, is illustrated below.

Putnam
Voyager Fund, Inc.

Cost of investment
April 1, 1968
$10,000

(Initial Net Asset
Value $9,150)

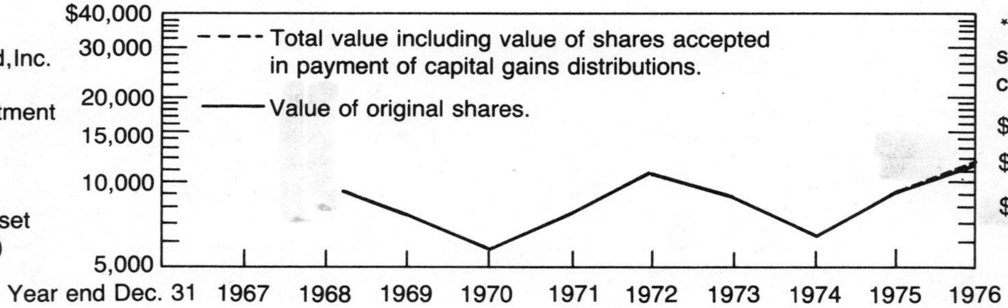

$40,000
30,000
20,000
15,000
10,000
5,000

- - - - Total value including value of shares accepted in payment of capital gains distributions.
——— Value of original shares.

Year end Dec. 31 1967 1968 1969 1970 1971 1972 1973 1974 1975 1976

December 31, 1976

*(Including $571 value of shares accepted as capital gains distributions)

$11,583 total value of investment*

$11,072 value of original shares

$282 total income dividends

Value of shares initially acquired through investment of $10,000	$7,477	$5,670	$7,583	$10,690	$8,838	$6,373	$9,016	$11,072
Value of shares accepted as capital gains distribution (cumulative)	—	—	—	—	—	—	—	511
Total value	7,477	5,670	7,583	10,690	8,838	6,373	9,016	11,583
Dividends paid from investment income	—	—	—	—	64	218	—	—

Dollar amounts of capital gains distributions accepted in shares were:

1969	$ —	1974	$ —
1970	—	1975	—
1971	—	1976	472
1972	—		
1973	—	Total	$ 472

Results taking all dividends and distributions in STOCK.

Initial investment at offering price, Apr. 1, 1969	$10,000
Total dividends from income reinvested	284
Total amount invested	10,284
Total value, Dec. 31, 1976	12,098*

*Includes value of shares received in payment of $493 capital gains.

Results taking all dividends and distributions in CASH.

Initial investment at offering price, Apr. 1, 1969	$10,000
Total value, Dec. 31, 1976	11,072
Distributions from capital gains	472
Dividends from investment income	282

SCUDDER DEVELOPMENT FUND

Scudder Development Fund was organized in 1970 and its shares first publicly offered on January 18, 1971. It is one of several investment companies under the management of Scudder, Stevens & Clark, some bearing the Scudder name and others such as Louisville Investment Co. and Savings Bank Investment Fund-Liquidity Series. A Canadian subsidiary manages Canadian Investment Fund Ltd. and Scudder North America Fund Ltd.

The fund seeks to achieve long-term growth of capital primarily through investments in marketable securities, principally common stocks, of relatively small, or little-known companies having prospects for a greater and more rapid rate of growth in sales and earnings than many larger and better established concerns. Current income is not a factor in the selection of equity securities.

At the 1976 year-end, the fund had 99 percent of its assets in common stocks, of which the major proportion was concentrated in five industry groups: food & beverage (17.8% of assets), merchandising (16.2%), electronics (10%), electrical equipment (9.4%), and construction (9.3%). The five largest individual investments were Flight Safety International (5.6% of assets), Taco Bell (5.1%), Hughes Supply (5%), Pittway Corp. (4.7%), and Ogilvy & Mather International (4.6%). The rate of portfolio turnover during the latest fiscal year was 30.3 percent of average assets. Unrealized appreciation was 3.6 percent of calendar year-end assets.

Special Services: All shareholder purchases are made in full and fractional shares. Minimum initial investment is $5,000; there is no minimum on subsequent purchases. Income dividends and short-term capital gains are automatically reinvested, unless shareholder elects otherwise.

Statistical History

	At Year-Ends							*Annual Data*				
					Percent of Assets in						*Offering Price ($)*	
Year	*Total Net Assets ($)*	*Number of Share-holders*	*Net Asset Value per Share ($)*	*Yield (%)*	*Cash & Equiv-alent*	*Bonds & Pre-ferreds*	*Com-mon Stocks*	*Income Div-idends ($)*	*Capital Gains Distribu-tion ($)*	*Expense Ratio (%)*	*High*	*Low*
1976	20,025,648	900	50.17	0.7	1	—	99	0.35	—	1.36	53.58	41.56
1975	17,278,560	971	41.16	0.5	2	—	98	0.21	—	1.41	47.16	23.55
1974	11,782,422	1,054	23.26	—	4	—	96	—	—	1.40	48.81	22.15
1973	24,152,690	1,174	43.98	—	2	—	98	—	—	1.24	82.20	41.07
1972	39,702,938	1,182	31.55	—	8	—	92	—	0.58	1.37	86.33	62.61
1971	13,959,202	550	62.72	0.1	8	2	90	0.035	—	0.97	61.72	44.82

Note: Initially 1/18/71 at $45.00 per share.

EXHIBIT 10 *(continued)*

Directors: Edmund R. Swanberg, Pres.; Eckley B. Coxe IV, V.P.; Daniel Pierce, V.P.; John L. Casey; Paul Bancroft III; George S. Johnston; Wilson Nolen.

Investment Adviser: Scudder, Stevens & Clark. Compensation to the Adviser is at an annual rate of 1 percent of average daily net assets.

Custodian: Brown Bros. Harriman & Co., Boston, MA 02109.

Transfer Agent: Investment Companies Services Corp., 99 High St., Boston, MA 02104.

Distributor: Scudder Fund Distributors, Inc., 175 Federal St., Boston, MA 02110.

Sales Charge: None; shares offered at net asset value. There is a 2 percent redemption fee.

Dividends: Income dividends and short-term capital gains, if any, will be paid annually.

Shareholder Reports: Issued quarterly. Fiscal year ends June 30. The 1976 prospectus was effective in December.

Qualified for Sale: In all states and D.C., except AL, AK, ID, IN, ME, MO, MT, NE, NH, ND, OR, SD, WV, WI and WY.

Address: 345 Park Ave., New York, NY 10022.

Telephone: (212) 350-8200.

An assumed investment of $10,000 in this fund, with capital gains accepted in shares, is illustrated below.

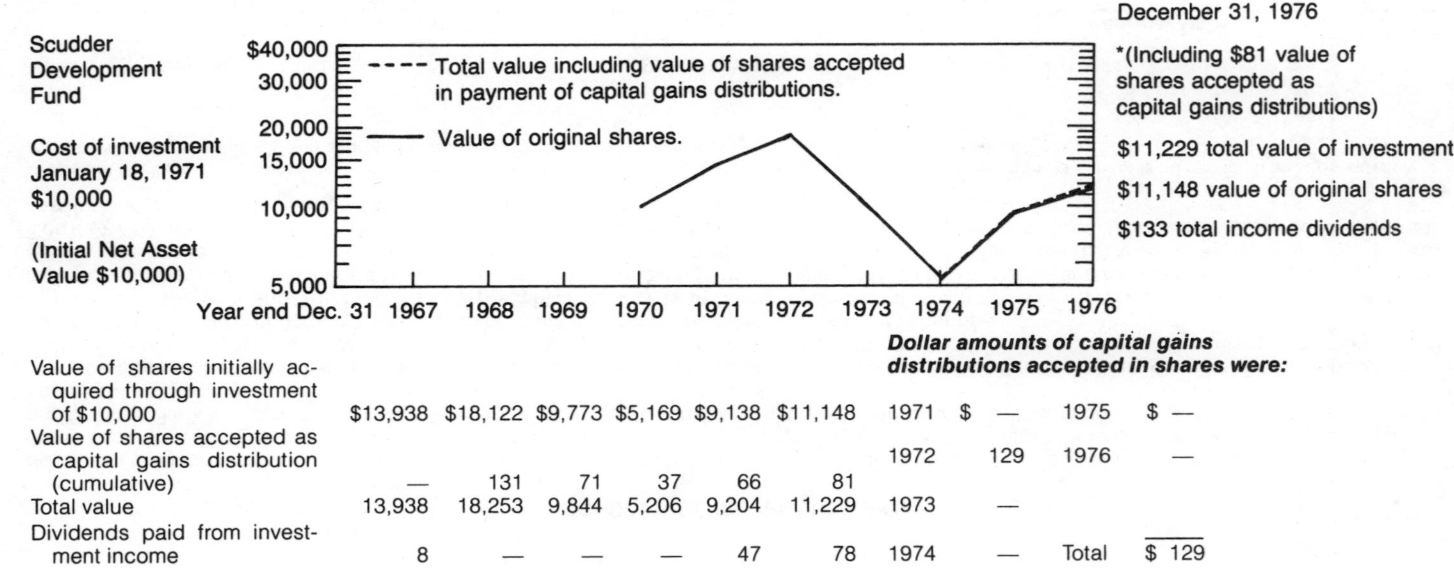

Value of shares initially acquired through investment of $10,000	$13,938	$18,122	$9,773	$5,169	$9,138	$11,148
Value of shares accepted as capital gains distribution (cumulative)	—	131	71	37	66	81
Total value	13,938	18,253	9,844	5,206	9,204	11,229
Dividends paid from investment income	8	—	—	—	47	78

Dollar amounts of capital gains distributions accepted in shares were:

1971	$ —	1975	$ —
1972	129	1976	—
1973	—		
1974	—	Total	$ 129

Results taking all dividends and distributions in STOCK.

Initial investment at offering price, Jan. 18, 1971	$10,000
Total dividends from income reinvested	134
Total amount invested	10,134
Total value, Dec. 31, 1976	11,381*

*Includes value of shares received in payment of $129 capital gains.

Results taking all dividends and distributions in CASH.

Initial investment at offering price, Jan. 18, 1971	$10,000
Total value, Dec. 31, 1976	11,148
Distributions from capital gains	129
Dividends from investment income	132

EDIE SPECIAL GROWTH FUND, INC.

Edie Special Growth Fund was one of two mutual funds launched in 1969 by Lionel D. Edie & Co., a firm which has been engaged in furnishing advisory and supervisory services to individuals with substantial investment portfolios and to a broad range of institutional investors since 1931. The other fund was Edie Special Institutional Fund which was merged into the Growth Fund on October 24, 1975, and added some $20 million of assets to the acquiring fund.

The Growth Fund seeks capital appreciation through investment primarily in small, quality growth companies. It may own over-the-counter issues, buy foreign securities up to 5 percent of its assets, and restricted issues up to 10 percent.

At the close of 1976, the fund had 95.4 percent of its assets in common stocks, of which the major proportion was concentrated in five industry groups: retail trade (14.8% of assets), building products (11.8%), education & leisure (11.4%), electronics & instrumentation (9.3%), and medical technology (7.4%). The five largest individual investments were Revco Drug (6.2% of assets), Tropicana Products (6%), Payless Cashways (5%), Longs Drug Stores (4.7%), and Petrie Stores (4.6%). The rate of portfolio turnover during the latest fiscal year was 9 percent of average assets. Unrealized appreciation was 7 percent of calendar year-end assets.

Special Services: An open account arrangement serves for voluntary accumulation and for automatic dividend reinvestment. Minimum initial investment is $1,000, but there is no minimum on subsequent purchases. Keogh Plans, corporate retirement plans, and Individual Retirement Accounts are available.

EXHIBIT 10 *(continued)*

Statistical History

Year	At Year-Ends							Annual Data				
					Percent of Assets in						Offering Price ($)	
	Total Net Assets ($)	Number of Share-holders	Net Asset Value per Share ($)	Yield (%)	Cash & Equiv-alent	Bonds & Pre-ferreds	Com-mon Stocks	Income Div-idends ($)	Capital Gains Distribu-tion ($)	Expense Ratio (%)	High	Low
1976	41,562,635	7,012	17.22	0.3	5	—	95	0.05	—	1.03	19.19	15.27
1975	48,024,000*	9,084	16.17	1.7	8	—	92	0.28	—	0.84	18.61	11.96
1974	21,406,765	8,621	11.74	2.1	15	—	85	0.25	—	0.91	18.76	11.11
1973	34,183,959	9,391	17.65	1.1	17	—	83	0.20	—	1.00	30.07	17.09
1972	59,988,824	9,500	29.94	0.6	26	—	74	0.17	—	0.85	32.20	27.97
1971	24,600,000	2,954	25.84	0.7	24	—	76	0.18	—	0.98	25.84	19.16
1970	7,930,480	524	19.38	1.7	20	—	80	0.33	—	1.05	30.31	14.19
1969	5,851,288	300	20.06	—	43	—	57	—	—	NM	20.56	19.57

*Includes assets of Edie Special Institutional Fund merged 10/24/75. Note: Initially offered 8/21/69 at $20.00 per share.
NM. Not meaningful; not a full year.

Directors: Ralph D. Creasman, Pres.; Robert F. Byran; John S. Cochran; Walter R. Good; Sherlock D. Hackley; George F. James; Sidney Lansburgh.

Investment Adviser: Edie Management Services, Inc. Compensation to the Adviser is at an annual rate of ¾ of 1 percent of average net assets.

Custodian and Transfer Agent: The Bank of New York, New York, NY 10249.

Distributor: Edie Funds Distributors, Inc., 530 Fifth Avenue, New York, NY 10036.

Sales Charge: None; shares are sold at net asset value. Minimum initial purchase $1,000; no subsequent minimum.

Dividends: Income dividends and capital gains, if, any, will be paid annually in quarter following end of fiscal year.

Shareholder Reports: Issued quarterly. Fiscal year ends June 30. The 1976 prospectus was effective in November.

Qualified for Sale: In all states and D.C.

Address: 530 Fifth Avenue, New York, NY 10036.

Telephone: (212) 575-4020.

An assumed investment of $10,000 in this fund, with capital gains accepted in shares, is illustrated below.

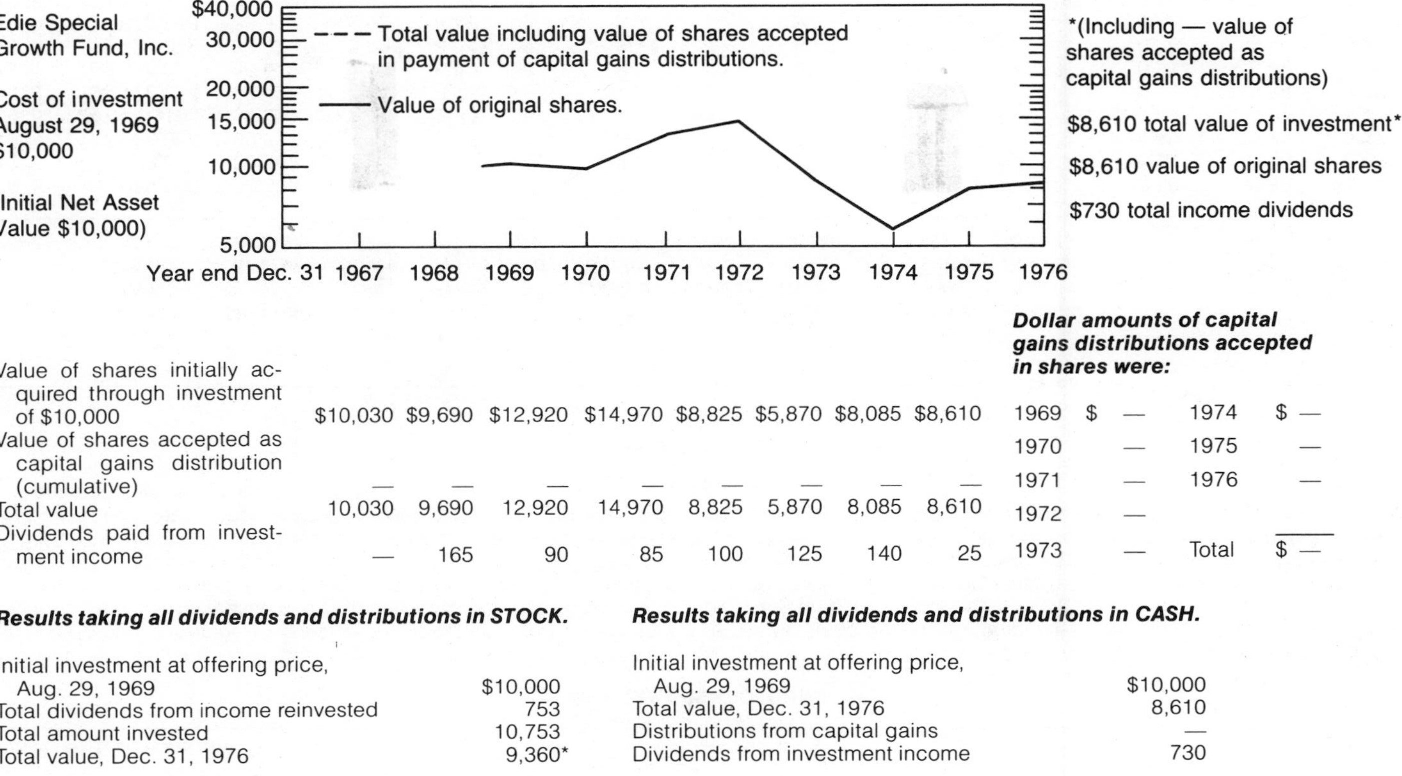

Value of shares initially acquired through investment of $10,000	$10,030	$9,690	$12,920	$14,970	$8,825	$5,870	$8,085	$8,610
Value of shares accepted as capital gains distribution (cumulative)	—	—	—	—	—	—	—	—
Total value	10,030	9,690	12,920	14,970	8,825	5,870	8,085	8,610
Dividends paid from investment income	—	165	90	85	100	125	140	25

Dollar amounts of capital gains distributions accepted in shares were:

1969	$ —	1974	$ —
1970	—	1975	—
1971	—	1976	—
1972	—		
1973	—	Total	$ —

Results taking all dividends and distributions in STOCK.

Initial investment at offering price, Aug. 29, 1969	$10,000
Total dividends from income reinvested	753
Total amount invested	10,753
Total value, Dec. 31, 1976	9,360*

*Includes value of shares received in payment of $— capital gains.

Results taking all dividends and distributions in CASH.

Initial investment at offering price, Aug. 29, 1969	$10,000
Total value, Dec. 31, 1976	8,610
Distributions from capital gains	—
Dividends from investment income	730

EXHIBIT 10 ***(continued)***

IDS NEW DIMENSIONS FUND, INC.

A diversified common stock fund, IDS New Dimensions Fund cites long-term growth as its primary objective, with any income produced regarded as a by-product thereof. In quest of its goal, management will invest in the common stocks of companies "believed to have a potential for significant growth by reason of a high degree of competence in technology, marketing or management."

At the 1976 year-end, the fund had 95 percent of its assets in common stocks, of which the major proportion was concentrated in five industry groups: chemicals & drugs (16% of assets), financial & related (13.8%), oil & gas (11%), business equipment (9.3%), and retail trade (8.5%). The five largest individual investments were IBM (3.6% of assets), Schlumberger (3.1%), Intel Corp. and Digital Equipment (each 2.8%), and Santa Fe International (2.4%). The rate of portfolio turnover during the year was 36 percent of average assets. Unrealized appreciation was 2.9 percent of year-end assets.

Statistical History

	At Year-Ends								Annual Data				
						Percent of Assets in						Offering Price ($)	
Year	Total Net Assets ($)	Number of Share-holders	Net Asset Value per Share ($)	Offer-ing Price ($)	Yield (%)	Cash & Equiv-alent	Bonds & Pre-ferreds	Com-mon Stocks	Income Div-idends ($)	Capital Gains Distribu-tion ($)	Expense Ratio (%)	High	Low
1976	232,035,050	53,300	4.92	5.34	1.1	5	—	95	0.056	—	0.59	5.38	4.74
1975	229,822,065	60,682	4.34	4.71	1.2	9	3*	88	0.054	—	0.54	5.40	3.52
1974	177,952,665	60,787	3.42	3.72	1.6	8	3	89	0.061	—	0.49	5.78	3.17
1973	247,447,105	58,225	5.33	5.80	0.5	4	1	95	0.031	—	0.47	8.27	5.71
1972	303,172,414	52,127	7.49	8.14	0.2	11	2	87	0.015	—	0.46	8.55	6.37
1971	186,934,097	36,672	5.91	6.42	0.3	3	2*	95	0.02	—	0.37	6.44	4.29
1970	118,324,079	33,929	3.99	4.34	1.5	3	4	93	0.064	—	0.26	5.54	3.31
1969	137,802,558	33,317	5.02	5.46	1.2	8	7	85	0.066	—	0.39	6.34	4.90
1968	99,168,512	22,719	5.84	6.34	NM	10	1	89	0.032	0.018	NM	6.66	5.43

Note: Initially offered Aug. 1, 1968 at $5.43 per share. NM: Not meaningful.
*Includes a substantial proportion in convertible issues.

An assumed investment of $10,000 in this fund, with capital gains accepted in shares, is illustrated below.

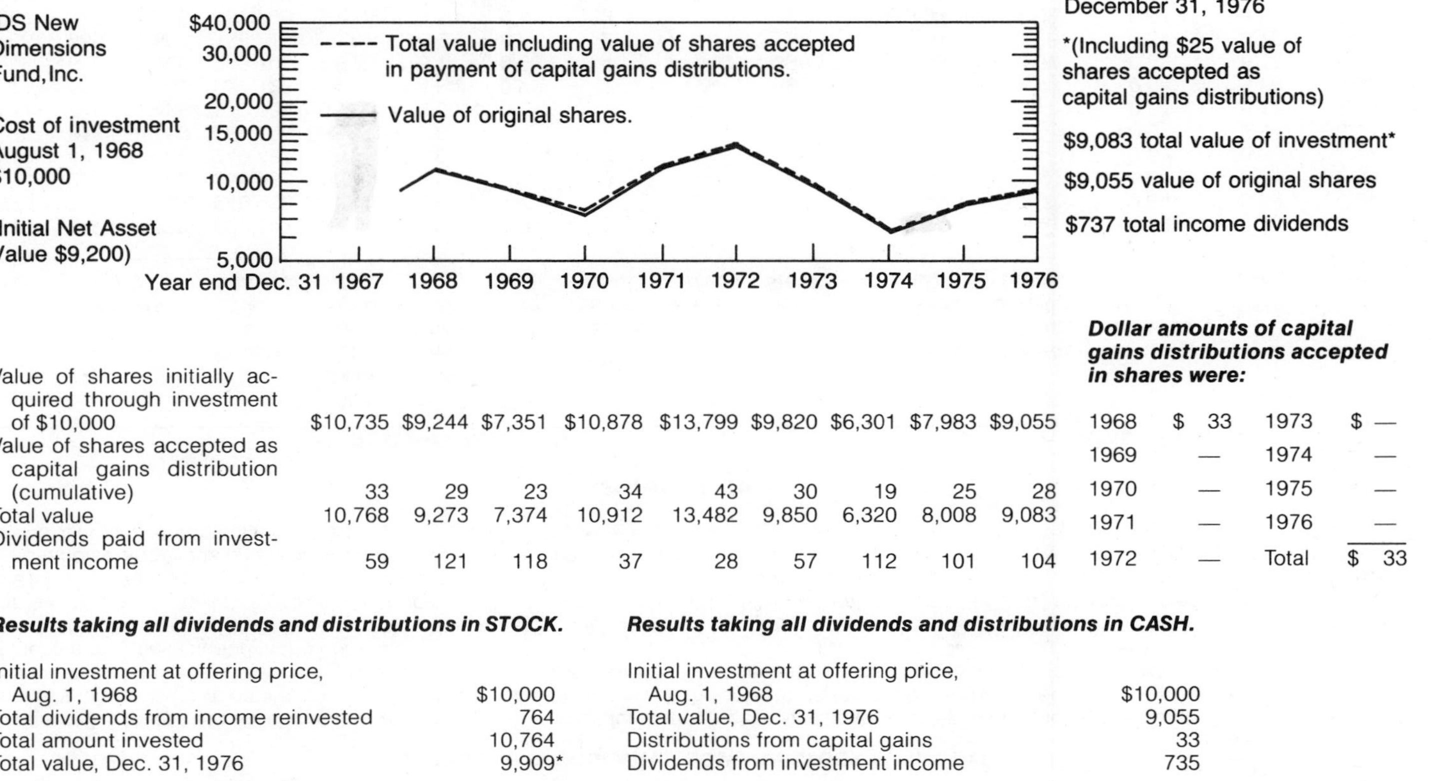

	1968	1969	1970	1971	1972	1973	1974	1975	1976
Value of shares initially acquired through investment of $10,000	$10,735	$9,244	$7,351	$10,878	$13,799	$9,820	$6,301	$7,983	$9,055
Value of shares accepted as capital gains distribution (cumulative)	33	29	23	34	43	30	19	25	28
Total value	10,768	9,273	7,374	10,912	13,482	9,850	6,320	8,008	9,083
Dividends paid from investment income	59	121	118	37	28	57	112	101	104

Dollar amounts of capital gains distributions accepted in shares were:

1968	$ 33	1973	$ —
1969	—	1974	—
1970	—	1975	—
1971	—	1976	—
1972	—	Total	$ 33

Results taking all dividends and distributions in STOCK.

Initial investment at offering price, Aug. 1, 1968	$10,000
Total dividends from income reinvested	764
Total amount invested	10,764
Total value, Dec. 31, 1976	9,909*

*Includes value of shares received in payment of $33 capital gains.

Results taking all dividends and distributions in CASH.

Initial investment at offering price, Aug. 1, 1968	$10,000
Total value, Dec. 31, 1976	9,055
Distributions from capital gains	33
Dividends from investment income	735

EXHIBIT 10 *(continued)*

KEYSTONE SPECULATIVE COMMON STOCK FUND (S-4)

Keystone S-4 invests its assets as fully as practicable, except for working cash positions, entirely in common stocks and equivalents selected primarily for prospective capital growth. The class of stocks from which the selections are made may be expected to experience wide fluctuations in price in both rising and declining markets. Income is not an objective, but securities appearing to offer attractive possibilities for future growth of income may be included in the portfolio.

At the close of the fund's fiscal midyear, November 30, 1976, about 47 percent of the fund's assets was concentrated in five industry groups: energy (14.8% of assets), electronic products (9.6%), finance & insurance (8%), natural resources (7.3%), and consumer products & services (6.9%). The five largest individual common stock holdings were Inexco Oil and Avnet (each 1.4% of assets), Mostek Corp. (1.3%), and Service Merchandise and Houston Oil & Minerals (each 1.1%). The rate of portfolio turnover during the latest fiscal year was 73.7 percent of average assets. Unrealized appreciation was 1 percent of calendar year-end assets.

Statistical History

	At Year-Ends									*Annual Data*				
						Percent of Assets in						*Offering Price ($)*	
Year	*Total Net Assets ($)*	*Number of Share-holders*	*Net Asset Value per Share ($)*	*Offer-ing Price ($)*	*Yield (%)*	*Cash & Equiv-alent*	*Bonds & Pre-ferreds*	*Com-mon Stocks*	*Income Div-idends ($)*	*Capital Gains Distribu-tion ($)*	*Expense Ratio (%)*	*High*	*Low*
1976	448,602,789	202,842	3.75	4.10†	1.0	3	—	97	0.04	—	0.62	4.15	3.18
1975	370,342,597	246,263	2.86	3.13	—	3	—	97	—	—	0.64	3.84	2.34
1974	274,872,702	258,636	2.09	2.29	—	3	—	97	—	—	0.64	4.24	2.09
1973	472,394,166	249,487	3.73	4.09	—	2	—	98	—	—	0.58	6.93	3.74
1972	813,568,000	261,724	6.27	6.87	—	1	—	99	—	—	0.51	7.94	6.04
1971	745,312,489	270,539	5.55	6.08	0.3	1	—	99	0.02	—	0.54	6.12	4.45
1970	553,150,000	267,123	4.12	4.50	0.7	1	2	97	0.03	—	0.54	5.80	3.32
1969	610,357,400	243,700	5.26	5.74	0.5	4	1	95	0.03	0.57	0.53	8.12	5.02
1968	665,421,937	198,210	8.07	8.07	0.4	2	—	98	0.04	1.28	0.54	9.72	7.10
1967	477,274,700	151,700	7.78	8.50	0.4	3	—	97	0.04	1.09	0.57	8.52	5.85
1966	272,751,900	137,000	5.48	5.98	1.3	2	—	98	0.08	0.70	0.56	8.13	4.63

†Reflects change in sales charge to 8½% from 8¾% effective 6/1/76; prior years' figures not adjusted for change.

An assumed investment of $10,000 in this fund, with capital gains accepted in shares, is illustrated below.

Keystone Speculative Common Stock Fund (S-4)

Cost of investment January 1, 1967 $10,000

(Initial Net Asset Value $9,150)

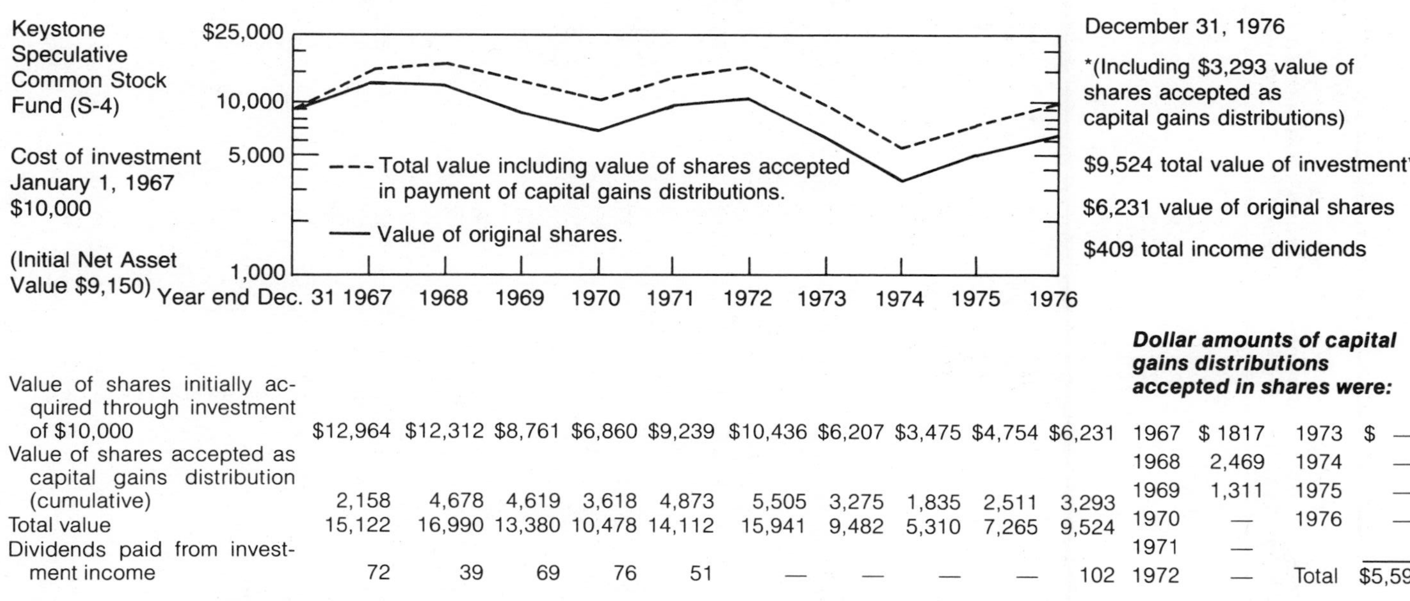

December 31, 1976

*(Including $3,293 value of shares accepted as capital gains distributions)

$9,524 total value of investment*

$6,231 value of original shares

$409 total income dividends

	1967	1968	1969	1970	1971	1972	1973	1974	1975	1976
Value of shares initially acquired through investment of $10,000	$12,964	$12,312	$8,761	$6,860	$9,239	$10,436	$6,207	$3,475	$4,754	$6,231
Value of shares accepted as capital gains distribution (cumulative)	2,158	4,678	4,619	3,618	4,873	5,505	3,275	1,835	2,511	3,293
Total value	15,122	16,990	13,380	10,478	14,112	15,941	9,482	5,310	7,265	9,524
Dividends paid from investment income	72	39	69	76	51	—	—	—	—	102

Dollar amounts of capital gains distributions accepted in shares were:

1967	$ 1817	1973	$ —
1968	2,469	1974	—
1969	1,311	1975	—
1970	—	1976	—
1971	—		
1972	—	Total	$5,597

Results taking all dividends and distributions in STOCK.

Initial investment at offering price, Jan. 1, 1967	$10,000
Total dividends from income reinvested	414
Total amount invested	10,414
Total value, Dec. 31, 1976	9,878*

*Includes value of shares received in payment of $5,619 capital gains.

Results taking all dividends and distributions in CASH.

Initial investment at offering price, Jan. 1, 1967	$10,000
Total value, Dec. 31, 1976	6,231
Distributions from capital gains	4,883
Dividends from investment income	300

Source: *Wiesenberger Investment Companies Service*, 37th edition, 1977, published by Wiesenberger Financial Services, New York, NY.

EXHIBIT 11
Quarterly Rates of Return

Year and Quarter	Opening Price	Cash Dividend	Capital Gain Dividend	Closing Price	Quarterly Rate of Return on Fund	Quarterly Rate of Return on Standard & Poor's 500 Index
1960: 3	$ 9.87	—	—	$ 9.79	− .81%	− 5.19%
4	9.79	—	—	10.92	11.54	9.59
1961: 1	10.92	—	—	12.62	15.57	12.81
2	12.62	—	—	12.24	− 3.01	.08
3	12.24	—	—	11.62	− 5.07	3.98
4	11.62	—	—	12.76	9.81	8.08
1962: 1	12.76	—	—	12.10	− 5.17	− 2.10
2	12.10	—	—	8.07	−33.30	−20.62
3	8.07	—	—	8.52	5.58	3.68
4	8.52	—	—	9.06	6.34	13.28
1963: 1	9.06	—	—	9.25	2.10	6.34
2	9.25	—	—	9.46	2.27	5.01
3	9.46	—	—	9.61	1.59	4.10
4	9.61	—	—	9.94	3.43	5.61
1964: 1	9.94	—	—	9.71	− 2.31	6.06
2	9.71	—	—	9.60	− 1.13	4.20
3	9.60	—	—	9.75	1.56	3.78
4	9.75	$.017	$.333	9.77	3.79	1.58
1965: 1	9.77	—	—	10.89	11.46	2.39
2	10.89	—	—	10.06	− 7.62	− 1.63
3	10.06	—	—	11.82	17.50	7.71
4	11.82	.042	.588	13.40	18.70	3.66
1966: 1	13.40	—	—	14.00	4.48	− 2.73
2	14.00	—	—	14.41	2.93	− 4.25
3	14.41	—	—	13.81	− 4.16	− 8.85
4	13.81	.09	.50	15.29	14.99	5.96
1967: 1	15.29	—	—	19.51	27.60	13.21
2	19.51	—	—	22.26	14.10	1.28
3	22.26	—	—	25.83	16.04	7.50
4	25.83	.15	1.43	26.97	10.53	.59
1968: 1	26.97	—	—	24.01	−10.98	− 5.72
2	24.01	—	—	29.69	23.66	11.24
3	29.69	—	—	31.52	6.16	3.89
4	31.52	—	—	33.24	5.46	1.96
1969: 1	33.24	.18	1.72	28.59	− 8.27	− 1.50
2	28.59	—	—	27.34	− 4.37	− 3.00
3	27.34	—	—	27.28	− .22	− 3.92
4	27.28	.18	1.72	29.15	13.82	− .31
1970: 1	29.15	.21	1.20	25.53	− 7.58	− 1.71
2	25.53	—	—	18.32	−28.24	−18.03
3	18.32	—	—	22.54	23.03	16.91
4	22.54	.21	1.20	24.36	14.33	10.43
1971: 1	24.36	—	—	28.42	16.67	9.70
2	28.42	.16	.46	29.96	7.60	.17
3	29.96	.16	.46	32.36	10.08	− .59
4	32.36	.16	.46	36.64	15.14	4.66
1972: 1	36.64	—	—	42.90	17.09	5.74
2	42.90	.11	.62	44.90	6.36	.67
3	44.90	.11	.62	55.61	25.48	3.91
4	55.61	.11	.62	43.76	−20.00	7.56

EXHIBIT 11 ***(concluded)***

Year and Quarter		Opening Price	Cash Dividend	Capital Gain Dividend	Closing Price	Quarterly Rate of Return on Fund	Quarterly Rate of Return on Standard & Poor's 500 Index
1973:	1	$43.76	$ —	—	$32.36	−26.05%	− 4.89%
	2	10.78*	.0419	.6923	8.84	−11.19	− 5.77
	3	8.84	.0419	.6923	10.72	29.57	4.81
	4	10.72	.0419	.6923	8.02	−18.34	− 9.16
1974:	1	8.02	—	—	7.57	− 5.61	− 2.82
	2	7.57	.0545	.0308	6.39	−14.46	−7.56
	3	6.39	.0545	.0308	4.60	−26.68	−25.16
	4	4.60	.0545	.0308	4.86	7.51	9.38
1975:	1	4.86	.0914	—	6.46	34.80	22.94
	2	6.46	.0914	—	7.62	19.37	15.37
	3	7.62	.0914	—	6.29	−16.25	−10.95
	4	6.29	.0914	—	6.66	7.34	8.65
1976:	1	6.66	.0742	—	7.57	14.78	14.97
	2	7.57	.0742	—	7.18	− 4.17	2.48
	3	7.18	.0742	—	7.09	− .22	1.92
	4	7.09	.0742	—	7.32	4.29	3.14
1977:	1	7.32	.0707	—	6.75	− 6.82	−7.44

*3 for 1 split.

Beta Analysis:

A. $\log(1 + R_p - R_F) = \alpha_p + \beta_p \log(1 + R_m - R_F)$

$\alpha = .00601$ (not statistically significant)

$\beta = 1.349$

$r^2 = .658$

$S_{y \cdot x} = .087$

$\sigma_p = .1434$

B. After Corchrane-Oroutt adjustment

$\alpha = .00512$ (not statistically significant)

$\beta = 1.208$

$r^2 = .607$

$S_{y \cdot x} = .0921$

$\sigma_p = .1434$

Part III

Capital Market Theory and Security Selection

The Little Professor Tackles the CAPM

If there was one thing that Rex King remembered about an executive seminar on the capital asset pricing model (CAPM) that he had recently attended at his (MBA) alma mater, it was the Little Professor, Dr. Willard Whitetower. Dr. Whitetower was all of five feet tall and nearly as wide. He lectured while looking at his feet so that his shiny bald dome predominated. His speed of delivery was as fast as it was monotoned, and the note-taking participants were hard-pressed to stay with him. Altogether, he proved unforgettable. Mr. King wondered, however, whether some of the ideas covered in the seminar might help him in his new job as manager of pension assets at Powerful Industries, Inc. Toward this end, he began reviewing some of the notes he had taken during the seminar, particularly those that related to the assumptions underpinning the CAPM.

Powerful Industries, Inc., manufactured and sold a diversity of products serving the heavy industrial equipment and agribusiness industries. Sales in the most recent year, 1982, had exceeded $2 billion. Profits were quite cyclical. Despite

This case was prepared by Robert F. Vandell, Charles C. Abbott Professor of Business Administration of the Colgate Darden Graduate School of Business Administration of the University of Virginia.

extensive cost-cutting efforts, Powerful had lost money (for the first time since the 1930s) in 1982. The severity of the recession had shocked management and shifted the strategic emphasis from moderately rapid expansion to consolidation. Several businesses had been sold, at near distress prices, in an effort to reduce high interest costs on short-term bank loans—a debt that had mounted with growing financial needs and with the unfavorable long-term fixed-income security issuing conditions. While interest rates were now declining, management was anxious to reduce its debt burden further, and to refinance it on a longer-term basis.

Powerful's pension fund amounted to nearly 40 percent of, and was growing more rapidly than, its equity position. Annual contributions had amounted to approximately 13 percent of payrolls in 1981, up from 10 percent in 1977, largely because Powerful's benefit plans were closely aligned with inflationary conditions. Actuaries assumed that payroll costs per employee would grow at 6 percent per year, a number that implied an inflation rate of 4.5 percent. At the same time, the actuaries assumed the pension assets would earn 8 percent per year.

Payroll costs and fringe benefits had tended to be regarded as a fixed (albeit growing) cost, when management made contingent, recessionary forecasts. The year 1982 called this into question. Employment had declined over 40 percent—more than sales—in part reflecting strenuous cost-cutting activities designed to reduce operating breakeven levels. Unlike other costs, pension benefits were accrued and paid on a one-year lag basis. These costs rose to 22 percent of 1982 payrolls. Given the emphasis on cost reduction, pension expenses tended to stand out in cost and financial analyses. Pressure was mounting to reduce these costs, if feasible, in the future.

At the end of 1981, the market value of the portfolio had exceeded the actuarial requirement by 12 percent. Because 1982 had been a good year in both the fixed-income and equity areas, the prospect was that overfunding would increase to the 20 percent range at year-end. Overfunding did not affect "normal" costs until it exceeded 25 percent of the actuarial required value.

In part because of conservative accounting practices, in which past-service costs were written off over a shorter period than required (20 years), unfunded liabilities of the pension plan were only about 20 percent of the fund's required value—a relatively low level compared to many other firms of similar size. Actuarial assumptions tended to be conservative also, and Mr. King believed that there was probably a valuation cushion built into them.

Recently, George Allsworth, Powerful's financial vice-president, had come to look upon unfunded liabilities as equivalent to long-term debt in the sense that the liability was real, and that there were scheduled payments, albeit tax-deductible, that would reduce the existing liability over the next 18 years (in declining amounts). This view had begun to influence his opinions about the appropriate amounts that Powerful could borrow without undue risk to finance operations and of the adequacy of burden coverage. Mr. Allsworth had raised the question whether Powerful's conservative funding and investing practices for pension assets were still appropriate.

As a matter of policy, pension funds were invested approximately as follows: 65 percent in equities, 30 percent in fixed-income securities, and 5 percent in real estate equity participations. While actual proportions changed with market conditions, inflows were used to rebalance the portfolio to these asset-mix targets. Powerful had four fixed-income managers, ten equity managers, and two real estate managers. Fees paid to these managers exceeded $3.5 million in 1982.

Cash inflows exceeded retirement and other outflow payments by a substantial amount in 1982, and this condition seemed likely to remain true well beyond the turn of the century. As a consequence, there was no need to consider portfolio liquidity, except for speculative reasons.

Mr. King had joined Powerful Industries in 1972 upon completion of his MBA. He had first served on the controller's staff evaluating major capital expenditure opportunities. Two assignments, as controller of a plant and then of a division, followed. His new assignment as manager of Powerful's pension assets was considered a significant advancement that carried with it a 20 percent salary increase.

Mr. King had one staff assistant and a secretary to help him with his task. Unfortunately, the assistant, Alfred Grand, had aspired to the job Mr. King now held and was clearly disgruntled. Mr. Grand tended to use, in a way meant to embarrass Mr. King, a lot of modern portfolio theory jargon—alphas, betas, and the like—that Mr. King was only vaguely familiar with. The CAPM seminar offered by Mr. King's alma mater seemed an ideal way to retool himself for his new job.

The most urgent task given Mr. King was to review the performance of each of the equity fund managers to see if they should be retained. Mr. King had available monthly total-return data for each fund manager for the period that they had managed Powerful's assets—a period that ranged from six months to 25 years. For recent hirings, Mr. King also had quarterly performance data for five years prior to their employment, for "representative" accounts managed by these firms. The market value for the portfolios of these equity managers averaged $52 million but ranged from $10 million to $160 million. There was no apparent rationale for these allocations. Over the last five years, there had been five equity management switches (firing and hiring).

To evaluate performance, Mr. King had access to two services. One service ranked the total-return performance of each manager relative to a large universe of other equity managers followed by the service. The ranking was done yearly for the previous 10 years, as well as quarterly for the most recent 12 months. Cumulative performance rankings were also made over the same period. However, the service covered only the span in which the equity manager had been retained by Powerful. Only two firms had data covering the full 10 years of analysis.

A consultant also provided Powerful with what appeared to be a modern portfolio theory evaluation of performance. Using quarterly data for the most recent five years (updated quarterly), the consultant constructed a "performance characteristic line" by regressing fund performance against the total rate of return for the Standard & Poor's 500 Index. In the case of newly added funds, "representative historic data" were used to permit a five-year analysis. Alpha, beta, R^2, and similar performance characteristic line statistics were then set forth and evaluated by the consultant.

The two services tended not to agree on performance rankings. One of the criteria previously used at Powerful for evaluating managers' performance was that they should each be in the top 25 percent of all managers. Only three managers met this criterion for both services, although each service recognized six firms as having met this goal.

As a group, the equity managers were characterized as having a wide diversity of styles. Each organization tended to restrict itself in scope as to the kinds of securities considered for the portfolio. One manager, for example, invested only in small growth firms; another only in international (non-U.S.) firms. No two firms were alike in their approach to investments.

As Mr. King began to review some of his notes (see Appendix A) from the CAPM seminar, he hoped that they might provide him perspective on the evaluation of performance. If the current services were inadequate, perhaps better services could be found. Alternatively, he might develop an internal evaluation system. What he didn't yet know was what he needed to know.

Appendix A

NOTES ON THE CAPITAL ASSET PRICING MODEL

The Capital Asset Pricing Model (CAPM) asserts:

$$E(\tilde{R}_i) = R_f + E(\tilde{\beta}_i)\ [E(\tilde{R}_m) - R_f] \qquad (1)$$

where:

$E(\tilde{R}_i)$ = The expected total rate of return for any security and specifically security i.

R_f = The risk-free total rate of return (assumed to be known).

$E(\beta_i)$ = The expected relative volatility (covariance) of security i compared against that of the market portfolio.

$E(\tilde{R}_m)$ = The expected total rate of return for the market portfolio.

$\sim$ = The variable is uncertain and must be estimated.

CAPM is an expectational model. All variables are forward-looking and must be estimated.

R_i is not restricted to equities. Any financial asset that is risky—bonds, real estate, antiques—should fit on the security market line (SML).

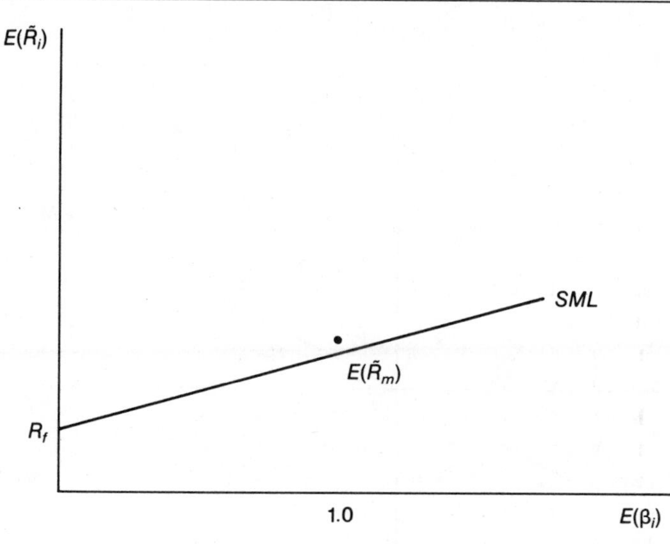

The market portfolio from which $E(R_m)$ is estimated should include all pertinent assets, weighted in proportion to their total value. (How?)

Some argue that things like human capital (present value of salaries) should be included in the market portfolio.

Mathematically, beta measures expected comovement as follows:

$$E(\tilde{\beta}_i) = \frac{E(\text{covariance } R_i, R_m)}{E(\text{variance } R_m)} \tag{2}$$

Covariance in turn (omitting the tildes, which are getting cumbersome) is measured by:

$$\text{Covariance } (R_i, R_m) = \rho_{im}\ \sigma_{Ri}\ \sigma_{Rm} \tag{3}$$

where:

ρ_{im} = Coefficient of correlation determined from regressing R_{it} against R_{mt}.
σ = Standard deviation of total returns.

All these quantitites are expectational.

Beta can be determined historically by regressing the risk premium of a security $(R_i - R_f)$ against the market $(R_m - R_f)$, using appropriate historic measures of the two variables (called the market model).

The regression equation is:

$$R_{it} - R_{ft} = \alpha_i + \beta_i(R_{mt} - R_{ft}) \pm \epsilon_i \tag{4}$$

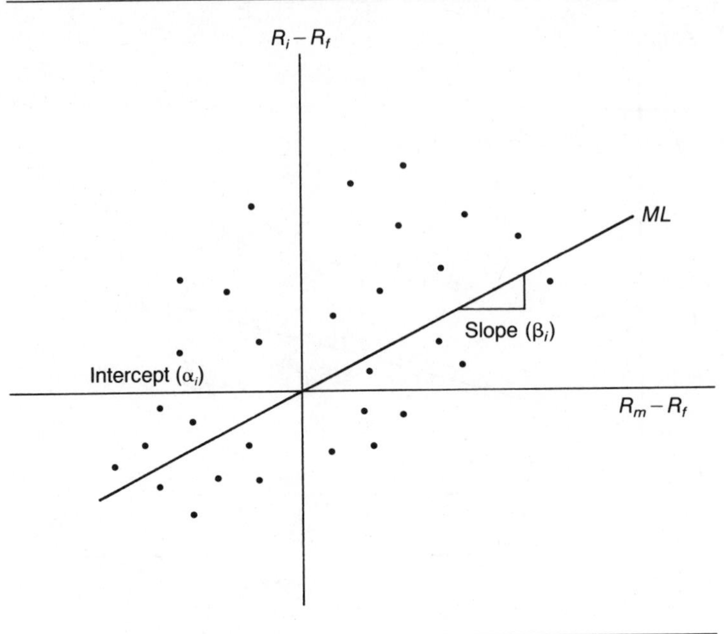

In interpreting the results of the regression analysis, the following symbols are often used:

$\rho_{im}{}^2 = R^2$ (coefficient of determination).

σ_{ϵ_i} = The standard error of the residuals.

ϵ_i = The residual error, a measure of vertical distance from each dot (R_{it}, R_{mt}) to the market line (ML).

Theoretically, α_i should be zero.

ϵ_i reflects the effect of unanticipated changes in the return for a security in a period relative to expectations of return for that security at the outset of the period. (These unanticipated changes are assumed to be non-forecastable.)

CAPM is a single-period equilibrium model or a static model.

The length of period is implicitly defined when the appropriate measurement for R_f is determined. Some argue this should be a very short period (hours, or even an instantaneous rate). Most practitioners tend to use the 90-day Treasury bill rate as the proxy for the risk-free rate.

All rates of return are expressed over the same time period. In most cases, returns are annual rates.

R_i and R_m are, in contrast, measures of total rate of return (per annum) over the long run (technically to infinity).

(*Question*) Does this imply that the expected value for R_i and R_m will be the same for the immediate period as for the long run? And will these estimates be the same at the end of the period? What if they are not?

(*Observation*) My economic training warns me to be skeptical of single-period equilibrium models. Dynamic models tend to allow for changing conditions.

The Assumptions Underlying CAPM

Instructor began by noting that all models simplify reality to some extent.

The test of a model is whether the implications of the model are acceptable.

(*Observation*) I think he means by this that the model's estimating power proves to be a reasonably reliable forecast of what, in fact, happens. Choosing a model is not a matter of taste but rather of reliability. Shades of "Positive Economics"?!

(*Observation*) Questionable assumptions often give some clue as to why a model may be unreliable.

Instructor seemed to argue that, even if not reliable, it serves (1) as a useful training device for students, (2) as a conceptual way of thinking about returns, or (3) a core or foundation model from which a better model can ultimately be built. (Why am I here?)

Now we come to the assumptions, which prove to be eight in number.

1. All investors seek to maximize the expected value of the utility of their terminal wealth.[1]

(*Observation*) Terminal wealth, while not defined explicitly, I presume refers to wealth at the end of the single CAPM period.

All investors are assumed to be risk-averse.

(*Observation*) I wonder if they are risk-averse always? Many of my friends seem to invest in equities looking for the big win, almost as if they had the gambling fever. If pressed, they might admit it was a risky opportunity too, although they often seem to think it's a sure thing in advance. Of course, they are pretty well off; they have good salaries, good prospects, good homes, good protection against risks through corporate pension plans, disability protection, insurance, etc. Perhaps they can afford to take flyers.

A utility function is a means of expressing an investor's risk preference for various possible wealth outcomes.

(*Observation*) This implies terminal wealth is uncertain. If so, the single-period portfolio model and its attendant capital market line (CML) is uncertain. In the diagram below, I have sketched out two *CMLs* to represent uncertainty (of R_m since R_f is fixed). Applying my crude concept of utility curves to the two asset mixes, I get two different optimal portfolios (R_p = return on portfolio).

---

[1]Omitted are notes on how an investor can determine his or her utility curve or function. Also, a discussion of various mathematical formulas (such as quadratic and power curves), which might be used as a proxy in defining utility curves, is omitted.

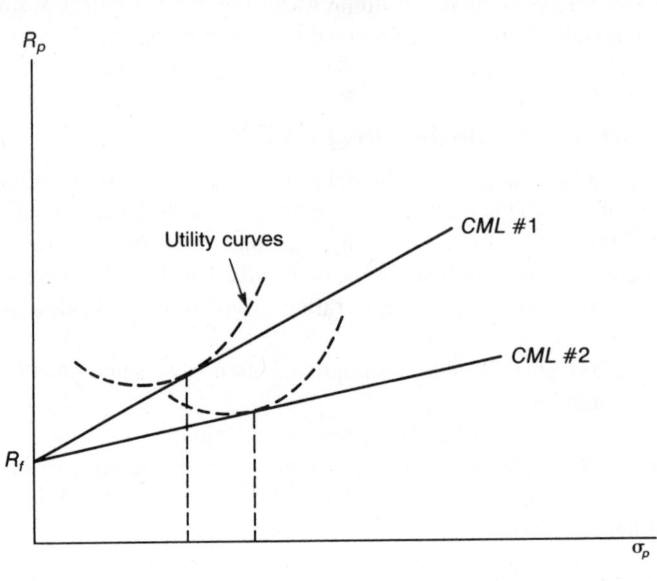

Two things puzzle me: (1) Does the underlying *SML* take these uncertainties of the *CML* and R_m's position fully into account? and (2) why should I want to be more aggressive (i.e., have a higher beta portfolio) when prospects for excess returns are more dismal?

The expected value of the utility of terminal wealth identifies the portfolio that will give me the greatest satisfaction (*ex ante*) from the wealth (risk) expectations I have (I think).

(*Question*) As the manager of the pension assets of Powerful Industries, do I use my utility curve? the president's? the stockholders'? If the latter, how is it determined?

(*Observation*) The exercise that we (*the students*) went through to determine our utility curve was to me a game. I have no idea whether my estimates of my preferences (by means of equivalent gambles) are anything close to what they would be if faced with real-world choices of this stark a magnitude. This stuff seems spongy. I've been investing for almost 20 years and never knew I had a utility curve. For that matter, I never tried to construct a probability distribution of my terminal wealth. Do people really do this sort of thing?

(*Question*) Given assumption #7 (no taxes), does this imply I am indifferent to the form incremental wealth takes (income versus gains)?

(*Question*) Given all my assets—home, car, pension fund, etc.—my equity investments are going to have a relatively small impact on my terminal wealth three months from now. If I'm lucky with the equity investments, my overall wealth may increase by 5 percent from what it otherwise would be; if unlucky, it might be off 5 percent. Frankly I feel relatively indifferent to these outcomes. Maybe my utility curve is flat for the discretionary investments I can make today, given the short horizon of the CAPM model.

(*Observation*) I guess my ultimate terminal wealth occurs when I die. I wonder what my utility curve will be then? The devil may care! Or Uncle Sam.

2. *Investors choose the portfolio they most want on the basis of their risk-and-return expectations. Risk and return are measured by the variance and mean of expected results for alternative portfolios.* (I hope I translated the jargon correctly.)

Variance is a measure of the probable dispersion of total rate of return results (presumably at the end of the shortish period of the model).

(*Question*) What happened to terminal wealth? Returns for a period are not wealth but wealth increments. I guess this would involve me in estimating the returns on my home, my car, and my wife's jewelry, among other things. My cup runneth over!

Variance is a complete measure of risk when probability distributions are normal. The Little Professor there asked us about our preference for the two distributions shown (one "skewed," one normal), both of which he assured us had the same mean and variance.

Someone said distribution B, and got a star on his forehead from the L.P. because B had a lower "downside risk," and higher "upside potential." Distribution B also seems to have a greater chance of losing, which I do not regard as attractive. Perhaps this is why I had such trouble with classic statistics in college. I still like A.

Normal and Skewed Distributions of Returns

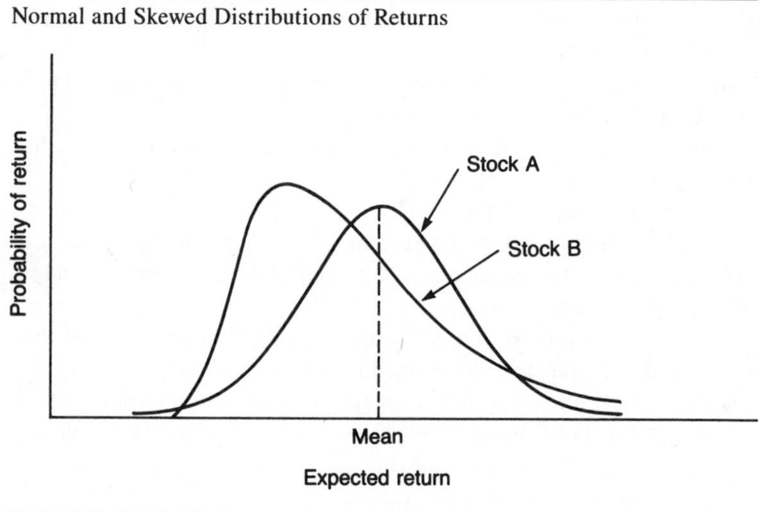

Some investors may be more concerned with achieving a target return and with semivariance downside risk of failing to achieve the target. The probability distribution of returns for the portfolio shown illustrates this:

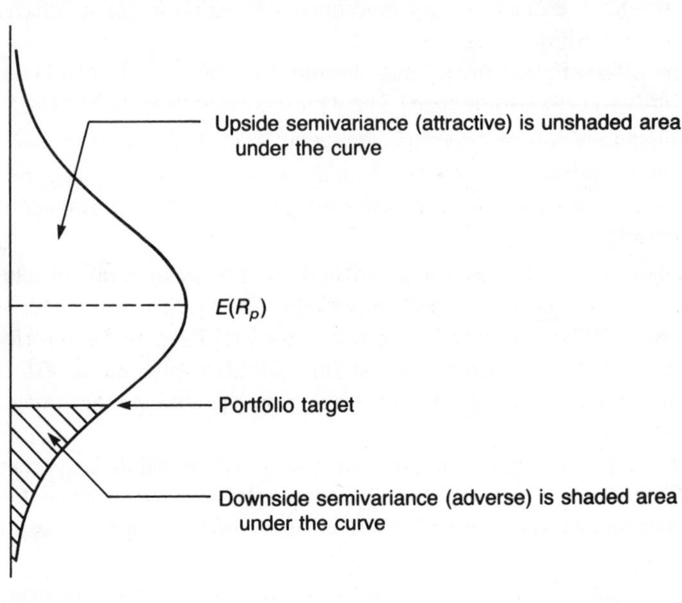

(*Observation*) Our actuaries give us a target return. In the assumption they make about how rapidly the pension fund will grow from its earnings (total return) as distinct from net new contributions, we gain one input to determine the adequacy of our fund. Perhaps semivariance is more germane to us. If this were true, how would CAPM be altered?

(*Question*) I vaguely remember another condition of abnormality, kurtosis (no relation to halitosis). We never discussed this condition.

(*Question*) Is variance another one of these *ex ante* variables that has to be forecasted?

(*Question*) What happened to beta?

The target seemed to affect the process of forming a utility curve in the eyes of the Little Professor. I must have been dozing off for I didn't understand why (too much starchy food at lunch).

Mean and variance make the model mathematically tractable, and that's why academics seem to prefer these measures to alternatives, I suppose.

(*Question*) Am I lost, or does beta equal variance? I don't see the relationship of variance to betas shown in equations (2) and (3) of this case in my earlier notes.

3. *All investors have homogeneous (identical) expectations of risk and return for each security among all those available.*

We clapped when somebody gave a responsive raspberry. The Little Professor seemed to accept that forecasts for individual securities were likely to be diverse. Expectations about risk and return prospects would not be identical (clearly they are not). He did not think the diversity would affect the model's validity.

If I understand his reasoning, he seemed to believe the consensus market price reflected a consensus of risk/return expectations as well. This sounded more like a hunch than a deduction—a hunch that I would think was unlikely.

4. All investors have identical time horizons (terminal dates to investment planning period of wealth accumulation).

(*Observation*) This assumption is obviously unrealistic. The market is made up of short-term speculators, of investors who buy and hold for long, long periods, and predominately of investors who buy for intermediate-term horizons.

The time horizon assumption of the model may be implicitly defined by the assumption about the holding period for the risk-free rate. If 90-day T-bills are used to represent the riskless asset, then the implied planning horizon of the investor would be 90 days. (This horizon would be unusually short.)

If an investor cannot anticipate changing expectations about market return or volatility prospects for the long run at the end of the first or any other period, then the horizon assumption may not be critical, says the Little Professor.

However, the riskless asset no longer has certainty associated with it. At what rate will risk-free funds be invested at the end of a single or a series of single holding periods? Change in expectations for R_f may also affect expectations for R_m. What are the implications of a variable R_f on the model?

As R_f becomes an uncertain quantity, then one must worry about covariance between R_f and R_m. the true *SML* may (1) become curved and (2) be understated by CAPM.

CAPM gives a misleading picture of longer-term risks.

(*Observation*) Suppose wealth risk was defined as uncertainty of wealth achievement relative to expected wealth for a stated time period—say annually. We could express relative risk as standard deviation divided by expected value. If we measure wealth at the end of (n) periods for example, wealth (W_{t+n}) will have grown as follows:

$$W_{t+n} = W_t \cdot \prod_{t=1}^{n} (1 + R_{p_t})$$

(where Π represents multiplication as Σ represents summation).

In logarithmic form:

$$\log(W_{t+n}) = \log(W_t) + \sum_{t=1}^{n} \log(1 + R_{pt})$$

If returns are independent through time with similar probability distributions, we could expect W_{t+n} to have the following expected value and risk (logarithmically):

$$E[\log(W_{t+n})] = \log(W_t) + (n)\, E[\log(1 + \mathrm{R}_{pt})]$$
$$\sigma[\log(W_{t+n})] = \sqrt{n} \cdot \sigma[\log(1 + R_{pt})]$$

In short, as the time horizon (n) lengthens, the relative risk ratio will decrease by the factor $\sqrt{n}/n$ in terms of our performance measure R_{pt} or annual return.

(*Question*) Do investors with longer planning horizons, like me (about 30 years until I retire), have different risk/return relationships to choose from (in the CAPM trade-off)? Supposing the axes of the portfolio model were wealth (Y axis) after n periods and risk were $\sigma_{W_{t+n}}$, what would the model look like for various n assumptions?[2]

(*Question*) What happens if distributions are not normal? Does risk cancel faster than is true for normal distributions under the law of large numbers? I've forgotten what I learned in Statistics.

(*Question*) Are risks independent over time? It seems to me the market has a cycle of about four years—similar to and anticipating the business cycle. If so, would not extremes of good and bad results tend to cancel out over a cycle so that average returns are less uncertain over four-year periods than one would expect if returns were completely independent?

The L.P. mentioned continuous CAPM models had been developed,[3] but implied that return expectations were assumed to follow a random walk.

(*Question*) Over time, is the forecasting uncertainty of security and/or portfolio total returns more critical than volatility in determining how well a portfolio will do? In my day we used to construct probability distributions of return expectations for a security over a five-year planning period and used these data to measure expected returns and their expected uncertainty. Why is this not a valid way of viewing risk?

(*Question*) How does dollar-averaging affect risks? I tend to invest at a steady (growing) rate. In bad markets I buy more shares than I do in strong markets for the same bucks. Over time, I end up with more shares and more wealth than if I invested the same sum at the average price.

(*Observation*) It seems to me that the single-period (short) model is valid only if:

a. Risk preferences are unaffected by how wealth and wealth uncertainties change over time (largely applicable to a small number of individuals who will be reducing wealth to finance current consumption).[4]

---

[2]Mr. King decided to test this on various data drawn from R. G. Ibbotson and R. A. Sinquefield's study, *Stocks, Bonds, Bills and Inflation: The Past and the Future*, The Financial Analysts Research Foundation, Charlottesville, VA, 1982.

Pertinent data:

	Annual Geometric Return	**Annual Standard Deviation (Arithmetic)**
Common stocks	9.1%	21.9%
Small stocks	12.1	37.3
Long-term corporate bonds	3.6	5.6
U.S. Treasury bills	3.0	3.1

[3]References:
Phil C. Merton, "An Intertemporal Capital Asset Pricing Model," *Econometric* (September 1973); Eugene Fama, "Multiperiod Consumption Investment Decisions," *American Economic Review* (March 1970).

[4]Perhaps this would not be important unless a shift in the size of investments between the risk-free and the market portfolio had no effect on return requirements for each.

b. Returns and uncertainties for the market portfolio are independent over time. Knowing the results of the performance in the initial or any subsequent capital-asset-pricing-model period will not change risk/return expectations for the next period. (These returns should probably be calculated in real, not nominal, terms to avoid the effects of changing inflation rates on expectations.) In short, the weak form of the efficient market hypothesis holds with respect to both risk and returns.

c. The semi-strong form of the efficient market hypothesis also holds. Expectations with respect to market risk and returns may be changed as the result of new information bearing on the economy or securities at large; however, these changes cannot be estimated today.

d. The risk-free rate does not covary with the return on the market portfolio.

Perhaps there are other assumptions as well.

5. Information is freely available.

Insiders may have special information. Presumably these individuals can make risk/return decisions that would lead to a portfolio other than the market portfolio.

(*Observation*) Even index funds involve modest management and transaction costs for large investors. Costs may be higher for smaller investors. If so, net R_m to the investor would not be the same.

This condition may be more true for large-capitalization stocks that are actually analyzed thoroughly by a large number of security analysts than for smaller companies that are not as broadly followed.

The market requires that enough analysts gather the available data (usually at a cost), process the data to form conclusions about the relative attractiveness of individual securities, and participate or cause participation in the market to the point the price reflects an equilibrium consensus about value.

While a large amount of information is generally available through annual reports, newspaper coverage, press releases, industry analysis, etc., security analysts often seem to seek edges by (1) enriching this information through field trips or (2) acquiring the information sooner than broad distribution allows. Are these edges of value? They are not costless.

Most security analysts will argue that it is the interpretation of the information that is of value. When prices change significantly for stocks or groups of stock, it must be because someone has caused them to change. Does analytical skill have no value, or insufficient value to cover the costs of acquiring, processing, and transacting? Why are the ranks of security analysts growing, not declining? Do not certain analysts have disproportionate influence, because their peers respect and seek out their opinions as a part of the analytical process?

The market portfolio will not be efficient unless people gather and analyze information at some cost so that prices reflect the (uniform) expectation of appropriate values.

6. There is a risk-free asset with a uniform rate of return for all. Investors can borrow and lend at the risk-free rate in sufficient quantities to meet their risk objectives. Short selling is feasible for all.

Certain investors are precluded from borrowing (pension plans, many eleemosynary institutions) and may not be able to achieve a portfolio beta above 1, using only the risk-free and market portfolios. Short selling is not permitted in many institutions, and has some cost disadvantages.

Most investors cannot borrow at the same rate (R_b) as can the U.S. Treasury (i.e., $R_b > R_f$). When this happens the security market line (SML) has a lower slope to the right of R_m, as illustrated.

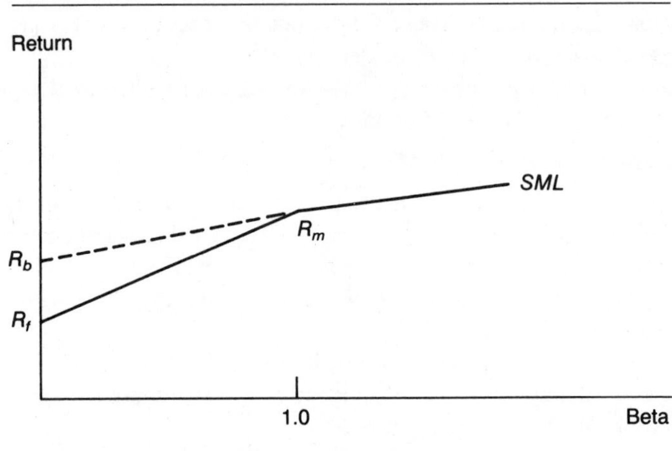

The change in slope to the right of R_m should affect the risk/return matrix considered more attractive by investors seeking higher than market risks. (Would this impact the market portfolio?) It also would seem to lead them to take more incremental risk for less incremental return relative to what would be feasible if they could borrow at the risk-free rate, if I understand how utility curves work.

More aggressive borrowing (leveraging of a portfolio) may cause R_b to rise as B_p rises. The SML to the right of R_m may be segmented to reflect increasing rates for R_b as the level of borrowing increases.

The borrowing rate may be quite different for investors of different wealth, and may change as wealth changes. R_b, like R_f, may also change with time.

The assumption that there is a risk-free asset with a uniform return is of more serious concern.

The rate will not be uniform unless

a. There is a uniform horizon (short).

b. There are no taxes.

c. There are no barriers (minimum investment requirements) or transaction costs.

Of these, perhaps taxes are the most crucial assumption. Income on Treasury bills is fully taxable. Alternative short-term tax-free investments, such as municipals, may not be risk-free and will have lower rates of return. In contrast, the differential taxes on income and gains (if realized) will have a different impact on total after-tax returns of the market portfolio.

If investors think in terms of after-tax results (and it is hard for me to conceive that they do not), wealthy investors will have an SML that has a different intercept and a different slope than would otherwise be the case for a tax-free investor. Which SML line amid the many, given the diverse tax interests of individuals and institutions, is the relevant one?

The risk-free rate of return is a nominal rate. The real risk-free rate of return is uncertain if the rate of inflation during the period to the investment horizon is uncertain. (While the real R_m may be affected, too, I'm not sure the uncertainty of R_m will be altered very much. In fact, it might even be reduced.)

Given the uncertainty of real T-bill return prospects, the next question is: How do T-bill returns covary with the returns on the market portfolio? (It seems to me an unexpected increase in inflation should tend to hurt the real returns for both R_f and R_m.) If the covariance is other than zero, the security market line would not be linear.

Given nonzero covariance, the risk/return relationships should look like this (I think):

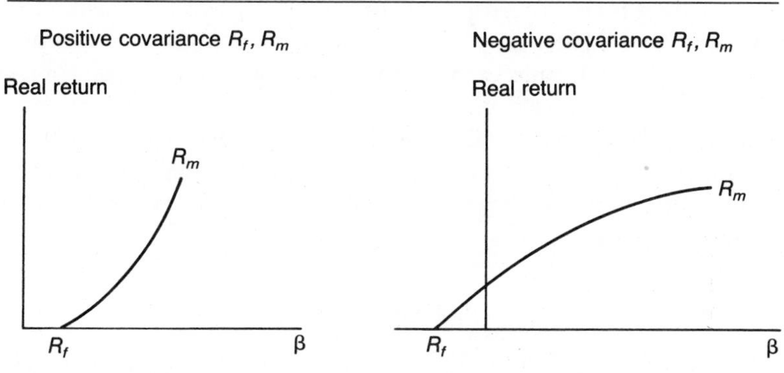

(I'm not sure I have plotted R_f on the correct side of the Y axis, but the point is that T-bills have a nonzero beta.

Here is a formula that the Little Professor says describes CAPM in an uncertain inflationary environment (see Exhibit 1), along with notes taken in an effort to explain the model to myself.

Taxes complicate this analysis further. Supposedly, nominal R_f tends to equal the inflation rate over the long run. In a world of taxes, however, the expected value of the after-tax real rate of return is negative. I don't consider a guaranteed loss of the purchasing power of my current wealth to be risk-free.

Add horizon to this taxable, inflation-uncertain world and, over the long run, I am trading off an almost certain loss of real wealth if I invest in riskless securities against an almost certain gain in wealth if I invest in risky equity securities.

(*Question*) Does inflation affect the calculation of stock betas? Do taxes?

(*Question*) The lending rate is tax-sheltered for some. If one could borrow at R_b and invest in short-term municipals, one might get a positive real after-tax rate of return for a 90-day investment. Unfortunately R_b is also uncertain in real terms (effect?) and more volatile than real R_f over time (effect?). Unfortunately, also, the IRS might question the tax deductibility of R_b if a direct or indirect source-application relationship with a municipal investment could be established.

7. There are no taxes, transaction costs, or other market imperfections.

This assumption is clearly not true, but, as the Little Professor queried, are market imperfections material to security pricing?

(*Observation*) It is hard for me to believe that taxes do not affect pricing. As a moderately well-off individual, the differential tax treatment between dividend income (now taxed at 56 percent—including state taxes—for me) and capital gains (now taxed at 21.5 percent—including state taxes) certainly influences my thinking about relative attractiveness of alternative investments.

The municipal bond market is a good case in point, indicating that there is a tax effect on pricing. Municipals sell at lower yields than comparable-risk corporate bonds of similar maturity because municipal interest income is tax-free.

(*Question*) Besides the tax differential on dividend or interest income and on capital gains, there is also a question as to timing of tax payments. Dividend income is taxed as realized. Capital gains taxes are only paid when the securities are sold. Until securities are sold, gains can be compounded on a pre-tax basis. For a longer term investor, such as myself, there is a present-value advantage to postpone the taking of gains. There are also still some step-up opportunities where gains can be avoided or reduced in estate planning that no doubt will be important to me.

To illustrate the nature of my dilemma, let me refer to a simple model of return expectations:

$$R_i = \frac{D_{it+1}}{P_{it}} + g_i$$

where:

R_i = Expected long-term total return for security i.

D_{it+1} = Expected dividends per share for the next 12 months for security i.

P_{it} = Today's market price for security i.

g_i = Expected long-term rate of capital appreciation, often related (correctly?) to the expected growth of dividends per share for security i.

The preceding formula may well be of interest to tax-free portfolios such as our pension fund. For me, however, after-tax return prospects are more material. Thus, I would be inclined to the formula:

$$\boxed{R_i} = (1-y_d)\frac{D_{it+1}}{P_{it}} + (1-y_c)g_i$$

where:

$\boxed{R_i}$ = After-tax expected long-term total rate of return for security i.
y_d = Tax rate on dividend income.
y_c = Tax rate on capital gains.

My dilemma is this: Given my ability to postpone capital gains, is y_c the proper number to use? Should it be zero? Should it be some present-value estimate of the tax effect?

(*Observation*) Taxes—really the ability to postpone capital gains—make horizon a very important issue for an investor subject to taxation. Also, the differential tax effect on short- and long-term capital gains makes it almost mandatory to have a horizon longer than the three months implicit in many CAPM analyses.

(*Observation*) I tend to think of capital gains liabilities as a transaction cost. Unless I foresee a price decline for a security that I own that is going to be more (relative to the market) than the tax liability, I tend to hold the security. The real question is: Can I sell the security, pay the taxes and transaction costs, and, finally, switch to a security that will have a more favorable impact on my wealth (tax considered) over a reasonable forward period?

(*Question*) This point is a little hard to explain even to myself. As I understand it, low-beta stocks often have high dividend yields. Electric utilities are a good example of this relationship. Low-yield/high-growth stocks, in contrast, tend to have high betas.

If we look at a security market line on a before- and after-tax basis, using R_i and $\boxed{R_i}$ as the two inputs, we should see something like shown in the sketch.

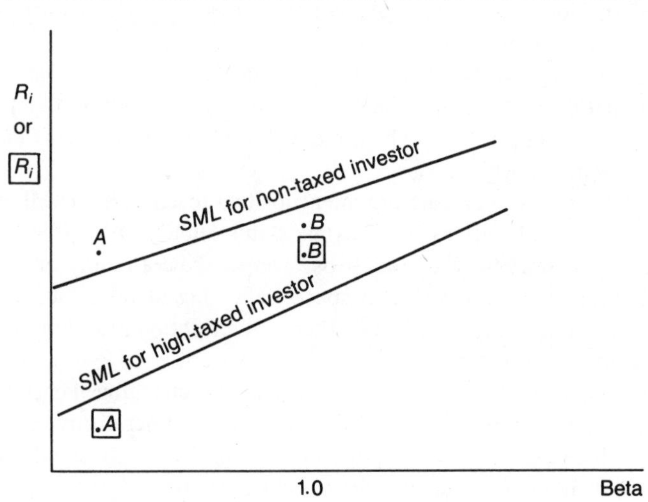

If my observation about the negative covariance between yield and beta is true, the $\boxed{R_i}$ for low-beta stocks should be more adversely affected by taxes than is true for high-beta stocks. Hence, the change in slope in the after-tax SML. (Note the change in intercept: perhaps one reason for the misspecification of R_f—the R_z problem—is taxes. CAPM may be more realistic when adjusted for taxes.)

Not only does this problem hold for SML, but it also should influence security selection. Consider security A, a slow-growing electric utility with a high yield. It may be undervalued to the non-taxed investor and considered overvalued to the high-tax-bracket investor. The reverse could be true for security B, a rapidly growing, low-yield company. Any tendency to correct for the pricing anomaly of A or $\boxed{B}$ by bidding up prices (moving these securities' plots in the direction of their respective SMLs) only makes A or $\boxed{B}$ look less and less attractive and should tend to generate compensatory selling pressures. Can a security ever be priced efficiently for all investors, given the diversity of tax circumstances? If not, what are the implications?

My mind's been wandering. The Little Professor has been talking about what he calls the "clientele effect." The clientele effect appears to refer to the individual circumstances of particular clients, including the tax effect. Investors who are exposed to taxes may hold different portfolios (more high-growth-potential securities). (By inference, so would non-taxed investors, since they could no longer hold the market portfolio, either, in the aggregate.)

The L.P. seems to minimize the significance of the clientele effect for two reasons. The first has to do with diversification. The high-tax-bracket individual would be exposed to extra market risk for which he would not be rewarded. This would cause him to diversify into lower beta securities. This argument misses the point of taxes, I think. The steep slope of the after-tax SML encourages the highly taxed investor to take more risk. Even if we were to substitute portfolio risk, as measured by σ_{Rp} for β_p (thus considering nonsystematic risk), the incentive to be a risk-taker should remain.

The second argument has something to do with the aggregate balance of investors with different clientele interests. The market portfolio impounds this balance at any moment in time. Thus, the SML still offers the most efficient way of composing portfolios.

I don't follow this aggregate argument for two reasons. The SML differential for R_i and $\boxed{R_i}$ should still hold. The tax status should still affect the relative willingness of investors to take risk. If one can imagine a family of utility curves in expected return-standard deviation space, reflecting identical attitudes towards risk, the point of tangency should be further to the right on a tax-adjusted chart for the high-tax-bracket investor.

Also, the balance of funds invested is constantly changing. Pension funds, for example, are big net equity investors in some years, and net disinvestors in others. Somehow, a changing mix of investor interests may well affect interim security returns. If so, it should be a factor influencing expectations.

(*Question*) Do taxes affect beta calculations? $\boxed{R_{it}}$ and $\boxed{R_{mt}}$ should not be the same as R_{it} and R_{mt}. Clearly R_{zt} and $\boxed{R_{zt}}$ are different. Is this important?

The Little Professor suggested that there is some empirical evidence to suggest that taxes do affect security pricing. He suggested that we follow the arguments between Litzenberger and Ramaswany[5] (pro-tax) and Miller and Scholes[6] (anti-tax). The issue is far from settled in his mind.

Transaction costs also exist. Given post-May Day transaction costs and the development of a block trading market, this market friction may have become less significant for large-portfolio managers. These costs may have risen for small investors.

There are two components to transaction costs: (1) brokerage fees, etc., associated with the transaction and (2) market impact. Market impact includes the price changes caused by buying and selling portfolio positions. Market impact is particularly important for managers of large portfolios.

Market impact can be quite significant. Apparently there are several measures of market liquidity. The most simple one is the total market value of the equity. The larger the total market value of a firm, the greater is its liquidity. Another measure is: the number of trading days necessary to accumulate or divest a portfolio position in a stock of *$X* assuming only *Y* percent of the average daily trading is used. The *X*'s and the *Y*'s would differ from investment firm to investment firm, depending on total funds under management and other factors. The lower the days are, the more liquid is the security. One service measures the amount of volume the market can absorb before a 1 percent extra-market price change takes place. And so on.

Some firms sort the stocks in their universe into liquidity classes and compute separate SMLs for each class as illustrated.

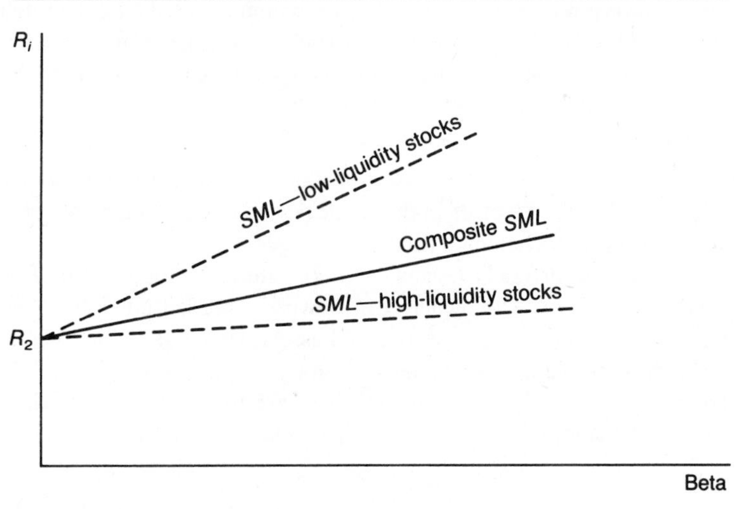

[5]R. Litzenberger and K. Ramaswany, "The Effect of Personal Taxes and Dividends on Capital Asset Prices: Theory and Empirical Evidence," *Journal of Financial Economics* (June 1979).

[6]M. Miller and M. Scholes, "Dividends and Taxes," *Journal of Financial Economics* (December 1978).

While the chart shows only two liquidity SMLs, most often there are three to five liquidity classes.

The area between the high- and low-liquidity SMLs is called the "liquidity fan." Apparently the liquidity fan can open and collapse under different market conditions and will be influenced by any changes in the composite SML.

The market liquidity return premium associated with low-liquidity stocks may be necessary to compensate for market-impact risks. Market impact may cause very sizable risks for the large-portfolio manager investing in illiquid stocks. If the large-portfolio manager tends to restrict investments to the most liquid stocks, he will have a tough time beating the market! (Is this point considered in portfolio evaluation?)

Transaction costs are a barrier to trading. So are capital gains. Do barriers to trading affect market efficiency? If so, how?

(*Question*) How do diverse liquidity SMLs affect identification of under- and overvalued stocks?

(*Observation*) If one invests in an index fund representing the market portfolio, transaction costs should be low. Does this condition affect the concept of market efficiency?

Many portfolio managers operate under policy or client constraints. There are prohibitions against selling short, borrowing, owning certain types of stocks (e.g., tobaccos), etc. Trust beneficiaries may be restricted from drawing down capital, and hence may strongly prefer to own dividend-oriented securities in their portfolios. And so on. If a number of investors *can't* behave as the capital asset pricing model says they should, what is the consequence?

(*Observation*) In high school physics, I remember calculating the rate at which a particular block would slide down a particular inclined plane in a frictionless world. My reaction was: So what? Are there sufficient frictions in the capital markets to justify the same reaction to CAPM?

8. The total asset quantity is fixed and all assets are marketable and divisible.

No firm issues new or repurchases outstanding securities, in short. Neither is true. Although quantity changes in the single period of CAPM may not be material, they may be very important over time.

Many firms are privately owned, and constitute disproportionate fractions of their owner's portfolio. The owners can't own the market portfolio. And no one can own the complete portfolio of financial assets. Home ownership may represent a similar sort of problem for the small investor.

(*Observation*) I don't know whether these are likely to be material considerations or not. Offhand, they seem to be of secondary importance.

Implications

(Written later) There seem to be a number of implications to CAPM that are not readily reflected in the discussion of assumptions.

The most important of these is that only systematic (beta) risk is relevant for individual securities while standard deviation risk is relevant for portfolios. Perhaps this is best illustrated by the difference between optimum portfolio composition in the context of the capital market line and the security market line.

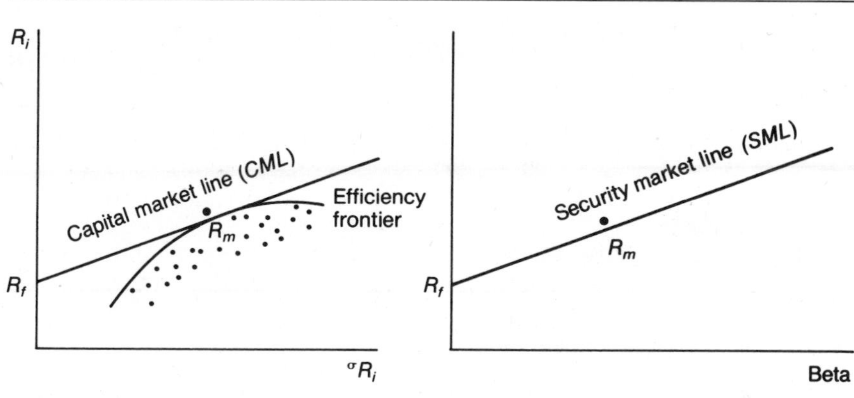

The security market line (SML) looks only at beta risk. The capital market line (CML) looks at both systematic and unsystematic risk.

The point of tangency for CML should be the market portfolio if CAPM theory is correct. In CML, the solution is arrived at by a risk/return trade-off process looking at portfolios built from the risk/return characteristics of individual securities.

In the SML model all stocks should be priced to fall on the security market line. In the CML all stocks are presumed priced below the efficient frontier line. The two representations are compatible if nonsystematic risk is truly irrelevant.

In the CAPM all investors are presumed to hold some mix of the market portfolio and the risk-free return asset (realistic?). The market portfolio is the only efficient portfolio, based on the CLM. It is a portfolio with no residual risk.

Only systematic relative volatility of securities affects pricing in the marketplace.

SML is forward-looking although its key inputs may have to be derived from the past.

The horizon is a single (often short) period.

EXHIBIT 1
The Effects of Inflation on CAPM

The Little Professor first exposited this model:

$$R_i = \text{real } R_f + \text{inflation rate} + \beta_i (R_m - R_f)$$

He then suggested a more complex model that took into account possible covariances:

$$E(\tilde{R}_i) = E(\tilde{R}_f) + \frac{\text{covariance } (R_i, R_m - R_f)}{\text{covariance } (R_m, R_m - R_f)} [E(\tilde{R}_m) - E(\tilde{R}_f)]$$

Still a more complex formulation is:

$$E(\tilde{R}_i) = R_f + \text{cov}(R_i, R_I) + \frac{E(R_m - R_f) - \text{cov } (R_m, R_I)}{\alpha\sigma R_m^2 - \text{cov } (R_m, R_I)} \cdot [\alpha \text{ cov } (R_i, R_m) - \text{cov } (R_m, R_I)]$$

where:

R_I = Rate of inflation.
α = Fraction of assets in risky assets.

Source: I. Frierd, Y. Lands Kroner, and E. Losq, "The Demand for Risky Assets under Uncertain Inflation," *Journal of Finance* (December 1976).

Central City Capital Advisors: Security Selection

[This is the first of two cases that describe how the Central City Bank adapted and used modern portfolio theory for portfolio composition and security selection. The first case focuses on the security selection process. How the security selection process was adapted to portfolio management is described in the second case.]

Central City Bank, through a wholly owned subsidiary, Central City Capital Advisors, began to systematically explore the use of modern portfolio theory in its investment activities in 1970. One aspect of this work involved security selection. By 1974 computer-based techniques using security analysts' fundamental forecasts and capital market and classical financial theories were put into operation. Evidence (presented later) showed that Central City's subsequent record of identifying firms that performed better or worse than the market was excellent—indeed, enviable. Mr. Vernon James, senior vice-president in charge of Central City's investment activities, was pleased with the lead his bank had established in its methodology and with its skill in security analysis. He wondered, however, to what extent Central City could repeat its past record.

As of September 1977, Central City employed 12 security analysts who regularly evaluated approximately 350 equity securities on the bank's approved list. The approved list included most of the country's 200 largest companies, as mea-

---

This case was prepared by a Professor of the Colgate Darden Graduate School of Business Administration of the University of Virginia with the cooperation of a company that wishes to remain anonymous.

sured by market capitalization, and was representative of a large number of industries. Each analyst was assigned several industries, which he or she followed closely. The analyst's task was very specific. Each was expected to develop the information necessary to calculate the long-term total rate of return that could be expected from each security and to review, and adjust where appropriate, an estimate of the riskiness of the security provided by an independent service organization.

Central City's security analysts had an established format for developing total-rate-of-return estimates for individual securities. The analysis was predicated on a well-developed financial theory, which states that the market price of a security should equal the present value of the security's future dividends when discounted at the rate of return required of securities of comparable risk. In practice, Central City solved for the internal rate of return necessary to equate estimates of dividend prospects and the stock's current market price.

The following equation was used to compute the internal rate of return:

$$MP = \frac{D_1}{(1+R)} + \frac{D_2}{(1+R)^2} + \ldots \frac{D_N}{(1+R)^N} + \ldots$$

where:

MP = Current market price for the stock.
D = Dividends per share (numeral refers to years in the future).
R = Internal rate of return (i.e., discount rate or expected return).

In projecting long-term dividends per share for a common stock, the Central City security analyst made five separate but interrelated estimates. First, the dividend per share for each of the next five years was forecasted by drawing on an analysis of historical trends and an analysis of prospects for the industry and firm. The security analyst next made the following additional estimates:

1. A fifth-year normalized earnings-per-share growth rate and normalized dividend-payout ratio;
2. The number of years before a steady-state growth and payout would be reached (i.e., the beginning of the terminal period, or maturity);
3. The pattern of growth to be expected between the fifth year and the year of maturity, as described by one of the following choices:
   a. A slow decay in the growth rate.
   b. A linear decay.
   c. A rapid decay.
4. A terminal growth rate, payout ratio, and implied return on equity.

These separate estimates were then translated into year-by-year, long-term forecasts of dividends per share for the firm. For simplicity, we will refer to these estimates as a security's "expected dividend stream."

The expected total return for a given security was then determined by solving for the internal rate that equated its expected dividend stream to its current market price. As the market prices of the security changed from day to day, so did the expected total return for the security. At any point, the security analyst could revise his or her estimate of the expected dividend stream to fit changing firm, industry, or general business circumstances. A computer program facilitated keeping these estimates up to date and making the required expected-return calculations.

Central City Capital Advisors' management believed that total-return expectations for securities could not be directly compared unless they were first put into equivalent risk classes. To achieve this end, Central City drew upon financial theory related to the capital asset pricing model (CAPM).

Capital asset pricing theory expresses security returns in relation to risk. The original CAPM is:

$$\tilde{R}_i = R_F + \tilde{\beta}_i (R_m - R_F)$$

where:

$\tilde{R}_i$ = The expected total rate of return for a security (i).

R_F = The risk-free rate of return, often equated with 90-day Treasury bills.

$\tilde{\beta}_i$ = The variability of total returns for a security (i) relative to those of the market, called the security beta.

$\tilde{R}_m$ = The expected total rate of return for a broadly based market index such as the Standard & Poor's 500 Index.

The tildes (~) over the variables indicate the uncertainties of the expected value estimates.

The CAPM asserts that the proper measure of risk is the relative volatility of a security's return, reduced by the degree to which the volatility can be diversified away. This measure of risk is called beta (β_i). Investors should expect to be compensated only for taking on that risk that cannot be diversified away, which is why expected return should be positively related to beta.

The historic beta for a security is usually determined by fitting a least squares regression to a series of total security and market returns. Although β_i can be determined by a number of procedures, investment professionals most commonly calculate it using monthly data for the most recent five-year period.

The beta for a security is usually measured historically; however, the CAPM's beta is expectational in concept. An immediate question arises as to how useful the historic beta is as an estimate of the future beta for the security. Unfortunately, in most cases, the historic beta for a security cannot be estimated accurately. The standard error of the beta coefficient is frequently about 30 percent of the beta estimate, and historic betas for the same security have proved unstable over time. In some instances the firm's risk characteristics have changed, but much of the variation can be ascribed simply to the inaccuracy of the historic beta measurements themselves.

At the time Central City was developing its use of modern portfolio theory, the academic community had been actively involved in trying to refine the historic measure of a firm's beta in order to obtain a more accurate predictor of future beta expectations. Of the work done, Central City had found the "fundamental" beta to be the most useful approach. This beta estimate combined fundamental firm financial ratios and variability of earnings with historic betas to project future betas for a security. Management at Central City regarded fundamental betas as an interim solution to the risk-estimation problem.

Central City subscribed to a service that provided fundamental beta predictions for all of the securities on its approved list. These estimates were turned over to the appropriate security analyst. The analyst had the option of accepting the beta estimate or revising it. Approximately 40 percent of these beta estimates were revised by the analysts, but in only 15 percent of the cases was the change more than 10 percent. The changes were made when the analyst expected future fundamental financial risks to be different from the past evidence used by the service. The resulting estimates of expected betas were then used as a measure of risk for the security.

The projected betas used by Central City were based on a value-weighted index of market performance. As a result, a high percentage of individual firms had betas greater than 1.0. Value-weighted indices are usually less volatile than equal-weighted indices. The average beta for the approved list was 1.18. The beta for the capitalization-weighted S&P 500 was set at 1.0.

When these tasks were completed, all securities in Central City's common stock universe were arrayed according to their risk/return prospects as shown in Exhibit 1. The universe was then subdivided into 10 roughly equal risk classes according to the beta measures. These classes were then summarized into five risk sectors. (Risk Sector 1 includes deciles 1 through 3; Sector 2, deciles 4 and 5; Sector 3, deciles 6 and 7; Sector 4, deciles 8 and 9; and Sector 5 is decile 10.) The averages of total security returns and betas for each sector are indicated as "*X*'s" in Exhibit 1.

A least squares regression line was then fit to the data as shown in Exhibit 2 (see heavy line). This line was called the "empirical" security market line to distinguish it from the "theoretical" security market line described by CAPM. The empirical security market line usually had a much higher intercept than the theoretical line. Other academic research (see Black *et al.*[1] in particular) had found this relationship in performance studies.

Stocks above the higher dashed line in Exhibit 2 were regarded as very attractive investment prospects and were categorized as P1 (P = positive). The least attractive were categorized as N2 (N = negative). The remaining securities were divided into three more classifications, P2, P3, and N1, in what was an approximate bell-shaped distribution. P3 securities were ones about which Central City was relatively neutral.

At any given time, there might not be a P1 security in a particular industry, yet it might be desirable to include this industry in a portfolio for diversification reasons. Exhibit 3 shows a comparative analysis of bank and chemical stocks as of a given date (the dots with circles represent securities). Other factors being equal,

[1]Fisher Black, Michael Jensen, and Myron Scholes, "The Capital Asset Pricing Model: Some Empirical Tests," in *Studies in the Theory of Capital Markets*, ed. Michael Jensen (New York: Praeger Publishers, 1972).

Central City would prefer the securities labeled A and B, if only one stock from each industry were to be selected.

Exhibit 4 shows the empirical security market line as of February 23, 1977. The break points in the risk classification on that date are indicated at the bottom of the exhibit.

P1 investments offered two features that were attractive. First, they promised high long-term total rates of return for the risk involved. Secondly, to the extent that any long-term market pricing "inefficiencies" became recognized in the short run, an additional return would be realized. This point can be illustrated by a simple example. Assume a stock is inefficiently priced to provide a total long-term return (*R*) of 15 percent (inefficient because stocks of similar risk offer 12 percent), given a dividend (*D*) of $1.00 and a stable growth rate (*G*) of 6 percent; its market price (*MP*) would then be:

$$MP = \frac{D}{R - G} = \frac{1.00}{.15 - .06} = \$11.11$$

When, a short time later, the market has bid up the price to a 12 percent total-return level (efficient, because stocks of similar risk offer 12 percent), the market price would then be:

$$MP = \frac{1.00}{.12 - .06} = \$16.67$$

The short-term return would be:

$$\frac{16.67 - 11.11}{11.11} \text{ or } 50\%$$

For other investment reasons, stocks were not only ranked by overall relative attractiveness (P1 to N2) but were also ranked again within risk sectors. There were consequently 25 different subclassifications. The rankings were revised monthly. Central City then kept score of the total return performance of each subclassification and summary classification. Exhibit 5 shows the results for 1976. Exhibit 6 shows the same data by quarters from the inception of the program.

Until 1977 portfolio managers had considerable discretion as to accepting or rejecting the recommendations of the Security Analysis Group. In addition, very demanding diversification constraints had been placed on portfolios. The result was that many equity portfolios did not perform as well as the security selection data indicated they could have. Performance only slightly above the Standard & Poor's Index was a typical achievement. Fortunately, this performance was well above the competition, and Central City was able to bring in a large amount of new business.

Mr. James had already made the decision to prevent the portfolio managers from "second-guessing" the security selection process. However, he was troubled as to whether or not he should reduce the organization's diversification constraints and loosen the requirements for broad industry representation. (This issue is discussed in the second case.) He was also concerned because the stock selection approach had not added much value in the past quarter. Mr. James was aware that several major money managers were now using similar approaches, partially because Central City was supplying its monthly, *The Security Market Line,* for a fee, to over 100 investment organizations—some of whom indicated that it was influencing their stock selection decisions. The publication reported total-return estimates and other key decision variables for all the stocks covered by the analysts.

Several issues perplexed Mr. James:

1. Although the security selection process at Central City was built around the CAPM, which in turn derived from efficient market theory, Central City was betting that the market was inefficient but would tend to become efficient.
2. As the CAPM gained currency—and Central City was abetting this process—the market might become more efficient and make it difficult to realize "excess" profits. Should Central City change its "service" policies and discontinue marketing *The Security Market Line?*
3. If competition improved, were there any refinements that Central City could devise that would help it retain a significant competitive edge?
4. A number of P1 securities dropped out from this classification within a few months after the point of initial identification. If portfolios were concentrated in P1 securities, a relatively high turnover might develop with attendant transaction costs. For personal trust accounts, extra taxes might also be involved.
5. Mr. James was aware that other models reflecting prevailing ideas had been used in security analysis work in the past but had been found to have drawbacks. For example, Benjamin Graham's Intrinsic Worth Model, which related market values to adjusted net asset values, was very hard to use successfully in a roaring bull market such as existed in the 1950s, although its record in other markets was good. Were there any limitations to the general usefulness of Central City's model? Were the results of the third quarter of 1977 a cause for concern?
6. The security line used by Central City differed from the theoretic line of the CAPM. The intercept (α) was continuously and significantly higher than the 90-day Treasury bill rate. The difference had been rationalized but not completely explained. Was this difference a cause for concern? Might not an explanation for the underspecification provide insights that would lead to further effective modification of the model?
7. The novelty of the model lay in its placing projected returns in the context of projected risk, which was intuitively appropriate. However, the effectiveness of the analysis lay in the proper definition of risk. Was the theoretical definition of risk, as modified by Central City, the most appropriate one?

8. Should the slope of the security market line affect security selection? If so, how? Should the risk category be used in security selection? Were there times when an N2 high-risk security might be better than a P2 low-risk security?
9. Experience had shown that the slope and intercept of the empirical security market line changed significantly over time. Were the movements of security returns relative to the security market line random or did they follow patterns? If the latter, how should this situation affect security selection?
10. Estimates of returns prepared by analysts were long-term in character and involved judgments. Similarly, risk measures involved judgments. How should the quality of the security analysts' work be judged?

EXHIBIT 1
Distribution of Expected Returns

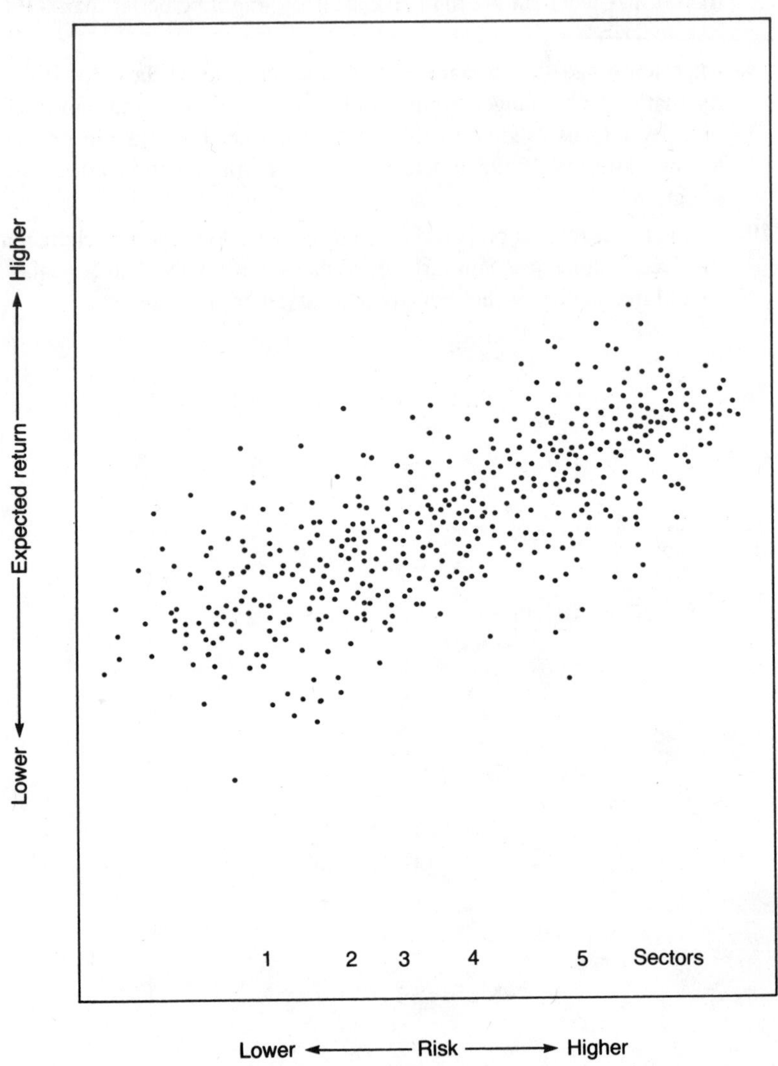

EXHIBIT 2
Distribution of Expected Returns with "Empirical" Security Market Line

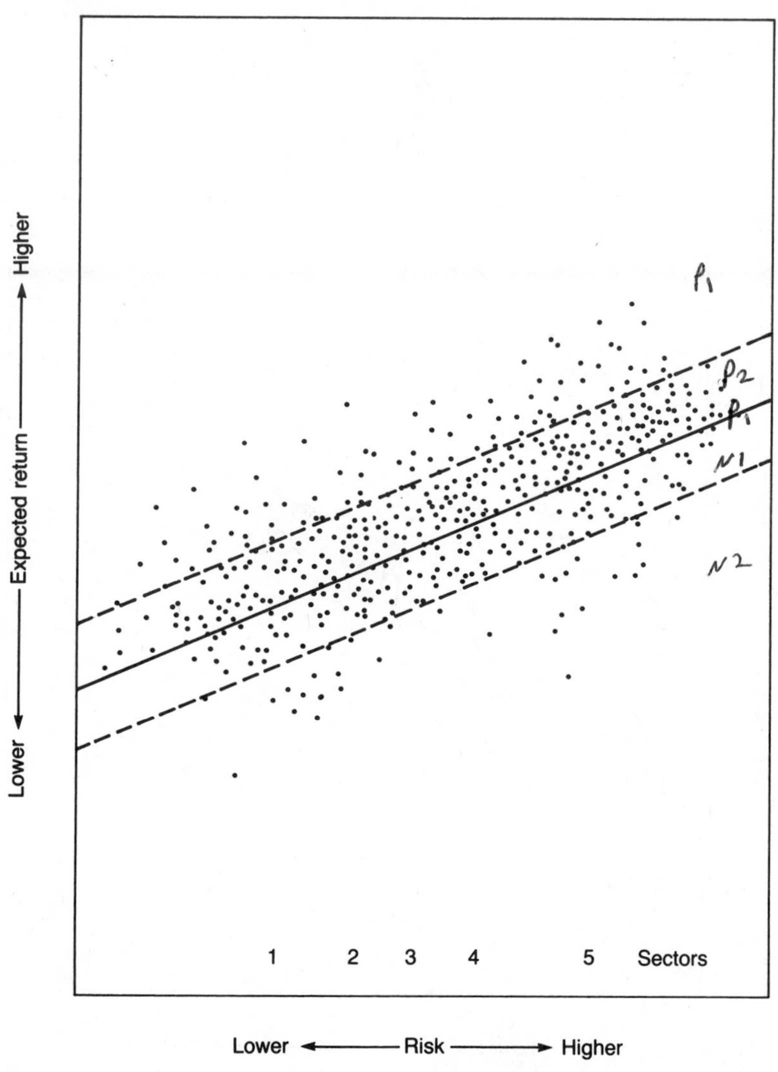

One Standard deviation above and below the line

EXHIBIT 3
Distribution of Expected Returns: Bank and Chemical Industries

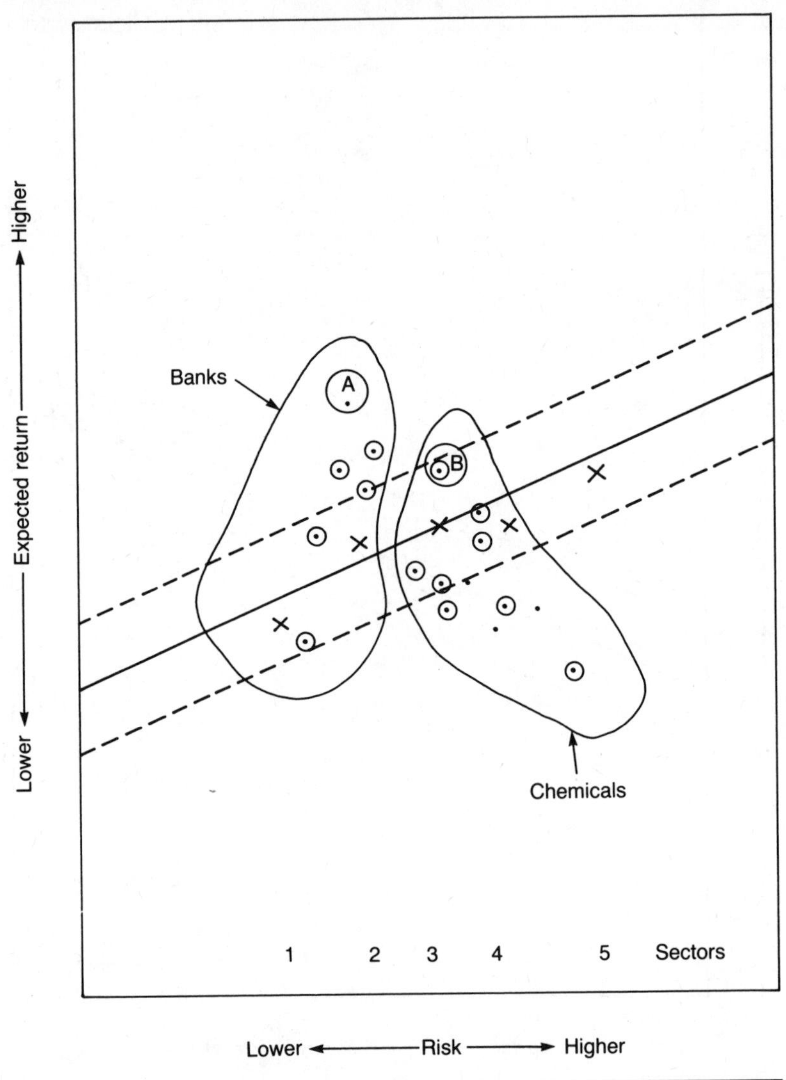

EXHIBIT 4
Security Market Line (*February 23, 1977*)

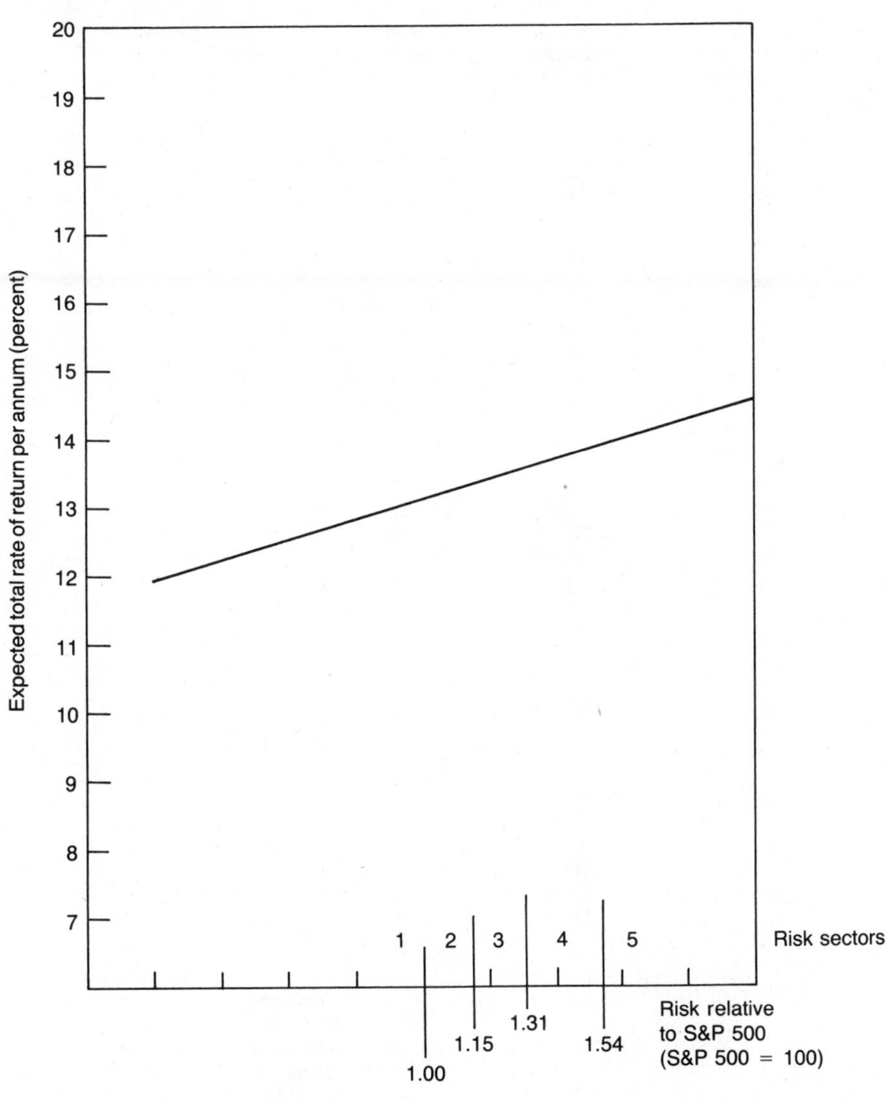

EXHIBIT 5
1976 Returns for Each Subclass of Securities

Code	Number of Securities	Rate of Return		Weighted Average Return for Risk Sector
Risk Sector 1				
P1	8	43.515		
P2	13	27.853		
P3	25	20.918		16.33
N1	21	5.211		
N2	17	1.731		
Total	84			
Risk Sector 2				
P1	7	70.982		
P2	11	37.093		
P3	21	22.134		20.52
N1	18	4.327		
N2	14	0.644		
Total	71			
Risk Sector 3				
P1	8	35.921		
P2	12	25.238		
P3	25	18.923		16.25
N1	20	11.704		
N2	16	1.194		
Total	81			
Risk Sector 4				
P1	7	60.977		
P2	10	40.911		
P3	20	27.259		28.88
N1	17	24.191		
N2	14	12.231		
Total	68			
Risk Sector 5				
P1	4	70.944		
P2	6	4.885		
P3	12	26.945		29.32
N1	10	32.738		
N2	8	26.149		
Total	40			
			Cumulative Rates of Return from 12/31/74 to Date	
Summary				
P1	34	55.933	218.796	
P2	52	29.006	113.727	
P3	103	23.078	89.635	
N1	86	12.955	58.957	
N2	69	6.045	36.903	
Total	344			

EXHIBIT 6
Quarterly Performance Stock Valuation Model* Stated as a Simple Return (%)

	P1	*P2*	*P3*	*N1*	*N2*	*All Stocks*
1975						
I	55.8	42.3	32.4	30.7	21.4	33.3
II	20.6	25.9	19.2	18.2	15.7	19.4
III	− 6.8	−14.5	−14.4	−14.9	−15.7	−14.0
IV	16.8	8.2	14.1	7.0	9.0	10.6
1976						
I	27.3	15.1	15.8	13.7	12.8	15.7
II	4.0	2.0	2.5	− .4	− 1.5	1.0
III	7.6	3.2	.8	.0	− 4.1	.6
IV	9.5	6.5	2.9	− .4	− .4	.3
1977						
I	1.7	− 6.2	− 8.4	− 9.4	−12.6	− 8.2
II	5.6	6.7	3.8	2.7	2.6	3.9
III	− 4.1	− 3.5	− 4.5	− 4.9	− 6.0	− 4.7
Total period	227.3	106.2	71.9	40.8	15.4	62.2

*Does not include transaction costs. Calculations based on price appreciation only. A regression of P1 returns against all stocks produced the following statistics:

Alpha = 6.0%/quarter $R^2 = .906$
Beta = 1.23 Standard error of residuals = 5.7% points/quarter
t alpha = 3.27

Bondsens

In early January 1978, Mr. Richard Dent, vice-president in the Trust Department of the Lee National Bank, a medium-size regional bank in the Southeast, learned of a computer program designed to help a fixed-income portfolio manager in selecting securities for a portfolio. The computer program, Bondsens (Bond Sensitivity Analysis), had been developed by Gifford Fong Associates "to examine fixed-income securities in a dynamic interest rate environment." Bondsens analyzed "the behavior of individual securities as well as the entire portfolio under conditions of change." Overseeing the investment of the fixed-income components of portfolios managed by the Lee Trust Department was Mr. Dent's responsibility, hence his interest in the program.

The Lee Trust Department had $1,247 million under management at the end of 1977. After allowing for market-value fluctuation, this sum had grown only slowly of late. The personal trust business continued to grow; however, the pension fund and profit-sharing business was suffering from competition from larger banks and other portfolio management organizations. Lee had lost several of its larger corporate pension accounts over the last few years. Overall performance in these accounts, compared with other pension fund portfolios of similar size, had proved to be relatively poor in the 1970s.

The one bright spot in this pattern was the performance of the fixed-income component of the portfolio, where the bank's performance was among the very best over the last decade. These bond portfolios had been actively managed; that is, bonds were not held to maturity but were traded in order to take advantage of anomalies in interest patterns. The portfolios might be shifted, for example, from longer-maturity issues to shorter maturities in an effort to gain superior short-term performance. A dramatic shift from long maturities to short ones in early 1973 and then a reversal in late 1974 had improved performance over a buy-hold, passive strategy. Similar changes between various classes of debt securities had also been made at points that seemed appropriate from an analysis of the market.

Two other trends were important: First, clients in many cases had become somewhat disenchanted with equity securities in recent years and now sought or were willing to permit investment of fractions of their portfolios in fixed-income securities. As a result, the portion of funds invested in fixed-income securities had grown from 34 percent to 57 percent of the total available over the past five years. Secondly, the performance of the bond portfolio had been helpful in salvaging parts of two pension accounts that would otherwise have been lost, and the bank had been able to win the fixed-income component of two new pension accounts. As a result of these factors, the relative importance of fixed-income investment in the complex of bank activities had grown.

Managers at Lee had recently attempted to step up their bond-analysis capability. Prior to 1974, Mr. Dent had managed all bond analysis and portfolio investment with the help of only one assistant and a secretary. He now had three bond analysts working for him. Still a fourth assistant had been authorized, and Mr. Dent had been searching for a qualified individual when he learned about Bondsens.

Asset-mix objectives for various classes of portfolios were decided by the policy committee of Lee Trust. This committee considered economic and market forecasts in deciding policy objectives. Mr. Dent was considered to be the "money market" expert in this group, and his inputs were among the important factors considered in deciding the target breakdown between fixed-income and equity securities. Once the targets were established, Mr. Dent had complete latitude, subject to certain diversification constraints, to determine the composition of the fixed-income portfolios. He did keep the senior vice-president informed of any major changes to be made in fixed-income portfolio composition and the reasons for changes before they were implemented.

Most of Mr. Dent's work was concentrated on understanding the dynamics of the fixed-income market, which involved looking at present and prospective spreads in the yield curve (time patterns), in risk classes (risk patterns), and in security classes (sectors) and trying to sense where superior opportunities might lie. Once a group of securities had been identified as attractive, the bank would search through recent recommendations from salesmen and services to narrow the search for particular security investment alternatives.

The bank undertook no original fixed-income security research and spent only a modest amount of time listening to or reading the recommendations of bond analysts. "Once a potential security has been identified," Mr. Dent noted, "we then read everything in sight about the issue that we can find before the final decision is made."

Mr. Dent believed that the strength of his section lay in its ability to come to a "conviction about the future course of the market," and, once the conviction was reached, "to move quickly and decisively to implement it." He added, "If we have a weakness, it is in our ability to select good securities to do the job we want done in the most effective manner. We just don't have the capability to look at very many securities in much depth and still move quickly."

It was in regard to this weakness that Mr. Dent had become interested in Bondsens. Gifford Fong Associates described Bondsens as a "powerful" tool to use in the construction of a bond portfolio. (See Exhibit 1 for a complete description of Bondsens.) The system was designed to measure the sensitivity of bond portfolios to changes in interest rates over specific periods of time. Particular benefits of Bondsens were described as allowing the user (1) to adjust future interest rates as well as time periods, in order to examine how these conditions could affect portfolio and individual security returns, (2) to restructure the portfolio in order to measure the impact of potential shifts in the maturity profile, coupon rate, quality, or terms, and thus to identify alternatives (swaps) under dynamic conditions, and (3) to measure duration to gain direct insight into the sensitivity of each security to interest-rate change.

Mr. Dent learned that the Bondsens program could be leased for under $10,000 a year for unlimited use, with the user being billed also for the computer costs involved. The run described subsequently cost $15 to $20 in computer time. The data base covered all publicly traded bonds on the New York Stock Exchange, as well as approximately 15,000 other corporate issues and over 1 million municipal issues. Gifford Fong Associates was willing to demonstrate the program for a nominal fee, and Mr. Dent decided to take advantage of this opportunity.

The portfolio chosen by Mr. Dent was a $2.64 million profit-sharing section of a bond portfolio of $5.1 million. This portfolio was less actively managed, on instructions from the client, and had a more diverse set of securities in it than was typical. Mr. Dent also included several bonds at zero face value that the bank was currently considering purchasing for one account or another.

Exhibit 2 shows the inputs required by the model. Mr. Dent elected to use assumptions that, while fairly representative of his expectations, also would tend to test the character of the model. Exhibit 3 shows the various printouts of Bondsens for the sample portfolio. Certain terms used in the model are defined in Appendix A, and Appendix B describes the concept of "duration."

As Mr. Dent reviewed the output of the sample run, he planned to answer several questions: What specific actions would I take on the basis of this information (accepting the validity of the assumptions for argument's sake)? How would these actions improve performance potential? How could Bondsens be used more effectively to help improve performance? Should there be a ceiling on the total budget for Bondsens, and if so, how much? Would I rather have Bondsens or another bond analyst in my department?

EXHIBIT 1

BONDSENS AT A GLANCE

Bondsens provides specific information regarding the securities that make up a bond portfolio as well as summary data concerning the portfolio as a whole.

Data Requirements
After the portfolio file is constructed, the user need only specify the time horizon over which he wishes to observe the portfolio or security behavior and specify the shift, if any, in yields to the future date.

Nature of the Output
Bondsens identifies the effect of time and interest rate shifts for each security examined. Each instrument's return is calculated over the projected time period. Return is partitioned by those environmental factors which influence it: the effect of moving through time, the effect of changing interest rates (market effect). Bondsens output also provides structural information which influences each security's behavior in a changing environment. The combined factors of maturity and coupon payments (duration), yield spread, calls, and coupon reinvestment rate (interest on interest) are provided. The relationship of these structural factors coupled with environmental changes leads to the price and return behavior of each security. The interrelationship allows the user to examine explicitly individual securities and their contribution to the portfolio. It also allows the user to make direct comparisons among various security holdings in order to determine whether alterations are appropriate, given a specified set of conditions.

The factors mentioned above are combined in a portfolio summary, thus allowing a transition from specific analysis to overall portfolio analysis.

Special Features
Bondsens provides for optional graphic displays that include a plot of the current and future yield curves as well as security returns plotted against duration. Portfolio summary data can be provided, reflecting time and interest shifts while suppressing individual security analysis output.

Hard Copy or Time-Sharing Computer Availability
Bondsens may be acquired as a customized printed report or accessed from a time-sharing computer.

Consultation
As a subscriber to Bondsens you will receive continuous systems support as well as personal consulting visits.

BONDSENS INPUT—KEY ELEMENTS

One year forecast, rising rates, quality spread.
Portfolio: Name of sample bond portfolio—x-xx-xx

Current Date (XX-XX-XX)	***Projection Date (XX-XX-XX)***

Interest rate projection.
Reinvestment is at average yield for each bond.
Yield shift profile:

Maturity Year	***Yield Shift XX-XX-XX***
1977.75	0.0 %
1978.00	0.6000
1978.75	0.5000
1980.75	0.4000
1987.75	0.2000
2007.75	0.1000

Quality Group	***Volatility Factor (%)***
AAA	0.0
AA	10.00
A	10.00
BAA	15.00
Other	15.00

EXHIBIT 1 *(continued)*

Projection Date
End date of yield shift projection.

Yield Shift Profile
User-specified shift in the yield curve is reflected from the present date to the future date. Yield shift represents the increase (decrease) in interest rates to the projection date and is representative of interest rate levels for the effective maturity year. For example, a new issue bond maturing in the year 2007 will have a current coupon 25 basis points higher on the projection date than it does on the current date (run date). Up to 30 points representing various maturity dates can be utilized to define the projected yield shift.

Volatility Factor Additional yield shift (in percent of nominal yield shift profile described above) applied to bonds in specified quality groups.

BONDSENS OUTPUT—INDIVIDUAL SECURITY ANALYSIS

Current Date (xx-xx-xx)	Projection Date (xx-xx-xx)

Face Value ($000)	Bond Description		Price (%)	Minimum Yield to (%)	Current Yield (%)	Total Return (%)
100	Allied Chemical Corp. Nts.	Curr:	103.250	7.640 mat.	8.111	
	8.3750% 4-1-83 A	Proj:	101.388	8.002 mat.	8.260	6.540

Impact on Price: Yield (%)	Time (%)	Total (%)	Effective Maturity Date	Duration (Yrs.)	Note
			4-1-83	4.37	
−1.366	−0.495	−1.862	4-1-83	3.70	

Face Value
The par value of the security of a corporate or municipal bond. If instrument is a mortgage (GNMA or other) face value is stated in dollars (thousands).

Price
Current price is either stipulated by the user or retrieved from the available database.

Minimum Yield
The lowest yield to maturity or yield to call (if available).

Total Return
Reflects the return earned by the instrument over the forecasted period including price impact, accrued interest and the reinvestment of coupons collected (interest on interest). (User may specify reinvestment rate.)

Impact on Price
Yield—projected price (with interest rate changes) less projected price (without interest rate changes).
Time—projected price (without interest rate changes) less present price.
Total—projected price (with interest rate changes) less present price.

Effective Maturity
Date to which a bond is priced to achieve minimum yield. If a bond becomes callable due to interest rate changes, effective maturity will be the date on which this occurs.

EXHIBIT 1 *(continued)*

BONDSENS OUTPUT—PORTFOLIO

Portfolio Summary

	Total Value ($000)	Residual Face Value ($000)	Residual Market Value ($000)	Bonds with Call Provisions (%)	Bonds Now Subject to Call (%)	Average Minimum Yield (%)	Average Current Yield (%)	Average Effective Maturity Date	Average Duration (Yrs.)	Average Quality Rating
Current (xx-xx-xx)	2903.3	2849	2903.3	0.0	0.0	7.778	7.987	11-29-87	5.22	A-1
Projected (xx-xx-xx)	3109.5	2599	2619.9	0.0		8.199	8.140	10-02-88	5.03	A-1

Projected Portfolio Performance (xx-xx-xx to xx-xx-xx)

Matured Bonds		Called Bonds			
Face Value ($000)	Reinvestment Interest ($000)	Face Value ($000)	Redemption Value ($000)	Reinvestment Interest ($000)	Earned Interest ($000)
250	0.931	0	0.0	0.0	230.747

Portfolio Return on Beginning Market Value (%)

Yield Change Impact	Time Impact	Earned Interest	Coupon Reinvstmt	Matured/ Called	Mat./Call Reinvstmt	Total	Annual Total
−0.942	−0.158	7.948	0.275	−0.052	0.032	7.103	6.986

EXHIBIT 1 *(continued)*

KEY ELEMENTS SUMMARY

Total Value
Current—market value of all bonds held.
Projected—market value of all bonds remaining (uncalled and unmatured) on evaluation date plus proceeds and interest from coupons, redemptions, principal payments, and matured bonds.

Residual Face Value
Total par value of all remaining bonds.

Residual Market Value
Total market value of all remaining bonds.

Portfolio Averages
Dollar-weighted averages over all remaining bonds.

Matured Bonds
Bondsens displays total face value and interest on reinvested cash from maturity to evaluation date for all bonds maturing before the evaluation date.

Called Bonds
Bondsens displays total face value, total cash realized from redemptions, and total funds generated from reinvestment of this cash from date of call to evaluation date.

Earned Interest
Actual total accrued interest from present date to earliest of evaluation date, call, or maturity.

Quality Rating
User can specify his own quality ratings or the system will supply Moody's ratings, where available.

Duration
Described in years, this is the weighted average of the present value of all coupon payments of a bond over the length of time to maturity plus the present value of the final payment.

Portfolio Return
The total buy-and-hold return on the beginning market value of the bond portfolio, including all reinvestment interest, is shown as of the evaluation date both as a total return and in its annualized (semi-annually compounded) form. In addition, this total return is broken down into the following components.

1. Yield change impact—price changes which may be assigned to designated yield shift change (zero if no change is expressed).
2. Time impact—due to passage of time only (assume interest rates remain unchanged).
3. Earned interest—actual coupon return without reinvestment.
4. Coupon reinvestment—"interest on interest" and interest on mortgage payments, current date to evaluation date.
5. Matured/called—return assignable to the difference between value at call or maturity and current market value for bonds which mature or are called prior to evaluation date.
6. Matured/called reinvestment—interest to evaluation date on funds received as a result of a bond's maturing or being called.
7. Total—return reflecting all elements above over the forecasted time period.

EXHIBIT 1 *(concluded)*

MATURITY PROFILE

One year forecast, rising rates, quality spread.
Portfolio: Name of sample bond portfolio—xx-xx-xx

	Current Date (xx-xx-xx)	Projection Date (xx-xx-xx)	
		Effective Maturity	
Year	Maturing ($000)	Current ($000)	Projected ($000)
1978	498.750	498.750	249.363
1979	448.800	448.800	447.222

Maturing
The current market value of instruments with stated maturity year per description.

Effective Maturity
Current—current market value of instruments with maturity to minimum yield (call or maturity) in year shown at current interest rates.
Projected—projected market value of instruments with maturity to minimum yield (call or maturity) in year shown based on yield shift at future date.

BONDSENS REVISITED

It is readily apparent that Bondsens provides the user with a substantial amount of information. This information provides insights into the following questions and more.

Under a given environment which securities provide the highest return, including the trade-off between coupon and maturity volatility?

Which securities have the greatest interest rate (market) risk?

What instruments will be affected by the terms of the indenture (call) under a changing interest rate environment?

Does a particular swap really improve future return?

To what extent do changing quality spreads influence portfolio return?

The questions above, and many more, are answered directly through Bondsens analysis. The answers provide a framework for the portfolio manager to better recognize the characteristics of his portfolio and to help implement change in order to improve portfolio performance.

EXHIBIT 2
Assumptions Made by Mr. Dent as Model Inputs

PORTFOLIO: "X" PROFIT SHARING PLAN—LEE (Identification of portfolio.)

CURRENT DATE	PROJECTION DATE	
1-31-78	12-31-78	(Projection date can be altered to suit interest of management.)

INTEREST-RATE PROJECTIONS

REINVESTMENT IS AT AVERAGE YIELD FOR EACH BOND

Applied to reinvestment of interest income and matured or called bonds from the date of receipt of funds. Other assumptions feasible.

YIELD-SHIFT PROFILE

Analysis focuses on change from existing yield curve. An upward interest shift is shown as a positive item. Forecast yield is equal to the current yield plus the forecast change with appropriate attention to sign. The model smooths these data into a yield curve.

Maturity Year	*Yield Shift (12-31-78)*	*Quality Group*	*Volatility Factor (%)*
1978.08*	0.0 %	AAA	0.0
1978.33	0.9000	AA	15.00
1979.08	0.7000	A	25.00
1983.08	0.5500	BAA	40.00
2008.08	0.2500	Other	40.00

The *yield shift* table should be read as follows: Time to maturity represents the difference between the stated maturity and the current date shown on the top line under the column heading; 1978.33 is thus a 90-day maturity. 1983.08 is a 5-year maturity. The Yield Shift column should be read as follows for the line 1978.33: as of 12-31-78, the yields for 90-day securities will have increased by 90 basis points from their level as of 1-31-78.

The yield curve generated above is for prime-grade securities. The yield on lower grade securities tends to change more. The *volatility factor* specifies how much more the change will be, in the opinion of the forecast. In computation the volatility factor is divided by 100, and 1 is added to the resultant. This factor is then multiplied by the yield-shift data to determine the yield curve for lower quality issues.

*Decimals refer to fractions of a year. A month $\doteq$ .08.

EXHIBIT 3
Sample Bond Portfolio Analysis

PORTFOLIO: "X" PROFIT SHARING PLAN—LEE

Current Date	Projection Date
1-31-78	12-31-78

Impact is decreasing because you are projecting rising interest rates.

Face Value ($000)	Bond Description		Price (%)	Minimum Yield to (%)	Current Yield (%)	Total Return (%)	Impact on Price: Yield (%)	Impact on Price: Time (%)	Impact on Price: Total (%)	Effective Maturity Date	Duration (Yrs.)	Note
100	ALLIED CHEM CORP	CURR:	100.000	8.375MAT	8.375					4-01-83	4.30	
	8.3750% 4-1-83 A	PROJ:	97.628	9.060MAT	8.579	5.652	−2.372	0.0	;2.372	4-01-83	3.65	
200	ARIZONA PUB SVC CO	CURR:	103.750	8.387MAT	9.157					2-15-82	3.46	
	9.5000% 2-15-82 A	PROJ:	101.016	9.119MAT	9.404	6.246	−1.991	−0.743	−2.734	2-15-82	2.78	
200	ASIAN DEV BK	CURR:	100.750	8.121MAT	8.437					4-15-80	2.06	
	3.5000% 4-15-80 AAA	PROJ:	99.670	8.776MAT	8.528	6.972	−0.785	−0.295	−1.080	4-15-80	1.25	
100	ATLANTIC RICHFIELD CO	CURR:	101.875	8.437MAT	8.466					4-01-00	10.33	
	8.6250% 4-01-00 AA	PROJ:	98.027	8.832MAT	8.799	4.332	−3.820	−0.028	−3.848	4-01-00	9.98	
250	COMMERCIAL CREDIT CORP	CURR:	100.000	8.375MAT	8.375					9-01-79	1.51	
	8.3750% 9-01-79 A	PROJ:	99.463	9.223MAT	8.420	7.553	−0.537	−0.000	−0.537	9-01-79	0.66	
100	CONSOLIDATED NAT GAS CO	CURR:	95.500	8.365MAT	8.246					12-01-95	9.68	
	7.8750% 12-01-95 AA	PROJ:	91.769	8.821MAT	8.581	3.870	−3.836	0.106	−3.731	12-01-95	9.30	
100	CONSUMERS PWR CO	CURR:	95.625	9.083MAT	9.020					11-01-00	10.07	
	6.6250% 11-01-00 BAA	PROJ:	91.536	9.555MAT	9.423	4.321	−4.146	0.057	−4.089	11-01-00	9.71	
100	GNMA	CURR:	96.999	7.851MAT	7.732					12-15-02	8.68	
	7.5000% 12-15-02 AAA	PROJ:	94.573	8.162MAT	7.930	4.913	−2.497	0.071	−2.426	12-15-02	8.35	
250	FEDERAL NATL MTG ASSN	CURR:	100.190	7.126MAT	7.436					9-11-78	0.61	
	7.4500% 9-11-78 AAA	PROJ:	100.000	7.450MAT	7.450	6.999	0.0	−0.190	−0.190	9-11-78	0.00	Matured

EXHIBIT 3 (*continued*)

Face Value ($000)	Bond Description		Price (%)	Minimum Yield to (%)	Current Yield (%)	Total Return (%)	Impact on Price: Yield (%)	Impact on Price: Time (%)	Impact on Price: Total (%)	Effective Maturity Date	Duration (Yrs.)	Note
200	FIRST PA CORP CAP NT	CURR:	97.875	8.204MAT	7.024					11-01-79	1.68	
	6.8750% 11-01-79 A-1	PROJ:	98.293	9.043MAT	6.994	7.102	−0.656	1.073	0.418	11-01-79	0.83	
200	FLORIDA POWER CORP	CURR:	100.000	9.000MAT	9.000					11-01-00	10.04	
	9.0000% 11-07-00 A	PROJ:	96.128	9.421MAT	9.363	4.702	−3.872	0.000	−3.872	11-01-00	9.70	
250	GENERAL AMERN											
	TRANSN CORP	CURR:	99.375	7.036MAT	6.289					12-01-78	0.82	
	6.2500% 12-01-78 A	PROJ:	100.000	6.250MAT	6.250	6.647	0.0	0.625	0.625	12-01-78	0.00	
200	HERCULES INC	CURR:	101.375	8.416MAT	8.631					4-01-83	4.27	
	8.7500% 4-01-83 A	PROJ:	98.785	9.101MAT	8.858	5.717	−2.287	−0.203	−2.590	4-01-83	3.63	
100	ONTARIO PROV CDA	CURR:	95.750	9.026MAT	8.982					3-15-04	10.50	
	8.8000% 3-15-04 AAA	PROJ:	93.028	9.323MAT	9.244	5.821	−2.761	0.040	−2.722	3-15-04	10.22	
100	UNITED STATES TREAS NTS	CURR:	98.500	7.331MAT	6.218					5-31-79	1.30	
	6.1250% 5-31-79 AAA	PROJ:	99.245	8.019MAT	6.172	6.602	−0.273	1.018	0.745	5-31-79	0.41	
200	SOUTHERN CALIF EDISON CO	CURR:	101.875	7.832CLL	8.834					11-01-79	1.66	
	9.0000% 11-01-81 AA	PROJ:	100.812	8.605CLL	8.972	6.845	−0.615	−0.949	−1.583	11-01-79	0.82	
0	MOUNTAIN STS TEL & TELEG CO	CURR:	107.813	8.801CLL	8.928					9-01-80	2.36	
		2-27-78:	107.684	8.913MAT						9-01-15	11.20	
	9.6250% 9-01-15 AAA	PROJ:	105.642	9.092MAT	9.111	6.620	−2.104	−0.067	−2.170	9-01-15	11.00	
0	UNITED STATES TREAS NTS	CURR:	101.068	7.741MAT	7.916					2-15-83	4.25	
	8.0000% 2-15-83 AAA	PROJ:	99.001	8.291MAT	8.081	5.600	−1.898	−0.164	−2.062	2-15-83	3.59	
0	AMAX INC	CURR:	96.375	8.642MAT	8.301					1-01-86	5.97	
	8.0000% 1-01-86 BAA	PROJ:	93.114	9.363MAT	8.592	4.394	−3.567	0.306	−3.261	1-01-86	5.43	
0	FORD MTR CR CO	CURR:	98.000	8.759MAT	8.673					3-15-91	8.10	
	8.5000% 3-15-91 A	PROJ:	94.061	9.325MAT	9.037	4.340	−4.018	0.079	−3.939	3-15-91	7.68	
0	PACIFIC GAS & ELEC CO	CURR:	66.344	8.803MAT	6.971					6-01-92	9.64	
	4.6250% 6-01-92 AA	PROJ:	64.536	9.307MAT	7.167	3.860	−2.940	1.132	−1.808	6-01-92	9.19	
0	NORTHERN NAT GAS CO	CURR:	103.500	8.166CLL	8.696					5-01-83	4.31	
	9.0000% 5-01-85 A	PROJ:	100.529	8.850CLL	8.953	5.389	−2.461	−0.509	−2.971	5-01-83	3.68	

Portfolio Summary

	Total Value ($000)	Residual Face Value ($000)	Residual Market Value ($000)	Bonds with Call Provisions (%)	Bonds Now Subject to Call (%)	Average Minimum Yield (%)	Average Current Yield (%)	Average Effective Maturity Date	Average Duration (Yrs.)	Average Quality Rating
Current (1–31–78)	2643.9	2649	2643.9	26.4	0.0	8.102	8.099	8–28–85	4.07	A-1
Projected (12–31–78)	2807.4	2148	2101.2	32.1		8.973	8.556	2–17–87	4.16	A-1

Projected Portfolio Performance (1–31–78 to 12–31–78)

Matured Bonds		Called Bonds			
Face Value ($000)	Reinvestment Interest ($000)	Face Value ($000)	Redemption Value ($000)	Reinvstmt Interest ($000)	Earned Interest ($000)
500	7.480	0	0.0	0.0	188.821

Portfolio Return on Beginning Market Value (%)

Yield Change Impact	Time Impact	Earned Intrst	Coupon Reinvstmt	Matured/ Called	Mat./Call Reinvstmt	Total	Annual Total
−1.574	−0.035	7.142	0.327	0.041	0.283	6.183	6.670

Maturity Patterns*

Year	Maturing ($000)	Effective Maturity Current ($000)	Effective Maturity Projected ($000)
1978	498.912	498.912	0.0
1979	544.250	748.000	745.111
1980	201.500	201.500	199.340
1981	203.750	0.0	0.0
1982	207.500	207.500	202.032
1983	302.750	302.750	295.197
1995	95.500	95.500	91.769
2000	397.500	397.500	381.819
2002	96.514	96.514	92.869
2004	95.750	95.750	93.028

*Current Date 1–31–78; Projection Date 12–31–78.

EXHIBIT 3 ***(concluded)***
Sample Profit Sharing Plan (*1–31–78 to 12–31–78*)

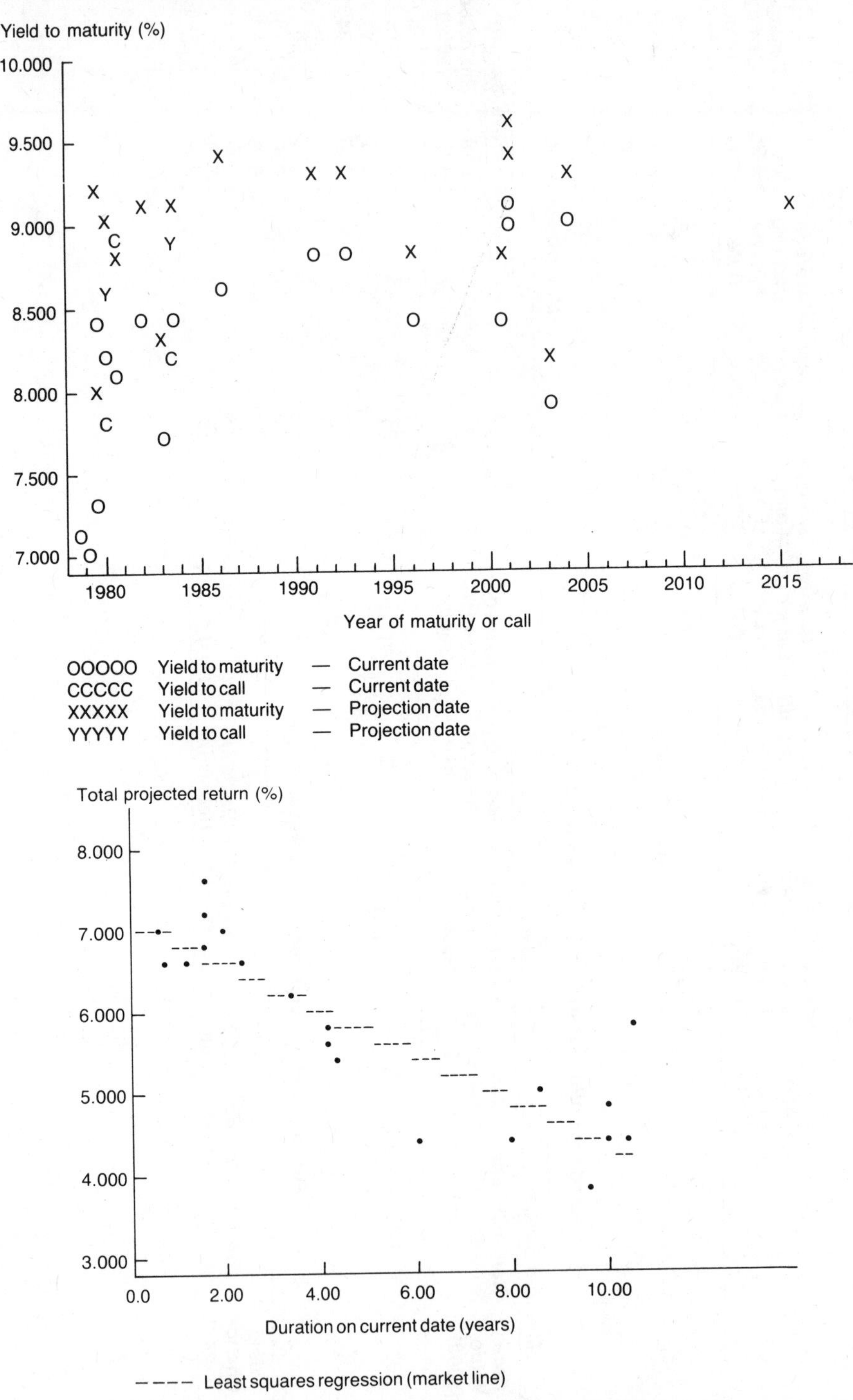

Appendix A

TERMINOLOGY

Term	Definition	Comment
Face Value	Bonds were usually denominated in $1,000 units. Face Value is the par value of the security. It is also the amount that will be paid upon maturity. The units represent the number of bonds in the portfolio.	Bonds with zero in the Face Value column were *NOT* in the portfolio. They represent items that Mr. Dent was considering for possible investment. These items are not included in portfolio summaries.
Bond Identification	Includes the name of the issuing agency, the stated interest rate, and the date of maturity. The stated interest rate (a percentage) when multiplied by the face value equals the dollar size of the annual interest payments.	
Price	Price is quoted as a percentage of the face value of the bond. Current prices are closing market quotations of the last trade. Projected prices are those prices expected to prevail on the projection date, given the forecast changes in interest rates.	
Minimum Yield to	The "internal rate" necessary to equate the prevailing bond price to the scheduled stream of interest. These calculations are very precise and take into account the specific date of payment.	1. Projected yields were determined from the model's yield-curve projections. These yields, when used to discount future cash flows from 12-31-78, determined the projected price.

Term	Definition	Comment
	MAT indicates yield to maturity. CLL indicates yield to prospective call date.	2. Certain bonds were subject to call at prices above the face value. Bondsens analyzed an issue to determine when, if at all, it might be economically attractive for the issuer to call the issue by refinancing. When it could be attractive to refinance at some point in the future, the prospective date of call was noted in the Effective Maturity Date column. Intervening interest payments and the call price were used to determine the yield to the call date.
Current Yield	The simple yield determined by dividing the annual interest payment by the current market price.	
Impact on Price, Total	The projected price minus the current price in the Price column.	This total price change was then decomposed into its two component parts. Some change in price was caused by the change in interest rates forecast. This change is shown in the Yield column. Price changes also occurred because a security was nearer to maturity. These are shown in the Time column. Time changes tended to be more pronounced when a security was nearing maturity, when it was selling at a more sizable premium or discount above its face value, or when the yield curve was more sloped.

Term	Definition	Comment
Total Return	The simple yield plus the total price change. Rates are annualized.	The evaluation period, in this instance, was only 11 months. Total returns were calculated on a 12-month or annualized basis, which complicates verification.
Effective Maturity Date	The actual maturity date or the estimated call date, if the security could be called economically.	
Note	Matured bonds are considered to be invested at their face value at the rate specified in the assumptions. They are omitted from the prospective maturity patterns data, but not from the total portfolio analysis.	

Appendix B

EXPLANATION OF DURATION[1]

The Duration Concept

The point of departure in evaluating portfolio performance, whether it be of bonds, stocks, or anything else, is the development of an adequate benchmark, or standard. Then the actual return can be compared to this "fair return" to determine the incremental benefits due to fund management. This logic underlies comparisons to a market index or a sample of other managers.

Just as the price behavior of stocks contains a strong market component, the price of all fixed-income obligations tends to be markedly affected by changes in the level of interest rates. For bond portfolios, a broadly based capitalization-weighted index such as the Salomon Brothers High Grade Corporate Bond Index or the Kuhn Loeb Bond Index can serve as the S&P 500 used for evaluating equity portfolios.

In recent years the idea of risk adjustment has been widely accepted with respect to stock portfolios: high risk, or high beta, portfolios appreciate faster in

[1]Excerpts from Dennis A. Tito and Wayne H. Wagner, "Definitive New Measures of Bond Performance and Risk," *Pension World*, May 1977.

rising markets and fall faster in declining markets. But would an analogous concept work for the measurement of bond sensitivity? The answer, not surprisingly, is that it would.

The customary way of computing beta coefficients for equity issues is to regress security returns against index returns. This approach does not work well for bonds, however, because bonds change their sensitivity characteristics as time passes and the market itself changes. For example, a bond about to mature is far less sensitive to interest-rate changes than a bond a long way from maturity. Furthermore, bonds are less sensitive to interest-rate changes when promised yields-to-maturity are high rather than low. The net effect is that the regression technique used for beta computations does not apply very well to the derivation of bond risk measures.

Actually, the computation of bond sensitivity measures is far simpler than the computation of beta coefficients for stocks. One relationship, derived by Frederick Macaulay in 1938, incorporates all the factors that relate sensitivity of bond price changes to changes in interest rates. Macaulay named it *duration*.

The duration of a bond measures the sensitivity of its price to changes in interest rates: the longer the duration, the greater the impact of yield changes on price. An increase in bond yields causes a percentage decrease in price equal to the duration times the change in yield. For example, the price of a bond with a 10-year duration will increase 10 percent in response to a 1 percent fall in yield to maturity.

Like time to maturity, bond duration—or mean term to maturity, as it is sometimes called—is measured in years. The difference between duration and time to maturity is that duration measures the average time to receipt of coupon income, principal repayment and any other cash flow. Sinking fund provisions and call features can be incorporated by properly identifying the timing of the expected cash flows. Evaluative factors such as quality, marketability, and tax status are reflected in the duration computation through the yield factor.

Figure 1 shows how three bonds with 20-, 10-, and 5-year maturities respond to changes in yield to maturity. Each bond is assumed to be selling at par to yield 9 percent per annum. The durations for the bonds are, respectively, 9.4, 6.7 and 4.2 years. The exhibit plots the expected price change for each bond for changes in interest rates up to 100 basis points in either direction. As an illustration of the duration concept, note that the price change for the 20-year maturity bond in response to a 100 basis-point fall in yield is 9.4 percent, equal to the computed duration multiplied by the negative of the change in yield on the bond.

The duration of an entire portfolio can be computed by weighting the durations of the individual bonds that comprise the portfolio by their relative dollar weights in the portfolio. Thus, by observing how the manager is responding to market expectations by varying the duration of the portfolio, it is possible to assess the impact of interim changes in holdings, interest rates, and time to maturity on the sensitivity of the portfolio. In addition (as we will see), it is also possible to relate the performance of a particular portfolio to the performance of bond markets in general, using the duration concept.

FIGURE 1

Expected price change for three different bonds when interest rates move up to 100 basis points in either direction.

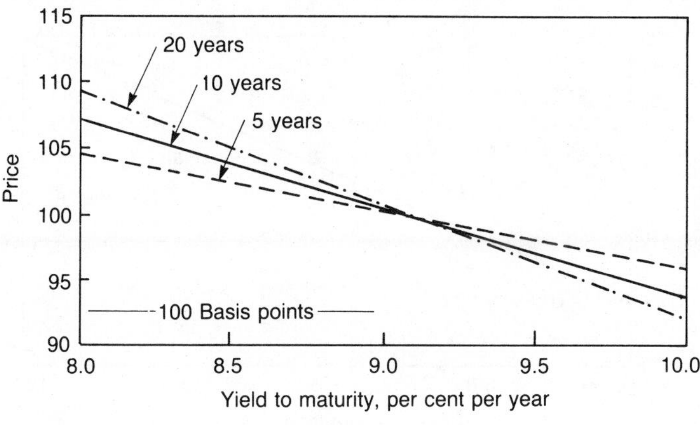

The Bond Market Line

One of the most valuable features of the beta concept for the analysis of equities and equity portfolios is the theory of the market line. The market line, which is customarily drawn between the return on a risk-free asset such as Treasury bills and the return on the S&P 500, shows the period-by-period returns for assuming equity risk. The stock portfolio manager would be credited with a positive net management effect if the return on his portfolio exceeded the "market return" at the beta of his portfolio.

The same concept applies to the bond market, except that the duration of the bond portfolios replaces the betas of stock portfolios. Figure 2 plots the rates of return on various bond indexes against their durations for the year ending September 30, 1976. The market line is drawn between 90-day Treasury bills with a return of approximately 5 percent and a duration of three months, and the Kuhn Loeb Bond Index with a return of approximately 22 percent and a duration of approximately 9.75 years. The Kuhn Loeb Index duration is computed by treating it as though it were a single bond with a schedule of cash flows equivalent to the sum of the cash flows of the bonds that comprise the index.

Several other industrial group indexes are shown. It is comforting to see that these collections of bonds lie close to the postulated bond market line. In general, it is our observation that this market line works well in practice: The results of other indexes and actively managed portfolios tend to lie close to the market line. In fact, the observations we have made of the bond market line indicate that it is a better descriptor of the bond market than the beta approach is of active stock portfolios.

FIGURE 2

Return versus duration for one year for several different indices and portfolios. "Total" refers to Kuhn Loeb Index. Note how closely the different portfolios lie to the bond market line.

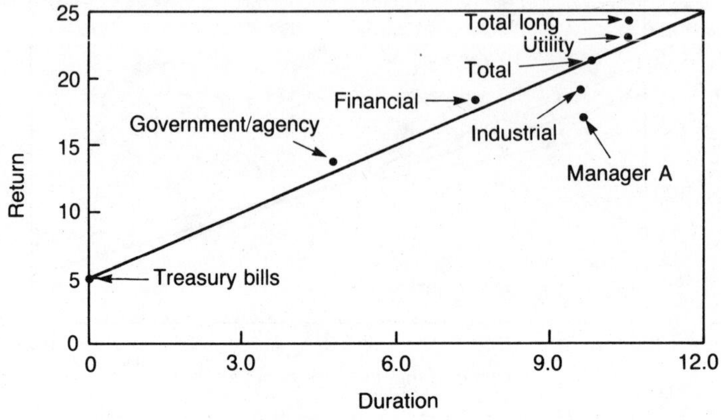

FIGURE 3

Return versus duration for the same indices as in Figure 2, but for the quarter ended September 30, 1976. Manager A's risk just matched his return for the three months.

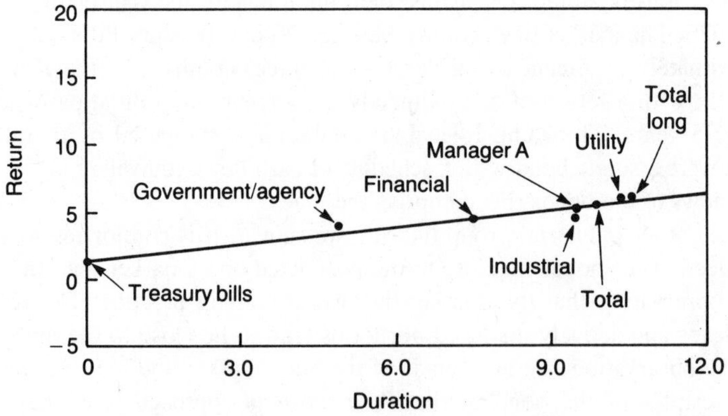

The actual performance of a particular fixed-income manager's portfolio is also plotted on the chart. Net management effect is represented by the vertical distance between the portfolio's return and the corresponding point on the market line at the same duration. Because the return on this actual portfolio was lower than the return on the total index, yet had approximately the same duration, this manager would be assigned a negative net management effect for the year.

Figure 3 shows an extremely good fit between predicted and observed return/duration relationships for the quarter ending September 30, 1976. During this three-month period, the fixed-income manager realized a bond portfolio return that just compensates for the level of duration risk undertaken. Hence, his net management effect for the quarter would be zero.

Part IV

Methods of Capitalizing on Market Anomalies

Down-Town Trust Department (A)

"For several years now, we have been selecting common stocks based upon perceived long-term pricing inefficiencies, taking both expected risks and returns into account," noted Mr. Thomas Mix, Chairman of the Senior Policy Committee of the Trust Department of the Down-Town Bank of New York. "Subsequent performance of the group that we identify as most attractive (top 15 percent of all stocks reviewed) has been outstanding on average—much better than we had reason to expect. The dispersion of returns within this group is still wide, of course. What I'd like to have us explore during this meeting is the cause of these errors. Can we learn something from this experience that will help us to improve estimating capacity? As you well know, a number of investment managers are developing systems similar to the ones we use for identifying more attractive stocks. I'm afraid that if we don't develop our systems further, other firms will be identifying the same inefficiencies we are, and the inefficiencies will tend to disappear."

The Down-Town Bank of New York was one of the 25 largest banks in the United States. Its commercial roots lay in retail, as distinct from wholesale, banking, although in the postwar years it had developed the kind of broad and quite competitive service capacity generally associated with strong money-center banks. In part because of its history, Down-Town's trust business did not have as large a share of the market as did the commercial side of the business.

This case was prepared by a Professor of the Colgate Darden Graduate School of Business Administration of the University of Virginia with the cooperation of a company that wishes to remain anonymous.

In the early 1970s, when many similar organizations were fighting the ideas associated with the rapidly developing field of modern portfolio theory, management of the Trust Department of Down-Town saw in these developments a potential competitive advantage. They thereupon began exploratory research into the feasibility of using some of the modern portfolio theory concepts toward practical ends.

By mid-1975 management was in the process of implementing the more successful models and approaches emerging from its experimentation. The timing was ideal. Poor equity market performance in the early 1970s and concern over the implications of ERISA were causing a number of employee-benefit-plan sponsors to reconsider their objectives and methods. Some of these sponsors were quite receptive to the ideas being used at Down-Town. Since 1975 the funds under active management at Down-Town had more than doubled. By early 1979 Down-Town had approximately $2.5 billion of managed accounts, of which better than 70 percent (in dollar value) were employee-benefit clients.

In his discussions with modern portfolio theorists, Mr. Mix had learned that all but the purists seemed to accept the fact that the market was not perfectly efficient at all times. Pricing "anomalies," as they were called, might develop and provide attractive buying or selling opportunities.

Down-Town's Security Analysis

Down-Town's approach to security analysis identified a significant number of potential under- or overvaluation pricing anomalies in the bank's common stock universe. Subsequent performance of securities identified as "strong buys" or "strong sells" by this system confirmed the fact that this identification system had a high "information content." Over the last five years, a portfolio of securities (equally weighted) identified as strong buys at the outset of each year outperformed the Standard and Poor's 500 Index by, on average, better than 10 percent per year in the ensuing 12 months. Similarly, the "strong sell" group underperformed this index by an average of about 8 percent per year. Both *ex ante* and *ex post*, the risk characteristics of these two portfolios were quite similar. Some of these results were achieved "on paper" in simulated portfolios. Within the last 18 months, Down-Town had taken steps to assure that the demonstrated security "selection" capability was more fully reflected in actual portfolio performance. In this 18-month period, those portfolios in which clients were willing to take more risks in order to achieve better return results had performed very well. The compound return was about 6 percent per year above the market, and risks were controlled at a level equivalent to a portfolio beta of about 1.15 (i.e., total risk, including unsystematic risk associated with this beta).

The research group at Down-Town followed 280 common stocks, a number that was increasing by about 20 per year (with about a 5 percent turnover as well). These securities were drawn from a representatively diverse number of industries.

In the security-selection process, the returns for each security were estimated by projecting its dividends per share into the future and then determining the internal rate of return which discounted this dividend stream to the current market price of the security. A security analyst was charged with making a number of specific decisions about prospective earnings-per-share growth, dividend payout, return on equity, and maturation process (changes in growth rates with product maturity) to develop the dividend stream forecasts. The security analyst also measured the risk for the security. The risk measure was somewhat comparable to a market beta estimate but tied more closely to estimates of the projected fundamental risk characteristics of the firm in question. More specific details on these estimating procedures were considered proprietary. As market prices or firm circumstances changed, estimates were updated.

Twice a month, the estimates of return/risk for each security were summarized into a "security market line," using least squares regression techniques (see an illustration in Exhibit 1). This line, called the "fitted security market line," was considered to represent the *ex ante* expectations of the market's risk/return relationships. Stocks that plotted above the fitted security market line were considered undervalued (i.e., had a positive alpha). Overvalued stocks fell below the line (i.e., had a negative alpha). The vertical distance between a stock's plot and the market line was used as a measure of its alpha.

Those stocks whose alpha estimates were in the top 15 percent of the universe were "strongly preferred" or "strong buys." Most portfolios were invested so that at least half the equity market weight of the portfolio was composed of stocks from this group. Other stocks were added for diversification purposes in an effort to control *ex post* portfolio risk. A portfolio composition model designed to achieve a prespecified portfolio alpha with minimal residual risk and an acceptable beta level was used to facilitate this objective. Portfolio turnover was also constrained by an algorithm to average less than 20 percent per year. Portfolio managers had the latitude to alter portfolios proposed by the composition model when a change was considered beneficial.

The universe was also subdivided into three "liquidity" categories (most to least liquid) based on the number of trading days necessary to accumulate or divest a significant position in each stock followed without putting pressure on the stock's price. Fitted security market lines were developed for each of these liquidity categories. These latter lines tended to be somewhat different in slope and intercept from the primary ("composite") fitted security market line (with the least-liquid line generally above the most-liquid line). Liquidity-line alphas were also calculated. This information was used subjectively by portfolio managers in making final portfolio change decisions and by the policy committee in specifying "portfolio tilt" objectives toward more or less liquid securities.

Mr. Mix was increasingly aware that other banks and fund management organizations had begun developing security-selection systems similar to those of the pioneers such as Down-Town. Therefore, the anomalies now being identified by Down-Town researchers might disappear. It was this concern that had led Mr. Mix to call a meeting of more knowledgeable Down-Town investment officers to discuss what might be done to stay ahead of the field.

Senior Policy Committee Meeting

At the meeting of the Senior Policy Committee and certain other trust department officers, Mr. Mix wanted them to consider: "How can Down-Town remain ahead of the competition in the use of modern portfolio theory?" His opening remarks made clear his concern that other institutions were beginning to develop procedures similar to those used at Down-Town. The quotes below are abstracted from the discussion that followed:

President of Trust Department: The growth of funds under management has certainly been most attractive over the last few years. It's beginning to cause a different kind of problem for us. Our total equity portfolio is now about $1.5 billion. A 2 percent position in a stock in all portfolios now involves a commitment of $30 million. Accumulating or divesting a commitment this size can only be done expeditiously in the more liquid stocks on our approved list. Our flexibility in developing portfolios is beginning to be compromised.

Quantitative Systems Manager: Our present system (based on alphas developed from the composite market line) is biased against the most liquid stocks. If we were to use the security market line for the most liquid group of stocks, the calculated alphas for this group would typically be higher. I believe that we can use a measure like the number of trading days necessary to accumulate a $30 million position in a stock as an additional dimension in our analysis. If we did this, we would end up with a security market "plane." Stock rates of return would be a function of both risk and liquidity. Alphas could then be measured relative to the plane. We could add a constraint to our composition model, such as keeping portfolio liquidity to an average of 45 days or some such constraint for large portfolios. In any case, the "revised" alphas should encourage more investment in high-liquidity stocks.

Portfolio Manager A: You're right in principle but wrong in purpose. The least liquid stocks have (with an occasional exception) a higher (liquidity) security market line than the most liquid stocks. In general, they should be preferred because they offer more return for less risk. My solution to this problem would be to increase the number of less liquid stocks we follow. By identifying, say, an additional 100 of the most promising companies from a diverse set of industries in non-Standard & Poor's 500 companies, we would probably pick up 20 or 30 firms with "strongly preferred" alphas. [This action was feasible inasmuch as the trust department was planning to increase its security-analysis work force in order to increase coverage.] We could end up investing less in each of these stocks (say 1 percent) and have both a more diversified portfolio and a higher expected rate of return.

Portfolio Manager B: That might be a little difficult to do if we all want the same low-liquidity stocks at the same time. We would have to control somehow the collective purchase and sales of these securities. Some of our competitors have set up pooled funds to facilitate controlled investment in low-liquidity stocks. Portfolio managers can then invest part of their funds in the pool up to a maximum fraction of their portfolio. The pool would then be treated as a single security in their portfolio analysis.

(Considerable discussion followed as to what others were doing and how accounts might invest more funds in less liquid securities. Several noted that turnover-minimization objectives made the simultaneous buying or selling of these stocks unlikely. Problems related to the death (really, price nose-dive) of "hot" issues were also discussed.)

Senior Security Analyst A: Now I am confused. I thought that one of the principles of modern portfolio theory was that one could only achieve excess returns by taking more risks. The simple capital asset pricing model does not consider liquidity as a risk. It assumes investors are "price-takers" and do not influence prices by their actions. Liquidity is a real risk for us. The "liquidity plane" seems to me to be an appropriate adjustment. My impression in that low-liquidity stocks tend to move together anyway. To use these stocks to any great degree in our portfolios would mean higher portfolio betas and higher residual errors, wouldn't it? If so, that may mean an unsatisfactory level of total risk.

Portfolio Manager A: You know, I don't think we really know the answer to your questions, both asked and implied. Modern portfolio theory also assumes you can't make excess returns unless you have superior information. With every few exceptions, we don't have superior information. We get our edge by using available information more fully and effectively in some judgmental sense of the word. I am beginning to wonder if the theory isn't wrong in other important respects. What troubles me most is the belief that superior returns can only be achieved by taking greater risks. We have been keeping track of how our portfolios perform in the subsequent quarter, assuming they are invested in the strongly preferred (top 15 percent) and the least preferred (bottom 15 percent) list in equal amounts [see Exhibit 2 for data on these results, which do not consider transaction costs]. Let me call your attention to the fact that the most preferred group has outperformed the market in every quarter. While the group's standard deviation is slightly higher than the S&P 500's, the superior performance is caused by very spectacular upside performance in one or two quarters. I can't see how anyone could say that this performance is more risky. If you ask me, we (and our composition models) are too preoccupied with diversification. Actual portfolio performance is, in any case, less than it should be because we load a lot of inferior stocks for their alleged diversification benefits.

Quantitative Systems Analyst: I've been worrying about this same point but in a different way. If we took our strongly preferred portfolio and mixed it with some corporate bonds—say 80 percent/20 percent—returns would be better than the market and risks less, I'm pretty sure. Our present composition model presumes the market portfolio is on the efficiency frontier. If it should not be—as our evidence tends to suggest—the whole notion of minimizing nonsystematic risk relative to the market may be wrong. [A more concrete testing of these ideas was encouraged.]

Security Analyst B: I think one of our problems relates to how we measure security risk. As you know, we measure return over the long run. It always seemed strange that we should measure risk in a very short-term context—one based upon relative stock-to-market monthly volatility. We've gone through several cycles now. First, we used a plain market beta [$R_i = a_i + \beta_i\ (R_m)$] based on five years of monthly data. This proved a poor predictor of future betas. In fact, the naive forecast that all stocks had a beta equal to one was almost as good a forecaster of future betas. We tried the risk-premium model [$R_i - R_f = a_i + \beta_i\ (R_m - R_f)$] without a material improvement in forecasting ability. We have tried several adjustments (Bayesian, Blume, etc.) to improve this measurement, again with modest benefits. Even at the portfolio level we could only get decent forecasts of future portfolio betas if the forecast was close to one. We have tried several other measures of risk and are now trying to project risk using estimates of future firm fundamental characteristics. I don't think we will find these results much better when we accumulate enough evidence to test their predictive ability. [The research department used a mean-square-error test of actual versus forecast for these evaluations.] Are we fooling ourselves? Is beta a useful measurement of risk? In my opinion, we overdiversify our portfolios because the composition model is largely diversified against our own measurement errors. This kills our demonstrated superior stock-selection capability.

Portfolio Manager A: Our fitted security market lines tend to be much flatter than theory says they should be. The intercept of the fitted line is much higher than the risk-free rate, and the slope, less. You guys [the quantitative systems group] call it misspecification. With a comparatively flat line, measuring risk shouldn't be that important. [Several noted that the line did become steeper in certain markets.]

Security Analyst B: Our basic strategy is to buy and hold. We try to keep portfolio turnover to about 20 percent per year, which implies an average investment period of five years. Why should we be worried about short-term portfolio volatility under these circumstances? Theory tends to assume that portfolios can be recomposed instantaneously and without cost. If this were feasible, perhaps we could trade in and out of the market as prices bobbled, but we know we can't. As a security analyst, I'm much more concerned about the problems of measuring security return. We make a single "point estimate" of a security's return. We all know that this estimate is uncertain—more so in some cases than in others. We ignore this uncertainty in our security-selection process, or perhaps we assume beta captures it all. I don't think so. Before we got hooked on this modern portfolio kick, we used to make probabilistic measures of return (reduced to a mean and a standard deviation). We then made security-selection decisions based on the coefficient of dispersion ($\alpha R_i/R_i$, as projected).

President: I remember those days all too well. One thing I think we can say for sure is that consideration of covariance is important in reducing portfolio risks. In my opinion, this is the single most important contribution theory has made. Portfolio risks, not stock risks, are paramount.

Security Analyst B: That's just the point. When we made forecasting errors, usually we made the same kind of error across all companies in the same industry. This result would now be called high positive covariance. We then reduced those risks by diversifying by industry so that our mistakes would tend to be offsetting (i.e., have high negative covariance) because we would be spreading out our bets. Modern portfolio theory misses this point.

President: Can we really diversify our bets? If the market goes off sharply, almost all the stocks in our universe drop in price too. We can't diversify this risk anyway. We can only control it, we hope, by having a low portfolio beta when the market is vulnerable on the downside.

Portfolio Manager A: Betas are useful for cyclical market-timing purposes. We do try to increase the portfolio beta when the market outlook is optimistic and decrease this beta when it is not. However, over the course of a cycle—four or five years—results are driven by how accurate—in a collective portfolio sense—our estimates of stock returns are, not by the market.

Senior Vice-President—Portfolio Management: Where have you been for the last dozen years? Our equity performance has been good relative to the market, but the market has been so poor that good is pretty bad.

Portfolio Manager A: But we beat the market because of our security-selection capability. Wouldn't we have done better if we had simply selected the stocks with the best returns from a somewhat diverse group of favored industries? In 1973–1974, when we ran a closet index fund in the belief that high portfolio R^2s were good, we got clobbered. Matching the market is a defeatist attitude.

Senior Security Analyst A: You've heard me express my concern before about the way we measure security returns. With the dividend model we are using, the most critical decisions (that is, the ones to which results are most sensitive) are the hardest to make. The terminal rate of return on equity (from which we determine dividend growth thereafter) tends to be the most critical. Earnings-per-share results five years out and the length of time before a firm reaches maturity are also very critical. These inputs aren't estimates, they are guesses. I'd rather be held accountable for estimates made in the first five years, where my diagnostic skills will count for more.

Mr. Mix: The one thing we can count on is that you will fight the new system to your dying breath, George. But it works. I'm too much of a pragmatist to abandon something that works. What concerns me is that it may not work as well in the future. Most of the comments made so far suggest we should develop a new theory. I'm skeptical about our capacity to do this. I was hoping for more practical ideas. Are there any other suggestions?

Quantitative Systems Analyst B: I was talking to my counterpart at another bank that uses a system similar to ours. They develop two alpha and beta estimates. One set is similar to the ones we use. The other set reflects the security analyst's judgment. The average of these estimates reportedly gives better results than either does separately. There are several articles to this effect in the literature also. Frankly, I'm intrigued by the coefficient of dispersion based on the uncertainty of security-return estimates. Would this second type of estimate improve our forecasting ability?

Senior Vice-President—Portfolio Management: One of our competitors adjusts return estimates—and perhaps risk estimates—for taxes. Our fitted capital market line is okay for our tax-free clients. It may not work as well for high-tax-bracket trust clients.

Quantitative Systems Analyst A: We are working on making tax adjustments. There are two problems: (1) because the pension market is so much more competitive now, this project keeps being pushed back in terms of priorities; (2) capital gains, which are not taxed until realized, are also a tough problem to deal with conceptually. But you're right, the after-tax market line for a high-bracket investor is different. It tends to have a higher slope (because many low-beta stocks also have high yields). Also, the stocks with the best alphas tend to be different. We can accelerate our work on this project if you think it will be useful. What I see coming out of this work is a "tax plane" similar to the "liquidity plane" we discussed earlier.

Quantitative Systems Analyst B: I have begun to study the time series of the monthly alpha estimates. [He thereupon presented the data for four companies, as shown in Exhibit 3.] These data don't look random to me. As you know, we make excess returns—assuming no change in estimates—when the alpha for a firm decreases. I have been wondering whether a more detailed study of such data could help us in predicting changes in alpha.

Portfolio Manager B: I've been wondering about the same problem. If we bought a portfolio of high-alpha stocks today, how long would it be before the information wore out—that is, before the portfolio ceased to generate excess returns? The information we use always seems to me to be better at identifying buys than sells. If we followed our buy recommendations (keeping only strongly preferred securities in the portfolio), we would have a very high turnover rate—more than 100 percent per year. We need better sell information.

Quantitative Systems Analyst A: We do have an algorithm to reduce trading. At the moment, we have to see a 2 percent (approximate) alpha differential (risk unaffected) before the composition model recommends a change in portfolio composition. Whether the algorithm is sufficient in light of this discussion is another matter.

Mr. Mix: We're going to have to adjourn this meeting about now. We have covered a lot of interesting ideas this morning. I'm going to have to do a lot of thinking about priorities—priorities for investigation or for action. We can't act upon all these ideas, and it's going to be tough deciding which ones are more promising. We have limited time in our quantitative systems group, and I'm going to have to consider the cost/benefit of these ideas very carefully. Let me know if you have any ideas after you've reflected on this discussion further.

EXHIBIT 1
Method of Estimating Security Market Line

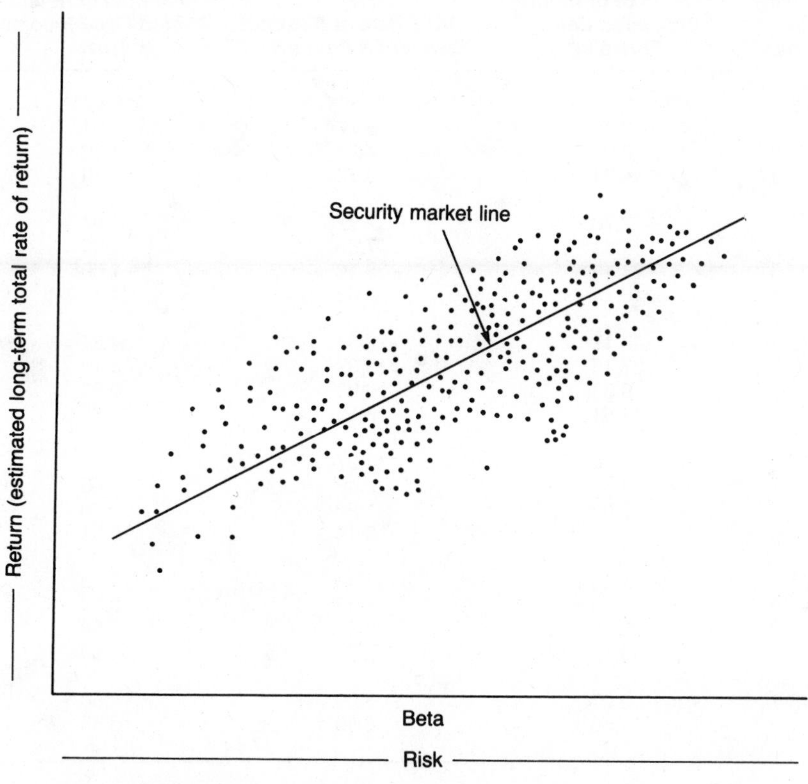

Note: Each dot represents the risk/return plot for one of the securities followed by Down-Town. The security market line is fitted to the plots for all stocks by least squares regression techniques.

EXHIBIT 2
Performance of Simulated Portfolio Relative to Two Benchmarks (*Jan. 1973–June 1978*)

Year and Quarter	Total Rate of Return Simulated Equity Portfolio*	Total Rate of Return Standard & Poor's 500	Total Rate of Return Pooled Fixed-Income Trust
1973-1	− 3.98%	− 4.89%	0.42%
2	− 2.18	− 5.77	0.51
3	6.01	4.81	1.30
4	− 4.31	− 9.16	1.19
1974-1	− 2.70	− 2.82	−1.63
2	4.81	− 7.56	−3.05
3	−23.16	−25.16	−1.60
4	16.14	9.38	1.41
1975-1	48.17	22.94	4.34
2	27.16	15.37	3.19
3	− 6.37	−10.95	−0.99
4	13.51	8.65	7.35
1976-1	23.15	14.97	4.75
2	3.84	2.48	2.40
3	2.02	1.92	0.00
4	4.47	3.14	6.51
1977-1	− 1.43	− 7.44	−1.20
2	5.16	3.32	3.57
3	− 2.02	− 2.82	1.54
4	0.15	− 0.13	−0.69
1978-1	− 2.03	− 5.00	−1.50
2	14.50	8.40	−0.45

*The stocks with the highest alphas (top 15 percent) were purchased and held throughout the subsequent quarter opening. Weights were equal. Subsequent total returns for the portfolio were monitored and are recorded here. No transaction costs have been assessed, although quarterly turnover averaged 30+ percent.

EXHIBIT 3
Examples of Alphas for Four Companies (*Jan. 1974–Oct. 1978*)

Year and Month	American Home Products	Anheuser-Busch	Baltimore Gas and Electric	Beneficial Corporation
1974– 1	−2.00	−1.90	1.60	−0.06
2	−2.53	−2.05	1.81	0.68
3	−2.59	−1.87	2.02	1.65
4	−2.67	−2.14	2.89	2.27
5	−3.29	−2.66	4.47	1.87
6	−3.31	−2.85	5.67	1.38
7	−1.81	−1.82	5.54	1.39
8	−2.02	−2.13	4.21	1.99
9	−1.01	−2.14	4.48	1.25
10	−1.95	−2.17	3.70	1.60
11	−1.22	−2.10	3.71	0.25
12	−1.72	−2.60	4.43	0.36
1975– 1	−0.14	−1.91	2.08	0.15
2	−0.00	−2.58	1.99	1.32
3	−0.08	−2.35	2.17	2.03
4	−0.00	−2.55	2.40	1.61
5	−0.11	−2.01	2.40	1.16
6	−0.10	−2.24	1.79	1.15
7	−0.31	−2.02	2.24	2.13
8	−0.51	−1.74	1.35	2.05
9	−0.19	−1.47	1.82	2.05
10	−0.44	−1.65	1.80	2.50
11	−0.45	−1.71	0.69	1.38
12	−0.20	−1.60	1.12	1.87
1976– 1	−0.13	−0.90	0.21	1.18
2	−0.13	−0.71	0.35	1.16
3	−0.20	−1.31	0.89	1.04
4	−0.01	−1.28	0.38	1.32
5	−0.14	−1.20	0.70	0.72
6	−0.29	−1.01	0.61	1.00
7	−0.12	−1.15	−1.65	0.25
8	−0.46	−1.07	−0.37	0.78
9	−0.54	−0.99	−0.57	0.95
10	−0.59	−0.53	−0.58	1.18
11	−0.25	−0.26	−0.30	1.42
12	−0.09	−0.85	0.01	0.82

EXHIBIT 3 ***(concluded)***

Year and Month	American Home Products	Anheuser-Busch	Baltimore Gas and Electric	Beneficial Corporation
1977– 1	0.40	−0.77	0.05	1.24
2	0.05	−0.99	0.24	1.79
3	0.19	−1.05	0.58	1.91
4	0.60	−1.12	0.41	2.20
5	1.01	−1.09	−0.32	2.75
6	0.41	−1.15	−0.31	2.13
7	0.54	−1.04	−0.71	2.05
8	0.30	−1.04	−0.80	3.20
9	0.63	−0.67	−0.40	2.77
10	0.71	−0.30	−0.25	3.38
11	0.71	−0.09	−0.50	3.01
12	0.69	−0.13	−0.15	3.36
1978– 1	0.50	−0.11	0.38	4.03
2	0.67	−0.04	0.78	3.12
3	0.81	−0.69	0.73	3.55
4	0.57	−1.01	1.03	3.54
5	0.27	−1.04	0.87	3.43
6	0.59	−1.45	0.75	3.09
7	0.15	−1.28	0.30	2.76
8	0.21	−1.19	0.14	2.01
9	0.41	−0.60	0.61	1.81
10	0.90	−1.25	1.18	3.82

Note: Alphas may change as the result of:
1. Changes in the market price of the stock.
2. Changes in the security market line.
3. Changes in analysts' estimates of returns for the stock.
4. Changes in analysts' estimates of risks for the stock.
5. Passage of time.

Down-Town Trust Department (B)

[The background information necessary to understand this case is reported in the Down-Town Trust Department (A) case.]

Following a meeting called to explore ways in which the Down-Town Trust Department could maintain the competitive edge the firm had developed in its security-selection process as others copied the system, Mr. Mix received the four memoranda set forth (in edited form) below. All the points seemed to merit further consideration.

MEMORANDUM

TO: Tom Mix
FROM: (Bond Analyst)

As you know, we have begun to use *duration* as one measure of bond security risk. Like betas for stocks, duration is believed by some people to be a measure of systematic risk for bonds. It is not a measure of total risk, of course.

Duration of a bond measures the sensitivity of its price to changes in interest rates. The longer the duration, the greater the impact on price of a given interest-rate change. Duration is the weighted average of the present value of all coupon

This case was prepared by a Professor of the Colgate Darden Graduate School of Business Administration of the University of Virginia with the cooperation of a company that wishes to remain anonymous.

and scheduled repayments over the length of time to maturity. (See note at the end of this memorandum.) Duration is usually measured in years (to two decimal points, in our shop). Price and return volatility are partially a function of duration. The longer duration is, the greater are the volatility risks.

Stock analysts have from time to time noted that low-beta stocks are often high-payout, slow-growth stocks, whereas high-beta stocks are often high-growth, low-payout securities. This is exactly what one might expect if duration were a factor influencing stock prices.

Duration risks are not independent of bond prices. If the yield of a bond rose significantly because its bond price fell, we would expect its duration (risk) measure to decrease.

The stock analysts have been very concerned about beta instability. Prices of stocks vary more dramatically, and *ex ante* risk expectations should change with those prices. Beta instability is to be expected. Duration, which can in principle be applied to stocks, would capture this change in perception of risk. *Ex post* betas (historical results) are likely to be distorted by the changes in perception of risk caused by price movements.

It would be simple to develop a program for calculating the duration of stocks and cheap to run it bimonthly (given data already in our computer). By a scaling process, duration estimates could be converted into beta estimates.

I suggest that we consider combining the security analyst's beta estimates with a duration-related beta. The resulting betas will not be stable over time but I do not believe that they should be.

Stocks tend to be more volatile than bonds. In part this may be because cash-recovery estimates are more uncertain and must be revised from time to time. Stocks also tend to have much longer durations than bonds. These factors could be a cause of the extra volatility.

Note: The formula for duration (D) at time, t_o, for a security is:

$$D_{t_o} = \frac{\sum_{j=1}^{n} (t_j - t_o) A_{t_j}}{\sum_{j=1}^{n} A_{t_j}}$$

where:

n = Number of periods to the maturity of the security.
t_j = A time period between $t=o$ and $t=n$.
A_{t_j} = Present value of income and capital recoveries forecast for the security in period j, discounted at the yield to maturity of the security.

and:

$$\frac{dP_{it}}{P_{it}} = (-D_{it})\,(dr_{it})$$

where:

dP_{it} = Change in security price for security i.
dr_{it} = Change in yield to maturity.

MEMORANDUM

TO: Thomas Mix
FROM: (Security Analyst)

Considerable attention yesterday was devoted to possible problems that could arise if more and more people copy our security-selection system. In an efficient market, our superior selection skill should tend to disappear. I don't believe this will happen.

I accept the fact that we (and others) seldom have "special" information—or at least have it long enough to execute buy-and-sell orders that are as large as ours. In this sense, the market is efficient. I do not, however, accept as fact that available information will be used with equal skill by all, as efficient market theory does.

As a matter of curiosity, I compared the market line information we use with those of two competitors. The date I happened to select (August 1978) was a period when we all foresaw a relatively flat "fitted" security market line. Under these circumstances, differences in estimating security returns would be largely responsible for any differences, since risk measures would be less influential.

The slopes were all similar; however, the beta or slope difference was about 6 percent. The estimated "market return" for a portfolio beta of 1 differed by as much as 177 basis points. We, incidentally, were in the middle.

All of the securities listed as strong buys for us on that date were also on their approved lists. Of the stocks we considered best bets, 57 percent were also considered best by [competitor A] and 43 percent by [competitor B]. Only 31 percent of our best bets were on both their preferred lists. Within this latter group, alpha estimates were noticeably different. (Incidentally, we seem to like "growth" stocks better than they do, and I think this can be traced to systematic causes.)

I also checked the beta estimates for about two dozen stocks. There were some similarities and some differences. In our system, betas affect portfolio composition (as handled by our composition model), which in turn affects what we buy and sell. The transaction cost algorithm further moderates actions. I doubt very much if the buy/sell orders placed or the portfolio mix on a given date are very similar to those of these competitors. Efficiency would only be affected by collective actions that were more or less concurrent.

While I have not looked into this question systematically, my impression from the many outside stock recommendations that we review is that we are more often selling than buying when others are recommending buys.

You may remember our discussions of the Miller article[1] and his ideas on pricing efficiency, when it first appeared. I won't review these arguments, but we thought his ideas fit better with experience than did "perfect market" theories.

All this means to me that our time would be better spent trying to improve what we are now doing rather than doing something new and perhaps throwing the baby out with the bath water.

---

[1]Edward W. Miller, "Risk, Uncertainty and Divergence of Opinion," *Journal of Finance,* September 1977.

As you know, we still have not developed a system to appraise the performance of security analysts. Until we can agree on a common performance-appraisal system, we have probably not wrung dry all the value added that our security analysts are capable of achieving.

MEMORANDUM

TO: Thomas L. Mix, Jr.
FROM: (Senior Security Analyst)

The average *ex ante* alpha in our preferred list (top 15 percent) tends to be about 2 percent per year. After the fact, this group is averaging performance better than 19 percent per year. Some sort of leverage factor is at work. The dispersion around this average is fairly large and appears to be asymmetrical with the median less than the mean.

There is, I think, a systematic reason for this multiplier or leverage effect. Our return estimates are very long term in character. Short-term returns tend to be higher because the market tends to correct for the undervaluation we have identified. We call this the "short" game.

The short game occurs because of a change in price/earnings ratios that our present analytical system fails to forecast.

It is hard to forecast dividends and dividend growth for the next five years. (I chose five years because we tend to think in terms of intermediate-term results.) Estimates beyond that point are, in all honesty, just intelligent guesses. These later estimates tend to account for over 80 percent of current market price, in present value terms, in our system. These hunches are obviously very important in determining relative value. We have several checks to make sure the collective estimates seem reasonable.

These checks do not make use of an important piece of information that security analysts tend to develop a useful feel for—the price/earnings ratio.

Using the same input information we now use but adding a price/earnings ratio, we would develop a system that we, the analysts, will feel more comfortable and confident about.

I have tried this system out on about a dozen stocks that I follow. This system causes different estimates of total returns and alphas. Security rankings change. Estimated alphas tend to be more in line with *ex post* results.

The dividend-stream approach we now use is based on a rather abstract theory for which I have seen no empirical proof. We know that it underestimates and misestimates alphas.

The terminal dividend stream (generally, dividends 15 or more years in the future) accounts for almost 50 percent of today's market price, typically. Our estimates of long-term dividend yield and growth are keyed to an estimate of a terminal rate of return on equity capital. I checked our estimates of this rate. They were X percent [confidential] ± .5 percent. In short, we all tend to make the same guess as to what this key estimate (terminal rate of return on equity) will be. (The uniformity of this guess is hardly surprising because the Standard and Poor's 500 terminal rate of return on equity is formally estimated and is provided to analysts as a "guide.") Heaven knows that it is hard to be more precise, dealing as we are with the distant future. The standard deviation of historical returns on equity for our universe tends to be about 12 percent. This should still be true 15 years from now. In short, we know that a key estimate in our return calculation will be wrong, but we don't know how. Sizable distortions result in our return estimates for stocks as a result. My system will reduce the seriousness of these misestimates.

A portfolio manager tells me that, if we develop more realistic estimates of alphas for our "strong-buy" stocks, this will change portfolio-composition decisions. Our composition models load the most desirable stocks into the portfolio on the basis of the ratio: alpha/standard error of the alpha estimate (i.e., residual error). Higher and more realistic alpha estimates would change this loading.

We have been charting relative price/earnings ratios for years (stock p/e ÷ Standard and Poor's 500 p/e). We have a good idea what these ratios will be in the future. The theory behind this analysis may not be formally developed, but it exists in our mind's eye.

I propose we proceed in two steps to determine an estimate of a security's short-term rate of return from which a more realistic alpha can be deduced.

The first step in this analysis would be to discount all dividends beyond five years to a "projected" market price at the end of five years. This market price could then be divided by our "normalized" (i.e., mid-cycle) earnings-per-share estimate to derive a projected price/earnings ratio. If the security analyst thought the price/earnings ratio was too high or too low relative to the Standard and Poor's 500 ratio (Down-Town's system would also provide this estimate), the analyst could correct the stock's price/earnings ratio and, through that, its market price at the end of the fifth year. These changes would have to be justified, just as our other estimates are.

At what rate would dividends beyond five years be discounted? Well, we often talk about a "normal" security market line. We could simply construct one that seems normal for the circumstances we foresee five years out. Given such a line, we would infer a rate for a single firm from our estimate of beta for the firm.

Once the fifth-year closing market price is established, the interim rate of return would be readily calculable from this price, the interim dividend estimates, and the price today. We would use these data in the same risk/return framework we now use to measure alphas.

The market price at the end of the fifth year would still account for more than 80 percent of the present value of the stock's market price. However, it would be keyed to two estimates—fifth-year earnings per share (eps) and p/e ratio—about which we feel more confident. The more realistic alphas will also favorably affect portfolio composition. There will be more concentration on winners and less diversification into losers.

MEMORANDUM

TO: Thomas L. Mix, Jr.
FROM: (Bond Portfolio Manager)

I have been impressed by how similar bond and stock analysis is becoming.

For example, we look at the spread between our value-weighted Standard and Poor's 500 Index estimate of total returns for stocks and the Utility AAA yield rate. When the spread looks unusually wide, we tend to go longer on stocks and shorter on bonds. We have, of course, been using similar spreads between yields in various sectors of the bond market to achieve improved risk/return results for many, many years.

Stocks, like bonds, seem to follow short-term return movements that are quite different from their long-term expected rate of return, or in bond terms, yield. We have developed a procedure that helps us to deal with the shorter aspects of investment performance.

Periodically, we project five economic scenarios for conditions, say, 12 months hence. Associated with each scenario is a yield-curve forecast and subsector risk-spread forecast for that terminal date. Each set of forecasts is used to estimate price on bonds (in our portfolio or the one that we are considering) at that point in time by discounting recovery streams beyond that date at the appropriate yield for that type of security to that date. Interim rates of return are then developed from intervening interest flows, the projected market price for the terminal date one year hence, and the current bond price.

For each scenario, we estimate a short-term total rate of return for every bond in which we have an interest. We assign probabilities to each scenario, which allow us to project an "expected" short-term rate of return for the bond and a crude measure of uncertainty (standard deviation). We can then spread out these estimates on a risk/return matrix and find those bonds with superior estimated returns for the risks foreseen over the forthcoming 12-month period.

The fitted security market line you use for stock selection is very transient. We have seen it change significantly in a short time (for example, from September 1974 to January 1975). In short, it behaves like a yield curve.

In each of our scenarios, we already estimate what the S&P 500 Index will be promising in the way of return a year hence. To project a future capital market line for that date, all we would have to add is an estimate of the slope of the line.

Given five estimates of "future" security market lines, the interim expected return and the risk associated with each stock could be readily estimated by the same procedures used for bonds.

If these short-term estimates of risks/returns for stocks are arrayed in a risk/return matrix, you can fit what I will call an "incremental" security market line to the data. When the market outlook is on balance poor, the line will even slope down to the right. In general, slopes will be much more unstable than those you now use. However, *ex post* security market lines for a year are similarly unstable.

I'm sure you will find that this new stock "incremental" risk measure will be different from and more descriptive than your current beta measures are. You will also find that the short-term "incremental" alphas will be different from the "long-term" alphas you now use. You will, in short, tend to identify different stocks as your winners and losers. This system will improve your discriminating capability, I feel sure.

I have outlined the bare bones of the analogy of our approach to bond investing to a possible approach to stock investing. As you know, we have made considerable refinements in our bond approach over the last several years. Many of these refinements also seem applicable to stocks as well.

If you have any questions about this approach, let me know. It is a little complicated, and the implications are hard to describe simply. It would not cost much to run out a set of data to see what happens.

Central City Capital Advisors: Equity Portfolio Composition

[This is the second of two cases setting forth how the Central City Bank adapted modern portfolio theory for investment purposes.]

During the past year (1976), Mr. Vernon James, manager of Central City Capital Advisors, a wholly owned subsidiary of Central City Bank, had established a requirement that the organization's institutional portfolio managers make full use of a portfolio-optimization program in an effort to get full value from the security-selection skills exhibited by the firm's Security Analysis Group. This latter group had been reorganized earlier and was making use of an improved security-valuation model. It had been very effective in its stock selection (see Exhibit 1).

Since Mr. James, over a period of years, had become less and less pleased with the performance results of the loosely structured investment management approach, in 1971 he had implemented an investment process in accordance with each client's risk-bearing capacity. Because back in 1971 there had been no strong evidence that his research group could "pick" stocks successfully, portfolios were highly diversified. As a result, Central City's portfolios had about one half as much non-market-related risk as the typical institutionally managed portfolio. Yet the performance of Central City portfolios placed them well up in the top half of money managers' results (see Exhibit 2).

This case was prepared by a Professor of the Colgate Darden Graduate School of Business Administration of the University of Virginia with the cooperation of a company that wishes to remain anonymous.

In establishing the recent portfolio diversification guidelines, Central City management had access to a number of academic studies on portfolio diversification. One finding of the studies was that even randomly selected portfolios had more stable performance than individual securities. This stability increased with the number of securities in the portfolio, but at a decreasing rate:

Number of Securities	*Average Return*	*Annual Range of Returns*	
		68% of Portfolios	*95% of Portfolios*
2	9%	−11 to 29%	−31 to 49%
8	9	−1 to 19	−11 to 29
16	9	2 to 16	− 5 to 23
32	9	4 to 14	1 to 19
128	9	7 to 11	4 to 14

Portfolios composed by randomly selecting from certain types of securities did not, however, reduce total risk by as much as risk was reduced for portfolios with forced industry diversification. Also, there was evidence that certain classes of stocks (for example, growth, income, and cyclical) had above-average covariance within the class and below-average or negative covariance between classes, so that efficient combinations of these stocks might lead to lower portfolio risks. This finding also meant that a simple beta approach, which assumes that there is no extra-market covariance, would not provide optimal portfolio risk control.

Central City therefore decided to find a practical way to capture some of the extra-market covariance. A statistical analysis sorted 58 industries into 10 "super industries." These 10 super industries (called economic/market sectors) then served as a means to control portfolio diversification.

The risk of the equity portfolio is determined by the portfolio beta, its residual risk, and risk of the market. Mathematically, the portfolio risk is stated as:

$$\sigma_{p^2} = \beta_{p^2}\sigma_{m^2} + \sigma_{r^2}$$

where:

σ_p = Standard deviation of portfolio returns.
β_p = Portfolio beta.
σ_m = Standard deviation of the market.
σ_r = Standard deviation of non-market-related risk, also called specific or diversifiable risk.

Central City reduced portfolio risk by reducing diversifiable risk.

Central City set up four categories of accounts reflecting different degrees of comparable risk aversion. For each category, a Policy Guidance Statement was issued monthly by the Policy Guidance Committee of Central City Capital Advisors. In the Policy Guidance Statement (see Exhibit 3), a target beta, a desired concentration in each of 5 risk sectors, and a desired concentration in each of 10 economic/market sectors was stated. Guidance ranges were also provided. A portfolio operating inside the guidance ranges was considered to have an appropriate beta and diversification. Subsequent portfolio performance met expectations in this regard.

With the development of the portfolio-optimization program, the policy-making process was integrated with security valuation. Based on the slope of the security market line, the Policy Guidance Committee used its judgment to establish a desired level of portfolio beta. The greater the slope of the security market line, the higher the beta. The portfolio-optimization program, which is a linear program, then sought out that portfolio which maximized the expected return from the valuation model, subject to the guidance range constraints. The program then determined where, within the guidance range, the current policy should be. By inspecting the dual of the linear programming solution, the "cost" of the constraints was evaluated. Constraints to control the level of portfolio turnover were also used.

At first, portfolio managers did not choose to use the linear program, preferring to deal manually with the many variables involved. However, with time and exposure, the program was shown to deal quickly with the complex effects of policy changes on the portfolio and began to be used routinely.

Now Mr. James was reflecting on how much portfolio management had changed at Central City over the past five years. He had transformed the management process from a "star" system to a system that more and more resembled a manufacturing operation. Someone had recently told Mr. James at a Financial Analysts Federation meeting that Central City was "the McDonald's of the money management business." The more he thought about it, the more he liked the analogy. The organization had standardized the product being delivered to the client. The organization had reduced its costs by routinizing portfolio reviews and raising the degree of utilization of its "high-priced" professionals. In some cases it had also been able to use "lower priced" individuals in specialized ways. Mr. James was convinced that the product delivered to the client had been significantly improved, and, at the same time, Central City Capital Advisors had never been more profitable.

Despite this success, Mr. James was preparing a lot of questions that he wished to discuss with Central City's principal modern portfolio theory consultants:

1. Even though Central City can control beta and specific risk within reasonable boundaries, how confident can we be that we know what the risk of the market is and, hence, what the target beta should be? This question seemed especially important because of the 1973–74 market decline.
2. How could the concepts of modern portfolio theory be used to describe to clients the risk/reward structure of alternative investment strategies?
3. Should clients be encouraged to formulate specific investment goals or objectives in the context of modern portfolio theory concepts?
4. Several of Central City's current portfolio managers had been security analysts prior to the evolution of capital market modern portfolio theory.

What would be the most appropriate way of communicating to the portfolio managers that it is necessary to integrate traditional and new (beta and specific) risk measures, that neither alone is sufficient?

5. Since Central City's security-market-line valuation model was successfully picking stocks, was beta theory deficient in some way? Mr. James had understood that beta theory and efficient market theory were the same thing. If so, what might this imply about portfolio composition?
6. Mr. James noted that the empirical security market line derived by Central City had a higher intercept and flatter slope than the theoretical security market line. Was the theory deficient, or had Central City incorrectly applied the theory?
7. The results of security-selection simulations were dramatic. Actual portfolio performance was not as good, although still superior. Did diversification policies interfere with performance now that Central City could pick stocks? Major accounts had as many as 70 securities in them, for example. Was this number so large that it was diluting the value of the firm's stock-selection capacity? How should a study be structured to determine optimum diversification, given superior selection capacity?
8. Central City had found that diversification was better when its super-industry groupings were used. What were the implications of this finding?
9. Concentration in P1 securities (other factors being equal) suggested low downside risk but high upside potential. Did (should) diversification reduce upside potential more than downside risk? If so, how should portfolio risk be evaluated?
10. The current security-selection process, using the security market line, ignored market liquidity of individual stocks. Had the system been biased against the more liquid stocks in favor of less liquid ones? Also, would investment volume rise to a point in the future when liquidity might be a severe problem and force curtailment of the approval list to the large, and perhaps more efficiently priced, stocks?
11. The selection process also ignored tax considerations. Could they be incorporated? Would it be worthwhile?
12. Did any of these questions really matter so long as the model worked? After all, McDonald's concentrated on the efficient delivery of a standardized product, not on product innovation. Didn't profits lie in scale?
13. How should performance-measurement techniques be incorporated? Mr. James noted that, in Exhibit 1, a number of statistical measures could be generated. Also, two performance measures had been around and promoted in academic circles for over 10 years:

$$\text{Treynor Measure: } \frac{\text{Portfolio return} - \text{Risk-free rate}}{\text{Portfolio beta}}$$

$$\text{Sharpe Measure: } \frac{\text{Portfolio return} - \text{Risk-free rate}}{\text{Portfolio standard deviation of returns}}$$

Which of the measures was most appropriate? Were there other dimensions to consider? Did the investment horizon of the client make a difference? How could the value-added of the security analysts be separated from that of the portfolio manager, and was such a separation desirable?

14. Did possible further innovations exist that would help Central City continue to maintain its competitive edge?

EXHIBIT 1

Quarterly Performance Stock-Valuation Model* (*stated as simple return*)

	P1	*P2*	*P3*	*N1*	*N2*	*All Stocks*
1975						
I	55.8%	42.3%	32.4%	30.7%	21.4%	33.3%
II	20.6	25.9	19.2	18.2	15.7	19.4
III	− 6.8	−14.5	−14.4	−14.9	−15.7	−14.0
IV	16.8	8.2	14.1	7.0	9.0	10.6
1976						
I	27.3	15.1	15.8	13.7	12.8	15.7
II	4.0	2.0	2.5	− .4	− 1.5	1.0
III	7.6	3.2	.8	.0	− 4.1	.6
IV	9.5	6.5	2.9	− .4	− .4	.3
1977						
I	1.7	− 6.2	− 8.4	− 9.4	−12.6	− 8.2
II	5.6	6.7	3.8	2.7	2.6	3.9
III	− 4.1	− 3.5	− 4.5	− 4.9	− 6.0	− 4.7
Total period	227.3	106.2	71.9	40.8	15.4	62.2

*Does not include transaction costs. Calculations based on price appreciation only. A regression of P1 returns against all stocks produced the following statistics:

Alpha = 6.01 percent/quarter
Beta = 1.23
t alpha = 3.27
R^2 = .906

Standard error of residuals = 5.7 percentage points/quarter

EXHIBIT 2
1976 Performance of 13 Major Accounts: *A–M*

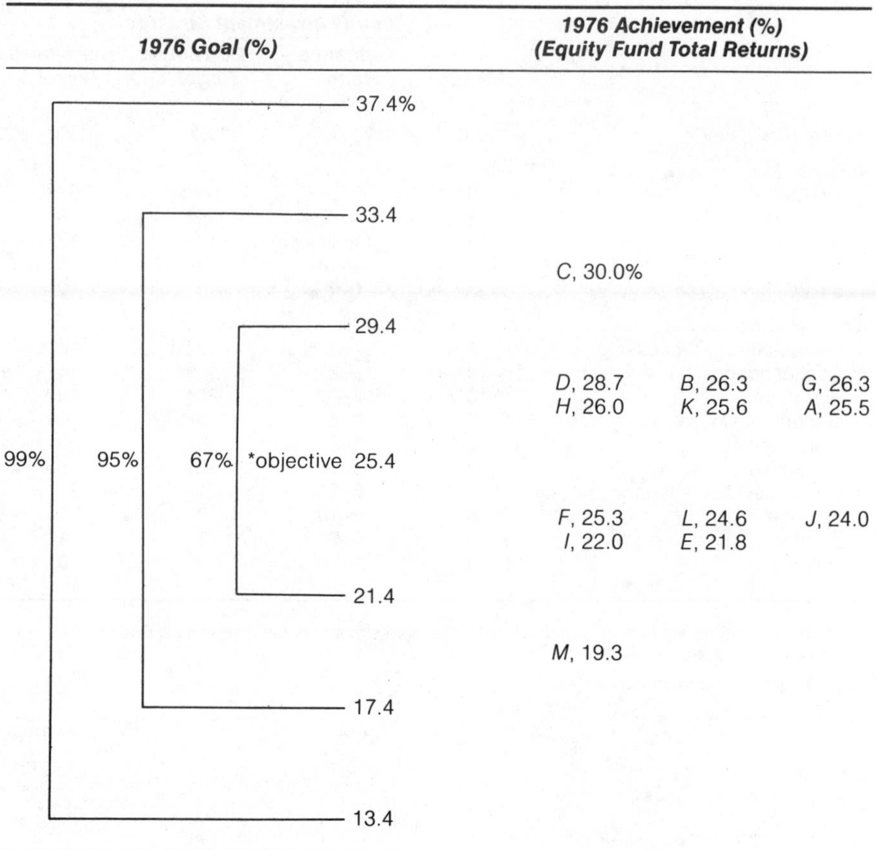

*S&P total return *plus 1.50 percentage points.* (23.9 + 1.50 = 25.4%)

Recap: Average performance was 25.0 percent, or 0.4 percentage points under the objective but 5.7 percentage points above the Becker median. 85 percent of the portfolios were within the 67 percent confidence range and 100 percent were within the 95 percent confidence range. The median variability for the Becker sample was 8.1 percentage points.

EXHIBIT 3
Policy Guidance Statement—Average Risk Objective

	Equity Investment Strategy			
	S&P 500	Guidance Range	Current Target	Prior Month Target
*Equity Risk Level**	1.00	1.00–1.04	1.02	1.00
Risk Sectors				
1 (LOW)	56%	50–58%	52%†	57%
2	18	14–22	20†	16
3	13	11–19	17	17
4	10	6–14	8	8
5 (HIGH)	3	0–7	3	2
Economic/Market Sectors				
Manufacturing-processing	9%	7–15%	13%†	14%
Capital goods	19	13–21	15†	14
Petroleum	18	14–22	20†	19
General business	1	0–5	0	0
Transportation	2	0–6	0	0
Consumer-basic	12	8–16	12†	15
Consumer-discretionary	17	15–23	21	21
Finance	6	2–10	7	7
Shelter		0–7	3†	1
Utilities	13	7–15	9	9

*Portfolios holding equities valued at $1 million or more should hold at least the equivalent of 40 equal-dollar-weighted issues.

†Changed from prior month target.

Southern States Bank and Trust Company (A)

In January 1980, Mr. Desmond Morris, senior vice-president and chief executive officer of the Trust Department of the Southern States Bank and Trust Company, was reviewing his firm's strategy of selecting equity securities following a year of somewhat disappointing equity performance results.

The Southern States Bank and Trust Company was the third largest statewide bank in one of the states of the old Confederacy. Even so, it was considered only a moderately sized regional bank. Southern benefited from the fact that both the southeast region in general and its state in particular were growing more rapidly than most other areas. In the last decade Southern also benefited from conservative policies that led to slower asset growth and lower loan-to-deposit ratios. Profits had not been as adversely affected by the high cost of borrowing during the credit crunches of 1974 and 1979 as they had for banks caught up in the real estate lending excesses of the mid-seventies. As a result, the bank's earnings-per-share growth rates over the seventies were among the more attractive in its region. Even so, very few people knew about the bank outside its home state, in which 85 percent of its stockholders resided.

The bank's headquarters were located in the second largest city of the state—a city known for its "old wealth." This location had been an asset to the Trust Department. Southern States had more individual trust accounts than any other bank in the state. Several national and regional firms were also headquartered in

---

This case was prepared by Robert F. Vandell, Charles C. Abbott Professor of Business Administration, of the Colgate Darden Graduate School of Business Administration at the University of Virginia.

this city, and Southern States had attracted somewhat more funds from employee benefit plans than was typical for a bank its size. Despite revenues of $1.1 million from these activities, Southern States' Trust Department did little more than break even on a fully allocated cost basis. Some growth in revenues remained necessary to offset rising operating costs.

Altogether, 26 individuals were employed in the Trust Department of the bank. Six of these people were located in other major cities within the state and were primarily responsible for maintaining good relations with individual clients in their areas and for seeking new accounts. Subject to review by headquarters, these field officers made investment decisions for the 20 to 40 accounts they each managed. All of the remaining people, 60 percent of whom were investment professionals, were located on one floor of the headquarters building.

Southern had been one of the first banks in its region to automate. Mr. Morris had seen in computerization the opportunity to make communications with clients more effective. Almost all clients now received a letter each quarter describing the performance of their accounts over several historic periods. Although these letters appeared personalized, large parts of them were substantially similar. Clients also received information explaining the reasons behind additions or deletions from their accounts. While some "hand holding" was still necessary, Mr. Morris believed that the bank's posture of being informative had helped sustain many relationships.

In the early 1970s Mr. Morris became increasingly aware of the problems that a small regional bank might experience in trying to compete against larger institutions with greater resources at their disposal. About this time, Mr. Morris had made a number of changes simplifying the investment processes of his firm and focusing more of management's attention on what were considered to be the key issues of portfolio management. Of these many changes, Mr. Morris believed that the de-emphasis of security analysis was probably the most controversial.

Mr. Morris had concluded that it would be hard for the small number of professionals in his organization, removed as they were from money centers, to compete with professional security analysts located in larger organizations. His conclusions were conditioned by the belief that the equity capital markets for big-capitalization stocks—the kind his firm preferred—were priced relatively efficiently. To identify market inefficiencies, one had to have either inside information or unusual insight. With the exception of a few firms with headquarters or major operations located nearby, sources of either were unlikely to be available to Southern States analysts. More likely, they would be considering information that was already thoroughly evaluated and digested by others and, consequently, likely to be already embedded in security prices.

At the same time, Mr. Morris believed that the typical field security analyst suffered from information overload. Too many people had too many opinions—some good, some bad—that they were all too ready to disgorge at the first sign of interest. The analyst's problem was to differentiate the good advice from the bad, but this was difficult given the avalanche of recommendations.

For this reason, Mr. Morris believed that it was desirable to restrict the number of sources from which recommendations were received. Each of these sources was to be very carefully monitored to ascertain the relative usefulness of its stock recommendations. In a few cases, the source was an expert in only a narrow portion of the market spectrum, such as an industry. These latter sources were ones particular professionals at Southern States had found especially helpful in the past. Four firms, however, were selected to provide a broad range of security advice to Southern States.

In one case, Quantum Investment Bank had provided monthly summary evaluations on better than 250 stocks since late 1973. Mr. Morris particularly liked the fact that the Quantum service provided a very specific forecast ranking for each of the stocks it followed. He had maintained a file of these forecasts dating back to January 1, 1974.

Mr. Morris also found it appealing that Quantum's universe of stocks was broad. In 1973 and 1974, Southern States had been hurt by what, in the clarity of hindsight, could only be described as an over-commitment to growth stocks. Growth stocks had failed to participate fully in the 1975 recovery, although by then the compositions of the bank's portfolio had already begun to change substantially. In the future, Mr. Morris wanted to avoid the risk of overly concentrating portfolios in just one type of security.

Mr. Morris' ideas had begun taking shape in mid-1975. It was not until late 1978 that Mr. Morris began limiting and focusing the sources of information flowing to the bank's security analysts—a delay caused in part by employee resistance. The analysts tended to fear that the restrictions might cost them potentially useful buy or sell ideas or might reflect adversely on their judgments.

Despite his general belief that most of the security information becoming available to Southern States was noise, Mr. Morris also believed that at least a part of these recommendations would prove valuable. The problem was in recognizing the difference between the wheat and the chaff.

Mr. Morris then recalled a concept espoused by Ambachtsheer[1] involving "information coefficients" (or ICs) to assess the potential value of analysts' estimates. Using this technique, actual total-return results for a set of securities followed by an analyst were regressed against the forecasts prepared for these same stocks at the outset of the measurement period. The IC for this set of data was simply the correlation coefficient (r). Mr. Morris had inferred that an IC of .15 ($R^2 = .0225$) was generally sufficiently good to be used successfully in achieving excess returns after (pre–May Day) transaction costs.

Mr. Morris had several problems in evaluating the forecasting skills of Quantum using information coefficients. (Another valuation technique will be described later.) These problems boiled down to the following:

[1] Keith Ambachtsheer, "Where Are the Customer's Alphas?" *Journal of Portfolio Management*, Fall 1977.

- What forecasts should be used?
- Over what period should returns be measured?
- In what form should returns be measured?
- What universe should be tested?
- How frequently should the tests be made?
- How should the results be interpreted?
- What were the action implications of the findings?

In addressing these issues, Mr. Morris realized that the limited time available for research sharply restricted the way he conceived alternatives. Each of these will now be discussed in more detail.

Estimated Returns

In its service, Quantum provided several forecasts that might be used for investment purposes. For each security, a total rate of return over the long run was estimated by a sophisticated dividend discount model that allowed for changing growth rates. Ranking could be done by total returns alone.

Quantum also provided a risk-adjusted alpha for each security. In addition to forecasting a security's total return, an analyst also estimated its beta risk. Initially, Quantum had used a "market" model that simply regressed total monthly returns against the Standard & Poor's 500 Index total returns for the most recent 60 months to estimate the stock's beta. Over time, the beta-measurement process became more sophisticated. In any case, measures of returns could be regressed against measures of risk to determine a central tendency, which Quantum called the security market line (SML). The relative attractiveness of any particular stock was measured vertically as the distance between the value of the plot for that stock and the security market line.

As Mr. Morris knew, the SML concept was derived from capital asset pricing theory. SML did not, however, mirror theory exactly. In his experience, the SML almost always had a higher intercept and a lower slope than did its theoretical counterpart. Mr. Morris was not sure he fully understood the implications of the persistent departure of empirical forecast evidence from theory. In some periods the empirical SML slope actually turned negative. (See Exhibit 1, where representative SML parameters are reported.) While a negatively sloped SML was counterintuitive, Mr. Morris had heard from others that negatively sloped SMLs were not at all uncommon among other firms that used an SML evaluation system.

The alphas from Quantum's SML data did provide an alternative ranking system. Stocks with positive alphas were considered to be undervalued; overvalued stocks had negative alphas. The extent of over- and undervaluation could also be measured. For convenience, Mr. Morris referred to these alphas as risk-adjusted alphas.

Quantum also provided an adjustment for the liquidity of a particular stock. Quantum measured liquidity based on the number of trading days necessary to accumulate or divest $2 million in stock. A stock's liquidity was determined by dividing \$2 million by the product of its current market price and its average daily trading volume over the last 12 months. The greater the time necessary to achieve the target position, the poorer was that stock's liquidity. All stocks were then sorted into five liquidity groups approximately even in number, ranked from most liquid (subgroup #1) to least liquid (subgroup #5). The security market line for each subgroup was then calculated in such a way that the intercept remained unchanged from that determined in the composite SML. In general, the most liquid stocks had an SML with a lower slope than the composite SML, and the least liquid stocks had an SML with a higher slope. The charts in Figure 1 illustrate two sets of SML lines.

As suggested in Figure 1, the liquidity "fan" could be very wide (on right) or very narrow (on left). The five liquidity subgroups were not always ranked from best (#1) to worst (#5) as suggested by these charts. When a subgroup was out of order, it was lumped with the adjacent numbered subgroup with the most similar slope, and the composite slope was recalculated. This process continued until all subgroups were ordered in a logical way. Alphas for individual stocks were then measured in relation to the appropriate liquidity SML.

Mr. Morris was never sure whether he liked the liquidity adjustment of alphas just described. The effect of the adjustment was, other factors remaining equal, to increase the alphas of the most liquid stocks and decrease the alphas of the least liquid stocks. Given Southern's size, liquidity was not the major consideration in investment decisions among the stocks in the bank's universe.

Recently, Quantum had also begun adjusting its return estimates to consider taxes. The theory behind this adjustment was simple. Because of tax differentials, wealthy investors would prefer capital gain prospects to dividend income prospects.

FIGURE 1
Security Market Lines for Two Liquidity Groups

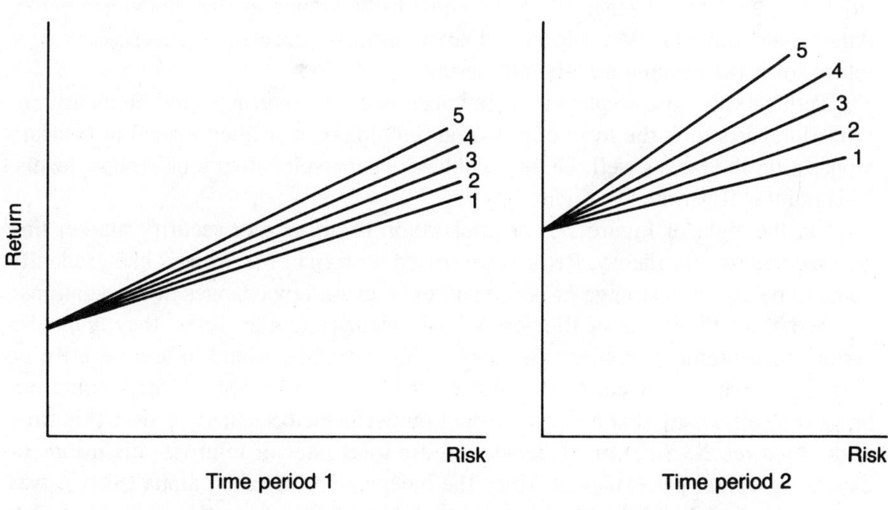

Not so, institutions that were not subject to taxation. Investors in higher tax brackets might assess the alphas of stocks quite differently from those in lower tax brackets.

As noted, Quantum provided *a* means of adjusting alphas for tax status. While Mr. Morris liked the idea embodied in the tax adjustment, he had not yet thought through the particular methodology employed at Quantum. In any event, this alpha evidence was too recent to use in evaluating Quantum's forecasting skill. With some reservations, Mr. Morris decided to use the risk-adjusted alphas, unadjusted for either liquidity or tax status, in his analysis of Quantum's ICs.

Other Measurement Issues

Mr. Morris decided to use the bank's, not Quantum's, universe. The number of stocks in the bank's universe had approximated 170 at any given recent time. He reasoned that Quantum's skill in forecasting the other companies which it followed was of academic interest only.

As Mr. Morris reviewed how the list of the top 10 percent of alpha forecasts changed from month to month, he found a fair turnover (about 25 percent) after three months. As market prices also changed significantly over most three-month periods, he thought that quarterly testing would afford perspective.

Mr. Morris puzzled at greater length over the appropriate time period for his measurements of results. On the one hand, he had always been an intermediate-term investor, purchasing securities on the basis of potential for the next business cycle of about four years. SML alphas also were long-term indicators of potential, at least theoretically. On the other hand, his impression was that Quantum's alphas had their greatest value in the short run. Their informational value might "wear out" after only three to six months. As he understood it, when undervalued stocks were more widely recognized, they would be bid up in price (thus reducing the stocks' alphas toward zero). This had come to be known as the short-term game. After some thought, Mr. Morris, at least initially, decided to measure *ex post* returns over the ensuing nine-month period.

Perhaps the most perplexing issue concerned how returns would be measured. Since forecasts took the form of risk-adjusted alphas, it seemed logical to measure alphas after the fact as well. Unfortunately, *ex post* results often took strange forms. This point is illustrated in Figure 2.

On the right of Figure 2 is an illustration of an *ex post* security market line that seemed to defy theory: Returns decreased with risk! Mr. Morris had gradually come to believe this strange *ex post* result to be caused by changes in expectations.

Whatever the cause of illogical *ex post* security market lines, they created a serious measurement problem. Security A, for example, would have a negative *ex post* alpha, whereas Security B's alpha would be positive. Mr. Morris could not bring himself to say that Security B had outperformed Security A over this time span. As a result, Mr. Morris decided to use total rates of return as his means of measuring actual performance. Since the independent variable, alpha (SML), was measured net of the SML, Mr. Morris decided to subtract from the measure of each

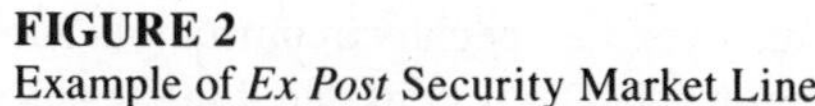

FIGURE 2
Example of *Ex Post* Security Market Line

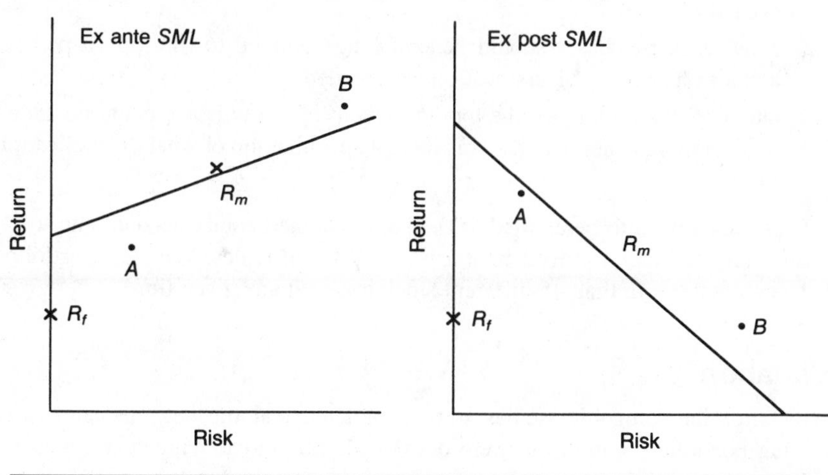

security's *ex post* return the comparable measure of its market return as measured by the Standard & Poor's 500 Index (*Rm*). These returns were annualized for comparison purposes.

Results

The initial IC correlation runs were completed in November 1978. Since nine months' *ex post* data were required in the calculation, the last forecast that could be used was the data available at the outset of the first quarter of 1978.

The evidence generated from this study is shown in Exhibit 2. In reviewing these data, Mr. Morris thought that it was too much to hope that the information coefficients be positive in all time periods. He was impressed that the information coefficients were infrequently negative and then only by small amounts.

The second quarter of 1976 drew his attention because the IC for that period was similar to the average and to the .15 IC threshold mentioned earlier. As he understood it, a portfolio with an average *ex ante* alpha of 2 percent, reasonably easy to achieve, could be expected to beat the market at a rate of better than 6.3 percent per year ($a+b=2\%$) over a nine-month period. A return of this magnitude seemed likely to remain attractive after transaction costs as well (about .35 percent one way before considering market impact).

While Mr. Morris was not sure he fully understood these results, he was, on balance, pleased. This led him to develop three decision rules which were implemented fully, starting January 1, 1979:

1. Any stock that did not have an alpha in the upper half of the universe must be sold. A portfolio manager could make an exception only after approval

by Mr. Morris. This exception was reserved for special circumstances such as announced terms of a tender offer not adequately considered in the stock evaluation.

2. New stock purchases should generally be confined to the top 15 percent alpha group unless diversification was needed.
3. Other stocks ranking in the top 35 percent of the universe could be added to diversify. (In neither case was there a specification of what diversification meant.)

These rules were to be applied to the bank's pooled equity account and to all portfolios large enough to invest in at least 25 different issues. Very few portfolios had, by contrast, more than 45 different stock issues at any given time.

A Variation

Shortly after the foregoing studies were completed and the new decision rules governing portfolio composition were developed, Mr. Floyd Wingett, the department's employee with the greatest statistical savvy, raised a new question. He pointed out that Southern was relying primarily on the data in the top 15 percent and top 35 percent groups. The analyses recorded in Exhibit 2, in contrast, assumed forecasting skill was uniform. This assumption need not be true, he argued.

Mr. Wingett illustrated his point with the graphs in Figure 3. Analyses of Exhibit 2 tended to assume an oval cloud-like relationship (symmetrical around the regression line), much as shown in Graph A. If Quantum was very good at picking winners but unable to pick losers, Graph B might represent the resulting "cloud." If, in contrast, Quantum was good at picking losers but not winners, the cloud in Graph C might pertain. All three graphs could produce the same statistical results as shown in Exhibit 2, although the interpretation could be quite different.

In order to test for Quantum's skill in identifying winners, Mr. Wingett had proposed the test illustrated in Figure 4.

Each forecast in the top 15 percent was entered as a separate independent variable (see x's in Figure 4). The remaining 85 percent were represented by their

FIGURE 3
Alternative Actual-to-Forecast Relationships

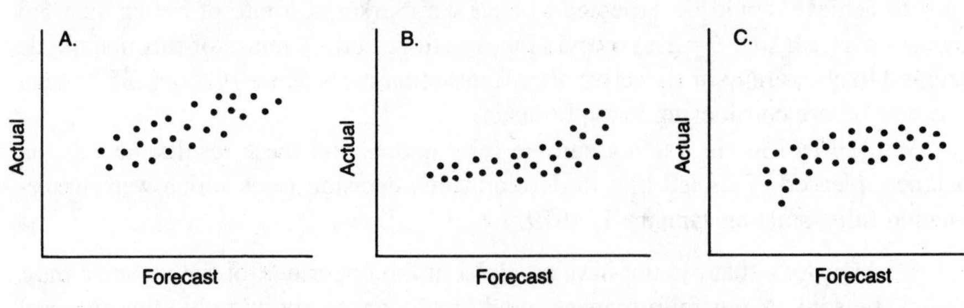

FIGURE 4

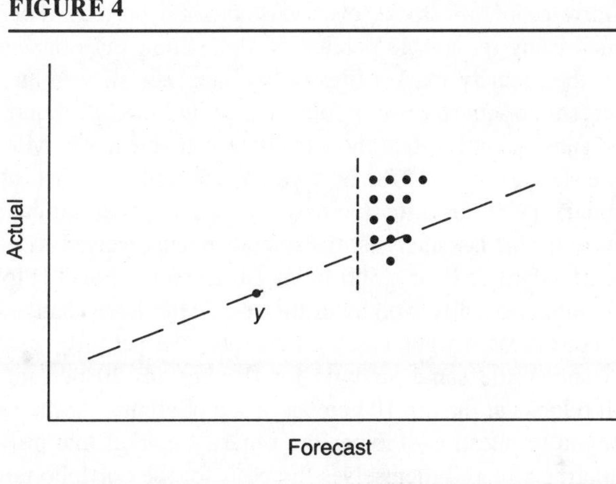

average forecasts *and* actual results (see *y* in Figure 4). In the regression equation, these latter averages were given a weight equal to the number of observations in the total (in this case, about 85 percent of the universe). The regression line tended to be forced through *y* as a consequence of its weight. Regressions were run for the top 15 percent alpha group as well as for the group in the next 20 percent. Except as noted, the forecasts and actual data were the same in these calculations as in Exhibit 2. The regression results are shown in Exhibit 3.

On the whole, Mr. Morris found these results supportive of his view that Quantum was quite good at identifying stocks with good prospects. He consequently entered 1979 in a buoyant mood.

Simulated Excess Return Performance

As 1979 progressed, Mr. Morris with the help of his staff developed still another way of looking at forecasting that seemed to provide additional perspective that he found helpful. He called his new analysis "skill simulation."

"Skill simulation" worked as follows. At the beginning of each quarter, the universe was broken down into specified subgroups; for example, the top 20 percent by alpha rankings. An equal amount was assumed to be invested in each security within that particular subgroup. The investment performance of the subgroup portfolio was then monitored for as long a time as feasible (up to four years). To simplify comparisons, the performance was first shown as a quarterly compound rate for all observations. Next, the corresponding performance of the universe (equally weighted) was subtracted from the performance of the subgroup so that only excess rates of returns were recorded.

Exhibit 4 shows the analysis for the top 20 percent group selected on the basis of SML alphas. The first column shows the date on which the portfolio was formed. The remaining columns show the amount by which the portfolio exceeded or failed to beat the universe of all stocks over various time periods. For example, the portfolio formed using the top 20 percent of alpha companies on January 1974 as determined by the security market line *ex ante* analysis showed an excess rate of return 2.95 percent per quarter over a four-year period (see 48-month column, first row). This and subsequent exhibits show the data available to Mr. Morris in January 1980. Only the data through 1978, however, were available when he first ran the analysis in January 1979, just after the new policies had been initiated.

Significantly in this last analysis, the reference had changed from performance relative to the Standard & Poor's 500 Index (in Exhibits 2 and 3) to performance relative to the bank's equally weighted universe. This later change had not been made without considerable argument, a controversy not yet fully resolved.

Exhibit 5 shows the same analysis for the bottom 20 percent of the alpha group. Exhibit 6 looks at the top 10 percent group of alphas. At the same time, Mr. Morris had begun to question whether the security market line provided the best basis for calculating alphas—themselves the basis for the portfolio rankings used in the analyses reported in Exhibits 2 through 6.

Mr. Morris had become increasingly skeptical of beta measures. Several studies he had seen suggested that the information value of beta forecasts (predicting future betas *or* future returns) was, at best, negligible. This led him to speculate whether total-return estimates (unadjusted) might be a better indication of stock potential. Exhibit 7 shows an analysis of the performance of the top 20 percent from the Quantum universe selected on the basis of total returns.

Exhibit 7 illustrates just one way of viewing value identification. Mr. Morris planned to consider alternative ways of ranking securities by their value prospects if the comparison of Exhibits 3 and 7 proved useful.

Subsequent Developments

Results in 1979 were disappointing, especially in view of expectations. For example, Southern's pooled equity fund underperformed the market, as represented by the Standard & Poor's 500 Index, by over 4 percent per year and the equally weighted universe by almost 2 percent per year. The performance of other large equity accounts ranged around these performance values. Exhibit 8 shows the information gained from extending the time period of Exhibit 2.

The Issue

What, Mr. Morris wondered, should he learn from this experience? Was 1979's performance just a stroke of bad luck or was it an indication that his system was not working? If the latter, did it fail because he wrongly relied upon the skill of Quantum or because his decision rules led to bad results? Analysis was, of course, only a step toward action. Mr. Morris now wondered what changes, if any, were likely to be in the interest of the bank's clients.

EXHIBIT 1
Ex Ante Security Market Lines (*1/1974 to 10/1979*)

Month and Year*	Coefficients			
	Constant (α)	Slope (β)	R^2	Market Return‡
1/1974	8.28	2.35	.08	10.63%
4/1974	8.25	2.77	.12	11.02
7/1974	8.83	2.96	.11	11.78
10/1974	11.61	3.15	.09	14.76
1/1975	12.47	1.26	.02	13.74
4/1975	13.70	− .40†	.00	13.30
7/1975	13.18	− .10†	.00	13.08
10/1975	14.25	− .75†	.01	13.50
1/1976	13.18	− .62†	.01	12.56
4/1976	12.60	.15†	.00	12.74
7/1976	12.79	.15†	.00	12.95
10/1976	12.92	.19†	.00	13.12
1/1977	12.01	.91	.04	12.92
4/1977	12.54	.78	.03	13.32
7/1977	12.41	1.02	.04	13.42
10/1977	12.61	1.43	.08	14.03
1/1978	13.18	1.23	.05	14.41
4/1978	13.73	.36†	.00	14.09
7/1978	13.79	.13†	.00	13.92
10/1978	14.18	.65†	.01	14.83
1/1979	14.14	.69†	.01	14.83
4/1979	14.10	.70†	.01	14.80
7/1979	14.73	.32†	.00	15.05
10/1979	15.60	− .54†	.00	15.06

*Beginning of month.

†Not significant at .01 level.

‡At a beta = 1.0.

EXHIBIT 2
Information Coefficients for 17 Periods (*all 170 stocks in universe*)

Beginning Year and Quarter	Information Coefficient (r)	Intercept (a)	Slope (b)	t-Statistic (Slope Coefficient)	Residual Error
1974–1	.147	.231	2.214	1.99	20.4%
2	−.061	−.129	−1.047	−0.82	22.8
3	.152	.514	3.235	2.07	30.9
4	−.000	−.013	−0.115	−0.05	60.4
1975–1	.172	.382	4.591	2.33	49.1
2	−.020	−.057	− .336	−0.26	30.1
3	.055	.021	.257	0.22	27.3
4	.244	.478	4.383	3.37	31.5
1976–1	.273	.479	5.004	3.79	27.7
2	.166	.265	3.061	2.25	24.0
3	.224	.329	3.472	3.07	21.3
4	.308	.330	5.193	4.33	23.3
1977–1	.206	.268	3.803	2.82	19.4
2	.240	.311	5.887	3.31	24.2
3	.076	.056	1.354	1.02	19.1
4	−.035	−.039	−0.848	−0.46	27.0
1978–1	.061	.128	1.409	0.81	27.8
Average	.130	.209	2.487	1.75	

Note: Forecast (alpha SML) versus actual (total market return over nine months).
Actual (net of Standard & Poor's 500 Index, both annualized) is the dependent variable.

EXHIBIT 3
Analysis of Forecasting Power of Top 15% and Next-to-Top 20% Groups
(*Quantum's forecasts, 1974 to 1978*)

Beginning Year and Quarter	Top 15 Percent				Next-to-Top 20 Percent			
	r	*a*	*b*	*t*	*r*	*a*	*b*	*t*
1974–1	.192	.174	1.668	2.62	.333	.736	7.048	4.73
2	−.442	−.394	−3.192	−6.24	.014	.047	.380	0.20
3	.315	.767	4.829	4.44	−.012	− .571	−3.594	−1.61
4	−.164	−.281	−2.520	−2.22	.299	1.848	16.561	4.18
1975–1	.174	.179	2.155	2.36	.445	2.137	25.671	6.63
2	−.178	−.236	−1.400	−2.42	−.033	− .180	−1.065	−0.44
3	.162	.138	1.698	2.20	−.184	− .430	−5.255	−2.50
4	.344	.464	4.258	4.91	.154	.584	5.350	2.08
1976–1	.359	.369	3.852	5.15	.379	1.214	12.688	5.47
2	.184	.186	2.154	2.50	.221	.516	6.480	3.03
3	.416	.302	3.192	6.11	.203	.531	5.609	2.77
4	.720	.474	7.466	13.86	−.000	− .014	−0.225	−0.77
1977–1	.488	.511	7.230	7.48	−.275	−4.100	−5.794	−3.82
2	.434	.479	9.056	6.45	−.079	− .103	−1.956	−1.06
3	.153	.090	2.173	2.07	.020	.018	.423	0.28
4	−.014	−.012	−0.262	−0.20	.000	.007	.156	0.07
1978–1	.162	.189	2.076	2.20	.010	.023	.261	0.13
Mean	.194				.088			

EXHIBIT 4
Ex Post Average Quarterly Rates of Excess Return* (*top 20% equally weighted portfolios*)

Beginning Year and Quarter	Average Quarterly—Compound—Excess Rates of Return for the Ensuing Time Periods (number of months)							
	(3)	(6)	(9)	(12)	(18)	(24)	(36)	(48)
1974–1	7.815	1.666	4.461	2.070	2.592	3.011	2.397	2.950
2	−6.578	2.773	.359	1.058	1.881	1.442	1.670	2.325
3	9.391	3.055	3.503	3.502	3.582	1.854	2.421	2.310
4	−7.389	−1.564	.352	1.557	1.156	.735	1.637	1.965
1975–1	9.792	7.660	5.775	5.575	3.150	2.942	2.886	3.098
2	3.079	2.331	2.238	1.924	2.383	2.482	2.428	2.590
3	.110	1.614	1.860	2.088	1.684	2.119	1.656	1.624
4	1.524	1.836	2.853	2.578	2.803	2.411	2.348	2.456
1976–1	− .569	2.780	2.571	3.036	3.702	2.672	2.264	3.042
2	2.420	3.695	4.117	3.866	3.508	2.790	2.308	
3	4.405	5.527	5.048	4.568	3.925	2.540	2.105	
4	5.795	4.741	3.719	2.727	2.470	1.832	1.339	
1977–1	2.629	2.057	1.380	1.722	1.286	1.214	1.284	
2	1.932	1.260	1.293	.960	1.083	.836		
3	− .888	.330	.407	.013	.165	.455		
4	1.730	.795	− .199	1.023	.496	.415		
1978–1	.185	.114	.691	.214	.681	.230		
2	−1.814	.041	− .844	− .211	− .078			
3	.817	−2.133	− .168	.366	− .387			
4	−4.750	− .919	− .154	− .392				
1979–1	2.919	2.708	1.510	− .167				
2	3.690	.955	−1.602					
3	−1.769	−3.320						
4	−8.936							
Mean	1.064	1.623	1.781	1.813	1.899	1.763	2.057	2.484
Std. Dev.	4.712	2.424	1.970	1.613	1.327	.931	.470	.469

*Formed by alpha rankings using security market line data.

EXHIBIT 5
Ex Post Average Quarterly Rates of Excess Return*
(bottom 20% equally weighted portfolios)

Beginning Year and Quarter	Average Quarterly—Compound—Excess Rates of Return for the Ensuing Time Periods (number of months)							
	(3)	(6)	(9)	(12)	(18)	(24)	(36)	(48)
1974–1	−6.018	−2.831	−4.531	−2.614	−2.142	−2.918	−2.447	−2.687
2	6.481	−2.890	−2.842	−1.204	−1.891	−1.500	−2.656	−2.832
3	−8.580	−6.992	−3.796	−3.347	−3.533	−2.766	−3.690	−2.964
4	8.807	1.549	.322	− .246	−1.916	−1.368	−1.754	−1.655
1975–1	−2.331	−3.337	−2.086	−2.925	−2.621	−2.446	−2.147	−1.918
2	−1.561	−1.528	−2.222	−2.056	−1.898	−1.983	−1.959	−2.110
3	− .038	− .988	−1.027	− .826	−1.120	−1.024	− .876	−1.449
4	−2.019	−1.878	−2.823	−2.999	−3.205	−2.651	−2.173	−2.653
1976–1	1.471	−1.070	−2.564	−2.204	−2.930	−2.642	−1.990	−2.826
2	−2.990	−4.163	−3.202	−3.830	−2.988	−2.440	−1.572	
3	−4.060	−3.483	−3.560	−3.009	−2.503	−1.727	−1.411	
4	−4.444	−4.405	−3.781	−2.635	−2.247	−1.615	−1.047	
1977–1	−2.597	− .926	− .742	− .400	− .112	.179	.515	
2	1.916	−1.119	−1.425	−1.413	− .862	− .511		
3	−1.428	− .564	− .278	− .157	.413	.079		
4	3.829	1.943	1.834	1.022	.745	.782		
1978–1	− .009	1.219	1.464	.728	.083	.960		
2	2.754	2.143	.949	.357	.493			
3	2.041	− .101	− .901	−1.463	.125			
4	2.722	− .670	− .194	.639				
1979–1	−3.632	−1.723	.545	2.310				
2	− .745	2.407	4.575					
3	5.751	6.601						
4	5.936							
Mean	0.374	−0.992	−1.195	−1.251	−1.479	−1.388	−1.785	−2.349
Std. Dev.	3.849	2.845	2.236	1.680	1.400	1.272	1.001	0.558

*Formed by alpha rankings using security market line data.

EXHIBIT 6
Ex Post Average Quarterly Rates of Excess Return* *(top 10% equally weighted portfolios)*

Beginning Year and Quarter	Average Quarterly—Compound—Excess Rates of Return for the Ensuing Time Periods (number of months)							
	(3)	(6)	(9)	(12)	(18)	(24)	(36)	(48)
1974–1	5.372	1.228	3.852	1.491	3.103	3.625	3.045	3.688
2	−5.793	3.811	.955	.904	2.354	1.838	2.283	3.073
3	12.108	1.872	3.822	4.187	4.589	2.823	3.264	3.509
4	−12.340	.949	2.052	2.629	2.146	1.820	2.669	4.047
1975–1	16.172	11.373	7.328	6.510	4.566	3.772	3.761	4.590
2	2.758	2.351	2.682	1.581	1.965	2.640	2.820	2.859
3	1.690	2.741	3.355	2.586	1.717	1.639	1.306	1.669
4	−2.250	1.381	2.952	2.017	2.763	2.433	2.647	3.119
1976–1	4.655	6.536	4.030	4.014	5.277	4.126	3.781	4.641
2	.166	1.343	2.313	3.310	3.225	2.842	2.651	
3	.923	3.671	4.590	4.095	3.996	2.465	2.410	
4	6.300	6.134	4.521	3.877	3.801	3.280	2.991	
1977–1	4.154	3.660	2.633	2.820	1.620	1.526	1.305	
2	2.827	1.569	2.051	.813	1.386	.763		
3	−.392	2.493	1.730	.897	.757	.991		
4	.765	1.891	1.190	3.096	2.002	1.786		
1978–1	.862	−.736	.443	−.586	−.144	−.865		
2	−2.943	.061	−1.464	−.673	−.189			
3	−1.350	−3.865	−1.855	−.950	−1.752			
4	−6.399	−2.288	−.290	−.749				
1979–1	3.604	2.894	.794	−1.559				
2	6.147	1.245	−3.253					
3	−1.949	−5.712						
4	−7.090							
Mean	1.167	1.939	2.020	1.920	2.273	2.206	2.687	3.464
Std. Dev.	5.955	3.380	2.349	2.050	1.761	2.203	.732	.928

*Formed by alpha rankings using security market line data.

EXHIBIT 7
Ex Post Average Quarterly Rates of Excess Return* *(top 20% equally weighted portfolios)*

Beginning Year and Quarter	Average Quarterly—Compound—Excess Rates of Return for the Ensuing Time Periods (number of months)							
	(3)	(6)	(9)	(12)	(18)	(24)	(36)	(48)
1974–1	6.322	2.048	4.090	1.284	2.536	2.880	2.471	2.974
2	−5.416	2.381	.132	1.487	1.779	1.695	1.741	2.495
3	9.136	2.489	3.892	3.818	3.710	2.045	2.380	2.344
4	−9.506	− .981	1.091	1.663	2.075	1.340	1.873	2.479
1975–1	7.921	7.589	5.550	5.476	3.489	3.114	2.993	3.419
2	3.489	2.368	2.189	1.919	2.392	2.561	2.527	2.656
3	.795	3.132	2.200	2.178	1.926	2.239	1.753	1.748
4	.125	.605	1.979	2.156	2.717	2.247	1.903	2.040
1976–1	− .843	2.646	2.645	3.114	3.830	2.765	2.328	3.072
2	2.420	3.095	4.117	3.866	3.508	2.790	2.308	
3	4.390	5.421	5.046	4.502	3.889	2.490	2.075	
4	5.795	4.741	3.719	2.727	2.470	1.832	1.339	
1977–1	1.770	1.723	1.057	1.372	1.064	.897	.686	
2	1.719	1.490	1.546	1.267	1.426	.901		
3	− .194	.982	.953	.602	.488	.899		
4	.000	.480	.411	1.568	.891	.765		
1978–1	− .153	− .308	.624	− .096	.446	− .377		
2	−2.019	− .003	−1.196	− .482	− .229			
3	.617	−2.133	− .168	.356	− .387			
4	−5.002	− .880	− .011	− .268				
1979–1	3.610	2.845	1.168	− .527				
2	3.355	.585	−1.878					
3	−1.925	−3.635						
4	−6.414							
Mean	.833	1.621	1.780	1.809	2.002	1.828	2.029	2.581
Std. Dev.	4.502	2.486	1.980	1.657	1.362	0.961	0.588	0.520

*Formed by rankings using security total rates of return.

EXHIBIT 8
Information Coefficients Based on Forecasts from April 1978 to April 1979

Year and Quarter	Information Coefficient (r)	Intercept (a)	Slope (b)
1978 : II	.084	.053	1.472
III	−.057	−.048	−1.067
IV	.001	.000	0.064
1979 : I	.089	.061	1.524
II	.024	.020	0.154

Note: Forecast (alpha SML) versus actual (total market return—nine months—net of the S&P 500 Index).

Southern States Bank and Trust Company (B)

In early 1980, as Mr. Desmond Morris, senior vice-president and chief executive officer of the Trust Department of the Southern States Bank and Trust Company, considered the issues before him that were raised in Southern States Bank and Trust Company (A), he became increasingly aware that the performance of the oil industry had contributed significantly to the relatively poor performance of the bank's equity portfolios in 1979. As oil shortages and increasing prices for international oil came to be accepted as important parts of American life, the short- and long-term expectations for the profits of oil firms increased significantly. Prices of most oil stocks responded accordingly. It was not uncommon to find among the exploratory firms (e.g., Helmerich & Payne) or service firms (e.g., Schlumberger) instances where prices had more than doubled.

While Mr. Morris had not personally checked this out, he had heard it said that the yearly total rate of return for the Standard & Poor's 500 Index in 1979 of 18.4 percent was almost entirely due to the strong performance of the oil group. Given the large weight of the oil industry in the Standard & Poor's 500 Index (an index giving more weight to large companies), Mr. Morris did not find this surprising.

The main problem affecting his bank's equity performance, as Mr. Morris now saw it, was Quantum's low alpha rankings for oil stocks. At the outset of 1979, Quantum was predicting below-average performance for the group, although some stocks were considered attractive. The following summary data illustrate this point.

This case was prepared by a Professor of the Colgate Darden Graduate School of Business Administration of the University of Virginia.

	Group Averages (Equally Weighted; January 1, 1979)	
	Beta	**Total Return**
Petroleum stocks	1.09	13.91
All stocks	1.21	15.07

By October of 1979 the forecasts were as follows:

	Group Averages (Equally Weighted; October 1, 1979)	
	Beta	**Total Return**
Petroleum stocks	1.12	12.86
All stocks	1.20	14.79

As the year progressed, Quantum's analysts' estimates of oil stock prospects did not rise as rapidly as did prices. As a result, alphas fell. The first groups dropped from consideration were the smaller firms, such as Baker International, whose performance in 1979 was—to say the least—spectacular.

As Mr. Morris reviewed these data, he reached two conclusions. First, the performance of the bank's equity accounts would have been considerably worse if the portfolio managers had not generally dragged their feet about selling oil-related stocks whose alphas had fallen out of the magical top 50 percent. (In fact, the portfolio manager with the worst record for the year—lower by 2–3 percent than the average—had been the most systematic in following the bank's new selling discipline.) Second, the results were not as bad as they could have been had not Quantum's analysts done a good job of forecasting performance for stocks outside the oil industry.

As Mr. Morris considered these various tentative conclusions, he became increasingly aware that the information coefficients he had used in some of his earlier analyses might be misleading. These coefficients tended to consider all forecasts as equally valid. Mr. Morris expected to find, in contrast, that the analysts employed at Quantum were not equally skilled. Some, perhaps like the oil analyst, were producing bad results. Could the good be distinguished from the bad and the indifferent?

More specifically, Mr. Morris hoped there might be some way that he could differentiate the skill levels of different analysts. He still had stored in his computer the forecasts and actual results for 170 stocks by quarters from 1974 forward. These data could be sorted or combined in almost any way considered useful for analytical purposes. What might he do—within reason—to understand the relative levels of skill reflected in the forecasts of Quantum's security analysts?

As he pondered these questions, he began to consider how he might use the data. As noted in the previous case, Southern had access to three other sets of forecasts covering most of the 170 stocks in Southern's universe (back-dated for three to five years, depending on the source). The bank also had access to additional industry forecasts in still other cases. Perhaps the oil analysts at one of the other firms might have been better. Could this be tested, he wondered. If forecasts from one source were not always comparable (i.e., average total returns and standard deviations differed considerably), how might forecasts from different sources be compared? Might not two forecasts be better than one? And so on? Mr. Morris' mind was racing; unfortunately, it was racing in too many directions at once.

Mr. Morris nevertheless recognized that his basic tenet—that the bank should use other sources' forecasts more efficiently rather than develop its own—demanded the development of a much better system to evaluate and differentiate those forecasts. He planned to outline a plan of attack in preparation for a strategy meeting of the portfolio managers scheduled for the next morning.

Southern States Bank and Trust Company (C)

Mr. Desmond Morris, senior vice-president for the Trust Department, had spent most of the day organizing his thinking about how he might evaluate the various suppliers of equity forecasts, especially Quantum, a firm whose general forecasting skill had been analyzed in some detail already. He had hoped that the day might lead to a plan of evaluation that would help identify those analysts who seemed best able to predict the fortunes of various companies and industries used for investment purposes by the bank. (The problem Mr. Morris was focusing on is described in more detail in the Southern States Bank and Trust Company (B) case.)

In some senses, Mr. Morris was pleased with his progress. Nevertheless, two things remained troubling. First, an analyst who could correctly forecast about 2 percent (R^2; $r \simeq .14$) of the excess-return results for the stocks he followed had enough skill to provide useful information. This skill level was so low, however, that Mr. Morris found it hard to distinguish its results from random performance. In any case, results were unlikely to be stable over time or across analysts. Second, it was hard to distinguish between group performance (e.g., all oil stocks) and individual stock performance (identifying stocks within the oil group that tended to perform better). Both of these skills, he recognized, could be valuable. No doubt, also, individual analysts had biases toward particular stocks that needed to be recognized.

This case was prepared by Robert F. Vandell, Charles C. Abbott Professor of Business Administration of the Colgate Darden Graduate School of Business Administration of the University of Virginia.

As was his wont, Mr. Morris stuffed some of his reading backlog into his briefcase at the end of the day. Nearly every evening and early morning he spent an hour reading. One article he read that night, "Can Active Management Add Value?" by Ambachtsheer and Farrell in the *Financial Analysts Journal* (attached as Appendix A), seemed particularly apropos. While almost all facets of this article were interesting, he found the portfolio-building rules most intriguing. First of all, they seemed very simple. Second, they appeared to help diversify against the most serious forms of forecasting mistakes without requiring elaborate optimization models. (Had Southern followed these rules in 1979, he thought it likely that portfolios would have done about as well as, if not better than, the Standard & Poor's 500 Index.) He also noted that this system looked through the problems of diverse forecasting skill within an organization, hoping to overpower the poor estimates of a particular analyst with forecast data from several sources.

All this led Mr. Morris to wonder if the day he had spent trying to devise a plan to analyze relative levels of forecasting skills within and across several firms had been worthwhile. Might he have better spent his time worrying how to protect against the inevitable forecast errors that would remain? Would diversification as set forth in the article prove to be a superior way of dealing with forecasting uncertainty?

Appendix A

CAN ACTIVE MANAGEMENT ADD VALUE?

by Keith P. Ambachtsheer and James L. Farrell, Jr.

To survive the onslaught of passive management, active management must produce returns large enough to offset its higher risks and fees. The authors identify the basic building blocks of a viable active management approach, shed light on the kinds of results that can be expected when these building blocks are integrated into an active management process, and suggest some reasons why active management, although viable in theory, has often failed to outperform passive management in practice.

The five basic building blocks of active management are (1) judgments on the degree to which securities are under- or overvalued, (2) assessments of the correla-

---

Keith Ambachtsheer is Director of Research for the investment management consulting firm Canavest House Inc., Toronto. James Farrell is a Vice President of Citibank, N.A., in New York.

The authors thank College Retirement Equities Fund, Citibank, N.A. and Canavest House for their financial support of this study.

Source: *Financial Analysts Journal*, November-December 1979, pp. 39–47.

tion between these judgments and subsequent security returns, (3) conversion of the judgments into expected returns that are both unbiased and scaled to reflect the judgments' predictive power, (4) portfolio building rules that generate changes consistent with diversification requirements, transaction costs and legal and other considerations, and (5) a mechanism for translating portfolio changes into actual buy and sell orders.

Tests suggest that existing research approaches are capable of generating judgments with low but significant predictive power, and that a combination of approaches will often yield results superior to those of any one approach. Superior results are forthcoming, however, only when the active manager devotes adequate attention to building blocks (2) through (5).

The passive management of security portfolios has been elevated over the last few years from an oddity with subversive overtones to a viable and even attractive option for buyers and sellers of portfolio management services. The attraction lies partly in the fact that the product characteristics of passively managed portfolios can readily be described by sellers and understood by buyers. More importantly, the promise of diversification combined with reduced management and brokerage fees has proved hard to resist, especially for those responsible for the administration of large pools of pension assets.

The success of passive management has provided a healthy perspective from which to reexamine active management. The viability of active management hinges on whether it can produce over the long term incremental returns large enough to more than offset its greater risks and higher fees. The passive and active approaches are contrasted graphically in Figure 1.

This article has three purposes—(1) to identify the basic building blocks of a viable active management approach, (2) to shed light on the kinds of results that can be expected when the building blocks are integrated into an active management "manufacturing process," and (3) to suggest a number of reasons why active management, while viable in theory, has often failed to succeed in practice.

Basic Building Blocks

It takes neither mysticism nor high-powered mathematics to list the basic components of successful active management. There are five—

1. *Judgments on the degree to which securities are under- or overvalued:* These can be judgments about individual securities (leading to "security selection"), groups of securities (leading to "group rotation"), or classes of securities (leading to "market timing").
2. *Predictive ability:* There must be some positive correlation between the judgments and their subsequent actual outcomes. Without predictive ability, there is no basis for active management.
3. *Scaling:* To be useful, the judgments must be converted into return increments (decrements) that are unbiased and scaled to reflect the level of predictive ability embodied in them.

4. *Portfolio building rules:* Converting even properly scaled valuation judgments into portfolio rebalancing decisions is a complex task—especially when diversification requirements, transaction costs, and other possible constraints must be considered. Portfolio building rules, which can be carried out by people, computers, or some combination of the two, can greatly simplify the task.
5. *Buy and sell orders:* It is not enough to know what ought to be done. Successful active management requires that what ought to be done in theory actually be carried out in practice.

Valuation Judgments

At least one aspect of past capital markets will surely apply in the future: Security prices will continue to fluctuate. Whether there exists some method of successfully predicting their fluctuations continues to be a subject of debate. Most of the currently used methods of predicting securities values fall into three broad categories.

The long-term fundamental approach (LTF) focuses on present value analysis. When applied to common stocks, LTF entails making long-term projections of dividends, earnings, or cash flow and then relating the resulting payments stream back to current market values through a discount rate. This approach has become extremely popular over the last few years, and a significant number of investment management organizations currently use it in one form or another.[1]

The short-term fundamental approach (STF) has myriad specific applications in current use. Most revolve around analyzing earnings, earnings momentum, and price-earnings multiples against a background of historical relations. For many years Value Line has used an STF method to derive one-year price appreciation expectations on a large list of common stocks.

The technical approach focuses on deriving the demand and supply for securities through such devices as charting price and volume relations over time. Adherents claim that success with this approach demands subjective evaluation of patterns, making it a highly individualistic exercise not easily reduced to simple formulas or rules.

Other methods that do not fit into these three categories include those that focus on certain corporate balance sheet items or analysis of insider trading reports.

Predictive Ability

Successful active management obviously requires valuation judgments (acquired by whatever method) that have some predictive content. There is no one correct method of measuring the predictive content of such judgments. Canavest House has

[1] Footnotes appear at end of article.

developed a method called "Information Coefficient Analysis" (or IC analysis), which is similar in spirit to the approach described by Treynor and Black.[2]

IC analysis is based on the thesis that, if a set of valuation judgments has predictive content, there should be some positive correlation between the judgments and subsequent stock price behavior. Figure 2 shows three possible cases: Case A suggests perfect predictive ability leading to an Information Coefficient (IC) of 1.0; Case B shows the logical consequence of no predictive ability at all—an IC of zero; Case C shows some predictive ability leading, in the example, to an IC of 0.15. In all cases the IC simply denotes the correlation between sets of codings denoting return expectations and sets of codings denoting subsequent return experience.

Results based on IC analyses of long-term and short-term fundamental valuation approaches (LTF and STF) suggest that carefully constructed valuation methods of both types appear capable of generating judgments having low but significant predictive content, with ICs typically in the 0.05 to 0.25 range.[3] These results are consistent with other scattered reports on the predictive content of appropriately designed and executed valuation methods.[4]

In the case of active management, the simple homily, "Two heads are better than one," takes the form, "Two valuation methods are better than one, as long as they approach the valuation problem through different perspectives."[5] It seems reasonable to assume that STF and LTF methods do provide different perspectives on the valuation of a given list of stocks. Insider trading data might provide a third perspective.

In statistical terms, composite forecasting means moving from simple ICs (denoting the correlation between valuation judgments based on a single method and actual results) to multiple ICs (denoting the correlation between valuation judgments based on multiple methods and actual results). Multiple ICs are higher than simple ICs as long as the valuation methods (i.e., the "explanatory variables") are not perfect substitutes for one another (i.e., perfectly correlated). In other words, predictive power can potentially be enhanced by using more than one valuation method. [A more rigorous statement of the concept is appended by the authors at the end of this article.]

Scaling

Valuation judgments with positive predictive content are a means, not an end—the raw material from which incremental portfolio returns can be produced. Effective integration of valuation judgments and portfolio rebalancing decisions is highly dependent on the proper expression of the judgments.

The final output of the valuation process is, ideally, a set of expected residual returns (or alphas, in portfolio theory language) that have been adjusted to reflect their assumed level of predictive content. Traditionally, valuation judgments have not been expressed in terms of adjusted alphas, but as a wide variety of coding schemes such as "buy," "hold" or "sell." But procedures can be devised to convert any coding or rating scheme into an estimate of IC-adjusted alphas.[6]

Portfolio Building Rules

With the valuation judgments converted into properly scaled residual return expectations, the existing portfolio becomes the focus of attention. At this point, appropriate buy and sell decisions flow from the answers to two critical questions: (1) Given the portfolio's current structure, how much residual return (alpha) can be expected at the cost of how much incremental, non-market related, risk? and (2) What can be done to improve the incremental reward-risk characteristics of the existing portfolio?

The computer can answer the first question, but the second is a different matter. On one hand, rebalancing portfolios "manually" can lead to improper decisions, since proper rebalancing judgments require simultaneous consideration of residual returns, transaction costs, and risk factors on a potentially very large list of securities. On the other hand, even highly sophisticated optimization programs cannot possibly deal with those subjective, qualitative aspects that are and will always continue to be part of the portfolio management function. The appropriate balance between man and machine can be struck by deriving a set of portfolio building rules that define the range of reward-risk characteristics desired, while permitting portfolio managers discretion in terms of specific securities and weights to be used.

An Application

We employed building rules along the lines proposed above to find out what a properly integrated active management process based on integrating the "basic building blocks" detailed above can produce. Our study began in September of 1973 with a "typical" institutional stock portfolio. We converted valuation judgments actually available at that time into IC-adjusted expected residual returns and used these expectations, along with transaction cost assumptions and a set of formal portfolio building rules, to rebalance the portfolio. We repeated the rebalancing procedure in March 1974, September 1974, March 1975, September 1975, and March 1976.

We began with two sets of valuation judgments—LTF judgments acquired from Wells Fargo and STF judgments from Value Line—and a selection universe of 200 of the largest capitalization stocks common to both services.[7] We then used IC analysis to measure the predictive ability of each set over each six-month period. The IC statistics, shown in Table A, indicate that both LTF and STF methods delivered predictive power in a reasonably consistent fashion.[8]

Tests of independence between the two sets of valuation judgments for all six forecast dates suggested virtually no correlation. To test the "two heads are better than one" concept, we combined the LTF and STF judgments, using a two to one weighting scheme that reflected their relative predictive powers over the entire observation period, to create a third set of judgments. The IC statistics on the combined judgments set, also shown in Table A, are on average higher than those of either the LTF or STF set alone.

TABLE A
Six-Month ICs

	9/73 to 3/74	*3/74 to 9/74*	*9/74 to 3/75*	*3/75 to 9/75*	*9/75 to 3/76*	*3/76 to 9/76*	*Mean*	*Std. Dev.*
LTF	0.12	0.16	0.01	0.13	0.08	0.31	0.135	0.100
STF	0.17	0.04	−0.09	0.16	0.11	0.01	0.067	0.100
Combined	0.17	0.18	0.00	0.16	0.10	0.30	0.152	0.099

The Value Line STF judgments came in the form of a one-to-five rating scheme. For consistency, we scaled the Wells Fargo LTF "differences" (that is, the difference between each security's projected long-term return and its risk-adjusted required return) to a one-to-five rating scheme and used the two rating schemes to create ratings for the combined judgments. The three rating sets were converted to IC-adjusted alphas, using IC assumptions of 0.15 for LTF, 0.075 for STF, and 0.17 for the two combined (the latter being mathematically derived from the first two).[9]

Ideally, the LTF and STF IC assumptions should have been based on information generated outside the test period. This was not possible at the time the study was performed. Recent IC analyses suggest that the orders of magnitude assumed continue to be realistic, although LTF-based ICs have deteriorated somewhat, while STF-based ICs have improved.[10]

While properly scaled residual return expectations can be used in all three areas of active management—market timing, group rotation, and security selection—our study focused exclusively on the security selection component. We accomplished this by maintaining (1) portfolio market risk (beta) levels close to 1.0, (2) market (Standard & Poor's 500) weighting between the growth, cyclical, stable, and oil sectors of the portfolio,[11] and (3) as a further risk-control measure, a 60-stock portfolio at all times, with no one stock exceeding three percent of the total value of the portfolio.

Within these risk-related guidelines, our objective was simply to maximize expected portfolio alphas by taking advantage of any switch opportunities that offered a return greater than the three percent round-trip transaction cost. With this objective in mind, we derived a set of portfolio building rules for a computer program that rebalanced the initial September 1973 portfolio and the resulting portfolios every six months thereafter.[12]

Study Results

Table B shows the three-year annualized rates of return (including income and after transaction costs but before management fees) for the following portfolios:

1. *The Combined Fund*—the "managed" fund based on the combined STF and LTF valuation inputs.

2. *The LTF Fund*—the "managed" fund based only on inputs from the long-term fundamental valuation method.
3. *The STF Fund*—the "managed" fund based only on inputs from the short-term fundamental valuation method.
4. *The S&P 500 Fund*—the unmanaged portfolio of 500 stocks as created by Standard & Poor's Corporation.
5. *The Universe (EW) Fund*—the unmanaged portfolio of 200 stocks used as the selection universe for the study, equally weighted.
6. *The Starting Fund*—a hypothetical portfolio of 60 stocks selected from our 200-stock universe and designed to meet the risk-related portfolio building rules created for the three "managed" funds but to have an alpha (given the September 1973 valuation judgments) of zero, in order to give performance equal to that of the universe.
7. *The Universe (CW) Fund*—the unmanaged portfolio of 200 stocks used as the selection universe for the study, capitalization weighted.
8. *The Becker Funds*—managed funds representing the 20th, 50th, and 80th percentile breaks in the universe of the Becker Pension Fund Evaluation Service.[13]

Table B shows that the LTF and STF Funds each earned sufficient excess return to more than justify the incremental management fee typically charged for active management. The Combined Fund produced an alpha that exceeded the better of the two single managed funds by 1 percent. At the same time, the performances of the Universe Funds and the Starting Fund suggest that the performances of the three managed funds were not aided by the 200 stocks chosen as the selection universe. All three unmanaged funds marginally underperformed the S&P 500 Fund.

TABLE B
Performance Results of Test Portfolios
(*September 30, 1973, to September 30, 1976*)

	Rates of Return*
The Combined Fund	10.0%
The LTF Fund	9.0
The STF Fund	5.5
The S&P 500 Fund	3.3
The Universe (EW) Fund	2.9
The Starting Fund	2.5
The Universe (CW) Fund	1.9
The 20th Percentile Becker Fund	0.8
The 50th Percentile Becker Fund	−2.9
The 80th Percentile Becker Fund	−5.6

*Annualized, including income and after transaction costs of 1.5 percent each way, but before management fees.

A detailed examination of performances within each of the six six-month subperiods revealed that the Combined and LTF Funds outperformed the S&P 500 in each period. The STF Fund had a superior performance in five of the periods, versus one out of six periods for the 50th percentile Becker Fund. Figure 3 shows the cumulative wealth indexes for these funds over the three-year period.[14]

Table C shows the results of an *ex post* evaluation of the risk characteristics of the three managed and three unmanaged funds, performed by regressing the 36 observations of monthly returns against the returns of the S&P 500. The *ex post* betas of the managed portfolios (in the 1.00 to 1.07 range) suggest that market risk was reasonably well controlled over the three-year evaluation period. At the same time, the risk-related building rules produced superior levels of diversification, as evidenced by the R-squared and standard error statistics of the managed funds. Comparable statistics for the average pension fund over the test period were roughly 0.90 and 7.0 percent, respectively.[15] The managed funds' results may be at least partially related to the conscious decision not to engage in either market timing or group rotation activity.

The somewhat higher specific, or non-market, risk of the LTF and Combined Funds (indicated by their standard errors) could reflect a tendency toward higher yield exposure over the period. The dividend yields on the LTF and Combined Funds averaged 120 and 90 basis points, respectively, over the S&P 500 Fund's yield. By contrast, the STF Fund's dividend yield approximated the S&P 500's.

The bias in favor of high yield stocks on the part of the LTF and Combined Funds was rewarded over the evaluation period since high yield stocks generally outperformed low yield stocks. The alpha contribution of the high yield bias in the LTF and Combined Funds should not be exaggerated, however. Separate IC tests

TABLE C
Time Series Risk Statistics (*September 1973 to September 1976*)

	Regression Results†			
	Percent Annualized Alpha	*Beta*	R^2	*Annualized Standard Error*
Combined Fund	6.7	1.03	0.93	6.0
LTF Fund*	5.7	1.00	0.93	5.8
STF Fund*	2.2	1.07	0.97	3.9
Starting Fund*	−0.6	1.03	0.95	5.3
S&P 500 Fund	0.0	1.00	1.00	0.0
Universe Fund (EW)	−0.4	1.07	0.98	3.5
Universe Fund (CW)	−1.3	1.02	0.99	2.1

*Adjusted monthly for dividends and transaction costs (Transaction costs equal 1.5 percent each way.)

†The monthly percentage change in the total return index for the portfolio minus the risk-free rate regressed against the monthly percentage change in the total return index for the S&P 500 minus the risk-free rate, using 36 observations.

TABLE D
Portfolio Turnover Rates

Date	*LTF*	*STF*	*Combined*
9/73	62%	27%	64%
3/74	30	22	31
9/74	34	23	36
3/75	32	32	33
9/75	24	23	25
3/76	25	23	25
Cumulative	207	150	214

on the high and low yield subcomponents of the selection universe showed that the LTF valuation judgments discriminated successfully between under- and overvalued securities within *both* subcomponents. Recall also that all the funds were constrained to carry market (S&P 500) weights in the growth, cyclical, stable, and oil sectors. Perhaps one percent of the realized alpha on the LTF Fund and one half percent on the Combined Fund can be attributed to the high yield bias in these two funds over the test period.[16]

Portfolio Turnover Experience

Table D shows period-by-period and cumulative turnover rates for the three managed funds. Initial turnover was high for all three funds, reflecting the rebalancing of the original portfolio in September 1973. "Reweighting" held securities required about a 7 percent turnover on each subsequent rebalancing date. The remaining turnover reflects switches out of held securities into new ones.

The turnover numbers reemphasize the need for realistic IC assumptions and transaction cost estimates.[17] Too conservative assumptions depress turnover below the level warranted and lead to foregone return opportunities. Too optimistic assumptions cause excessive turnover, which can transform potential gains into losses.

Can Active Management Add Value?

The results of our study reveal that successful active management is not dependent on the use of any one specific valuation approach. Indeed, some combination of approaches can yield results superior to those of any one approach. Nor does successful active management require valuation judgments with high levels of predictive content. The Information Coefficients reported in this article imply that only 1 to 2 percent of the variance of residual returns on the 200-stock universe was "explained" by the STF and LTF judgments employed.

The alphas realized by the active management approaches used in our study arose purely from security selectivity within the growth, cyclical, stable, and oil sectors of the sample stock universe. Market timing and group rotation strategies played no part in the superior results achieved by active management.

Successful active management is obviously not dependent on the use of sophisticated optimization models, as the relatively simple portfolio building rules used in the study demonstrate. Successful active management *is* dependent on (*a*) the availability of valuation judgments with some predictive content, (*b*) reasonable assumptions about the degree of predictive content embodied in each valuation judgment employed, (*c*) the conversion of valuation judgments into unbiased, properly scaled residual return expectations, (*d*) the existence of portfolio building rules that deal adequately with transaction costs and risk control, and (*e*) the availability of computer aids to look after the very real data processing needs that the proper integration of the first four factors implies.

Some Caveats

Our STF, LTF, and Combined Funds produced positive annual residual returns of 2.2, 5.7, and 6.7 percent, respectively, with residual risk exposure equal to or less than that of actual equity components of pension funds. These results were achieved using valuation judgments with only modest predictive content (mean ICs of 0.067, 0.135, and 0.152 for STF, LTF, and Combined Funds, respectively, over the test period).

Should these realized alphas be taken as targets for investment management organizations that assume they can make valuation judgments with Information Coefficients in the 0.067 to 0.152 range? First, consider that the reported results suffer from *ex post* bias, in the sense that we knew beforehand what order-of-magnitude ICs to assume for the STF and LTF methods over the September 1973 to September 1976 period. This luxury does not exist for the investment manager looking ahead. All he can practically do is to make informed IC judgments based on sound *a priori* reasoning and available *ex post* IC data. The availability of such data over an extended period of time clearly constitutes highly useful information on which to base *ex ante* judgments.

Furthermore, our study results were based on instantaneous implementation, in the sense that the valuation judgments for each six-month interval were assumed to have been received, turned into buy or sell decisions, and executed all on the same day. This is hardly possible in reality (although a three-day turn-around time has been shown to be practical in one organization that uses the integrated building block approach outlined here).

The above arguments suggest that an organization using valuation methods with ICs in the 0.15 range should not necessarily promise clients a 6 percent alpha; 2 to 3 percent might be more realistic.[18] The real question at issue, however, is why actively managed funds are not achieving even this realistically modest level of return. The Becker results reported in Table B suggest that, during the 1973–76 period at least, over 80 percent of actual funds realized *negative* alphas. This experience is likely to continue as long as investment management organizations fail to define the "product characteristics" of their active management services and to establish an integrated "manufacturing process" capable of converting low-grade valuation judgments into positive portfolio alpha realizations.[19]

Much of the active-passive debate over the last few years has focused on technical issues such as market efficiency. This article suggests that process design and organizational design considerations are at least equally important. Unless these issues are given the attention they deserve, active management will continue to lose ground to passive management in the years ahead.

Appendix: Combining Forecasts

This appendix illustrates the generalized procedure for combining forecasts from two different methods. In this regard, it might be easier to demonstrate the process by working with forecast errors, or the unexplained portion of realized return, rather than with the explained portion of returns, or correlation coefficient, on which the text focuses. Error reduction is the converse of maximizing correlation.

To begin with, we can designate the two forecasting methods as F_1 and F_2, and denote the variance of errors associated with each as $VAR\ F_1$ and $VAR\ F_2$ and the correlation between the errors of the two methods as P_{12}. Note that the method with the smaller error would be the one with the higher IC. In addition, the objective in combining forecasts would be to minimize forecast errors (which as noted would be equivalent to maximizing correlation). We can let k represent the weight of the first method and $(1-k)$ the weight of the second, thereby ensuring that the combined forecast is unbiased. The variance of errors in the combined forecast, $VAR\ C$, can then be written:

$$VAR(C)=k^2\ VAR\ F_1+(1-k)^2\ VAR\ F_2+2P_{12}\ k(VAR\ F_1)^{1/2}\ (1-k)(VAR\ F_2)^{1/2}. \quad (1)$$

Note that the extent of error reduction depends on the correlation between methods (P_{12}). We can best illustrate this by analyzing two extreme cases mentioned in the body of the study—zero correlation and perfect correlation between methods.

First, assume that the forecasting methods have the same predictive power, or that $VAR\ F_1$ equals $VAR\ F_2$. Assume also that both forecasts carry the same weight in the combining formula, or that k equals one half. Substituting in Equation (1) produces Equation (2):

$$VAR(C)=\tfrac{1}{2}\ VAR\ F+2P_{12}(\tfrac{1}{4})VAR\ F, \quad (2)$$

where $VAR\ F$ is a general representation of the error from both methods.

Note that when the methods are independent, the variance of the combined forecast is one half that of each individual forecast. This is because the zero correlation ($P_{12}=0$) eliminates the covariance term in the expression. On the other hand, when the correlation is perfect ($P_{12}=+1$), the variance of the combined forecast is the same as that of each individual forecast. This is because the covariance term becomes equivalent to the error of an individual forecast.

Weighting forecasting methods in proportion to their forecasting power is optimal. We can specifically illustrate this by first differentiating Equation (1) with respect to k, then equating to zero. This provides Equation (3), where the combined error is minimal (combined IC is greatest):

$$k = \frac{VAR\ F_2 - P_{12}(VAR\ F_1)^{1/2}\ (VAR\ F_2)^{1/2}}{VAR\ F_1 + VAR\ F_2 - 2P_{12}\ (VAR\ F_1)^{1/2}(VAR\ F_2)^{1/2}} \tag{3}$$

In the case where P_{12} equals zero, this reduces to:

$$k = \frac{VAR\ F_2}{VAR\ F_1 + VAR\ F_2} \tag{4}$$

In the case where each method has equal forecasting power, the errors will be equal, and the numerator will be one half the denominator. This indicates that equally powerful methods should be weighted equally to obtain the optimal reduction in forecasting error. In the case in the text, the LTF dividend discount method appeared to have about twice the forecasting power (IC) of the STF relative value/earnings momentum method, implying that the forecasting error of the LTF method was one half that of the STF method, or that *VAR* STF equaled 2 *VAR* LTF. Using the preceding formula would indicate that the STF method should receive a weighting, k, of one third and the LTF method a weighting of $(1-k)$ or two thirds. This was precisely the weighting used in our study.

FIGURE 1
The Two Basic Portfolio Management Styles

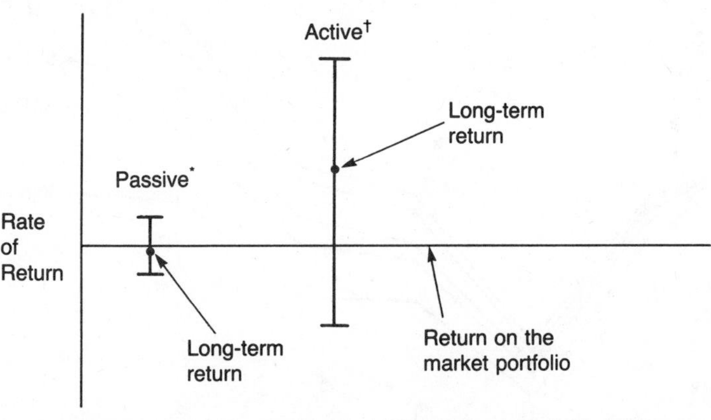

*Passive Management leads to a long-term return slightly below that on the market portfolio because of management and brokerage charges. There is some period-to-period return variability, since it is typically not feasible to match the market portfolio exactly. This variability is represented by the bar.

†Successful Active Management leads to a long-term positive increment of return (net of all fees) at the cost of greater period-to-period return variability.

FIGURE 2
Information Coefficients

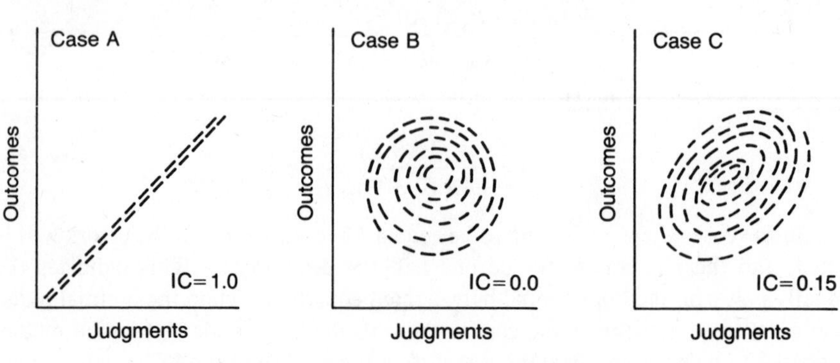

FIGURE 3
Cumulative Wealth Indexes (*September 30, 1973, to September 30, 1976*)

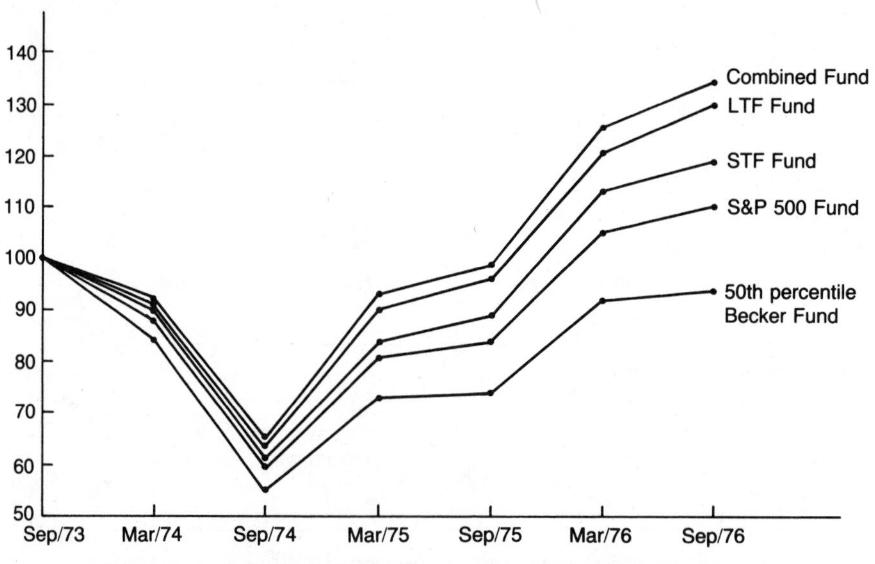

Footnotes

1. The long-term fundamental approach has been popularized through the efforts of the Wells Fargo Research Group. See, for example, William Fouse, "Risk and Liquidity Revisited," *Financial Analysts Journal*, January/February 1977.
2. Jack Treynor and Fischer Black, "How to Use Security Analysis to Improve Portfolio Selection," *Journal of Business*, January 1973. See also Robert Ferguson, "How to Beat the Index Funds," *Financial Analysts Journal*, May/June 1975; and Stuart Hodges and Richard Brealey, "Dynamic Portfolio Selection," *Financial Analysts Journal*, March/April 1973 for further exposition of these ideas.
3. Keith Ambachtsheer, "Where Are the Customers' Alphas?" *Journal of Portfolio Management*, Fall 1977, and "Profit Potential in an Almost Efficient Market," *Journal of Portfolio Management*, Fall 1974.
4. See, for example, Fischer Black, "Yes, Virginia, There is Hope: Tests of the Value Line System," *Financial Analysts Journal*, September/October 1973; Charles Dubois, "Insider Trading Information and Superior Portfolio Performance" (Institute for Quantitative Research in Finance, Spring Seminar, 1978); and Benjamin Korschot, "Measuring Research Analysts' Performance," *Financial Analysts Journal*, July/August 1978.
5. Robert T. Falconer and Charles M. Sivesind ("Dealing with Conflicting Forecasts: The Eclectic Advantage," *Business Economics*, September 1977) discuss this approach with respect to improving economic forecasts.
6. For a description of one such procedure, see Ambachtsheer, "Where Are the Customers' Alphas?"
7. Both Wells Fargo's Security Market Line Service and Value Line's One Year Price Appreciation Rankings were in existence prior to the test period and during the test period and continue to be available today. Both services have made some revisions to their methodologies over time.
8. We tested for the significance of the ICs from each model within each of the six subperiods of the test. For a universe of 200 stocks (sample size), a correlation coefficient of 0.10 is significant at the 0.05 level. The LTF and combined approaches showed "t" statistics in excess of two (0.05 significance level) in five of the six periods of the test, while the STF model proved to be significant at the 0.05 level in three of the six periods.
9. The conversion process used is described in Ambachtsheer, "Where Are the Customers' Alphas?"
10. This deterioration was found to relate to industry group valuation and not to security valuation within industry groups.
11. James Farrell has shown that stocks within each of these four groups tend to move together even after the overall market effect has been removed. See "Analyzing Covariation of Returns to Determine Homogeneous Stock Groupings," *Journal of Business*, April 1974; and "Homogeneous Stock Groupings: Implications for Portfolio Management," *Financial Analysts Journal*, May/June 1975.
12. This computer program is part of the Equity Management and Control System of Canavest House.
13. We wish to thank Gil Beebower of A.G. Becker for providing this information.

14. Detailed period-by-period performance results are shown in Table E below.
15. Gil Beebower, A.G. Becker.
16. The IC within the higher yielding class of securities was 0.13 versus 0.06 within the lower yielding class of securities. These results compare with an IC of 0.14 across the entire selection universe. These numbers suggest that some of the overall predictive power resulted from the LTF approach correctly identifying high yield stocks as undervalued relative to low yield stocks. However, the weighted average of the two "within" class ICs was 0.11, suggesting significant predictive power even after the "across" class IC effect had been removed.
17. See Wayne Wagner and Larry Cuneo, "Reducing the Cost of Stock Trading," *Financial Analysts Journal*, November/December 1975.
18. Ambachtsheer, "Where Are the Customers' Alphas?" and "Profit Potential."
19. This statement does not imply that the "zero sum" nature of the active management game can be repealed. Instead, it suggests that steps can be taken to be a "winner" rather than a "loser" if the decision is made to play the game.

TABLE E
Detailed Performance Results

	9/73 to 9/76 Annualized Rate of Return	*3/76 to 9/76*	*9/75 to 3/76*	*3/75 to 9/75*	*9/74 to 3/75*	*3/74 to 9/74*	*9/73 to 3/74*
Combined Fund	10.0	7.8	28.0	5.5	44.4	−28.9	− 9.0
LTF Fund	9.0	8.9	25.9	4.9	42.7	−28.3	−10.1
STF Fund	5.5	5.6	28.5	6.1	34.8	−31.4	− 9.8
S&P 500 Fund	3.3	4.4	25.0	2.7	34.5	−30.8	−11.7
Starting Fund (Zero Alpha)	2.5	6.3	20.3	3.0	35.4	−31.5	− 9.8
20th Percentile Becker Fund	0.8	5.3	26.2	3.1	44.2	−32.2	−14.1
50th Percentile Becker Fund	−2.9	2.5	22.3	−0.3	39.2	−35.2	−17.2
80th Percentile Becker Fund	−5.6	0.8	18.9	−3.4	35.2	−38.4	−20.5

Part V

Asset-Mix Determination

Lockwood Corporation (A)

In early April 1982, Mr. Robert Malverne, manager of Employee Benefit Plans at Lockwood Corporation, was considering a major shift in the asset mix of the firm's pension portfolio. Two outside directors who were members of the Board's Pension Fund Advisory Committee had been urging that Lockwood dramatically increase the fraction of assets invested in fixed-income securities to take advantage of the high prevailing interest rates on quality bond portfolios. In response, Mr. Malverne was now considering how large a shift, if any, in asset mix he should make, and how the changes should be implemented.

Lockwood was a rapidly growing processor and distributor of branded food and related products marketed through supermarkets and similar outlets. (Exhibit 1 summarizes Lockwood's recent financial statements.) Retained earnings and outside borrowings had proved sufficient to finance rapid expansion; however, as debt utilization approached the firm's policy limitation of 40 percent long-term debt to long-term capitalization, it had been necessary to retain a higher fraction of earnings. Top management, Mr. Malverne knew, had been concerned that the low payout ratio might be adversely influencing the price/earnings ratio, which seemed low for a rapidly growing firm with relatively predictable earnings prospects and with low cyclicality around the earnings-per-share trend line.

Tight cost control was one of the hallmarks of Lockwood's management. These efforts had resulted in generally rising operating margins. Of late, the net profit margin had not shown the same rate of increase, however, in large part because of

This case was prepared by a Professor of the Colgate Darden Graduate School of Business Administration of the University of Virginia.

rising interest and pension-funding costs. Inflation had necessitated liberalization of pension benefits and had therefore significantly increased the past-service component of annual pension costs, which ran at a rate equal to 12.8 percent of payroll in 1981 (as against 9.1 percent in 1977). This problem had been made worse because earnings on pension assets had not been adequate in real terms over the last decade.

The market value of pension fund assets at the end of 1981 was $20.1 million. A requirement of $19.9 million had been determined by the firm's actuary. Assets were invested as follows:

Assets	*Percent*
Cash equivalents	9.8%
Fixed income	20.3
Equities	64.5
Equity real estate	5.1
Other (convertibles)	0.3
Total	100.0%

Real estate equities had been a recent addition designed to provide more protection against inflation.

One outside manager was responsible for handling fixed-income securities (including cash equivalents). Of the $6.05 million in fixed-income securities, approximately $200,000 was required to balance the timing of fund inflows and outflows.

Three outside managers handled the equity investments, which were required to stay as fully invested as possible (usually about 96 to 98 percent). Mr. Malverne believed that market timing had tended to hurt portfolio performance in the past, and the fully-invested stricture was designed to provide protection against judgment errors. One manager employed a "growth" style, tending to invest in firms with higher-than-average earnings-per-share growth records and prospects. A second was value-oriented, tending to invest in firms with low price/earnings ratios. The third was dividend-oriented, investing in stocks with higher yields. The three managers had the following funds under management at the end of 1981:

Style	*Funds' Management ($ millions)*
Growth	$ 3.7
Value	5.2
Dividend	4.1
Total	$13.0

In 1972 all the assets of the fund (then considerably smaller) were managed by a local bank. The equity-management record of the bank had been poor in the mid-1970s, and in 1978 assets were transferred to two new equity managers. One had since been fired, and two new managers hired. The bank continued to manage the fixed-income component of the portfolio. At the time the equity managers were hired, all three had minimum commitment requirements of $1 million. The growth-fund manager had since raised his minimum new commitment requirement to $5 million and the dividend-oriented fund manager had raised his to $10 million. Neither was likely to be sanguine about a significant fund withdrawal at this time.

Lockwood had 3,905 employees at the end of 1981. All employees with more than two years' service were covered by the plan, and vesting, started in the fifth year, was full by the tenth year. Following a 1972 strike, relations with employees were excellent, and turnover was low. Only 407 former employees were currently receiving retirement benefits.

Women constituted over half of the work force. Because of their longer life expectancy, women upon retirement did not receive the same dollar payments per unit of accumulated pension benefits as men. Although the issue had not been raised by any of the unions representing Lockwood's employees, Mr. Malverne was concerned about recent national agitation by Women's Liberation groups to equalize benefits. Equal benefit requirements would add considerably to funding costs.

The current plan had been designed by an employee-benefits consulting firm. Benefits were based on the years of service and the average salary over the last five years of service. This latter requirement provided good protection against inflation for the employees, but added to funding requirements for the firm in inflationary periods.

An actuary determined annual funding requirements according to a complex formula that considered employee age and sex, turnover, and life expectancy. Expected benefit payments for active workers were scheduled out until the last current employee was statistically likely to die. These estimated payments were then discounted at 7 percent, the assumed actuarial rate of return on the pension fund portfolio. Salaries for current employees were also scheduled out to retirement at a growth rate of 5 percent per year and discounted at 7 percent to determine their present value. The ratio of these two present-value estimates was used to determine the normal-cost percentage to be applied to current payrolls. Certain other adjustments, which considered past-service liabilities and the adequacy of current funding levels, influenced the determination of annual costs.

Mr. Malverne was not in a position to evaluate most of the assumptions used by the actuary. Two, however, seemed critical: (1) the increase in salaries, which consisted of two components, an inflation rate of 4 percent per year and a productivity increase of 1 percent per year, and (2) the assumed rate of return on the portfolio, which also had an inflation component of 4 percent factored into it. These assumptions suggested that the portfolio must earn at the real rate of 3 percent per year if the fund was to be considered adequate by the actuary.[1] The low present ratio of market value-to-current funding requirement concerned Mr. Malverne, especially in the face of a weak equity market in early 1982.

Given recent high inflation rates, Mr. Malverne had several times questioned the appropriateness of the 4 percent inflationary assumption. Because inflation tended to affect both salaries and benefits, he was told, the impact of the inflationary assumption tended to cancel out. Mr. Malverne concluded that the key number he should focus upon was the real rate of return earned by the portfolio.

The problem was that the portfolio had not earned a real rate of return of 3 percent per year over the last 10 years. Exhibit 2 includes some data Mr. Malverne had collected on the performance of key indicators used by the Pension Advisory Committee to evaluate manager performance. These data suggest that it would have been difficult to earn a real rate of return of 3 percent per year on any prudent portfolio during this period.

Exhibit 3 shows the results of Lockwood's fixed-income and equity portfolios over this same decade, as well as the composite results. Under-performance was evident in these data. Exhibit 4 reports the 10-year investment record of Lockwood's three current equity managers. Mr. Malverne was aware that this last decade had not had markets that supported a "growth" manager, whereas this style had tended to produce very attractive results in the two preceding decades.

The Asset-Mix Issue

On April 1, 1982, quality corporate bonds were yielding 15.75 percent to maturity. Under active pressure from the Federal Reserve Bank, under Mr. Volker's leadership, inflation rates had begun to decline, as shown on an annualized basis below:

Year and Quarter	*Inflation Rate*
1980	12.4%
1981:1	10.8
2	9.7
3	12.3
4	3.5
1982:1	3.2 (estimated)

Forecasts of inflation for the next 12 months tended to be in the 5–6 percent range. Many speculated that the Fed would act to reduce inflation more permanently, and that we would not experience double-digit rates again for the foreseeable future.

[1] The actuary computed the market value-to-fund requirement ratio each year. The average ratio of the most recent five years was then used to determine current funding adequacy (a resulting figure of 1 being the minimum requirement before additional funding proved necessary). This method tended to smooth out some of the effects of short-term marketplace volatility.

Appendix A contains a recent economic commentary of the sort Mr. Malverne was seeing with increasing frequency.

These circumstances prompted two directors to urge that a substantial part of the pension portfolio be invested in fixed-income securities. They both saw the opportunity to "lock up" a real rate of return of about 10 percent for a considerable period into the future, and thereby "guarantee" a comfortable margin of safety with respect to achieving the actuarial target real rate of 3 percent per year. They noted that inflation rates would have to average more than 12.75 percent per year before the real rate of return would be jeopardized. One of these directors wanted to shift all the pension assets into fixed-income securities as quickly as possible. The second preferred to increase the fixed-income mix to 60 percent, on the theory that nothing was ever perfectly certain and that an equity/real estate hedge of approximately equal amounts would be desirable.

These proposals did not meet with enthusiastic acceptance among the three other members of the Pension Fund Advisory Committee (all on the Board of Directors). Nevertheless, there seemed to be a sentiment for a considerable shift into fixed-income securities at this time.

One Committee member, doubtful that inflation had really been cured, did not want to go overboard. A shift to, say, a 50 percent fixed-income position seemed most suitable to him.

The financial vice-president of Lockwood (a Committee member) pointed out that a fixed-income portfolio would not necessarily produce steady rates of return at the level of 15.75 percent per year. Much depended on the reinvestment rate. If this was below 15.75 percent, as seemed probable—say 10 percent per year—the realized rate of return might only be 12–13 percent. He asked Mr. Malverne to check his hunch by using a hypothetical 20-year bond selling at its par value with a 15.75 percent coupon rate and no sinking funds. He suggested three reinvestment rates be tested: 8 percent, 10 percent, and 12 percent. Sinking funds or refundings (a real possibility if interest rates fell sharply) would only worsen the comparison, he noted. He did not oppose the idea of increasing the fixed-income component, but thought action should be taken cautiously.

One of the proponents of a dramatic change to an enlarged fixed-income component responded tartly that interest rates had already begun to fall (to 15.45 percent). The "iron was hot," he claimed, and prompt action was mandatory if they were to capitalize upon a once-in-a-lifetime opportunity.

One Committee member who was an investment banker felt less sure that any change was advisable. Equities, he noted, tend to promise higher rates of return than long-term bonds.[2] He had seen estimates of long-term rates of return on the Standard and Poor's 500 Index ranging from 18 to 21 percent per year from various services in the last few months. If interest rates fell, he thought stocks were likely to appreciate in market value to a greater extent than bonds. Finally, he was

---

[2]Over the 56 years prior to 1982, the Standard & Poor's 500 Index had a compound total rate of return of 9.1 percent, according to estimates made by his source. Corresponding rates of return for T-bills and the Salomon Brothers Bond Index were only 3.0 percent and 3.6 percent, in contrast.

impressed with the performance record of the three current equity managers and would, for this reason, hate to see the investments in equity reduced. When pressed by one of the proponents of change, the investment banker admitted that equity-return estimates were not as certain as bond yields. He thought, however, that stocks were reasonably sure to return at least 15.75 percent per year over the next five years and the uncertainty lay in how much they would return above that level. He liked this kind of uncertainty.

The most active proponent argued that a shift to fixed-income securities now could be very beneficial if interest rates fell sharply, as he expected would happen. A 400 basis-point decline of interest rates over the next 12 months would, he estimated, produce a total rate of return of about 50 percent as the result of price appreciation. If so, the Committee could then consider redeploying capital to equities, having locked up a good part of the benefits he foresaw in one fell swoop. He believed that the interest-rate decline would exceed 400 basis points. If he was right, funding costs would decrease one year from now.

Discussion also covered a number of alternative ways the changes could be made. The Advisory Committee agreed that some further analysis of the asset-mix issues raised would be appropriate. Mr. Malverne was asked to undertake this task. It was not clear what precisely the Advisory Committee members wanted, but it was clear they wanted the analysis fast. A telephone conference call was arranged for the following week. Mr. Malverne had already decided to focus on the policy issue first: that is, on how much of the portfolio, if any, should be shifted into fixed-income securities in the immediate future. Later, he would consider the tactical questions relating to how best to achieve the policy objectives.

EXHIBIT 1
Recent Financial Data

Income Statement Summary (most recent ten years)

Year	Sales ($ millions)	Operating Margin	Net Profit ($ millions)	Net Profit Margin	Earnings per Share	Dividends per Share	Average P/E Ratio
1972	$193	2.2%	$ 0.9	0.5%	$ .30*	$ .30*	19.0x*
1973	228	3.3	2.1	0.9	.68	.30	6.4x
1974	264	3.4	2.3	0.9	.76	.32	5.6x
1975	278	4.7	4.5	1.6	1.52	.34	3.3x
1976	305	5.0	6.0	2.0	2.07	.40	5.1x
1977	348	5.6	7.4	2.1	2.48	.50	6.1x
1978	420	5.4	8.9	2.1	2.98	.64	6.9x
1979	507	5.2	9.8	1.9	3.26	.78	6.1x
1980	612	5.9	12.5	2.0	4.14	.92	5.8x
1981	729	6.3	16.2	2.2	5.34	1.14	7.5x

*Earnings per share in 1971 were $.72; a strike adversely affected results in 1972. Dividends were maintained. The price/earnings ratio was probably unrealistically high in 1972.

EXHIBIT 1 *(concluded)*

Balance Sheet
December 31, 1981
($ millions)

Assets		Liabilities and Net Worth	
Cash assets	$ 13.7	Accounts payable	$ 54.2
Receivables	52.2	Other payables	12.9
Inventories (FIFO)	34.2	Current portion LT debt	2.9
Other	3.9	Total current liabilities	$ 70.0
Total current assets	$104.0	Long-term debt	34.2
Fixed assets (net)	77.2	Deferred taxes	5.7
Other assets	5.9	Net worth	77.2
Total assets	$187.1	Total liabilities & net worth	$187.1

EXHIBIT 2
Ten-Year Performance Record of Key Market Indicators

Year	Treasury Bills	Salomon Brothers Corporate Bond Index	Standard & Poor's 500 Index	Consumer Price Index
1981	14.7%	−1.0%	− 4.9	8.9%
1980	11.2	−2.6	32.4	12.4
1979	10.4	−4.2	18.4	13.3
1978	7.2	−0.1	6.6	9.0
1977	5.1	1.7	− 7.2	6.8
1976	5.1	18.7	23.6	4.8
1975	5.8	14.6	37.3	7.0
1974	8.0	−3.1	−26.5	12.2
1973	6.9	1.1	−14.7	8.8
1972	3.8	7.3	19.0	3.4
Compound rate of return	7.8%	3.0%	6.4%	8.6%
Standard deviation (compound basis)	3.1%	7.6%	22.7%	3.1%

Source: R. G. Ibbotson and R. A. Sinquefield, *Stocks, Bonds, Bills and Inflation: The Past and the Future* (Charlottesville, Va.: Financial Analysts Research Foundation, 1982).

EXHIBIT 3
Total Rate of Return on Lockwood Portfolio

Year	Fixed-Income Portfolio	Stock Portfolio	Total Portfolio (Composite)
1981	9.2%	− 2.3%	2.0%
1980	4.5	29.8	15.2
1979	3.7	19.0	10.8
1978	3.5	7.1	5.5
1977	3.0	− 8.0	2.4
1976	11.8	21.2	16.8
1975	10.0	25.7	17.3
1974	− 1.0	−28.0	−13.5
1973	− 1.4	−17.2	−12.0
1972	6.8	21.0	17.1
Compound rate of return	5.2%	5.0%	5.6%
Standard deviation (compound basis)	3.9%	22.0%	12.1%

EXHIBIT 4
Ten-Year Performance Record of Lockwood's Three Equity Managers

Year	Growth	Value-Oriented	Dividend-Oriented
1981	− 7.4%	− 5.2%	5.2%
1980	38.3	16.7	27.3
1979	29.3	23.9	28.9
1978	11.6	10.5	3.0
1977	− 3.2	12.4	− 0.7
1976	14.0	43.4	42.3
1975	26.7	40.8	39.5
1974	−24.7	−20.6	− 7.7
1973	−10.0	−21.1	−10.4
1972	26.1	18.8	11.7
Compound rate of return	8.2%	9.8%	12.5%
Standard deviation (compound basis)	21.7%	23.3%	18.3%

Appendix A

HITTING INFLATION AT THE ROOTS

Inflation is finally on the wane. Twice before in the last couple of years, double-digit inflation in consumer prices melted away and then built right back up (see chart). That won't happen now. It's taken two recessions, not one, but this time the root of inflation has been hit hard.

The most recent numbers, such as the 1.1% decline in producer prices in February, are nevertheless too good to last. Indeed, what has been happening lately has very little to do with the improved fundamentals that matter for the longer run. Much of the slowdown so far is accounted for by the unwinding of the previous spurt. Last summer, consumer prices soared because several elements speeded up all at once: food prices, which had been nearly flat during the spring, jumped at an 8% annual rate; mortgage rates rebounded, pushing home-financing costs up at a 33% pace; used-car prices climbed at a 44% rate as buyers turned away from the stickers on the new models; and gasoline prices, which had taken a breather in the spring, accelerated again.

Vanishing Pressures

By early winter all this extra pressure on prices had dissipated. Food prices have moved up at less than a 4% pace during the most recent three months (despite an up-tick from bad weather in January); home-financing costs retreated to a 3.5% rate of increase; and used-car prices fell back to a 13% pace. Even though these volatile components of consumer prices aren't going to explode again, somewhat larger increases should be counted on in the months ahead.

Gasoline prices, on the other hand, have a bit more give. In January, service stations dropped prices by 1.7% and followed that with a much larger cut in February, estimated at about 5%, bringing prices down to the level of early 1981. With margins squeezed badly, declines at the pump will be more gradual now. World oil prices have dropped 6% already from the peak early last year. The speculation is that Saudi Arabia will curb the oil glut by cutting its production to 6.5 million barrels a day from the 7.5 million current rate. But that will still leave an overhang, and some analysts are expecting a further 10% drop in world prices, down to about $30 a barrel. Allowing for some catch-up in margins, that would translate into a 3% to 4% further slippage at the service stations over the next 10 months, to a weighted average of $1.23 per gallon by year-end. Of course, a new

---

Chief Economist: Todd May, Jr.; Associate Economist: Vivian Brownstein; Staff: Edward Boyer, Catherine Comes Haight, Lenore Schiff.

tax, imposed at the import level or at the cash register, would wipe out at least some of the reduction. Both have been talked about lately.

The recent low numbers on the CPI also reflect some transitory effects of the recession. Price increases for all consumer goods other than food and energy averaged only a 2% rate of rise over the last few months, while producer prices for the same items rose at a 5% rate. Retailers won't be able to tolerate that kind of a profit squeeze for long. Once they get rid of the extra inventory piled up last autumn, some catching up is bound to occur. Home-purchase prices, too, will show some renewed life now that sales have stopped falling.

At the same time, however, inflation will finally begin to reflect the better long-term fundamentals. The personal-consumption deflator, which excludes mortgage-interest costs, never bounced as high as the CPI last summer and is showing slightly larger gains now. Both measures should move up as the recovery begins—but only to the neighborhood of a 6.5% to 7% annual rate. That is way below last year's 9% rise in the CPI, and a significant improvement from last year's gain of 7.6% in the

Inflation Tumbles

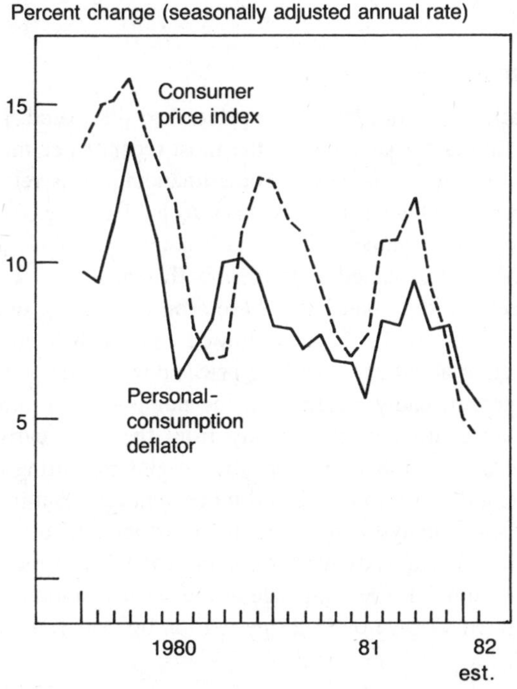

Inflation has slowed to half last summer's double-digit pace. Increases in the CPI, which gives large weight to recent swings in mortgage costs, slipped below the rate shown by the Commerce Department's less volatile personal-consumption deflator. Both series are charted as three-month moving averages.

personal-consumption deflator. What's changed is the outlook for the core of inflation—unit labor costs.

Fortune estimates that gains in hourly compensation are slowing in a major way this year. Compensation slipped under a 7% rate in the fourth quarter during the worst of the recession, and there won't be much rebound because unemployment will stay high. Unit labor costs, on the other hand, shot up last quarter, at a 14% rate for all nonfarm business and at a 20% rate in manufacturing. The slowdown in hourly compensation couldn't make up for the fact that output dropped much more sharply than the number of hours worked—that is, productivity collapsed.

Productivity was bound to fall. Even during earlier decades, when better performance was routine, there were reverses during business contractions. Last quarter's decline was larger than expected for the amount of production loss, and that is a bit worrisome. But for a couple of years prior to last quarter, output per hour was tracking closely with an underlying 2% rate of growth, so *Fortune* still expects productivity gains on that order to start showing up after the recovery is under way. There won't be any extra kick as in past recoveries, however, because growth will be slow. If productivity is off only slightly in the first quarter, inches up at a 1% rate in the second, and reaches a 2% pace in the second half, then unit labor costs should go up by 6.5% or 7% this year, compared with 10% during 1981.

Though profits were down, cash-flow margins held up surprisingly well last quarter despite the run-up in unit labor costs. Cash flow is getting another boost from accelerated depreciation now. So with margins not likely to swell and a better outlook for costs, there is good reason to expect that inflation pressures are down to stay.

The Payoff from Labor's New Mood

It's no April Fools' joke: wage gains will slow dramatically this year despite a crowded bargaining calendar for organized labor. Contracts covering 3.6 million of the 9 million workers in major bargaining units expire during 1982, compared with contracts covering only 2.5 million last year. But over one quarter of the 3.6 million workers are in the hard-pressed auto and trucking industries, where large layoffs and mounting losses are forcing labor to accept wage freezes and less frequent cost-of-living increases. The UAW's give-backs to Ford in the contract signed in late February will probably influence the negotiations with General Motors, which resumed last week. The imminent United Parcel Service settlement, covering more than 70,000 Teamsters, should benefit from the modest example of recent trucking pacts.

Rubber and electrical machinery—the other big industries due to negotiate contracts this year—aren't in great shape either. Labor concessions lately in Firestone and Goodyear plants may signal restraint in the contracts that come due next month. Moderation is likely among the electrical-machinery workers as well. Negotiations under way at General Electric and Westinghouse cannot ignore the drop in demand for major appliances.

A Break in Wages

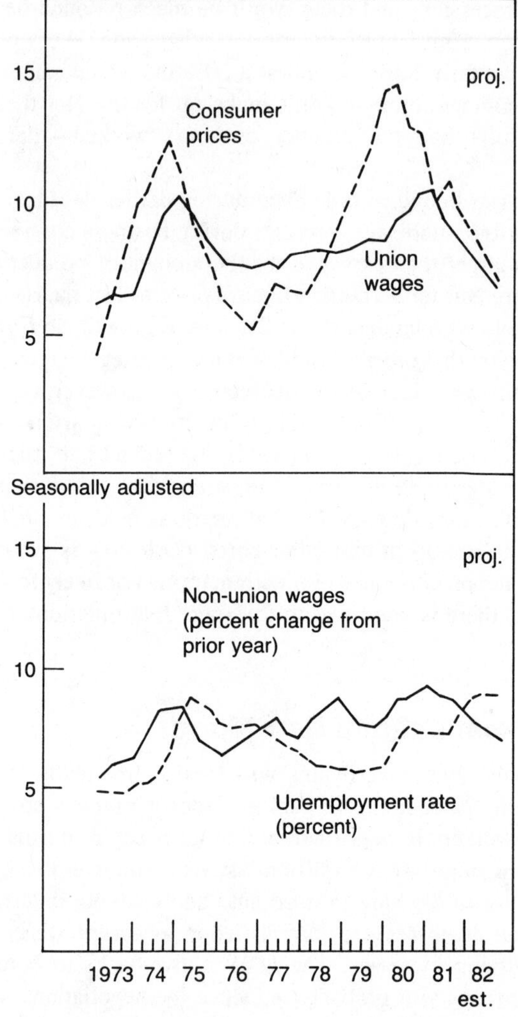

To facilitate a comparison with changes in wage trends, this chart shows the change in the CPI from the same quarter in the prior year. Union wages generally track inflation, but fell behind in 1979–80. Non-union wages are strongly influenced by labor-market conditions.

It can be argued, says Audrey Freedman, a labor economist at the Conference Board, that labor's tractability is long overdue, a return to "rational bargaining for the first time in 10 years." Still, the departure from past patterns is breathtaking. After the severe 1974–75 recession, for instance, new contracts were just as fat as ever. Even last year, when the competitive problems of American industry were becoming abundantly clear, first-year increases under new contracts averaged 10%. That figure will drop by almost half this year, to only about 6%.

The deceleration is so sudden that, in a reversal of the norm, increases due in 1982 under contracts negotiated in earlier years will actually be higher than first-year hikes. Some 4.3 million workers—versus 6.3 million last year—will take home deferred raises averaging 6.3%. This figure doesn't include the cost-of-living adjustments (COLAs) that a third of all union workers will get this year. The COLAs, on average, are expected to make up for about 60% of the rise in consumer prices this year. Assuming that the CPI will increase by 7% in 1982, pay hikes from COLAs should average about 4.2%. All in all, union wages should rise by an average of about 7%, well below last year's 9%.

The Scare Effect

While union wages have tended to track inflation (see charts), non-union pay is strongly influenced by the unemployment rate. With unemployment likely to stay around 9% through 1982, gains for non-union workers (80% of the labor force) will be held down. Lower inflation will help here, too, and there won't be an upward push from workers at the lower end of the pay scale because the minimum wage will hold steady at $3.35 an hour. The Reagan tax cut, by increasing take-home pay, should also have some ameliorative effect. Non-union wage gains, which slowed from a 9% rate in the first nine months of 1981 to 8.1% with the recession late last year, will slow further to 7% in 1982.

Fringe benefits won't add much to total compensation. The rise in Social Security taxes is increasing employers' costs by only .2%, compared with .6% in 1981. Other fringes should add no more than last year's .6% and possibly even less if the recent UAW concessions—less time off with pay, for instance—are followed in other agreements. The average rise in hourly compensation, then, will decline from 9.2% in 1981 to 7.5% to 8% this year, the lowest since 1977 and the best news yet for inflation.

de Vechio Industries, Inc.

Mr. Rolf Linstrom, Treasurer of de Vechio Industries, Inc., let his exasperation show as he addressed Mr. Rob Pinches, Vice President of Seldon and Lait, Actuaries:

> As I understand your analysis, you take very precise demographic information on our existing employee population by age and sex, attrition rates, death rates, and so on, to project the benefits that will accrue to these people to the point of retirement and then schedule the benefits to be paid each year over their actuarially determined life, or, as appropriate, to determine residual benefits, under our plan. This is then coupled with the actuarially determined fixed (actuarial) commitments to employees already retired or those who have left the company with vested benefits. The cash stream of future benefits is then discounted to its present value. From this amount are deducted: (1) the adjusted market value of our portfolio and (2) unfunded past service liabilities, which we are already scheduled to work off at predetermined amounts over the next 20-odd years. The residual is our unfunded liability for future employee services. Concurrently, you schedule out the payrolls we will pay these current employees year by year until the youngest ones finally retire, and then present-value this payroll stream. Our normal cost rate is then determined by relating the present value of the unfunded liability to the payroll present value. The result is then multiplied by the total payroll of participants to determine the dollar normal cost. To this figure, we add the scheduled payments of the past service liability to determine our annual pension costs. All this sounds very precise. What I don't

---

understand is why you use such ridiculous assumptions about key variables to screw up the usefulness of this analysis!

Mr. Linstrom continued,

Let me be specific. Four things in particular concern me. First, you assume payrolls will increase at a rate of 5 percent per year in the future. This assumption affects both the present value of benefits and future payrolls. Since 1970, our payrolls have increased at a rate of 8.1 percent per year assuming a static work force. About 6 percent of this number is directly attributable to inflation; the balance reflects seniority/productivity increases and the like. Most forecasters seem to be expecting inflation to continue at about 6 percent into the foreseeable future. A 5 percent assumption looks silly in this perspective. Moreover, as best I can see, looking back through our records for the last 30 years, wage increases of less than 5 percent are the infrequent exception, not the rule.

Next, I'm worried about your treatment of the social security wage ceiling: As you know, an employee accrues retirement benefits equal to 1.2 percent of wages up to the social security ceiling and 2.4 percent of wages above that ceiling. You assume this ceiling will grow at 3 percent. Congress has already enacted legislation increasing this ceiling at a rate more than double your assumption well into the future. If anything, the consensus seems to be that the changes in the new law are inadequate. All else equal, the changes enacted—which we anticipated when our plan was last revised—should lead to lower accrual of benefits than you have projected. Our normal cost is, as a result, overstated.

Next, you assume that our portfolio will earn at a rate of 6 percent per annum into the future. Right now I can buy solid corporate bonds promising yields of 8.5 percent to 9 percent. From what I can learn, investment experts seem to be forecasting long-term rates of return of 12 percent to 15 percent for the Standard & Poor's 500 Stock Index. A 6 percent assumption looks awfully conservative in this light. A higher discount rate would pull down the present value of unfunded benefits faster than the present value of future payrolls. Normal costs would then drop.

Finally, I am worried about the adequacy of our plan in the event of continuing rapid inflation. To a large extent, our benefits are tied to the average wages an employee earns during his or her career here. If terminal wages for this employee have increased solely as the result of inflation to a level well above the average, the benefits may be quite inadequate in real terms. We may later have to increase benefits and funding. It is this potential "bombshell on the horizon" that most worries me. It could be big and hurt us badly. Your assumptions, in short, seem to lull us into thinking everything is OK when it is not.

The best way to reduce the risks of this bombshell is to shoot for superior performance on our pension portfolio. This will involve more risks, however. The use of "adjusted market" values in determining current costs helps. As I understand it, if the total market value is between 100 percent and 120 percent of the actuarial requirement, we use the actuarial requirement in the cost calculation. Fortunately, our market value is 111.7 percent of the actuarial requirement at the moment, which serves as a cushion to reduce some of the dangers of volatility inherent in the market values of risky securities. If, however, the market value falls below the actuarial value in the future, we are faced with increased funding costs (even if spread over 15 years). This risk is putting a severe constraint on how I think about our portfolio objectives. The realities of the marketplace are such that the portfolio should fluctuate around actuarial requirements. What worries me is that we may be hit with higher costs (because of bad business conditions, which tend to follow bad equity market conditions). We are being placed in the bind between the need for high returns on our portfolio and achieving them with low risks. This situation makes the task of setting portfolio goals and determining portfolio strategies impossible. The adjustment, while helpful, is inadequate and unrealistic.

Mr. Pinches' reply to these comments did not afford Mr. Linstrom much comfort. Mr. Pinches first talked about the importance of long cycles in determining actuarial requirements. History illustrated well that it was a mistake to overreact to short-term problems, no matter how serious they might seem at the moment. For example, he noted that, compounded from 1928 to 1977, inflation had averaged 2.3 percent per year—well below recent experience. Mr. Pinches did make two concessions. First, his firm would change the assumption about the rate of payroll increase from 5 percent to 8 percent if they also changed the assumed rate of return on investment from 6 percent to 10 percent. Also, his firm would increase the ratio of market value to actuarial value (now at 20 percent) to 30 percent, before annual funding cost decreases would be permitted. This increase would facilitate a larger cushion against market volatility in the future, assuming market values rose in the interim.

Mr. Pinches offered one further suggestion, to wit:

> You could build up this cushion immediately. Here's how: You have an unchangeable contractual obligation to retired employees and to former employees with vested benefits. You could purchase fixed-income securities with appropriately spaced maturities to satisfy the benefit requirements for these people, say, to yield close to 9 percent. If you did this, we would remove these obligations from the funding requirement by discounting the benefits at the actual return on the securities purchased (say 9 percent). Similarly, these securities would be removed from the market value of the portfolio. The net result would be to increase the ratio of remaining funding requirements to about 125 percent. This would give you a 25 percent cushion against adverse market developments. Perhaps you could then plan your portfolio investments more beneficially.

Although the latter idea seemed to Mr. Linstrom worthy of some consideration, he was concerned by the change in the required rate of return to 10 percent should he choose a more realistic assumption about payroll increases (8 percent). First, there would be no appreciable change in annual funding. It seemed to Mr. Linstrom as if the actuary had decided on a solution and then worked out the assumptions necessary to achieve this end, rather than selecting appropriate assumptions first. Secondly and more importantly, a return of 10 percent per year seemed to be a very high target for future portfolio performance.

All of these issues had become more important to Mr. Linstrom as a result of a charge given him at the outset of 1978 by Mr. Floyd Little, Financial Vice President of de Vechio Industries. Mr. Little had said,

> To date we have given no guidance to the manager of our $25 million-plus pension funds. Although we do not want to get involved in day-to-day management (security selection, etc.), it seems to me we should spell out our objectives with regard to income and risk and define some major policies with respect to target percentage investments in major categories of investments. I am also wondering if we should spell out any guidelines about, say, the types of equity securities that should be purchased. I'd like to have you make a definitive study of this subject and present some concrete, supported recommendations for our directors to consider by the June board meeting.

Although Mr. Linstrom was only in the first weeks of this assignment, it seemed harder and harder to achieve. His attempts to get clarification from Mr. Little had been frustrating. Mr. Little had responded, "You and I know that our board has been itchy since the enactment of ERISA (Employee Retirement Income Security Act of 1974). They want us to define our investment policies more clearly. I'm not sure what this means, and I don't think they do either. Do the best you can."

The Wilshire Long-Range Pension Planning Service

In late January 1978, Mr. Linstrom learned of a long-range pension planning service offered by Wilshire Associates, Inc., a consulting firm specializing in providing analytical assistance to "retirement systems, endowments, and investment managers." The following excerpt from Wilshire's promotional literature described the basic purposes and benefits of their service:

> Wilshire Associates' Long-Range Pension Planning Service examines prospective investment policies and determines appropriate investment mixes.
>
> The major benefits provided to corporate management include:
>
> - A financial planning tool for corporate pension funds.
> - A forecast of future pension costs and future actuarial liabilities.
> - A quantitative analysis and documentation of the fact that management has discharged its corporate fiduciary responsibility as defined by ERISA.
>
> The basis of the Pension Planning Service is a tailor-made computer forecasting model that integrates the three components of a company's retirement system: (1) the future growth of the company, (2) a forecast of future pension liabilities, and (3) a simulation of future investment market conditions and their financial impact on the trust and the company.
>
> The Wilshire planning model computes the likelihood of future outcomes resulting from different investment policies. The model portrays the probabilities of the very best along with the very worst results. Therefore, the model is especially beneficial in identifying the prospective risks of different investment policies.

As these benefits appealed to Mr. Linstrom, he arranged to have Mr. Louis Kingsland of Wilshire make a presentation to Mr. Little and himself in early February.

The Nature of the Wilshire Asset Allocation Service

As preparation for their forthcoming meeting, Mr. Kingsland sent Mr. Linstrom copies of the brochure, "Pension Planning: An Asset Allocation Service for Pension Plan Sponsors." Excerpts from this brochure follow:

The Asset Allocation Question . . .

The future growth of pension liabilities, retirement benefit payments, and trust assets are of major concern in the management of corporate pension finance.

As a result of this concern, pension trust officers and fiduciaries have turned to Wilshire Associates to seek meaningful guidance in the selection of an asset mix and an investment policy that will be suitable to the needs of their pension plans. Wilshire created the first full-scale pension forecasting model in 1972 and is nationally recognized as a leader in pension forecasting services.

The Pension Planning Approach . . .

Wilshire Associates has pioneered the application of analysis techniques to the projection of pension plan funding requirements that must be anticipated in the prudent management of trust assets. These capabilities are available in an investment planning service designed to assist corporate pension plan sponsors in the formulation of long-range investment policy.

The major purpose of the Wilshire Pension Planning Service is to analyze future pension costs and levels of funding resulting from investment policies that are established today.

The key to the Wilshire Pension Planning Service is that it pulls together the two major components of corporate pension finance, i.e., the actuarial evaluation and the trust investment programs, and develops written investment policies and objectives that are appropriate to the needs and risk tolerances of your pension plan.

The Wilshire Pension Planning Service does not replace the services of your current actuary, but simply incorporates and extends their treatment of actuarial liabilities.

Future Demographics and Liabilities . . .

Beginning with the data contained in your pension plan census, plan documents, and actuarial valuation report, plus the most current projection of inflation and work force growth rates, Wilshire develops a detailed projection of the demographics and liabilities of the pension plan for up to 20 years into the future.

In developing these projections, we develop a very detailed specification of the characteristics of the pension plan being modeled, including the funding method, the asset valuation method, contributory provisions, average attained age, actuarial interest rate assumptions, variable inflation and growth rate assumptions, and the relation of benefits to pay. The result is a projection which is tailored precisely to the conditions of your plan. This precision is essential because the credibility of the projections will be critical to any conclusion to be derived from them.

The Investment Environment . . .

Next we develop, in conjunction with you, a set of capital market assumptions describing the expected investment environment. We also develop with you a set of potential investment policies and then calculate the expected range of investment returns that can be expected from those alternative policies.

These capital market assumptions and investment policies are then used to develop a set of 300 simulated 20-year time sequences which are chosen so as to fully depict the full range of possible scenarios which could conceivably occur.

Pre-Experiencing the Future . . .

The next step is the heart of the pension financial projection process. It involves the evaluation of the behavior of the pension plan for each alternative investment policy and investment strategy, in each of the 300 simulated market scenarios. This evaluation applies the detailed funding and asset valuation methods and other actuarial assumptions to identify the full range of costs and asset values that could be expected for each year of the projection.

The methodology used to model possible investment experiences is called "simulation," because it allows one to pre-experience the complete statistical range of future possible capital market behavior.

Using this technique, we can portray the likelihood of future outcomes resulting from different investment policies, including the probability of the very best results along with the very worst results.

The Full Range of Possible Outcomes . . .

The results of the full simulation of possible investment experience allow the range of possible asset market values to be projected, expressed in terms of probability percentiles. These ranges of market values can then be compared with corresponding levels of plan liability to determine the likelihood that assets will be sufficient to cover those liabilities. By expressing the results in terms of probabilities, it is then possible to evaluate possible expected gains against the additional risks that may be involved.

The results of these possible investment scenarios are also depicted in terms of the range of possible employer contributions that will be required to comply with the funding requirements of the pension plan, in response to those scenarios. This range of costs, stated both in dollars and as a percentage of pay, can then be evaluated to determine not only the expected costs, but also the level of costs that could result in the event of adverse investment performance.

The Conclusion of the Process . . .

After we have documented the financial forecast in the form of a printed statistical report, we begin the process of personal consultations with you in the development of the detailed conclusions.

Following these deliberations, Wilshire Associates will make its recommendations to you regarding optimal investment policies. Our staff will be available for special presentations to your Pension Committee or Board of Directors, if desired.

The final step in the pension planning process will be for Wilshire consultants to assist in the development of specific investment guidelines for your investment managers.

At the completion of the project, a full-scale model of your pension plan will be available to you as part of a separate ongoing service for the analysis of the effect of future variations in actuarial assumptions or investment policies. The use of Wilshire's Pension Planning Service, however, does not require retention of this or any other ongoing Wilshire consulting service.

Fee Schedule . . .

The cash fees for the Wilshire Pension Planning Service are as follows:

First Pension Plan
(One Liability Model) $20,000
Additional Pension Plans
(Added Liability Models) . . . . $10,000 each

There are no additional costs for the Pension Planning Service other than those listed above. However, if you wish to further test the effects of changes in inflation, growth rates, demographic trends, etc., then the fee for each additional run of the model is $2,666 in cash.

Directed brokerage commissions, the brochure noted, could be used in lieu of cash payments.

Mr. Kingsland's Presentation

After a general description of Wilshire's long-term pension planning service, Mr. Kingsland illustrated a sample application as follows:

A pension fund sponsor is faced with several realities:

1. The growth in work force, payrolls, and retirement liabilities under the existing plan.
2. The determination of annual funding costs by the actuary.
3. The actual market performance of the portfolio with all the future uncertainties associated therewith.

All these factors can influence what is an appropriate pension fund investment strategy. The Wilshire simulation model deals explicitly with all three.

The Wilshire model uses the same tapes as does your actuary in determining funding adequacy and annual funding requirements. It is based on your specific plan and the demography of your work force. However, you can build in the specific assumptions you want in terms of work force growth, wage growth due to productivity, and wage growth due to inflation. Exhibit 1 shows the kind of data our clients receive summarizing the actuarial and liability projection assumptions. (Explanation of details omitted.)

The current status of your pension plan is taken from the actuarial valuation report and serves as the starting point for the simulation. Exhibit 2 illustrates the nature of data used. . . .

The next report concerns the projection of the number of active and inactive members of the plan over a 20-year forward period. A sample projection is shown in Exhibits 3 and 3a.

These data are used to project your firm's future payroll costs and the related benefit payments. Exhibits 4, 4a, and 4b illustrate the kind of data our clients receive on these forecasts. . . .

The projected pension fund liabilities are next projected for both active and inactive plan members. Exhibits 5 and 5a show a sample of the summary results of this analysis. . . .

One of the critical parts of the analysis involves specifying the returns and the variability of returns that you anticipate can be achieved on the various assets in your portfolio. At the moment, your fund manager is investing in only three classes of assets—Treasury bills and similar liquid assets, long-term bonds, and common stocks. Exhibit 6 indicates the kind of assumptions that might be made about returns realizable in the capital markets and their uncertainties. We have considerable experience based on extensive analysis to help you formulate useful assumptions that mesh with the performance achievements of your fund manager. . . .

We next work with you to develop a set of investment policies that you consider potentially appropriate. We then test the implications of these policies on portfolio performance and funding requirements. Exhibit 7 illustrates a sample of these policies developed for one client. We will help you develop a set of strategies that seem most suitable for you to explore. . . .

Our simulation model tests the implications of these strategies over a 20-year period based on the assumptions that seem most appropriate. The model goes through two steps in each simulation. It first determines the effects of the simulated market conditions on portfolio values. Then, given these developments, it uses actuarial data to determine the funding requirement at the end of each year.

Altogether, 300 separate simulations are run so that we can determine the range of portfolio returns under a variety of market conditions. These results are then summarized in a way that allows you to see what could happen from near worst (5th percentile) to near best (95th percentile). Exhibit 8 reports the type of performance results our clients receive. These are further illustrated graphically in Exhibits 8a, 8b, and 8c. . . .

The financial implications of the various strategies are next analyzed. Exhibits 9 and 9a show the effects of median portfolio performance on various key financial parameters. Termination liabilities represent the past service (actuarial) liabilities of the plan in the event the plan is terminated. The total liability represents the actuarial determination of the present value of past and future service liabilities. . . .

The annual net cash flows of the plan, based on median results, are developed in Exhibits 10, 10a, and 10b.

The ranges of possible market values for your portfolio for representative years are then developed, as shown in Exhibits 11, 11a, and 11b.

In your firm and in the firm we have been analyzing, market values are not necessarily used for determining funding requirements. What you refer to as adjusted market value, used in your cost determinations, means the same thing as applied assets as shown in Exhibits 12, 12a, and 12b. These tables and charts show a range of possible determinations. . . .

Annual pension costs in dollar terms are then worked out for a range of possibilities as shown in Exhibits 13, 13a, and 13b. Where applicable (as would be true for de Vechio), these data are converted into costs as a percentage of payroll in the appropriate year, as shown in Exhibits 14, 14a, and 14b. . . .

As you can see, the risks and rewards associated with various strategies are displayed not only in terms of the market values but in terms of their financial and cost implications. At this point we would work with you in selecting the strategy that best meets your circumstances. We will work with you in preparing presentations to management and directors, and be available to help you answer any questions.

The actual presentation lasted over an hour and the foregoing excerpts do not do full justice to it.

Questions and Answers

Mr. Kingsland then answered management's questions. Considerable time was spent describing the de Vechio pension plan to determine if the Wilshire simulation model would fit the plan specifics. The determination was that it would. A brief summary of other questions and answers follows:

Q: As I understand it, you use realistic assumptions to determine payroll growth and the newly accrued retirement benefits. Then, however, you use actuarial assumptions to determine funding requirements. Isn't this inconsistent?

A: You are not alone in being skeptical about the accuracy of actuarial assumptions. Our model permits you to make whatever assumptions you consider appropriate. However, actuaries will continue to determine the adequacy of portfolios and the size of annual contributions. As you have found, actuaries make changes very slowly and very gradually. We can't change this. However, if these differences are material, their effects should show clearly by the 20th year.

Q: Some of the model's assumptions require judgments that seem difficult to make. I can't honestly say I know what inflation will be this year, let alone over the next 20 years.

A: Yes, I agree. First of all, the inflation assumption should be somehow related to your investment assumptions. An error in one would to some extent be offset by an error in the other. Secondly, you can test for sensitivity by requesting several simulation runs. There is a small additional cost for more than one study.

Q: Can the inflation rate be varied? Could we assume 7 percent for the first 5 years and then 5 percent?

A: Yes, but the other assumptions should be kept consistent.

Q: Our actuaries have suggested that we fund inactive beneficiaries separately [for reasons explained earlier in the case]. Can this be done in your analysis?

A: Yes, in part. We could easily omit all existing inactive membership data and assume that these liabilities would be funded separately at the current long-term interest rate. As new members become inactive we would keep their liabilities in the plan. This might cause the results to be slightly conservative. We might be able to remove the liabilities for future newly inactive people by presuming they are funded at the prevailing interest rate. However, this rate could be below the target rate in some years, and the removal could be an unlikely action. This is one question I'd like to do more thinking about.

Q: Our fund manager has achieved equity performance that is slightly above average over the last 12 years according to the Becker study. His performance in managing the bond portfolio, in contrast, has been outstanding. Can this manager's relative performance capability be considered?

A: Yes. We would study both the return and risk data available and help you reach assumptions that you feel comfortable with.

Q: Can you tell briefly how the simulation works?

A: The median return and the standard deviation are used to develop a probability distribution for the asset class. The probability distribution can then be used to determine the odds of each return possibility. A random generator selects a return for each year. Given the odds of its occurrence, any particular return has the same chance of being selected as appropriate. Returns for each asset class are determined independently in each and every year by this random selection process. This is consistent with the efficient market hypothesis. We make 300 separate simulations of 20 years of investment results so that you can determine what the range of future possibilities might be. If we only looked at one or two simulations, we might get distorted results. These methods are consistent with modern portfolio theory, applied in a realistic context.

Q: How do you determine these probabilities?

A: We have made historic studies of results for the last 52 years. We also will study the performance of your portfolio manager. We will discuss these findings with you and we will work out assumptions that make the most sense in your circumstances.

Q: I have told you about our dispute with the actuaries over Social Security regulations. Is your program flexible enough to handle these costs as they are likely to be?

A: Yes, as it relates to termination value. We, of course, have to live in the world of actuaries when it comes to determining period costs.

Q: We have been considering moving our equity portfolio to two separate managers—one a "growth" fund manager and the other an "underevaluation" fund manager. Can we use your program for this purpose?

A: Well, I would encourage you to study results achievable by your present manager first. We can later set up separate asset classes for two different fund managers and run the simulation. You might, for example, choose two mutual funds who run their funds the way you would like your new managers to run theirs. This would take a little further working out of details, but it can be easily done.

Q: We are afraid that, given continued rapid inflation, our present plan will provide inadequate real benefits. Does your simulation model help in this case?

A: No, not directly. However, there are some simple analytical techniques that can be used to explore the meaning of these risks for "typical" employees. We could describe how this can be done.

Q: The strategies you illustrated don't seem appropriate to us. I doubt that we would consider an equity strategy below 40 percent or above 80 percent, for example. Are we restricted in any way by your model?

A: No. It does help to spread the strategies out over a wide range of possibilities you might consider appropriate. We will work with you to help determine policies you might seriously want to consider.

Throughout this discussion, a member of de Vechio's computer staff had been in attendance. He thereupon asked a number of technical questions concerning the program. Later he reported to Mr. Linstrom that the program appeared technically sound. He was particularly impressed with the number and quality of clients that had already used the program.

Mr. Linstrom's Problem

On the whole, Mr. Linstrom was quite impressed with the presentation. In fact, the Wilshire program seemed an answer to a prayer. Nevertheless, he had had poor experience with some computer programs in the past because they had hidden assumptions that greatly oversimplified the realities and led to distorted results. He could not think offhand of any that concerned the Wilshire model, but he wanted to think more about it.

There were three other issues he wanted to consider. First, could the output really be used to formulate pension fund portfolio strategy? He decided to use the sample information (in the exhibits) to see if he could, in fact, select an appropriate strategy for the firm illustrated.

Second, the value of the study would depend on the usefulness of the assumptions. Could realistic assumptions be made? If not, how could he be sure a range of possible consequences could be apropriately considered? What specific assumptions should be tested?

The third issue involved cost. Several possibilities might be tested for about $30,000. This cost seemed reasonable, even if it had to be paid in cash rather than with "soft" dollars. He wondered, however, if additional runs would have to be made in the future as conditions or outlooks changed. If different optimum solutions developed over time would not this in itself cast doubt on the value of the findings of the present study? Several Wilshire clients appeared to use the program frequently. These firms, however, had much more sizable portfolios than did his firm and could afford higher internal pension administrative costs. Was this first purchase simply the razor for which a stream of blades would be required in the future? If so, it was unlike other consulting arrangements made by his firm. Consultants tended to be used by de Vechio only to solve problems in areas where management's technical competence was limited.

The alternative was to try to do something internally. Would this task be difficult? Would the results be as useful? Were there still other alternatives, as yet undiscovered? Mr. Linstrom had promised to give the Wilshire model more thought as Mr. Kingsland was departing. Time was moving by, and Mr. Linstrom realized he would have to make a decision soon.

EXHIBIT 1
Sample Output of Wilshire Pension Simulation: Actuarial and Liability Projection Assumptions

This page provides a summary of the key assumptions that are input to PENSIM to be used in the generation of demographic and liability projections. The format of this table is tailored to the specific conditions of the plan.

Benefit type: Pay-related

Funding provided by: Employer contributions

Funding method: Entry age normal, with frozen initial liability

Asset valuation method: Adjusted actuarial value

Interest rate: 6.00%

Wage growth due to inflation: 5.00%

Wage growth due to productivity: 0.0%

Work force growth rate: 2.00%

EXHIBIT 2
Sample Output of Wilshire Pension Simulation: Plan Status (*as of 9/30/75*)

This table summarizes the initial conditions of the pension plan as of the start of the projection, as obtained from the actuarial valuation report. The format of this table is tailored to the specific funding method and the condition of unfunded liabilities, if any, being amortized.

Plan census		
Number of active members		2,370
Number of inactive members		742
	Total:	3,112
Payroll and benefits ($000)		
Valuation payroll		$29,491.1
Annual benefits		$ 1,368.3
Plan liabilities ($000)		
Present value of benefits for active members		$70,318.2
Present value of benefits for inactive members		14,195.7
	Total:	$84,513.8

EXHIBIT 2 ***(concluded)***

Plan assets ($000)	
Market value of fund	$12,658.1
Applied asset value	$13,341.7
Unfunded frozen initial liability ($000)	$28,713.1
Employer cost for plan-year beginning 10/01/75 ($000)	
Normal cost	$2,938.40
Payment on unfunded	2,055.10
Employer cost if paid 10/01/75	$4,993.50
Employer cost if paid 9/30/76	$5,293.11

EXHIBIT 3
Sample Output of Wilshire Pension Simulation: Projection of Active and Inactive Members

The projected membership of the pension plan is summarized in this table, based on the initial conditions, work force growth rates, and average age of active members of the pension plan. These values are shown for each of 10 years into the future and also for the 15- and 20-year points. Inactive members include both retired and terminated vested employees.

Year		Active		Inactive		
Begins	**Number**	**Members**	**As Percent of Total**	**Members**	**As Percent of Total**	**Total Members**
10/75	0	2,370	76.16%	742	23.84%	3,112
10/76	1	2,417	76.32	750	23.68	3,167
10/77	2	2,466	76.47	759	23.53	3,225
10/78	3	2,515	76.61	768	23.39	3,283
10/79	4	2,565	76.70	779	23.30	3,344
10/80	5	2,617	76.81	790	23.19	3,407
10/81	6	2,669	76.87	803	23.13	3,472
10/82	7	2,722	76.94	816	23.06	3,538
10/83	8	2,777	76.99	830	23.01	3,607
10/84	9	2,832	77.02	845	22.98	3,677
10/85	10	2,889	77.06	860	22.94	3,749
10/90	15	3,190	77.09	948	22.91	4,138
10/95	20	3,522	76.97	1,054	23.03	4,576
Increase		1,152	—	312	—	1,464
Percent increase		48.6%	—	42.0%	—	47.0%

EXHIBIT 3a
Sample Output of Wilshire Pension Simulation: Plan Participants Growth Pattern

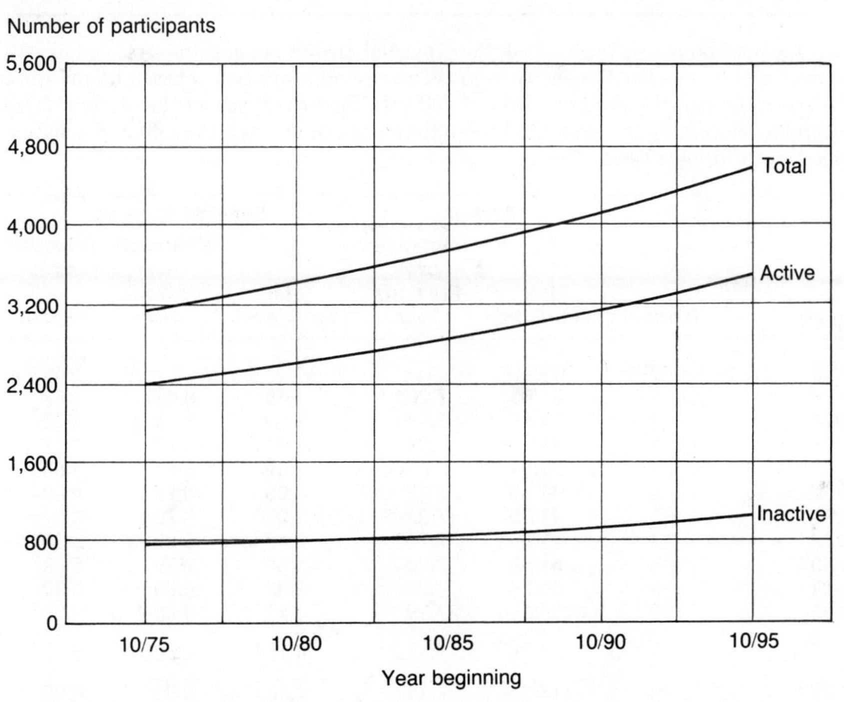

EXHIBIT 4
Sample Output of Wilshire Pension Simulation: Projection of Payroll and Benefit Payments

If the pension plan is pay-related, the projected growth in annual payroll and benefit payments will be tabulated as shown below. The payroll projection is based on the work force and wage growth rates provided to PENSIM. The benefit payouts are derived from projections concerning the growth in the retired population, plus the effect of inflation on the benefit formula basis, if any.

Year		Payroll		Benefit Payments		
Begins	Number	Total ($ millions)	Increase over Previous Year	Total ($ millions)	% Increase over Previous Year	Benefits as % of Payroll
10/75	0	$ 29.49	—	$1.37	—	4.64%
10/76	1	31.63	7.26%	1.48	8.03%	4.67
10/77	2	33.92	7.25	1.60	8.28	4.72
10/78	3	36.38	7.24	1.74	8.47	4.77
10/79	4	39.01	7.23	1.89	8.61	4.83
10/80	5	41.83	7.22	2.05	8.72	4.90
10/81	6	44.85	7.22	2.23	8.79	4.97
10/82	7	48.08	7.21	2.43	8.83	5.05
10/83	8	51.55	7.20	2.64	8.85	5.12
10/84	9	55.26	7.20	2.88	8.85	5.20
10/85	10	59.23	7.19	3.13	8.83	5.28
10/90	15	83.76	7.17	4.75	8.62	5.67
10/95	20	118.33	7.15	7.13	8.33	6.03
Increase		88.84	—	$5.76	—	—
Percent increase		301.2%	—	421.1%	—	—

EXHIBIT 4a
Sample Output of Wilshire Pension Simulation: Annual Payroll

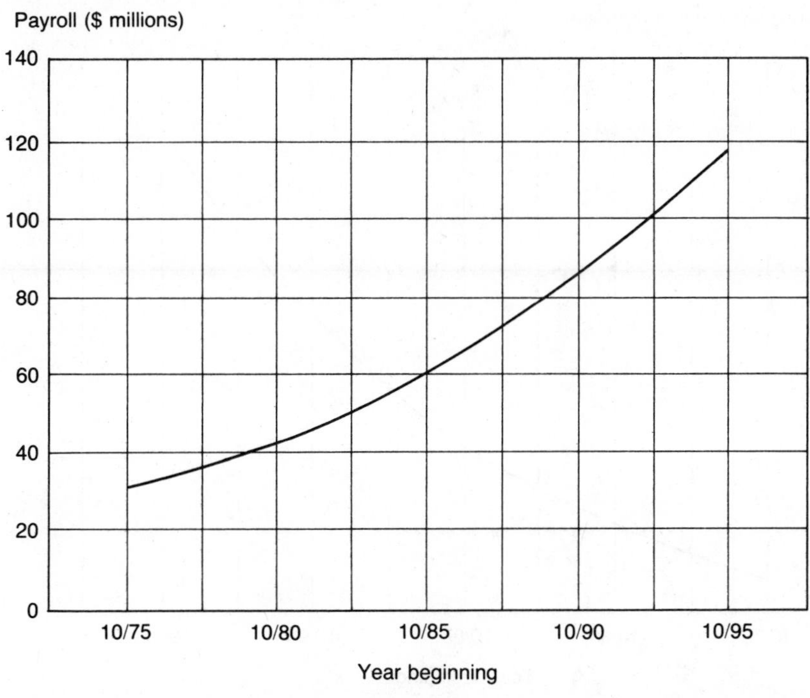

EXHIBIT 4b

Sample Output of Wilshire Pension Simulation: Annual Benefit Payments

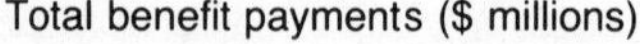

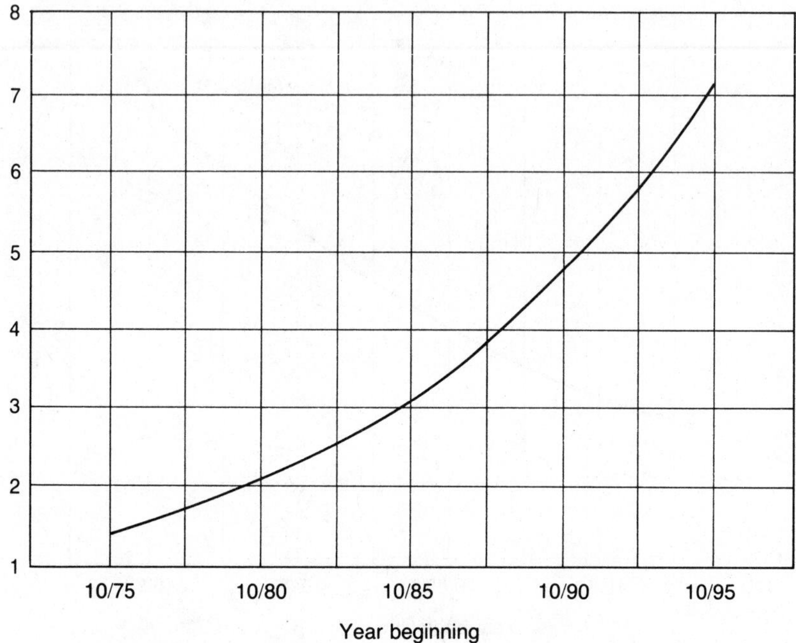

EXHIBIT 5
Sample Output of Wilshire Pension Simulation: Projection of Total Pension Liabilities

This table summarizes the expected growth in liabilities for both active and inactive members. The format of this table is tailored to the specific funding method of the plan being analyzed. The growth in these liabilities will provide the basis for comparison with fund asset value in the determination of yearly funding requirements.

Year		Active Members		Inactive Members		Total
Begins	Number	Pension Liabilities ($ millions)	As Percent of Total	Pension Liabilities ($ millions)	As Percent of Total	Pension Liabilities ($ millions)
10/75	0	$ 70.32	83.20%	$14.20	16.80%	$ 84.51
10/76	1	76.21	83.25	15.34	16.75	91.54
10/77	2	82.53	83.25	16.60	16.75	99.13
10/78	3	89.32	83.22	18.01	16.78	107.33
10/79	4	96.60	83.16	19.56	16.84	116.16
10/80	5	104.42	83.08	21.27	16.92	125.69
10/81	6	112.81	82.98	23.14	17.02	135.94
10/82	7	121.81	82.87	25.18	17.13	146.99
10/83	8	131.46	82.75	27.41	17.25	158.87
10/84	9	141.81	82.62	29.83	17.38	171.65
10/85	10	152.92	82.49	32.47	17.51	185.38
10/90	15	221.66	81.80	49.31	18.20	270.98
10/95	20	318.91	81.17	73.97	18.83	392.88
Increase		$248.59	—	$59.77	—	$308.37
Percent increase		353.5%	—	421.1%	—	364.9%

EXHIBIT 5a
Sample Output of Wilshire Pension Simulation: Composition of Liabilities

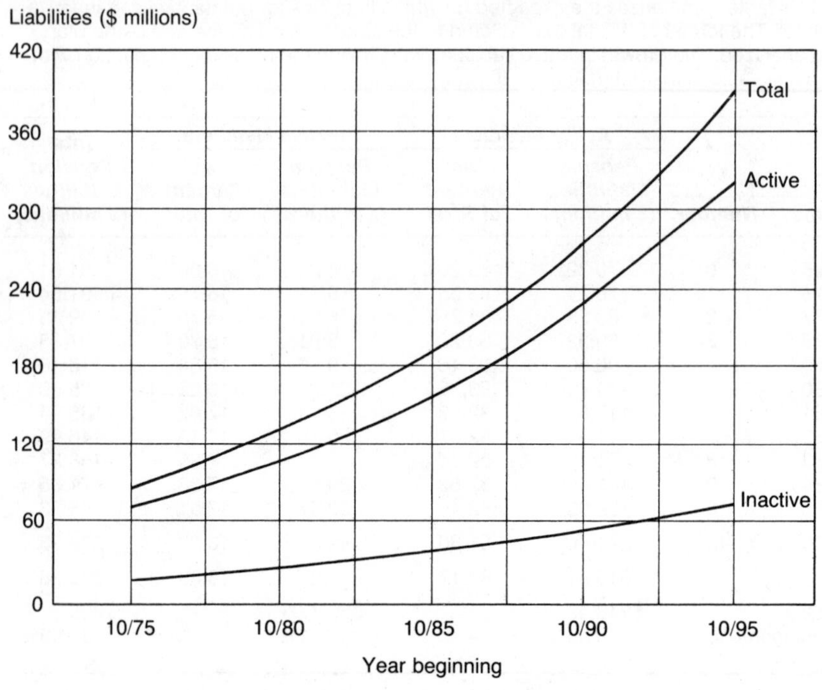

EXHIBIT 6
Sample Output of Wilshire Pension Simulation: Capital Market Assumptions

This page summarizes the expected capital market environment that was assumed for the purpose of analyzing the possible future financial condition of this pension plan. The parameters on this page are output exactly as they were specified to PENSIM in the setup of the analysis.

Annual rate of inflation:	5.00%
Annual Treasury bill return:	5.00%
Distribution of long-term bond returns	
Median:	8.00%
Standard deviation:	9.50%
Distribution of annual equity market returns	
Median:	12.00%
Standard deviation:	22.00%

EXHIBIT 7
Sample Output of Wilshire Pension Simulation: Portfolio Risk/Return Characteristics

This page summarizes the characteristics of each investment policy that was specified to be analyzed for this case. The characteristics of each major component of the portfolio as well as those of the overall composite portfolio for each investment policy selected are described here.

	Policy					
	A	***B***	***C***	***D***	***E***	***F***
Equity segment						
% Equities	0.0 %	0.0 %	25.00%	50.00%	75.00%	100.00%
Portfolio return	12.43%	12.43%	12.43%	12.43%	12.43%	12.43%
Beta	1.06	1.06	1.06	1.06	1.06	1.06
Portfolio yield	5.00%	5.00%	5.00%	5.00%	5.00%	5.00%
Diversity	95.30%	95.30%	95.30%	95.30%	95.30%	95.30%
Bond segment						
% Bonds	50.00%	100.00%	75.00%	50.00%	25.00%	0.0 %
Return	8.00%	8.00%	8.00%	8.00%	8.00%	8.00%
Beta	0.26	0.26	0.26	0.26	0.26	0.26
Yield	8.00%	8.00%	8.00%	8.00%	8.00%	8.00%
T-bills segment						
% T-bills	50.00%	0.0 %	0.0 %	0.0 %	0.0 %	0.0 %
Yield	5.00%	5.00%	5.00%	5.00%	5.00%	5.00%
Total portfolio						
Expected return	6.50%	8.00%	9.11%	10.22%	11.33%	12.43%
Total beta	0.13	0.26	0.46	0.66	0.86	1.06
Portfolio yield	6.50%	8.00%	7.25%	6.50%	5.75%	5.00%
Std. deviation	4.64%	9.50%	11.49%	14.96%	19.26%	24.10%

EXHIBIT 8
Sample Output of Wilshire Pension Simulation: Portfolio Compound Annual Return Characteristics

This table summarizes the range of possible annualized returns that could be achieved from each investment policy for four time periods into the future. Note that the range of possible variability is greater over shorter periods and for more volatile portfolios.

	Policy					
	A	***B***	***C***	***D***	***E***	***F***
Expected return (%)	6.50	8.00	9.11	10.22	11.33	12.43
Std. deviation (%)	4.64	9.50	11.49	14.96	19.26	24.10
Total beta	0.13	0.26	0.46	0.66	0.86	1.06
1-year percentiles						
5th	−1.16%	−6.98%	−8.77%	−12.37%	−16.68%	−21.18%
10th	0.49	−3.84	−5.07	− 7.79	−11.15	−14.72
25th	3.29	1.58	1.38	0.32	− 1.15	− 2.81
50th	6.50	8.00	9.11	10.22	11.33	12.43
75th	9.81	14.82	17.42	21.09	25.38	30.08
90th	12.87	21.30	25.41	31.75	39.48	48.23
95th	14.75	25.39	30.49	38.62	48.74	60.38
5-year percentiles						
5th	3.00%	1.02%	0.72%	− 0.53%	− 2.20%	− 4.08%
10th	3.77	2.53	2.52	1.76	0.65	− 0.64
25th	5.05	5.08	5.58	5.68	5.56	5.34
50th	6.50	8.00	9.11	10.22	11.33	12.43
75th	7.97	11.00	12.75	14.95	17.41	20.01
90th	9.30	13.76	16.12	19.37	23.14	27.23
95th	10.12	15.46	18.20	22.12	26.73	31.79
10-year percentiles						
5th	4.02%	3.02%	3.11%	2.51%	1.58%	0.49%
10th	4.56	4.10	4.41	4.17	3.66	3.03
25th	5.47	5.93	6.60	6.99	7.22	7.37
50th	6.50	8.00	9.11	10.22	11.33	12.43
75th	7.54	10.11	11.67	13.55	15.59	17.74
90th	8.47	12.04	14.02	16.61	19.55	22.70
95th	9.04	13.22	15.46	18.51	22.01	25.80
20-year percentiles						
5th	4.74%	4.45%	4.83%	4.71%	4.34%	3.85%
10th	5.13	5.23	5.76	5.91	5.85	5.70
25th	5.77	6.53	7.33	7.92	8.41	8.83
50th	6.50	8.00	9.11	10.22	11.33	12.43
75th	7.23	9.49	10.91	12.56	14.33	16.16
90th	7.89	10.84	12.56	14.70	17.08	19.60
95th	8.29	11.67	13.56	16.02	18.78	21.73

EXHIBIT 8a
Sample Output of Wilshire Pension Simulation: Distribution of One-Year Returns

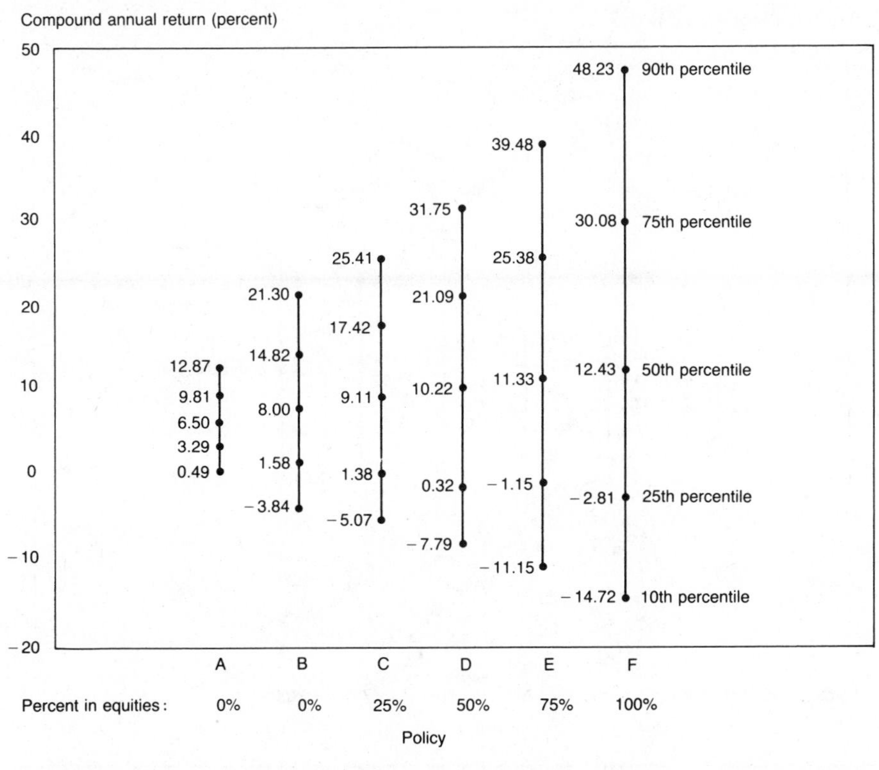

EXHIBIT 8b
Sample Output of Wilshire Pension Simulation: Distribution of Five-Year Returns

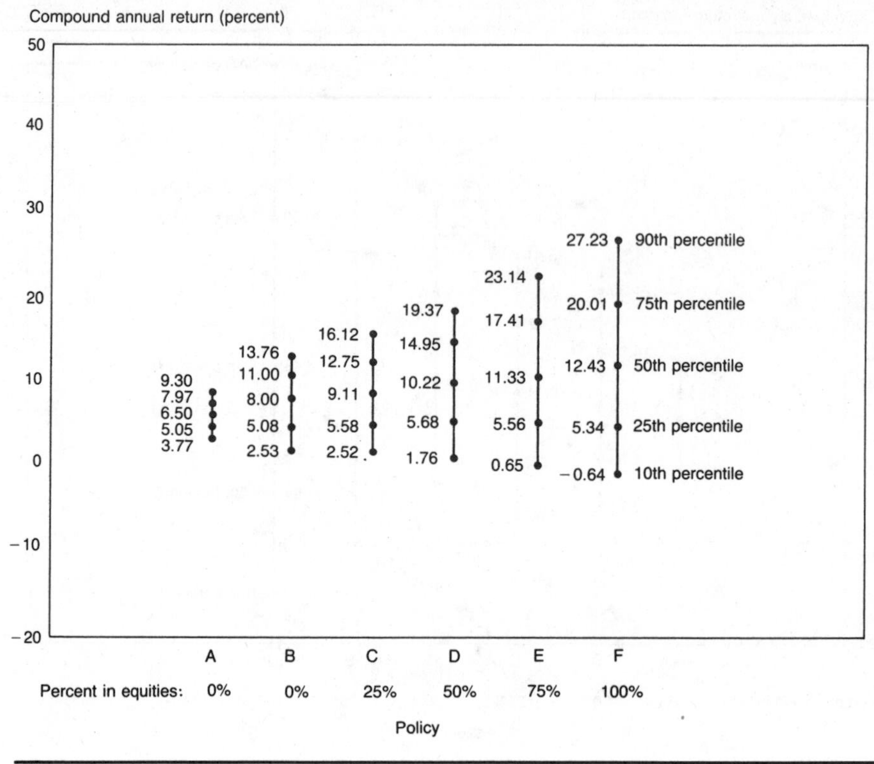

EXHIBIT 8c
Sample Output of Wilshire Pension Simulation: Distribution of Ten-Year Returns

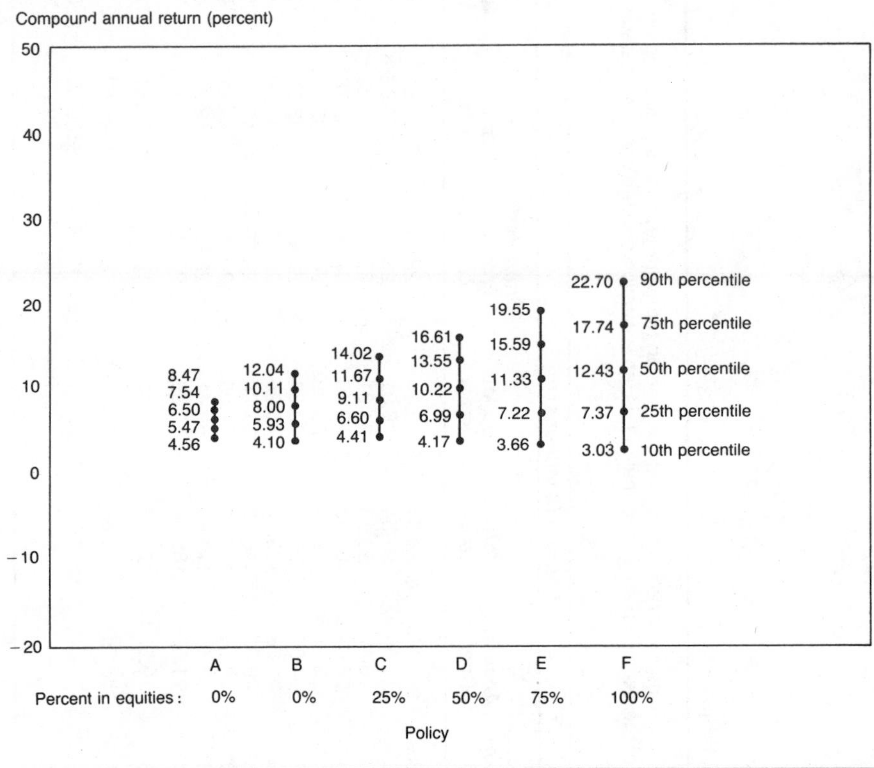

EXHIBIT 9
Sample Output of Wilshire Pension Simulation: Financial Projections

A financial projection table is provided for each specified investment policy, showing the median (or average) results that could be expected from that policy for the key financial parameters of the pension plan. The format of this table is tailored to the specific characteristics of the pension plan.

Year		Policy A ($ millions)								
			Employer Cost							
Begins	Number	Payroll	Total	As Percent of Pay	Accum. Cost	Total Liab.	Applied Assets	Unfunded Frozen Liab.	Termin. Liab.	Market Value
10/75	0	$ 29.49	$ 5.14	17.43%	$ 5.14	$ 84.51	$ 13.34	$ 28.71	$ 25.81	$ 12.66
10/76	1	31.63	5.40	17.08	10.54	91.54	16.91	28.26	27.92	17.23
10/77	2	33.92	5.63	16.58	16.17	99.13	21.91	27.84	30.23	22.22
10/78	3	36.38	5.87	16.13	22.04	107.33	27.29	27.40	32.76	27.60
10/79	4	39.01	6.13	15.71	28.16	116.16	33.09	26.92	35.51	33.40
10/80	5	41.83	6.41	15.32	34.57	125.69	39.33	26.41	38.51	39.65
10/81	6	44.85	6.71	14.96	41.28	135.94	46.05	25.87	41.76	46.37
10/82	7	48.08	7.03	14.63	48.32	146.99	53.28	25.28	45.29	53.61
10/83	8	51.55	7.38	14.32	55.70	158.87	61.05	24.66	49.11	61.40
10/84	9	55.26	7.76	14.04	63.46	171.65	69.41	23.99	53.25	69.78
10/85	10	59.23	8.16	13.78	71.62	185.38	78.39	23.28	57.71	78.78
10/90	15	83.76	10.66	12.73	119.57	270.98	134.34	18.92	85.91	134.87
10/95	20	118.33	14.21	12.01	183.04	392.88	214.05	12.87	126.62	214.79
Increase		$ 88.84	$ 9.07	—	—	$308.37	$200.71	$ − 15.84	$100.82	$202.13
Percent increase		301.2%	176.5%	—	—	364.9%	1,504.4%	− 55.2%	390.7%	1,596.8%

Year		Policy B ($ millions)								
			Employer Cost							
Begins	Number	Payroll	Total	As Percent of Pay	Accum. Cost	Total Liab.	Applied Assets	Unfunded Frozen Liab.	Termin. Liab.	Market Value
10/75	0	$ 29.49	$ 5.14	17.43%	$ 5.14	$ 84.51	$ 13.34	$ 28.71	$ 25.81	$ 12.66
10/76	1	31.63	5.39	17.05	10.53	91.54	17.04	28.26	27.92	17.45
10/77	2	33.92	5.60	16.51	16.14	99.13	22.25	27.84	30.23	22.73
10/78	3	36.38	5.82	16.00	21.96	107.33	27.94	27.40	32.76	28.49
10/79	4	39.01	6.05	15.52	28.01	116.16	34.13	26.92	35.51	34.76
10/80	5	41.83	6.30	15.06	34.31	125.69	40.86	26.41	38.51	41.56
10/81	6	44.85	6.56	14.62	40.87	135.94	48.16	25.87	41.76	48.95
10/82	7	48.08	6.83	14.21	47.70	146.99	56.08	25.28	45.29	56.95
10/83	8	51.55	7.12	13.82	54.83	158.87	64.67	24.66	49.11	65.62
10/84	9	55.26	7.43	13.45	62.26	171.65	73.95	23.99	53.25	75.00
10/85	10	59.23	7.76	13.10	70.02	185.38	83.99	23.28	57.71	85.15
10/90	15	83.76	9.71	11.60	114.44	270.98	147.52	18.92	85.91	149.28
10/95	20	118.33	12.36	10.44	170.62	392.88	239.73	12.87	126.62	242.34
Increase		$ 88.84	$ 7.22	—	—	$308.37	$226.39	$ − 15.84	$100.82	$229.68
Percent increase		301.2%	140.4%	—	—	364.9%	1,696.9%	− 55.2%	390.7%	1,814.5%

EXHIBIT 9 *(continued)*

Year		Policy C ($ millions)								
			Employer Cost					Unfunded		
Begins	Number	Payroll	Total	As Percent of Pay	Accum. Cost	Total Liab.	Applied Assets	Frozen Liab.	Termin. Liab.	Market Value
10/75	0	$ 29.49	$ 5.14	17.43%	$ 5.14	$ 84.51	$ 13.34	$ 28.71	$ 25.81	$ 12.66
10/76	1	31.63	5.38	17.01	10.52	91.54	17.21	28.26	27.92	17.61
10/77	2	33.92	5.59	16.49	16.12	99.13	22.36	27.84	30.23	23.10
10/78	3	36.38	5.81	15.98	21.93	107.33	28.05	27.40	32.76	29.15
10/79	4	39.01	6.04	15.48	27.97	116.16	34.30	26.92	35.51	35.80
10/80	5	41.83	6.28	15.01	34.25	125.69	41.15	26.41	38.51	43.08
10/81	6	44.85	6.52	14.54	40.77	135.94	48.66	25.87	41.76	51.05
10/82	7	48.08	6.78	14.10	47.55	146.99	56.86	25.28	45.29	59.75
10/83	8	51.55	7.04	13.66	54.59	158.87	65.80	24.66	49.11	69.25
10/84	9	55.26	7.32	13.24	61.91	171.65	75.54	23.99	53.25	79.59
10/85	10	59.23	7.60	12.84	69.52	185.38	86.15	23.28	57.71	90.85
10/90	15	83.76	9.22	11.01	112.25	270.98	154.40	18.92	85.91	163.30
10/95	20	118.33	11.21	9.47	164.14	392.88	255.72	12.87	126.62	270.89
Increase		$ 88.84	$ 6.06	—	—	$308.37	$242.38	$ – 15.84	$100.82	$258.23
Percent increase		301.2%	118.0%	—	—	364.9%	1,816.7%	– 55.2%	390.7%	2,040.1%

Year			Policy D ($ millions)							
			Employer Cost							
Begins	Number	Payroll	Total	As Percent of Pay	Accum. Cost	Total Liab.	Applied Assets	Unfunded Frozen Liab.	Termin. Liab.	Market Value
10/75	0	$ 29.49	$ 5.14	17.43%	$ 5.14	$ 84.51	$ 13.34	$ 28.71	$ 25.81	$ 12.66
10/76	1	31.63	5.37	16.98	10.51	91.54	17.37	28.26	27.92	17.76
10/77	2	33.92	5.59	16.46	16.10	99.13	22.48	27.84	30.23	23.48
10/78	3	36.38	5.81	15.96	21.90	107.33	28.16	27.40	32.76	29.83
10/79	4	39.01	6.03	15.45	27.93	116.16	34.47	26.92	35.51	36.88
10/80	5	41.83	6.26	14.96	34.19	125.69	41.46	26.41	38.51	44.67
10/81	6	44.85	6.49	14.46	40.67	135.94	49.17	25.87	41.76	53.26
10/82	7	48.08	6.72	13.98	47.40	146.99	57.65	25.28	45.29	62.73
10/83	8	51.55	6.96	13.50	54.35	158.87	66.98	24.66	49.11	73.13
10/84	9	55.26	7.20	13.03	61.55	171.65	77.22	23.99	53.25	84.54
10/85	10	59.23	7.44	12.56	68.99	185.38	88.43	23.28	57.71	97.04
10/90	15	83.76	8.67	10.36	109.89	270.98	161.97	18.92	85.91	179.15
10/95	20	118.33	9.89	8.36	156.93	392.88	273.99	12.87	126.62	304.39
Increase		$ 88.84	$ 4.75	—	—	$308.37	$260.65	$ – 15.84	$100.82	$291.74
Percent increase		301.2%	92.3%	—	—	364.9%	1,953.6%	– 55.2%	390.7%	2,304.7%

EXHIBIT 9 *(concluded)*

Year		Policy E ($ millions)								
			Employer Cost							
Begins	Number	Payroll	Total	As Percent of Pay	Accum. Cost	Total Liab.	Applied Assets	Unfunded Frozen Liab.	Termin. Liab.	Market Value
10/75	0	$ 29.49	$ 5.14	17.43%	$ 5.14	$ 84.51	$ 13.34	$ 28.71	$ 25.81	$ 12.66
10/76	1	31.63	5.36	16.94	10.50	91.54	17.54	28.26	27.92	17.93
10/77	2	33.92	5.58	16.44	16.08	99.13	22.59	27.84	30.23	23.86
10/78	3	36.38	5.80	15.93	21.87	107.33	28.27	27.40	32.76	30.53
10/79	4	39.01	6.02	15.42	27.89	116.16	34.65	26.92	35.51	38.00
10/80	5	41.83	6.23	14.90	34.12	125.69	41.76	26.41	38.51	46.33
10/81	6	44.85	6.45	14.38	40.57	135.94	49.69	25.87	41.76	55.59
10/82	7	48.08	6.66	13.85	47.24	146.99	58.48	25.28	45.29	65.88
10/83	8	51.55	6.87	13.33	54.11	158.87	68.22	24.66	49.11	77.28
10/84	9	55.26	7.07	12.80	61.18	171.65	78.98	23.99	53.25	89.88
10/85	10	59.23	7.27	12.27	68.45	185.38	90.85	23.28	57.71	103.79
10/90	15	83.76	8.07	9.64	107.34	270.98	170.30	18.92	85.91	197.10
10/95	20	118.33	8.38	7.08	148.90	392.88	294.89	12.87	126.62	343.82
Increase		$ 88.84	$ 3.24	—	—	$308.37	$281.55	$ – 15.84	$100.82	$331.16
Percent increase		301.2%	63.0%	—	—	364.9%	2,110.3%	– 55.2%	390.7%	2,616.2%

Year		Policy F ($ millions)								
			Employer Cost							
Begins	Number	Payroll	Total	As Percent of Pay	Accum. Cost	Total Liab.	Applied Assets	Unfunded Frozen Liab.	Termin. Liab.	Market Value
10/75	0	$ 29.49	$ 5.14	17.43%	$ 5.14	$ 84.51	$ 13.34	$ 28.71	$ 25.81	$ 12.66
10/76	1	31.63	5.35	16.90	10.49	91.54	17.71	28.26	27.92	18.09
10/77	2	33.92	5.57	16.42	16.06	99.13	22.70	27.84	30.23	24.25
10/78	3	36.38	5.79	15.91	21.85	107.33	28.39	27.40	32.76	31.25
10/79	4	39.01	6.00	15.39	27.85	116.16	34.82	26.92	35.51	39.16
10/80	5	41.83	6.21	14.85	34.06	125.69	42.08	26.41	38.51	48.06
10/81	6	44.85	6.41	14.29	40.47	135.94	50.22	25.87	41.76	58.05
10/82	7	48.08	6.60	13.73	47.07	146.99	59.34	25.28	45.29	69.24
10/83	8	51.55	6.78	13.15	53.85	158.87	69.51	24.66	49.11	81.73
10/84	9	55.26	6.94	12.56	60.79	171.65	80.83	23.99	53.25	95.66
10/85	10	59.23	7.08	11.96	67.88	185.38	93.41	23.28	57.71	111.14
10/90	15	83.76	7.41	8.85	104.59	270.98	179.50	18.92	85.91	217.46
10/95	20	118.33	6.65	5.62	139.95	392.88	318.86	12.87	126.62	390.36
Increase		$ 88.84	$ 1.51	—	—	$308.37	$305.52	$ – 15.84	$100.82	$377.70
Percent increase		301.2%	29.4%	—	—	364.9%	2,289.9%	– 55.2%	390.7%	2,983.9%

EXHIBIT 9a
Sample Output of Wilshire Pension Simulation: Matching Assets* and Liabilities

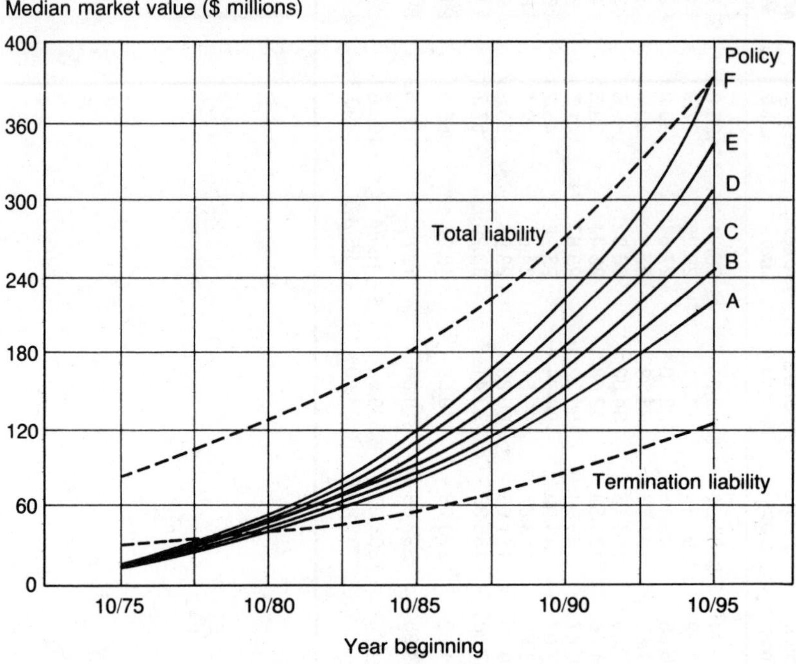

*Assumes the median return experience is realized.

EXHIBIT 10
Sample Output of Wilshire Pension Simulation: Net Cash Flow

A breakdown of the expected net cash flows resulting from each specified investment policy is summarized in these cash flow tables. Again, the values shown in these tables are for median levels of investment performance and provide a means of obtaining a year-by-year comparison of the expected results for each investment policy. By means of these cash flow tables, it is possible to project whether cash inflow via contributions and investment income will be sufficient to cover the cash outflow for benefit payments, or whether assets will have to be liquidated to provide the cash for such benefit payments.

Year		Policy A ($ millions)			
Begins	**Number**	**Median Cost**	**Interest and Dividends**	**Benefit Payments**	**Net Cash Flow***
10/75	0	$ 5.14	$ 0.80	$1.42	$ 4.52
10/76	1	5.40	1.09	1.54	4.96
10/77	2	5.63	1.41	1.67	5.37
10/78	3	5.87	1.75	1.81	5.81
10/79	4	6.13	2.12	1.97	6.28
10/80	5	6.41	2.52	2.14	6.78
10/81	6	6.71	2.94	2.33	7.33
10/82	7	7.03	3.40	2.53	7.90
10/83	8	7.38	3.90	2.76	8.52
10/84	9	7.76	4.43	3.00	9.19
10/85	10	8.16	5.00	3.27	9.90
10/90	15	10.66	8.56	4.96	14.27
10/95	20	14.21	13.64	7.42	20.43
Increase		$ 9.07	$ 12.83	$6.00	$15.90
Percent increase		176.45%	1,596.8%	421.7%	351.7%

Year		Policy B ($ millions)			
Begins	**Number**	**Median Cost**	**Interest and Dividends**	**Benefit Payments**	**Net Cash Flow***
10/75	0	$ 5.14	$ 0.97	$1.42	$ 4.69
10/76	1	5.39	1.34	1.54	5.20
10/77	2	5.60	1.75	1.67	5.68
10/78	3	5.82	2.19	1.81	6.20
10/79	4	6.05	2.68	1.97	6.76
10/80	5	6.30	3.20	2.14	7.36
10/81	6	6.56	3.77	2.33	8.00
10/82	7	6.83	4.38	2.53	8.68
10/83	8	7.12	5.05	2.76	9.42
10/84	9	7.43	5.77	3.00	10.20
10/85	10	7.76	6.65	3.27	11.05
10/90	15	9.71	11.49	4.96	16.25
10/95	20	12.36	18.66	7.42	23.59
Increase		$ 7.22	$17.68	$6.00	$18.90
Percent increase		140.41%	1,814.6%	421.7%	402.8%

*Net cash flow = Annual cost + Interest and dividends − Benefit payments.

EXHIBIT 10 ***(continued)***

Year		Policy C ($ millions)			
Begins	Number	Median Cost	Interest and Dividends	Benefit Payments	Net Cash Flow*
10/75	0	$ 5.14	$ 0.89	$1.42	$ 4.61
10/76	1	5.38	1.24	1.54	5.08
10/77	2	5.59	1.62	1.67	5.55
10/78	3	5.81	2.05	1.81	6.05
10/79	4	6.04	2.51	1.97	6.59
10/80	5	6.28	3.03	2.14	7.16
10/81	6	6.52	3.59	2.33	7.78
10/82	7	6.78	4.20	2.53	8.44
10/83	8	7.04	4.86	2.76	9.15
10/84	9	7.32	5.59	3.00	9.91
10/85	10	7.60	5.38	3.27	10.72
10/90	15	9.22	11.47	4.96	15.73
10/95	20	11.21	19.03	7.42	22.81
Increase		$ 6.06	$18.14	$6.00	$18.20
Percent increase		117.97%	2,040.2%	421.7%	395.1%

Year		Policy D ($ millions)			
Begins	Number	Median Cost	Interest and Dividends	Benefit Payments	Net Cash Flow*
10/75	0	$5.14	$ 0.80	$1.42	$ 4.52
10/76	1	5.37	1.13	1.54	4.96
10/77	2	5.69	1.49	1.67	5.41
10/78	3	5.81	1.89	1.81	5.89
10/79	4	6.03	2.34	1.97	6.40
10/80	5	6.26	2.84	2.14	6.95
10/81	6	6.49	3.38	2.33	7.54
10/82	7	6.72	3.98	2.53	8.17
10/83	8	6.96	4.64	2.76	8.84
10/84	9	7.20	5.37	3.00	9.56
10/85	10	7.44	6.16	3.27	10.34
10/90	15	8.67	11.37	4.96	15.09
10/95	20	9.89	19.33	7.42	21.79
Increase		$4.75	$18.52	$6.00	$17.27
Percent increase		92.34%	2,304.7%	421.7%	381.9%

*Net cash flow = Annual cost + Interest and dividends − Benefit payments.

EXHIBIT 10 ***(concluded)***

Year		Policy E ($ millions)			
Begins	Number	Median Cost	Interest and Dividends	Benefit Payments	Net Cash Flow*
10/75	0	$5.14	$ 0.72	$1.42	$ 4.44
10/76	1	5.36	1.02	1.54	4.84
10/77	2	5.58	1.35	1.67	5.26
10/78	3	5.80	1.73	1.81	5.72
10/79	4	6.02	2.16	1.97	6.20
10/80	5	6.23	2.63	2.14	6.72
10/81	6	6.45	3.15	2.33	7.28
10/82	7	6.66	3.74	2.53	7.87
10/83	8	6.87	4.39	2.76	8.50
10/84	9	7.07	5.10	3.00	9.17
10/85	10	7.27	5.89	3.27	9.89
10/90	15	8.07	11.18	4.96	14.30
10/95	20	8.38	19.51	7.42	20.47
Increase		$3.24	$18.79	$6.00	$16.03
Percent increase		63.01%	2,616.2%	421.7%	361.3%

Year		Policy F ($ millions)			
Begins	Number	Median Cost	Interest and Dividends	Benefit Payments	Net Cash Flow*
10/75	0	$5.14	$ 0.63	$1.42	$ 4.35
10/76	1	5.35	0.90	1.54	4.71
10/77	2	5.57	1.21	1.67	5.11
10/78	3	5.79	1.56	1.81	5.54
10/79	4	6.00	1.96	1.97	5.99
10/80	5	6.21	2.40	2.14	6.47
10/81	6	6.41	2.90	2.33	6.99
10/82	7	6.60	3.46	2.53	7.53
10/83	8	6.78	4.09	2.76	8.11
10/84	9	6.94	4.78	3.00	8.72
10/85	10	7.08	5.56	3.27	9.37
10/90	15	7.41	10.87	4.96	13.33
10/95	20	6.65	19.52	7.42	18.74
Increase		$1.51	$18.89	$6.00	$14.39
Percent increase		29.37%	2,983.9%	421.7%	330.8%

*Net cash flow = Annual cost + Interest and dividends − Benefit payments.

EXHIBIT 10a
Sample Output of Wilshire Pension Simulation: Median Cost*

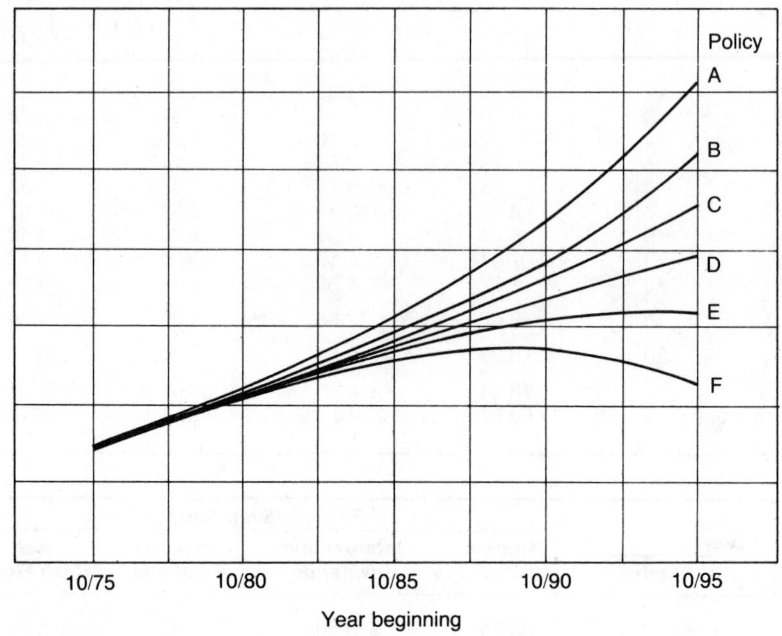

*Assumes the median return experience is realized.

EXHIBIT 10b
Sample Output of Wilshire Pension Simulation: Net Cash Flow*

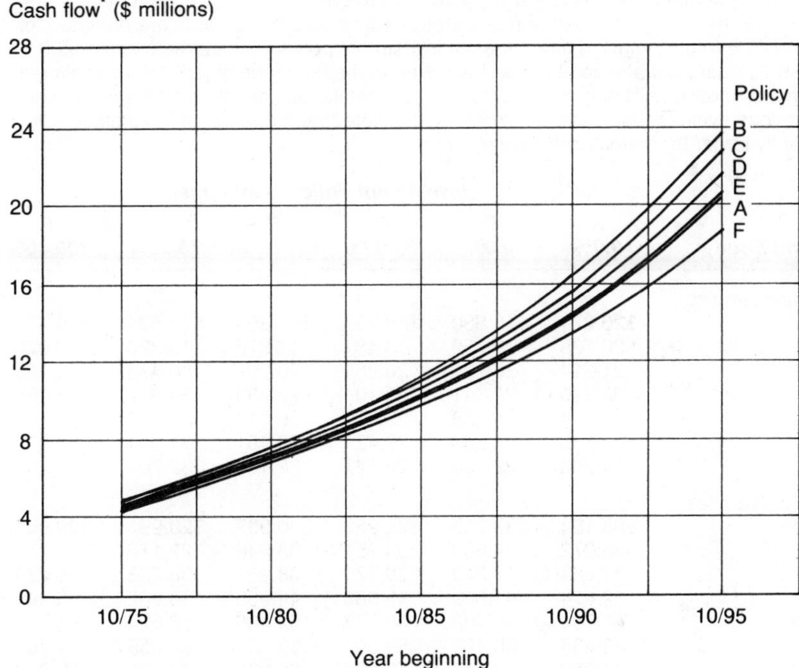

*Assumes the median return experience is realized. Net cash flow equals contribution plus dividends and interest less benefit payments.

EXHIBIT 11
Sample Output of Wilshire Pension Simulation: Market Value of Assets (*$ millions*)

This table summarizes the expected levels of fund asset market values that could be achieved over the range of possible market returns. The data in this table are provided for three specified future points in time for each investment policy and are the result of 200 simulated 20-year capital market scenarios covering the full range of potential investment experiences, showing not only median "expected" results, but also the whole range of best and worst case values that could be experienced. Note that the range of possible results is significantly larger for more aggressive policies.

	Investment Policy ($ millions)					
	A	***B***	***C***	***D***	***E***	***F***
Percent Equity	***0.0%***	***0.0%***	***25.00%***	***50.00%***	***75.00%***	***100.00%***
2-year percentiles						
5th	$20.274	$18.880	$18.737	$18.398	$17.534	$16.432
10th	20.728	19.750	19.481	18.875	18.326	17.620
25th	21.314	20.891	20.969	20.707	20.475	20.368
50th	22.220	22.741	23.104	23.483	23.867	24.255
75th	23.174	24.758	25.529	26.717	27.928	29.160
90th	23.835	26.233	27.421	29.401	31.364	33.683
95th	24.398	27.500	28.727	30.119	32.703	36.106
5-year percentiles						
5th	$35.154	$32.355	$32.253	$30.997	$28.991	$26.954
10th	36.272	34.600	34.751	33.948	32.176	30.114
25th	37.664	37.348	38.370	38.257	38.223	38.274
50th	39.674	41.659	43.085	44.900	46.682	48.940
75th	41.780	46.403	48.476	52.498	56.624	61.835
90th	43.433	50.462	54.001	60.323	69.259	81.709
95th	44.957	58.946	59.203	66.333	77.081	89.958
10-year percentiles						
5th	$67.590	$60.957	$62.344	$60.105	$56.399	$51.837
10th	70.506	66.902	66.261	65.503	65.405	63.290
25th	74.171	76.847	79.624	80.105	80.090	79.309
50th	78.782	85.474	91.009	97.621	104.584	112.127
75th	83.827	97.177	104.276	120.423	138.704	162.303
90th	88.570	110.831	126.384	149.921	180.621	218.228
95th	92.716	122.330	142.358	167.339	202.556	263.420

EXHIBIT 11a
Sample Output of Wilshire Pension Simulation: Distribution of Fund Market Values—Fifth Year (10/80)

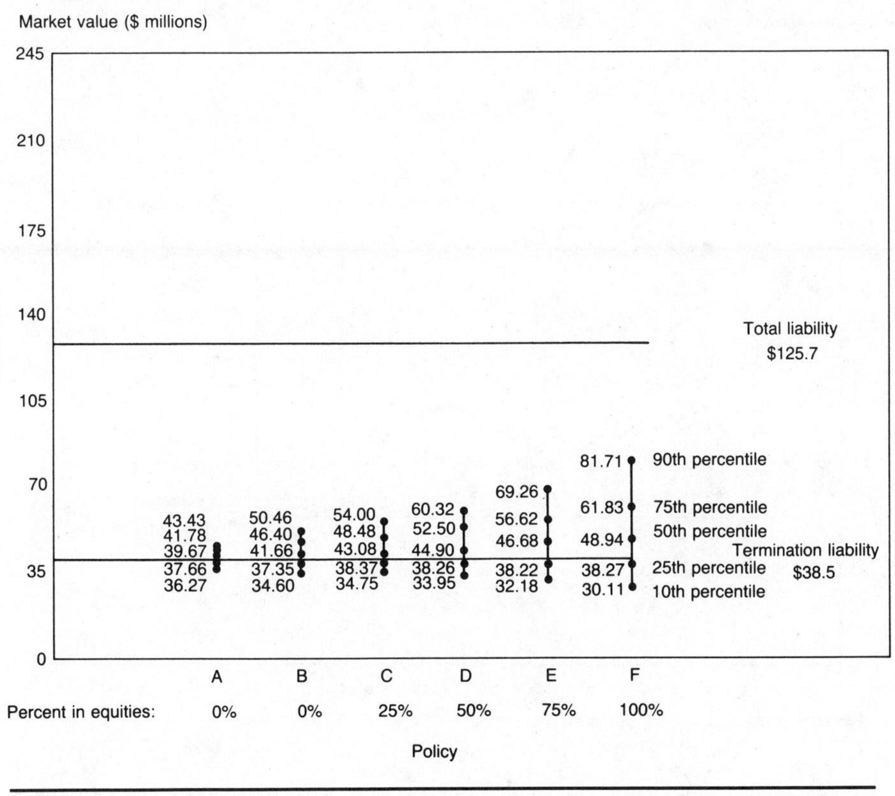

EXHIBIT 11b
Sample Output of Wilshire Pension Simulation: Distribution of Fund Market Values—Tenth Year (10/85)

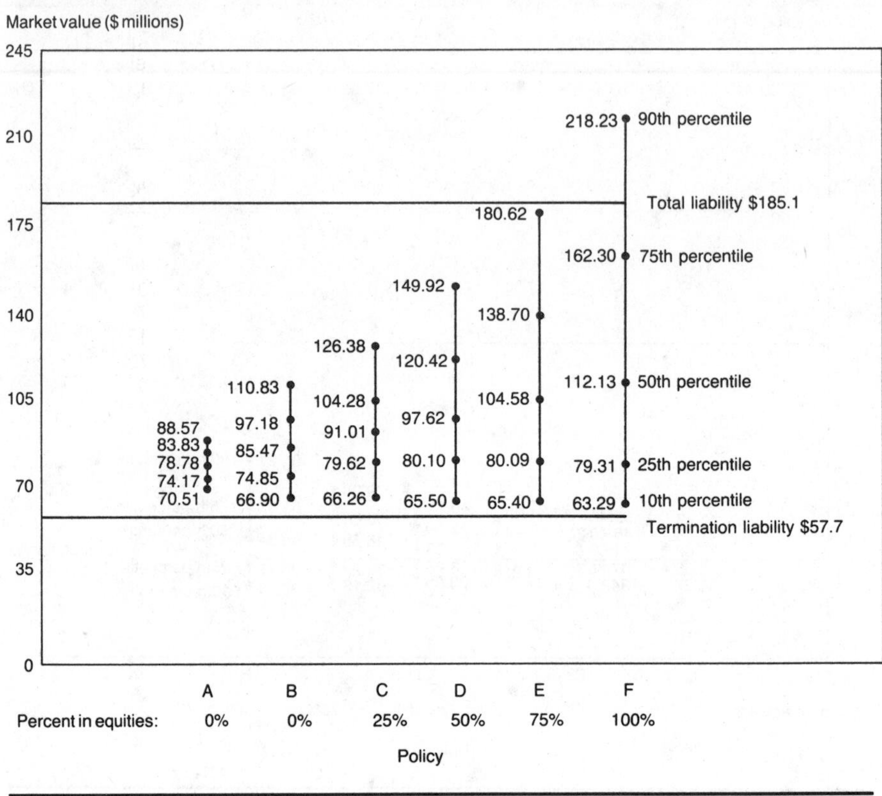

EXHIBIT 12
Sample Output of Wilshire Pension Simulation: Applied Asset Values (*$ millions*)

The asset value used in determining the annual funding costs is calculated by the actuary by gradually, rather than immediately, recognizing the effect of portfolio market value changes. This is designed to reduce short-range fluctuations in funding requirements so as to provide more stable and predictable year-to-year funding levels. The range of asset values that would be calculated via this method is summarized here.

	Investment Policy ($ millions)					
	A	***B***	***C***	***D***	***E***	***F***
Percent Equity	***0.0%***	***0.0%***	***25.00%***	***50.00%***	***75.00%***	***100.00%***
2-year percentiles						
5th	$20.696	$21.307	$21.159	$20.988	$20.747	$20.501
10th	20.981	21.451	21.347	21.212	21.006	20.825
25th	21.354	21.791	21.806	21.748	21.678	21.545
50th	21.914	22.266	22.372	22.530	22.613	22.750
75th	22.495	22.768	23.000	23.333	23.670	24.111
90th	22.914	23.189	23.585	24.052	24.702	25.273
95th	23.252	23.389	23.865	24.375	25.075	25.995
5-year percentiles						
5th	$36.453	$38.080	$37.273	$35.876	$34.464	$33.160
10th	37.112	38.440	37.856	36.947	35.864	34.608
25th	38.050	39.577	39.312	38.776	38.400	37.757
50th	39.349	40.976	41.293	41.575	42.066	42.381
75th	40.718	42.560	43.532	44.964	46.952	49.723
90th	41.877	44.082	45.557	47.833	51.071	55.285
95th	42.665	44.884	46.780	49.905	54.059	59.423
10-year percentiles						
5th	$71.671	$76.860	$75.423	$72.036	$67.702	$63.914
10th	73.371	78.610	77.968	75.186	72.286	69.275
25th	76.128	81.545	82.095	81.664	80.741	80.464
50th	78.496	84.913	87.083	89.330	92.539	95.828
75th	81.662	88.823	92.807	98.761	107.242	116.385
90th	85.307	94.726	101.916	111.783	125.383	146.329
95th	87.727	97.973	106.735	122.465	143.997	172.938

EXHIBIT 12a
Sample Output of Wilshire Pension Simulation: Distribution of Applied Assets—Fifth Year (10/80)

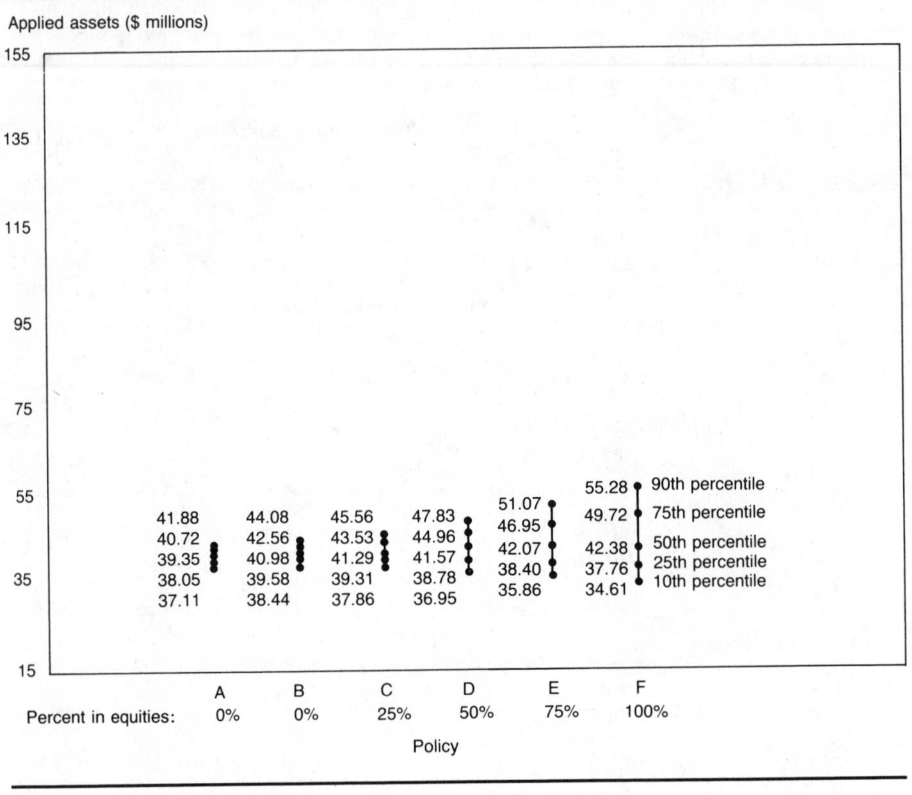

EXHIBIT 12b
Sample Output of Wilshire Pension Simulation: Distribution of Applied Assets—Tenth Year (10/85)

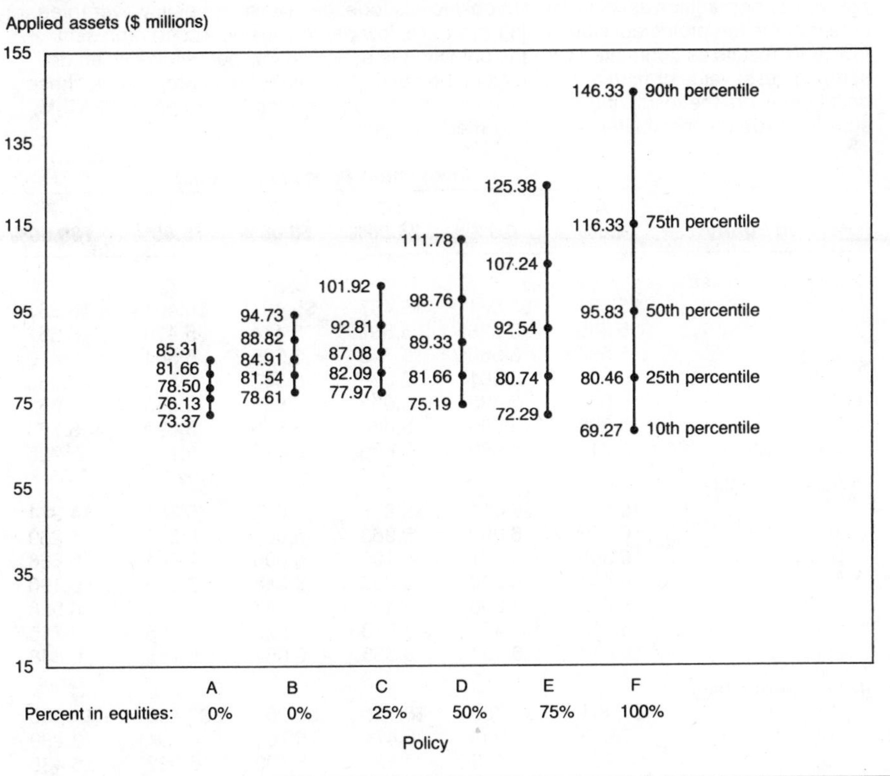

EXHIBIT 13
Sample Output of Wilshire Pension Simulation: Annual Cost

The expected range of annual funding costs is summarized in this table. Again, the probability percentiles associated with cost levels for each investment policy over three time periods are projected. Note that in this case, low percentiles (low cost) represent *favorable* results as contrasted with the unfavorable aspect of low percentiles when describing asset value or market return. As in the case of the asset value projections, these cost figures are the result of the full range of simulated scenarios generated by PENSIM, showing extreme possibilities as well as median results.

	Investment Policy ($ millions)					
	A	***B***	***C***	***D***	***E***	***F***
Percent Equity	***0.0%***	***0.0%***	***25.00%***	***50.00%***	***75.00%***	***100.00%***
2-year percentiles						
5th	$5.531	$5.521	$5.487	$5.451	$5.401	$5.336
10th	5.555	5.535	5.507	5.474	5.428	5.387
25th	5.584	5.565	5.549	5.525	5.501	5.470
50th	5.626	5.601	5.593	5.582	5.576	5.566
75th	5.666	5.635	5.633	5.638	5.643	5.652
90th	5.692	5.659	5.666	5.676	5.690	5.703
95th	5.712	5.669	5.679	5.692	5.709	5.726
5-year percentiles						
5th	$6.170	$6.011	$5.876	$5.653	$5.357	$4.974
10th	6.226	6.069	5.963	5.801	5.570	5.269
25th	6.309	6.177	6.108	6.006	5.864	5.666
50th	6.406	6.290	6.268	6.248	6.213	6.190
75th	6.499	6.390	6.409	6.447	6.474	6.520
90th	6.566	6.471	6.513	6.578	6.655	6.745
95th	6.613	6.497	6.555	6.654	6.755	6.848
10-year percentiles						
5th	$7.491	$6.756	$6.128	$5.000	$3.456	$1.180
10th	7.665	6.989	6.474	5.766	4.791	3.289
25th	7.926	7.413	7.127	6.700	6.092	5.436
50th	8.153	7.693	7.537	7.376	7.146	6.910
75th	8.323	7.934	7.895	7.926	7.992	8.012
90th	8.521	8.145	8.191	8.390	8.598	8.814
95th	8.642	8.270	8.373	8.616	8.927	9.199

EXHIBIT 13a
Sample Output of Wilshire Pension Simulation: Distribution of Annual Costs—Fifth Year (10/80)

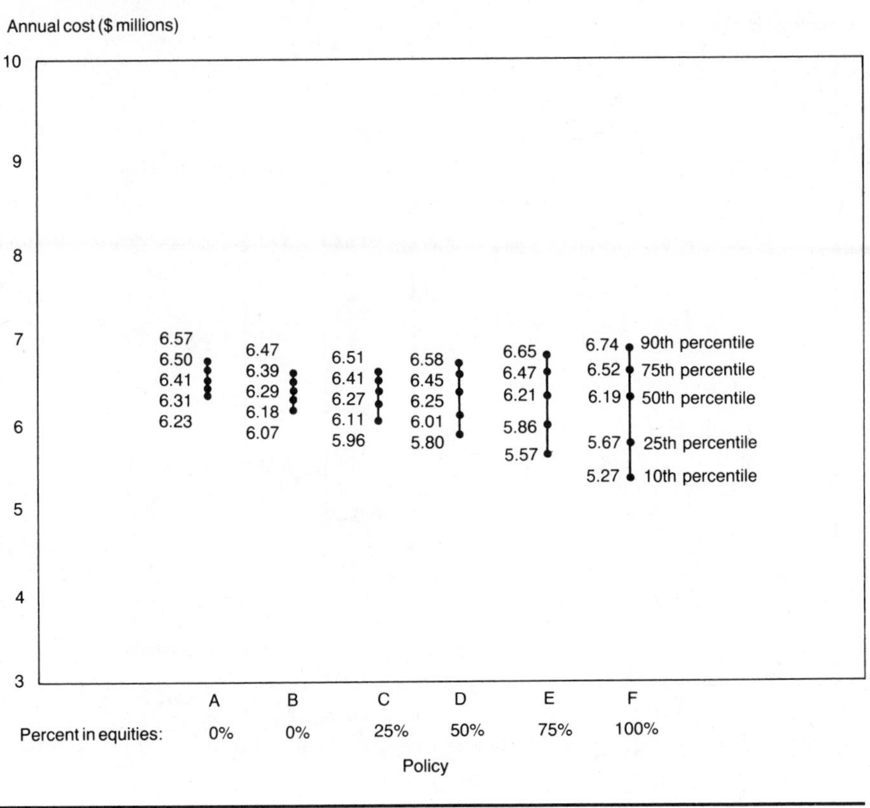

EXHIBIT 13b

Sample Output of Wilshire Pension Simulation: Distribution of Annual Costs—Tenth Year (10/85)

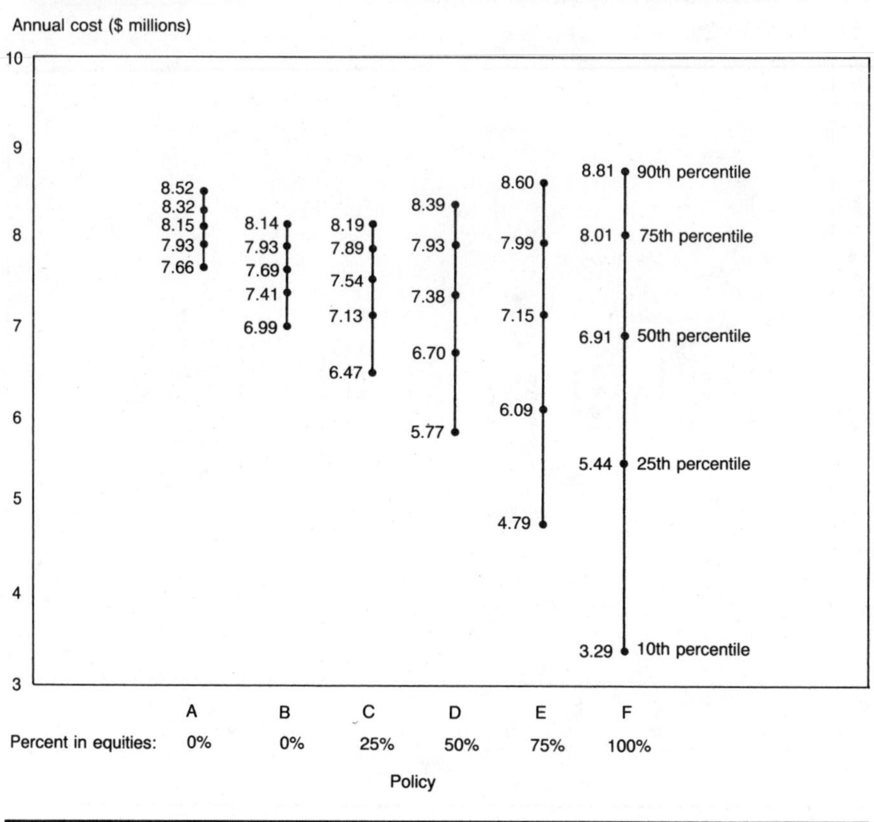

EXHIBIT 14
Sample Output of Wilshire Pension Simulation: Annual Cost as a Percent of Pay

When a pension plan is pay-related, cost projections are more meaningful when stated as a percent of pay, especially when payroll is growing as a result of inflation. This table shows the same cost figures summarized in the Annual Cost table, except now as a percent of pay. Note that the range of costs that might be required varies quite significantly as a function of investment policy.

	Investment Policy ($ millions)					
	A	B	C	D	E	F
Percent Equity	0.0%	0.0%	25.00%	50.00%	75.00%	100.00%
2-year percentiles						
5th	$16.303	$16.274	$16.174	$16.067	$15.921	$15.728
10th	16.373	16.316	16.233	16.135	15.999	15.879
25th	16.461	16.404	16.355	16.286	16.215	16.123
50th	16.583	16.509	16.487	16.454	16.437	16.408
75th	16.700	16.609	16.606	16.618	16.632	16.660
90th	16.779	16.680	16.702	16.730	16.773	16.811
95th	16.838	16.710	16.741	16.777	16.828	16.879
5-year percentiles						
5th	$14.750	$14.371	$14.048	$13.515	$12.806	$11.891
10th	14.884	14.508	14.256	13.868	13.316	12.597
25th	15.082	14.768	14.602	14.358	14.018	13.546
50th	15.315	15.038	14.984	14.936	14.852	14.798
75th	15.537	15.276	15.322	15.413	15.477	15.587
90th	15.697	15.470	15.570	15.725	15.910	16.124
95th	15.809	15.532	15.670	15.908	16.149	16.371
10-year percentiles						
5th	$12.648	$11.407	$10.347	$ 8.442	$ 5.836	$ 1.992
10th	12.941	11.800	10.930	9.735	8.089	5.553
25th	13.382	12.515	12.033	11.312	10.285	9.178
50th	13.765	12.988	12.726	12.454	12.065	11.667
75th	14.052	13.396	13.329	13.382	13.494	13.527
90th	14.386	13.751	13.829	14.166	14.517	14.882
95th	14.591	13.963	14.137	14.547	15.072	15.531

EXHIBIT 14a

Sample Output of Wilshire Pension Simulation: Distribution of Annual Costs as Percent of Pay—Fifth Year (10/80)

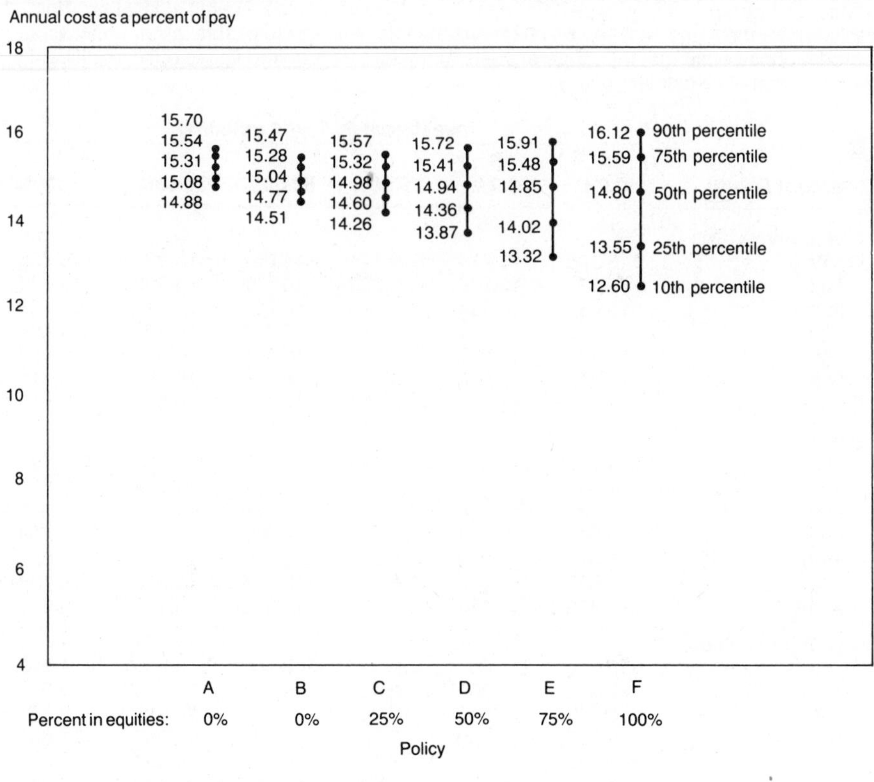

EXHIBIT 14b
Sample Output of Wilshire Pension Simulation: Distribution of Annual Costs as Percent of Pay—Tenth Year (10/85)

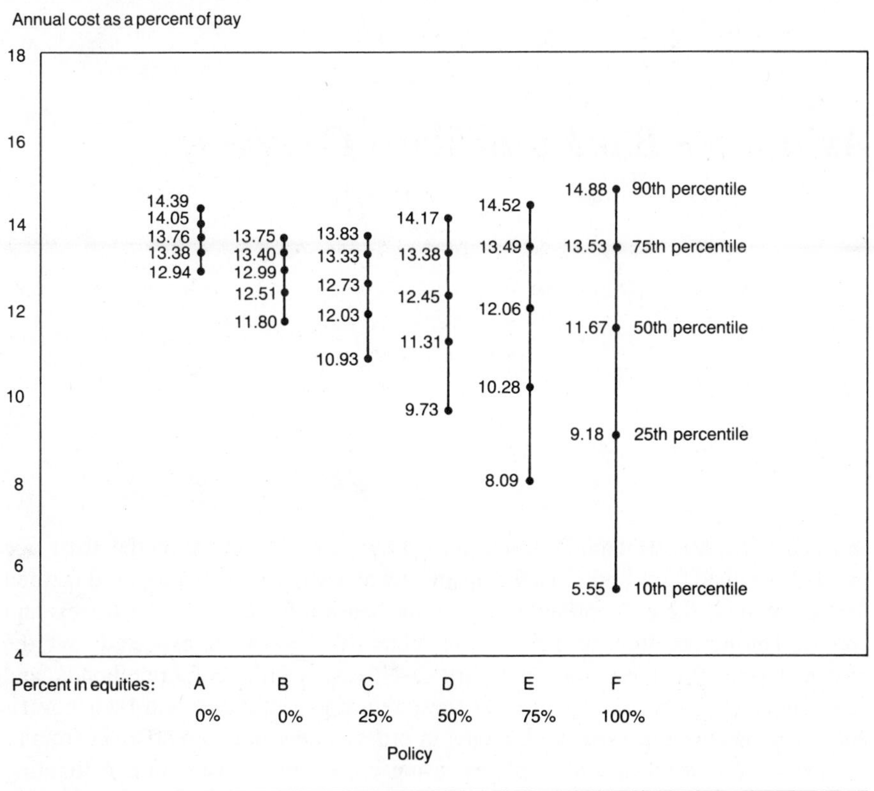

Assurance Bank and Trust Company

In April 1978, Ms. Barbara Peterson in the Research Department on the Trust side of the Assurance Bank and Trust Company was reviewing a newly proposed method for determining the appropriate asset mix for pension funds or similar tax-exempt clients. The model drew on forecasts of returns that might be expected over the next four years for three types of securities—Treasury bills, corporate bonds, and common stocks—the uncertainties of these return expectations, and their covariance. The model processed these inputs in order to determine an efficient frontier for the various asset-mix alternatives, using conventional risk/return estimating procedures. What was novel about the simulation was the way the inputs were determined.

Assurance Bank and Trust Company, a major money center bank and one of the 20 largest banks in the country, had always benefited from a comparatively strong Trust Department, in the broadest and most modern sense of this term. At the outset of 1978, the bank had nearly $4 billion of client business under active management and performed important advisory services for a substantial number of additional clients. Employee-benefit-plan clients represented over $2 billion of the funds under management.

Over the last decade, employee-benefit-plan accounts had become extremely competitive. A number of factors had caused clients to be much more concerned with the risk/return performance of funds under management. Fund managers were more frequently changed of late if performance was, for one reason or another, disappointing. There were more opportunities to gain new accounts and more problems in holding on to existing clients as the result of these changes.

In this period, the client's confidence in the manager's ability to achieve desired portfolio performance became a more important element in selling new or servicing old accounts. Historic performance of representative accounts was just one element considered by a client or prospective client. These individuals also considered the procedures used by the fund manager in assuring the continued ability of the manager to achieve the desired type of performance in the future, as well as the caliber of the people involved.

A number of the larger and more important clients were increasingly familiar with the ideas involved in the rapidly emerging Modern Portfolio Theory with its Index Fund concepts, betas, R^2s, and the like. Advisers seeking this business not only had to show considerable understanding of these concepts but also often had to demonstrate that they were using some of the more important models in a meaningful way in their decision-making processes.

Four years previously, Assurance had launched an intensive effort to develop systems that would facilitate the investment decision-making process. These systems were built upon some of the more practical concepts of Modern Portfolio Theory. A number of these systems had been in place now for a sufficient period of time to demonstrate their practical value. Assurance's management considered their position to be relatively strong in this area—well ahead of most of the competition, although somewhat behind the pathfinders.

Servicing clients' interests had also become more important and more task-oriented. Several of the systems developed at Assurance were designed to help clients participate in or make judgments that would strongly influence subsequent portfolio risk/return performance. The Assurance asset-mix model was designed to provide perspective on one of the more critical portfolio management decisions.

Asset-mix policy decisions were handled in different ways by different clients. In some cases the client determined the appropriate asset mix, and then parceled out funds to various managers who would be responsible for managing one part or subpart of the mix. At the other extreme, a manager might receive a pool of funds with no, or very loose, mix instructions. Assurance hoped to be able to use its asset-mix model in ways that would be considered useful in the entire spectrum of potential client applications.

Asset-mix policy refers to determining the target percentage of portfolio funds to be invested in various sectors of the market on average over the course of a cycle. Specific circumstances might, of course, warrant departure from targets in order to position the portfolio mix more satisfactorily, given short-term market outlooks.

Most asset-mix models focused on determining the target mix for key sectors such as common stocks, bonds, Treasury bills, and sometimes real estate, by estimating the risk/return market performance of several alternative asset-mix strategies. The Assurance model was of this nature. A few consulting firms had developed more elaborate models that also considered the future actuarial cost consequences of necessary funding action as well as portfolio market performance and related uncertainties. The range of sophistication designed into available models varied enormously.

The inputs to the models were similar in concept, although each required judgment. The median long-term return (from a symmetrical distribution) for each sector was estimated. The current yield to maturity of AA utility bonds might, for example, be used in the bond sector. The variability of these returns, stated as a standard deviation, was usually developed from historical information such as the data of Ibbotson and Sinquefield.[1] Covariance estimates were developed from similar historical analyses.

Ms. Peterson had undertaken an analysis of the Ibbotson and Sinquefield data as shown in Exhibit 1. Over four-year periods, the relationship between the returns of Treasury bills, corporate bonds, and common stocks had varied considerably. In some periods, these relationships were perverse; that is, lower risk securities provided higher returns. In other periods, the return benefits from riskier types of securities were extremely large. In hindsight, these outcomes did not seem to be random; rather they appeared to be the result of intervening structural changes in the capital markets.

The more Ms. Peterson thought about it, the more she began to believe that the long-term assumptions typically used in asset-mix decisions might be seriously misleading in intermediate-term planning periods. Certainly this would have been the case in the last decade. In her opinion, asset-mix decisions should be geared to the particular return opportunities existing in the intermediate future and the particular uncertainties associated with the returns. For example, capital market uncertainties, looking forward from April of 1978, appeared, if anything, larger than was normally the case, simply because economic uncertainties—inflation, growth, dollar instability—were larger. These uncertainties, she reasoned, should influence asset-mix decisions.

It occurred to Ms. Peterson that significant value might be added to the process by having the Bank explicitly forecast risk/return characteristics for the various asset classes over the intermediate term. The Economics Department was currently preparing "most likely" economic forecasts for the next 18 months, but she reasoned that this effort could be greatly expanded to encompass

1. A four-year period (assumed to be a proxy for a market cycle).
2. Alternate possible economic scenarios.

Once these economic forecasts were completed, the objective would be to forecast returns for each asset class within each scenario. This information would be sufficient to allow the Bank to derive overall expected return forecasts for each asset as well as to estimate the variability of returns and the correlation of returns among asset classes. All of these data would come directly from the underlying scenario forecasts. Ms. Peterson felt strongly that this was a better approach than simply extrapolating variability and correlation from the historic data.

---

[1] *Stocks, Bonds, Bills and Inflation: The Past (1926–1976) and the Future (1977–2000)*, Charlottesville, Va.: The Financial Analysts Research Foundation, 1977.

This approach was implemented by the Bank. A sample set of economic scenarios, dated March 15, 1978, is attached as Appendix A. A description of the capital-market-forecasting process, together with the associated data for these economic scenarios, is attached as Appendix B.

Summary data on the capital market forecasts are shown at the end of Appendix B. Forecasted data on return, standard deviation, and correlation are labeled as current. Historic data, provided by Canavest House, are given for comparative purposes.

The efficient frontier derived from these data is shown on the last page of Appendix B. This efficient frontier depicts the array of asset mixes offering the highest possible expected return for a given level of portfolio standard deviation.

In two weeks' time, Ms. Peterson was scheduled to present her approach to asset-mix determination to the Senior Policy Committee of the Bank. The last few months had been quite hectic, as the models were refined. Now she wanted to rethink several questions:

1. Was the approach appropriate and was the methodology consistent with the purpose?
2. How should the proposal be packaged for presentation to the Senior Policy Committee? Specifically, this approach took considerably more time and effort than simply forecasting return and risk by extrapolating from the past. Was the process worth it?
3. In determining the efficient frontier, was it appropriate to work from the current asset mix and factor in transaction costs? If so, how?
4. The efficient frontier depicts an array of "optimal" portfolios. How could the Bank work with each client to determine which mix was appropriate in each case?
5. All forecasts in this process were for a four-year period. Should the Bank adjust if shorter-term forecasts were at variance with market-cycle forecasts? If so, how?
6. What problems lay ahead in trying to train portfolio managers about how to use this tool in their client relationships?

EXHIBIT 1
Four-Year Average Compound Rates of Return of Treasury Bills, Corporate Bonds, and Common Stock (*compound annual rate of return*)

From Beginning of	To End of	Treasury Bills	Corporate Bonds	Common Stocks
1926	1929	3.6%	5.2%	19.2%
7	1930	3.4	5.4	8.0
8	1	2.9	3.0	−0.4
9	2	2.3	4.9	−27.0
1930	3	1.2	6.7	−11.9
1	4	0.6	8.1	−5.7
2	5	0.4	11.2	19.8
3	6	0.2	10.1	31.6
4	7	0.2	8.2	6.1
5	8	0.2	5.8	13.9
6	9	0.1	4.6	3.2
7	1940	0.1	4.1	−6.5
8	1	0.0	4.0	1.0
9	2	0.1	3.2	−1.1
1940	3	0.2	2.9	4.8
1	4	0.3	3.2	12.5
2	5	0.3	3.6	25.4
3	6	0.3	3.3	17.3
4	7	0.4	2.0	12.3
5	8	0.5	1.9	8.8
6	9	0.7	1.7	5.1
7	1950	0.9	1.8	14.9
8	1	1.2	1.7	19.6
9	2	1.4	1.5	23.1
1950	3	1.5	1.6	17.6
1	4	1.5	2.4	22.0
1952	1955	1.5	3.2	23.9
3	6	1.7	0.5	20.6
4	7	2.0	1.8	17.5
5	8	2.2	−0.1	15.7
6	9	2.5	−0.5	11.1
7	1960	2.6	3.5	9.5
8	1	2.3	2.6	19.6
9	2	2.6	5.1	6.8
1960	3	2.7	6.0	9.3
1	4	2.9	4.9	13.5
2	5	3.3	3.6	10.1
3	6	3.8	1.7	9.7
4	7	4.1	−0.2	9.9
5	8	4.5	−0.7	8.6
6	9	5.2	−2.7	3.2
7	1970	5.6	1.5	7.0
8	1	5.7	5.5	4.8
9	2	5.3	6.7	6.7
1970	3	5.4	9.3	4.8
1	4	5.8	3.9	− 3.9
2	5	6.1	4.8	0.6
3	6	6.4	7.5	1.6

Source: Ibbotson and Sinquefield, *Stocks, Bonds, Bills, and Inflation.*

Appendix A

ECONOMIC PROSPECTS FOR THE NEXT FOUR YEARS

The U.S. economy faces a multitude of uncertainties over the coming four-year period. The current inflation psychology and the high level of inflation that persists point to an inherent instability in the economy that is likely to take many years to overcome. The risk of error in government policy, given these inflationary pressures, plus the strong expectation of relatively high rates of unemployment, seem to be greater today than they have been for quite a while. Our national energy policy—now more than four years in the making—is still somewhat of an unknown, even with a group of energy proposals now poised to be enacted into law; as such, the threat of a cutoff of our crude oil supplies—be it due to OPEC government action, rebel sabotage of the OPEC oil fields, disruption along the supply lines, or any other factor that interrupts the flow of any of our energy supplies—continues to be a nagging uncertainty. And, perhaps the area most difficult to assess is the international sphere, where the high cost of energy and the slow economic growth in the developed world are combining to maintain strong pressure on the non-oil less developed nations.

Near term, the coal strike has created an additional uncertainty facing the economy. To begin with, there is question as to when the mines will return to full production; should they stay out much longer, or should they return to work for 80 days and then walk out again, the secondary effects of reducing coal supplies would produce a general business downturn. If recognized as such, and no massive government program is introduced to aid in the recovery, then the longer-term prospects should not be altered materially.

A more meaningful repercussion could develop in terms of impacting inflation, inflation psychology, or energy supplies. One of the immediate results of an ultimate labor agreement will be a significant increase in wages, which will not be offset by productivity gains and will be passed on to the consumer. This had been anticipated and should not come as a surprise. But, if the government actions are viewed by other unions as supportive of large wage increases, a more concerted push toward bigger settlements could develop in the major negotiations coming up next year. In addition, the question of reliability of coal sources could present more of a cloud over the plan to encourage coal utilization as the key means to satisfy growing energy demands.

While the current unknowns place a high risk premium on new investment programs—either in the securities markets or in physical plant and equipment—the most likely course upon which the economy is to travel is one that will be relatively slower and somewhat smoother than our experience over the past decade. The sharp decline in output and the surge in inflation during the 1973–75 recession have left the entire world in a state of extreme caution. Despite the still-high level of unemployment, there seems to be no great pressure to stimulate the economies much beyond trying to compensate for the damages caused by inflation. Recognition that excessive government stimulation via massive spending programs does not go very far in solving the unemployment problem is fairly widespread. This basically cautious position on the part of governments—and businessmen and consumers as well—combined with the relatively large pool of unutilized plant and human capacity, should lead to a prolonged expansion of economic activity which could persist through the next four years.

The prospects for an extended business cycle into the 1980s—our most likely scenario—depends, in large measure, on government fiscal and monetary policy not becoming overly exuberant in the face of expected slower economic growth during the coming year. By now it is becoming increasingly clear that the extremely rapid increases that have taken place in consumer spending over the past three years cannot continue for much longer. The recent holiday spending season was exceptionally strong, and with employment and incomes still headed upward, consumer outlays should post further gains into 1978. But, with much of the previously postponed demand in automobiles and housing—the two most cyclical consumer areas—being satisfied, slight declines should now be experienced for the next year or so.

To some extent the slowing in consumer outlays should be offset by the accelerating capital goods and government sectors, as is already quite evident. The leading indicators of capital goods demand—new orders, contract awards, appropriations and surveys of anticipations—are all pointed strongly upward, confirming the basic forces of rising capacity utilization rates and improving cash flow, which also suggest higher capital outlays. Government spending, meanwhile, has begun to show signs of life, reversing the weakness that has been prevalent for the past several years.

On balance, then, and with the absence of additional government stimulus, economic growth would likely taper off during the coming year and may well be even slower in 1979. Faced with these prospects, and the attendant rise in the highly political and visible unemployment rate, there is a growing push to adopt the Administration's tax-cut proposals while rejecting much of the reform aspects. As it appears currently, the prospective boost in take-home pay should be in excess of the hike in Social Security taxes, so as to provide a boost to overall business activity. Assuming that a further cut is enacted by 1979 or 1980 to offset the effects of "fiscal drag" and that the total tax reduction is not excessive, the economy could well avoid a recession over the next several years.

The general caution that is being displayed by governments, businessmen, and consumers should not only temper the real economic expansion over the next few years, but it should also limit the inflationary pressures that would otherwise develop. Near term, the rate of price increases is expected to accelerate from the good performance seen since mid-1977. This would reflect the higher minimum wage that went into effect January 1, the increase in Social Security taxes, the higher energy costs that are anticipated to stem from actions of the Congress or the Department of Energy, the expected upturn in food prices following the flat pattern seen since June and the effects of the decline in the value of the dollar, vis-à-vis other currencies.

Because of the faster-than-anticipated decline in the dollar in the latter part of 1977 and the now apparent less concern over inflation on the part of the Administration, prospects for inflation this year have worsened. Longer term, however, there is a reasonable chance for some moderation in the rate of inflation. This is not to suggest that inflation will cease to be a problem. Energy prices are expected to grow rapidly as the U.S. price of crude oil rises to world levels, as natural gas prices are raised high enough to spur increased production, and as the more expensive sources of energy begin to play a significant role in the total picture. Food prices should also remain a troublesome factor; further sharp gains in agricultural productivity will be difficult to achieve and the worldwide demand for food will continue to expand. Offsetting these upward pressures, though, will be the relative slack in the labor markets which should be a moderating influence on wage rates—the most significant of all business costs. And, with a chance for overall productivity to improve in the early 1980s, as more efficient plant and equipment are installed, pressures on inflation could well be eased during the later years of the forecasted period.

As the modest-growth [MG] scenario unfolds, corporate profitability will likely experience a modest uptrend. The emphasis being placed on the "bottom line" appears to be a bit more than a cyclical reaction to disappointing earnings levels of the past recession. This does not suggest, however, that profits will be rising throughout the next four years on a steady path. The cyclical nature of profitability will remain; as the economy slows, profits will tend to be hit harder than other economic [sectors]. Should a downturn in business activity occur, earnings are likely to fall faster, although it would appear that the extent of the decline should be more modest than past experience would indicate. Following the period of sluggish growth, margin improvement will once again be in evidence, resulting in faster gains in profits than in total business output.

While our forecasts do not go beyond early 1982 at this time, the modest-growth scenario could be perceived as continuing for several more years, as the lower inflation rates and stable world markets rebuild consumer confidence and encourage business investment sufficient to maintain longer-term economic growth. Expectations as of 1982 could well point to an economy that will be unable to generate enough momentum in the early 1980s to sustain itself longer term, and real growth will be slowly eroding into the mid-1980s.

Under the conditions in the MG scenario, the demand for funds remains relatively soft. With inflation on a downtrend and no real rebound in economic activity anticipated, there is little pressure to build inventories, and short-term rates remain low with a very small premium on inflation. The long-term markets are similarly soft, with corporations having little incentive to invest in major capital projects. Risk is prevalent in some low-quality issues but there is no real impact on AAA securities.

In this scenario, dividends grow a bit faster than corporate profits over the next four years. In MG, the intermediate-term dividend growth rate slows to 6.5 percent (versus the assumed long-term rate of 7.0 percent) to reflect the slower earnings potential of the mid-to-late 1980s. The required return on stocks in MG is assumed to be 12.5 percent and 12.0 percent for the intermediate and longer term, respectively. The higher required return used in MG reflects the higher risks associated with a scenario that continues to deteriorate in the mid-1980s.

Alternative Scenarios

In an effort to detect possible deviations from the most likely economic projections, alternative assumptions regarding government policy and, more important, business and consumer response to government stimulus have been developed. These are summarized in the following sections.

Growth Recession [GR]. While a recession, or something close to one, is not envisioned in the "modest growth" environment, an expansion extending from early 1975 to early 1982 or beyond (at least 7 years) would be unprecedented for a peacetime economy. Given the massive recession that took place just prior to the current growth period, no recession before the early 1980s is clearly a good possibility, but a marked slowdown in output into what could be called a "growth recession" is a viable offshoot of an economy that is expanding at a moderate pace.

At this point in time one can project a growth recession, or worse, stemming from a prolonged coal strike. More likely, though, would be a natural slowing of the growth path later this year in response to relatively high inflation rates and rising rates. This slowdown could continue into 1979 despite the attempt at fiscal stimulus through a tax cut this fall. Since excesses have not been built to any major degree in this environment, there is no evidence yet that would suggest anything more severe than a 6-month-or-so period of no growth in total output. Beyond that time, the natural growth forces would again emerge, but the advance would proceed along a slower-than-normal pace, since there would be no cyclical rebound from a depressed level.

Reflecting the relatively calm economic pattern, the capital markets should behave fairly positively in this scenario. Looking out four years from today, one can reasonably expect a slow-to-moderate growth pattern, perhaps nearing the next cyclical slowdown, with an inflation rate a bit below the current level and trending downward. Long-term bond rates would also be slightly below current rates, at an estimated 8.0 percent. Dividends would have grown by almost 9 percent annually and would be winding down toward the longer-term 7 percent growth rate. The required return for common stocks in this scenario is projected to be a modest 11 percent, reflecting the relative stability of expected economic conditions beyond 1982.

Stagflation [SF]. While consumer spending rebounded in the fourth quarter of 1977, the current year started off on a very weak note. To a large degree, the softness can be attributed to the impact of the weather and the coal strike. Still, it is conceivable that weakness will persist even after the temporary restraints are alleviated. At the same time, business outlays for new plant construction could be delayed further in response to a perceived inability in Washington to attack the problems facing the country today—energy, capital formation, inflation, unemployment. Also, government outlays could slow, business inventories could be reduced in the face of disappointing demand, housing construction could well decline at a faster pace than is currently foreseen, and our net foreign trade position could continue posting large negative numbers as foreign economies maintain their drifting course or decline into recession. In general, then, the near-term outlook could turn out to be weaker than is anticipated under the most likely set of conditions.

The response to this stagnating environment, no doubt, would be an even quicker move to enact some sort of stimulus program—probably in the form of a larger tax cut, but it could also include additional government spending programs. Given the uncertainties that prevail in the minds of businessmen and consumers, the response to the government initiatives in this scenario would be perverse. Real activity would not accelerate, but given the large deficit and the likelihood that the Federal Reserve will monetize at least part of it, the stimulus would result in a more rapid inflation rate than would otherwise be the case. Meanwhile, the higher energy and food price pressures would continue and boost the pace of inflation even further.

Faced with this discouraging set of events—stagnant real growth and high inflation—the government policymakers would be in a quandary. Additional stimulative actions may be attempted, but the fear of igniting the inflation fires to an even greater extent would limit the government moves. As such, the economy would limp along—perhaps as long as two years or so—but the pressure of excessive rates of inflation over a prolonged period is likely to lead to a sharp break in the level of output in the form of a recession by 1980. Despite the severity of the recession, the recovery to follow would be relatively slow, as all sectors of the economy would display even more caution than currently exists.

Under this scenario, the credit markets would become extremely tight, with many corporations finding long-term funds unavailable and being forced to finance their activities in the short-term markets, causing an unstable inverted yield curve. AAA securities would remain reasonably priced, although high by historical standards. Under these conditions, dividends would grow at an average of only 2½–3 percent from the current rate of $4.95 to $5.51 in early 1982. The estimated 6 percent growth in dividends during the intermediate period is below our long-term 7 percent assumption. The required return on stocks peaks at 15 percent for the intermediate period and declines to 13 percent in the long term. This scenario would generate conditions in the capital markets that are extremely unstable and precarious.

Renewed Growth [RG]. Starting with the premise that the 1978 economy gets off to the relatively poor start as outlined in the stagflation scenario, there is a reasonable chance that after an extended period of time, an effective stimulus program would be proposed and would, in fact, produce the desired results as far as real growth is concerned. Over the past few years there has been growing recognition that capital formation will have to be spurred in order to achieve significant progress on the problems of unemployment and inflation. Key members of the Administration and the Congress have spoken about the need to stimulate new construction of efficient plants, to expand the ability to produce energy domestically, and to return to historical rates of growth in research and development and technological progress. While the achievement of these goals may sound like a lot of wishful thinking, the pressure to provide business with incentives to invest in these vital areas—so as to assure a steady growth in employment opportunities without a rekindling of inflation—remains strong.

Given that there is growing disenchantment with the effects of traditional government spending programs to stimulate the economy, a reasonable chance exists that an attempt will be made to provide more direct incentives to investment. This could be achieved through tax credits for specific types of investment, as seems to be taking place as part of the energy program, or it could be gotten a bit more indirectly through the already-proposed corporate tax cut that would increase the rate of return on all new investments. In either case, the result would be a renewed expansion of real economic activity. While this expansion would not produce an immediate benefit in terms of lower inflation rates, the more productive facilities that would come on stream a few years out would allow an easing of inflationary pressures in the early 1980s.

This very favorable scenario would yield positive capital market implications. Dividend growth would start off rather slowly until the renewed expansion of the economy gets under way. Annual increases may well only average 6¾ percent over the next four years, but an above-average dividend growth rate of 7½ percent could well persist throughout the intermediate period before slowing to our 7.0 percent longer-term growth assumption. The corresponding required return on stocks should be relatively low for both the intermediate and long term, averaging 10.5 percent as investors become reasonably sanguine on the outlook for stocks. Conditions in the credit markets would also be positive, with a 150 basis point spread between long- and short-term issues. Most corporations would be fairly liquid and the demand for funds should remain stable longer term.

Boom-Bust [BB]. The risk of government overstimulation is manifested in the boom-bust scenarios. As 1978 unfolds, the inherent strength of the economy that is present due to previous expansive monetary and fiscal policies is masked by another temporary lull in activity. Government policymakers—concerned over the threat of higher unemployment rates as the Congressional elections near—adopt a stimulative program that turns out to be much stronger than is actually needed. As a result, consumer spending once again accelerates in response to the hefty tax cut, and is quickly reinforced by rapid gains in business spending for inventories and capital expansion, while government outlays continue to post strong advances.

While the renewed growth tends to reduce the level of unemployment, it also leads to a relatively quick absorption of the excess labor and plant capacity that currently exists. As the economy pushes toward heightened capacity utilization rates, the growing shortages rekindle memories of the 1973–74 experience, producing another scramble for inventories and excessive inflationary pressures. The rapid expansion phase of the cycle carries with it a confrontation with the monetary authorities who attempt to control the rampant inflation by reining in sharp growth of the monetary aggregates. Following this period of money tightness, a fairly severe recession occurs by late 1979 and persists through 1980.

As the economy begins to recover from the depths of the recession, two scenarios are envisioned. The first (BB_1) presumes that the instability of the economy will remain into the 1980s, with the government inducing sharper swings in activity—both upward and downward—without any success in bringing about any degree of stability. The second possibility (BB_2) allows for a return to a more cautious attitude throughout the key sectors of the economy—consumers, businessmen, and government leaders—leading to a more subdued economic recovery in the early 1980s.

In either of the boom-bust scenarios, the rapid expansion and high rates of inflation produce big gains in corporate earnings. These profits, however, are of questionable quality, reflecting a marking up of inventory valuations and a failure to adequately depreciate assets that need replacement. Recognizing that a good deal of the earnings are "phantom," companies would be reluctant to increase their dividend payments as fast as the growth in reported profits.

The more pronounced cyclical swings within the BB_1 scenario during the 1980s causes greater concern in the capital markets. Under these conditions, interest rates tend to rise to fairly high levels, with investors demanding an inflation premium of 8½ percent on both short- and long-term instruments. Stocks are similarly perceived as high-risk instruments, commanding a required return of 14.5 percent and 12.5 percent for the intermediate and long term, respectively. Dividend growth during the intermediate period is also perceived to decline below long-term expectations as corporations become more aware of the impending problems within the economy and develop a skepticism in their own profitability.

Capital market conditions under BB_2 (less cyclicality within future business cycles) are expected to be somewhat more positive. Although interest rates are relatively high, there is stability to the structure, with long-term rates 150 basis points higher than short rates. The required return on stocks is also somewhat lower than in BB_1 as investors' perceptions for 1982 reflect the less volatile nature of future cycles. Dividend growth for both intermediate and long term is stable at 7 percent as businessmen prepare themselves for a somewhat difficult, yet manageable environment.

Dollar Crisis [DC]. In order to capture the possibility of some exogenous factor (a future oil embargo, irresponsible fiscal or monetary policies, a world liquidity crisis, social and political turmoil, or worldwide terrorism), we have included an extreme scenario. This scenario could be an outgrowth of the current lackluster demand that persists throughout the world and the downward slide that the value of the U.S. dollar has undergone. Should the dollar weaken substantially from present depressed levels, more money would flow toward the stronger currencies. This would raise the risk of capital controls being imposed, to be followed by investment and trade barriers in an effort to protect domestic industries throughout the world. World trade would then be cut severely, unemployment would move higher, a more restrictive trade barrier would be erected, leading to a further curtailment of trade and the cyclical downturn would continue to spiral downward. While wages would be slow to respond even in this negative scenario, they are likely to finally crack as a result of the extremely poor employment opportunities. This, combined with the prospect of declining commodity prices as demand dries up, is likely to produce lower consumer prices before too long. Near term, however, the impact of the declining value of the dollar would drive the U.S. inflation rate upward.

Whereas the ultimate outcome of the deflation scenario would be beneficial in that it would wipe out the problem of inflation and would cleanse the system of excessive monetary imbalances, the road upon which the world economies would have to travel would produce major hardships and dislocations. Realizing the human suffering and the political turmoil that could develop should this scenario unfold, there is a high probability that the political and monetary authorities would do their utmost to prevent it from happening. Increased discussions among the world's leaders are likely to produce a more stable monetary system and a more balanced growth pattern than exists today.

In the event that this scenario does unfold, however, equity prices should experience sharp declines even from today's low levels. And, while the total return from stocks would be aided by the current high dividend yield, payouts would likely be cut as total earnings decline. At the same time, the lower rate of inflation and, ultimately, declining prices should result in lower interest rates (i.e., higher bond prices) for those companies strong enough to survive the weakened economic environment. The inflation premium four years from now would be markedly below current levels. The required return on stocks, meanwhile, would move sharply higher—toward the 15–16 percent range in the intermediate term, before settling down to a still-high 12–13 percent range, longer term.

Summary of Economic Scenarios to 1982

	Modest Growth	**Growth Recession**	**Renewed Growth**	**Stagflation**	**Boom-Bust$_1$**	**Boom-Bust$_2$**	**Dollar Crisis**
Probability	25	20	10	22.5	10	10	2.5
Average growth range	3–4	2.5–3.5	4–5	1–2	3.5–4.5	3–4	−0.5–0.5
Average CPI	5–6	5.5–6.5	5.5–6.5	7–8	7.5–8.5	7–8	0.2
Growth pattern	Declining, with some cyclical rebound. However, longer-term growth continues to erode.	Slowdown developing followed by modest cyclical move upward and then tapering off.	Short-term weakness followed by sustained growth longer term.	Sluggish growth deteriorating into severe recession.	Short-term growth followed by cyclical decline followed by very high unsustainable growth.	Short-term growth followed by cyclical decline followed by a less volatile cycle.	After modest improvement deteriorating into severe and prolonged decline.
Inflation pattern	Secular decline extending beyond forecast period reflecting slower growth pattern.	Fairly flat at relatively high rates.	Slowly declining rates fueled by capacity expansion.	Persistent high rates with a very slow decline following recession.	Increasing rates despite cyclical downturn ultimately peaking in mid-80s.	Increasing rates despite cyclical decline ultimately declining as cycle becomes less volatile.	Acceleration followed by extreme weakness with prices falling.

Summary of Scenarios

	Modest Growth	Growth Recession	Renewed Growth	Stag-flation	Boom-Bust$_1$	Boom-Bust$_2$	Dollar Crisis
GNP growth							
1978	4.2%	4.1%	3.3%	3.3%	4.1%	4.1%	3.8%
1979	3.3	1.9	2.1	2.1	6.3	6.3	−0.2
1980	4.0.	3.2	3.7	0.5	−0.5	−0.5	−3.1
1981	3.6	4.0	6.2	−1.5	1.7	1.5	0.3
Average	3.8	3.3	3.8	1.1	2.9	2.9	0.2
CPI growth							
1978	6.1%	6.3%	6.3%	7.2%	6.2%	6.2%	6.6%
1979	5.8	6.0	6.0	8.7	8.4	8.4	5.0
1980	5.6	6.3	6.2	7.8	8.4	8.4	−2.2
1981	4.8	6.1	5.9	6.4	7.1	6.5	−0.5
Average	5.6	6.2	6.1	7.5	7.5	7.4	2.2
Profits growth							
1978	8.8%	8.8%	−1.8%	10.5%	14.9%	14.9%	8.3%
1979	7.5	−1.6	−7.0	9.3	21.7	21.7	−3.9
1980	12.4	9.6	8.0	−1.2	−0.1	−0.1	−30.5
1981	10.0	15.0	24.8	−3.5	1.9	2.5	−7.3
Average	9.7	8.0	6.0	3.8	9.6	9.8	−8.4
Level in IQ 1982							
Real GNP	$1,583	$1,552	$1,604	$1,415	$1,571	$1,528	$1,379
Profits	155	145	137	126	158	154	75
Rate in IQ 1982							
Real GNP	3.0%	3.0%	5.0%	3.0%	8.0%	3.0%	4.0%
CPI	4.0	5.0	5.0	6.0	9.0	6.0	2.5
IQ 1978							
Real GNP growth	4.0%	3.0%	2.0%	3.0%	3.0%	3.0%	3.0%
CPI growth	7.0	7.5	7.5	8.0	7.5	7.5	7.0
Profits	107	107	102	108	108	108	106

Note: IQ = Initial quarter.

Appendix B

DESCRIPTION—CAPITAL MARKET FORECASTING PROCESS

Assurance Bank and Trust Company attempts to calculate returns on three different assets—common stock, corporate bonds, and Treasury bills—over a four-year period. (This four-year period is a proxy for the market cycle.) The forecasting process begins with our economists' supposition of a number of economic scenarios. Values for real GNP, profits, and the CPI are projected on a quarterly basis for each scenario over the next four years. It is from this information that the Senior Policy Committee postulates a number of factors which will determine the returns on the assets for each scenario. This committee also attaches a probability of occurrence to each scenario.

An integral concept is that of an inflation premium. This is the investor's perception of inflation longer term, as he views it in four years. This perception is assumed to be a function of inflation over the intervening period, and is a key factor in projecting asset-class returns. For our seven scenarios, inflation premiums range from 2.0 percent to 10.0 percent.

The holding period return on commercial paper is a function of average future quarterly rates and the current rate. By adding required real returns (which vary from 0.5 percent to 1.5 percent) to inflation estimates on a quarterly basis, it is a simple calculation to obtain an average future rate.

To predict the holding period return on a bond, it is necessary to estimate the yield to maturity on the bond in four years. This yield is the sum of an inflation premium and the required real rate. For bonds, the real rates are assumed to vary within a range of 1.5 percent to 2.5 percent. Given that the bond today has a 20-year maturity and is purchased at par, and given an estimate of yield to maturity in four years, it is relatively simple to calculate its price four years hence. The holding period return is then calculated as price appreciation plus reinvestment of coupon income. If the bond is callable, its price and return given that it will be called are calculated. The probability of its being called is estimated and the return is the weighted average of its return if called and if not called.

In order to forecast holding period returns on common stock, we use a dividend discount model to solve for future price. The model calculates the future price given a particular level of future dividend payments, the required rate of return, and the projected dividend growth rate. The dividend payments are a function of corporate profits, which can vary significantly across scenarios. The dividend growth rate is estimated both intermediate and long term, with the long-term rate set at 7.0 percent across all scenarios. The required rate of return is also estimated intermediate and long term. The holding period return is then calculated as price appreciation plus income, reinvested quarterly.

The overall return on each asset is determined by multiplying the projected return on a given asset for each scenario by the probability of that scenario occurring. The standard deviation of returns and correlations among asset-class returns is also derived from the underlying scenario returns.

Capital Market Assumptions

	Modest Growth	***Growth Recession***	***Renewed Growth***	***Stag-flation***	***Boom-Bust$_1$***	***Boom-Bust$_2$***	***Dollar Crisis***
Probability	25%	20%	10%	22½%	10%	10%	2½%
Inflation premium	4.5%	5.5%	5.5%	7.5%	10.0%	9.0%	2.0%
Treasury bills							
Real rate	0.5%	0.5%	0.5%	1.5%	0.5%	0.5%	0.5%
Nominal yield	5.0	6.0	6.0	9.0	10.5	9.5	3.0
Long-term bonds							
Real rate	2.0%	2.5%	2.0%	2.5%	1.5%	1.5%	1.5%
Nominal yield	6.5	8.0	7.5	10.0	11.5	10.5	3.5
Common stocks							
EPS IQ 1982	$16.52	$15.45	$14.60	$13.43	$16.83	$16.41	$7.99
Dividend IQ 1982	7.27	6.95	6.42	5.51	6.90	6.73	4.39
Payout IQ 1982	44.0	45.0	44.0	41.0	41.0	41.0	55.0
Increase from historic EPS	10.1%	8.9%	6.7%	2.7%	8.6%	8.0%	−3.0%
Price 1981	$129	$153	$191	$68	$97	$113	$41
P/E	7.8%	9.9%	13.1%	5.1%	5.8%	6.9%	5.1%
Yield	5.6	4.5	3.4	8.1	7.1	6.0	10.7
Dividend growth							
Intermediate	6.5%	7.0%	7.5%	6.0%	6.5%	7.0%	4.0%
Long-term	7.0	7.0	7.0	7.0	7.0	7.0	7.0
Required return							
Intermediate	12.5%	12.0%	10.5%	15.0%	14.5%	13.5%	16.0%
Long-term	12.0	11.0	10.5	13.0	12.5	12.0	13.0

Four-Year Holding Period Returns

	Modest Growth	***Growth Recession***	***Renewed Growth***	***Stag-flation***	***Boom-Bust$_1$***	***Boom-Bust$_2$***	***Dollar Crisis***
Probability	0.20	0.25	0.10	0.23	0.10	0.10	0.02
Stocks	18.24%	14.56%	23.70%	−0.92%	7.55%	10.96%	−11.95%
Bonds	11.15	9.47	11.15	7.20	5.22	6.51	12.32
T-bills	6.18	6.89	6.43	7.70	7.60	7.60	4.50

Note: Developed from Appendix A.

Summary of Capital Market Forecasts

	Expected Return	
	Current	***Historic***
Stocks	11.00%	7.80%
Bonds	8.81	3.50
T-bills	6.97	5.00

	Standard Deviation	
	Current	***Historic***
Stocks	8.75%	5.40%
Bonds	2.11	3.20
T-bills	0.71	1.30

Correlation Matrix

	Current			***Historic***		
	Stocks	***Bonds***	***Paper***	***Stocks***	***Bonds***	***Paper***
Stocks	1.00			1.00		
Bonds	0.57	1.00		0.30	1.00	
T-Bills	−0.43	−0.91	1.00	−0.40	−0.10	1.00

Note: Historic data are for four-year periods ending 1960 through 1976. Current = 1981.

The Efficient Frontier

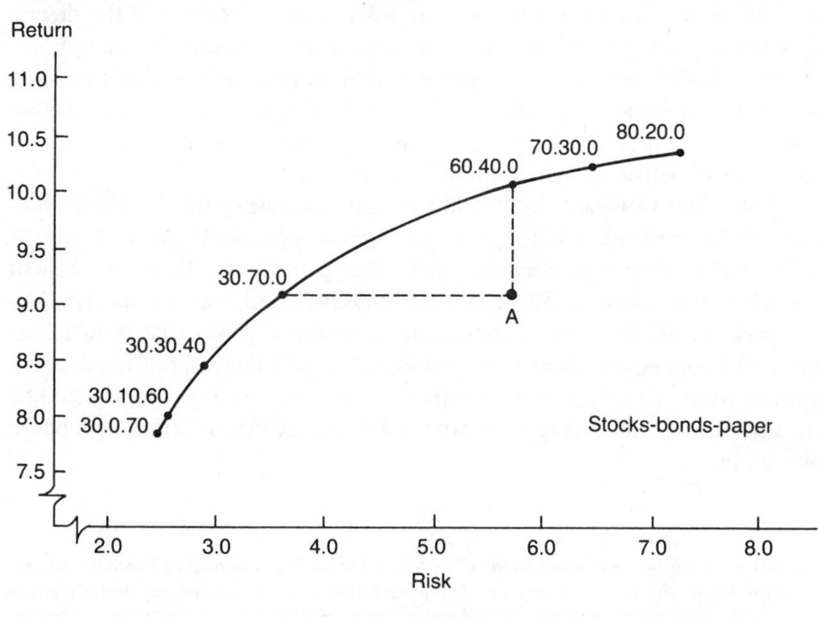

Illini Trust Company

In the late 1960s, the Illini Trust Company had begun exploring the possible application of modern portfolio theory to various aspects of the bank's investment decision process. The first several years were spent developing data that might be used for this purpose. In 1973 management, under Rodrick Grange, director of research, began running paper portfolios in order to assess the use of the theory. Based on the success of these programs, management had already introduced procedures for security selection and portfolio composition into normal operating practices of the investment operation. Management was now considering whether or not to formalize procedures for repositioning the asset mix of the portfolio to take advantage of perceived market-timing opportunities.

The Illini Trust Company, located in Chicago, was one of the 50 largest commercial banks in the United States. The bank's trust department managed over $4 billion in employee benefit, personal, and other trust funds. Employee benefit plans, which now amounted to $2.4 billion in funds managed, were the most rapidly growing part of this business. Unlike many competitor banks that were losing pension fund business, the Illini Trust had experienced a doubling of funds under management from this source in the last four years. A part of this success could be directly attributed to the management style the bank had evolved from its modern portfolio studies.

The impetus for these studies had been the close connections between members of the trust department and faculty at the University of Chicago. A number of the computer programs and many of the initial ideas had come from this source. As technical in-house competency grew, Mr. Grange found that the more practical ideas for using theory as a basis for making money came from the experienced money managers on the bank's staff.

The process had started with individual assessments of the return and risk prospects of 410 common stock securities regularly followed by the bank's 14 security analysts. The analyst first forecast the dividends for a stock over the long run using various procedures set forth by the bank. An internal rate-of-return program was then used to solve for the rate that would equate the forecasted dividend stream to the stock's current market price. These total-return estimates were updated monthly, or more frequently if market conditions changed significantly. An analyst had to present the logic underlying his analysis to a review committee at least once a year or whenever a significant interim change was proposed. Presentations were made on a rolling basis so that about one industry and ten securities were considered each week throughout the year.

Initially, the stock's market beta, as determined by regressing monthly total-return data for the most recent 60 months (updated quarterly) against comparable returns for the Standard & Poor's 500 Index, was used as the measure of risk. The equation used was

$$R_i - R_f = \alpha_i + \beta_i (R_m - R_f)$$

where:

R_i = Monthly total return for security i.
R_f = Monthly *ex post* risk-free rate of return as measured by 90-day Treasury bills.
R_m = Monthly total rate of return for the Standard & Poor's 500 Index.
β_i = Measure of relative volatility.
α_i = A constant with an expected value of zero.

The foregoing market-beta measurement of risk proved too unstable, however. The bank consequently developed a multivariate program that forecasted overall security risk (with output measures similar in magnitude to the market beta) on the basis of forecasts of firm fundamental characteristics such as interest coverage, earnings-per-share instability, rate of return on equity, debt-to-net worth ratios, and the like. Despite changing firm characteristics, these estimates proved more stable and seemed to be more useful than the market-beta risk measure. The analyst also had available a time series of quarterly market betas from 1970 forward to use as perspective. On the basis of these data, the analyst decided on the risk measurement for the security that seemed most representative of its risk characteristics. These judgments were also presented to the review committee at the time of the annual review.

Given the measures of the risk and return for individual securities at any point in time, an array could be developed for all 410 securities along the twin dimensions of estimated return and risk. A least squares regression line was then fit to these data to develop an "estimated security market line" (ESML). This program was also used to develop a "forecasted alpha" for each security. The forecasted alpha represented the vertical distance between the plot for an individual security and the point on the ESML for the same level of "beta" risk. Securities with plots above the ESML had positive alphas, indicating the potential for favorable excess return, whereas those below the line had negative alphas. The security alphas and betas became the input data for the portfolio-composition process.

The task of the portfolio manager at Illini was different from that at most other competitors. The portfolio manager worked out with the client certain target portfolio objectives and a discretionary range within which the objectives might be achieved. The objectives were specified in terms of target averages for the portfolio over a four-year-forward period. The statements of objectives included the desired mix of debt and equity securities in the portfolio, the portfolio beta, the target alpha for the equity portfolio, the maximum variability for the total portfolio returns (stated as a standard deviation), the approximate number of securities in the equity portfolio, and any special constraints (e.g., no tobacco stocks) of importance to the client. These statements were worked out in such a way that they seemed collectively attainable.

Often the statements allowed for some discretion on the part of the portfolio manager to reposition the portfolio to capitalize on the short-run state of the market. For the most part, these changes were small. The most important exception was the target asset mix (debt/equity) for the portfolio. A client might, for example, specify a target equity commitment of 50 percent of the portfolio, but allow the portfolio manager to change this position at his discretion between 30 and 70 percent.

The portfolio manager was assisted in the process of composing a portfolio by an optimizing model. The existing portfolio, the client specifications and constraints, and the portfolio manager's judgment as to asset mix were the inputs. The optimizer then suggested a portfolio that would best meet the client's objectives. The portfolio manager had some opportunity to modify the proposed portfolio provided constraints were not violated.

A senior policy committee, meeting monthly, suggested appropriate target debt/equity mixes. Currently, these mixes were specified on a scale of 0 to 100 percent. The portfolio manager could then calibrate where, within the asset-mix range for a specific client, the current mix should be. For example, if the range was 30 to 70 percent for a client, and the suggested equity position was 60 percent according to the policy committee, the appropriate mix position would be 54 percent (60 percent of the range of 40 percent equals 24 percent, plus the base of 30 percent equals 54 percent). A portfolio manager was not bound to accept the suggestion of the senior policy committee and often did not.

Both the senior policy committee and the portfolio managers had access to considerable economic and market information to help them reach these decisions. The decisions were nevertheless subjectively derived.

In mid-1978, a more formal look at the value added by the market timing of asset-mix positions took place. Mr. Grange first studied the discretionary asset-mix limits of a number of key accounts and concluded that an account with a target average equity position of 60 percent was representative of the universe. Typically, the account manager had the discretion of changing this position between 40 and 80 percent, depending on the market outlook. Mr. Grange consequently decided to focus on an account with these discretionary limits.

The study had to be limited to the five-year period 1973 to 1977 because data prior to that time were insufficient to test the effects of recorded decisions. The study was subsequently extended to cover the first half of 1978 as that information became available.

Although the policy committee had suggested target policies monthly, and portfolio managers could and did change the asset mix of individual accounts more frequently, Mr. Grange decided to focus on decisions at the beginning of each quarter. In his simulation analysis, he assumed that portfolios would be recomposed to the desired mix at the outset of each quarter. No intervening changes were made.

Mr. Grange first sought to establish a basis for eliminating all effects except the asset-mix market-timing ones and to establish a standard for comparisons. To do this, he decided that the assets should be invested either in a corporate bond index or in a common stock index (S&P 500). The total-return information for each of these indices was derived from the Ibbotson and Sinquefield study.[1] In this manner, he would eliminate the effects of security selection and other management inputs.

The standard was developed by assuming that the portfolios would be maintained at the target debt/equity mix of 40/60 at the time of quarterly recomposition. Transaction costs of .25 percent for bond and .50 percent for equity transactions were assumed necessary to achieve recomposition. No management fees were assessed.

The inputs and the results of this simulation are shown in Exhibit 1. Certain statistics are summarized in Exhibit 2.

Unfortunately, the study period chosen was an unusual one. Corporate bonds had realized a substantially higher total return than had common stocks, reflecting an inverted risk/return environment. Therefore, Mr. Grange also looked at the results from the beginning of the fourth quarter of 1974 to see what might happen under more typical *ex post* circumstances. These data are also shown in Exhibit 2.

Mr. Grange next simulated the performance of a portfolio, had it followed the asset-mix recommendations from the senior policy committee. Five of the bank's six current portfolio managers had been employed throughout the period. From a representative portfolio managed by each of these five individuals, Mr. Grange determined the actual opening asset-mix positions for each quarter and used these data as inputs for other runs of the simulation model. Again using total-return data

---

[1]R. G. Ibbotson and R. A. Sinquefield, *Stocks, Bonds, Bills and Inflation: The Past (1926–1976) and the Future (1977–2000),* (Charlottesville, Va.: The Financial Analysts Research Foundation, 1977).

for corporate bond and stock indices, Mr. Grange determined the consequences of following these positions (after transaction costs). The results of these analyses are shown in Exhibit 3.

On the basis of this evidence, Mr. Grange concluded that only one manager (C) had demonstrated that value had been added as a result of actual historic market-timing decisions of the asset mix. When this report was presented to the individuals involved, they were extremely critical of the methodology involved for four basic reasons: (1) The period covered was highly unusual and not representative of the normal conditions in which these decisions had to be made; (2) the asset-mix question could not be examined apart from knowledge of the detailed characteristics of the portfolio (knowledge of the makeup of the debt and equity subportfolios); (3) as proof of this point, they noted that the actual portfolio performance over this period tended to be better than the simulated performance (see results reported at the bottom of Exhibit 3); and (4) the model failed to recognize changes made within a quarter—changes that were considered important.

Some of these criticisms, Mr. Grange recognized, could be valid. The work necessary to correct his analysis for the issues raised would be considerable, however. He suspected that the reaction was more to the implied criticism involved in the findings than to the methodology. In any case, his thinking was already following a different tack.

On the basis of returns estimated for individual securities in the bank's universe at any point in time, Mr. Grange's staff had computed an expected rate of return for the S&P 500 Index. These estimates had been prepared from 1973 forward. Each estimate of return from the equity markets had then been compared with the prevailing quoted yield to maturity for AA Utility Bonds to determine a risk premium available from long-term stock ownership (as shown in Exhibit 4). The calculated risk premium had then been adjusted (for somewhat arbitrary reasons) by adding 20 basis points when interest rates were expected to fall over the next six months and by subtracting 20 basis points when they were expected to rise.

Mr. Grange had been using these adjusted risk-premium data to determine an appropriate asset-mix strategy. Whenever the adjusted risk premium was less than 2.5 percent, Mr. Grange believed that equity commitments should be at a minimum (represented by 0 percent in the last column in Exhibit 4). Whenever the risk premium was greater than 6.5 percent, the maximum equity commitment seemed appropriate. For a risk premium (X) between these extremes, a position equal to (X − 2.5 percent) ÷ 4.0 percent was recommended. Using this approach, target equity positions had been determined for each quarter in the study period, as recorded in Exhibit 4.

Mr. Grange had applied these decisions to simulate portfolio results using the format already discussed. These results are reported in Exhibit 5. Mr. Grange was very pleased with these findings, but when he showed the findings to a portfolio manager with whom he was particularly friendly, the reaction was not what he expected. He heard, "You were just lucky!" and, "These results may be okay for your indices, but our portfolio results are designed to be better than the market; will these conclusions fit our circumstances?"

Mr. Grange had been running a simulated equity portfolio since 1973. As inputs, he used about 15 percent of the stocks in the bank's universe with the highest alphas. The model was designed to produce a portfolio each quarter of 50 stocks with the highest estimated portfolio alpha subject to constraint on total estimated portfolio volatility. The *ex post* results of the simulated portfolios were extremely good, and this result had led the bank to institute similar procedures for composing actual equity portfolios beginning in 1975. Mr. Grange thought the output from these studies might represent the kind of performance that could be expected from managed equity portfolios in the future. Similarly, the bank had run a pooled fixed-income fund, the results of which might represent actual results for the bond part of the portfolio.

The returns for these "representative" bond and equity portfolios, as shown in Exhibit 6, reflect the transaction costs necessary to achieve them. This exhibit also shows the results that would have been achieved had a stable asset-mix strategy of 40/60 debt/equity been used. This new simulation followed methods already outlined. Mr. Grange then resimulated performance following his own asset-mix strategy, and these results are shown in Exhibit 7.

With these data at hand, Mr. Grange turned to preparing a report for the senior policy committee outlining his recommendations as to whether or not the bank should continue to time market cycles through asset-mix changes, and if so, how. The subject had already proved to be unexpectedly controversial, and he wanted to be sure his ducks were lined up in advance.

EXHIBIT 1
Results of Simulation of a Stable 40/60 Debt/Equity Asset Mix

Year and Quarter	Target Opening Equity Position	Rate of Return Quality Corp. Bond Portfolio	Rate of Return S&P 500 Index	Rate of Return Balanced Portfolio	Cumulative Value of $1 Invested in		
					Quality Bond Index	S&P 500 Index	Balanced Portfolio
1973-1	60%	0.14%	−4.89%	−2.90%	1.0014	.9511	.9710
2	60	−0.34	−5.77	−3.61	.9980	.8962	.9360
3	60	2.14	4.81	3.74	1.0194	.9393	.9710
4	60	−0.78	−9.16	−5.82	1.0114	.8533	.9144
1974-1	60	−3.50	−2.82	−3.09	.9760	.8292	.8862
2	60	−5.18	3.18	−0.18	.9254	.8556	.8846
3	60	−3.08	−32.96	−21.06	.8969	.5736	.6983
4	60	9.30	9.38	9.35	.9804	.6274	.7635
1975-1	60	4.75	22.94	15.63	1.0269	.7713	.8829
2	60	3.59	15.37	10.64	1.0638	.8899	.9768
3	60	−3.28	−10.95	−7.90	1.0289	.7924	.8997
4	60	9.22	8.65	8.87	1.1238	.8610	.9794
1976-1	60	4.21	14.97	10.65	1.1711	.9899	1.0838
2	60	0.30	2.48	1.60	1.1746	1.0144	1.1011
3	60	5.57	1.92	3.37	1.2400	1.0339	1.1382
4	60	7.52	3.14	4.88	1.3333	1.0613	1.1938
1977-1	60	−2.31	−7.44	−5.40	1.3025	.9870	1.1293
2	60	3.86	3.32	3.54	1.3527	1.0198	1.1693
3	60	1.09	−2.82	−1.26	1.3675	.9918	1.1545
4	60	−0.82	−0.13	−0.41	1.3563	.9897	1.1498
1978-1	60	−4.12	−5.00	−4.65	1.3004	.9402	1.0963
2	60	−0.40	8.40	4.90	1.2952	1.0192	1.1500

EXHIBIT 2
Summary Statistics for Stable Asset-Mix Simulation

	Corporate Bond Index	Standard & Poor's 500 Stock Index	Stable 40/60% Asset-Mix Simulation
Jan. 1973 to June 1978			
Mean return (quarterly)	1.18%	0.09%	0.64%
Standard deviation	.0418	.1213	.0815
Oct. 1974 to June 1978			
Mean	2.48%	3.91%	3.38%
Standard deviation	.0423	.0878	.0652

Note: Mean computed using log (1 + R_i) as quarterly inputs. Results are equivalent to the average quarterly compound rate of return, and are stated as percentages. Standard deviations were computed from these data, and are stated in their original log format.

EXHIBIT 3
Summary Statistics from Actively Managed Asset-Mix Portfolios (*January 1973 to June 1978*)

	Average Opening Equity Position	Mean	Standard Deviation
Simulated Results			
Senior policy committee	58.4%	0.67%	.0832
Portfolio managers			
A	61.2	0.65	.0821
B	54.6	−2.36	.0942
C	60.2	1.37	.0798
D	58.1	−0.30	.1102
E	55.7	0.58	.0921
Actual Portfolio Results			
Portfolio managers			
A	61.2%	1.37%	.0843
B	54.6	−3.07	.0874
C	60.2	4.61	.0842
D	58.1	1.01	.1090
E	55.7	0.60	.0907

EXHIBIT 4
Determination of Risk Premiums and Target Equity Commitments (*January 1973 to July 1978*)

(1) Year and Quarter	(2) Expected Equity Return S&P 500 Index	(3) AA-Bond Interest Rate		(2) − (3) Risk Premium Equity	Adjusted Risk Premium	Equity Target
1973-1	9.75%	7.43%	R	2.32%	2.12%	0%
2	10.13	7.53	R	2.60	2.40	0
3	10.47	7.59	R	2.88	2.68	5
4	10.65	7.96	R	2.69	2.49	0
1974-1	11.03	7.91	R	3.12	2.92	11
2	11.47	8.13	R	3.34	3.14	16
3	11.72	8.54	R	3.18	2.92	11
4	14.54	9.08	S	5.46	5.46	74
1975-1	15.44	9.01	F	6.43	6.63	100
2	13.94	8.88	F	5.06	5.26	69
3	13.30	8.80	F	4.50	4.70	55
4	14.23	8.96	F	5.27	5.47	74
1976-1	14.06	8.80	F	5.26	5.46	74
2	13.47	8.34	F	5.13	5.23	68
3	13.60	8.52	S	5.08	5.08	65
4	13.73	8.09	F	5.64	5.84	84
1977-1	13.86	7.94	F	5.92	6.12	91
2	14.32	8.00	S	6.32	6.32	96
3	14.48	7.96	S	6.52	6.52	100
4	14.79	7.90	R	6.89	6.69	100
1978-1	15.05	8.30	R	6.75	6.55	100
2	15.69	8.73	R	6.96	6.76	100
3	15.26	8.93	R	6.33	6.13	91

S = Stable interest rates expected.

R = Rising interest rates expected.

F = Falling interest rates expected.

EXHIBIT 5
Simulated Portfolio Results Using Mr. Grange's Asset-Mix Strategy (*January 1973–June 1978*)

Year and Quarter	Opening Equity Position	Simulated Rate of Return on Portfolio	Cumulative Value of $1 Invested
1973-1	40.0%	−1.88%	.9812
2	40.0	−2.54	.9563
3	42.0	3.24	.9873
4	40.0	−4.18	.9461
1974-1	44.4	−3.23	.9155
2	46.4	−1.31	.9034
3	44.4	−16.56	.7534
4	69.6	9.30	.8239
1975-1	80.0	19.17	.9818
2	67.6	11.49	1.0947
3	62.0	−8.10	1.0060
4	69.6	8.82	1.0947
1976-1	69.6	11.66	1.2224
2	67.2	1.75	1.2438
3	66.0	3.10	1.2823
4	73.6	4.27	1.3371
1977-1	76.4	−6.25	1.2535
2	78.4	3.42	1.2964
3	80.0	−2.04	1.2699
4	80.0	−0.28	1.2664
1978-1	80.0	−4.83	1.2052
2	80.0	6.60	1.2848

Summary Data

Jan. 1973 to June 1978		*Oct. 1974 to June 1978*	
Mean	1.14%	Mean	3.62%
Standard deviation	.0779	Standard deviation	.0723

EXHIBIT 6
Simulation of Stable Asset-Mix Results Using Company Return Estimates

Year and Quarter	Total Rate of Return Fixed-Income Pooled Trust	Total Rate of Return Simulated Equity Portfolio	Rate of Return on Simulated Stable 40/60% Asset-Mix Portfolio	Cumulative Value of $1 Invested		
				Bond Fund	Equity Fund	Balanced Fund
1973-1	0.40%	−0.11%	0.09%	1.0040	.9989	1.0009
2	0.53	−1.18	−0.50	1.0093	.9871	.9964
3	1.29	12.26	7.84	1.0223	1.1081	1.0745
4	1.23	−4.13	−2.00	1.0349	1.0624	1.0536
1974-1	−1.64	1.02	−0.04	1.0179	1.0732	1.0531
2	−3.02	6.24	2.53	.9872	1.1402	1.0797
3	−1.60	−25.07	−15.75	.9714	.8543	.9096
4	6.30	15.18	11.58	1.0326	.9840	1.1049
1975-1	4.35	50.13	31.62	1.0775	1.4773	1.3358
2	3.30	24.28	15.82	1.1131	1.8360	1.5470
3	−0.96	−9.73	−6.25	1.1024	1.6574	1.4504
4	7.31	13.49	10.97	1.1830	1.8809	1.6094
1976-1	4.75	22.20	15.15	1.2392	2.2985	1.8533
2	2.41	4.03	3.37	1.2690	2.3911	1.9157
3	0.03	6.36	3.81	1.2694	2.5432	1.9887
4	6.47	9.01	7.96	1.3515	2.7723	2.1470
1977-1	−1.20	−1.34	−1.29	1.3353	2.7352	2.1192
2	3.62	7.21	5.75	1.3862	2.9324	2.2410
3	1.51	2.80	2.27	1.4046	3.0145	2.2919
4	−0.67	3.05	1.61	1.3951	3.1065	2.3289
1978-1	−1.59	−3.03	−2.46	1.3730	3.0123	2.2716
2	−0.40	14.59	8.56	1.3675	3.4518	2.4659
Summary Totals Jan. 1973 to June 1978						
Mean	1.43%	5.79%	4.18%			
Standard deviation	.0290	.1328	.0881			
Oct. 1974 to June 1978						
Mean	2.31%	9.76%	6.88%			
Standard deviation	.0299	.1219	.0834			

EXHIBIT 7
Simulation of Cyclical Timing of Debt/Equity Asset Mix Using Company Return Data (*January 1973–June 1978*)

Year and Quarter	Target Opening Equity Position	Rate of Return on Simulated Portfolio	Cumulative Value of $1 Invested
1973-1	40.0%	0.20%	1.0020
2	40.0	−0.17	1.0020
3	42.0	5.86	1.0589
4	40.0	−0.91	1.0492
1974-1	44.4	−0.46	1.0444
2	46.4	1.26	1.0576
3	44.4	−12.23	0.9282
4	69.6	12.40	1.0433
1975-1	80.0	40.92	1.4703
2	67.6	16.39	1.7113
3	62.0	−6.47	1.6005
4	69.6	11.60	1.7862
1976-1	69.6	16.85	2.0872
2	67.2	3.49	2.1600
3	66.0	4.16	2.2499
4	73.6	8.32	2.4371
1977-1	76.4	−1.15	2.4091
2	78.4	6.43	2.5640
3	80.0	2.54	2.6291
4	80.0	2.23	2.6877
1978-1	80.0	−2.74	2.6141
2	80.0	11.59	2.9170

Summary Data

Jan. 1973 to June 1978		*Oct. 1974 to June 1978*	
Mean	4.99%	Mean	7.93%
Standard deviation	.0954	Standard deviation	.0982

T. David Brown and Sons

Bob Whitney, the new options strategist for the investment management firm of T. David Brown and Sons, gazed out his office window, overlooking the inner harbor in Baltimore, and thought about the job he had been asked to accomplish. T. David Brown managed a family of mutual funds and accounts for corporate pension plans. Bob had been asked by senior management to design and implement several specific option-related investment strategies that would appeal to pension plan sponsors in today's particularly turbulent equity markets. Bob knew he would not be able to sacrifice much return potential in his product development plans.

Bob noted that employee benefit plan sponsors typically traded well-diversified portfolios of stocks that tracked the major indexes quite well. Brown's clients often diversified across mutual funds, and pension fund clients in particular tended to invest in multi-managed portfolios that tracked the market closely. In fact, plan sponsors had popularized the idea of "indexing" early in the 1970s when some sponsors believed that it was difficult to outperform the market and they did not want to increase their risk exposure in excess of the market through active management. Bob's objective, taking the current market environment into account, was to design strategies to add value and reduce the risk of these portfolios.

The past months had seen increasing short-term volatility in the stock market and Bob sensed that a further decline was likely. In Bob's opinion, the Dow had peaked at 1850 and he had been surprised to see it approach 2000 in early September 1986. He noted that there had been major corrections of 3 to 5 percent in June,

This material was prepared by Michael A. Berry, Assistant Professor of Business Administration of the Colgate Darden Graduate School of Business Administration of the University of Virginia.

July, and September; he did not expect to see the stock market return to these dizzying heights for some time.

Portfolio Insurance

Beginning in 1984 the major "sell-side" institutions on Wall Street had popularized a number of strategies using the options and futures markets to protect the value of an equity or bond portfolio. These strategies, collectively known as portfolio insurance, had been implemented in various ways. (See Exhibit 1 for a comprehensive description of these strategies.) For instance, a plan sponsor might buy an index put against a portfolio, buy puts on individual stocks, buy index calls and money market securities, buy individual calls and money market securities, sell stock index futures to create a synthetic put, or sell the individual stocks, and "go to cash."

In the past, an equity portfolio manager sensing a market decline in the making could only increase cash by selling stocks or shift from more aggressive to more defensive securities. A plan sponsor could draw capital from equity managers and shift the funds to money market or similar funds or move funds from more aggressive to more defensive managers. For sponsors, meeting infrequently, timing changes was more difficult. The new synthetic instruments offered both managers and sponsors the opportunity to move more capital, often more expeditiously and usually with lower transactions' costs.

All these new strategies seemed to have different advantages and disadvantages in Bob's view. For instance, portfolio insurance, like any other insurance policy, was not free. If the plan trustees were not uncomfortable with the level of volatility in the market, they might consider the cost of the insurance too great for the decrease in expected return from the premium. Most employee benefit plans had either used or considered the "buy-write" strategy or the covered-call "overwrite" for modification of the risk/return profile on their plan. In addition, numerous mutual funds had incorporated these strategies into their product lines. Exhibit 2 provides an example of the performance of some of these funds.

Finally, Bob turned to the documentation that Nick Hanson at Salomon Brothers had produced. He wanted to understand the portfolio insurance phenomenon better, and Nick's work seemed to provide a good summary of an application (shown in Exhibit 1).

Plan Sponsors

Throughout the 1980s pension plan sponsors had discovered and utilized equity options to an extent not before contemplated. From its modest beginnings with options listed on 25 stocks in 1973, the CBOE had innovated a number of products including calls and puts on individual equities and indexes. In particular, the option on the S&P 100 Index (the famous OEX) had been extremely successful and plan sponsors were becoming more aware of its potential. Historically over 40 percent of large (over $1 billion) employee benefit plans used equity options both to control risk and create "extra" return. This meant that options were not strangers to these plan sponsors. Index options, however, were a more recent innovation and Bob wondered how to proceed with his product development ideas.

He was scheduled to present a strategy to the plan sponsors for the Monsanto Employee Benefit Fund in mid-October. This client had been invested in several of the Brown mutual funds and performance had been hurt in the market declines in June, July, and September. This sponsor wanted to explore some approaches to the choppy markets that had hurt its investment results.

Employee Benefit Plans' Risk Exposure

Many pension plans had grown to enormous size, with the median plan in the $500 million range. However, a large number of plans had grown to several billion dollars in assets by the mid-1980s. This necessarily meant the insurance programs would have to cope with a need for liquidity in the implementation of their plans. On the other hand, most funds were quite well diversified with exposure in stocks, fixed-income instruments, real estate, and the money market. With this much size and diversification, active management was difficult and plan sponsors were often faced with the task of diversifying across money managers and styles rather than across the individual financial instruments themselves. In short, many plans found themselves approaching "closet indexed"—i.e., closely tracking the market in composite.

In the 1980s some sponsors began to experiment with overwrite (selling calls against stocks owned) and buy/write programs. These programs promised to reduce downside risk exposure for a part of the portfolio at modest sacrifice of upside potential. Since sponsors tend to be risk conscious in exercising their fiduciary responsibilities, limiting downside risk was attractive to them during periods of adverse equity market movements.

These strategies had been sold to the sponsors as "free lunches." The option-related programs promised to increase average returns over a typical market cycle while reducing downside risk. Unfortunately, the equity markets of the mid-1980s were very strong and the strategies did not work as well as had been hoped. Reaction to the tests was therefore mixed and only a small part of equity portfolios were protected through the option strategies.

In the 1980s both the fixed-income and equity markets were strong. By the mid-1980s most pension funds had become significantly overfunded relative to actuarial requirements. Pension funding costs, relative to payrolls, were declining sharply. After a trying decade of rising pension costs and inadequate funding during the 1970s, pension sponsors were increasingly conscious of protecting the sound funding levels now achieved.

As the equity market continued to rise sharply in early 1986, sponsors increasingly questioned whether a significant market correction might be forthcoming. From June to September, daily and weekly market volatility increased and there were several sharp, although short-lived, market breaks that added to this concern.

In the previous decade, fixed-income securities—particularly those with long maturities—had become substantially more volatile and the covariance between long-term fixed-income and equity returns had increased. Fixed-income alternatives no longer appeared to be an attractive way of reducing exposure to an adverse equity market. The growing and active promotion of portfolio insurance as an alternative way of reducing potential market exposure found an increasingly receptive audience among the more nervous plan sponsors. Bob estimated that the market for portfolio insurance in one form or another was $75 billion and was growing rapidly.

Finally, the overriding impetus for a new view on portfolio insurance had come from tremendous volatility in the markets over the past year. From September 1985 to the present, Dow had increased by more than 500 points—about 33 percent. During that period there had been eight major declines followed by recoveries. Clearly, short-term volatility in the equity markets had increased dramatically and index options, priced on volatility, might be the best vehicles to offset these impacts for Brown's client base. Bob wanted to devise both an active and a passive investment strategy in this regard.

Index Options

The market for index options had increased in volume by more than 500 percent in 1984 alone. The growing liquidity of the index option market, particularly in the near-term contracts, had encouraged more plan sponsors to consider these instruments for use in the insurance plans. In addition to the innovation of broad market options, numerous other industry and sector option products had been introduced in 1984 and 1985. In September of 1986 it was clear that institutional investors were intrigued by these products.

Several characteristics differentiated stock index options from their equity counterparts. First, index options were settled in cash. Active investors liked this feature because it reduced the turnover of traditional portfolios when the stock was called away. Some believed that it would increase the dividend income. The cash settlement was equal to the difference between the option's strike price and the closing price of the index. Second, Bob believed that the index option was priced somewhat differently than the individual equity option. He was familiar with the Black Scholes option pricing model (OPM), which derived prices based on estimates of volatility and interest rates. Bob believed that market expectations were a pricing determinant in the case of index options. In fact he resolved to determine if a relationship existed between the index futures and the index options. He wondered if perhaps the index options were somehow priced "off" the index futures.

On the other hand, stock index futures and stock index options appeared to offer distinct advantages. By buying index puts, a sponsor knew in advance the cost of the insurance and the benefits that could develop. By selling stock index futures (creating a synthetic put), the seller could not determine the actual cost in advance and had to accept the pricing risk of the futures contract. This fact alone seemed to weigh heavily in favor of the index options in these markets. Bob did realize, however, that the futures contract allowed creation of both a strike price and an expiration date if one was willing to accept its pricing risk. Index options had to be rolled forward in this regard.

Index options seemed to have several other significant advantages but Bob was not sure how to quantify them. Instant diversification was one advantage that was difficult to achieve with a "buy/write" strategy. Index options seemed to offer higher option premiums than their equity counterparts written on the same portfolio. Finally, index options seemed to offer improved performance—especially in volatile markets. Bob did not believe that this fact had been appreciated by corporate sponsors currently involved in buy-and-write programs.

Bob Whitney

Bob returned to his Stockfacts terminal. He noticed that the market had become more volatile in the past few weeks. This had been variously attributed to interest-rate concerns and the impact of institutional buy-and-sell programs on the equity markets. He noted that a record two-million-plus options had traded in the past week with the popular OEX accounting for almost 1.5 million contracts. Puts had soared in price, reflecting expectations of the future course of the stock market. The OEX September 235 had risen to 15½ from 2¾. The put/call ratio at 1.04 seemed to indicate minimal downside risk in the short term. Bob didn't feel comfortable with an optimistic forecast of the market, given these facts. He was certain that the increased market volatility had turned the psychology of the market sour.

Given the performance of the market in the past quarter and the accompanying performance of the Monsanto portfolio, Bob began to sort out his thoughts on a strategy to manage risk and return more effectively, using stock or stock index options. Exhibit 3 shows recent weekly closing prices for the two indexes and Exhibit 4 reveals the performance and tracking characteristics of the Monsanto portfolio. Bob had obtained these data from Salomon Brothers Stockfacts system. Now was the time to put it to use.

Bob's first objective was to develop a systematic investment program that might meet Monsanto's concern about untoward volatility in their equity account.

EXHIBIT 1
Portfolio Insurance

Introduction

In recent years there has been increasing interest in the concept of portfolio insurance, brought about by two major developments in the investment community. The first was the introduction of dynamic portfolio insurance, a methodology based on the theory that

Source: Salomon Brothers report, by H. Nicholas Hanson, Ph.D. Vice President, Futures and Options Research, Stock Research Department, 1984.

EXHIBIT 1 ***(continued)***

stock options can be replicated with a continuously changing mix of stock and cash.[1] The second major development was the introduction last year of options on stock indexes and stock index futures. The availability of exchange-traded index puts and calls offers a simpler and perhaps more efficient way of achieving the desired pattern of portfolio returns.

In this paper, we present our findings that, from the middle of 1970 (near a market bottom) until the end of 1983, an S&P 500 Index fund protected by three-month index put options would have actually outperformed the S&P 500.

The Put Option—An Insurance Policy

Consider an investor who buys 100 shares of a stock at a price of $50 and simultaneously purchases a put option on that stock with a strike price of $50. The buyer of the put has the right to "put" the stock to the seller for $50 any time until its expiration.[2] If the stock increases in value, he will not exercise the put and thus will be entitled to the entire capital gain of the stock (less the price he paid for the put). Should the stock decrease below $50, he can exercise his option and receive $50 per share for the stock. The pattern of returns at expiration of the put is shown in Figure 1.

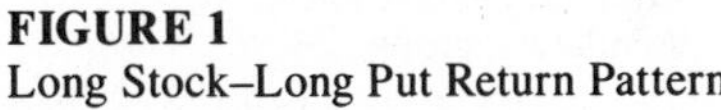

FIGURE 1
Long Stock–Long Put Return Pattern

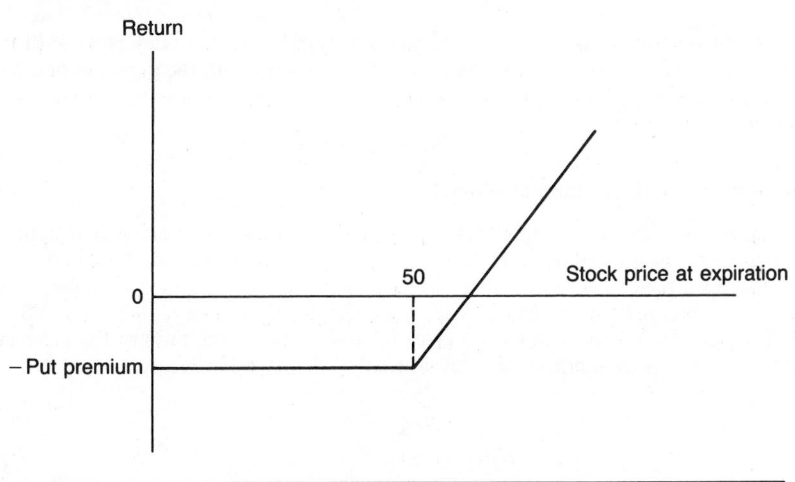

For every stock price above $50 the stock-put position will underperform the stock by the put premium. For stock prices below $50, the investor's loss will be limited to the cost of the put. The investor has thus insured his stock position against a price decline in

[1]M. Rubinstein and H. E. Leland, "Replicating Options with Positions in Stock and Cash," *Financial Analysts Journal,* July/August 1981.

[2]An option contract that allows its holder to exercise before expiration is termed an "American" option. In contrast, a "European" option may not be exercised before expiration. Therefore, an American option will always be worth at least as much as a European option.

EXHIBIT 1 ***(continued)***

the same way that a homeowner insures his house against loss due to fire. The purchase of an out-of-the-money put—one with a strike price of $45 for example—gives the investor insurance against a decline in stock price below $45. This put will cost less than the put with a $50 strike price in the same way that an insurance policy with a deductible costs less than one with no deductible. The more out-of-the-money the put, the larger the deductible and, therefore, the lower the premium. Thus, the purchase of a put on a stock is functionally the same as the purchase of a casualty insurance policy, and it is often helpful in understanding a put option to think of it as such. This analogy is displayed in Figure 2.

FIGURE 2
The Analogy between an Insurance Policy and a Put Option

Insurance Policy	*Put Option*
Premium	Time premium
Value of asset	Price of stock
Face value	Strike price
Amount of deductible	Stock price less strike price
Duration	Time until expiration
Likelihood of loss	Volatility of stock

The pattern of results shown in Figure 1 is similar to that obtainable with a call option. Thus, we note that the purchase of a stock coupled with the purchase of a put—a "protective put"—is functionally equivalent to the purchase of a money market instrument and a call option.

Option Pricing—The Binomial Model

An investigation of the binomial pricing model[3] provides some valuable insights into option pricing theory and dynamic portfolio insurance programs. The binomial process, as its name suggests, is a process that can have only two outcomes. For example, suppose a stock currently sells for **S,** and its next trade will be either at a higher price, **uS,** or at a lower price, **dS,** where **u** and **d** are price relatives, that is, the ratio of the price at the next trade to the current price. This "event tree" is displayed in Figure 3.

FIGURE 3
Event Tree for Stock

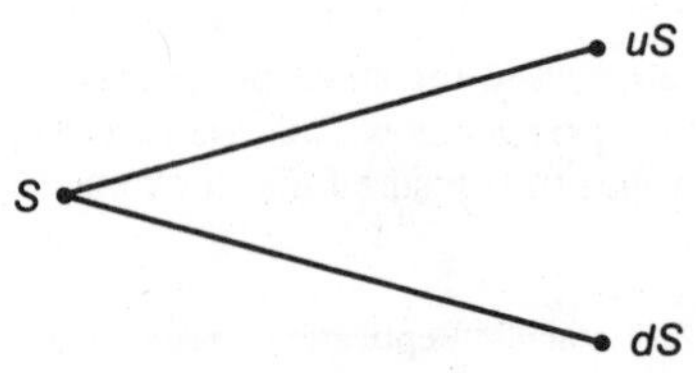

[3] J. C. Cox, S. A. Ross, and M. Rubinstein, "Option Pricing: A Simplified Approach," *Journal of Financial Economics*, September 1979.

EXHIBIT 1 *(continued)*

A call option on the above stock with strike price **E,** which currently sells for price **C,** and which will expire with the next trade of the stock, will have a corresponding event tree, as shown in Figure 4. For mathematical simplicity, we have assumed that stock price **dS** is below the strike price of the call.

FIGURE 4
Event Tree for Call Option

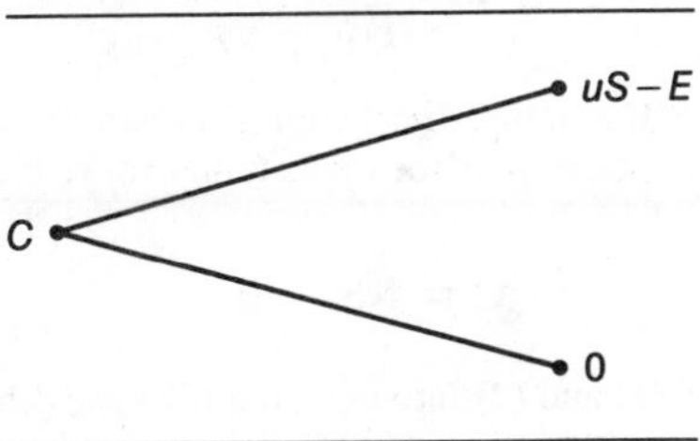

Suppose we now form a portfolio with **N** shares of the above stock and **B** dollars of cash. If **R** is the risk-free rate of interest and **r = (1 + R),** the event tree for this portfolio is shown in Figure 5. We call this portfolio the hedging portfolio.

FIGURE 5
Event Tree for Hedging Portfolio

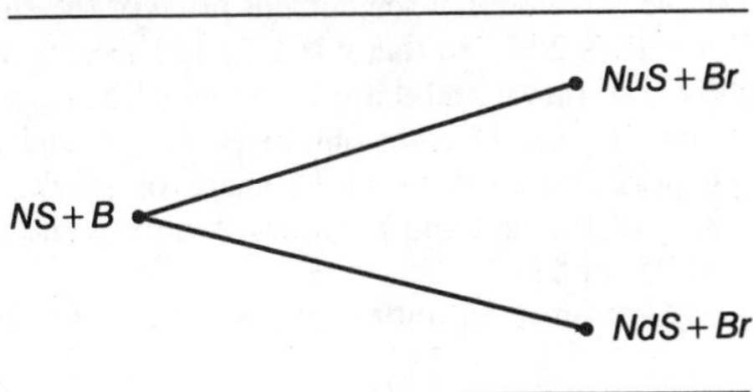

Figure 6 summarizes the values of the hedging portfolio and the call position at each node of the event tree.

FIGURE 6
Values at Event Tree Nodes

	Initial	***Positive Outcome***	***Negative Outcome***
Hedging portfolio	NS + B	NuS + Br	Nds + Br
Call option	C	uS − E	0

The quantities **S, E, r, u,** and **d** are known. We thus have two "free" parameters, **N** and **B.** Therefore, it will always be possible to choose **N** and **B** so that the values of the hedging portfolio and those of the call option will be equal given either outcome:

$$\mathbf{NuS + Br = uS - E}$$
$$\mathbf{NdS + Br = 0.}$$

EXHIBIT 1 ***(continued)***

There are two equations and two unknowns, **N** and **B,** which may be solved to give the following:

$$\mathbf{N} = \frac{\mathbf{uS - E}}{\mathbf{S(u - d)}} \tag{1}$$

$$\mathbf{B} = \frac{\mathbf{-d(uS - E)}}{\mathbf{r(u - d)}} \tag{2}$$

Since the payoffs are the same, the hedging portfolio and the call option must initially have the same value; otherwise the opportunity for riskless arbitrage would exist. Therefore,

$$\mathbf{C = NS + B.} \tag{3}$$

Substituting equations (1) and (2) into equation (3) yields the following:

$$\mathbf{C} = \frac{\mathbf{(r - d)(uS - E)}}{\mathbf{r(u - d)}} \tag{4}$$

Note that the call price depends on the stock price, the strike price, the risk-free rate of interest, and the possible outcomes **u** and **d.** It is, however, independent of the probabilities of these outcomes, and therefore, the call price does not depend on the expected return of the stock.

As a numerical example, assume that the current price of the stock is $60, the strike price is $60, the risk-free rate is 20%, so that **r** is 1.2, and the possible outcomes for the stock price are $75 and $45, so that **u** and **d** are 1.25 and 0.75, respectively. Substituting these values into equations (1) and (2), we obtain **N** = 0.5 and **B** = −18.75. This means that the hedging portfolio consists of ½ share of stock, of which $18.75 is borrowed. The initial value of the hedging portfolio, which is the fair value of the call option, is 0.5 × 60 − 18.75, or $11.25.

If we had two periods left until expiration, the event tree for the stock would be as shown in Figure 7.

The generalization to an event tree of many periods is straightforward. By starting at expiration and working backward through the tree, the fair value of a call with any

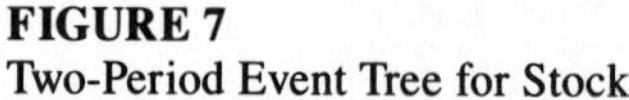

FIGURE 7
Two-Period Event Tree for Stock

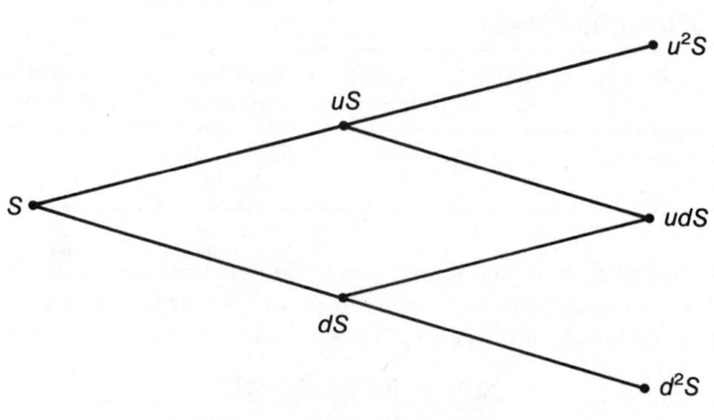

EXHIBIT 1 ***(continued)***

number of periods until expiration can be obtained. This is the binomial option pricing model.

It is instructive to compare equation (3) with the Black-Scholes option pricing formula,[4] which is:

$$\mathbf{C = N(x_1)S - N(x_2)Ee^{-rT}} \tag{5}$$

$$\mathbf{x_1 = \frac{\ln(S/E) + (r + 1/2s^2)T}{s\sqrt{T}}}$$

$$\mathbf{x_2 = x_1 - s\sqrt{T}}$$

where:

$\mathbf{T}$ = Time until expiration of the call.
$\mathbf{s}$ = The standard deviation of the continuously compounded stock price returns.
$\mathbf{r}$ = The continuously compounded risk-free rate.
$\mathbf{N(x)}$ = The cumulative normal density function.

The arithmetic form of each equation is the same. In fact, if we let the number of periods in the binomial model's event tree go to infinity and let the changes in stock price get very small, with the requirement that the continuously compounded stock price returns be normally distributed (stock prices log-normally distributed), the binomial model reduces to the Black-Scholes formula for the case of European options. **Thus, we can interpret the Black-Scholes formula as the instantaneous value of the hedging portfolio.** The first term, $\mathbf{N(x_1)S}$, is the amount of money invested in stock, with the hedge ratio $\mathbf{N(x_1)}$ being the fraction of a share that must be purchased. The second term, $\mathbf{-N(x_2)Ee_{-}^{rT}}$, is the amount invested in the risk-free asset. The negative sign means that a negative amount is invested in the risk-free asset, or in other words, borrowed. In the above example, borrowing was required to replicate a call option with the hedging portfolio. If the number of shares of stock held in the hedging portfolio is continuously adjusted, the replication can be perfect. This is the essence of dynamic portfolio insurance. To insure a portfolio in the absence of purchasing a put option, the hedge ratio must be determined at each node of the event tree, and the portfolio rebalanced accordingly.

Put-Call Parity

A formula relating the price of a European put and a European call may be easily derived. Consider a portfolio that consists of one share of stock XYZ, a short call with strike price **E** on stock XYZ, and a long put with strike price **E** on stock XYZ, with both options expiring in time **T**. Since the short call–long put combination is functionally equivalent to a short position in stock XYZ, the portfolio is riskless, and therefore, must earn the risk-free rate of interest. If **S, C,** and **P** are the current prices of the stock, the call, and the put, respectively, the current value of the portfolio is:

$$\mathbf{V = S + P - C} \tag{6}$$

Assume that at time **T** later the options expire with stock XYZ worth $\mathbf{S' > E}$. The put will expire worthless, and the call will be worth $\mathbf{(S' - E)}$. The value of the portfolio will then be

[4]F. Black and M. Scholes, "The Pricing of Options and Corporate Liabilities," *Journal of Political Economy*, May/June 1973.

EXHIBIT 1 ***(continued)***

$$V' = S' - (S' - E) = E \tag{7}$$

Since the portfolio is riskless

$$V' = Ve^{rT} \tag{8}$$

Substituting equations (6) and (7) into equation (8) and rearranging gives

$$C - P = S - Ee^{-rT} \tag{9}$$

Equation (9) is called the put-call parity equation. Notice that it depends only on the European nature of the options and not on any particular option pricing model. If a pricing model, such as the Black-Scholes model of equation (5), is used to find the fair value of the call, the fair value of the put may then be determined from equation (9). If the stock is expected to go ex-dividend before the options expire, equation (9) can still be used with the present value of the dividend subtracted from the stock price.

Historical Test of Portfolio Insurance

We ran a simulation of a portfolio insurance program using an S&P 500 Index fund protected by three-month at-the-money European index puts from mid-1970 until year-end 1983. It was assumed that the puts were purchased at the beginning of each quarter and held until the end of the quarter, at which time they were exercised if their intrinsic value was positive. Put prices were generated using a dividend-adjusted Black-Scholes model,[5] with perfect knowledge of the next quarter's dividend and annualized standard deviation of the daily price returns assumed at the beginning of the quarter.[6] The annualized standard deviation ranged from 7 percent to 26 percent, as is shown in Figure 8.

FIGURE 8
Volatility of S&P 500 (*quarterly data*)

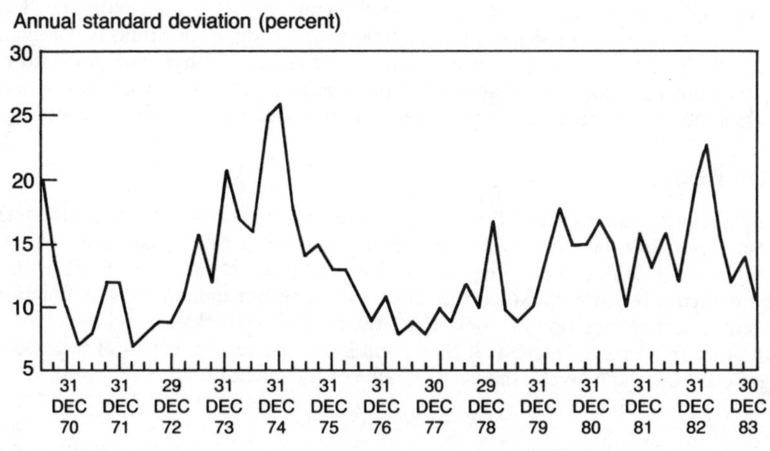

[5]The present value of the quarter's dividend (assumed paid continuously) was subtracted from the index price.

[6]This was done so that the puts would always be fairly priced.

EXHIBIT 1 ***(continued)***

Dividends were reinvested at the end of each quarter. For the risk-free rate, we used the bond-equivalent yield on a three-month Treasury bill at the beginning of the quarter. The results of this simulation are displayed in Figure 9.

The insured index fund outperformed the uninsured index fund by nearly 200 basis points per year on a compound annual basis, resulting in approximately 25 percent more wealth at the end of the 13.5-year period. We believe that this was particularly significant since the overall market was in a larger-than-average uptrend over this time span. Evidently, the ability to avoid the small number of disastrous quarters that did occur during this period made it possible for the insured index fund to outperform the uninsured index fund, even though its downside risk was obviously less, and an average quarterly premium of 2.2 percent was paid for the puts. In Figure 10, a comparison between the insured and uninsured index funds over various calendar-year periods is given.

The simulation was then repeated using the previous quarter's standard deviation as an estimate for the next quarter's standard deviation. As can be seen from Figure 9, the results are substantially the same.

It is interesting to investigate the sensitivity of these results to the prices paid for the puts, especially since listed index puts are American and theoretically would be expected to be more expensive than European puts, *ceteris paribus*. Figure 11 shows the results of repeating the backtest with put prices increased in increments of 5 percent from those shown in Figure 9.

Thus, prices nearly 20 percent higher than those shown in Figure 9 could have been paid for the puts, and the cumulative return of the insured index fund would still have nearly matched that of the uninsured index fund. Over the time period of our simulation, the average risk-free rate, quarterly dividend yield on the S&P 500, and annual standard deviation of the S&P 500 were 7.9 percent, 1.1 percent, and 13.2 percent, respectively. Using these numbers and an S&P 500 price of $100, we obtain theoretical values of 2.45 for a three-month at-the-money American put and 2.20 for a similar European put. Thus, it is not unreasonable to expect that had listed index puts been trading over the entire time period, they might have cost, on average, approximately 10 percent more than those shown in Figure 9. Nevertheless, from Figure 11, we see that the insured index fund would still have outperformed the uninsured index fund by 90 basis points on a compound annual basis.

Dynamic versus Static Insurance

In this section, we compare dynamic portfolio insurance programs with static insurance programs. By static we mean purchasing listed (or over-the-counter) index put options to protect the portfolio. An example of a dynamic insurance "tree" to protect a stock (or portfolio) initially priced at $100 for 13 weeks is shown in Figure 12. The numbers at each "node" of the tree—in the boxes—represent the amount of stock and cash held in the replicating portfolio, and are determined as follows. Using the Black-Scholes formula, the fair value of a European put struck at $100 is determined for the stock price and time until expiration represented by that particular box. The fair value of the put is then added to the stock price to determine the static portfolio value. The hedge ratio gives the number of shares required in the dynamic portfolio. Since both the dynamic and static portfolios must have the same value, the amount of cash to be held is found by subtracting the amount invested in stock (hedge ratio times stock price) from the static portfolio value. For example, assume that the stock is initially at $100 and will pay no dividend over the next 13 weeks. The fair value of a European put struck at $100 using a risk-free rate of zero and an annual standard deviation of 14.42 percent (2 percent per week) and having 13 weeks until expiration is $2.88. The cost of establishing the static portfolio (long one share of stock plus long one put) is $102.88. The hedge ratio is

EXHIBIT 1 *(continued)*

FIGURE 9
S&P 500 Index Fund Insured with Put Options

	S&P 500				Insured Index Fund 1*			Insured Index Fund 2†		
	Quarter-End Price	Qtr. Div.	Quarter Return	Annual Return	Put Price	Quarter Return	Annual Return	Put Price	Quarter Return	Annual Return
1970										
2	72.72	—	—		1.83	—		2.83	—	
3	84.21	0.78	16.9%		1.46	14.0%		2.12	12.5%	
4	92.15	0.79	10.4	29.0%‡	1.11	8.5	23.7%‡	1.65	7.7	21.1%‡
1971										
1	100.31	0.75	9.7		1.53	8.4		1.33	7.7	
2	99.70	0.78	0.2		2.13	−0.7		1.35	−0.5	
3	98.34	0.77	−0.6		2.17	−1.3		2.17	−0.6	
4	102.09	0.77	4.6	14.2	1.33	2.3	8.6	2.34	2.3	9.0
1972										
1	107.20	0.75	5.7		1.59	4.4		1.37	3.4	
2	107.14	0.78	0.7		1.78	−0.7		1.57	−0.5	
3	110.55	0.78	3.9		1.77	2.2		1.77	2.4	
4	118.05	0.84	7.5	19.0	2.22	5.8	12.1	1.76	5.8	11.4
1973										
1	111.52	0.77	−4.9		3.08	−1.2		1.99	−0.8	
2	104.26	0.83	−5.8		1.96	−2.0		2.77	−1.0	
3	108.43	0.83	4.8		4.04	2.9		2.13	2.1	
4	97.55	0.95	−9.2	−14.7	2.81	−2.7	−3.1	3.58	−1.1	−0.9
1974										
1	93.98	0.83	−2.8		2.47	−2.0		2.66	−2.7	
2	86.00	0.89	−7.5		3.90	−1.6		2.39	−1.8	
3	63.54	0.92	−25.0		3.24	−3.3		3.12	−1.7	
4	68.56	0.96	9.4	−26.3	2.28	4.1	−2.9	3.36	4.3	−2.1
1975										
1	83.36	0.90	22.9		2.20	18.9		2.85	17.2	
2	95.19	0.93	15.3		2.60	12.3		2.41	11.5	
3	83.87	0.92	−10.9		1.94	−1.7		2.27	−1.5	
4	90.19	0.93	8.6	37.1	2.19	6.2	39.5	2.19	5.8	36.1
1976										
1	102.77	0.91	15.0		2.10	12.2		2.50	12.2	
2	104.28	1.00	2.4		1.67	0.4		2.08	0.0	
3	105.24	1.01	1.9		2.19	0.3		1.78	−0.1	
4	107.46	1.13	3.2	23.8	1.64	1.1	14.2	2.28	1.5	13.8

EXHIBIT 1 *(continued)*

1977										
1	98.42	1.05	−7.4		1.77	−0.5		1.58	−1.1	
2	100.48	1.17	3.3		1.53	1.5		1.73	1.7	
3	96.53	1.15	−2.8		1.84	−0.4		1.46	−0.6	
4	95.10	1.30	−0.1	−7.2	1.55	−0.5	0.0	1.74	−0.2	−0.2
1978										
1	89.21	1.18	−5.0		2.03	−0.4		1.50	−0.6	
2	95.53	1.28	8.5		1.68	6.1		2.06	6.7	
3	102.54	1.26	8.7		3.11	6.8		1.71	6.4	
4	96.11	1.35	−5.0	6.5	1.47	−1.7	11.0	2.78	−0.3	12.5
1979										
1	101.59	1.31	7.1		1.36	5.5		1.56	4.1	
2	102.91	1.42	2.7		1.63	1.3		1.43	1.1	
3	109.32	1.43	7.6		2.45	5.9		1.61	6.1	
4	107.94	1.54	0.1	18.5	3.00	−0.8	12.3	2.18	−0.1	11.6
1980										
1	102.09	1.46	−4.1		2.10	−1.4		2.68	−0.7	
2	114.24	1.56	13.4		3.03	11.1		3.03	10.5	
3	125.46	1.56	11.2		3.28	8.3		2.80	8.3	
4	135.76	1.58	9.5	32.4	2.60	6.7	26.6	3.11	7.1	27.4
1981										
1	136.00	1.58	1.3		1.61	−0.6		2.88	−0.9	
2	131.25	1.67	−2.3		2.81	0.0		1.37	−0.9	
3	116.18	1.69	−10.2		1.91	−0.8		2.56	0.2	
4	122.55	1.69	6.9	−4.9	3.06	5.2	3.8	2.36	4.6	3.0
1982										
1	111.91	1.67	−7.3		1.79	−1.1		2.64	−0.6	
2	109.61	1.76	−0.5		3.28	−0.0		1.81	−0.8	
3	120.42	1.73	11.4		5.16	8.2		4.22	9.6	
4	140.64	1.71	18.2	21.5	3.92	13.4	21.3	5.85	14.2	23.6
1983										
1	152.96	1.71	10.0		2.91	7.0		4.10	5.6	
2	168.11	1.79	11.1		3.76	9.0		3.11	8.2	
3	166.07	1.79	−0.1		2.45	−1.1		3.74	−0.8	
4	164.93	1.80	0.4	22.5	—	−0.4	14.8	—	−1.1	12.0
Cumulative return				311.0%			414.3%			403.3%
Compound annual return				11.0			12.9			12.7

*Using actual standard deviation for quarter. †Using previous quarter's standard deviation. ‡Six-month return.

EXHIBIT 1 *(continued)*

FIGURE 10
Cumulative Return for Insured and Uninsured Index Funds (*percent*)

Insured S&P 500 Index Fund

Until Year-End	From Year-End												
	1970	1971	1972	1973	1974	1975	1976	1977	1978	1979	1980	1981	1982
1971	8.6												
1972	21.7	12.1											
1973	18.0	8.6	−3.1										
1974	14.5	5.5	−5.9	−2.9									
1975	59.8	47.1	31.3	35.5	39.5								
1976	82.5	68.0	49.9	54.7	59.3	14.2							
1977	82.5	68.0	49.9	54.7	59.3	14.2	0.0						
1978	102.6	86.5	66.4	71.7	76.8	26.8	11.0	11.0					
1979	127.5	109.5	86.8	92.8	98.6	42.4	24.7	24.7	12.3				
1980	188.0	165.2	136.5	144.1	151.4	80.2	57.8	57.8	42.2	26.6			
1981	198.9	175.2	145.5	153.4	161.0	87.1	63.8	63.8	47.6	31.4	3.8		
1982	262.6	233.9	197.8	207.4	216.5	126.9	98.7	98.7	79.0	59.4	25.9	21.3	
1983	316.3	283.3	241.9	252.9	263.4	160.5	128.1	128.1	105.5	83.0	44.5	39.3	14.8

Uninsured S&P 500 Index Fund

Until Year-End	From Year-End												
	1970	1971	1972	1973	1974	1975	1976	1977	1978	1979	1980	1981	1982
1971	14.2												
1972	35.9	19.0											
1973	15.9	1.5	−14.7										
1974	−14.6	−25.2	−37.1	−26.3									
1975	17.1	2.6	−13.8	1.0	37.1								
1976	45.0	27.0	6.7	25.1	69.7	23.8							
1977	34.6	17.8	−1.0	16.1	57.5	14.9	−7.2						
1978	43.3	25.5	5.5	23.6	67.7	22.4	−1.2	6.5					
1979	69.8	48.7	25.0	46.5	98.8	45.0	17.1	26.2	18.5				
1980	124.8	96.9	65.5	94.0	163.2	92.0	55.1	67.1	56.9	32.4			
1981	113.8	87.2	57.3	84.5	150.3	82.6	47.5	58.9	49.2	25.9	−4.9		
1982	159.8	127.5	91.2	124.1	204.1	121.8	79.2	93.1	81.3	53.0	15.5	21.5	
1983	218.3	178.7	134.2	174.6	272.5	171.7	119.5	136.5	122.1	87.4	41.5	48.8	22.5

FIGURE 11
Sensitivity of Insured Index Fund Returns to Put Prices

Increase in Put Price	Cumulative Return	Compound Annual Return
0%	414.3%	12.9%
5	384.9	12.4
10	357.2	11.9
15	331.1	11.4
20	306.5	10.9
S&P 500	311.0	11.0

EXHIBIT 1 *(continued)*

FIGURE 12
Dynamic Insurance Tree

Weeks until Expiration	Stock Price												
	88	**90**	**92**	**94**	**96**	**98**	**100**	**102**	**104**	**106**	**108**	**110**	**112**
13 **S**	3.63	6.93	12.08	19.32	28.61	39.55	51.44	63.44	74.78	84.88	93.43	100.40	105.96
C	96.48	93.29	88.35	81.44	72.65	62.41	51.44	40.57	30.58	22.00	15.12	9.92	6.23
12 **S**	3.09	6.17	11.15	18.36	27.80	39.06	51.38	63.82	75.51	85.80	94.40	101.29	106.69
C	96.99	94.01	89.22	82.33	73.37	62.79	51.38	40.08	29.75	21.00	14.09	8.99	5.46
11 **S**	2.56	5.39	10.16	17.31	26.90	38.52	51.32	64.26	76.32	86.82	95.44	102.22	107.43
C	97.50	94.76	90.15	83.30	74.17	63.22	51.32	39.53	28.84	19.89	12.98	8.02	4.69
10 **S**	2.05	4.60	9.11	16.15	25.88	37.90	51.26	64.76	77.25	87.95	96.56	103.19	108.18
C	98.00	95.52	91.15	84.38	75.09	63.72	51.26	38.91	27.81	18.68	11.79	7.00	3.92
9 **S**	1.57	3.79	8.00	14.88	24.74	37.19	51.20	65.34	78.31	89.22	97.78	104.20	108.92
C	98.46	96.30	92.22	85.57	76.13	64.31	51.20	38.21	26.64	17.33	10.51	5.95	3.15
8 **S**	1.13	3.00	6.82	13.47	23.42	36.37	51.13	66.04	79.54	90.64	99.10	105.23	109.64
C	98.89	97.07	93.35	86.91	77.34	65.01	51.13	37.38	25.30	15.82	9.14	4.88	2.41
7 **S**	0.74	2.22	5.58	11.89	21.90	35.39	51.06	66.88	80.98	92.25	100.52	106.28	110.31
C	99.27	97.82	94.55	88.41	78.76	65.85	51.06	36.40	23.73	14.12	7.66	3.79	1.72
6 **S**	0.43	1.51	4.30	10.13	20.09	34.20	50.98	67.93	82.72	94.09	102.03	107.32	110.91
C	99.58	98.52	95.79	90.11	80.45	66.89	50.98	35.21	21.88	12.20	6.10	2.73	1.10
5 **S**	0.20	0.88	3.01	8.15	17.91	32.71	50.89	69.27	84.84	96.19	103.61	108.28	111.41
C	99.80	99.13	97.04	92.02	82.52	68.23	50.89	33.71	19.63	10.01	4.47	1.75	0.60
4 **S**	0.07	0.40	1.79	5.96	15.21	30.75	50.80	71.07	87.52	98.60	105.20	109.11	111.76
C	99.94	99.60	98.23	94.15	85.10	70.03	50.80	31.73	16.84	7.54	2.84	0.91	0.24
3 **S**	0.01	0.11	0.77	3.61	11.79	28.00	50.69	73.65	90.99	101.27	106.64	109.69	111.94
C	99.99	99.89	99.23	96.44	88.41	72.59	50.69	28.96	13.24	4.80	1.37	0.31	0.06
2 **S**	0.00	0.01	0.15	1.40	7.34	23.71	50.56	77.78	95.62	103.98	107.66	109.96	112.00
C	100.00	99.99	99.85	98.62	92.75	76.69	50.56	24.63	8.49	2.04	0.34	0.04	0.00
1 **S**	0.00	0.00	0.00	0.10	2.03	15.54	50.40	85.82	101.47	105.82	107.99	110.00	112.00
C	100.00	100.00	100.00	99.90	97.99	84.62	50.40	16.35	2.55	0.18	0.01	0.00	0.00
0 **S**	0.00	0.00	0.00	0.00	0.00	0.00	50.00	102.00	104.00	106.00	108.00	110.00	112.00
C	100.00	100.00	100.00	100.00	100.00	100.00	50.00	0.00	0.00	0.00	0.00	0.00	0.00

S = Dollars invested in stock.
C = Dollars held in cash.

Risk-free = 0%.
Weekly standard deviation = 2%.

EXHIBIT 1 *(continued)*

0.5144, so that the dynamic portfolio will contain 0.5144 share of stock worth $51.44. Since the value of the dynamic portfolio must also be $102.88, the amount of cash held is simply $102.88 minus $51.44, or $51.44. This procedure is repeated at each box.

In comparing dynamic insurance with static insurance, we first note that dynamic insurance is path-dependent while static insurance is not. To see this, consider the following extreme case. Suppose over the next 13 weeks, the stock price were to remain constant at $100. Each week a small amount of stock would be sold and the proceeds held as cash. By the end of the thirteenth week, the dynamic portfolio would still have a value of $102.88 ($50 in stock and $52.88 in cash). In effect, the insurance would have cost nothing, since the stock exhibited zero volatility. The actual cost of the insurance in a dynamic strategy will depend on the experienced volatility, whereas that of the static strategy is fixed by the initial cost of the put, which is a function of the anticipated volatility. In cases in which the experienced volatility is greater than the anticipated volatility, the dynamic strategy will cost more. And this neglects the transaction costs associated with rebalancing, which can be formidable and rise with increasing volatility. To be sure, these transaction costs may be greatly reduced by using index futures, and we would argue that using futures is the only way that a dynamic insurance program has any real hope of successfully matching a static program over time. The use of futures, with their lower transaction costs, allows the investor to rebalance more often. Remember that, theoretically, the portfolio must be rebalanced continuously in order to perfectly replicate a protective put. However, this applies in the case of fairly valued futures. The deviation from fair value of the futures has historically been substantial. A dynamic program that exploits the mispricing of the futures is an interesting and perhaps potentially attractive product.

Certainly, some general statements regarding the relative merits of using a dynamic strategy instead of a static strategy can be made. If the volatility implied by the put price is believed to be too high (that is, the listed put is overpriced), the dynamic strategy might be preferable, since its cost for insurance will depend on the actual experienced (and presumably lower) volatility. However, if the listed put is fairly priced, or better yet, cheap relative to volatility expectations, then it is most probably superior to the dynamic strategy.

Of course, it is much easier to implement a static insurance program. Options on the S&P 100 Index are currently the most liquid contracts, trading on average nearly 100,000 put contracts per day. With the S&P 100 Index at 160, an at-the-money put option will insure $16,000 ($100x160). To insure a $10-million S&P 100 portfolio, one would have to purchase 625 put options. The growth of these markets over the past seven months is shown in Figure 13. Although there is currently very little trading in puts on the S&P 500 Index, there is a growing amount of liquidity in puts on the S&P 500 futures contract. Investors wishing to insure the market component of a portfolio may find these contracts attractive. Furthermore, when the S&P 500 futures are overvalued, puts on the futures may at times be undervalued relative to the S&P 500 Index, as a result of traders engaging in reversals—that is, selling the overvalued futures and simultaneously creating a synthetic long futures by purchasing the call and selling the put. This activity creates downward pressure on the put price.

Finally, with a dynamic strategy the investor can tailor insurance to his specifications. For example, one can dynamically replicate a one-year European put, an instrument that currently is not traded on any exchange. However, one must be careful not to make the argument that one-year puts are superior to three-month puts for insurance purposes. While the premium paid per year by rolling three-month puts is higher than would be paid initially for a one-year put, it must be remembered that rolling three-month puts provides a more comprehensive insurance policy, because the investor has the right to exercise four times per year instead of just once. Thus, comparing a rolling

EXHIBIT 1 ***(concluded)***

FIGURE 13
Average Daily Volume of Various Capitalization-Weighted Index Options
(*number of contracts traded*)

	S&P 100 Index*		S&P 500 Futures†		NYSE Index‡	
	Calls	Puts	Calls	Puts	Calls	Puts
Sept. 83	27,000	32,000	520	360	3,400	1,900
Oct. 83	28,000	31,000	650	290	4,600	4,100
Nov. 83	34,000	36,000	650	360	4,400	4,100
Dec. 83	39,000	39,000	1,100	1,200	6,000	4,400
Jan 84	57,000	52,000	1,800	1,700	8,000	7,800
Feb. 84	81,000	99,000	1,900	1,400	10,500	8,800
Mar. 84	86,000	95,000	1,200	1,000	7,800	6,900

*Approximate size of an at-the-money contract is $16,000 ($100 × Index).
†Approximate size of an at-the-money contract is $80,000 ($500 × Index).
‡Approximate size of an at-the-money contract is $9,000 ($100 × Index).

three-month put strategy with a one-year put strategy is comparing two entirely different types of insurance.

Conclusion

We have found that from the middle of 1970 until the end of 1983, an S&P 500 index fund protected by three-month at-the-money index puts would have significantly outperformed the uninsured index fund. Over the time period investigated, the S&P 500 rose from 72.72 to 164.93, so these results were obtained in a market with a strong upward bias. In our view, these results suggest that portfolio insurance should be considered seriously as a viable investment product.

EXHIBIT 2
Performance of Option Funds *(risk and diversification 3/83 to 3/86; percent return 3/83 to 3/86)*

Name of Fund	Management Co.	Assets (mil$)	Load Fee	Alpha	Beta	R^2	Std. Dev.	Annual ROR
Colonial Option Inc TR	COLONL	1,383	Yes	−1.9	0.73	82	2.9	15.3
Analytic Optioned Equity	ANALYT	86	No	−1.8	0.55	89	2.1	13.3
Putnam Option Income I	PUTNAM	1,191	Yes	−5.0	0.78	79	3.1	12.3
First Invest. Option	FSTINV	195	Yes	−4.2	0.64	52	3.2	11.6
Kemper Option Income FD	KEMPER	783	Yes	−3.4	0.52	81	2.1	11.0
Gateway Option Income	GATEWY	28	No	−2.9	0.47	79	1.8	11.0
Unweighted averages		611		−3.2	0.62	77	2.5	12.4
Weighted averages					0.69	79	2.8	
Standard & Poor's 500				0.0	1.00	100	3.6	21.1
Salomon Bros. Corp bonds				4.5	0.52	35	3.1	20.0

Note: Alpha expressed per annum; standard deviation expressed per month. Six entries reported.

EXHIBIT 3
Closing Weekly Prices of the OEX and SPX
(*1/10/86 to 9/05/86*)

"Date"	*S&P 100 Index OEX*	*S&P 500 Index SPX*
860110	200.61	205.96
860117	202.35	208.43
860124	199.93	206.43
860131	204.00	211.78
860207	207.49	214.56
860214	212.38	219.76
860221	217.57	224.62
860228	217.57	226.92
860307	215.05	225.57
860314	225.44	236.55
860321	222.22	233.34
860327	227.60	238.97
860404	218.41	228.69
860411	224.58	235.97
860418	230.40	242.38
860425	233.01	242.29
860502	225.84	234.79
860509	228.02	237.85
860516	222.14	232.76
860523	230.26	241.35
860530	236.05	247.35
860606	235.69	245.67
860613	235.17	245.73
860620	235.88	247.58
860627	236.57	249.60
860703	238.20	251.79
860711	229.21	242.22
860718	224.16	236.36
860725	226.14	240.22
860801	220.46	234.91
860808	222.67	236.88
860815	231.57	247.15
860822	234.42	250.19
860829	237.32	252.93
860905	236.41	250.47

EXHIBIT 4

Performance of the Monsanto Plan versus the OEX and SPX (*statistical analysis 1/3/85 to 9/15/86; daily returns*)

Versus OEX

	Average	***Std. Dev.***	***Beta***	***RSQR***	***Corr. Coeff.***	***Durbin Watson***	***Track Error***
(Number of observations—429)							
DEP: Monsanto Eq. Portfolio	0.083	0.95	0.84	0.56	0.75	1.99	0.63
IND: S&P 100 Index	0.077	0.86					5.08

Versus SPX

	Average	***Std. Dev.***	***Beta***	***RSQR***	***Corr. Coeff.***	***Durbin Watson***	***Track Error***
(Number of observations—429)							
DEP: Monsanto Eq. Portfolio	0.083	0.95	0.92	0.59	0.77	2.03	0.6
IND: S&P 500 Index	0.083	0.80					4.9

Part VI

Investment Strategies for Individual Clients

The Charles Andrews Trust

In early December of 1978, Ms. Gertrude Leiberman, Vice President of Santa Maria National Bank, met with Richard Pritchett, husband of Ellen Andrews Pritchett, the beneficiary of the Charles Andrews Trust. Their discussion centered on the bank's management of the entrusted funds. Ms. Leiberman had recently been assigned responsibility for managing this trust, and the funds in the trust had just increased substantially. These two factors together warranted thorough reconsideration of the objectives and approaches in managing these funds. Mr. Pritchett, on behalf of his wife, had suggested some approaches that were quite different from the bank's normal style of investing. Ms. Leiberman had now to resolve how she would manage the entrusted funds for the benefit of Ellen and her children.

Basic Terms of the Charles Andrews Trusts

When Charles Andrews died in 1968, his will had established three interrelated trust funds on behalf of his beneficiaries. Half of his gross estate was given to his second wife, Audrey, to take advantage of the "marital deduction" (this part of the estate was not subject to estate taxes at that time). A trust fund was established to administer these funds. The remainder of the estate, after estate taxes, was then established in two equal trusts to benefit Mr. Andrews' two children from his first marriage, William and Ellen. The management of the three trusts, which amounted

This case was prepared by Robert F. Vandell, Charles C. Abbott Professor of Business Administration of the Colgate Darden Graduate School of Business Administration of the University of Virginia.

to approximately $350,000, $110,000, and $110,000, respectively, was assigned to the Santa Maria National Bank of Columbus, Ohio, where Mr. Andrews had lived.

The children's trusts were both "remainderman" trusts. Each child was entitled to the income earned by his trust during his or her lifetime. Upon the death of either child, that trust would be distributed in equal shares to the children of that child outright. There would be no further estate taxes at the time of the distribution. This "generation skipping" feature of estate tax law was an attractive means of preserving family capital over time.

Mr. Andrews' will also specified that, should either William or Ellen die without children, the deceased child's trust would be closed into the surviving child's trust (again without being subject to estate taxation). Each child had previously been given outright about $100,000 upon the death of Mr. Andrews' first wife, Georgia, in 1960.

The circumstances surrounding Audrey's trust were somewhat more complicated. First of all, Audrey had two children of her own from her previous marriage. She had also accumulated capital of her own in the amount of about $200,000, as the beneficiary of her first husband's estate. The intent of Charles and Audrey Andrews was to leave to each other half of the estate of the spouse who died first for the other spouse's lifetime use. But upon the death of the second spouse the residual of the estate would revert to the children of the first spouse. To take advantage of the marital deduction, however, the funds in the estate going to either spouse had to be left outright to him or her. The income from the "marital" trust established would flow to the surviving spouse during his or her lifetime. This spouse also had the right of "invasion"—that is, the right to draw against the capital as needed or wanted for any reason. Finally, the surviving spouse had the right to designate the beneficiaries of the residual estate of the marital trust in his or her will.

To deal with these circumstances, Charles and Audrey Andrews had drawn up parallel conditions in their wills. Since Charles had died first, the terms of his will had become applicable. His will set forth that, should Audrey not specifically redesignate the beneficiaries of the "marital" trust funds, these funds would revert to his children's trusts in equal amounts, after paying any incremental estate taxes caused by the addition of this capital to the base of Audrey's personal estate. Audrey's will, in turn, explicitly confirmed this intention not to redesignate the beneficiaries of the marital trust. Despite her right to do so, Audrey had neither invaded the trust's principal nor redesignated the beneficiaries.

Each of the trusts was managed differently. William, who had moved to Hollywood to pursue an acting career with only modest success, needed a high income to support his bachelor's life. Ellen, whose circumstances are described more fully below, did not need the income and therefore sought capital appreciation in her trust. Audrey, whose combined investment income met her lifestyle's needs, sought modest income with sufficient income growth to protect against inflation. Because of the remainderman features of the trust agreements, the trustee also had to concern himself with the principal's safety in a "prudent man" context.

Subsequent Developments

In late 1977 William died unexpectedly. Because he had had neither a wife nor children, after due process his trust account was closed into Ellen's. William had also died intestate, and Ellen, as his nearest surviving relative inherited his net estate. The only asset in the estate was William's home, but this had appreciated significantly in value. However, a number of debts and expenses reduced the value of the estate to approximately $50,000.

In early 1978 Audrey passed away after a short illness. The Andrews marital trust, after paying the appropriate taxes, was also subsequently closed into Ellen's trust, effective October 31, 1978.

These two events changed significantly the amount of capital to be managed by the Trust Department of Santa Maria National Bank on behalf of Ellen and the remaindermen. Ms. Gertrude Leiberman, who had joined Santa Maria as a Vice President in the Trust Department in January of 1978 after holding similar responsibilities in a smaller Cincinnati bank, had taken over the management of the remaining Andrews trust. She had undertaken to learn more about Ellen's needs and circumstances as the first step in fulfilling her responsibility.

Ms. Leiberman was aware that the basic trust agreement allowed Ellen to change the trustee once. About a dozen trusts managed by the Santa Maria were larger than the Andrews trust. Nevertheless, this trust comprised almost 2 percent of the funds managed under trusts by Santa Maria (excluding employee benefit plans). It was not an account the bank could lose with equanimity.

Ellen's Financial Circumstances

In 1978 Ellen was 46. She had married Richard Pritchett in 1954, following his discharge from the armed services. Their three children, Charles Andrews, Robin Lambert, and Richard Drew, were 22, 21, and 19, respectively. The family now lived in a suburb near Greensboro, North Carolina.

Richard, a Harvard MBA, had risen to become financial vice president of a $300 million firm headquartered in Greensboro. Among other responsibilities, he oversaw management of the firm's $80 million pension trust. In the last five years, Mr. Pritchett had read several books and articles on the newer investment theories. He had frequent contact with the investment community through the five investment organizations that managed pieces of his firm's pension trust and through his position as a member of the advisory committee of the trust department of a large North Carolina bank similar in size to the Santa Maria National Bank. His contacts with investment and commercial bankers and his other responsibilities, such as overseeing the management of his firm's portfolio of marketable securities, kept him close to the capital markets.

Mr. Pritchett's salary exceeded $100,000 and was more than sufficient to meet the living requirements of his family. Both Richard and Ellen were somewhat frugal by nature and had always been able to save a significant part of their income beyond such forced savings programs as mortgages, pension funds, and the like. The net income after taxes from investments was also reinvested. As a result, the Pritchetts had become, by some standards, quite wealthy.

Initially, investments had been made in Ellen's name. As a woman four years younger than her husband, she would probably outlive him. If he should survive her, either his salary or his pension income would support his likely needs. The simplest way of reducing the taxes on an estate to be transferred to his wife was to have her own the investments before his death.

This strategy had worked almost too well. Ellen's common stock ownership had a market value of almost \$2.5 million in late 1978. Ellen had also maintained liquid assets of \$25,000 in savings accounts and tax-exempt securities as a cushion against unexpected needs. She also owned antiques, coin collections, jewelry, and the like, valued at several hundred thousand dollars. She and her husband jointly owned their house and furniture. Her investment income in 1978 was expected to be about \$75,000.

Richard had advised Ellen on most of her investments. Aside from odd-lot leftovers (from stock dividends, dividend accumulation plans, etc.) from investments sold, her portfolio was concentrated in a dozen carefully selected stocks, each with different reasons for Richard's hopes for its future. The largest investment, for example, amounted to almost \$500,000 (acquired for \$50,000 in 1971). This firm was relatively small (sales of \$30 million), but was growing very, very rapidly. When listed on the American Stock Exchange in 1978, the stock had begun to attract broader interest. Two large brokerage firms had recently forecasted a doubling of this stock's earnings by 1981. Other investments currently were in firms of similar size and promise.

These investments were made for an intermediate time horizon of five to eight years. Mr. Pritchett consequently only had to come up with about two good investment ideas per year. He tended to limit investments to industries that he knew well, and he usually spent several days, scattered over several months, carefully analyzing a potential opportunity.

His basic strategy had also changed with the times. In the late 1960s, when prices for growth stocks in general and small growth stocks in particular seemed too high relative to prospects and risks, he invested elsewhere in the market. He also had sold out some or all of his portfolio when he thought the market was near a peak (as in late 1972), only to repurchase when the market seemed low (as in mid-1974).

Over his desk was a bankrupt company's stock certificate, for which he had paid \$65,000. It bore this superimposed legend: "Minimize Risk before you Maximize Gain." Another sign read: "Buy promising stocks when their downside risk is low; Sell promising stocks when their downside risk is high; And don't be greedy."

In recent years more of the family savings had been channeled into Richard's name. He now owned a few stocks with an aggregate market value of \$400,000. This sum, however, excluded about \$200,000 in stock of his employer; as an insider he did not wish to sell these shares, and acquired new holdings only through stock options. About $120,000 of his total holdings had come to him upon the death of his mother in 1976. His life insurance amounted to $300,000, of which $120,000 was earmarked to retire all family debt at his death. His company benefits for retirement, health, disability, and so on, were also more than satisfactory.

The family's investment income was now being taxed at the margin at 70 percent. Capital gains, which were taxed at a lower rate and only if realized, were thus much preferred to investment income. He did not hesitate to take gains when a stock seemed too high: sharing gains with Uncle Sam seemed to him better than losing them to the market.

In 1972 the Pritchetts had established a remainderman trust for their three children in the amount of $60,000 ($30,000 from each parent), which was managed by a local bank. Mr. Pritchett had suggested that these funds be invested only in equity securities, and that investments be made in no more than the 10 stocks that the bank considered most promising. Mr. Pritchett had studied the bank's stock evaluation system and helped to work out explicit buy/sell criteria. He reviewed the account's status with the responsible trust officer once every two months. The account had grown in value to about $150,000 in late 1978 despite payment of all income to the children.

In 1974 each parent had also begun giving each child $3,000 per year, first under the uniform gifts to minors law—Richard's brother serving as trustee—and later outright. Each child's funds had grown in value to about $70,000 in late 1978.

Each child now received an income of about $5,500 from these sources, which helped to finance their college educations. Charles Andrews and Robin Lambert were now seniors in college. Upon graduation, Charles planned to work in business for several years before returning for his MBA. Robin planned to seek employment as a biomedical technician. The youngest child, Richard Jr., has just entered college.

Richard's will left his estate to his children in a remainderman trust in which the children would be equal-income beneficiaries. Ellen's will left one third of her estate to Richard in the form of a marital deduction. The balance of her funds were left to the children in a separate remainderman trust. The trusts would remain in effect for 17 years beyond the death of the last of their three children, and would then be distributed to their grandchildren *per stirpes*. Each trust was to be managed by a different institution. Richard and Ellen had written letters instructing the future trustees to invest the funds for long-term growth of the principal.

Santa Maria National Bank's Trust Department Operations

Santa Maria National Bank employed four account executives, including Ms. Lieberman. The account executive was responsible for liaison between the client and the investment operation. An account executive discussed each client's interests and needs with the client, and translated these needs into an investment program within the legal framework of the trust document. The account executives periodically reviewed the portfolio to make sure that it met the client's interests, and personally approved in advance any suggested changes in a portfolio. Formal reports were made to the client at least once a year. A good part of the account executives' work involved providing personal services (tax advice, accounting) and answering questions for clients.

The bank employed four stock analysts and one bond analyst. The stock analysts worked from an approved list of 130 companies that the bank actively followed. The analysts digested the industry and stock research information of supplier firms and made decisions as to whether stocks should be bought, sold, or held. If a stock was changed into the sell category, the analysts would screen accounts to determine holdings. They would select an appropriate stock from the buy list to replace the stock being sold. These changes were reviewed by the account executive before being executed. The bank maintained two pooled-equity funds (conservative, aggressive), a bond fund, a tax-exempt fund, and a money market fund (much like mutual funds). These pools were managed by the security analysts. Clients with smaller capital bases often were predominantly invested in the pools. Turnover of equity funds averaged less than 10 percent a year for most accounts.

The bank concentrated its commissions in six brokerage firms that it had found provided the most helpful research. In addition, two money-center commercial banks provided security research under a compensating-balance umbrella. About once every two weeks, a representative from one of these institutions would call on the bank to discuss investments or investment strategy. The analysts read broadly and talked with others to form their opinions about the potential of individual securities. New buy-and-sell recommendations required formal review by a committee before action was taken.

A policy committee considered portfolio strategies. Clients were categorized in several ways and separate strategies were developed for each category. This committee established guidelines concerning debt/equity mixes. It also suggested such things as which industries should be emphasized or avoided (regarding equities) or whether short or long maturities should be emphasized (regarding fixed-income securities). Certain diversification guidelines were also set forth. In short, the policy committee suggested general investment strategies that seemed appropriate, given money market outlooks, for various types of clients.

The Trust Department of the Santa Maria broke even on a "fully allocated" basis. The direct costs were, however, only 60 percent of total costs. The senior management of the bank tended to regard the operation as a necessary but not very attractive activity for a "full-service" bank.

The Bank and the Andrews Trust: The Historic Relationship

Ms. Leiberman, upon graduation from high school, had gone to work as a secretary to two trust account executives in a Cincinnati bank. She quickly demonstrated an aptitude for mastering the many legal, accounting, and other technical problems associated with account management. She also showed a flair for handling client relationships. Several years later one of her bosses suffered a protracted illness, and she assumed his responsibilities as an interim measure. When this person later died, she was named Assistant Vice President and Account Officer. But while the senior management at the Cincinnati bank seemed extremely pleased with her work, they continued to think of her in some respects as a glorified secretary. This problem led her to consider a change. The opportunity as Vice President at Santa Maria seemed ideal, and at age 28 she found herself in an upper-middle-management position with a salary approaching $35,000. Her experience with investments was limited, however, and she had never had to analyze a security, although she was a CFA.

In February of 1978 when she had called to introduce herself to Ellen Pritchett, she had found it easy to establish a warm friendship. Mr. Pritchett was another matter. Ms. Leiberman was quickly intimidated by his knowledge of investments. In her opinion, he would also have intimidated her colleagues—including the most senior executives. She had, however, gotten him to agree to set forth in a letter (included below) how he would like to see Ellen's account managed.

Prior to making this first call, she had reviewed the history of Ellen's trust. The account had been managed by the most conservative account executive (Mr. Strong, now retired) in a generally conservative banking group. Mr. Pritchett described him as "an ostrich with sand in his eyes who thought with his rump because it was his most elevated part." The correspondence file made clear that the relationship had been severely strained.

In 1968 the Pritchetts had indicated their interest in long-term capital appreciation and their preference for an all-equity portfolio. They had opposed investments in tax-exempt securities. Mr. Strong had then proceeded to invest about 40 percent of the account in long-term tax exempts, whose subsequent market performance was poor. Mr. Pritchett had complained that the account was invested in too many small equity investments (the average commitment was $2,000), that too few securities seemed promising as long-term investments, that the very low turnover indicated an absence of management, and so on. Very few of Mr. Pritchett's buy/sell suggestions had been acted upon, although many looked perceptive from hindsight.

In spite of this, the account had had good performance. Its market value had increased to $150,000 by early 1978, despite the tax-exempt commitment and despite the fact that the stock market indices had declined over the decade. (Income on the account was paid out to Ellen Pritchett.) No other account in the bank had done as well. Notwithstanding the disagreements, Mr. Strong had clearly spent much more time on the account than was typical. It was also clear that performance would have been better if more of Mr. Pritchett's suggestions had been followed.

This latter circumstance was potentially very awkward. The bank's responsibility for prudence remained even if it followed bad advice from a client. If advice was not followed, however, and it happened to look like good advice in hindsight, the bank might also be exposed, legally. For many reasons, then, trust officers generally did not like clients like the Pritchetts.

Mr. Pritchett had commented to Ms. Leiberman in February of 1978, "Ostriches don't have ears; I gave up talking to myself in 1972. The account was a small part of our wealth, and I had much better ways of spending my time. The amount you are now managing for Ellen and the children is no longer peanuts, and I hope that you will give it the kind of attention it deserves." The file indeed contained no correspondence after June 1972. Mr. Strong had told her, "If you weren't a lady, I'd tell you what an SOB Pritchett really is. He's all yours now, and the nicest part of retirement will be not having to listen to his wild ideas anymore."

The Pritchetts' Letter

In May of 1978, Ms. Leiberman received the following letter cosigned by Richard and Ellen Pritchett.

Dear Ms. Leiberman:

As you manage the Charles Andrews Trust on behalf of me and my children, please bear the following considerations in mind:

1. In many instances, a trustee manages the entire family wealth for an individual. This situation encourages conservatism. In our situation, the trust will be (after estate taxes are paid) only about 15 percent of our capital. The rest of the estate is suitably diversified, and the family is already protected against most likely needs. Normal conservatism need not enter your thinking.
2. We do not need income. All dividend and interest income will be taxed at 70 percent. If Ellen receives a monthly income of $2,000 from this trust, she will be pleased. Hopefully, this income will grow over time with inflation.
3. Fixed-income securities are inappropriate for this account, particularly during a period of inflation. Short-term principal safety is not an important consideration. We are willing to take the risks of market volatility in the short run in order to enhance long-term capital appreciation.
4. This principle applies to tax-free municipals as well. We are familiar with the arguments that a 6 percent tax-free yield for a 70 percent tax-bracket individual is equivalent to an 18 percent before-tax return on capital. However, an after-tax return of 6 percent in these inflationary times is a negative real return on capital. Other investments promise better prospects of protecting income and capital against the erosive effects of inflation.
5. Funds in the Charles Andrews Trust should be managed exclusively for long-term capital appreciation in a prudent manner. There is no conflict between the lifetime beneficiary and the remaindermen.
6. Ellen, at 46, has a life expectancy of about 30 years. A long-term view is appropriate. Short-term price volatility of securities is expected and is not a problem.
7. Even if Ellen dies prematurely, there will be no taxes when the trust is distributed to her children. There will be no need to sell assets if the market is temporarily down.
8. For these reasons, the trust should be entirely invested in common stocks.
9. The return on common stocks has been disappointing over the last decade, we are well aware. Price/earnings ratios have fallen in order to provide stockholders with satisfactory future return expectations. The long-term rate-of-return expectation for the market at large (e.g., Standard & Poor's 500 Index) has increased

from about 9 percent in 1968 to about 15 percent in 1978. This expectation appears to provide a satisfactory protection against the levels of inflation now foreseen.

10. Sooner or later inflation will be brought under control. If inflation falls back to historic levels of 2–3 percent, the market return requirements will decrease. Prices would about double. Some improvement in inflation rates in the 1980s seems probable.

11. Your bank follows 130 stocks. We would guess that at least half of these stocks have below-average growth expectations, and would be unsuitable for this trust under most circumstances. It is our experience that managers must concentrate the holdings in the top 10 percent or 15 percent of the stocks that they follow if they are to gain superior performance. This means that the Charles Andrews Trust should ideally be invested in 6 to 9 securities, and certainly no more than 10.

12. This portfolio may seem overly concentrated to you, but it will increase the diversification of the total family portfolio.

13. In selecting particular stocks, please pay attention to fundamentals. The earnings-per-share growth of stocks over the next three to five years—provided the growth can be purchased at a reasonable price—should be your first consideration. The certainty and durability of this growth should concern you next.

14. The stocks that you follow are categorized as "buy," "hold," and "sell," depending on their relative attractiveness. Holding stocks never has made sense to us. The portfolio should be concentrated in stocks categorized as "buys."

15. Establishing performance evaluation criteria may help. In any 12-month period, the trust portfolio should perform better than the Standard & Poor's 500 Index, measured as follows:

$$R_t = (1-t_1) \times \left(\frac{dps_t}{MP_{t-1}}\right) + (1-t_2) \times \left[\left(\frac{eps_t}{eps_{t-1}}\right) - 1\right]$$

where

R_t = Fundamental performance potential.
t_1 = Marginal tax rate on income (now 70%).
t_2 = Marginal tax rate on capital gains (now 25%).
dps_t = Dividends per share in the current 12-month period for the index (or portfolio).
MP_{t-1} = Market value of the index (or portfolio) at the outset of the current year.
eps_t = Earnings per share for the index (or portfolio) for the most recent 12 months.
eps_{t-1} = Earnings per share for the index (or the portfolio) for the previous 12 months.*

Portfolio calculations should be weighted by the fraction of the portfolio invested in each security.

16. The *R* for the trust portfolio should be at least 3 percent higher than the *R* for the index. Consistent performance of this order should produce very attractive portfolio performance over the long run.

17. In implementing this program, a turnover of 25 percent per year may well be necessary. A low turnover would indicate inadequate management.

18. At the moment, growth stocks appear attractively priced. This appears to be an ideal time to implement the program. If circumstances should change dramatically so that the programs set forth above no longer seem suitable, we would welcome your suggestions for change.

Sincerely,

Mr. & Mrs. R. Pritchett

---

*After studying this equation and reviewing Richard's point #13, Ms. Leiberman wondered whether the second element, incorporating earnings per share, was an appropriate substitute for appreciation.

Further Developments

The Pritchetts' letter proved disturbing in many respects. No other account at Santa Maria was invested only in equities. In a portfolio the size of the Andrews Trust, the equity part of the portfolio was usually invested in 30 or 40 securities. The Pritchett letter did not absolve the bank from its prudent-man responsibilities. If a significant fraction of the portfolio were invested in a few stocks that happened to do poorly after the fact, management could be criticized.

Ms. Leiberman had discussed the letter at length with Mr. Culbert, Senior Vice President and head of the trust department, and with legal counsel. Mr. Culbert's initial reaction was: "No way!" He later backed off, conceding to an all-equity portfolio, but one with 15 or 20 stocks in it. Legal counsel had waffled; they finally admitted, but not in writing, that an all-equity portfolio of 15 to 20 stocks probably would be considered prudent under the circumstances, but the undertone of their advice was a warning.

Ellen Pritchett had been quite understanding of the necessary changes in the Pritchetts' plan when Ms. Leiberman had called. Richard, however, only later grumpily agreed to a maximum of 15 equity securities.

In October of 1978 the Pritchetts bought a new home for $161,000. This house had an assumable mortgage of $34,000 with an interest rate of 6¼ percent. To close the purchase, the Pritchetts' needed to borrow an additional $90,000. After considering alternatives, they applied to the Charles Andrews Trust for a second mortgage loan. Instead, a collateralized (with marketable common stocks) loan of $90,000 at 9¾ percent was worked out. The loan was to be repaid at the rate of $1,000 per month, a rate that would amortize the loan in a little over 10 years' time. Terms were considered to be "arm's length" by outside counsel of the bank.

While Ms. Leiberman was on her honeymoon in late October and early November, the taxes on Audrey Andrews' estate were determined, and the trust paid its share. Unfortunately, the person handling the account in Ms. Leiberman's absence sold equity securities to provide the necessary cash, despite explicit instructions in the file as to how taxes should be paid. A status report on the trust as of October 3, 1978, after the tax payments, is shown in Exhibit 1.

When she returned to work in mid-November, Ms. Leiberman found on her desk a sharply critical letter from Richard Pritchett. He pointed out that "flower bonds,[1] which were obviously being held to pay Audrey Andrews' estate taxes, had not been used for this purpose." The balance of his comments related to: her failure to sell the tax-exempts to gain the remaining tax funds, and her selling the wrong stocks. The account, in his opinion, was far from the one that had been agreed to.

Ms. Leiberman learned with relief that the flower bonds could still be used at par value to replace the cash already paid in estate taxes. It would, however, take several months to effect the transaction.

She telephoned the Pritchetts, explaining the circumstances of the earlier sale. Ms. Leiberman agreed to complete the transition of the account by December 31, 1978.

In the course of this discussion, Ms. Leiberman mentioned that one of the services available to Santa Maria's security analysts was provided by Wells Fargo Investment Advisors, a division of Wells Fargo Bank. Mr. Pritchett had responded, "That's perfect. I know exactly how you should manage Ellen's funds now. Let me come to Columbus next month and explain to you what you should do."

It was clear to Ms. Leiberman that Mr. Pritchett was well informed about the Wells Fargo system. She decided to learn more about it.

The Wells Fargo System

Wells Fargo, Ms. Leiberman understood, had begun experimenting with the applied use of modern portfolio theory in 1970. In the mid-1970s Wells Fargo began to use various ideas emerging from this work to manage active portfolios.

Although the Wells Fargo system included several integrated elements, the "security market line" was an important part of the whole. For each of the (currently 376) securities followed by Wells Fargo's analysts, the analysts estimated the long-term rate of return and the risk. The return and risk of each security could then be arrayed in a scatter diagram similar to that shown in Exhibit 2.

A straight line, called the security market line, could then be fit to these data, using conventional least-squares techniques. The following formula was used:

$$R_i = R_z + x_i(\beta_i) + \epsilon_i$$

where:

R_i = The estimated total rate of return for a security, *i*.
β_i = The estimated risk (beta) associated with security *i*.
R_z = Intercept of the least-squares equation with the *Y* axis.
x_i = Slope of the least-squares equation.
ϵ_i = Error factor for security *i*.

[1] "Flower bonds" are certain deep-discount government bonds of long maturity. These bonds, which typically sell well below par, can be used in payment of any estate taxes due (upon the death of a holder) at their par value. The name "flower bonds" connotes their unique value to estates.

This equation resembled the conventional capital asset pricing model. Experience, however, had shown that the intercept, R_z, was usually considerably above the rate of return on risk-free securities (R_f).

The inputs to this equation were very carefully prescribed. Each security's total rate of return was estimated by the "dividend discount" model. Dividends per share were forecasted over the long run. The internal rate of return that equated the forecasted "dividend stream" to the existing market price represented that security's estimated total rate of return. The procedures for determining a security's dividend stream were spelled out in considerable detail. Given the specified dividend inputs, a computer program facilitated the calculation of total rate of return for that security.[2]

Initially, Wells Fargo had determined the stock's beta by a least squares regression that related the historic monthly total rate of return for a stock to that of the market index (for the most recent 60 months), using the following formula:

$$R_{it} = \alpha_i + \beta_i(R_{mt}) \pm \epsilon_i$$

where:

R_{it} = Total rate of return for a security, i, in a historic month, t.
R_{mt} = Total rate of return on the market index (S&P 500) in month t.
α_i, β_i, and ϵ_i = Coefficients determined by the regression equation.

After considerable further experimentation, Wells Fargo's analysts found that historic betas from this and similar equations were less reliable than they desired. Beta was now estimated from projections of firm fundamentals (such as debt-to-capital ratios), using formulas that were proprietary. Beta was described in Wells Fargo literature as "*the analysts' estimate of a stock's volatility*. The S&P 500, as a proxy for the market, has a volatility of 1.00; a stock with a beta of 1.15 is expected to be 15 percent more volatile than the market."

The security market line provided a basis for determining the relative attractiveness of various securities. Those stocks falling above the security market line were considered undervalued, and the vertical distance between the stock's plot and the security market line (called its alpha) was a measure of that stock's relative attractiveness. Stocks falling below the security market line had negative alphas. Exhibit 3 shows the security market line for four dates, including November 30, 1978.

Wells Fargo had subsequently expanded its analysis to include liquidity. Liquidity measured a stock's ability to absorb trading volume with only modest price change. Stocks that could absorb high trading volumes (such as American Telephone and Telegraph or International Business Machines) were considered highly liquid. Wells Fargo had found that stocks with lower liquidity tended to sell at premiums relative to stocks with higher liquidity (that is, they offered higher rates

---

[2]The specific means of calculating these inputs are set forth in W. L. Fouse, "Risk & Liquidity: The Keys to Stock Price Behavior," *Financial Analysts Journal* 32 (May–June 1976), p. 35.

of return for the same risks). The universe of stocks followed by Wells Fargo was divided into five liquidity categories, from 1 (highest) to 5 (lowest). Exhibit 4 shows the effect of liquidity on security market lines for four representative dates.

Of more immediate importance to Ms. Leiberman was a new concept promoted by Wells Fargo for the first time in 1978. This concept was called the "yield tilt."

The original security market line constructed by Wells Fargo did not consider the effects of personal taxes on investors' expectations (taxes were assumed away likewise in the capital asset pricing model). This assumption might be appropriate for tax-free clients such as pension funds or charitable foundations, but might not be suitable for wealthy individual clients in high tax brackets.

Ms. Leiberman was aware that several academic studies had shown that low-beta stocks tended to have a higher fraction of their total returns in the form of current yield rather than capital growth. The reverse was often true for high beta stocks. If the security market line was adjusted for personal taxes, it might look something like the line shown in Exhibit 5. The after-tax line for wealthy investors was below the security market line for tax-free investors. The after-tax line also had a steeper slope. As illustrated in this exhibit, certain stocks might look attractive to one type of investor and unattractive to another.

Wells Fargo had approached the problem somewhat differently. Analysts added yield as an additional "pricing" factor in the capital markets (yield = dividends per share for the forthcoming 12 months, divided by current market price). They then determined a "security market plane," using the following least-squares regression equation:

$$R_i = R_z + x_1 \beta_i + x_2 Y_i + \epsilon_i$$

Historical analysis indicated that the yield coefficient, x_2, was positive. A stock's expected return, in short, was positively related to its yield. This point is illustrated schematically in Exhibit 6.

The implications of the yield effect are illustrated in Exhibit 7. The middle line in the chart in Exhibit 7 isolates this effect. As the stock's yield increases (see the security yield line) from 0 to 12 percent, the expected total rate of return required in the marketplace also increases.

A tax-free investor would be indifferent to whether or not return was received in the form of dividends or capital growth. The indifference line for the tax-free investor would consequently be flat. This investor would prefer to invest in securities with higher-than-average yields (above 5.4 percent in this exhibit). The indifference line for the high-tax investor would be comparatively steep. All else equal, this investor would prefer investments with lower-than-average yields, as also illustrated in Exhibit 7.

While Ms. Leiberman wasn't sure exactly how this was done, Wells Fargo used these data to adjust the alphas for securities to consider the tax circumstances of four different types of investors. Exhibit 8 illustrates this adjustment for two securities. Mr. Pritchett, she believed, would be interested in the alphas for the highest tax bracket.

Ms. Leiberman had abstracted from the latest Wells Fargo report (November 30, 1978) the data on 116 of the companies followed by Santa Maria that were also followed by Wells Fargo. These data are shown in Exhibit 9.

Mr. Pritchett's Observations

During their meeting in early December 1978, Mr. Pritchett showed that he was very familiar with the Wells Fargo system. Apparently, one of the managers of his firm's pension trust used a similar system but without the "yield tilt" adjustment. This yield adjustment made a great deal of sense to him.

He thereupon suggested the following investment approach:

1. Identify each month the 25 stocks (from those followed by Santa Maria) with the highest alphas in the 70 percent tax column.
2. Invest in the 15 stocks from this list of 25 that had the best five-year earnings-per-share growth prospects, according to analyses made by Santa Maria's other analysts.

Mr. Pritchett also requested, "Now that the portfolio includes the secured $90,000 loan made to us, I hope that you can consider reducing the number of equity securities back to ten."

When Ms. Leiberman reported this meeting to Mr. Culbert, he made the following observations:

1. "Our security analysts don't rely on any one forecasting source for their return estimates and I don't think we should now."
2. "The Wells Fargo 'yield-tilt' system, to the best of my knowledge, has not yet been tested, and we don't know what sort of results it may produce for a high-tax-bracket investor."

He did not, however, suggest an alternative approach.

Ms. Leiberman had now to construct a portfolio of securities appropriate for the Charles Andrews Trust.

EXHIBIT 1

Santa Maria National Bank "Review of Investments" for Ellen Andrews Pritchett (*October 31, 1978*)

Description	Shares or Face Value	Carrying Value of Investment	Current Price	Approximate Market Value	% of Total Market Value	Estimated Income	% Yield on Market
Savings Accounts							
Local Savings & Loan	$ 6,647.11	$ 6,647.11	—	$ 6,647.11	1.14%	$ 348.97	5.25%
Government Bonds							
U.S. Treasury Bond 4.25 percent of 1992	130,000.00	130,000.00	$ 84.250	109,525.00	18.71	5,525.00	5.05
Municipal Bonds							
Columbus Civic Center 4.80 percent of 1997	50,000.00	47,508.00	85.858	42.928.00	7.33	2,400.00	5.59
Convertible Preferred							
International Tel. & Tel. CP $4.00	600	31,098.75	47.25	28,350.00	4.84	2,400.00	8.47
Common Stocks							
Bendix Corporation	400	19,983.33	5.625	14,250.00	2.43	1,024.00	7.19
Ford Motor Company	250	10,963.88	40.000	10,000.00	1.71	1,000.00	10.00
Hubbell (Harvey) Class A	686	15,254.41	25.500	17,493.00	2.99	1,070.16	6.12
Hubbell (Harvey) Class B	688	15,316.02	24.500	16,856.00	2.88	1,073.28	6.37
Minnesota Mining & Manufacturing	350	17,998.75	57.125	19,993.75	3.42	840.00	4.20
United Technology	700	24,791.48	37.750	26,425.00	4.52	1,540.00	5.83
Manufacturers Hanover Trust	800	31,150.00	34.000	27,200.00	4.65	1,824.00	6.71
American Home Products	500	13,510.00	27.125	13,562.50	2.32	750.00	5.53
K mart Corporation	850	20,387.81	25.000	21,250.00	3.63	714.00	3.36
RCA Corporation	500	12,670.31	23.875	11,937.50	2.04	800.00	6.70
Conoco	1,000	32,144.61	25.625	25,625.00	4.38	1,700.00	6.63
Exxon Corporation	700	35,459.41	48.000	33,600.00	5.74	2,520.00	7.50
International Business Machines	100	26,331.50	264.250	26,425.00	4.52	1,376.00	5.21
Raytheon Co.	300	14,092.50	43.125	12,937.50	2.21	480.00	3.71
Utah Power & Light	1,400	24,956.40	17.825	24,955.00	4.26	2,464.00	9.87
Miscellaneous							
Collateral Value of Note		1.00		1.00		—	
Promissory Value of Pritchett Note		90,000.00		90,000.00	15.38	8,775.00	9.75
Furniture & Fixtures*		5,022.00		5,022.00	0.86	—	
Cash		286.39		286.39	0.05	—	6.60
Total		$625,563.66		$585,269.75		$38,624.41	

*To be distributed to Ellen Pritchett.

EXHIBIT 2
Illustration of a Security Market Line

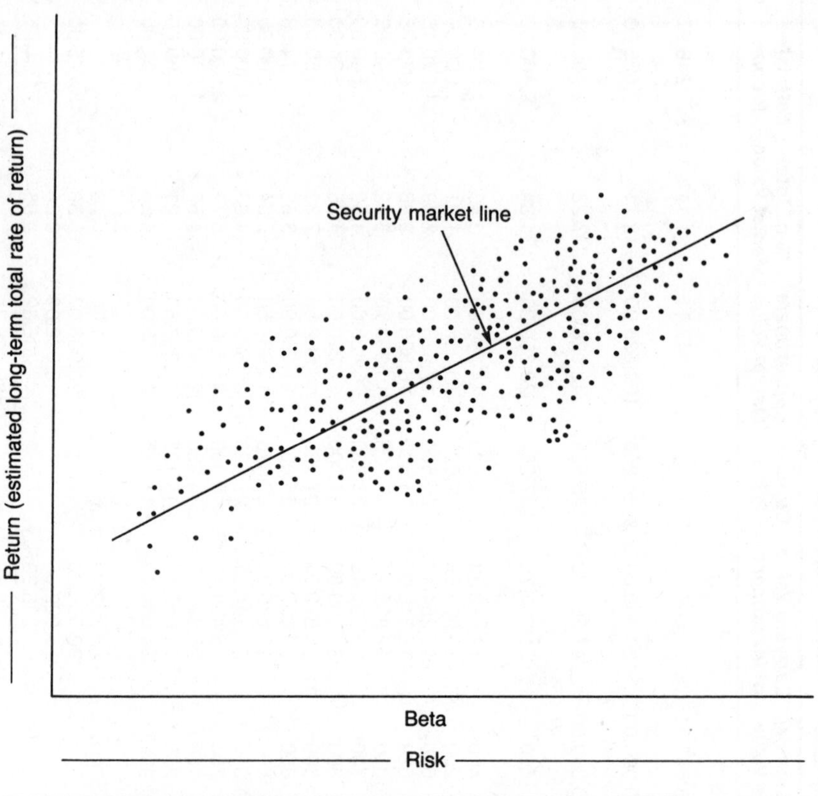

Note: Each dot represents the risk/return plot for one of the securities followed by Wells Fargo. The security market line is fit to the plots for all stocks by least squares regression techniques.

EXHIBIT 3
Illustration of Wells Fargo's Security Market Lines for Four Dates

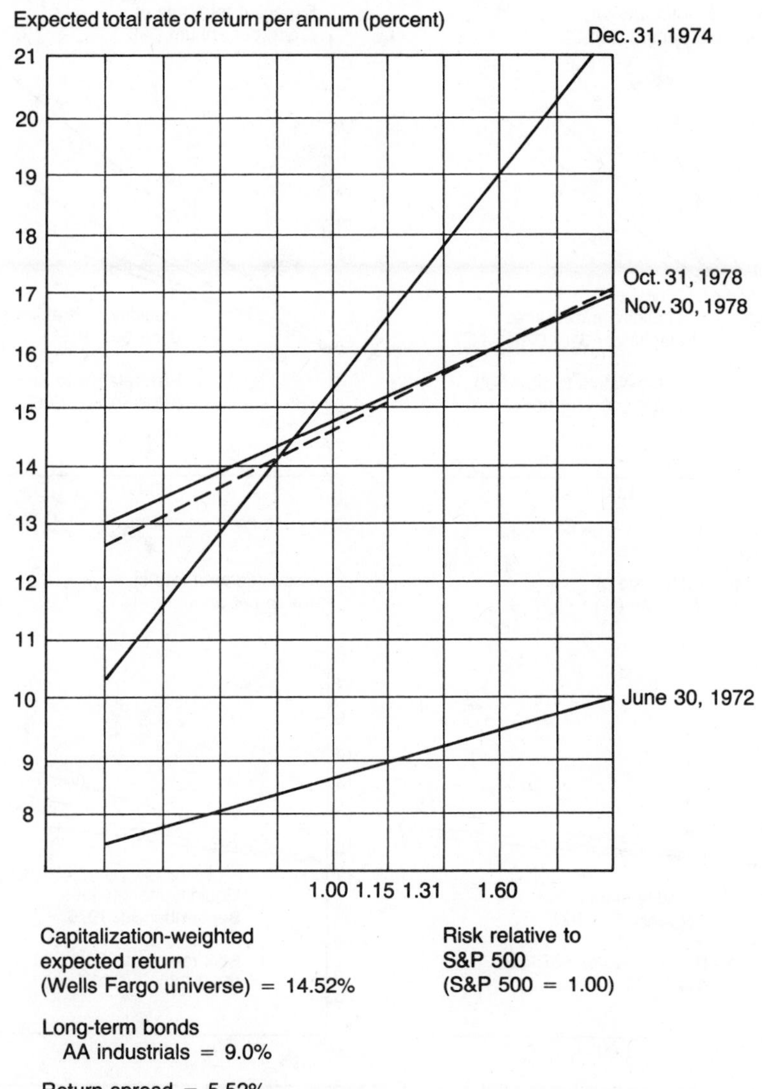

Capitalization-weighted
expected return
(Wells Fargo universe) = 14.52%

Long-term bonds
AA industrials = 9.0%

Return spread = 5.52%

Risk relative to
S&P 500
(S&P 500 = 1.00)

EXHIBIT 4
Illustration of Wells Fargo's Liquidity Market Lines

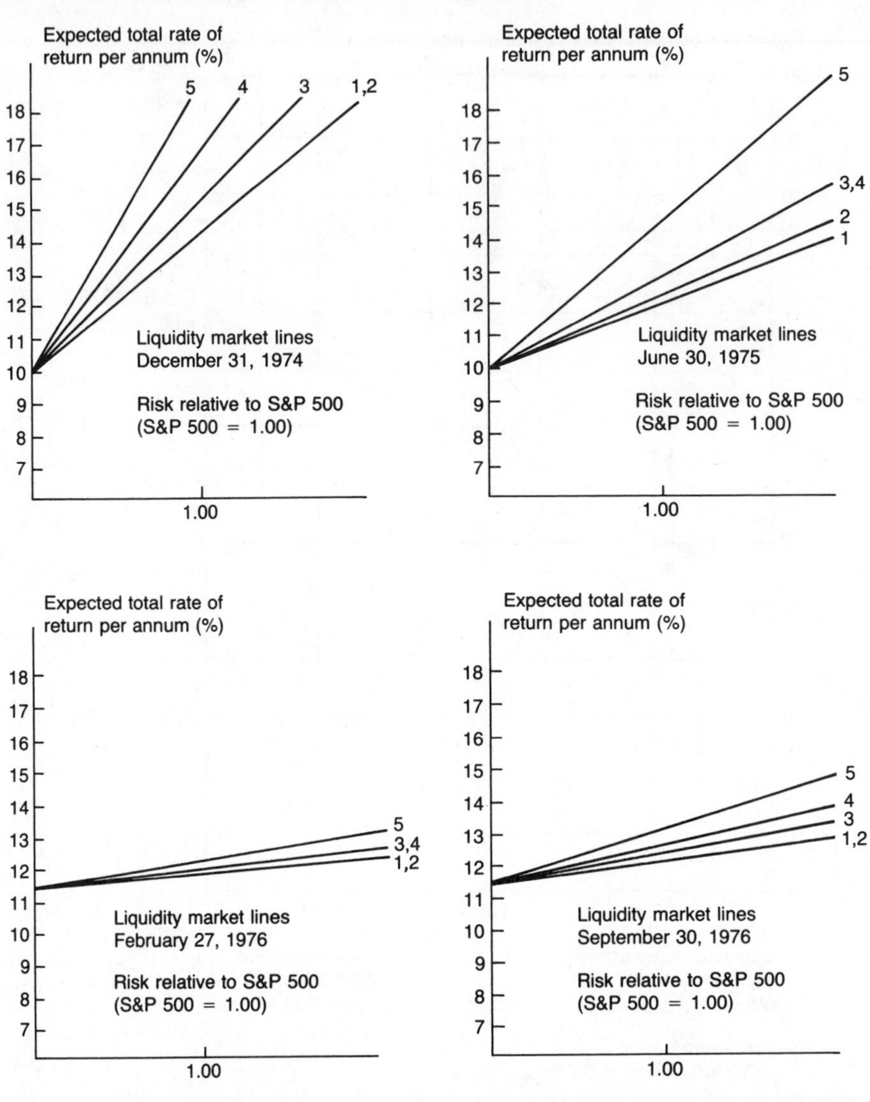

Note: These charts refer to five liquidity groups ranked from 1 (highest liquidity) to 5 (lowest liquidity). The spread is called the liquidity fan; the fan opens and closes over time.

EXHIBIT 5
Illustration of the Effects of Taxes on the Security Market Line

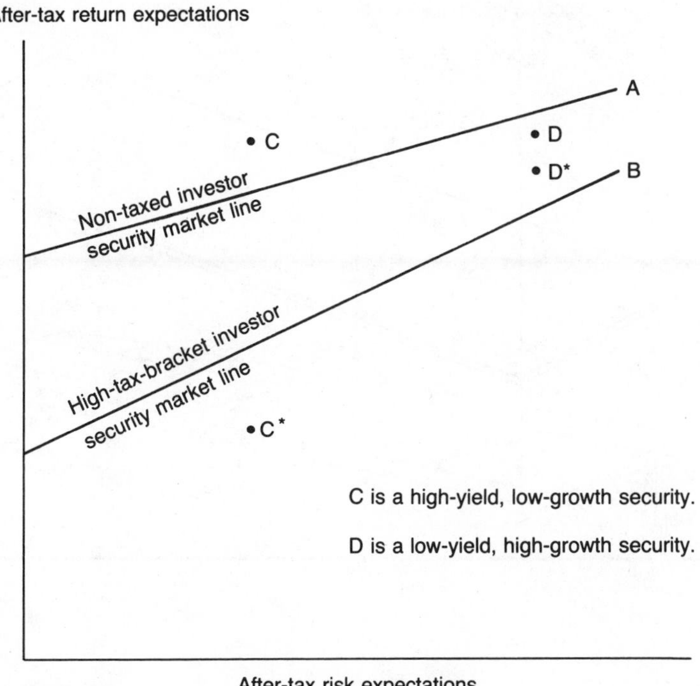

Note: Asterisk indicates security position relative to high-tax-bracket market line.

EXHIBIT 6
Illustration of Wells Fargo's Security Market Plane

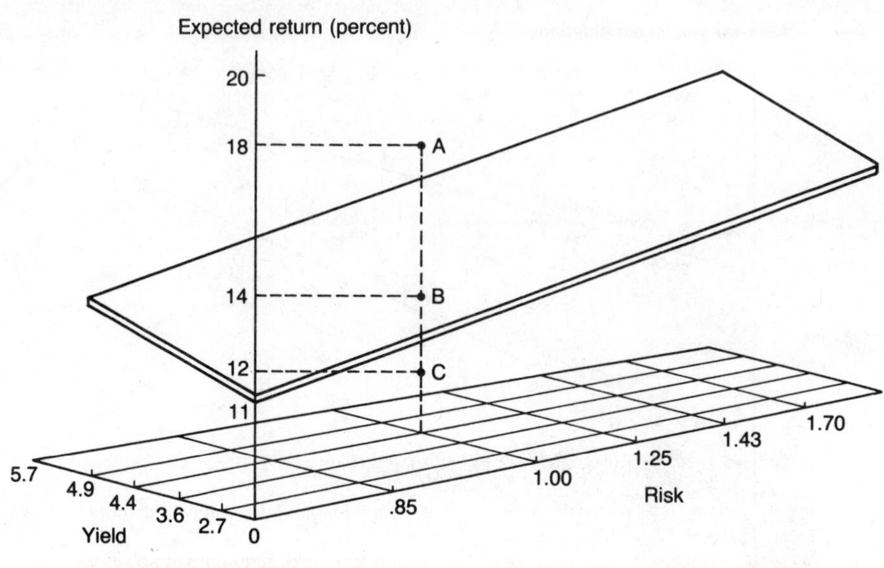

EXHIBIT 7
Illustration of Wells Fargo's Security Yield Line (*at market risk, November 30, 1978*)

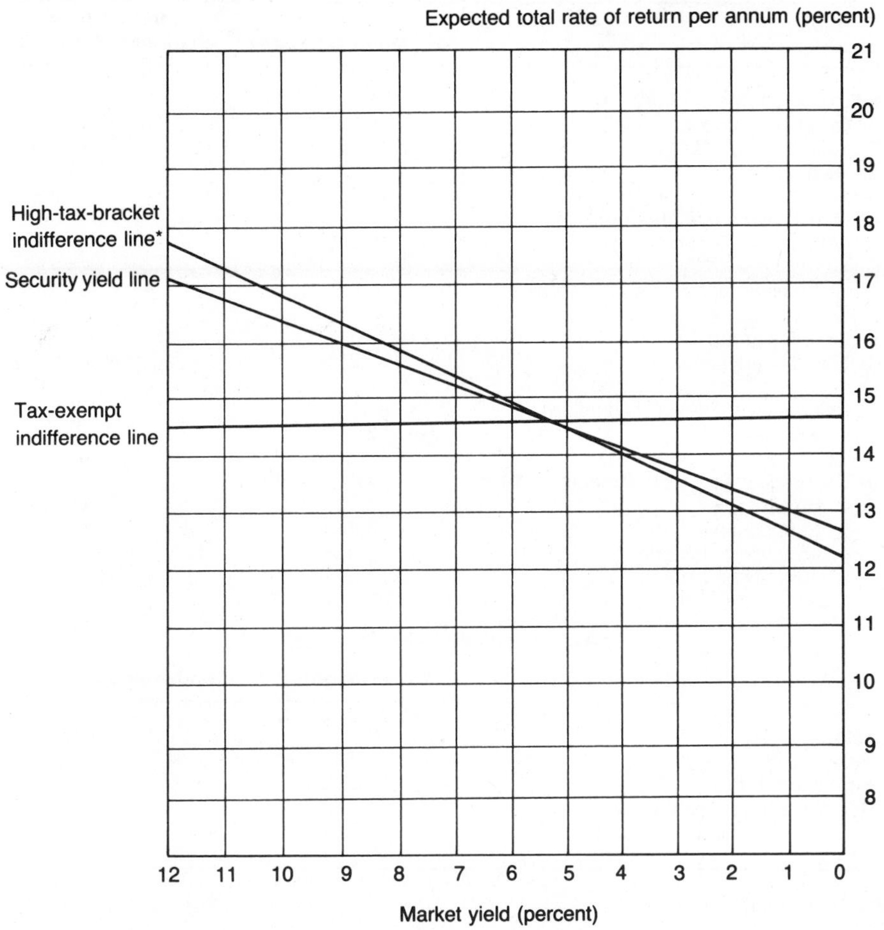

*High tax bracket.
Tax rates illustrated: income tax rate 60 percent; capital gain tax rate 28 percent.

EXHIBIT 8
Illustrative Examples of Alpha Adjustments for Two Companies* (*Wells Fargo Investment Advisors, November 30, 1978*)

	Ford Motor Company	International Business Machines
1. Expected rate of return (dividend discount model)	18.0 %	13.3 %
2. Yield	8.75%	4.27%
3. Beta	1.06	0.91
4. Market plane rate of return (for same beta and yield)	16.2 %	14.3 %
5. Unadjusted alpha (line 1 − line 4)	1.8 %	−1.0 %
6. Liquidity group	1	1
7. Liquidity adjustment	.35%	.69%
8. Relative mispricing (unadjusted) (line 5 + line 7)	2.2 %	−0.2 %
9. Tax bracket alpha adjustments		
a. No taxes	3.70%	−0.36%
b. 25% tax on income	3.14%	−0.31%
c. 45% tax on income	2.56%	−0.27%
d. 70% tax on income	1.59%	−0.19%

Market Averages (Wells Fargo Universe)

	Value-Weighted	Equal-Weighted
Beta	1	1.21
Yield	5.2 %	4.7 %
Expected return	14.52%	15.02%
Market plane for same yield and beta (liquidity adjustment)	14.76%	15.02%

*Some rounding errors.

EXHIBIT 9
Selected Data from Wells Fargo Stock Analysis Report (*November 30, 1978*)

	Expected Return	Beta	Yield	Liquidity Group	Market Plane Estimate of Return	Alpha Tax-Exempt	Alpha 70% Tax	1978 eps (E)	1979 eps (E)	5-Year eps Growth Forecast
Manufacturing/Processing										
Aluminum Company of America (aluminum)	14.0%	1.05	4.36%	2	14.7%	−0.47%	−0.52%	$ 7.70	$ 7.40	10.4%
American Cyanamid (chemicals)	16.9	.95	6.12	2	15.3	2.58	1.38	3.15	3.50	14.5
Koppers Company (chemicals)	17.0	1.15	6.04	4	15.4	1.94	1.17	2.80	3.25	11.4
Union Carbide (chemicals)	15.9	1.25	7.89	1	16.2	1.12	−0.41	5.50	5.25	4.4
du Pont (chemicals)	14.2	1.07	4.08	1	15.1	−0.14	−0.71	11.06	15.25	11.4
Dow Chemical (chemicals)	14.1	1.20	5.33	1	15.1	−0.65	−0.80	3.05	2.95	8.9
American Can Company (containers)	15.7	0.67	7.61	3	15.0	1.89	0.30	5.95	6.10	6.8
Pittston Company (mining)	16.5	1.35	6.53	3	15.9	1.25	0.45	0.50	2.40	21.4
Hanna Mining (mining)	19.2	1.04	5.83	5	15.2	4.30	3.56	2.50	5.00	16.5
Cyrus Mines (nonferrous metals)	19.0	1.22	0.00	5	15.0	3.66	3.74	5.00	1.50	79.4
Inco Ltd. (nonferrous metals)	16.3	1.30	2.67	2	14.4	1.13	2.32	0.40	0.40	26.4
Kennecott Copper (nonferrous metals)	14.0	1.20	2.65	2	14.1	−0.87	0.42	0.15	1.25	82.9
Homestake Mining (nonferrous metals)	13.1	0.55	4.18	3	13.3	−0.51	−0.04	2.50	2.50	11.9
Crown Zellerbach (paper products)	16.5	1.18	6.26	3	15.6	1.49	0.59	3.40	5.00	10.8
International Paper (paper products)	15.6	1.20	5.21	2	15.3	0.82	0.41	4.50	5.50	9.9
Union Camp Corporation (paper products)	14.6	1.08	5.08	2	14.7	−0.02	−0.01	5.10	5.40	11.8
U.S. Steel (steel)	15.6	1.20	7.03	1	15.7	0.82	−0.26	3.00	3.50	28.9
Armco (steel)	14.6	1.20	7.55	3	15.9	−0.36	−1.70	4.00	3.25	12.2
Capital Goods										
Rockwell International (aircraft)	14.7	1.02	6.72	2	15.5	0.18	−1.04	4.61	4.80	9.9
Raytheon (aircraft)	13.2	1.31	2.57	2	14.5	−1.88	−0.77	4.80	5.50	16.3
Caterpillar Tractor (construction & mining)	14.7	1.01	3.72	1	14.3	0.46	0.92	6.40	7.00	12.6
Gardner Denver (construction & mining)	14.6	1.37	5.44	5	15.5	−0.95	−1.15	2.75	2.80	22.4
General Electric Co. (electric equipment)	14.7	1.00	5.52	1	14.8	0.58	0.23	5.30	5.75	9.8
International Tel. & Tel. Co. (elect. equip)	17.0	1.16	7.05	1	16.0	2.37	0.85	4.80	5.45	13.3
Minnesota Mining & Manufacturing (elect. equip.)	14.1	1.08	3.37	1	14.3	−0.37	0.19	4.85	5.50	16.5
Black & Decker Company (elect. equip.)	14.4	1.31	3.56	3	15.0	−0.85	−0.50	1.58	1.75	14.6
Emerson Electric Co. (elect. equipment)	13.9	1.03	3.54	2	14.3	−0.59	−0.07	2.93	3.15	11.5
Motorola (electronics)	14.2	1.60	2.51	2	15.1	−1.44	−0.39	4.00	4.20	13.9

EXHIBIT 9 *(continued)*

	Expected Return	Beta	Yield	Liquidity Group	Market Plane Estimate of Return	Alpha Tax-Exempt	Alpha 70% Tax	1978 eps (E)	1979 eps (E)	5-Year eps Growth Forecast
Texas Instruments (electronics)	13.8%	1.39	2.11%	2	14.5%	−1.37	−0.08	$ 6.00	$ 7.00	15.0%
John Deere Co. (farm machinery)	14.0	1.24	4.27	2	14.8	−0.91	−0.56	4.30	4.75	7.0
Ingersoll Rand (industrial machinery)	16.0	1.28	6.30	2	15.8	0.89	−0.05	6.60	7.00	12.5
Clark Equipment (industrial machinery)	15.4	1.26	6.02	4	15.8	−0.59	−0.73	5.60	5.75	9.0
Hewlett Packard (instruments)	13.9	1.34	0.71	2	13.7	−1.19	1.08	5.10	6.10	16.6
Tektronix (instruments)	13.2	1.44	1.46	2	14.1	−2.29	−0.29	3.19	3.75	16.7
Digital Equipment (office machines)	14.7	1.42	0.00	1	13.6	−0.50	2.22	3.40	3.85	19.9
International Business Machines (office equipment)	13.3	0.91	4.27	1	14.3	−0.36	−0.19	20.00	22.50	10.6
Xerox Corporation (office machines)	13.8	1.16	3.76	1	14.6	−0.83	−0.42	5.70	6.45	11.7
Burroughs (office machines)	13.5	1.12	2.23	1	13.8	−1.02	0.40	6.10	6.95	13.3
Petroleum										
Exxon Corp. (international)	14.3	0.66	6.92	1	14.5	0.92	−0.08	5.80	6.75	10.6
Texaco (international)	14.3	0.74	8.38	1	15.3	0.60	−1.20	2.75	3.25	4.1
Mobil (international)	14.5	0.84	6.90	1	15.0	0.57	−0.56	10.30	10.75	6.8
Continental Oil (domestic)	15.5	1.02	5.38	1	14.9	1.08	0.70	4.00	5.50	14.7
Standard Oil—Ind. (domestic)	14.3	0.63	5.27	1	14.1	0.84	0.44	7.40	8.00	7.9
Atlantic Richfield (domestic)	15.1	1.06	4.39	1	14.7	0.73	0.72	6.50	7.50	11.9
Standard Oil—Ohio (domestic)	13.1	1.12	2.35	2	13.9	−1.48	−0.18	3.75	4.75	23.4
Louisiana Land Expl. (domestic)	13.8	1.01	6.32	3	15.1	−0.72	−1.45	2.65	2.90	5.8
Dresser Ind. (services)	14.8	0.98	2.68	2	13.9	0.44	1.40	5.25	6.00	11.0
Helmarich & Payne (services)	12.3	1.12	1.16	5	13.4	−2.74	−0.66	4.26	4.65	13.7
Schlumberger, Ltd. (services)	12.8	0.81	1.64	1	12.9	−1.08	0.70	5.90	6.75	15.2
Sedco, Inc. (services)	13.0	1.24	1.61	4	13.9	−2.19	−0.54	4.26	4.75	4.7
General Business										
CBS, Inc. (broadcasters)	15.3	1.30	5.10	2	15.3	0.24	0.14	7.00	7.20	7.9
ARA Services (bus. services)	16.8	1.33	4.60	4	15.1	1.47	1.73	5.00	6.00	17.3
Dunn & Bradstreet (bus. services)	11.8	1.02	3.94	4	14.3	−2.87	−2.49	2.45	2.80	11.3
Gannett (newspaper)	13.6	1.02	3.29	3	13.9	−0.96	0.12	3.00	3.30	13.5
Times Mirror (newspaper)	13.7	1.25	3.67	3	14.7	−1.43	−0.87	2.90	3.20	7.8
McGraw-Hill (publishing)	14.0	1.17	4.28	3	15.0	−0.96	−1.09	2.60	2.80	12.8

Transportation										
Southern Railway (railroad)	13.9%	1.05	6.03%	2	15.1%	−0.76%	−1.41%	$7.95	$8.00	6.0%
Union Pacific (railroad)	12.3	1.08	3.79	2	14.5	−0.68	0.08	5.30	5.60	9.1
Roadway Express (trucking)	15.2	1.48	2.73	3	14.9	−0.44	0.58	2.70	3.40	16.1
Consumer—Basic										
American Home Products (health care)	14.3	0.66	4.75	1	13.9	0.67	0.65	2.15	2.40	10.6
Warner Lambert (health care)	15.0	0.94	5.03	2	14.6	0.71	0.51	2.60	3.00	10.8
Baxter Travenol (health care)	13.8	1.13	1.00	2	13.4	−0.91	1.14	2.75	3.25	17.1
Johnson & Johnson (health care)	13.9	0.74	2.20	1	13.1	0.15	1.46	5.10	5.85	11.4
Bristol Myers Co. (health care)	13.7	0.98	3.86	2	14.3	−0.68	−0.33	3.00	3.30	10.1
Merck & Co. (health care)	13.1	0.88	2.85	1	13.6	−0.93	0.05	4.00	4.35	11.2
Beatrice Foods (food)	14.8	0.84	4.67	2	14.2	0.65	0.70	2.55	2.80	10.4
Kraft, Inc. (food)	14.9	0.83	5.83	2	14.8	0.76	−0.13	6.20	6.65	9.6
General Foods Corp. (food)	14.4	0.89	5.36	2	14.8	0.28	−0.40	4.25	4.40	10.9
General Mills (food)	13.9	0.88	4.00	2	14.0	−0.26	0.25	2.90	3.20	10.5
Nabisco, Inc. (food)	13.8	0.83	6.12	3	14.6	−0.40	−0.96	3.15	3.35	8.7
Safeway Stores (food stores)	14.7	0.88	6.48	2	15.0	0.46	−0.47	5.40	5.50	13.8
Clorox Co. (household)	14.2	1.44	5.85	4	15.9	−1.39	−1.89	1.53	1.55	8.3
Procter & Gamble (household)	11.7	0.74	3.50	1	13.5	−2.02	−1.23	6.19	6.75	10.6
Philip Morris, Inc. (tobacco)	14.0	0.17	2.97	1	13.5	0.24	1.10	6.50	7.60	14.9
Consumer—Discretionary										
Delta Airlines (air transp.)	15.4	1.54	2.34	2	14.7	−0.21	1.26	6.75	6.60	11.7
United Airlines (air transp.)	13.8	1.76	2.57	2	15.4	−2.26	−1.08	10.00	5.50	11.8
Levi Strauss (apparel)	16.1	1.24	4.60	3	15.1	1.02	1.05	6.50	7.00	9.8
Pepsi Company (beverage)	14.4	0.94	3.85	1	14.1	0.24	0.79	2.45	2.75	12.9
Coca-Cola (beverage)	12.8	0.76	4.22	1	13.9	−1.00	−0.75	2.95	3.27	11.2
Anheuser-Busch (beverage)	12.8	1.05	3.50	2	14.1	−1.85	−1.05	2.40	2.75	12.3
Avon Products (cosmetics)	13.8	1.11	5.01	1	15.0	−0.69	−0.96	4.00	4.50	13.3
Gillette Co. (cosmetics)	14.0	1.28	6.00	2	15.7	−1.02	−1.85	3.05	3.25	8.9
Mohasco (furniture)	17.2	1.37	8.37	5	16.6	1.50	−0.30	1.65	1.50	9.8
Hilton Hotels (hotel)	15.9	1.42	2.89	4	15.1	0.33	0.81	5.15	5.75	26.6
Holiday Inns (hotel)	13.1	1.66	3.03	3	15.5	−2.92	−2.27	2.15	2.55	14.7
RCA (brown goods)	14.4	1.29	5.41	2	15.3	−0.57	−0.74	3.50	3.80	9.6
Sunbeam Corp. (white goods)	17.0	1.19	7.62	5	16.0	1.76	0.24	3.15	3.30	7.6
Disney, Walt (leisure time)	14.1	1.44	0.84	2	14.1	−1.28	0.78	3.05	3.45	16.4
General Motors (motor vehicle)	17.4	0.94	12.22	1	16.7	3.47	0.16	12.10	8.50	10.5
Ford Motors (motor vehicle)	18.0	1.06	8.75	1	16.2	3.70	1.59	13.50	9.50	−4.1

EXHIBIT 9 *(concluded)*

	Expected Return	Beta	Yield	Liquidity Group	Market Plane Estimate of Return	Alpha Tax-Exempt	Alpha 70% Tax	1978 eps (E)	1979 eps (E)	5-Year eps Growth Forecast
Dana Corporation (motor vehicle)	15.8%	1.35	4.99%	4	15.5%	0.41%	0.19%	$4.22	$4.70	11.1%
Eastman Kodak (photographic)	13.7	1.09	4.26	1	14.6	−0.65	−0.43	5.20	5.60	13.5
K mart Corporation (retail—general)	16.2	1.25	3.15	2	14.5	1.32	2.22	2.85	3.10	13.6
Sears Roebuck (retail—general)	15.7	1.19	5.24	1	15.6	1.00	0.12	2.90	3.20	9.6
Federated Dept. Stores (retail—general)	15.1	1.22	5.08	2	15.4	0.21	−0.30	4.25	4.60	8.1
McDonald's Corporation (retail specialist)	16.3	1.38	0.77	1	13.9	1.15	3.31	4.20	5.00	21.0
Goodyear Tire (rubber)	17.1	1.19	8.25	2	16.4	2.22	0.24	2.90	2.40	9.1
Burlington Industries (textile)	16.6	1.07	8.12	2	16.0	1.84	0.04	2.50	3.00	5.7
Finance										
BankAmerica Corp. (bank)	15.5	0.88	4.38	2	14.2	1.32	1.50	3.00	4.00	14.1
Manufacturers Hanover Corp. (bank)	17.1	1.09	6.42	2	15.5	2.44	1.44	5.70	6.50	10.7
Citicorp (bank)	16.0	1.02	4.78	1	14.6	1.69	1.71	3.70	4.25	13.7
Morgan, J. P. (bank)	14.6	0.95	4.78	2	14.5	0.34	0.32	5.90	6.45	9.9
Beneficial Finance (finance company)	17.1	1.46	7.96	4	16.8	1.51	−0.25	4.40	4.90	10.5
American Express (insurance)	16.2	1.37	5.10	1	15.4	1.09	1.07	4.40	5.10	13.6
Travelers Corp. (insurance)	15.9	1.26	4.96	2	15.5	0.92	0.38	7.70	7.10	7.0
Shelter										
Johns Manville (construction)	19.5	1.21	7.83	2	16.1	4.61	3.11	5.75	5.70	11.4
Georgia Pacific (forest)	15.1	1.06	4.36	2	14.5	0.50	0.79	2.80	2.60	12.9
Weyerhauser Co. (forest)	14.3	1.13	3.92	2	14.4	−0.39	0.24	2.75	2.70	13.3
Utility										
Houston Industries (electric)	15.9	1.05	7.64	2	15.9	1.28	−0.52	4.40	4.85	5.4
Cincinnati Gas & Electric (electric)	14.7	0.76	9.86	4	15.9	0.58	−2.00	2.50	3.06	4.1
Florida Power Corporation (electric)	14.4	1.02	8.00	2	16.0	−0.12	−2.13	4.40	4.35	2.5
Commonwealth Edison (electric)	13.5	0.68	9.01	1	15.6	−0.13	−2.55	3.25	3.35	6.5
Public Service of Colorado (electric)	13.8	0.84	9.41	4	15.9	−0.53	−2.86	1.72	2.08	10.6
Columbia Gas System (gas)	15.1	0.80	9.00	3	15.8	0.91	−1.41	3.90	4.15	5.1
American Tel. & Tel. (telephone)	13.6	0.56	7.57	1	14.8	0.62	−0.99	7.60	7.95	5.2
General Tel. & Tel. (telephone)	15.0	0.72	8.70	1	15.4	1.31	−0.75	4.00	4.20	5.0
Average: Wells Fargo Universe	15.02	1.21	4.70	3	15.02					13.0

Part VII

Investment Strategies—Inefficient Markets

Delphi Investment Management Corporation

In late May 1983, Mr. George Seer, executive vice president of Delphi Investment Management Corporation, was contemplating what policy decisions, if any, should be made in response to the continued strength of the current bull market, which had begun in August 1982, and had already run longer and advanced more than any similar market during the last 25 years. By many criteria, a correction was long overdue. In the last few days, the market had weakened somewhat and a number of prophets were predicting a market pullback to the mid-1100 range or lower on the Dow Industrial Average. This recent market action was likely to be the focal point of the Investment Policy Committee meeting he was about to attend, where several key policy questions that had divided the Committee over the last several months would be raised.

Delphi Investment Management (DIM) was a subsidiary of the Delphi Management Company. The parent company had begun as a personal investment counselor in 1923 and had subsequently initiated several mutual funds. Oracle Income Fund, a mutual fund managed in a style similar to DIM (except that somewhat more freedom in market timing was permitted in Oracle) was the first of these funds. In 1971, DIM was established as a wholly owned subsidiary to provide investment services to separately managed accounts for tax-exempt institutions. Exhibit 1 provides an organization chart for DIM, and Exhibit 2 indicates the experience of certain key employees. In early 1982, DIM had 135 clients for which it managed

---

This case was prepared by a Professor of the Colgate Darden Graduate School of Business Administration of the University of Virginia.

$3.7 billion in equities and $.5 billion in fixed-income securities. DIM was owned by the active management group and the professional staff.

Goals and Management Style

Delphi Management Company had evolved a distinctive management style that permeated the organization and reflected its philosophy about the equity market. Over the last 20 years, equity market movements had become increasingly erratic: stocks had become sensitized to fiscal and monetary policies, which had resulted in progressively higher peaks for interest rates, unemployment, and inflation. As a result, old concepts about the relationship between the economic cycle and the market cycle had frayed. Investment strategy had to adapt to the new frequency and severity of these market cycles by broadening its dominant concern with company and industry valuation to include analysis of the fundamental economic and political trends profoundly affecting profit and market cycles; that is, investment philosophy had to move beyond return-performance boundaries to consider new standards of risk tolerance related to growing risk aversion among investors.

As a result of these views, DIM had established the following goals for its all-equity accounts—goals against which the group sought to be judged:

1. An investment style, and performance results, less volatile than those of the market.
2. An annual rate of return more consistent over time than the wide range of performance swings that characterized some investment managers.
3. Superior protection in bear markets.
4. A risk-adjusted rate of return that over a three- or five-year period would provide an incremental return over inflation during the same period.

These goals formalized a fundamental management belief: Long-term performance is not determined by how much is made in rising markets, but by how much of the gains achieved is preserved in falling markets.

Management believed that the best way to achieve these goals was through adoption of a total-rate-of-return methodology, requiring that dividends be a significant portion of the total expected rate of return. In short, the firm's management style was "yield oriented." Every equity security in a client portfolio had to possess one fundamental characteristic: The stock must offer a yield greater than that of the Standard & Poor's 500 Index. Overall, portfolio yields tended to be considerably higher.

This investment style seemed likely to provide, and had historically demonstrated, defensive characteristics and low volatility without sacrificing return prospects. The yield orientation produced a universe of stocks for investment consideration that tended to be characterized by low price-to-earnings ratios and low market-to-book-value ratios. Over time, this universe tended to be dominated by interest-rate-sensitive, consumer, capital-intensive, cyclical industry groups. The dividend discriminator tended, in contrast, to eliminate groups like the high-technology companies.

Many investors were appreciation oriented. Over the last 50 years, however, studies like those of Ibbotson and Sinquefield[1] had shown that the dividend component of total equity-market returns about equaled the capital gains component. During extended economic periods, such as depressions and the stagflation period from 1965 to 1981, dividends were the dominant component in total market returns. Over shorter periods, the mix of dividends/capital gains varied considerably; management, however, had achieved a rather consistent 50/50 mix of income and gains over periods of 8 to 10 years. By constructing portfolios with higher-than-average yields, management hoped to guarantee permanent higher-than-average yield performance. At the same time, portfolios were composed in ways that did not seem likely to sacrifice gains prospects, and portfolio results had over time tended to provide an above-average capital gains increment relative to the market.

The Decision-Making Process: The Eligible Universe

To be considered for investment, a stock had to meet all of the following tests:

1. The market capitalization for the stock must exceed $100 million (liquidity screen).
2. The stock must have a quality rating of B+ or better, as measured by Standard & Poor's (quality screen).
3. The stock must provide a current market yield greater than the current yield on the Standard & Poor's 500 Index (dividend screen).
4. The stock must have a total return prospect 300 points above the prevailing yield on Aa new issues of industrial bonds, or 500 basis points above the weighted, experienced inflation rate,[2] whichever the Investment Policy Committee considered to be more appropriate in the circumstances.

Forecasted total rates of return for each security were calculated by the following formula:

$$\text{Unadjusted total return} = \frac{\text{(Hard book value per share)(return on book value)(reinvestment rate)}}{\text{Price/share}} + \frac{\text{EPS}(1 - \text{reinvestment rate})}{\text{Price/share}}$$

---

[1]R. G. Ibbotson and R. A. Sinquefield, *Stocks, Bonds, Bills and Inflation: The Past and the Future* (Charlottesville, Va.: Financial Analysts Research Foundation, 1982).

[2]Calculated as follows: 2/3 weight: GNP deflater index, 3-year trend growth annualized, calculated quarterly; 1/3 weight: GNP deflater change, 12 months out, Investment Consensus.

where:

Hard book value per share eliminated intangibles from stated common equity book values at the most recent reporting date.

Rate of *return on book value* was determined by forecasted profits available to common stockholders, divided by the current or forecasted hard book values.

Reinvestment rate was equal to 1 minus the dividend payout ratio (i.e., the fraction of forecasted earnings estimated as likely to be retained).

Dividends were forecasted levels of payments per share.

Price/share was the current market price.

The Investment Policy Committee from time to time imposed more stringent criteria for determining eligible stocks.

Forecasts were prepared for three years into the future and adjusted for their time value. Unadjusted total returns for a stock (stated as a percentage) were then adjusted for their risk characteristics by dividing by that security's beta.

The Sales Discipline

Perhaps the most important element affecting portfolio composition was the sales discipline imposed on the portfolio manager. Each manager, first, had the right to sell any stock in the portfolios he/she was responsible for whenever an analysis of the macro or micro fundamentals suggested, in his/her judgment, that a sale was appropriate. A stock had to be sold, however, in the following instances:

1. The current estimate of total return (unadjusted for risk) was less than the prevailing Aa new industrial long-term yield to maturity.
2. The current yield on the stock was below the yield on the Standard & Poor's 500 Index.
3. Liquidity or quality tests failed to be met.

The Investment Policy Committee could and did sometimes impose more restrictive constraints, forcing the automatic sale of certain portfolio securities.

While other factors could come into play, the following elements tended to prove most critical in the sales discipline:

The automatic sales requirement influenced portfolio managers to pay considerable attention to the safety of the current dividend when selecting securities. (A dividend reduction might often trigger the yield-sales criterion at an unpropitious moment in the market for that firm's stock.) A security that was too near a sales trigger-point would be avoided, therefore, because it had little appreciation potential in view of the transaction costs incurred in the purchase and sale. A qualifying firm that seemed likely to increase its dividend in the near future or to show improving reinvestment prospects was likely to be preferred.

Stocks were most often sold because they had appreciated to the point where they no longer met guidelines. The sales discipline thus tended to lock in realized appreciation potential. Because dividends tended to be more forecastable and were often cushioned against micro-shocks by firm payout policies, "surprise" dividend decreases forced sales only infrequently.

Interest-rate volatility could affect sales decisions. Rising interest rates—often preceding a business recession—might force greater selectivity but often came at a time when defensive strategies were appropriate. Falling interest rates, in contrast, facilitated long holding periods and greater appreciation potential.

Finally, downward reevaluation of growth (reinvestment) potential could force a sale. Although many times the sales discipline forced sales of securities that seemed to the portfolio manager otherwise attractive (based on fundamental and technical prospects), the discipline, while sometimes painful, was nevertheless considered important to the overall achievement of objectives.

The Role of the Investment Strategy Committee

Delphi Investment Management followed a top-down approach to investing. The firm's emphasis was *not* on security selection per se, with the attendant dominance of the portfolio manager. The guidance of the Investment Strategy Committee was viewed as critical to the success of portfolio performance.

After analyzing economic and political trends, money market conditions and outlook, and industry data, the Strategy Committee suggested concentration/diversification guidelines to the portfolio managers. These guidelines covered selection of industries, their propensity for cyclicality, investment size and liquidity objectives, and other, broader economic concerns such as energy, natural resources, interest-rate sensitivity, and similar types of investment considerations.

The Role of the Investment Policy Committee

The Investment Policy Committee established—and altered according to prevailing market conditions—a total-rate-of-return goal for all portfolios and determined how much of this goal should be achieved in the form of dividend yield. Portfolios were monitored to assure that these goals were being achieved. Finally, as circumstances warranted, the Policy Committee also altered either the universe-eligibility criteria or the sell criteria.

Research

Delphi Investment Management held portfolio managers responsible for security research, an activity that was shared in weekly meetings. In management's view, there had been a manifold increase in both the quality and availability of financial, industrial, and political analyses. Analysts thus concentrated on evaluating qualitatively the readily available quantitative information.

In the evaluation, management was less concerned with the relative accuracy of the data than with the impact the information would have on the financial community. How pervasive was a given forecast and whom would it influence most? How long would the influence last? These and similar assessments seemed to affect appreciation performance most in the long run. Investment fashions, according to management, changed quickly; anticipating and recognizing these changes was viewed as critical. Analysts, in short, sought to ascertain how the world perceived the intrinsic worth of an investment idea. They ascertained opinion, examining the contrary point of view on every security, in order to anticipate and detect broad shifts in investment sentiment.

Portfolio Characteristics

A client's portfolio typically contained between 40 and 45 individual securities. Investments tended to be more equally weighted than value weighted. Portfolio turnover averaged about 35 percent per year, which suggested an average holding period of about three years.

Because of management style and the guidelines from the Investment Policy Committee, portfolios tended to be quite different in composition from those of a "market portfolio" as represented by the Standard & Poor's 500 Index. Exhibit 3 presents a portfolio prepared for presentation to a potential client seeking an all-equity portfolio on April 29, 1983, based upon an actual client account established November 15, 1976. A new account would tend to have more nearly equal weightings, but would hold similar securities.

Portfolio Management

Each account was assigned to a portfolio manager, who typically managed 13–15 accounts. Each security manager had considerable freedom to select the individual securities composing a portfolio—within the boundaries and guidelines established by the Investment Policy Committee. Because research was pooled, portfolios tended to be somewhat similar. Although performance of individual accounts might vary in a given year by as much as 2.75 percent (in standard deviation terms), over longer periods performance tended to be similar.

Investments were selected with a time horizon of six months or longer, depending on the market outlook. In more volatile or adverse markets, portfolio turnover tended to increase. Emphasis was placed on total-return prospects, with some consideration for current under- or overvaluation.

The firm did not regard itself as a market timer. However, to the degree that rising interest rates coincident with a rising stock price level reduced the number of stocks in the opportunity universe, the firm had the tendency to raise cash, de facto. As more stocks were sold that no longer met objective criteria, reinvestment of the proceeds often became more difficult, since replacement candidates were increasingly difficult to identify. During such environments cash positions of 15 percent were not uncommon.

Customer Service

With the growth of funds under management, Delphi now sought clients willing to invest $10 million or more initially. Management believed that close communication between the investment manager and the client was important. A quarterly letter setting forth an analysis of recent trends and the current outlook (including a 12-month rate-of-return estimate) was sent to clients (an example is shown in Exhibit 4). Semi-annual meetings of clients, the portfolio manager, and a member of the Investment Advisory Committee were encouraged. These meetings tended to emphasize the outlook governing the current portfolio composition.

Performance

Exhibit 5 contains an analysis of the yield and capital gains component of total return over various time periods, using internal and external studies of market performance. In this and the exhibits that follow, DIM's equity performance is based on the equity-only performance of the Oracle Income Fund (mutual fund), a portfolio managed in an identical style with similar performance results—results that were available over a longer period.

Exhibit 6 contains a further analysis of yield/gain relationships based on an internal DIM study. Exhibit 7 reports the cumulative performance of DIM's equity account over the past 10 years in a format used by A. G. Becker in its performance evaluation service. Exhibit 8 shows the low variability of DIM's total-return performance. DIM's dividend-yield ranking is shown in Exhibit 9. The performance of DIM's equity account in the four major down markets from 1969 to 1982 is shown in Exhibit 10. The composite equity performance of DIM's managed portfolios, along with contrasting yardsticks, is illustrated in Exhibit 11 for the last seven years.

Annualized total rates of return for DIM equities for all 10-year periods beginning in 1959 and extending to 1982 are shown in Exhibit 12. Exhibit 13 shows the relative performance of DIM equities against inflation for the 10-year period 1973 to 1982.

Exhibit 14 reports the quarterly rates of return for DIM equities for the 25-year period ending March 31, 1983. The portfolio characteristic line relating to those quarterly data (with supporting portfolio characteristic information) is shown in Exhibit 15. Note the low beta and the high alpha (quarterly) inherent in this record.

Policy Issues

As shown in Exhibit 16, the first phase of the bull market that began in August 1982 had already run longer and advanced more sharply than was characteristic of other recent market upturns. Exhibit 17 shows details of performance of the Standard & Poor's 500 Index from August 1982 up to and including a recent price weakening. Investors often attempted to correct the first phase of a bull market by giving back roughly one third of the advance to the market. Others chose to think in terms of a 10–15 percent price correction. The recent price weakening was likely to reawaken policy controversies among the members of Delphi's Investment Policy Committee, scheduled to meet the next day. It was for this meeting that Mr. Seer was currently preparing.

The issues had arisen because of DIM's flexible policy concerning perceived market risks, which were increasing as a result of cyclical or secular growth in market values when compared to fundamentals such as yield and total-return prospects. To preserve capital, a firm could react in a number of ways to periods of price vulnerability that were perceived as serious. DIM, like others, attempted to moderate risk during periods of anticipated market risk through appropriate industry and stock selection. Moderating the portfolio beta, and selling stock and raising cash wherever this discretion was allowed by their clients, were further options available to DIM portfolio managers.

As noted, the Investment Policy Committee could also set directives for the preservation of capital. DIM could increase minimum-yield requirements for purchasing new securities in order to preserve some premium over prevailing market yields. The greater the perceived market risk, the higher this premium would tend to be. Similarly, the Investment Policy Committee could raise the minimum-yield selling point for securities in the portfolio and force a paring of more issues likely to be vulnerable. The Investment Policy Committee had, as noted, other options at its disposal when reduction of potential portfolio vulnerability seemed appropriate.

For well over two years, the Investment Policy Committee had insisted upon a large-yield entry premium to the market yield because of worldwide financial risk, large federal deficits, sky-high real interest rates, and so on. At the moment, the Standard & Poor's 500 Index was yielding 4.6 percent. Nonetheless, the Investment Policy Committee had seen fit to require a 100-basis point premium for new stock purchases (currently 5.6 percent). Stocks could be held in the portfolio if yields exceeded those of the market index.

Because of the dramatic changes in equity market values since August 1982, portfolio managers had felt increasingly pinched by the lack of variety and (relative) attractiveness of stocks qualifying in the purchase universe. They had been seeking reductions in the yield required for investment purposes.

No exact weighting of the critical elements could be given, nor could the degree of financial risk exposure inherent in the equity market—or in any particular policy of the Investment Policy Committee—be evaluated scientifically. Instead, this Committee based its judgment on the following criteria, which had proven reliable during their 20 years of working together:

- Absolute and nominal level of short-term and long-term interest rates.
- The spread between interest rates and market dividend yield.
- The perceived cyclical and secular direction of interest rates.
- Current inflation level and forecasted trend.

- Outlook for corporate profits over next 18 months.
- Prevailing investor psychology.
- System-wide liquidity.
- Stock market valuation levels.
- Technical market factors.

Current Options

The primary issue at the moment was whether the Investment Policy Committee should become more aggressive in its policy structures, and if so, when—now, or after the market reversal that was being forecasted by many professional investors. The following notes from Mr. Seer's file provide a synopsis of the main arguments in the debate taking place within the company:

> Let's take the argument for becoming more aggressive. Mr. X argues, "DIM has a 20 percent yield premium to the market. This is too high, for clearly we are in a bull market. Of course, interest rates remain high, but they have dropped mightily from prevailing levels earlier this year. Inflation has become a very positive market force and is likely to remain so. What matters most is that this is obviously a bull market, not a bear market. If one perceives a long-lived up cycle, one should lower the yield guidelines closer to the market now, not react after a potential new market upleg. Likewise, we shouldn't be selling stocks right at the market yield; we should be lowering this as well. Too many good stocks might be lost by an arbitrary sell discipline, only to find them back in our universe when we drop the guidelines. Since we're all agreed the guidelines must be eventually liberalized, why wait?"
>
> Mr. Y counters, "The most critical element in performance during a bull market is to be invested. We are. True, we have sold some stocks early, insofar as they continued to rise after we sold them. But in the main, they were replaced by other securities which have also done well, or which we anticipate will do well in the next market phase. As to our yield premium, it's obviously high. But then again, real interest rates are still numbingly high. In fact, the spread between real interest rates and the market yield has seldom been as much as it now is, at least in modern times. In fact, short-term rates are not far removed from the 1974 cyclical tops and they are above the 1970 highs. Nominal long-term rates are well above the 1974 cyclical high. Interest rates must come down for further material progress until rates do come off. True, DIM believes rates will be coming down, but it's not our job to anticipate this decline. Our job is primarily a defensive one, and although we don't want to sit out a bull market, and don't intend to, we shouldn't be leading the way. That's for the more aggressive managers. Finally, although the market has so far fooled everyone by its refusal to experience a meaningful correction, such retrenchment is only a matter of time. Therefore, it would be premature to lower our yield guidelines, because this might only encourage some of our managers to move into stocks that have had the biggest runups, and which might experience the biggest setbacks. We should wait for interest rates to decline and/or a market correction to become more aggressive."

The debate did not extend to the fundamental policy precepts that had guided DIM's investment success in the past.

EXHIBIT 1
Organizational Chart of Delphi Investment Management Corporation

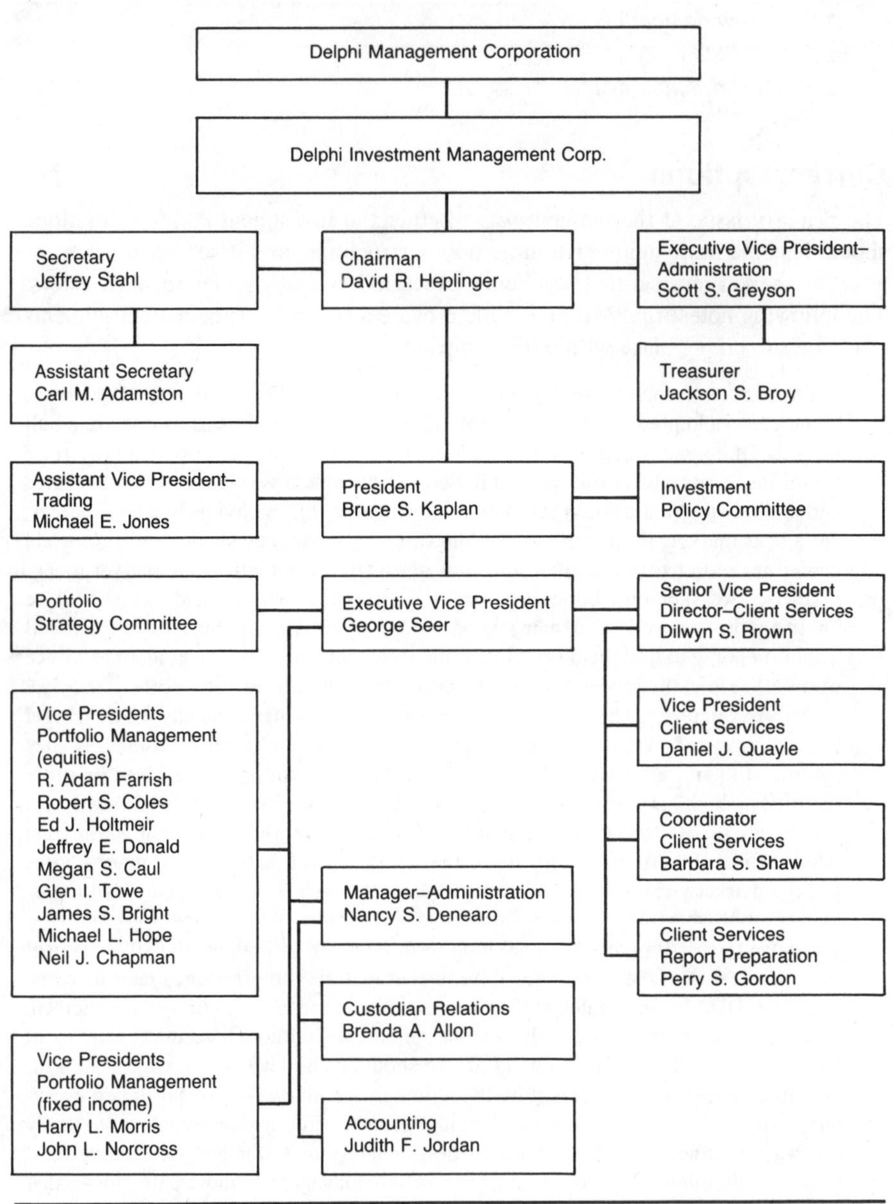

EXHIBIT 2
Background of Key Personnel

David R. Heplinger, Chairman
Mr. Heplinger, who is also president and chief executive officer of Delphi Management Corporation and chairman and chief executive officer of the Delphi Group of Mutual Funds, holds both BS and JD degrees from the University of Pennsylvania. He joined the Delphi organization in 1953 as in-house counsel, subsequently becoming involved with operations and long-range planning before being named executive vice president in 1965. A World War II naval officer, Mr. Heplinger is a member of the Navy League as well as the Financial Analysts of Philadelphia, the National Association of Security Dealers, the Investment Companies Committee of the Securities Industry Association, and the Investment Company Institute, where he serves on the Board of Governors.

Bruce S. Kaplan, President
Mr. Kaplan holds an AB in Economics from Queens College and an MBA in Finance from the University of Pennsylvania's Wharton School. He joined Delphi in 1960 as a securities analyst, becoming portfolio manager for Oracle Income Fund and Oracle Fund. In 1975 he was named executive vice president/policy, Delphi Management Company, and president of the Delphi Group of Mutual Funds in 1977. Dr. Kaplan is on the board of directors and is a past president of the Financial Analysts of Philadelphia. He belongs to the National Association of Business Economists and is a Chartered Financial Analyst.

George Seer, Executive Vice President
A graduate of Brown University, Mr. Seer also attended the NYU Graduate School of Business Administration while a senior transportation analyst at the Irving Trust Company. He came to Delphi in 1962 as a securities analyst covering a wide range of industry groups and eventually became co-manager of Delphi Fund. He was appointed investment vice president of Delphi Management Company in 1974 and was named to his present DIM position in 1978. He coordinates all portfolio management and analytical activities. Mr. Seer is a member of the Institute of Chartered Financial Analysts and the Financial Analysts Federation.

Portfolio Management/Equities

R. Adam Farrish, Vice President/Portfolio Manager
After receiving a BA in Business Administration from Westminster College, Mr. Farrish joined the investment department of a major eastern bank. After several years' experience as a portfolio analyst, he left to continue his education, and subsequently received an MBA in Finance from the University of Southern California. Mr. Farrish joined Delphi in 1976. He was made a vice president in 1978.

Robert S. Coles, Vice President/Portfolio Manager
Mr. Coles holds a BA in Accounting from St. Francis College and an MBA in Finance from the University of Maryland. An assistant vice president and asset

EXHIBIT 2 ***(continued)***

manager with the Mellon Bank NA, Mr. Coles, who was appointed a vice president in 1978, joined Delphi in early 1977, bringing with him 10 years of analytic and portfolio experience. He is a Chartered Financial Analyst.

Megan S. Caul, Vice President/Portfolio Manager
A graduate of Stanford University, BA Economics, Ms. Caul pursued an investment career with two major eastern institutional investment firms before attending Harvard Business School, where she received an MBA in Finance. Ms. Caul joined DIM in 1976 and was appointed vice president in 1978. She is a Chartered Financial Analyst.

Ed J. Holtmeir, Vice President/Portfolio Manager
Mr. Holtmeir earned his BS in Economics and Political Science from the University of Vermont and an MA in International Affairs from the University of Pennsylvania's Wharton School. Prior to joining DIM in 1978, he was responsible for portfolio management and institutional sales with two NYSE member firms.

Jeffrey E. Donald, Vice President/Portfolio Manager
Mr. Donald earned his BS in Accounting from Florida State University. Upon completing a tour of duty with the Navy, he received an MBA from Harvard Business School. He joined the Delphi organization in 1972, advancing from portfolio analyst to co-manager of Oracle Income Fund and portfolio manager of Delchester Bond Fund. He became an investment officer in 1976 and was subsequently named portfolio manager for DIM. Mr. Donald is a member of the Financial Analysts of Philadelphia. He is a Chartered Financial Analyst.

Glen I. Towe, Vice President/Portfolio Manager
A graduate of the University of Wisconsin, Mr. Towe also holds MA and MBA degrees from the University of Chicago. He joined DIM in 1978 as a research analyst and was named vice president in 1981. Prior to this, Mr. Towe was a research officer with Citibank.

James S. Bright, Vice President/Portfolio Manager
Mr. Bright is a graduate of Pennsylvania State University and holds an MBA in Finance from Temple University. A member of the New York Society of Security Analysts, he served as an investment analyst for two large Philadelphia banks and was portfolio manager at Philadelphia National Bank prior to joining DIM in 1978.

Michael L. Hope, Vice President/Portfolio Manager
A graduate of the University of Illinois with a BS in Finance, Mr. Hope has also pursued graduate studies at the University of Massachusetts and Northwestern University. He joined DIM early in 1980 after 17 years of investment management experience, most recently serving as Vice President, Equity Research for Commercial Credit Securities, Inc., a subsidiary of Control Data, Inc.

Neil J. Chapman, Vice President/Portfolio Manager
A graduate of Colgate University, Mr. Chapman received his MBA in Finance from the University of Pennsylvania's Wharton School. He joined Delphi in 1972 as a

EXHIBIT 2 ***(continued)***

portfolio analyst; later he became an investment officer and portfolio manager for Delta Trend Fund and was named to his present position in DIM in 1978. He is a Chartered Financial Analyst.

Portfolio Management/Fixed Income

Harry L. Morris, Vice President/Portfolio Manager
A 1968 graduate of American University, Mr. Morris also received his MBA in Finance from the same institution. He began his business career with the Provident National Bank and was head of the bank investment division, which included the bank portfolio and liability management functions. Mr. Morris assumed direction of DIM's fixed-income obligation operations in 1977 and was named vice president in 1978.

John L. Norcross, Vice President/Portfolio Manager
A graduate of the College of William and Mary with a BA in Economics, Mr. Norcross began his career in the municipal bond and institutional sales departments of White Weld & Co., Inc. He subsequently spent eight years as a corporate bond specialist with Salomon Brothers and Kidder, Peabody & Co., Inc., before joining DIM's fixed-income department as a vice president in 1978.

Administrative Services

Scott S. Greyson, Executive Vice President/Administration
A graduate of the University of Pennsylvania's Wharton School, BS Economics and a CPA, he joined Delphi in 1969 as operations vice president/treasurer. He has over 20 years experience in the application of data processing, accounting, and control procedures of large-scale investment operations. He was named to his position with Delphi Management Company in 1971 and assumed similar responsibilities with DIM in 1972.

Jeffrey Stahl, Secretary
Mr. Stahl received a BA from Washington and Jefferson College and a JD from the University of Pennsylvania Law School. Following several years experience with the legal department of a Philadelphia bank, Mr. Stahl came to Delphi in 1956. He is a member of the Philadelphia Bar Association and the Law and State Liaison Committees of the Investment Company Institute.

Jackson S. Broy, Assistant Secretary
Mr. Broy is a graduate of St. Joseph's College and a Certified Public Accountant. After several years with Arthur Young & Company, he joined Delphi as controller in 1967 and became treasurer in 1972.

Carl M. Adamston, Assistant Secretary
Mr. Adamston holds a BA in Economics from the University of Delaware and a JD from Georgetown University Law Center. Prior to joining Delphi in 1977, he was with a large Philadelphia law firm and a major financial publication. He is a

EXHIBIT 2 ***(concluded)***

member of the Federal, Pennsylvania, Philadelphia, and American Bar Associations and the Lawyers' Club of Philadelphia.

Trading and Custodian Relations

Michael E. Jones, Assistant Vice President/Trading
A graduate of Temple University, BS in Business Administration, Mr. Jones joined Delphi in 1962 as a trainee, becoming a trader for the Delphi Group of Mutual Funds in 1966. He was named to his present position in 1977.

Nancy S. Denearo, Manager—Administration
Ms. Denearo joined Delphi in 1968 after receiving a BA from Centenary College. Named to her present position in 1979, she is responsible for all custodian bank relationships and DIM accounting.

Client Services

Dilwyn S. Brown, Senior Vice President/Director—Client Services
Mr. Brown joined the Irving Trust Company in 1960 after receiving a BA from the University of Notre Dame. Following active service as a naval officer, Mr. Brown was associated with the Securities and Exchange Commission and a quasi-government agency. During this period he received an MBA in Finance from American University. Mr. Brown joined Delphi in 1974, assuming client services responsibilities, and was named senior vice president in 1978.

Daniel J. Quayle, Vice President/Client Services
Mr. Quayle is a graduate of Brown University where he majored in economics. He began his career with Kidder, Peabody & Company in 1968 where he was a vice president in charge of institutional equity sales. Mr. Quayle joined DIM in 1977 as vice president/client services.

EXHIBIT 3
Sample Portfolio *(April 29, 1983)*

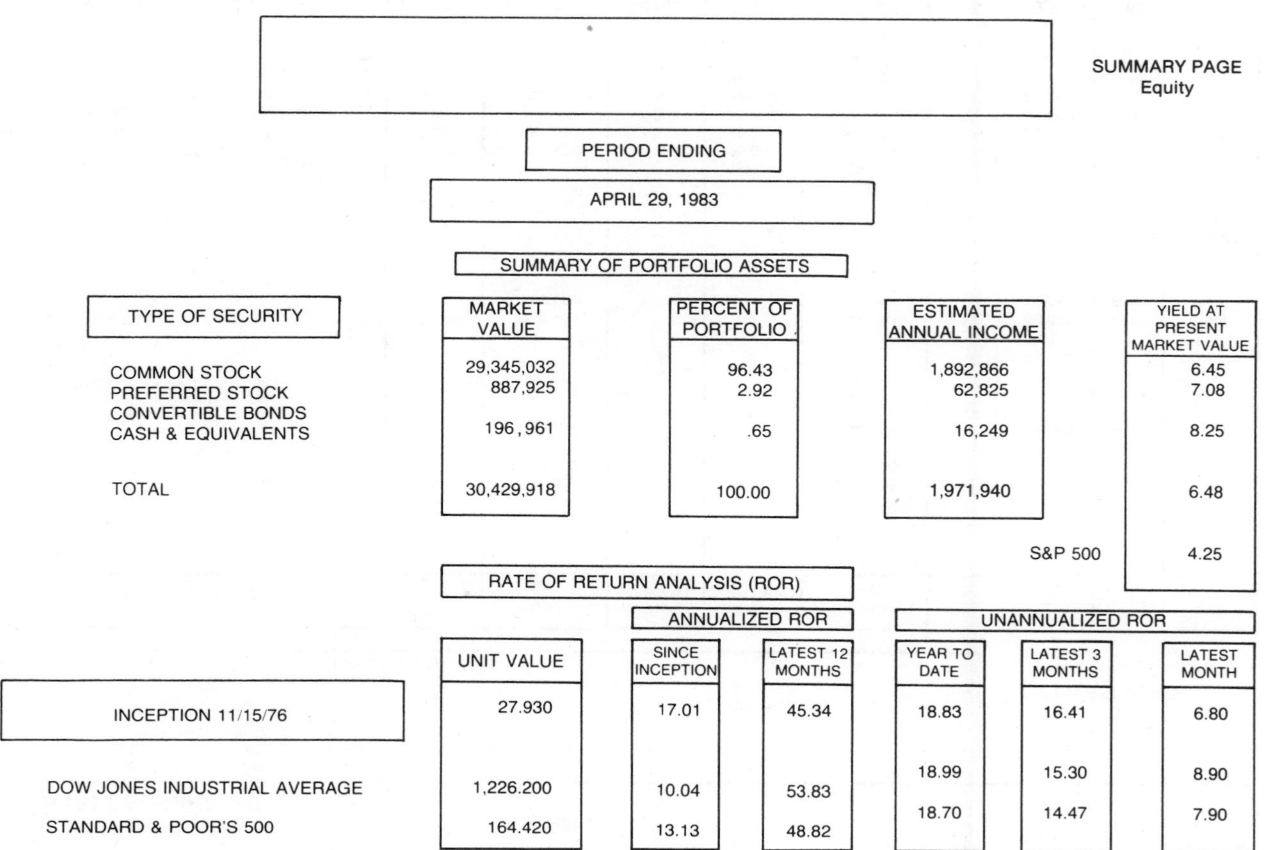

SUMMARY PAGE
Equity

PERIOD ENDING

APRIL 29, 1983

SUMMARY OF PORTFOLIO ASSETS

TYPE OF SECURITY	MARKET VALUE	PERCENT OF PORTFOLIO	ESTIMATED ANNUAL INCOME	YIELD AT PRESENT MARKET VALUE
COMMON STOCK	29,345,032	96.43	1,892,866	6.45
PREFERRED STOCK	887,925	2.92	62,825	7.08
CONVERTIBLE BONDS				
CASH & EQUIVALENTS	196 ,961	.65	16,249	8.25
TOTAL	30,429,918	100.00	1,971,940	6.48
S&P 500				4.25

RATE OF RETURN ANALYSIS (ROR)

		ANNUALIZED ROR		UNANNUALIZED ROR		
	UNIT VALUE	SINCE INCEPTION	LATEST 12 MONTHS	YEAR TO DATE	LATEST 3 MONTHS	LATEST MONTH
INCEPTION 11/15/76	27.930	17.01	45.34	18.83	16.41	6.80
DOW JONES INDUSTRIAL AVERAGE	1,226.200	10.04	53.83	18.99	15.30	8.90
STANDARD & POOR'S 500	164.420	13.13	48.82	18.70	14.47	7.90

EXHIBIT 3 *(continued)*

DATE: APRIL 29, 1983

STATEMENT OF INVESTMENTS

DESCRIPTION OF SECURITIES	SHARES OR FACE VALUE	TOTAL COST	AVERAGE UNIT COST	MARKET PRICE	TOTAL MARKET VALUE	ANNUAL		YIELD ON MARKET VALUE	% OF PORTFOLIO
						INCOME RATE	TOTAL INCOME		
UNASSIGNED EQUITIES									
HIRAM WALKER RES. LTD.	3,500	68,862	19.675	19.625	68,688	1.32	4,620	6.72	.23
		68,862			68,688		4,620	6.73	.23
****TOTAL		68,862			68,688		4,620	6.73	.23
EQUITY CASH AND EQUIVALENTS									
CASH - EQUITY -									
EQUITY CASH		196,961			196,961	8.25	16,249	8.25	.65
		196,961			196,961		16,249	8.25	.65
****TOTAL		196,961			196,961		16,249	8.25	.65
CREDIT SENSITIVE									
BANKS									
BANKAMERICA CORP.	24,500	557,455	22.753	25.000	612,500	1.52	37,240	6.08	2.01
CITICORP	12,000	288,559	24.047	45.250	543,000	1.88	22,560	4.15	1.78
FIRST ALABAMA BANKSHARES	5,000	140,000	28.000	31.000	155,000	1.80	9,000	5.80	.51
MANUFACTURERS HANOVER	9,000	285,187	31.687	51.000	459,000	3.04	27,360	5.96	1.51
J. P. MORGAN	8,000	432,132	54.017	83.000	664,000	3.70	29,600	4.45	2.18
		1,703,333			2,433,500		125,760	5.17	7.99
BUILDING/HOUSING									
LONE STAR IND.	17,000	552,500	32.500	32.375	550,375	1.90	32,300	5.86	1.81
		552,500			550,375		32,300	5.87	1.81

STATEMENT
OF
INVESTMENTS

DATE: APRIL 29, 1983

DESCRIPTION OF SECURITIES	SHARES OR FACE VALUE	TOTAL COST	AVERAGE UNIT COST	MARKET PRICE	TOTAL MARKET VALUE	ANNUAL INCOME RATE	ANNUAL TOTAL INCOME	YIELD ON MARKET VALUE	% OF PORTFOLIO
FINANCIAL SERVICES									
CONTINENTAL CORP.	15,000	451,573	30.105	35.250	528,750	2.60	39,000	7.37	1.74
TRANSAMERICA	18,000	324,865	18.048	28.500	513,000	1.50	27,000	5.26	1.69
		776,438			1,041,750		66,000	6.34	3.43
LIFE INSURANCE									
AETNA LIFE & CAS.	15,000	599,635	39.976	42.500	637,500	2.64	39,600	6.21	2.09
COLONIAL PENN GROUP	30,000	561,460	18.715	22.875	686,250	1.40	42,000	6.12	2.26
COMBINED INTERNATONAL CORP.	24,000	516,696	21.529	34.750	834,000	2.00	48,000	5.75	2.74
		1,677,791			2,157,750		129,600	6.01	7.09
****TOTAL		4,710,062			6,183,375		353,660	5.72	20.32
CONSUMER GROWTH									
COSMETIC & SOFT DRINKS									
AVON PRODUCTS	15,000	476,789	31.786	31.750	476,250	2.00	30,000	6.29	1.57
COCA COLA	12,800	435,898	34.055	55.625	712,000	2.68	34,304	4.81	2.34
REVLON INC.	8,000	250,042	31.255	33.625	269,000	1.84	14,720	5.47	.88
		1,162,729			1,457,250		79,024	5.42	4.79
HEALTH CARE									
AMERICAN HOME PRODUCTS	13,000	344,804	26.523	46.250	601,250	2.40	31,200	5.18	1.98
RICHARDSON VICKS INC.	12,000	289,600	24.133	27.250	327,000	1.48	17,760	5.43	1.07
WARNER LAMBERT	19,400	383,931	19.790	33.625	652,325	1.40	27,160	4.16	2.14
WHITTAKER CORP.	27,000	692,221	25.638	30.250	816,750	1.60	43,200	5.28	2.68
		1,710,556			2,397,325		119,320	4.98	7.87
****TOTAL		2,873,285			3,854,575		198,344	5.15	12.66

EXHIBIT 3 ***(continued)***

DATE: APRIL 29, 1983

STATEMENT OF INVESTMENTS

DESCRIPTION OF SECURITIES	SHARES OR FACE VALUE	TOTAL COST	AVERAGE UNIT COST	MARKET PRICE	TOTAL MARKET VALUE	ANNUAL		YIELD ON MARKET VALUE	% OF PORTFOLIO
						INCOME RATE	TOTAL INCOME		
CONSUMER CYCLICALS									
RETAIL TRADE									
CARTER HAWLEY HALE	24,100	425,582	17.659	23.750	572,375	1.22	29,402	5.13	1.88
		425,582			572,375		29,402	5.14	1.88
MISCELLANEOUS									
AMR. CORP. CUM. CV PFD	17,000	425,000	25.000	31.125	529,125	2.125	36,125	6.82	1.74
HOUSEHOLD INTERNATIONAL CORP.	7,000	134,260	19.180	25.500	178,500	1.65	11,550	6.47	.59
SCM	7,100	235,881	33.223	38.250	271,575	2.00	14,200	5.22	.89
		795,141			979,200		61,875	6.32	3.22
****TOTAL		1,220,723			1,551,575		91,277	5.88	5.10
CAPITAL GOODS									
ELECTRIC EQUIPMENT									
GOULD	8,000	198,000	24.750	35.250	282,000	1.72	13,760	4.87	.93
SQUARE D CO.	3,880	114,239	30.063	35.750	135,850	1.84	6,992	5.14	.45
		312,239			417,850		20,752	4.97	1.38
OFFICE EQUIPMENT									
BURROUGHS CORP.	12,700	469,862	36.997	48.750	619,125	2.60	33,020	5.33	2.03
XEROX CORP.	13,000	517,234	39.787	47.750	620,750	3.00	39,000	6.28	2.04
		987,096			1,239,875		72,020	5.81	4.07
MISCELLANEOUS									
INTERNATIONAL TEL. & TEL. CORP.	13,000	434,720	33.440	40.750	529,750	2.76	35,880	6.77	1.74

STATEMENT OF INVESTMENTS

DATE: APRIL 29, 1983

DESCRIPTION OF SECURITIES	SHARES OR FACE VALUE	TOTAL COST	AVERAGE UNIT COST	MARKET PRICE	TOTAL MARKET VALUE	ANNUAL		YIELD ON MARKET VALUE	% OF PORTFOLIO
						INCOME RATE	TOTAL INCOME		
MC DERMOTT INTERNATIONAL	13,000	233,997	18.000	19.625	255,125	1.80	23,400	9.17	.84
MOORE LTD.	7,800	235,906	30.244	50.000	390,000	2.00	15,600	4.00	1.28
		904,623			1,174.875		74,880	6.37	3.86
****TOTAL		2,203,958			2,832,600		167,652	5.92	9.31
BASIC INDUSTRY									
CHEMICALS, FIBERS, FERTILIZERS									
ALLIED CORP.	7,000	232,596	33.228	45.500	318,500	2.40	16,800	5.27	1.05
CELANESE CORP.	8,300	398,109	47.965	62.125	515,638	4.00	33,200	6.43	1.69
W. R. GRACE	11,000	447,986	40.726	44.500	489,500	2.80	30,800	6.29	1.61
INTERNATIONAL MINERAL & CHEM.	10,500	336,000	32.000	39.500	414,750	2.60	27,300	6.58	1.36
PENNWALT	10,000	380,000	38.000	38.625	386,250	2.20	22,000	5.69	1.27
		1,794,691			2,124,638		130,100	6.12	6.98
CONTAINERS									
AMERICAN CAN	8,440	266,904	31.624	38.250	322,830	2.90	24,476	7.58	1.06
CONTINENTAL GROUP	14,000	426,709	30.479	43.875	614,250	2.60	36,400	5.92	2.02
DENNISON MFG.	9,500	203,560	21.427	31.875	302,813	1.44	13,680	4.51	1.00
		897,173			1,239,893		74,556	6.01	4.08
PAPER									
KIMBERLY CLARK CORP.	7,000	376,848	53.835	87.875	615.125	4.20	29,400	4.78	2.02
		376,848			615,125		29,400	4.78	2.02
TRANSPORTATION & MISCELLANEOUS									
FRUEHAUF CORP. $2 CUM. CV PFD	6,700	167,500	25.000	29.000	194,300	2.00	13,400	6.89	.64
I U INTERNATIONAL	6,500	113,998	17.538	22.125	143,813	1.15	7,475	5.19	.47

EXHIBIT 3 *(concluded)*

DATE: APRIL 29, 1983

STATEMENT OF INVESTMENTS

DESCRIPTION OF SECURITIES	SHARES OR FACE VALUE	TOTAL COST	AVERAGE UNIT COST	MARKET PRICE	TOTAL MARKET VALUE	ANNUAL		YIELD ON MARKET VALUE	% OF PORTFOLIO
						INCOME RATE	TOTAL INCOME		
NORTON CO.	4,600	163,622	35.570	43.500	200,100	2.00	9,200	4.59	.61
		445,120			538,213		30,075	5.59	1.77
****TOTAL		3,513,832			4,517,869		264,131	5.85	14.85
DEFENSIVE CONSUMER STAPLES									
FOODS									
ARA SERVICES	12,400	419,213	33.808	47.250	585,900	2.05	25,420	4.33	1.93
GENERAL FOODS	12,000	396,966	33.081	44.625	535,500	2.40	28,800	5.37	1.76
LUCKY STORES	10,000	145,417	14.542	22.000	220,000	1.16	11,600	5.27	.72
NABISCO BRANDS	11,000	352,000	32.000	37.000	407,000	2.28	25,080	6.16	1.34
		1,313,596			1,748,400		90,900	5.20	5.75
NON-FOOD									
AMERICAN BRANDS	10,000	343,050	34.305	54.625	546,250	3.50	35,000	6.40	1.80
COLGATE PALMOLIVE	26,000	469,802	18.069	24.750	643,500	1.28	33,280	5.17	2.11
GILLETTE	12,000	319,120	26.593	46.375	556,500	2.30	27,600	4.96	1.83
REYNOLDS INDUSTRIES	12,000	339,640	28.303	53.625	643,500	3.00	36,000	5.59	2.11
		1,471,612			2,389,750		131,880	5.52	7.85
****TOTAL		2,785,208			4,138,150		222,780	5.38	13.60
ENERGY									
OIL									
PENNZOIL	15,000	531,959	35.464	38.375	575,625	2.20	33,000	5.73	1.89
STANDARD OIL OF CALIF.	11,000	350,663	31.878	40.750	448,250	2.40	26,400	5.89	1.47

STATEMENT
OF
INVESTMENTS

DATE: APRIL 29, 1983

DESCRIPTION OF SECURITIES	SHARES OR FACE VALUE	TOTAL COST	AVERAGE UNIT COST	MARKET PRICE	TOTAL MARKET VALUE	ANNUAL		YIELD ON MARKET VALUE	% OF PORTFOLIO
						INCOME RATE	TOTAL INCOME		
STANDARD OIL OF OHIO	6,300	254,759	40.438	47.250	297,675	2.60	16,380	5.50	.98
		1,137,381			1,321,550		75,780	5.73	4.34
****TOTAL		1,137,381			1,321,550		75,780	5.73	4.34
UTILITIES									
ELECTRIC									
CINCINNATI GAS & ELECTRIC	16,300	295,437	18.125	17.750	289,325	2.16	35,208	12.16	.95
COMMONWEALTH EDISON	22,000	566,500	25.750	26.875	591,250	3.00	66,000	11.16	1.94
DUKE POWER CO.	16,000	321,128	20.071	23.125	370,000	2.28	36,480	9.85	1.22
FLORIDA PROGRESS CORP.	20,000	305,960	15.298	19.875	397,500	1.92	38,400	9.66	1.31
GULF STATES UTILITIES	45,000	539,267	11.984	14.875	669,375	1.56	70,200	10.48	2.20
NIAGARA MOHAWK POWER	20,000	254,511	12.726	17.250	345,000	1.80	36,000	10.43	1.13
NORTHERN IND. PUB. SVC. CO.	44,000	488,805	11.109	13.625	599,500	1.50	66,000	11.00	1.97
PUBLIC SERVICE OF NEW MEXICO	19,000	470,250	24.750	28.375	539,125	2.80	53,200	9.86	1.77
PUBLIC SERVICE ELECTRIC & GAS	20,000	460,000	23.000	23.625	472,500	2.56	51,200	10.83	1.55
SOUTHERN CALIFORNIA EDISON	16,000	430,795	26.925	37.375	598,000	3.52	56,320	9.41	1.97
		4,132,653			4,871,575		509,008	10.45	16.01
TELEPHONE									
AMERICAN TEL. & TEL. CO.	9,500	492,219	51.813	68.000	646,000	5.40	51,300	7.94	2.12
		492,219			646,000		51,300	7.94	2.12
****TOTAL		4,624,872			5,517,575		560,308	10.15	18.13
ACCOUNT TOTAL ****		23,335,144			30,182,918		1,954,801	6.48	99.19

EXHIBIT 4
An Economic/Market Outlook—Second Quarter 1983

Disinflation Prospects Are Still the Key to a Long-Lasting Bull Market

Despite moments of transitory weakness, the eight-month-old stock market advance persists in precedent-setting duration and intensity. It thereby confounds market strategists, and each day breaks with old rules and past observed correlations which have signaled for months that a substantial correction was overdue. Important information is conveyed by the rupturing of "rules" previously useful in identifying interim market tops.

Although a bull market's initial thrust stems from rising multiples, not earnings, we believe that the two most critical elements that cause P/E's to change (the contemplated investment time horizon and the required discount rate) diverged in the post-1965 bull markets because the period was characterized by seemingly ineluctable inflation. Although multiples rose and fell cyclically, there was a secular downward trend; the market multiple at the end of this period was less than one half what it was at the beginning. This was the dominant umbrella trend which caused a 20-year trading range market. However, since 1980, indications are increasingly persuasive that we have commenced a period of disinflation. We believe that the stock market has begun to recognize this, and that now both components that determine P/E's are moving synchronously. If this be so, this not only explains the historic dynamism of this market rebound, but also suggests that in the eventual second bull market phase, which is typically dominated by earnings results, multiples can continue to move ahead, thereby enhancing return expectations. Therefore, the focus of investment strategy should be on the prospects for, and beneficiaries of, an enduring reduction of inflationary forces.

The End of the Beginning of a New Bull Market

A bull market is best defined as a period when most stocks are rising most of the time. All bull markets have a beginning, a middle, and an end. The stock market's price action during these three stages is dominated, first, by hope, then by reality or fundamentals, and finally, by speculation. Profits come easiest in the initial stage when all securities rebound from compressed price levels, typically pushed by overexuberance to valuations unjustified by realistic earnings estimates. There then follows a market correction or consolidation phase, proximate to the time the economy discernibly passes from contraction to expansion; a transition wherein the reality of fundamentals supplants emotions as the market's motive force. One now must become an investor rather than merely being "in the market" for the ride. Selectivity is more critical. Ultimately, forgetting that cycles are finite, investors become overconfident, bidding stock prices to excess levels just when the economy is peaking, thus setting the stage for the next bear market. Timing the onset and conclusion of each of these acts is difficult, perhaps impossible, but the rewards for success are so great that guessing market reversals is one of Wall Street's favorite pastimes.

A bull market emerges from the ashes of a bear market, not when fundamentals turn positive, but rather, when conditions materialize which are perceived to be requisite for such a turn later. These conditions include: declining short-term and

EXHIBIT 4 ***(continued)***

long-term interest rates; improving systemwide liquidity; ameliorating inflation; a technically oversold stock market; and a significant percentage of investors who are bearish. Fundamentals such as earnings, unemployment and GNP growth matter little during the first third of a bull market, since bear market reversals occur many months before a recession's end.

This market cycle has been no exception. Stock prices began soaring in August 1982, though the recession didn't end until December. Since then, economic progress has been muted save in a few industries. Plummeting inflation numbers, sharply lower interest rates and financial reliquification induced the market rise and sustained prices which are now up more than 50 percent from their August lows. But, how long can this initial market phase exist on hope alone—the prediction that these circumstances will ultimately create favorable fundamentals until the market insists that improved earnings materialize? Although no one wants to leave the table too early, a transition period during which most stocks will give back some of their gains is certain. New leadership must emerge and selectivity will be critical to future results. The longer this first phase endures, the more keen will be the preoccupation with identifying the end of this first bull market act. The portfolio manager's job is to get off stage early, if he can, to go backstage and change costume and reappear when the curtain rises on the second act.

How Does One Recognize the End of the First Phase of a Rising Market?

No bull market keeps rising from beginning to end without interruptions along the way. There is an ongoing, progressive deterioration in fundamentals that begins fairly early in the economic cycle which underlies several corrective interludes. This degenerative process doesn't explain the first serious challenge to a new bull cycle because a bull market arrives while fundamentals are still deteriorating. Thus, economic conditions are steadily improving when the interim market reversal occurs. Therefore, analysts look for certain critical readings on a number of technical indicators and cycle relationships that were associated with market peaks during past transition phases to help in timing a cyclical reversal. Two measures often cited are the average duration of the first leg of previous cycles and the average price gain during these periods. Other indicators that provide benchmark readings which correlate well with the corrective phase of past bull markets are: the number of stocks selling at prices above their 200-day moving average, specialist short-selling, price gains on the AMEX and OTC relative to the senior averages, the completeness of rotational group leadership, and institutional cash positions. However, the readings of these indicators at past tops are merely correlative phenomena. Correlation doesn't prove causation.

This current market advance has decisively broken the reasonably expected boundaries predicted by the litmus tests cited above. We are in new territory at this price level, seeking new standards of comparison, attempting to reinterpret old rules. Most market observers have fallen back on intuition. What accounts for the stock market's aberrant behavior?

EXHIBIT 4 *(continued)*

The first phase of a bull market is explained by rising P/E's, not improving earnings. P/E's may be altered by a change in investors' time horizons or by a change in the required rate of return. Previous expansion in multiples dating to the mid-1960s was due to the confidence factor; that is, a willingness to look farther into the future. The multiple expansion that's now occurring may be different and may explain why market setbacks have thus far been modest.

The price of a common stock is a function of a company's earnings and the multiple investors are willing to place on them. Although the degree of earnings cyclicality varies according to company size and the industry of which it is a part, the return on equity and the growth rate of each mature enterprise are remarkably constant over time. Good security analysis can produce a fairly accurate earnings estimation. However, the appropriate earnings multiplier is not constant, but results from complex relationships which change. The two most important elements that influence changes in the P/E are confidence, which is reflected in the number of years buyers are willing to project a given growth rate, and the required rate of return, which is the discount rate that must be applied to the earnings stream over the selected time horizon. Confidence is elusive, and there's no scientific way to equate a given level of optimism with the correct time horizon. Determining the required discount rate obliges investors to predict future inflation and the associated long-term interest rate.

Stocks rise in the first third of a bull market because multiples expand. But the reason multiples are more generous is that when the dominant psychology affecting the market turns from negative to positive, investors implicitly lengthen the contemplated holding period for new stock purchases. During the depth of a bear market, buyers might only be willing to project earnings three or four years into the future, even for rapidly growing companies. As confidence builds, perhaps that time horizon is extended to six or seven years. Changes in the discount rate also critically impact P/E's. If the inflation rate or its proxy, the long-term bond rate, remains relatively constant over time, there is no P/E effect. Similarly, even though inflation and interest rates cyclically rise and fall, there is no P/E effect, provided inflation and interest rates are centered on some constant level that persists over time. This was the situation from 1955 to 1965.

However, since 1965, inflation and interest rate volatility increased. Although inflation and interest rates fluctuated cyclically, a secular trend became evident wherein we experienced higher troughs and higher peaks in both measures over successive business cycles. Thus, there has been a steady decline in market P/E's throughout the last 18 years. Therefore, we may deduce that the multiple expansion that typified the initial stage of bull markets post-Vietnam derived from only one component that influences changes in P/E's—the confidence factor. One may infer that there was a concomitant negative multiple effect from a steadily increasing discount rate, though this negative influence was obscured in bull markets.

EXHIBIT 4 ***(continued)***

This distinction is relevant to the current situation. Although it is recognized that initial bull market gains derive from expanding multiples, we contend that in recent years this phenomenon was solely due to a rising confidence factor rather than a lowering of the interest assumption. To the degree that there now exists a consensus view that there has been a secular inflation reversal, then the multiple expansion during this entire bull market may be positively impacted by the lowering of the required discount rate as compared to the negative influence previously operative. Thus, many statistical correlations based on the 1965–81 market experience that argue for a substantial market correction might not apply in the present circumstances.

The Current Debate Over Possible Excess Money Supply Growth is Primarily of Academic Interest and Should Not Be a Great Concern at this Point in the Business Cycle

There are innumerable variables that influence stock prices. The investment manager must separate the critical issues from the sub-critical. Because we believe that a probable secular inflation reversal is the key to investment strategy, we disagree with Wall Street's current angst over interest rates that accompanies the *sturm und drang* surrounding recent monetary policy. Seemingly endlessly debated are charges that the Fed is promoting excess money supply growth, the possibility, timing, and size of an increase in short-term interest rates; and the long-term bond market's possible reaction to perceived inflationary implications of rapid money growth.

These concerns reflect elements of a technical debate dominated by a handful of economists who comprehend the concatenation of interest rates, reserve availability, and the demand for money. Since there is wide disagreement among these experts, how are money managers who are much less informed to discern whether this ongoing debate is truly significant, or merely a sort of mental gymnastics that fascinates academics? Obscuring the issues further is the static created by the impact of structural financial changes which makes doubtful the relevance of various measures of money. Those who are negative are monetarists, convinced that too much money, however defined, is a bad thing in and of itself. They dismiss the possibility that monetary deregulation means that the bond market will henceforth be an effective governor, through the interest rate mechanism, which will prevent excess money creation from fueling inflation. And what of the hand wringing over the failure of bond yields to decline further. After decades of dismal performance, professional bond buyers (who should never be credited with being endowed with economic wisdom) have concluded pragmatically that only a gloomy atmosphere is good for fixed income. The bond market tends to greet, willy-nilly, a recovery encouraged by Fed supplied liquidity as, ipso facto, inflationary and portending rising interest rates. Thus, a simplistic interpretation and overreaction to Fed policy might tend to force long-term interest rates up, though we think there is little danger this will occur. But in the event, should we accept the bond market's reaction as indirect confirmation that current monetary policy is inherently inflationary? Our answer is no!

EXHIBIT 4 *(continued)*

While we concede that a jump in interest rates might shake market complacency, are we not fighting the last cycle's battles by overemphasizing the importance of monetary policy at this juncture. Consider current money supply growth in the context of these questions:

. . . Do you believe that real interest rates are too low to inhibit excessive loan demand and speculation?

. . . Do you believe that a modest uptick in interest rates will abort the recovery, propelling the United States into an unprecedented triple-dip recession?

. . . Do you believe the Federal Reserve will allow short-term interest rates to rise so high that a liquidity crisis materializes?

. . . Do you fear an imminent inflation revival from current monetary policy given: a weak domestic recovery, a foreign dependency on a revival of U.S. import demand to pull Europe out of its own slump, and the existence of a strong dollar which will inhibit the pace of our domestic snapback?

. . . Do you believe there is a clear and present danger of current monetary policy re-igniting demand-pull inflation given: high unemployment, low capacity utilization, declining energy prices and persistently high level interest rates?

If your answer to all these questions is no, then you should neither fear an imminent resurgence of inflation nor rising interest rates.

A Sharp Increase in Short-Term Interest Rates Is Unlikely

The Fed's primary objective is to support the integrity of the current embryonic recovery and to make possible continuing non-inflationary growth. Interest rate stabilization is essential in effecting this policy. Thus, the Fed has put aside, at least temporarily, strict monetarism and has adopted a more "pragmatic" approach which embraces interest rate targeting. However, given recent money supply growth, many predict that if a strong economic recovery collides with rising government credit needs, the Fed will be forced to pull back, allowing interest rates to rise to maintain its anti-inflation credibility. But we are convinced that a *modest* increase in short rates won't undermine the recovery. Further, we don't believe the Fed will passively allow a recovery-threatening *significant* increase.

Short-term interest rates *always* uptick early in the business cycle when business loan demand picks up, after which rates either stabilize or retreat, the business recovery being unaffected. Since this is a normal occurrence, why is this temporary interest rate blip traumatic for the stock market? A possible answer is that this event represents a convenient milestone, the first real negative that has surfaced in many months, a rallying point for diverse negative opinions—an *excuse* for the market to correct rather than a *reason*. This early cycle interest rate upturn is merely another correlation; a prophecy which is self-fulfilling because money managers have "learned" that an early bull market shakeout almost always accompanies the appearance of this interest rate "hiccup." Thus, investors don't fear the fundamental consequences of the event, but rather, the market risk typically associated with the event.

EXHIBIT 4 ***(continued)***

Nevertheless, psychology counts more in the short run than reality in determining the stock market's direction. There does exist a real fear that inflation will reappear if the Fed continues current monetary ease. The counter view is that the Fed still has ample time and latitude before one need fear inflation because of low capacity utilization rates, the existence of still high real interest rates which inhibit speculation, and moderating labor demands. Three recent developments suggest that the Fed has been granted more time before it will have to choose between clamping down or risking hard-won inflation gains. The most important is the OPEC reduction of crude prices and indications that energy prices will remain weak. Thus, near-term inflation statistics should get even better, thereby strengthening the argument that inflation trends are so favorable that the risk of maintaining an easy money policy is diminished. The second development is that it now appears the 1983 recovery will be modest, in contrast to the more ebullient outlook suggested by the first quarter "flash" GNP growth report. This will tend to defer a pickup in private credit demand. Third, the dollar remains firm, which tends to suppress economic activity in the United States and which is an indirect validation that the Fed's monetary policy isn't inflationary relative to the policies of foreign central banks.

Will Long-Term Interest Rates Decline?

Although one can make a fundamental case for declining long-term interest rates if inflation remains subdued, no one knows for sure what will transpire since psychology plays such an important role. But there are two positives that should be noted. There is currently a 400–700 basis point real return implicit in current long-term government bond yields (depending on which inflation measure you use). Many argue that this historically generous risk premium is deserved because of greater bond volatility in recent years.

Since the Fed began de facto interest rate targeting, there has been a sharp, sustained decline in interest rate volatility. A combination of lower inflation and the continuation of "pragmatic monetarism" should bring about a reduction of the substantial risk premium embodied in the term structure of interest rates. Also, a normal, positively sloped yield curve makes it much less advantageous to remain in the shortest maturities. If you believe that we will experience a period of relative interest rate stability, then the market timing incentive to stay out of the long bond market to avoid whipsaws is less valid. Since there is a substantial penalty associated with being invested short, the virtuous bond cycle could become operative as positive conviction increases. An increased willingness to extend maturities creates more credit supply, enabling corporations to fund in the long bond market, thus reducing pressure in the short-term market. This tends to create downward pressure on rates across the maturity spectrum.

There are some who believe that long-term interest rates *must* decline for the stock market to move ahead. This is not necessarily true. Even if long rates don't decline from current levels, the economy will continue to improve and corporate earnings will grow. If inflation remains subdued, moderately rising multiples and earnings could fuel an extension of the current market advance. The stock market

EXHIBIT 4 *(continued)*

might conclude that the maintenance of high interest rates effectively precludes inflation from recurring, thus enabling this to be a long-lived recovery. This scenario might be interpreted positively.

The Direction of Economic Fundamentals Counts Most, Not the Degree of Change

There are few clear trends which indicate how vibrant the current expansion will be although all the critical elements are positive: improving consumer confidence; enhanced personal, corporate, and banking liquidity; much lower interest rates than existed a year ago; the lagged, positive effect of the last nine months' monetary policy; and, firm prospects for sharp increases in real personal income. February's rise in the leading economic indicators was the sixth consecutive monthly increase, but the index of coincident indicators fell after rising 1.1 percent in January. A smooth acceleration of economic growth throughout 1983 is unlikely because each quarter will be affected by large changes in inventories and exports. Private and public estimates for 1983 real GNP growth fluctuate from day to day. Whereas a few weeks ago initial conservative estimates were raised, they have now been pulled back to 2–3 percent real growth. Whether this forecast is accurate or not is moot. Expectations regarding the contour and intensity of economic revival are still modest and likely revisions in the economic model over the next few quarters will be up, not down. The critical factor is direction, not magnitude of change.

It is likewise impossible to get a firm fix on corporate profits at this time. Not only is the dimension of the rebound unknown, but the favorable earnings impact from the leverage that exists at low operating rates, as well as the salutary effect of declining short-term interest rates, are difficult to quantify. Therefore, a 15–25 percent range for expected profit growth is appropriate.

Have You Missed the Bull Market?

A bull market exists when most stocks are rising most of the time. This being a bull market, there are only three critical concerns: how much longer it's going to last, how much further it's going to go, and, which stocks and groups will do best? The first two questions are the most important.

The stock market is up 50 percent from its August 1982 low and 15 percent above the 1,000 Dow level that proved to be a redoubtable barrier for 18 years. But the United States still faces formidable problems. Many industries such as steel and autos face structural difficulties that will endure despite recovery. The domestic banking industry has extended billions of dollars in loans to foreign countries who cannot repay that debt. Unemployment will remain high for the next few years. Government deficits mean heavy public borrowing. Thus, even if long-term interest rates don't increase from this level, there might not be enough savings to finance much private growth for the foreseeable future.

EXHIBIT 4 ***(concluded)***

There are partial answers to these concerns. Although some industries have structural problems, they account for a small portion of total GNP. The lesson provided by industries which have become non-competitive in a global economy due to past excessive wage settlements might prevent other, still healthy companies from duplicating such errors. The Fed won't allow the foreign loan problem to create a large-scale banking liquidity crisis. From a longer perspective, these problem loans will probably be rewritten over the next few years for much longer terms and at reduced, affordable interest rates. It's much too early to know to what degree government credit demands will impact private needs. At present, there's enough liquidity to accommodate both the private and the public sector. Though only a partial solution, economic growth will reduce currently projected outyear deficits.

Wall Street's favorite conundrum (a question which has no satisfactory answer) is this: How are we going to finance both an awesome public deficit and private credit demands and, at the same time, keep inflation under control, sustain stable interest rates and increase GNP growth enough to impact unemployment meaningfully? You *can't* achieve all those goals simultaneously. You can attain *most* of those objectives if you overinflate the money supply and keep interest rates cheap. However, the end result of such a policy is a high core inflation rate and, ultimately, punishingly high interest rates.

The stock and bond market suffered such consequences during the last 20 years. The ultimate enemy is inflation—not slow economic growth, not high interest rates, not rational money-supply growth. A period of stringency is needed in which we must learn to live within our means. If the payoff is lower inflation and a long-lived, slower, but sustainable economic expansion—earnings will grow modestly, multiples will expand, and the stock market will prosper.

George Seer
Executive Vice President

EXHIBIT 5
Analysis of the Importance of Yield as a Component of Total Returns (*selective time periods and studies*)

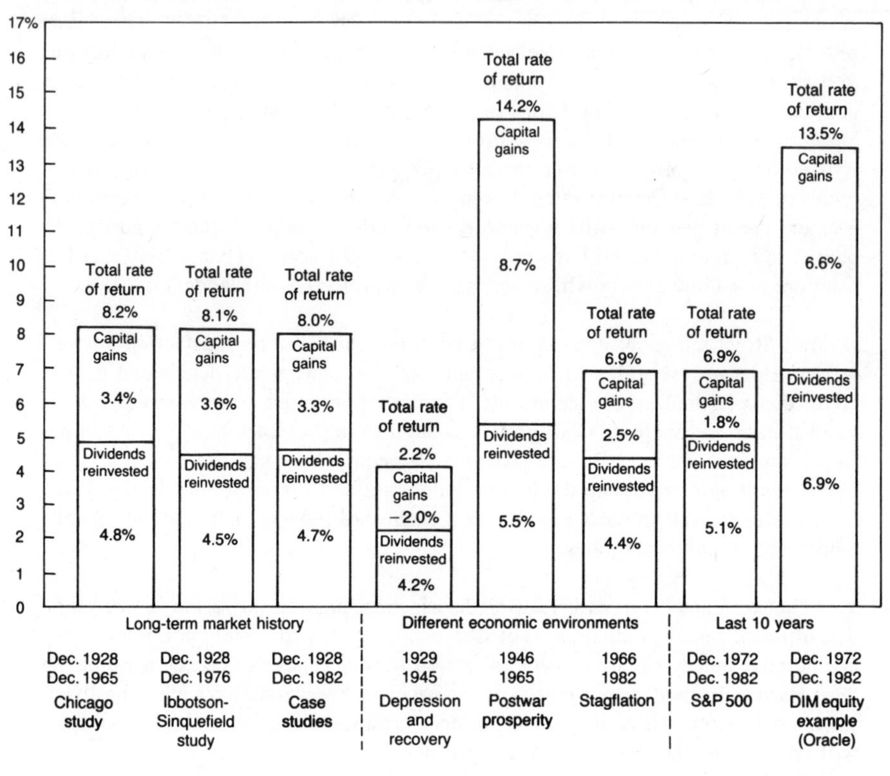

EXHIBIT 6
Analysis of Returns on Yield Quintiles (*1929–1982*)

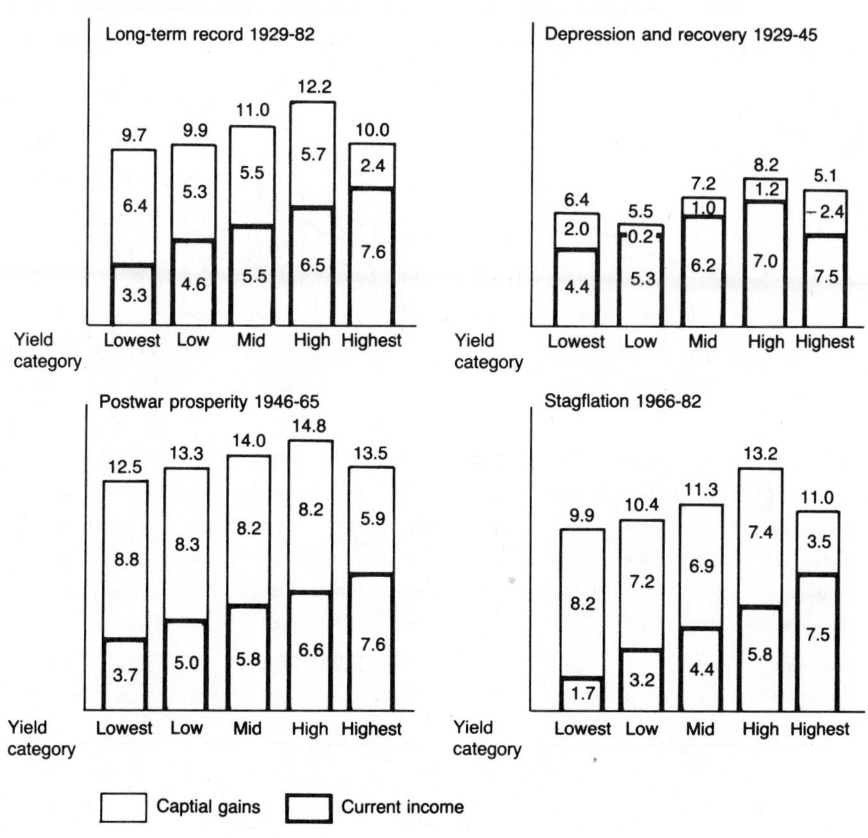

This study covers all dividend-paying common stocks listed on the NYSE for the period 1929 through 1982. It was undertaken to determine the investment results that would have been achieved by arbitrarily pursuing an investment policy based on dividend yield. At the beginning of each year, all securities were rank ordered from low to high yield, based on the dividends paid in the preceding year divided by current price. At the beginning of each year, five portfolios were constructed based on the prior year's yield. The five groups were selected by breaking the securities into quintiles. The annual return on each yield category was determined by giving equal weight to each security in the portfolio. Compound returns were constructed for each yield category by linking the annual returns of each category.

EXHIBIT 7
Ten-Year DIM Equity Performance Evaluation (*A. G. Becker prototype; for periods ending December 31, 1982*)

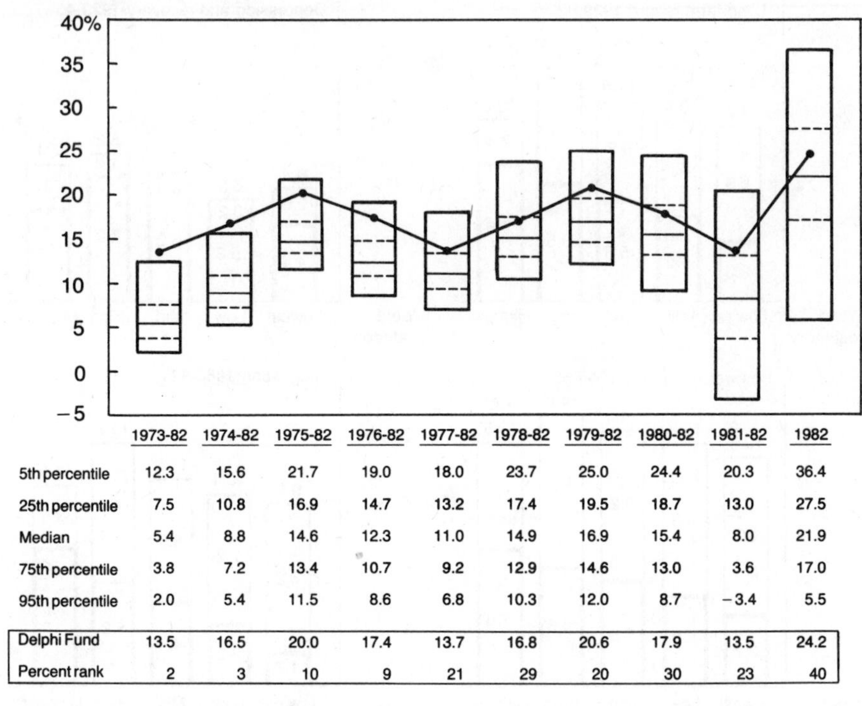

	1973-82	1974-82	1975-82	1976-82	1977-82	1978-82	1979-82	1980-82	1981-82	1982
5th percentile	12.3	15.6	21.7	19.0	18.0	23.7	25.0	24.4	20.3	36.4
25th percentile	7.5	10.8	16.9	14.7	13.2	17.4	19.5	18.7	13.0	27.5
Median	5.4	8.8	14.6	12.3	11.0	14.9	16.9	15.4	8.0	21.9
75th percentile	3.8	7.2	13.4	10.7	9.2	12.9	14.6	13.0	3.6	17.0
95th percentile	2.0	5.4	11.5	8.6	6.8	10.3	12.0	8.7	−3.4	5.5
Delphi Fund	13.5	16.5	20.0	17.4	13.7	16.8	20.6	17.9	13.5	24.2
Percent rank	2	3	10	9	21	29	20	30	23	40

EXHIBIT 8

DIM Equity Volatility Rankings* (*A. G. Becker prototype; for moving five-year periods ending December 31*)

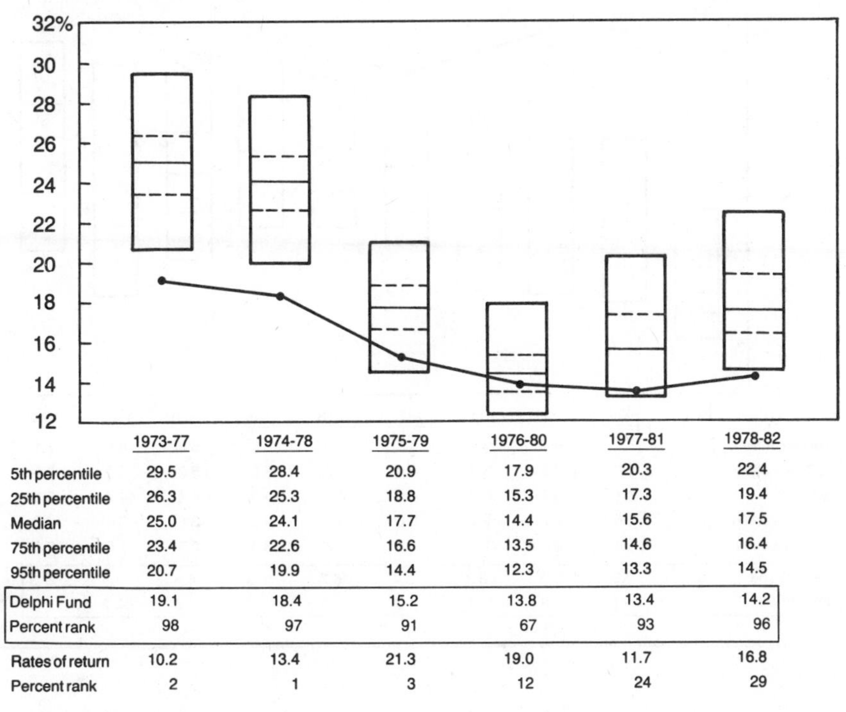

	1973-77	1974-78	1975-79	1976-80	1977-81	1978-82
5th percentile	29.5	28.4	20.9	17.9	20.3	22.4
25th percentile	26.3	25.3	18.8	15.3	17.3	19.4
Median	25.0	24.1	17.7	14.4	15.6	17.5
75th percentile	23.4	22.6	16.6	13.5	14.6	16.4
95th percentile	20.7	19.9	14.4	12.3	13.3	14.5
Delphi Fund	19.1	18.4	15.2	13.8	13.4	14.2
Percent rank	98	97	91	67	93	96
Rates of return	10.2	13.4	21.3	19.0	11.7	16.8
Percent rank	2	1	3	12	24	29

*Annualized values.

EXHIBIT 9
DIM Equity Yield Rankings (*A. G. Becker prototype; for years ending December 31*)

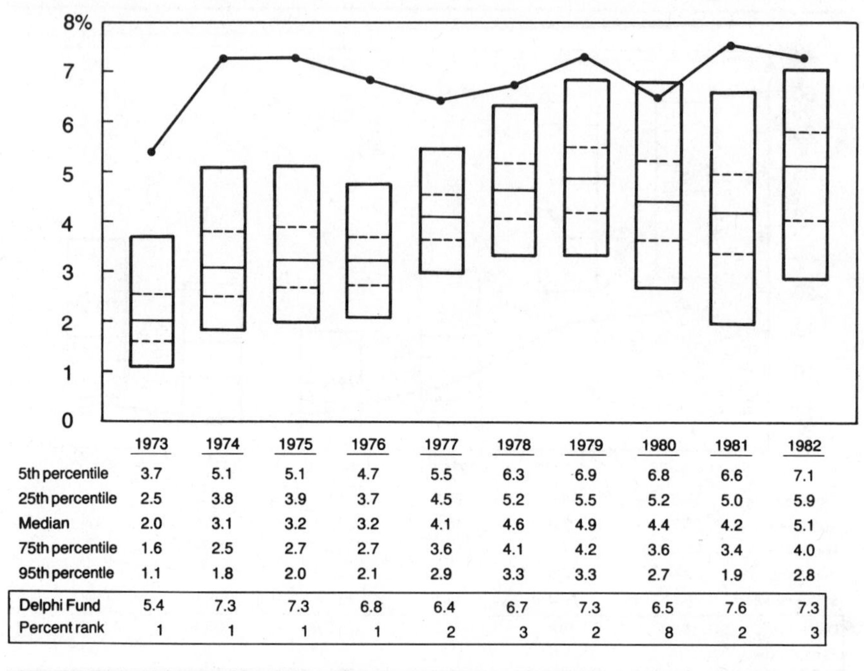

	1973	1974	1975	1976	1977	1978	1979	1980	1981	1982
5th percentile	3.7	5.1	5.1	4.7	5.5	6.3	6.9	6.8	6.6	7.1
25th percentile	2.5	3.8	3.9	3.7	4.5	5.2	5.5	5.2	5.0	5.9
Median	2.0	3.1	3.2	3.2	4.1	4.6	4.9	4.4	4.2	5.1
75th percentile	1.6	2.5	2.7	2.7	3.6	4.1	4.2	3.6	3.4	4.0
95th percentile	1.1	1.8	2.0	2.1	2.9	3.3	3.3	2.7	1.9	2.8
Delphi Fund	5.4	7.3	7.3	6.8	6.4	6.7	7.3	6.5	7.6	7.3
Percent rank	1	1	1	1	2	3	2	8	2	3

EXHIBIT 10
DIM Equity Performance Relatives (*four major market downturns; 1969–1982*)

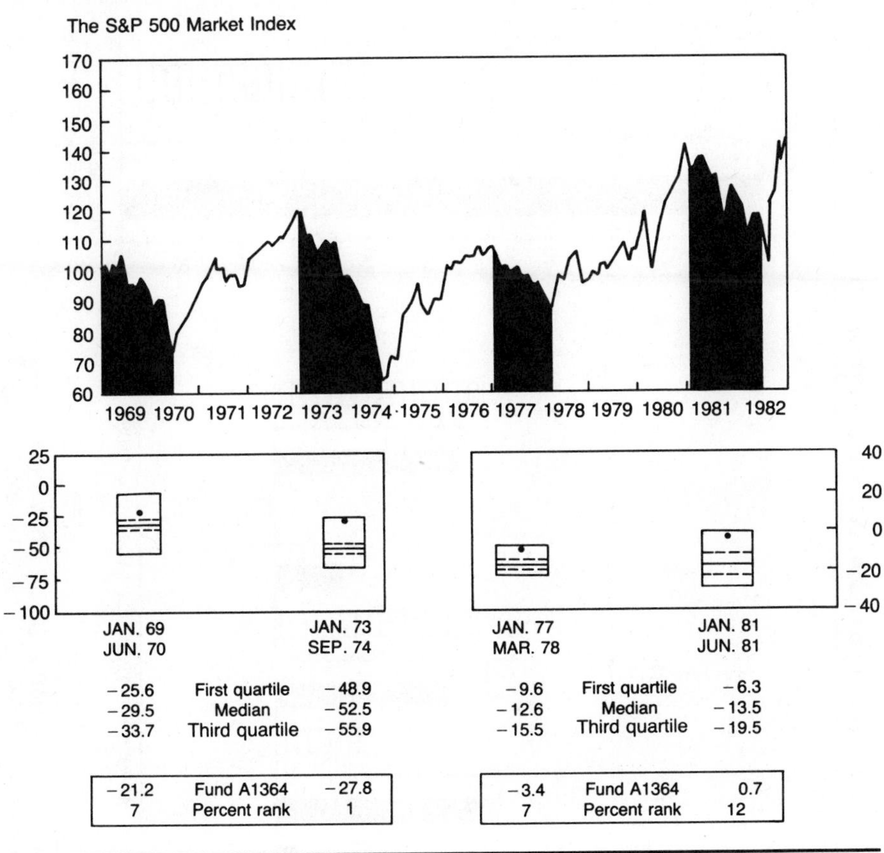

EXHIBIT 11
Relative Performance of DIM's Equity Composite (*for periods ending December 31; 1976–1982*)

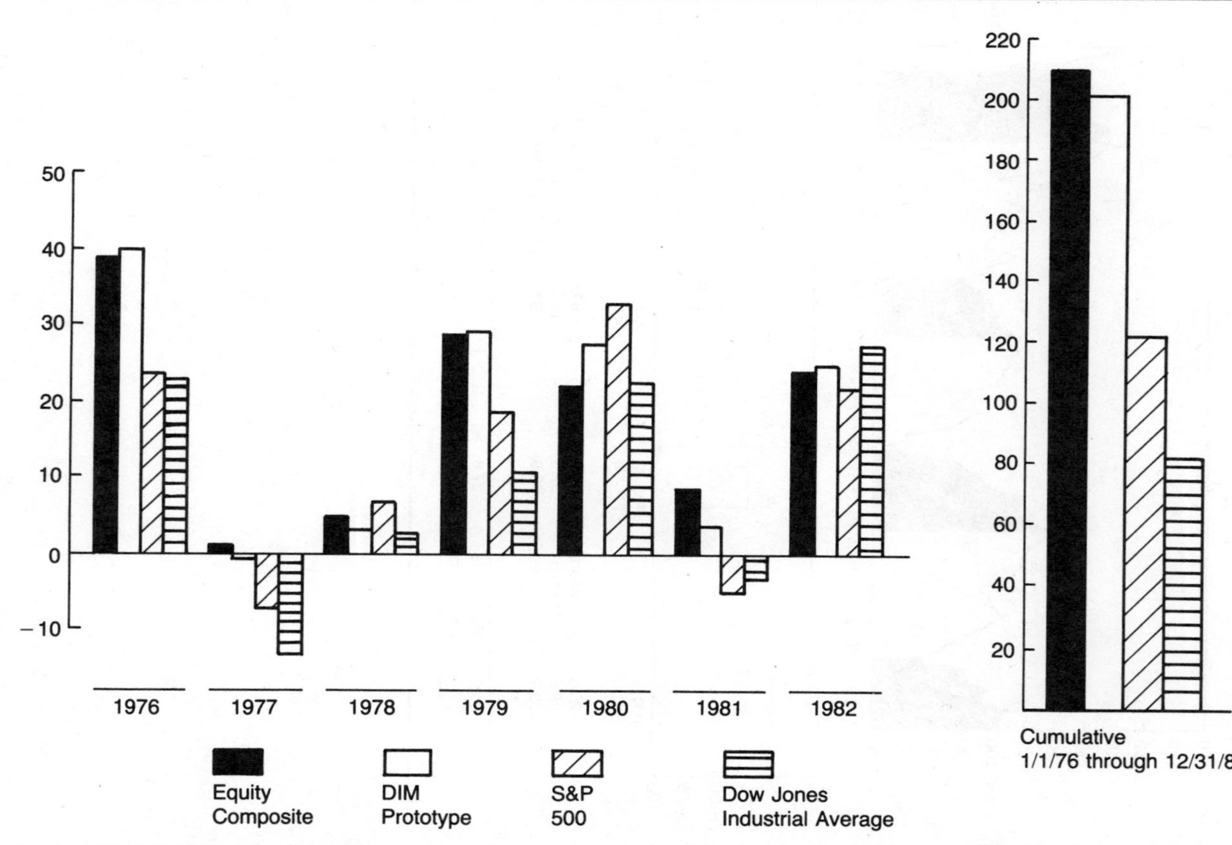

EXHIBIT 12
Ten-Year Relative Performance Records for DIM Equities (*1959–1982*)

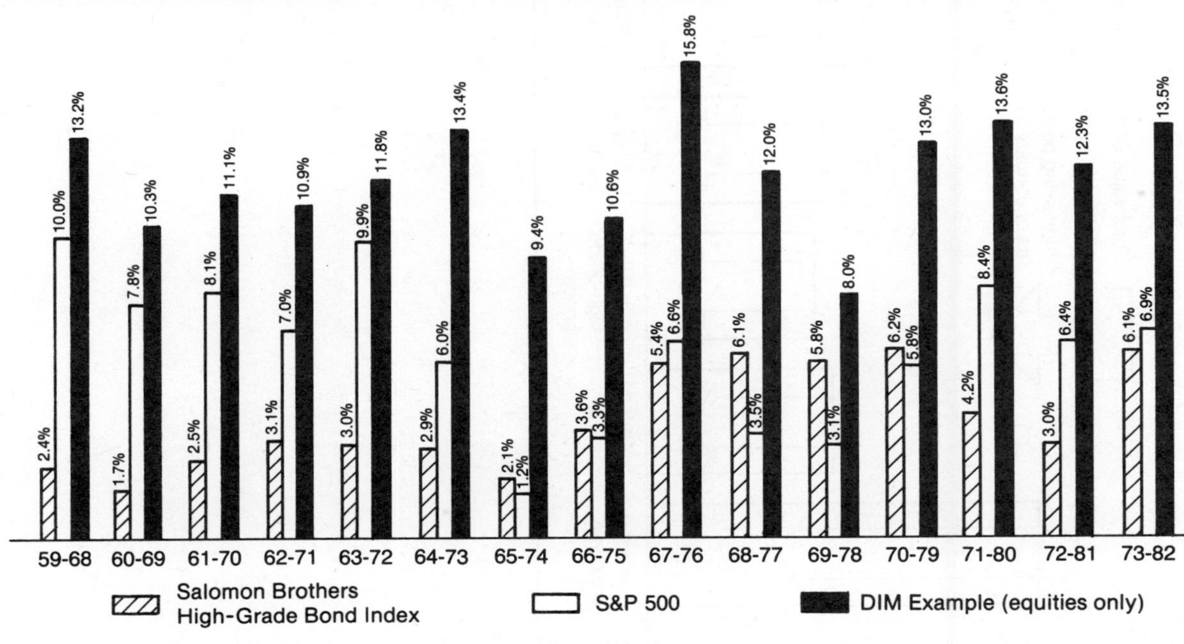

EXHIBIT 13
DIM Relative Equity Performance after Inflation (*1973–1982*)

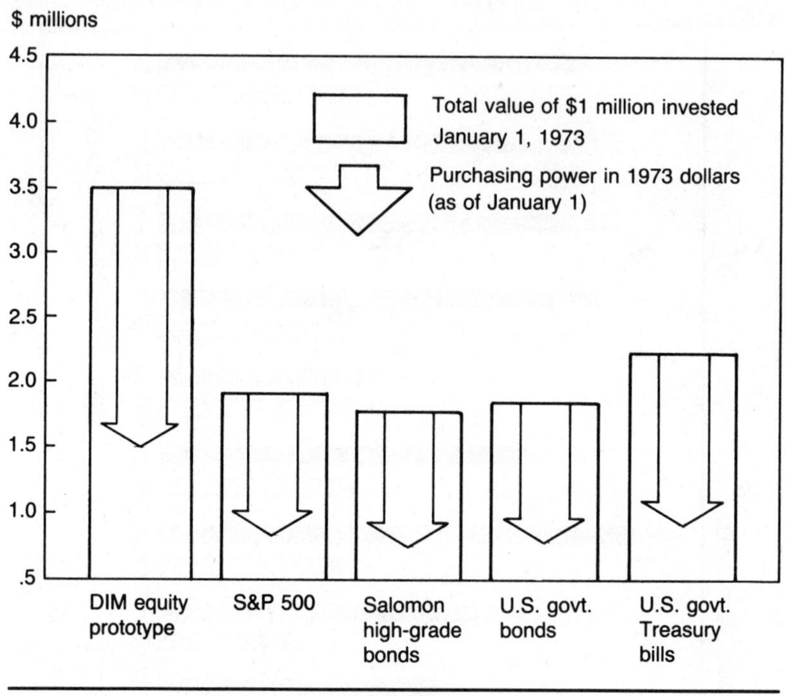

EXHIBIT 14
Oracle Income Fund Performance (*equities only*)

Year	1st Quarter	2nd Quarter	3rd Quarter	4th Quarter
1967	11.20	7.07	21.20	(2.44)
1968	5.12	18.90	7.29	8.79
1969	(4.24)	(9.55)	(4.53)	(.58)
1970	9.38	(12.60)	11.93	11.56
1971	12.16	(.27)	1.86	1.69
1972	4.72	(3.51)	2.41	7.72
1973	(5.47)	(9.18)	7.85	(3.89)
1974	2.04	(10.83)	(11.17)	13.51
1975	16.12	20.04	(5.17)	6.20
1976	19.09	6.08	1.95	8.66
1977	(2.24)	6.53	(5.11)	.63
1978	(2.70)	5.80	7.50	(7.10)
1979	8.90	6.10	9.85	1.57
1980	(4.50)	15.70	10.80	3.98
1981	6.00	1.05	(10.28)	7.80
1982	(2.00)	1.10	12.00	12.00
1983	7.60			

EXHIBIT 15
Oracle Income Fund Portfolio Characteristics (*equities only; five-year moving average, annualized quarterly 1967–1982*)

	Beta	Alpha
1967–71	.90	10.56
1968–72	.85	6.24
1969–73	.84	.42
1970–74	.74	5.42
1971–75	.75	4.13
1972–76	.79	7.29
1973–77	.80	8.92
1974–78	.78	8.10
1975–79	.84	7.02
1976–80	.98	4.79
1977–81	.91	3.35
1978–82	.86	2.93

Source: A. G. Becker

EXHIBIT 16
Price Trends in First Phase of Bull Markets

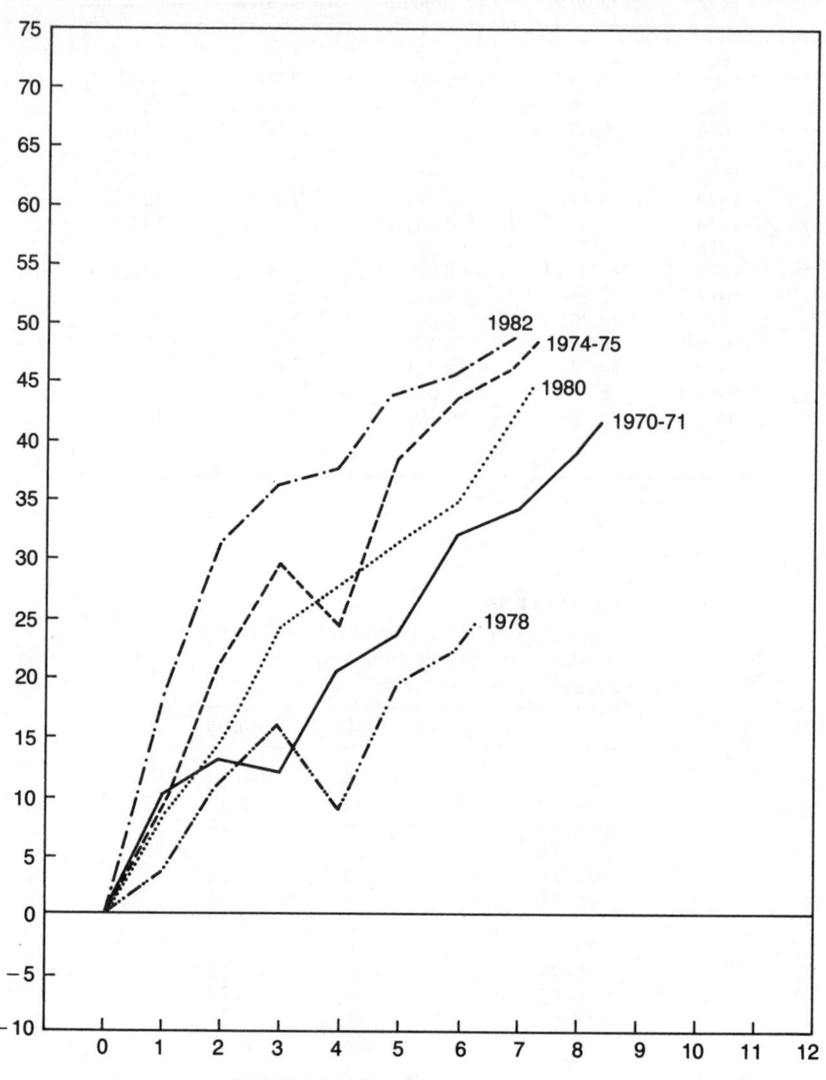

EXHIBIT 17
Recent Price Action

End of Month	***Standard & Poor's 500 Index***			
	1980	***1981***	***1982***	***1983***
January	115.12	129.55	120.40	145.30
February	113.66	131.27	113.11	148.06
March	102.09	136.00	111.96	152.96
April	106.29	132.87	116.44	164.42
May	111.24	132.59	111.98	*
June	114.24	131.21	109.61	
July	121.67	130.92	107.09	
August	122.38	122.79	119.51	
September	125.46	116.18	120.42	
October	127.47	121.89	133.71	
November	140.52	126.35	138.54	
December	136.76	122.55	140.64	

*Weekly close: May 6, 1983 166.10
May 13, 1983 164.90
May 20, 1983 162.14

Commonwealth State Retirement System Internally Managed Equity Account

In April 1978 the trustees of the Commonwealth State Retirement System (CSRS) approved a plan to bring a portion of the system's equity investments under the direct management of their in-house staff. This decision was made on the recommendation of James R. Grey, the CSRS portfolio manager, whose long career in portfolio management had included the presidency of a major mutual fund.

In May 1981 after three years' experience managing the internal equity account, Mr. Grey began a review of its performance with his assistant David Britton, to see what revisions, if any, might be appropriate. Mr. Britton was scheduled to present his analysis and findings first to the Investment Advisory Committee, consisting of three experienced portfolio managers, the State Treasurer, and an academic, and then to the trustees, only a few of whom had experience in handling significant amounts of financial assets. The Investment Advisory Committee limited its recommendations to the deployment of financial assets of the pension fund. The trustees were responsible for all policies and procedures relating to the successful operation of CSRS.

The Objectives of the Internal Equity Account

Mr. Grey had designed a stock-selection system around the following basic concepts:

- The account should be diversified, usually fully invested in a portfolio of common stocks of companies with large market capitalizations.
- Strict guidelines would be established for the purchase, retention, and sale of each stock.
- A large in-house research staff would not be used because it would not be as cost-beneficial as a computer-based system that had information readily available, at no direct cost, from the investment reports of the brokerage firms chosen to execute portfolio transactions.
- On the premise that earnings are the prime determinant of stock prices, the account would purchase and hold only those stocks with distinctly favorable current earnings. However, because even good earnings do not always produce good price results, the account would dispose of issues that did not react favorably to an upward trend of earnings.
- Little attempt would be made to predict future trends or turning points in the economy, the financial markets, or the stock market. Emphasis would be placed on identifying current firm-related trends and then taking appropriate action to benefit from them, or to lessen the chance of future losses.

Account Guidelines

Portfolio

The portfolio would normally consist of 48 stocks with an initial investment position of 2 percent in each issue (96 percent stock) and a 4 percent cash operating balance.

Diversification

Not more than 10 percent (at market) would be held in any one industry, as determined by the *Value Line* industry classification. Not more than 3 percent (at market) would be held in any one stock.

Research

The investment staff had the following responsibilities:

1. Evaluate earnings projections received from outside sources.[1]
2. Maintain on each company in the stock universe a file of research reports from the outside research organizations.
3. Monitor computer reports to ensure the accuracy of data input.

---

[1]Investment information, including earnings projections, was obtained from at least two of the following sources for each company in the stock universe: Merrill Lynch, Goldman Sachs, Kidder Peabody, Smith Barney.

Stock Universe

All companies considered for the account had to meet the following basic criteria:

1. Be listed on the New York Stock Exchange.
2. Have a market capitalization at time of purchase in excess of $200 million.
3. Be incorporated in the United States.[2]
4. Be registered with Depository Trust Company.
5. Be included in the monthly publication of Securities Research, Boston.

The common stocks of companies conforming to the criteria listed above were established as the stock universe in a computer system maintained by an outside vendor.

Stock Screening

Using a program designed specifically for this portfolio, the computer determined for each company:

1. Rate of change in earnings for each of the past four quarters (i.e., earnings per share for the four quarters preceding the date mentioned).
2. The price/earnings ratio based on the present price and the latest reported 12-month earnings.
3. The yield determined by the latest dividend payments and the present price.
4. Five-year rate of growth of annual earnings.

These figures constituted the seven factors that were then ranked individually within the stock universe. Subsequently, the individual rankings were combined into a composite rank called the DEP (dividends, earnings, price) index, which was computed as follows:

Factor	*# Rank*	×	*Weights**	=	*Subtotal*
3-month earnings change rank (1)	#		a		a#
6-month earnings change rank (2)	#		b		b#
9-month earnings change rank (3)	#		c		c#
12-month earnings change rank (4)	#		d		d#
P/E ratio change rank	#		e		e#
Yield rank	#		f		f#
5-year earnings growth rate	#		g		g#
Total			1.00		Weighted total

*Weights are confidential.
(1) = Ranked earnings change for most recent 4 quarters.
(2) = Ranked earnings change for 4 quarters preceding the 2nd quarter back.
(3) = Ranked earnings change for 4 quarters preceding the 3rd quarter back.
(4) = Ranked earnings change for 4 quarters preceding the 4th quarter back.

[2]A legal requirement.

Finally, the DEP index numbers were used to determine a composite rank from best to worst within the stock universe. The DEP rank served as the initial screen in the decision to purchase or sell an individual stock. (For sample calculations of the DEP index, see Appendix A.)

The DEP rank provided one number that indicated each stock's position within the stock universe and determined those stocks that were currently showing:

1. The greatest increase in reported earnings.
2. The lowest price in relation to those earnings.
3. The highest yield in relation to price.

For stocks already held in the portfolio, the system also computed a relative price index (RPI), which showed the price performance of the stock since purchase, relative to the price performance of the Standard & Poor's 500 Stock Index. The RPI was computed as follows:

$$\text{RPI} = \frac{\text{Percent increase in stock price since purchase}}{\text{Percent increase in S\&P 500 index since purchase}}$$

Trends in the RPI could influence decisions on the sale of individual stocks.

Sales Criteria

Selling a stock was considered when any of the following events occurred:

1. The DEP ranking fell into the lower half of the ranked universe.
2. The company had two consecutive quarters of down earnings (5 percent or more each quarter).
3. The stock had an RPI trending downward for six months.
4. The holding of an individual stock amounted to 3 percent or more of the total account at market value; under these circumstances, the issue was automatically reduced to 2 percent.
5. Overinvestment by more than 1 percent occurred in any one industry. Generally, the least attractive stock in the industry would be trimmed first.

When a stock was sold because it failed to meet any of the first three criteria listed, then the entire holdings of that stock would be liquidated and a new issue purchased to take its place. The new stock would be purchased until it constituted 2 percent of portfolio holdings. Discretion in selling those stocks that failed to meet any one of the first three criteria was limited; a very convincing case had to be made for retaining the issue.

If a stock or stocks had to be sold because a single issue exceeded 3 percent of portfolio holdings, or because any industry group exceeded 11 percent, the stock(s) would be trimmed back until they met the target holdings (2 percent or 10 percent) and the proceeds reinvested in those stock issues already held in the portfolio with holdings of less than 2 percent. Temporary variances in these two rules were allowed only if additions to the internal equity portfolio were shortly to be made that would keep the issues or industry within the limit.

Investment Decisions

At regular intervals the computer produced a report of the stocks that should be considered for sale and for purchase. A flow diagram of the investment decision process is shown in Exhibit 1. When an issue was recommended for liquidation, the investment officer then looked for a replacement issue, using the following criteria:

First, the computer selected those stocks with a DEP rating in the top 200 (approximately top 40 percent) of the stock-selection universe and listed them according to ranks. It then listed[3] those stocks within this subsample that failed to meet either of the other primary selection criteria:[4]

1. Current quarter's earning rank in top half of universe.
2. Estimated earnings-per-share growth for next 12 months greater than 5 percent.

In addition to the primary criteria, the computer also listed the stocks that failed to meet each of the following secondary selection criteria:

3. *Value Line* ratings of timeliness *and* safety of 1, 2, or 3.
4. Six-month RPI within 1 *negative* standard deviation of the mean of the top 200.
5. Five-year EPS growth rate greater than S&P 500 average growth rate.
6. The $\dfrac{\text{(est. EPS growth for the next 12 months)} - \text{(5-year EPS growth)}}{\text{(5-year EPS growth)}}$ in the top 200 of the stock-selection universe.

A stock considered for investment had to meet all primary criteria and, with only rare exception, all secondary criteria. Variances from secondary criteria could be allowed, but only where unusual circumstances existed.

After eliminating those stocks that failed to meet the primary or secondary criteria, the computer then sorted those stocks qualifying for purchase by industry group. Stocks already owned or stocks in industries where further investment was not feasible were then eliminated from consideration. Finally, using the detailed information provided by the DEP ranking program, information in the company file including research reports, and Security Research's 3-Trend (prices, earnings, dividends) security charts for visual anlysis of trends, the investment officer made

[3]The report first listed the criteria and then those stocks in the top 200 DEP rankings that failed to meet it. A stock was listed only once, even if it failed to meet several criteria.

[4]These primary and secondary criteria are similar to but not identical to those used in the portfolio. Actual criteria are confidential.

his purchase decisions. Usually only a few stocks were available for consideration in each replacement decision.

The CSRS was designed so that stocks would be considered for sale or purchase based on formal analysis done in a systematic way. For this reason, Mr. Grey asked the brokerage firms that provided CSRS with investment information not to pass on to the investment officers any "street talk" or "hot tips." Mr. Britton was also asked to disregard any of this type of information when making an investment recommendation.

Other Considerations

Prior to implementing the system, Mr. Grey backtested the concept by using four years of historical data on the stock universe to simulate the operations of the system. The backtest indicated that the system had the potential to outperform the S&P 500 Index by at least 1 percent per year (CSRS target). These backtests did not allow for judgment in selecting securities. Based on these results, the CSRS trustees authorized the establishment of a portfolio with an initial investment of $25 million, to be managed as outlined. The initial investments were executed in early May 1978.

One of the advantages of bringing equity funds in-house to be managed was the possible saving of management fees. A $100 million account often required the payment of $200 to $500 thousands in fees annually. The CSRS internal fund, in contrast, was designed to be managed with the input of only three to five days of time per month on the part of investment officers. Mr. Grey had initially played an active role in the selection of investments and the execution of decisions. Increasingly, however, Mr. Britton had assumed these responsibilities, and Mr. Grey grew more confident that when he retired (within a year's time) the account would continue to be managed effectively.

CSRS

CSRS was the agency for accumulating, investing, and paying retirement and other benefits for most Commonwealth employees, and a number of local government or other government-related agencies had joined the plan voluntarily. Funding for state employees was provided for in the annual budget, based on cost determinations made by a reputable actuary. Other agencies participating in the plan paid in appropriate amounts, determined by an agency, based on individual pension programs and employment records. Ultimately, the greatest portion of the plan was funded by state and local taxpayers.

By most standards, the state retirement plan was a relatively attractive one, providing significant annual benefits in relation to terminal wages (immediately before retirement) and some protection against inflation in the post-retirement years. The provision for inflationary protection made it important that the pension portfolio earn a real rate of return of at least 2 percent on available investment funds.

The market value of the portfolio was approximately $1.8 billion in May 1981. Until recently, law had restricted equity investments to less than 50 percent of the book value of the portfolio. "Book value" referred to the cost basis of securities held in the portfolio, not to contributions (adjusted for the assumed actuarial rate of return). Thus, when securities were sold for a capital gain and then reinvested, the capital gains or losses were impounded in the cost basis.

CSRS had recently been given the authority, beginning two months hence, to increase the equity investments (based on cost) to 60 percent of the portfolio value. Various forecasts indicated that the fund would double in market value in the next three to five years, as the result of reinvestment of income and gains and of net new inflows of funds. Equity investments might, therefore, grow from their current level of approximately $0.8 billion to over $2.2 billion in a relatively short period.

The CSRS fixed-income portfolio had been managed largely in-house for a long time. This account, representing about 80 percent of available fixed-income assets, was predominantly invested in long-term securities of high quality. As the result of rising interest rates, the market value of this portfolio was significantly below its cost basis. The CSRS investment officer responsible for managing this account engaged in some "sector" swapping, but more frequently in "security swapping" whenever he foresaw some improvement in cash yield without compromising safety or yield to maturity. Compared with most actively managed bond portfolios, the "duration" of the in-house bond portfolio tended to be quite long. The average maturity of this account was over 17 years in May 1981. An outside manager handled the balance of the fixed-income portfolio. This manager was more active than the in-house management in changing the "average maturity" composition of the portfolio to maintain its range from 6 to 15 years, and at this time the portfolio was invested at the short end of the average maturity range. The outside manager also was active in making sector and security changes according to his assessment of the present and future status of the money markets.

CSRS employed five outside equity managers in addition to those responsible for the in-house portfolio. Two of three managers had been employed at the beginning of 1981 and only two of the current outside managers had been working with CSRS for more than 18 months.

The Investment Advisory Committee had expressed some concern about allocating more than $250 million to any single manager. When a new manager was hired, the initial commitment tended to be $25 million. If the new manager performed according to expectations, additional funds were then allocated to that manager. It was clear, however, that funds would have to be allocated to new managers more rapidly in the immediate future than had been true in the past, and several new managers would have to be located and hired.

Equity fund managers were expected to provide total-return performance that exceeded the S&P 500 Index total return by 1 percent per year over a typical market cycle, and to earn a real rate of return of 3 percent per year over a somewhat longer period. CSRS trustees provided explicit guidelines for each of the managers, which constrained overconcentration and mandated that practice conform with Commonwealth law and "prudent man" requirements. The only constraint that caused controversy was the requirement that at least 75 percent of the funds allocated to a manager be invested in equity securities at all times. The outside managers had indicated occasionally that they would like more leeway in investing in money-market securities when the equity market outlook was unfavorable. The Investment Advisory Committee, in contrast, was concerned about the evidence that managers in general, and its managers in particular, had not proven to be good market timers in the past. As a consequence, several advisors were pressing to require managers to be at least 90 percent invested in equities at all times.

The In-House Equity Account Performance

Exhibit 2 provides a summary of the total-rate-of-return performance as of April 30, 1981, of the CSRS in-house equity portfolio, divided by periods in the manner most frequently reviewed by the advisors and trustees. Exhibit 3 shows this same information graphically. Exhibit 4 provides data on the performance of each equity fund manager.

Using a somewhat different period breakdown, Exhibit 5 compares the performance of the Commonwealth Stock Portfolio (CSP) universe (equally weighted) against certain other indices. Exhibit 6 shows the performance of the universe, subdivided by quintiles based on DEP rankings. At the beginning of each six-month period, paper portfolios based solely on DEP rankings (by quintile) were formed on an equally weighted basis, and *performance* of the total rate of return for each quintile was monitored.

The CSP portfolio as of April 30, 1981, is shown in Exhibit 7, with individual stocks ranked by percentage invested, yield, year-to-date gain, and the RPI calculation explained earlier. The characteristics of this portfolio are summarized by industry in Exhibit 8.

The volatility of the CSP in-house portfolio in various short-term up and down markets from May 1978 to April 1981 is shown in Exhibit 9. Exhibit 10 summarizes the DEP printouts on the stocks held by CSP on May 1, 1981.

The Issues

As the result of reinvestment of income, capital gains, and the allocation of new funds to the account, the market value of CSP was now in excess of $180 million, and the advisors were urging that further funds be allocated to it.

While Mr. Grey was pleased with the past performance of CSP, he believed that now was an excellent time to sit back and examine the system to determine what components of it were contributing to the above-average results and what, if any, changes in the system might produce even better results.

While reviewing the information, Mr. Grey considered a number of questions:

- Do elements of individual judgment help or hurt the system?
- Is the above-average performance due to luck? Investment officer skill? The system? Or some combination of all these?

- How does the general action of the stock market affect the system? Is the system working with or counter to the market in general?
- What effect would a major change in market conditions have on the system?
- Are our self-imposed restrictions too tight? Should we change some of them?
- Has our stock turnover rate been too high?
- Are we outperforming the market by making better decisions or by taking more risk?
- Is there some upper limit to the amount of money CSP can manage without impairing performance?
- Does the growing number of equity managers hired by CSRS suggest too much diversification? Should the number of securities in the portfolio be reduced to 33? To 25?
- Should the capitalization constraint be loosened to permit investment in more securities?

He knew the data at hand would not give an answer to all of these questions. Therefore, after he first drew whatever conclusions he could from the data, he wanted to devise tests that would allow him to analyze the remaining issues.

EXHIBIT 1
Flow Chart of Portfolio Decisions

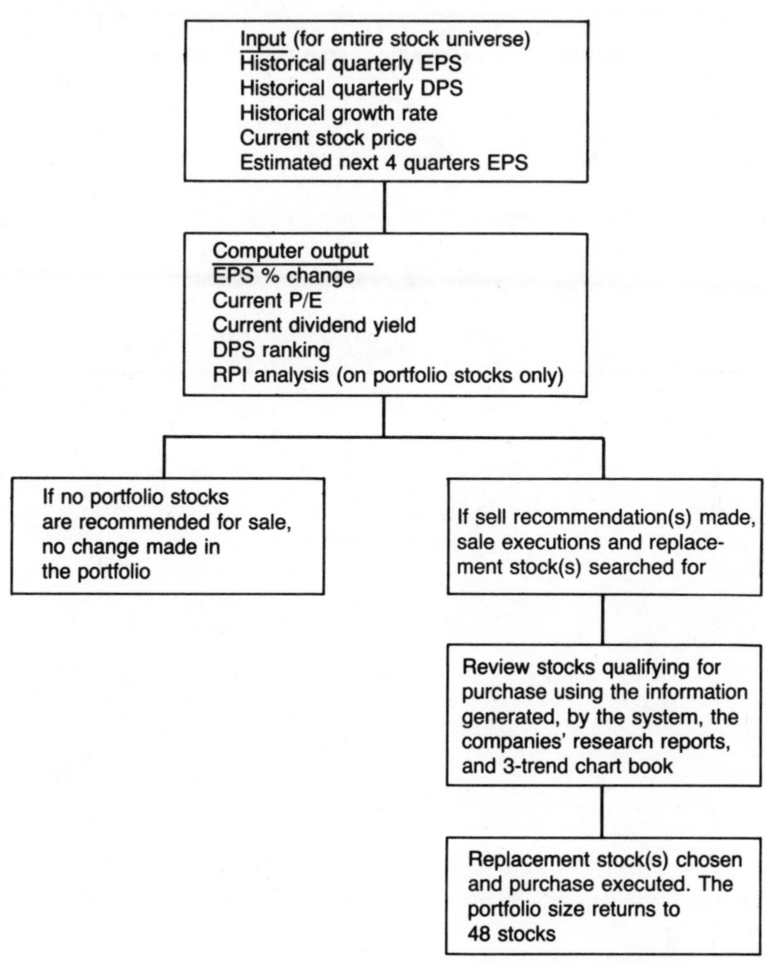

EXHIBIT 2
Commonwealth Stock Portfolio (CSP) Performance (*percent change in unit value total return; April 30, 1981*)

	3 Months	Year to Date	12 Months	24 Months	36 Months
CSP	6.8	−1.1	45.5	69.5	89.5
S&P 500	3.5	−1.0	30.0	42.0	56.0
CSP versus S&P	3.3	−0.1	15.5	27.5	33.5

Turnover Rate (12-month periods ending April 30)

1979	1980	1981	36-Month Average
24%	31%	38%	31%

EXHIBIT 3
Commonwealth Stock Portfolio (CSP) Performance
(*total return, quarterly basis*)

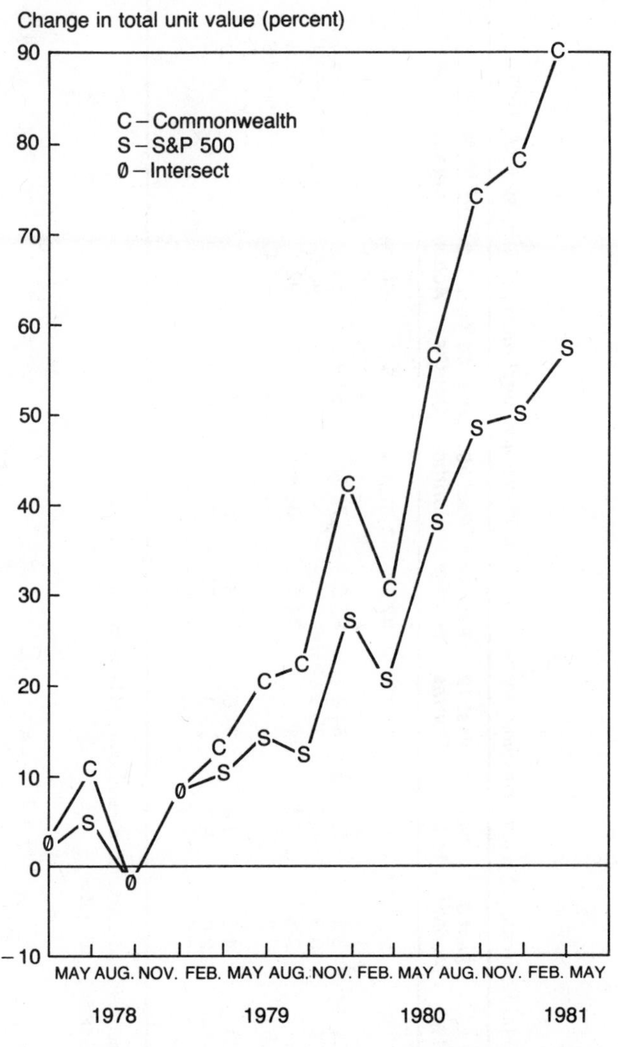

EXHIBIT 4

Commonwealth Supplemental Retirement System (*common stock managers' performance; total rate of return, May 31, 1981*)

Manager Style	May	Past 3 Months	Year to Date	Past 12 Months	Past 24 Months	Past 36 Months	Past 60 Months	Since Inception Actual	versus	S&P†	Inception Date
A Growth/rotation	0.7%	2.2%	−1.4%	25.7%	47.3%	57.3%	—%	60.4%		4.2%	7/1/77
B Small growth	4.3	11.3	9.3	—	—	—	—	9.3		10.1	1/1/81
C Growth	1.1	3.5	−0.9	34.2	62.2	72.7	85.9	85.2		9.8	7/14/72
D Value	0.7	10.3	14.7	30.3	—	—	—	43.5		7.4	.4/1/80
E CSP	1.4	7.3	0.3	40.2	74.9	88.8	—	92.1		35.9	5/1/78
F Asset/growth	−0.5	−2.8	−5.4	—	—	—	—	−5.4		−4.6	1/1/81
Total stocks*	1.0	4.2	0.2	31.8	55.8	65.7	71.0				
S&P 500	0.1	2.0	−0.8	23.9	45.5	55.0	62.9				
Total versus S&P	0.9	2.2	1.0	7.9	10.3	10.7	8.1				

*Includes managers whose services had been discontinued; composite performance of total fund.

†Actual (cumulative) minus S&P 500 (cumulative).

EXHIBIT 5
CSP Universe versus Market Indices

Period	*CSP Universe*	*S&P 500*	*DJIA*	*NYSE Index*
July–Dec. 78	−3.4%	−.5%	−1.7%	−.1%
Jan.–June 79	11.2	7.1	4.6	9.1
July–Dec. 79	5.6	4.9	−.4	6.0
Jan.–June 80	5.6	5.8	3.5	6.3
July–Dec. 80	14.7	18.8	10.9	19.2
Compounded return	37.4	41.6	17.7	45.2

EXHIBIT 6
Record of DEP Rank Quintiles* (*percent return*)

	1	**2**	*3*	*4*	**5**	*CSP Universe*	*Actual CSP Portfolio*	*S&P 500 Index*
July–Dec. 78	−2.0%	−1.9%	−2.5%	−4.2%	−6.2%	−3.4%	0.4%	0.6%
Jan.–June 79	11.4	9.8	10.6	11.0	13.2	11.2	10.0	7.1
July–Dec. 79	9.3	8.0	2.7	2.6	5.2	5.6	15.3	4.9
Jan.–June 80	9.8	6.4	6.5	3.1	2.4	5.6	4.3	5.8
July–Dec. 80	28.0	22.6	11.6	7.8	3.8	14.7	34.9	18.8
Average	11.3	9.0	5.7	4.1	3.7			
Compounded total return	67.7	51.6	31.4	21.2	18.8			

*Quintile 1: DEP ranks 1–100, with DEP rank 1 being most favorable.
Quintile 5: DEP ranks 401–500, with DEP rank 500 being least favorable.

EXHIBIT 7
CSP Portfolio (*April 30, 1981*)

Total Market Value			Current Yield			Year-to-Date Gain			Relative Gain/Loss		
$	%	Security	$	%	Security	$	%	Security	$	%	Security
$2,851,184	100.0	CASH EQUIV	$417,772	14.5	CASH EQUIV	$1,285,875	32	TANDY CORP	$3,730,410	341	TANDY CORP
5,424,048	3.3	HOSP CORP OF AM	199.500	6.5	CONSOL. FOODS	1,071,702	29	WARNER COMM	2,679,129	198	HOSP CORP OF AM
5,322,525	3.3	WAL-MART	183,600	8.0	NABISCO	1,154,075	28	WAL-MART	2,040,834	194	HELMERICH & PAY
5,285,250	3.2	TANDY CORP	188,760	5.8	AMER STANDARD	458,437	22	TRAVELERS	2,571,631	193	WAL-MART
4,790,000	2.9	WARNER COMM	135,160	5.2	TRAVELERS	524,375	21	REVCO	1,367,658	152	SMITHKLINE
4,215,200	2.8	HELMERICH & PAY	133,210	5.1	WESTERN BANCORP	557,700	20	AMER STANDARD	1,248,801	152	BAKER INTL
3,997,350	2.4	WHEELABRATOR-F	142,080	4.7	STD OIL-OHIO	572,125	20	SUPER-VALU	1,558,201	148	WARNER COMM
3,977,375	2.4	SMITHKLINE	128,280	4.5	ATLANTIC RICH	875,184	19	HOSP CORP OF AM	1,122,782	149	HILTON HOTELS
3,810,000	2.3	RAYTHEON	86,520	4.1	BOEING COMPANY	449,250	17	PHILIP MORRIS	1,139,854	143	RAYTHEON
3,802,925	2.3	HARRIS CORP	135,280	4.1	CHESEBRGH-PONDS	534,625	15	WHEELABRATOR-F	1,099,859	141	McGRAW-HILL
3,788,200	2.3	McGRAW-HILL	113,750	4.0	AMER BRANDS	445,000	15	HILTON HOTELS	1,082,046	140	HARRIS CORP
3,680,600	2.3	HUGHES TOOL	119,800	3.9	PHILIP MORRIS	339,187	11	AMP INC	1,103,685	138	WHEELABRATOR-F
3,648,700	2.2	BAKER INTL	99.600	3.8	LEVI STRAUSS	306,062	10	CONTROL DATA	961,092	136	DIGITAL EQUIP
3,628,050	2.2	DIGITAL EQUIP	91,520	3.7	PIONEER CORP	306,000	10	HEWLETT-PACKARD	973,932	136	HUGHES TOOL
3,558,750	2.2	SUNDSTRAND CORP	135,408	3.6	McGRAW-HILL	231,000	8	1ST INTL BANCSH	799,943	135	FOSTER WHEELER
3,500,000	2.1	BAXTER TRAVENOL	108,000	3.5	SANTA FE IND	193,827	8	BAXTER TRAVENOL	784,117	129	COOPER INDUST
3,494,937	2.1	SUPER-VALU	91,500	3.3	HOUSTON NAT GAS	217,375	8	SMITHKLINE	728,178	127	AMP INC
3,487,250	2.1	AMP INC	113,920	3.3	HILTON HOTELS	198,550	6	DIGITAL EQUIP	585,892	124	STD OIL-OHIO
3,453,200	2.1	COOPER INDUST	100,800	3.3	1ST INTL BANCSH	148,750	5	AMER BRANDS	660,872	124	ABBOTT LABS
3,453,200	2.1	HILTON HOTELS	104,000	2.9	SUNDSTRAND CORP	148,982	4	HARRIS CORP	620,044	122	AMER STANDARD
3,436,312	2.1	BAUSCH & LOMB	95,940	2.8	BAUSCH & LOMB	111,967	4	DOVER CORP	413,043	122	FLUOR CORP
3,407,250	2.1	ABBOTT LABS	83,900	2.8	REVCO	73,750	2	ABBOTT LABS	598,959	121	BAUSCH & LOMB
3,378,375	2.1	AMER STANDARD	88,288	2.6	COOPER INDUST	62,500	2	BIG THREE IND	604,195	121	SUPER-VALU

3,363,100	2.1	PETROLANE	105,280	2.6	WHEELABRATOR-F	60,450	2	McGRAW-HILL	525,348	119	PETROLANE
3,349,000	2.1	HEWLETT-PACKARD	84,960	2.5	ABBOTT LABS	27,150	1	WESTERN BANCORP	386,635	115	REVCO
3,293,000	2.0	CHESEBRGH-PONDS	91,440	2.4	RAYTHEON	−14,658	0	SUNDSTRAND CORP	367,123	114	PHILIP MORRIS
3,260,250	2.0	AMER HOSP SUP	90,240	2.3	SMITHKLINE	−69,672	−2	AMER HOSP SUP	384,897	114	CONTROL DATA
3,231,812	2.0	CONTROL DATA	79,600	2.3	SUPER-VALU	−74,075	−2	DELTA AIR LINES	363,927	113	BIG THREE IND
3,208,875	2.0	LITTON IND	73,140	2.2	AMER HOSP SUP	−105,823	−3	CHESEBRGH-PONDS	262,362	108	HEWLETT-PACKARD
3,173,375	1.9	DOVER CORP	68,000	2.2	DELTA AIR LINES	−180,075	−6	CONSOL. FOODS	214,747	108	1ST INTL BANCSH
3,182,500	1.9	BIG THREE IND	72,360	2.1	AMP INC	−197,690	−6	SANTA FE IND	224,156	107	SUNDSTRAND CORP
3,111,900	1.9	FOSTER WHEELER	60,720	2.0	FOSTER WHEELER	−215,800	−8	LEVI STRAUSS	108,863	104	ATLANTIC RICH
3,107,812	1.9	DELTA AIR LINES	68,884	2.0	PETROLANE	−265,100	−8	NABISCO	79,716	103	AMER HOSP SUP
3,100,500	1.9	SANTA FE IND	60,000	1.9	BIG THREE IND	−381,000	−9	RAYTHEON	63,496	102	DOVER CORP
3,085,500	1.9	NABISCO	60,200	1.9	LITTON IND	−373,800	−10	COOPER INDUST	52,318	102	AMER BRANDS
3,058,125	1.9	CONSOL. FOODS	44,000	1.9	FLUOR CORP	−376,687	−10	BAUSCH & LOMB	55,434	102	LITTON IND
3,039,925	1.9	PHILIP MORRIS	55,120	1.7	DOVER CORP	−513,600	−12	BAKER INTL	33,924	101	BAXTER TRAVENOL
3,041,375	1.9	REVCO	58,060	1.5	HARRIS CORP	−670,600	−14	HELMERICH & PAY	−18,931	99	WESTERN BANCORP
3,010,000	1.8	1ST INTL BANCSH	51,360	1.4	BAKER INTL	−592,093	−16	FOSTER WHEELER	−47,171	99	CHESEBRGH-PONDS
3,011,800	1.8	STD OIL-OHIO	47,500	1.4	BAXTER TRAVENOL	−612,750	−16	LITTON IND	−74,049	98	DELTA AIR LINES
2,601,250	1.8	AMER BRANDS	65,144	1.4	WARNER COMM	−549,000	−17	HOUSTON NAT GAS	−68,723	97	TRAVELERS
2,834,125	1.7	ATLANTIC RICH	37,350	1.2	CONTROL DATA	−768,150	−19	PETROLANE	−93,962	97	LEVI STRAUSS
2,745,000	1.7	HOUSTON NAT GAS	32,504	0.9	HUGHES TOOL	−938,075	−20	HUGHES TOOL	−124,135	96	CONSOL. FOODS
2,633,550	1.6	WESTERN BANCORP	42,763	0.8	HOSP CORP OF AM	−637,000	−21	PIONEER CORP	−140,728	96	SANTA FE IND
2,639,400	1.6	LEVI STRAUSS	35,828	0.7	WAL-MART	−817,950	−22	ATLANTIC RICH	−207,258	94	NABISCO
2,575,125	1.6	TRAVELERS	13,600	0.4	HEWLETT-PACKARD	−625,725	−23	BOEING COMPANY	−308,620	89	PIONEER CORP
2,444,000	1.5	PIONEER CORP	10,538	0.3	HELMERICH & PAY	−1,250,600	−29	STD OIL-OHIO	−294,028	88	BOEING COMPANY
2,318,675	1.4	FLUOR CORP	0	0.0	TANDY CORP	−983,125	−30	FLUOR CORP	−487,728	85	HOUSTON NAT GAS
2,101,200	1.3	BOEING COMPANY	0	0.0	DIGITAL EQUIP						

EXHIBIT 8

Analysis of CSP (*April 30, 1981*)

		Total Market		Total Cost		Income			Total Gain/Loss		Ytd Gain/Loss*		Rel.
		$	%	$	%	$	%	Yld	$	%	$	%	Pct.
	Cash and Equity	2,881,194	1.7	2,881,184	2	417,772	9	14.5					
3.5	CHEMICALS	3,182,600	1.9	2,419,550	2	80,000	1	1.9	742,950	31	62,500	2	113
1.8	AEROSPACE	2,101,200	1.3	1,843,803	2	86,520	2	4.1	257,597	14	−625,725	−23	88
1.1	BUILD. & CONSTRUCT	3,378,375	2.1	2,112,048	2	188,780	5	5.6	1,266,320	80	557,700	20	122
0.2	ENVIRON. CONTROL	3,997,350	2.4	2,302,948	2	105,280	3	2.8	1,094,404	74	534,825	15	138
2.5	MACHINERY	13,297,225	8.1	9,843,742	9	308,128	8	2.3	3,450,483	35	−808,564	−8	118
0.7	APPAREL, TEXTILE	2,039,400	1.8	2,127,541	2	99,600	2	3.8	511,859	24	−215,800	−8	97
0.8	FOOD SERV/LODG	8,948,137	4.3	4,369,846	4	193,520	5	2.9	2,578,291	50	1,017,125	17	133
2.0	LEISURE TIME	10,075,250	8.2	4,074,798	4	85,144	2	0.8	5,400,454	116	2,357,837	31	211
1.5	PHOTO. & OPTICAL	3,436,312	2.1	2,332,588	2	95,940	2	2.8	1,103,724	47	−376,687	−10	121
1.3	PRINTING & PUBLISH	3,788,200	2.3	2,059,038	2	135,408	3	3.8	1,729,164	84	80,450	2	141
2.4	RETAIL-GENERAL	3,041,375	1.9	2,085,175	2	83,900	2	2.8	978,200	47	524,375	21	115
4.3	DRUGS	7,384,625	4.5	4,142,148	4	170,800	4	2.4	3,242,477	78	281,125	4	138
2.8	FOODS	6,143,625	3.9	6,580,800	6	383,100	9	8.2	−445,175	−7	−445,175	−7	95
2.2	HOSPITAL SUPL + SERV	12,184,296	7.5	8,275,813	7	103,403	4	1.3	3,908,883	47	999,339	9	130
1.0	SOAPS & TOILETRIES	3,293,000	2.0	3,396,823	3	135,280	3	4.1	−105,823	−3	−105,823	−3	99
1.4	TOBACCO	5,901,175	3.8	4,308,720	4	233,550	6	4.0	1,594,455	37	598,000	11	108
1.7	COAL & GAS	2,745,000	1.7	3,104,441	3	91,500	2	3.3	−359,441	−12	−549,000	−17	85
4.5	OIL-SUPLS & CONSTR	17,224,475	10.5	9,333,428	8	205,266	5	1.2	7,891,047	85	−3,871,550	−18	143
9.0	OIL-DOMESTIC	5,845,925	3.8	3,938,037	3	288,380	7	4.6	1,907,888	48	−2,088,550	−28	113
2.2	BANKS	5,643,550	3.5	4,404,320	4	234,018	8	4.1	1,179,230	26	258,150	5	104
2.3	INSURANCE	2,575,125	1.6	2,082,824	2	135,180	3	5.2	512,501	25	450,437	22	97
3.3	ELECTRONICS	14,429,175	8.8	9,443,409	8	233,480	8	1.6	4,985,788	53	413,149	3	129
8.2	OFFICE EQUIPMENT	6,859,802	4.2	4,738,294	4	37,350	1	0.5	2,121,568	45	504,612	8	124
0.8	UTILITY-GAS, PIPEL	2,444,000	1.5	2,418,843	2	91,520	2	3.7	27,157	1	−637,000	−21	89
0.4	AIRLINES	3,107,812	1.9	3,181,888	3	88,000	2	2.2	−74,076	−2	−74,075	−2	96
2.1	RAILROADS	3,100,500	1.9	3,298,190	3	108,000	3	3.5	−197,690	−8	−197,890	−6	98
2.5	DIVERSIFIED	3,208,875	2.0	3,122,863	3	60,200	1	1.9	88,012	3	−612,750	−18	102
	NOT CLASSIFIED	5,322,525	3.3	2,212,085	2	35,828	1	0.7	3,110,440	141	1,154,075	28	193
	TOTAL EQUITIES	163,278,869	98	114,182,395	98	4081,413	91	2.5	49,098,475	43	−859,110	−1	122
	TOTAL PORTFOLIO	166,160,053		117,083,579		4499,185		2.7	49,096,475	42	−859,110	0	

S&P		Total Market $	Total Market %	Total Cost $	Total Cost %	Income $	Income %	Income Yld.	Total Gain/Loss $	Total Gain/Loss %	Ytd Gain/Loss* $	Ytd Gain/Loss* %
9.0	BASIC MATERIALS	3,162,500	1.9	2,419,550	2	60,000	1	1.0	742,950	31	62,500	2
9.4	CAPITAL GOODS/CONSTR	22,774,150	13.9	16,105,337	14	688,688	17	3.0	6,668,813	41	−401,984	−2
12.8	CONSUMER CYCLICAL	29,926,075	18.3	17,628,982	15	673,512	17	2.3	12,299,692	70	3,367,100	13
15.1	CONSUMER STAPLES	34,906,721	21.4	26,712,104	23	1090,533	27	3.1	8,194,617	31	1,337,468	4
24.4	ENERGY	25,815,400	15.8	16,375,908	14	555,128	14	2.2	9,439,494	58	−8,489,100	−20
5.2	FINANCIAL	8,218,875	5.0	6,526,944	6	369,176	8	4.5	1,691,731	28	714,587	10
9.5	TECHNOLOGY	21,289,037	13.0	14,181,703	12	270,830	7	1.3	7,107,334	50	917,761	5
9.1	UTILITIES	2,444,000	1.5	2,418,843	2	91,520	2	3.7	27,157	1	−837,000	−21
2.9	TRANSPORT & SERVICES	8,208,312	3.8	6,480,078	6	176,000	4	2.8	−271,705	−4	−271,705	−4
2.5	MISCELLANEOUS	8,531,400	6.2	5,334,948	5	96,028	2	1.1	3,196,452	60	541,325	7

	Least Squares Growth						Profitability								Risk					
	EPS				DPS		Return on				Reinvest Rate		Operating Margin		Price as %	P/E		Debt to	5-Yr Pay-	Mkt Cap
	5-Year		10-Year		5-Year		Equity		Capital								5-Yr			
	Rate	Stab	Rate	Stab	Rate	Stab	1 Yr	5 Yr	1 Yr	5 Yr	1 Yr	5 Yr	1 Yr	5 Yr	Book	Cur	Avg	Capt	Out	MMS
CSP	23.7	92.1	20.8	90.4	23.8	87.6	21.2	18.7	15.0	13.8	16.2	14.8	17.3	18.8	324.2	13.5	14.8	24.9	24.9	24.1
% WITH DATA	100.0	100.0	97.8	97.9	100.0	100.0	100.0	100.0	95.0	95.0	100.0	98.1	95.0	95.0	100.0	100.0	100.0	95.0	98.1	100.0
S&P 500	15.1	75.8	13.3	83.2	14.3	87.2	16.5	15.8	12.9	12.2	11.3	10.2	18.8	19.5	180.4	10.3	12.1	25.1	30.3	84.9

*Ytd means year-to-date.

EXHIBIT 9

Commonwealth Stock Portfolio (*interim volatility*)

	Total Return							
	3 Mo. May 78- Aug. 78	***2 Mo. Sept. 78- Oct. 78***	***10 Mo. Nov. 78- Aug. 79***	***2 Mo. Sept. 79- Oct. 79***	***2 Mo. Nov. 79- Jan. 80***	***2 Mo. Feb. 80- Mar. 80***	***7 Mo. Apr. 80- Nov. 80***	***4 Mo. Dec. 80- Apr. 81***
CSP	+15.0	−14.5	+32.0	−6.3	+17.4	−11.8	+52.7	−1.5
S&P 500	+ 8.3	− 8.8	+21.9	−6.2	+13.4	− 9.8	+41.6	−4.0
CSP versus S&P	+ 6.7	− 5.7	+10.1	− .1	+ 4.0	− 2.0	+11.1	+2.5

EXHIBIT 10
Summary Data on Stocks in CSP (*May 1, 1981*)

Portfolio Stocks (Company)	Earnings per Share					EPS % Change					Cur	Div	DEP Rankings								Price	
	Cur	3 Mo	6 Mo	9 Mo	12 Mo	5 Yr	3 Mo	6 Mo	9 Mo	12 Mo	P/E	Yld	5 Yr*	3 Mo	6 Mo	9 Mo	12 Mo.	P/E	Yld*	Total Decile†	Cur	Rel Chn Ytd
AMP INC	3.54	3.65	3.62	3.61	3.54	26	−3	−2	−1	0	16	2.1		350	319	315	288	454		7	57.8	14
ABBOTT LABS	3.60	3.48	3.32	3.21	3.08	19	3	8	12	17	16	2.5		157	140	124	113	450		3	57.2	4
AMER BRANDS	14.20	14.02	14.31	14.38	13.76	24	1	−0	−1	3	6	4.0		241	300	306	258	57		4	81.6	8
AMER HOSP SUP	3.16	3.03	3.00	2.88	2.83	15	4	5	9	12	15	2.3		134	198	157	163	434		5	46.3	−1
AMER STANDARD	5.69	5.42	5.23	5.15	4.76	27		8	10	20	7	5.8		125	129	147	93	131		1	39.0	21
ATLANTIC RICH	6.31	6.64	6.43	6.16	5.47	28	−4	−1	2	15	8	4.4		373	315	256	126	214		3	50.1	−19
BAKER INTL	2.64	2.38	2.11	1.91	1.76	19	11	25	38	50	16	1.4		47	28	25	22	453		1	42.8	−10
BAUSCH & LOMB	3.32	4.20	4.19	3.99	3.74	22	−20	−20	−16	−11	17	2.8		465	446	404	373	457		9	55.0	−9
BAXTER TRAVEN	3.79	3.72	3.49	3.46	3.36	18	1	8	9	13	15	1.4		219	135	161	154	433		5	55.5	7
BIG THREE IND	2.19	2.04	1.88	1.74	1.61	19	7	16	25	36	15	1.8		81	57	47	39	436		2	32.6	8
BOEING COMPAN	6.23	6.01	5.94	5.58	5.25	38	3	4	11	19	5	4.1		153	207	131	101	38		1	34.1	−21
CHESEBRGH-PON	3.23	3.10	3.01	2.79	2.69	15	4	7	15	20	11	4.2		137	158	90	90	356		3	36.5	33
CONSOL. FOODS	4.54	4.40	4.23	4.12	3.96	22	3	7	10	15	6	6.4		169	157	151	134	113		1	29.5	28
CONTROL DATA	8.49	8.32	7.75	7.54	7.35	27	2	9	12	16	9	1.2		212	113	117	125	263		2	75.7	10
COOPER INDUST	4.38	4.27	4.09	3.98	3.84	20	2	7	10	14	11	2.5		191	164	155	139	346		3	48.6	−7
DELTA AIR LIN	6.80	5.82	4.68	3.69	4.23	13	16	45	84	61	10	2.3		28	12	7	12	328		1	70.5	22
DIGITAL EQUIP	6.27	5.78	5.56	5.41	5.08	25	8	12	15	23	16	0.0		67	85	89	76	449		1	99.7	7
DOVER CORP	4.27	4.10	3.91	3.64	3.44	21	4	9	17	24	14	1.7		140	121	81	72	423		2	60.0	−2
1ST INTL BANC	6.30	5.85	5.55	5.32	5.11	15	7	13	18	23	9	3.4		77	75	73	77	240		2	53.6	11
FLUOR CORP	2.87	2.73	2.61	2.42	2.12	19	5	9	18	35	14	1.9		122	105	72	40	429		2	41.5	−29
FOSTER WHEELE	1.64	1.62	1.54	1.51	1.44	24	1	6	8	14	12	2.0		244	180	173	141	384		4	20.3	−15
HARRIS CORP	2.92	2.83	2.73	2.62	2.55	30	3	6	11	15	19	1.5		168	167	132	135	465		3	54.1	6
HELMERICH & P	2.05	1.85	1.70	1.57	1.40	22	10	20	30	40	22	0.2		52	41	37	28	482		1	44.5	−11
HEWLETT-PACKA	4.61	4.47	4.08	3.82	3.58	23	3	12	20	29	21	0.4		172	80	65	57	478		2	97.8	12
HILTON HOTELS	4.02	4.00	3.91	3.84	3.68	32	0	2	4	9	12	3.3		268	245	227	179	377		4	49.1	19
HOSP CORP OF	1.87	1.74	1.63	1.54	1.45	21	7	14	21	29	23	0.8		80	69	60	56	487		2	43.2	22
HOUSTON NAT G	5.56	5.29	5.06	4.87	4.42	15	5	9	14	26	8	3.4		124	106	104	68	217		2	44.3	−16
HUGHES TOOL	6.14	5.23	4.85	4.57	4.24	20	17	28	34	45	13	0.9		26	24	33	30	391		1	77.7	−18

EXHIBIT 10 *(continued)*

Portfolio Stocks (Company)	Earnings per Share					EPS % Change					Cur	Div	DEP Rankings								Price	
	Cur	3 Mo	6 Mo	9 Mo	12 Mo	5 Yr	3 Mo	6 Mo	9 Mo	12 Mo	P/E	Yld	5 Yr*	3 Mo	6 Mo	9 Mo	12 Mo.	P/E	Yld*	Total Decile†	Cur	Rel Chn Ytd
LEVI STRAUSS	5.10	5.37	5.19	5.07	4.92	23	−5	−1	0	4	8	3.8		374	311	280	253	198		6	39.5	−6
LITTON IND	7.29	7.10	6.96	6.28	5.70	69	2	4	16	28	10	1.9		184	210	87	61	313		2	73.6	−15
McGRAW-HILL	3.57	3.48	3.36	3.23	3.17	19	2	6	10	13	13	3.6		189	183	146	156	403		4	47.1	4
NABISCO	4.21	3.96	3.75	3.32	3.21	15	6	12	26	31	7	6.1		98	89	45	48	140		1	29.3	13
PETROLANE	1.71	1.59	1.45	1.39	1.34	15	7	17	23	28	12	2.0		79	50	55	62	373		2	20.7	−18
PHILIP MORRIS	4.85	4.88	4.78	4.47	4.18	18	−0	1	8	16	10	3.9		298	267	177	120	329		5	50.7	20
PIONEER CORP	2.44	2.25	2.23	2.08	1.78	23	8	9	17	37	10	3.7		70	115	80	36	303		1	24.0	−17
RAYTHEON	6.98	6.80	6.59	6.31	6.08	21	2	5	10	15	14	2.4		187	193	143	133	424		3	99.3	−8
REVCO	3.21	3.08	2.98	2.88	2.77	20	4	7	11	16	12	2.7		136	151	133	122	362		2	37.2	27
SANTA FE IND	10.92	10.34	9.42	8.37	8.24	18	5	15	30	33	8	3.5		111	61	38	46	213		1	88.7	−13
SMITHKLINE	4.97	4.04	4.37	4.12	3.96	31	7	13	20	26	17	2.3		86	74	66	89	460		1	84.2	8
STD OIL-OHIO	7.65	7.37	7.30	7.04	5.92	46	3	4	8	29	7	4.7		151	209	171	53	124		2	51.1	−27
SUNDSTRAND CO	4.64	4.54	4.42	4.36	4.34	20	2	4	6	7	12	2.9		201	205	200	207	363		3	54.2	−2
SUPER-VALU	3.05	2.88	2.78	2.69	2.50	22	5	9	13	22	11	2.3		105	111	111	81	361		2	35.0	22
TANDY CORP	2.86	2.61	2.35	2.23	2.00	25	9	21	26	43	23	0.0		56	39	42	33	486		1	65.5	39
TRAVELERS	8.63	8.85	9.05	8.99	9.03	23	−2	−4	−4	−4	5	5.3		343	348	336	325	32		5	46.8	23
WAL-MART	1.73	1.58	1.49	1.42	1.34	27	9	16	21	29	22	0.7		57	59	58	54	485		1	38.5	30
WARNER COMM	2.38	2.21	2.09	2.02	1.98	27	7	13	17	20	21	1.3		78	73	76	92	479		2	50.6	34
WESTERN BANCO	6.03	5.84	5.53	5.67	5.67	21	3	9	6	6	6	5.2		165	123	201	217	67		2	35.5	1
WHEELABRATOR	4.45	4.31	4.23	4.04	3.90	16	3	5	10	14	14	2.6		166	201	154	138	411		4	60.3	17

*Omitted to protect company confidentiality.

†Decile rankings of total DEP used to protect confidentiality.

Commonwealth Stocks (Company)		Price					Rel. to S&P			P/E Ratios			EPS			Interim EPS				EPS, DPS Growth		Indicated Dividends	
					Year			P/E		5Yr						Date		12Mo.					
		Cur	Wk Chn	Ytd Chn	Hi	Lo	Ytd Chn	80	Lst 12M	Hi Lo	80	Lst 12M	1979	1980E	1981E	Mo	Q	$	Chn	Lst 5Yr	Lst 5Yr	$	Yld
AMP INC.		58	−2	12	61	33	14	170	178	24–17	16	16	3.38	2.65A	3.70	MR	1	3.54	0	26	20	1.20	2.1
ABBOTT LABS		57	−3	1	61	37	4	177	173	19–13	17	16	2.94	3.46A	4.10	MR	1	3.60	17	19	23	1.44	2.5
AMER BRANDS		82	1	5	83	58	8	66	66	9– 7	6	6	12.00	14.02A	14.90	MR	1	14.20	3	24	17	3.25	4.0
AMER HOSP SUP		46	−3	−4	49	31	−1	164	160	19–13	15	15	2.78	3.03A	3.55	MR	1	3.16	12	15	20	1.06	2.3
AMER STANDARD		39	−2	19	40	24	21	76	78	9– 6	7	7	4.76	5.69A	5.95	DC	4	5.69	20	27	29	2.20	5.8
ATLANTIC RICH		50	7	−21	59	41	−19	83	89	15–10	8	8	4.74	6.64A	7.25	MR	1	6.31	15	28	21	2.20	4.4
BAKER INTL	09	43	4	−12	46	27	−10	216	177	21–12	20	16	1.62	2.11A	2.85	MR	2	2.64	50	19	26	0.60	1.4
BAUSCH & LOMB		55	−5	−11	59	37	−9	141	180	15– 8	13	17	3.49	4.19A	5.05	MR	1	3.32	−11	22	26	1.56	2.8
BAXTER TRAVENOL		56	−3	5	59	41	7	160	160	22–15	15	15	3.24	3.72A	4.35	MR	1	3.79	13	18	24	0.76	1.4
BIG THREE IND		33	3	5	38	19	8	170	163	20–14	16	15	1.49	2.05A	2.35	MR	1	2.19	36	19	27	0.60	1.8
BOEING COMPANY		34	−4	−23	38	32	−21	62	63	13– 7	5	5	5.25	6.23A	5.50	DC	4	6.23	19	38	37	1.40	4.1
CHESEBRGH-PONDS		37	−5	30	39	21	33	127	125	15–11	12	11	2.56	3.10A	3.50	MR	1	3.23	20	15	12	1.52	4.2
CONSOL. FOODS	08	30	−4	23	31	20	26	79	74	27–20	7	6	3.60	4.12A	4.65	MR	3	4.54	15	22	5	1.90	6.4
CONTROL DATA		76	−4	7	80	47	10	100	99	12– 7	9	9	6.86	8.29A	9.37	MR	1	8.49	16	27	53	0.90	1.2
COOPER INDUST		49	−3	−10	51	29	−7	124	122	13– 8	11	11	3.67	4.26A	4.30	MR	1	4.38	14	20	24	1.24	2.5
DELTA AIR LINES	06	71	−7	19	77	31	22	161	115	12– 8	15	10	6.34	4.69A	7.00	MR	3	6.80	61	13	15	1.60	2.3
DIGITAL EQUIP	06	100	−8	5	112	59	7	195	173	28–19	18	16	4.10	5.45A	6.30	MR	3	6.27	23	25	0	0.00	0.0
DOVER CORP		60	−0	−4	64	33	−2	157	154	14– 9	15	14	3.20	4.10A	5.15	MR	1	4.27	24	21	21	1.04	1.7
1ST INTL BANCSHS		54	−2	8	56	35	11	100	95	11– 9	9	9	4.89	5.85A	7.00	MR	1	6.30	23	15	13	1.80	3.4
FLUOR CORP	10	42	−2	−31	55	24	−29	163	158	18– 9	15	14	2.01	2.73A	3.25	JA	1	2.87	35	19	27	0.80	1.9
FOSTER WHEELER		20	−2	−17	25	11	−15	136	136	14– 7	13	12	1.43	1.62A	1.95	MR	1	1.64	14	24	20	0.40	2.0
HARRIS CORP	06	54	−5	4	60	29	6	219	201	37–29	21	19	2.32	2.63A	3.15	MR	3	2.92	15	30	18	0.80	1.5
HELMERICH & PAYN	09	45	3	−13	50	23	−11	253	234	21–11	24	22	1.31	1.86A	2.65	DC	1	2.05	46	22	29	0.11	0.2
HEWLETT-PACKARD	10	98	−5	9	104	51	12	232	229	28–19	22	21	3.43	4.47A	5.35	JA	1	4.61	29	23	23	0.40	0.4

EXHIBIT 10 *(concluded)*

Commonwealth Stocks (Company)		Price					Rel. to S&P			P/E Ratios			EPS			Interim EPS				EPS, DPS Growth		Indicated Dividends	
					Year			P/E		5Yr						Date		12Mo.					
		Cur	Wk Chn	Ytd Chn	Hi	Lo	Ytd Chn	80	Lst 12M	Hi Lo	80	Lst 12M	1979	1980E	1981E	Mo	Q	$	Chn	Lst 5Yr	Lst 5Yr	$	Yld
HILTON HOTELS		49	−1	16	50	26	19	133	134	16– 9	12	12	3.42	4.00A	4.30	MR	1	4.02	9	32	30	1.60	3.3
HOSP CORP OF AM		43	−1	20	44	20	22	265	249	18–10	25	23	1.34	1.73A	2.22	MR	1	1.87	29	21	28	0.34	0.8
HOUSTON NAT GAS	07	44	−9	−18	51	36	−16	98	90	14– 8	9	8	3.57	5.06A	6.00	JA	−2	5.56	26	15	20	1.50	3.4
HUGHES TOOL		78	6	−20	83	51	−18	158	139	17–10	15	13	3.88	5.27A	6.50	MR	1	6.14	45	20	29	0.68	0.9
LEVI STRAUSS	11	40	−15	−8	50	31	−6	82	87	9– 6	7	8	4.58	5.36A	6.15	FB	1	5.10	4	23	36	1.50	3.8
LITTON IND	07	74	−6	−17	79	44	−15	113	112	47–30	10	10	4.11	7.06A	7.50	JA	2	7.29	28	69	79	1.40	1.9
McGRAW-HILL		47	−1	2	48	27	4	146	145	13– 9	14	13	3.10	3.48A	3.95	MR	1	3.57	13	19	20	1.68	3.6
NABISCO		29	−7	10	33	19	13	82	79	11– 9	7	7	3.10	3.96A	4.45	MR	1	4.21	31	15	8	1.80	6.1
PETROLANE	09	21	1	−20	25	46	−18	153	133	14– 8	14	12	1.20	1.46A	1.85	MR	2	1.71	28	15	20	0.42	2.0
PHILIP MORRIS		51	−5	17	54	34	20	119	116	13–10	11	10	4.08	4.63A	5.45	MR	1	4.85	16	18	24	2.00	3.9
PIONEER CORP		24	−2	−19	27	18	−17	107	109	14– 7	10	10	1.79	2.44A	3.00	DC	4	2.44	37	23	21	0.88	3.7
RAYTHEON		99	−3	−10	105	63	−8	157	156	15– 9	15	14	5.83	6.80A	8.00	MR	1	6.98	15	21	28	2.40	2.4
REVCO	05	37	−4	24	40	22	27	139	128	14– 9	13	12	2.61	2.88A	3.30	FB	3	3.21	16	20	32	1.00	2.7
SANTA FE IND		87	−4	−15	97	40	−13	91	89	10– 8	8	8	8.08	10.42A	12.50	MR	1	10.92	33	18	8	3.00	3.5
SMITHKLINE		84	−1	5	86	45	8	193	184	24–14	18	17	3.76	4.65A	5.65	MR	1	4.97	28	31	28	1.92	2.3
STD OIL-OHIO		51	5	−29	60	41	−27	77	76	23–14	7	7	4.91	7.37A	8.50	MR	1	7.65	29	46	31	2.40R	4.7
SUNDSTRAND CORP		54	−2	−4	58	36	−2	128	129	12– 7	12	12	4.03	4.57A	5.30	MR	1	4.64	7	20	26	1.60	2.9
SUPER-VALU	02	35	−3	19	37	18	22	124	126	13– 8	11	11	2.50	3.05A	3.33	FB	4	3.05	22	22	22	0.80	2.3
TANDY CORP	06	66	−4	33	74	14	36	310	247	19– 8	29	23	1.61	2.23A	2.95	MR	3	2.86	43	25	0	0.00	0.0
TRAVELERS		47	−5	20	50	36	23	61	62	9– 6	5	5	9.03	8.63A	7.50	DC	4	8.63	−4	23	14	2.48	5.3
WAL-MART	01	39	−1	27	39	15	30	236	240	21–12	22	22	1.34	1.73A	2.20	JA	4	1.73	29	27	31	0.28	0.7
WARNER COMM		51	−5	30	55	33	34	226	230	22–13	21	21	1.97	2.38A	3.10	DC	4	2.38	20	27	25	0.68	1.3
WESTERN BANCORP		36	−5	−1	38	28	1	67	67	8– 6	6	6	5.68	5.91A	6.35	MR	1	6.03	6	21	11	1.84	5.2
WHEELABRATOR-F		60	−5	15	65	32	17	150	148	14– 9	14	14	3.72	4.31A	5.06	MR	1	4.45	14	16	23	1.60	2.6

Appendix A

SAMPLE DEP CALCULATIONS

Exhibit A–1 provides a sample page from the CSRS DEP report for its stock universe. Atlantic Richfield Company serves as the example for calculating DEP data in this appendix.

Earnings per Share

Using historical quarterly EPS for Atlantic Richfield, a rolling annual EPS was computed (see Exhibit A–2 for details). This EPS information along with the current stock price of $44.6 was then used to compute all the necessary inputs to the DEP index.

EPS Percent Change

The five-year EPS percent change was computed by using a regression line fitted through the 20 quarterly EPS figures (Note: in order to compensate for the upward curve normally found in EPS data, the regression was computed by using base-10 log data.)

For the Atlantic Richfield Company, the fitted regression equation is as follows:

$$Ln\ EPS = .28409 + .02634\ \text{(time period)}$$

Using the equation, the computer then solved for the first and last points on the regression line. The detailed calculation of the five-year growth rate is shown below for Atlantic Richfield:

Period 1

$\text{LnEPS}_1 = .28409 + .02634\ (1)$

$\text{LnEPS}_1 = .31043$

$\text{EPS}_1 = 1.31043$

$\text{EPS}_1 = 2.043760$

Period 20

$\text{LnEPS}_{20} = .28409 + .02634\ (20)$

$\text{LnEPS}_{20} = .81089$

$\text{EPS}_{20} = 1.81089$

$\text{EPS}_{20} = 6.4697.87$

$$\frac{\text{EPS Period 20}}{\text{EPS Period 1}} = \frac{6.469787}{2.043760} = 3.165630$$

$$\text{Growth per quarter} = 19\sqrt{3.165630} = 1.062527$$

$$\text{Compounded annualized growth rate} = (1.0626)^4 = 1.2749, \text{ or } 27.5 \text{ percent}$$

The 3-month, 6-month, 9-month, and 12-month EPS percent change was computed by using the most recently published annualized EPS figure as the base. The computer then calculated percentage changes in earnings per share for the comparable earnings-per-share level during the 2nd through 5th quarters back. For example:

$$\text{3-month EPS percent change} = \frac{\$6.31 - \$6.64}{\$6.64} = -4.94 \text{ percent}$$

$$\text{12-month EPS percent change} = \frac{\$6.31 - \$5.47}{\$5.47} = +15.35 \text{ percent}$$

P/E Ratio

The P/E ratio was computed using the current stock price (shown in 2nd column from end of DEP report) and the EPS figure for the most recently published period:

$$\text{P/E ratio} = \frac{\$44.6}{6.31} = 7.07$$

Dividend Yield

Using the assumption that the most recent quarter's dividend rate is the best indication of the future dividend flow, the dividend yield was found by multiplying the current dividend by 4 and dividing it by the current stock price:

$$\frac{.55 \times 4}{\$44.6} = 4.93 \text{ percent}$$

DEP Ranking

Each of the seven data points calculated above was then ranked individually to show how Atlantic Richfield stood within the stock universe. A ranking of 1 indicated the best and a ranking of 474 indicated the lowest rank.

Each of the rankings for the Atlantic Richfield Company was then multiplied by the assigned weights to establish a DEP value, as follows:

	Rank		*Weight*		*Rank × Weight*
5-Yr. EPS	23	×	a	=	(Confidential)
3-Mo. EPS	371	×	b	=	"
6-Mo. EPS	321	×	c	=	"
9-Mo. EPS	257	×	d	=	"
12-Mo. EPS	121	×	e	=	"
P/E	153	×	f	=	"
Yield	253	×	g	=	"
		Total	1.00		169.8

The total DEP-weighted values for each firm in the universe were then ranked from best (lowest) to worst (highest) to determine the composite DEP ranking. The Atlantic Richfield DEP value of 169.8 ranked the company 71st in the stock universe on June 5, 1981.

3-Trend Charts

If the responsible investment officer was considering a stock for purchase as a replacement for a stock to be sold, the investment officer evaluated the possibilities using the 3-trend (price, earnings, dividends) security charts published by Securities Research of Boston. A sample 3-trend chart is shown in Exhibit A–3.

EXHIBIT A–1
Sample Page from CSRS DEP Report

Common Stocks (Company)	Earnings per Share					EPS % Change							Rankings									
	Cur	3 Mo	6 Mo	9 Mo	12 Mo	5 Yr	3 Mo	6 Mo	9 Mo	12 Mo	Cur P/E	Div Yld	5 Yr	3 Mo	6 Mo	9 Mo	12 Mo	P/E	Yld	Tot	Cur	Rel Cng Ytd
ACE INDUSTRIE	4.88	4.72	6.20	5.64	5.28	8	3	−21	−13	−7	10	5.7	*	*	*	*	*	*	*	*	48.1	8
AMP INC	3.54	3.65	3.62	3.61	3.54	26	−3	−2	−1	0	17	2.0									61.5	22
ABBOTT LABS	1.80	1.74	1.66	1.80	1.53	19	3	8	12	18	16	2.6									28.0	2
AETNA LIFE	5.98	6.30	6.35	6.75	6.92	24	−5	−5	−11	−14	7	5.8									40.1	17
AIR PRODUCTS	4.20	4.11	4.07	4.17	4.10	15	2	3	0	2	10	1.9									43.1	7
ALLEGHENY POW	2.92	2.59	2.24	2.13	2.09	0	12	30	37	40	5	13.0									15.1	13
ALLIED CORP	8.01	7.75	8.08	7.61	7.26	3	3	−0	5	10	7	4.1									53.7	3
ALLIED STORES	4.37	4.12	3.92	4.00	4.17	5	8	11	9	5	7	6.0									28.5	40
ALLIS-CHALMER	3.14	3.59	4.21	4.52	5.14	7	−12	−25	−30	−39	8	7.6									26.2	−28
ALCOA	5.88	8.36	6.88	7.37	7.19	32	−7	−14	−20	−18	8	5.5									32.8	13
AMERADA HESS	6.15	6.21	6.38	6.77	6.68	32	−0	−3	−9	−8	5	3.9									28.3	−33
AMER AIRLINES	−3.05	−3.15	−3.64	−3.99	−0.23	112						0.0									21.0	140
AMER BRANDS	7.10	6.99	7.14	7.18	6.87	24	1	−0	−1	3	6	7.6									42.8	13
AMER BROADCAS	4.77	5.18	5.41	5.50	5.52	24	−7	−11	−13	−14	8	5.2									30.8	18
AMER CAN	4.04	4.28	4.54	5.52	6.17	2	−5	−11	−26	−35	10	7.2									40.1	30
AMER CYANAMID	3.51	3.32	3.26	3.24	3.46	3	5	7	8	1	10	4.4									36.2	14
AMER ELEC PWR	2.28	2.74	2.69	2.73	2.60	−2	−16	−15	−13	−12	7	14.0									16.1	−2
AMER EXPRESS	5.32	5.27	5.12	4.98	4.90	17	0	3	8	9	10	3.9									51.2	31
AMER GEN CORP	6.46	6.58	6.34	6.42	6.62	19	−1	1	0	−2	7	4.6									43.5	20
AMER HOME PRO	2.93	2.84	2.75	2.66	2.59	12	3	6	10	13	12	5.5									34.3	26

AMER HOSP SUP	3.16	3.03	3.00	2.88	2.83	15	4	5	9	12	15	2.3	46.1	−2
AMF INC	2.76	2.60	2.69	2.64	2.59	9	6	2	4	7	9	4.9	25.3	19
AMAX INC	6.07	7.54	8.01	8.14	7.55	25	−19	−24	−25	−20	9	4.5	53.5	33
AMER NATRL RE	5.41	5.10	5.03	5.03	5.13	−0	6	7	7	5	7	8.7	39.3	−18
AMER STANDARD	5.54	5.68	5.43	5.24	5.18	27	−2	2	5	7	7	5.5	39.7	24
AMER TEL & TE	8.21	8.18	8.07	8.01	8.03	9	0	1	2	2	7	9.5	58.8	22
AMSTED INDUST	5.35	6.16	6.60	7.16	6.89	17	−13	−18	−25	−22	9	5.2	47.6	13
ANDERSON CLAY	3.66	3.68	3.78	4.00	3.83	10	−0	−3	−8	−4	6	5.2	23.2	16
ARCHER-DAN-MI	2.82	2.35	2.15	2.01	1.75	10	11	21	30	50	7	0.7	19.2	−20
ARIZ PUB SERV	2.65	2.75	2.90	2.87	2.99	2	−3	−8	−7	−11	6	12.8	16.5	−4
ARKANSAS LA G	2.86	2.92	3.02	3.12	2.94	12	−2	−5	−8	−3	12	4.1	34.5	−0
ARMCO INC.	4.23	4.83	4.68	4.29	4.47	12	−12	−9	−1	−5	7	5.2	31.5	−15
ARMSTRONG WOR	1.62	1.94	1.98	2.27	2.79	8	−16	−17	−28	−42	10	6.7	16.5	19
ASARCO	3.48	7.16	9.10	10.71	11.85	51	−51	−61	−67	−71	11	5.8	37.6	−11
ASHLAND OIL	3.86	4.34	5.43	6.79	6.78	16	−11	−28	−43	−43	8	7.8	30.6	−23
ASSOC DRY GOO	3.99	3.86	3.80	3.53	3.39	3	3	10	13	18	7	5.8	28.3	19
ATLANTIC CITY	3.02	2.62	2.38	2.35	2.39	1	15	26	28	28	8	11.7	16.7	9
ATLANTIC RICH	6.31	6.64	6.43	6.16	5.47	28	−4	−1	2	15	7	4.9	44.6	−28
AUTOMATIC DAT	1.40	1.34	1.28	1.24	1.24	17	4	9	12	13	22	1.5	30.2	26
ARA SERVICES	5.15	5.16	5.08	5.00	4.82	9	−0	1	3	7	6	5.9	32.8	8

*Confidential data.

EXHIBIT A–2
Atlantic Richfield Company Quarterly EPS Data

	Period	Quarters Back 4th	3rd	2nd	Most Recent Quarter	Recent 4 Quarters
Most current	20	1.75	1.57	1.60	1.39	6.31
3 mo. back	19	1.72	1.75	1.57	1.60	6.64
6 mo. back	18	1.39	1.72	1.75	1.57	6.43
9 mo. back	17	1.30	1.39	1.72	1.75	6.16
12 mo. back	16	1.06	1.30	1.39	1.72	5.47
15 mo. back	15	.99	1.06	1.30	1.39	4.74
	14	.90	.99	1.06	1.30	4.25
	13	.91	.90	.99	1.06	3.86
	12	.87	.91	.90	.99	3.67
	11	.62	.87	.91	.90	3.30
	10	.69	.62	.87	.91	3.09
	9	.80	.69	.62	.87	2.98
	8	.79	.80	.69	.62	2.90
	7	.60	.79	.80	.69	2.88
	6	.55	.60	.79	.80	2.74
	5	.79	.55	.60	.79	2.73
	4	.59	.79	.55	.60	2.53
	3	.59	.59	.79	.55	2.52
	2	.50	.59	.59	.79	2.47
	1	.43	.50	.59	.59	2.11

EXHIBIT A–3
A 3-Trend Chart

The Earnings Line

Earnings per share are shown on a 12-months-ended basis and are read from the left-hand scale. Earnings below the range of the charts, and deficits, are shown in typed notations.

The Dividend Line

Dividends are charted on an annual rate basis and are also read from the left-hand scale. Extras, year-end, or other special dividend payments appear in typed notations. Payments below the range of the charts also appear in typed notations. The "●" on the small dividend line indicates the week of the ex-dividend date and the small open circle appears on the week that the dividend payment is made.

The Ratio-Cator Line

The plottings for this line are obtained by dividing the closing price of the stock by the closing price of the Dow-Jones Industrial Average on the same day. The resulting percentage is multiplied by a factor of 7.0 to bring the line closer to the price bars and is read from the right-hand scale. The plotting indicates whether the stock has kept pace, outperformed, or lagged behind the general market as represented by the DJIA.

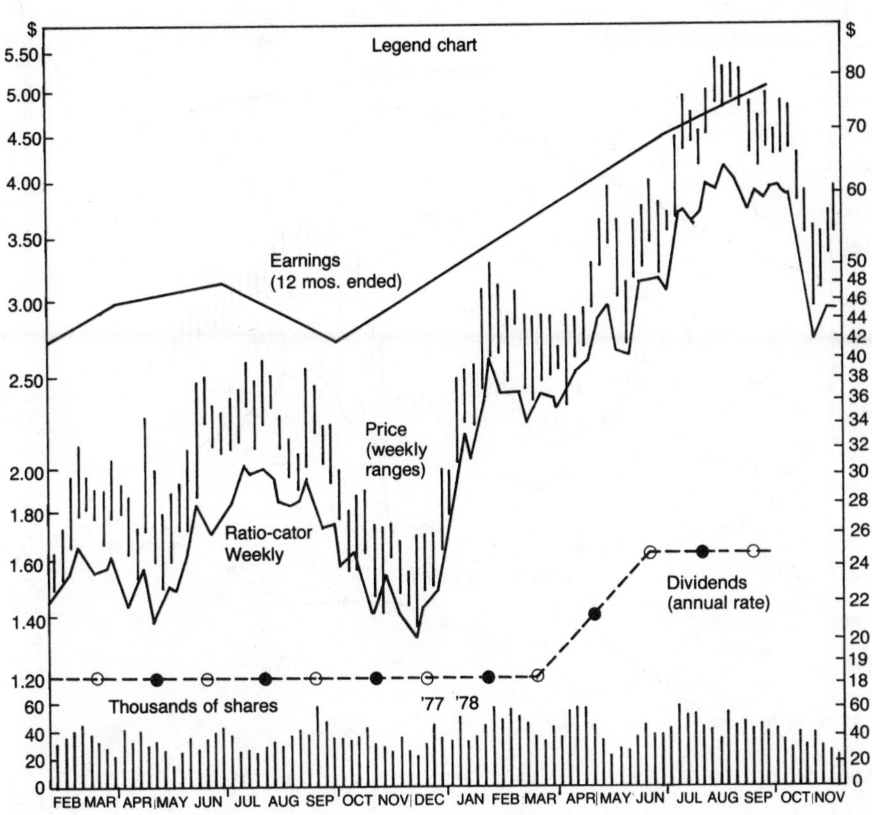

The Weekly Price-Range Bars

The vertical bars depict the range of the week's highest and lowest trading prices.

Ratio Scale

The Price Range, Earnings and Dividend data of all stocks are plotted on uniform ratio scale (semi-logarithmic) grids. In this scale, the vertical linear distance for a 100 percent move is the same any place on the chart—irrespective of whether the rise is from \$5 to \$10, \$20 to \$40, etc. The price pattern of any stock, its earnings trend, and the relationship of price to earnings, as well as the margin of earnings coverage over the dividend payment rate can thus be directly compared with any other stock in the book. Percentage advances or declines, price/earnings ratios, and percentage yields can be more closely measured with the rulers of the transparent "Market Diagram Comparator" sheet.

The Price Range scale at the right side of each chart is equal to 15 times the Earnings and Dividend scale at the left. Thus, when the price bars and the earnings positions coincide, the price is 15 times earnings. When the price pattern is above

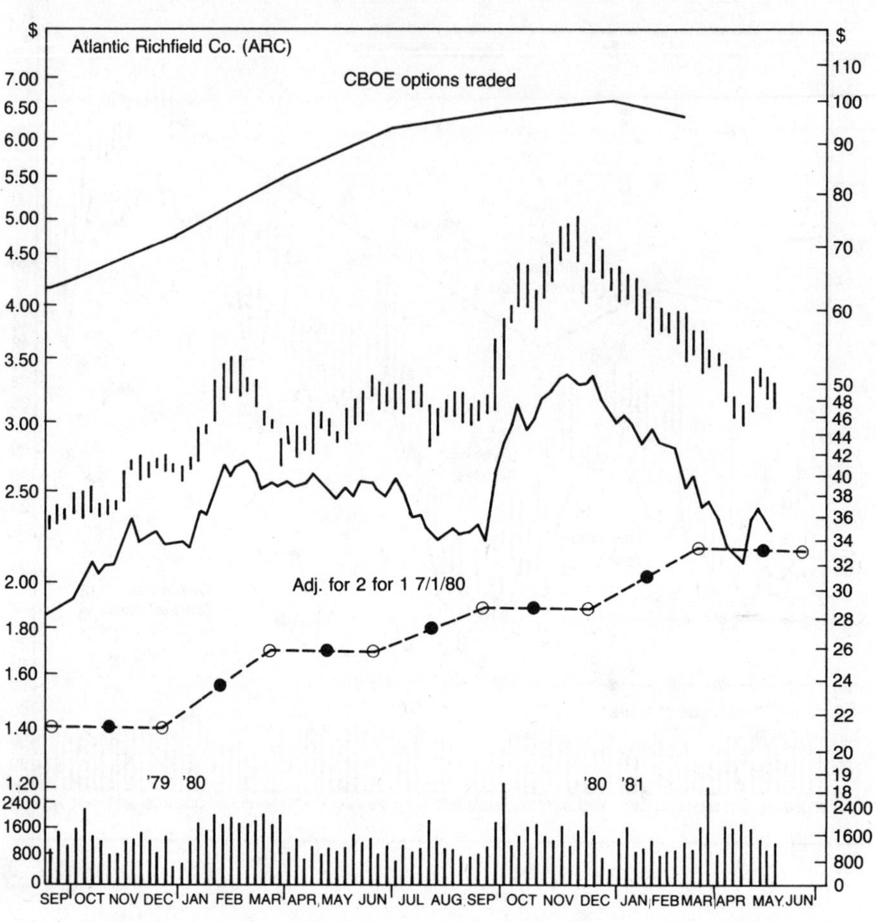

the position, the ratio of price/earnings is accordingly greater than 15 times; when below, it is less.

Volume

The number of shares traded each week is shown by the vertical bars at the bottom of each chart on an arithmetical scale in thousands (unless otherwise designated).

A Purposeful Stride Down Wall Street

In September 1983, George Straight, adviser to the Midwest State Retirement System (MSRS) trustees, visited Abel/Noser Corporation, a Wall Street financial service organization, in order to develop a means of testing a proposed in-house investment strategy for MSRS. Mr. Straight had been invited by Abel/Noser's Vice President Clement Ogden, who wanted to illustrate his firm's simulative capability by allowing Mr. Straight to test his strategy. The results, which far exceeded those of the Standard & Poor's 500 Index for the same period, were spectacular enough to cause Mr. Straight to examine the methodology more closely. Was this strategy worthy of more consideration, or was it just a fluke? What did this simulation imply about market efficiency, he wondered?

The Abel/Noser Model

Abel/Noser had developed a data base that allowed them to sort and rank firms retroactively, using various criteria. They had maintained consensus estimates of firms' earnings-per-share prospects for each of the four succeeding quarters at the outset of each quarter from 1974 forward. These estimates were updated as new consensus information arose. The ability to work retroactively from security analysts' actual consensus estimates for nearly 10 years provided Abel/Noser with an

This case was prepared by Robert F. Vandell, Charles C. Abbott Professor of Business Administration of the Colgate Darden Graduate School of Business Administration of the University of Virginia.

ability to test alternative investment strategies on a data base involving over 1,000 securities.

The data base consisted of 10 measures for each company: price/earnings ratio, market/book value ratio, yield, dividend payout percent, growth rate, earnings momentum, earnings surprise factor, rate of return on equity, relative price/earnings ratio, and relative market/book ratio. At the outset of each period, each firm was ranked by each of these ratios from best to worst. The rankings were then converted into a measure of relative attractiveness using normalized curve techniques.

Anyone wishing to test a theory could develop a composite ranking of securities by assigning whatever weights seemed appropriate to each of the factors. Thus, a portfolio composed of high-yield, low-price/earnings ratio stocks could be constructed, if that is what the testers wanted. Once the appropriate weights for the test were developed, securities could be ranked by their weighted-average value at the outset of any historic quarter.

The testers also had the ability to exclude certain types of securities, if that was their preference. For example, a tester could exclude the lowest 30 percent of stocks, using the growth criterion if he/she wanted to keep a growth orientation to the portfolio beyond the primary weighting factors. A security that was excluded would not be allowed as an investment in the portfolio irrespective of its weighted rank.

The tester also had to develop a set of sales criteria. Any security in the portfolio that failed to meet established criteria at the outset of the next quarter would be automatically sold. Use of the exclusion power thus tended to create turnover. In addition, the weighted rank could be used as a sales criterion. For example, if a security fell to, say, a weighted rank below the median it could be automatically sold.

The simulation model was sales-driven. At the outset of any new quarter, the program would first identify any securities that must be sold. These securities would then be replaced by securities from the top of the current weighted ranks from among those securities eligible. Stocks already in the portfolio were not eligible for additional purchase.

The tester could redeploy capital from the more successful investments to the less successful investments by making use of trimming criteria. For example, if a particular investment increased by more than X percent—say 100 percent—but was still eligible to be held in the portfolio, it could be trimmed back to the level of the initial investment. Similarly, a stock that fell more than, say, 25 percent from its initial investment level, yet was still considered attractive, could be "filled" back to its initial investment level. (The model results were trimmed first and filled if feasible.)

Remaining proceeds from sales were then invested in equal dollar amounts in the new securities to be purchased. All purchases were made in round lots of 100. Funds that could not be invested (usually small in dollar amount) were held as cash and no interest was paid on cash balances.

The tester could specify a number of other investment criteria: the minimum size of a security to be considered for investment (market liquidity constraint), number of securities in the portfolio (rough diversification constraint), cost of one-way transactions, management fee to be paid, and so on.

Because MSRS had certain diversification constraints that limited the amount that could be invested in any one industry, the model couldn't handle these constraints without additional programming. Thus, there was some possibility that a particular strategy might lead to a heavier-than-desired industry concentration. The way portfolios were constructed (emphasizing certain factors, excluding others) made it unlikely that a portfolio of 100 or more securities would have characteristics similar to those of the Standard & Poor's 500 Index, or even broader indices.

Using the "rank/buy/sell constraints" inputs, the Abel/Noser simulator would automatically buy and sell securities quarterly from the initiation point, January 1, 1974, through to the termination point. Performance of each stock in the portfolio in each quarter was then monitored and reported, and performance after transactions costs and fees was summarized for a quarter. Dividends received on stocks in the portfolio were put into the cash account and held for investment at the outset of the new quarter. Because the simulation took place only by quarter, interim buy/sell actions could not be initiated. More frequent and timely actions might normally be expected to improve performance somewhat beyond those of the simulation.

Background

The Midwest State Retirement System had assets of approximately $3.2 billion, of which approximately $1.9 billion were invested in equity funds, $.2 billion in real estate, and the balance in fixed-income securities. Most of the fixed-income investments were managed in-house or by the State Treasurer's Office in the case of shorter-term maturities. In contrast, only $.3 billion of the equity portfolio was managed by the financial staff of MSRS.

The trustees of MSRS, who were appointed by the Governor, reflected the major constituencies of the state and municipal employees. The Trustees had the responsibility for overall administration of the fund. A number of non-financial issues commanded a major part of their attention. The Trustees appointed an Investment (Advisory) Committee, the members of which generally had considerable experience in managing portfolios. The Investment Committee, in concert with the Trustees, reviewed portfolio performance, and made both policy and tactical recommendations to the Trustees. The in-house investment staff consisted of six professionals. The Chief Investment Officer prepared reports and made recommendations to the Investment Committee and the Trustees.

In 1977 the Chief Investment Officer of MSRS developed a highly disciplined system of investing, driven by a computer-screening process. The portfolio characteristics (number of securities, weight of securities, trimming redistribution rules) were all prespecified in a way that could be automatically implemented. Sales decision rules were also prespecified: a security could not be sold unless it failed a hold criterion and then it would be automatically sold. Securities were only purchased to replace securities sold. A small buy list was automatically generated once a month, using the screening rules. The portfolio manager had limited discretion in selecting new securities from within the buy list, but even these choices were more mechanical than judgmental. Decisions were made only on the first business day of the month and implemented the next day.

In mid-1977 the portfolio was implemented, and its subsequent performance was, on balance, better than that of any of the 10 active equity managers (most of whom outperformed the market [S&P 500] on a risk-adjusted basis) also employed by the fund. The cost of operating the in-house fund was unusually low (even relative to professionally managed index funds). Once training was completed, ongoing management of the in-house fund was accomplished with two man-days a month for a medium-level employee. No particular problems were experienced even when the fund grew in size to $300 million. However, management did not want to invest any new monies in this account for fear that the portfolio might be approaching a point where market illiquidity might become a problem.

The success of the initial in-house fund led management to consider developing a second strategy with the same, relatively mechanical features as the first, but a strategy with an orientation very different from the first fund. Management had had good experience with value-oriented managers and was impressed with the long-term (30-year) record of the managers who had followed this style. The new fund was therefore to have a strong "value tilt."

Briefly, the back test, routinely implemented in a reasonably realistic way, produced results of 28.3 percent/year over a 9½ year period, a period when the Standard & Poor's 500 Index performance was at the rate of 11.2 percent per year. Risk-adjustment did not materially change the attractiveness of this strategy, and in any case, management was interested in types of risk other than beta, standard deviation, residual error, and other conventional risk measures portrayed.

Developing the Model

The purpose of the model was relatively clear: (1) to develop an investment system with an emphasis on value, (2) one that could be implemented relatively mechanically and quickly, with low managerial inputs, and (3) in a way that would produce superior returns relative to a market index (the S&P 500 Index), (4) over an intermediate period of four years, and (5) to complete the analysis, including back tests, within a reasonable period of time (tentatively six months), (6) within time and money budgets that were modest. The matrix of trade-offs implicit in these criteria were left to be worked out subjectively as the investigation proceeded.

Collectively, these purposes required a very different approach to the research/development/testing phases of the analysis than might be suitable for academic research. There was no interest in seeking an optimum solution; rather, a pretty good solution, implemented sooner and refined with time and experience, was much preferred. The staff was more concerned with the surety of a satisfactory achievement over an intermediate horizon than with the short-term volatility of the portfolio (for reasons that will be developed later), inasmuch as experience had convinced them that short-term and intermediate results were unrelated. There was no time to test the possible predictive elements of individual factors (and alternative measurement of these factors) upon the desired outcome; the staff would instead have to build a multi-factor model and hope that all elements would contribute positively to the outcome. Only limited experimentation would be feasible. They did not have the time or the talent to build a model to back-test the investment strategy developed. They would have to live within the constraints of a model available from some supplier's shelf. Many of the factors would have to be defined in a very simplistic way. The more complicated the definition, the less likely the staff would be to find an easy means of testing the theory. And so on. Most notably, of course, they believed that they could construct a model that would routinely work even without any special knowledge or judgments external to the model (analytic skill), or without very complicated mispricing theories. They were, in short, willing to bet their experience against the empirical evidence that had been produced to support efficient market theory.

No one in the firm or in the small advisory group had direct experience with managing a value-oriented fund. There was a significant risk that the staff might overlook, through ignorance, factors that value-oriented managers have found to be important in general or in specific markets. On the other hand, the Chief Investment Officer expected that the discipline of the model would protect MSRS against the emotion of the marketplace—a factor that all too often, in his opinion, hurt managed portfolio results. And the staff did have the opportunity to talk with value-oriented managers.

Attention was focused on the price/earnings ratio, one of two popular but crude measures of relative value that are influenced by accounting treatment in ways that limit direct comparability across firms. The other, the market-to-book-value ratio, seemed less reliable as a measure of comparable value. The staff was also aware of practitioner and academic studies that suggested price/earnings ratios could be used to identify excess return prospects.

Price/earnings ratios can be defined in many ways. For the staff, today's price was the relevant input in the denominator of the ratio. They were also interested in a forward-looking measure based on estimated earnings, despite the uncertainties this might entail, rather than a backward-looking one based on recently reported earnings. A model relating to consensus expectations, as best they could be measured, seemed likely to entail less risk than one built from a single source of unknown quality. Some sources of forecasts might be better than others, but no one at MSRS knew which ones they would be, and any attempts to find the more reliable estimators seemed like a major chore and one more suitable for the refinement phases of implementation if the basic concept proved out.

Price/earnings ratios by themselves are not necessarily good discriminators. Some firms have consistently low price/earnings ratios, whereas others have consistently high price/earnings ratios. Discriminating on the basis of price/earnings alone might not provide a good indication of potential, since both groups had "moments in the sun" in the marketplace. To make money, something positive would have to happen. In the simplest terms, either earnings-per-share expectations would have to rise and/or the market would have to capitalize earnings at a higher level if this fund were to achieve superior investment results.

The staff briefly considered a relative price/earnings ratio measured as follows:

$$\text{Value index} = \frac{\text{Current stock p/e}}{\text{Current market p/e}} \div \frac{\text{Historic average stock p/e}}{\text{Historic average market p/e}}$$

The lower this value index was, the more attractive the stock would seem. Two things warned the staff away from this index. Changed corporate circumstances might make today's pricing different from the past, and appropriately so. Historic relationships had undergone some radical changes in the 1970s as a result of changed inflation expectations, but these expectations seemed in the process of changing again. Recent history, in short, might not be a good indicator of relative valuation. And so attention turned to earnings improvement prospects as the additional discriminator that might be needed.

As the staff initially envisioned it, the model depicted in Figure 1 would enable them to identify superior values. The dots in Figure 1 represented the combined assessment of relative value for individual securities. The solid line, *AB*, represented a "least-squares-fit" to the data. The staff would concentrate MSRS's bets on those securities furthest above the fitted line. Note, this model did not exclude from consideration stocks with above-average price/earnings ratios. To implement the model, the staff needed only to develop some explicit means of measuring "earnings prospects."

There were more ideas than agreement about the appropriate measure. Among those more actively considered were total return prospects, as measured by some variant of the dividend growth model; trend line earnings-per-share growth, using a combination of recent history and future estimates (in log form); and a ratio of earnings/per share several years out divided by today's market price (future earnings yield). Each of these alternatives required finding a reliable source of estimates

FIGURE 1
Framework for Identifying Values

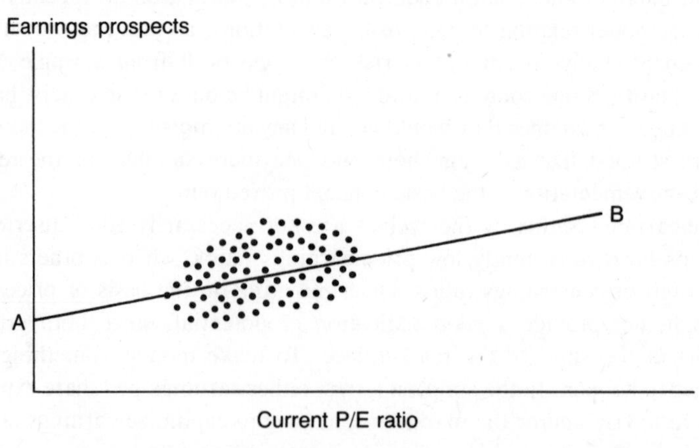

to drive the measurement process. Combined measures were also considered. The staff was intrigued with quality measures as well, such as Value Line Estimating Accuracy Index, in relation to its historic forecasting skills.

While all of these measures had some obvious appeal, little empirical or experimental evidence supported the idea that any one of them might add value to a portfolio. The staff considered the following questions: how quickly, if at all, would the market adjust to longer-term prospects? How reliable (good, or subject to serious misestimates) would these estimates be? An alternative "earnings prospect" theory, or "earnings momentum," pushed its way into attention because there was some empirical and experimental support for its use as a predictor of future market movements.

Earnings momentum is a measure of recent or prospective rates of change (growth) in earnings per share reported or estimated for a company. Earnings momentum might be measured by taking the sum of the four most recent quarters' earnings per share and dividing this number by the corresponding annual calculation of a year earlier. However measured, there is a time series of recent and prospective changes in earnings-per-share growth rates that, through some weighting process, could be used to measure and rank the earnings momentum index for every firm in the universe. Firms with a higher earnings momentum index would be preferred.

Value Line's timeliness rankings are heavily influenced by earnings momentum, and these rankings have been shown to contain forecast content. Other sources of evidence from experience suggested that earnings momentum was a useful indicator of price movements. Other than indicating a bias toward future earnings momentum, the particular weights that the staff was most attracted to could not be readily tested, and will not be reported because they remain confidential.

Because of the potential size of the portfolio, market liquidity was an important consideration (one that could only be proxied in the test) and a minimum liquidity test was established. (While the staff was aware of the favorable evidence on the "small firm" effect, and this could, in theory, be dealt with by buying two or three stocks in lieu of one large stock, the consensus was that these stocks had become overvalued in the marketplace at the time. Experimentation that might include smaller capitalization stocks was consequently postponed.)

Diversification was also a consideration. The earlier in-house portfolio restricted investment in any industry to the larger of X percent or S&P 500 industry weight plus Y percent.[1] This practice was adopted for the new portfolio. The number of items in which MSRS would invest was discussed, and at this stage was left at a maximum of 50. Initial investments and reinvestment of proceeds from sales would be equally weighted. Existing "timing" rules would be followed. Because the model was to be sales-driven, stocks failing to meet prespecified tests would be automatically sold. New purchases would only be made in the event of and in the amount of sales.

---

[1]X and Y are confidential.

With these somewhat flexible guidelines, the staff turned to the problem of back-testing analysis. After a somewhat cursory search of alternatives, the Abel/Noser Corporation appeared to have the most acceptable data structure and programs for assisting them.

The Initial Test

Abel/Noser Corporation's data file, which captured consensus earnings-per-share forecasts for the following four quarters for each quarter from the outset of 1974 forward, provided estimates that were continuously revised and kept current. The universe consisted of at least 1,000 of the more widely followed securities at any time. Mergers and the like caused some turnover in the universe. The test was run with the then-current universe. The files also contained such other data as market prices needed to calculate company statistics (such as the price/earnings ratio).

Abel/Noser tracked 10 commonly used investment statistics, such as the dividend yield and the reinvestment rate for each firm in its universe. Measures were forward-looking, in general. Thus, the price/earnings ratio was the ratio of current price to estimated earnings per share for the next 12 months. Among these measures were two of importance to this study: "earnings momentum" and "earnings surprise." At the time of the test, earnings momentum was measured simply (as a growth rate) by dividing the four most recent quarterly earnings-per-share information reported by a firm by the same measure reported one quarter earlier. (Subsequently, earnings momentum was found by Abel/Noser to have more value if measured on a forward basis.) Earnings surprise was measured by the ratio ([actual EPS − estimated EPS] ÷ estimated EPS) for the most recently reported quarter.

At the outset of each quarter, all companies could be ranked from 1 to 1,000 by each of Abel/Noser's 10 measurement criteria. Raw ranks were then converted to ranks that tended to reflect degrees of difference by using normal distribution equivalents. Thus, significantly less than 10 percent of the firms in each sample had a rank in the top 100 once the scaling transformation was completed.

Abel/Noser had also constructed a simulation model that facilitated testing certain investment strategies with respect to any one or a combination of the 10 factors available as inputs. The model required developing explicit buy-and-sell criteria in relation to these factors. The model would then automatically reformulate the portfolio each quarter on the basis of the input instructions. Over the test period, performance was monitored quarterly for the entire portfolio and stock-by-stock. At the time of this test, the test period covered nine and one half years from January 1974 to June 1983, a total of 38 quarters. The simulation period was a relatively long one (by comparison with alternatives) and covered a diverse and representative market period.

The Abel/Noser model was not a perfect one for the theories the staff wished to test, and some modifications of MSRS's half-formed theories were necessary. Similarly, the printed-out performance information met most but not all of their interests. While Abel/Noser could adapt their model to their needs, the cost in time, and to a lesser extent in money, made this alternative seem unattractive. Considering alternatives, the model seemed like a remarkably fine one for the purposes at hand.

Aside from the fact that Abel/Noser measured earnings momentum and market liquidity somewhat differently than the staff had planned to do, two major changes in the plan were necessary. The Abel/Noser model could not evaluate investment alternatives in the framework of Figure 1. Rather, it could assign weights to any of its 10 factor rankings (normalized) and determine a weighted average ranking. The composite weighted averages were then ranked from 1 to 1,000 at the outset of each investment quarter. In the initial run, Mr. Straight and two staff members who had accompanied him decided to rank the price/earnings factor (low being best) and the earnings momentum factor equally. Ranks subsequently reported were based on these composite weights (and were not scaled).

The Abel/Noser model did not permit forced diversification constraints such as the ones that had been envisioned. There were no diversification constraints in the test run. To compensate for this, the study group elected to compose portfolios of 50 stocks each (equally weighted, at the time of purchase, given proceeds from sales). Later, the group might consider whether the absence of diversification constraints hurt performance by crude means, given a somewhat larger portfolio size than would suit their ultimate purpose.

The Abel/Noser model did permit negative screens. The staff was able to eliminate low-market-capitalization stocks from consideration for investment purposes (although these stocks were ranked) at each decision point.

Abel/Noser's experience with the "earnings surprise" factor led the study group to one spur-of-the-moment change in MSRS's investment model. Even though the earnings surprise measure was often several months "old" at the time a portfolio was to be composed, Abel/Noser had found that the beneficial or adverse effects of favorable or unfavorable surprises lasted into the quarter (and beyond) following the initial news (and despite any forecast revisions made). For this reason, the study group elected to exclude from investment consideration any security that ranked in the bottom 20 percent (most adverse) of the earnings surprise ranking factor.

Even though the MSRS model (and the Abel/Noser model) were to be driven by sales, the group had not developed explicit sales criteria in advance of the first test. Again, an *ad hoc* adjustment was made to facilitate the initial run. A stock was to be sold if either (1) it no longer ranked in the top 25 percent of the universe, or (2) its most recent earnings surprise factor ranked in the bottom 20 percent of the universe. The study group was warned that these rules in combination and the first rule in particular might cause a high turnover rate for MSRS's portfolio. It did.

The staff also elected to "trim back" the portfolio's "big winners." The rules for doing so did not prove to be a material factor in the performance of the portfolio during the test run.

When stocks were sold, new stocks were added to the portfolio from the top of the ranking list of those eligible for consideration and not already in the portfolio.

The number of stocks in the portfolio was held constant at 50. Available dollars were distributed equally among new purchases. A 1 percent transaction charge was automatically levied against each purchase and sale. The size of the transaction charge was determined by the staff, and accorded with MSRS's experience (1.1 percent one way).

Dividends and other cash distributions were not reinvested at the time of their receipt. Rather, they were held uninvested until the outset of the next quarter, where they formed a part of the pool of dollars available for investment. The portfolio was kept as fully invested as round lot trading would permit. The model was unusually efficient in keeping the portfolio cash balances to a minimum. The initial portfolio size was $50 million (although for reporting purposes here it is represented as $50 thousand).

Once the buy/sell and other decisions were put in, the model automatically executed the decisions in accordance with the revised ranking/screening information available at the outset of each quarter. No additional judgments influenced the results.

Performance results by quarters are shown in Table 2. (A sample of details for a sample period are available as shown in Exhibit 1. The total portfolio's return performance (including cash receipts) is stated after transaction costs. Individual stock performance is shown on an appreciation-only basis.) The total return for the Standard & Poor's 500 Index is shown for each quarter in Table 2. (Table 1 explains the codes associated with buying and selling securities.)

The results were almost too good to be believed. The test portfolio provided a compound rate of return of 28.25 percent per year over the 9½ year test period. In the same time span, the total rate of return for the Standard & Poor's 500 Index was 11.22 percent. The investment of $1 in the S&P 500 would have created $2.75 in wealth at the end of the simulation period; Mr. Straight's strategy, in contrast, developed wealth of $10.62 over the same period. These results were all the more surprising given the *ad hoc* action criteria, the high portfolio turnover, and the relatively large numbers of securities in the portfolio. It did not take a statistical analysis to see the promise of the model. In fact, the initial sentiment of the Investment Committee was to implement the strategy exactly in accord with the simulation (no discretion, quarterly trading only, etc.) and to do so right away.

TABLE 1
Code to Portfolio Actions

BO	=	Buy.
HO	=	Hold.
H+	=	Hold and trim up.
H−	=	Hold and trim down.
S1	=	Sell because value rank fell below 250.
S2	=	Sell because earnings surprise report fell in bottom 20 percent.
S3	=	Sell for both reasons.
S0	=	Sell because firm no longer meets minimum capitalization requirements.

A Preliminary Evaluation of the Simulation Results

Table 2 summarizes by quarter the test model's total-return performance relative to the Standard & Poor's 500 Index. The model outperformed the index in 28 of the 38 quarters. If the chances of beating the market were truly 50/50 for each quarter, then the odds that the model portfolio contained a skill component were more than 100 to 1. Table 2 also reports the portfolio standard deviations. The Abel/Noser portfolio was more risky by this performance criterion.

TABLE 2
Abel/Noser Simulation versus Standard & Poor's 500 Index
(*total-rate-of-return quarterly performance*)

Year	*Quarter*	*Abel/Noser Simulation*	*S&P 500 Index*	*Difference*
1974	1	9.0	−2.8	11.8
	2	−13.8	−7.5	−6.3
	3	−14.9	−25.2	10.3
	4	11.3	9.4	1.9
1975	5	44.9	22.9	22.0
	6	20.2	15.3	4.9
	7	−10.3	−11.0	0.7
	8	7.2	8.6	−1.4
1976	9	30.2	15.1	15.1
	10	3.6	2.5	1.1
	11	0.0	1.8	−1.8
	12	10.0	3.2	6.8
1977	13	−2.7	−7.4	4.7
	14	9.8	3.3	6.5
	15	−5.5	−2.9	−2.6
	16	3.1	−0.1	3.2
1978	17	5.2	−4.9	10.1
	18	17.4	8.5	8.9
	19	15.1	8.7	6.4
	20	−14.4	−4.9	−9.5
1979	21	13.2	7.1	6.1
	22	4.1	2.8	1.3
	23	13.6	7.7	5.9
	24	5.6	0.1	5.5
1980	25	−7.8	−4.1	−3.7
	26	22.5	13.5	9.0
	27	20.6	11.3	9.3
	28	6.3	9.5	−3.2
1981	29	8.2	1.3	6.9
	30	9.0	−2.3	11.3
	31	−12.1	−10.3	−1.8
	32	8.9	7.0	1.9
1982	33	−5.1	−7.3	−2.2
	34	−2.4	−0.5	−1.9
	35	7.7	11.5	−3.8
	36	20.6	18.3	2.3
1983	37	15.8	10.0	5.8
	38	17.9	11.0	6.9
Average		7.16	3.14	4.02
Standard deviation		12.66	9.35	6.16

FIGURE 2
Portfolio Performance Characteristic Line versus S&P 500 Index

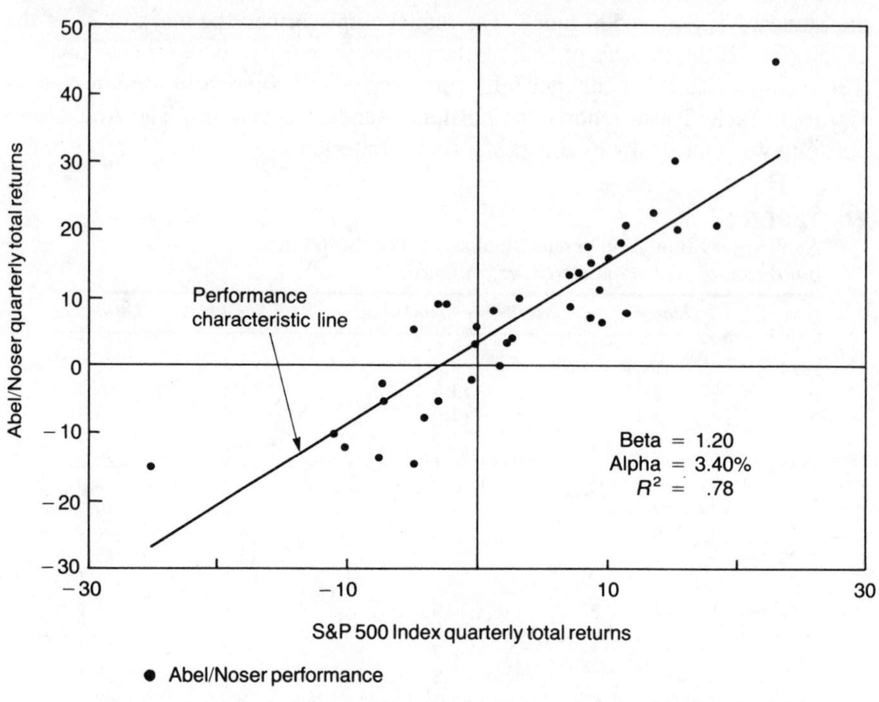

Figure 2 shows the performance characteristic line of the portfolio relative to the Standard & Poor's 500 Index (as one representation of the market portfolio). The portfolio beta of 1.20 indicates a moderately more risky portfolio.[2] The alpha of 3.40 percent per quarter is statistically significant at the .01 level (*t* test = 3.3). Given the high level of excess returns, the R^2 of .78 proved surprisingly high.

Table 3 contains a one-year moving average (geometric, annualized) total return for these performance data. There were only two subperiods of one year when performance risks did not cancel out. The consistency of good performance within a relatively short span of time added to the model's appeal.

Figure 3 depicts the time series of residual errors associated with the performance characteristic line, along with a four-quarter smoothing factor. There is no significant evidence that the worth of the model has depreciated over time, despite broader awareness of the potential market inefficiencies that the model was designed to capture.

[2]When an equal-weighted S&P 500 Index is regressed against a value weighted S&P 500 Index, beta tends to be about 1.17. Most of the high beta is thus owing to composing an equally weighted portfolio.

TABLE 3
Abel/Noser Simulation versus Standard & Poor's 500 Index
(moving one-year average (geometric) of total returns)

End of Period	*Abel/Noser Simulation*	*S&P 500 Index*	*Difference*
4	−11.01%	−26.43%	15.42%
5	18.30	−6.97	25.28
6	64.97	15.96	49.01
7	73.88	37.97	35.91
8	67.48	36.96	30.52
9	50.49	28.27	22.22
10	29.71	14.03	15.68
11	44.60	30.43	14.17
12	48.38	23.94	24.43
13	10.88	−0.28	11.17
14	17.52	0.49	17.03
15	11.06	−4.15	15.20
16	4.09	−7.21	11.30
17	12.54	−4.71	17.25
18	20.33	0.09	20.24
19	46.56	12.05	34.51
20	21.68	6.66	15.02
21	30.94	20.12	10.81
22	16.10	13.81	2.29
23	14.59	12.77	1.82
24	41.36	18.69	22.67
25	15.14	6.28	8.86
26	35.49	17.34	18.15
27	43.84	21.27	22.57
28	44.79	32.66	12.14
29	69.92	40.12	29.80
30	51.19	20.62	30.58
31	10.20	−2.79	12.99
32	12.89	−5.01	17.90
33	−0.98	−13.07	12.09
34	−11.34	−11.47	0.13
35	8.63	10.04	−1.41
36	20.30	21.66	−1.36
37	46.80	44.37	2.43
38	77.33	61.06	16.28
Average	30.25	13.30	16.94
Standard deviation	23.50	18.51	11.11

Figure 4 shows the cumulative wealth index for the model relative to the S&P 500 Index. The benefits of compounding excess returns even for a short period (in the life of a pension fund) can be spectacular. When (see Figure 5) a trend line was fit to these data (in log-normal wealth format), the model and the Standard & Poor's Index achieved compound annualized returns of 27.36 percent and 11.14 percent, respectively; and standard errors (quarterly, log) of .127 and .114, respectively.

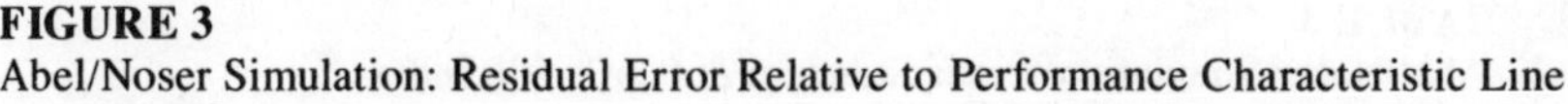

FIGURE 3
Abel/Noser Simulation: Residual Error Relative to Performance Characteristic Line

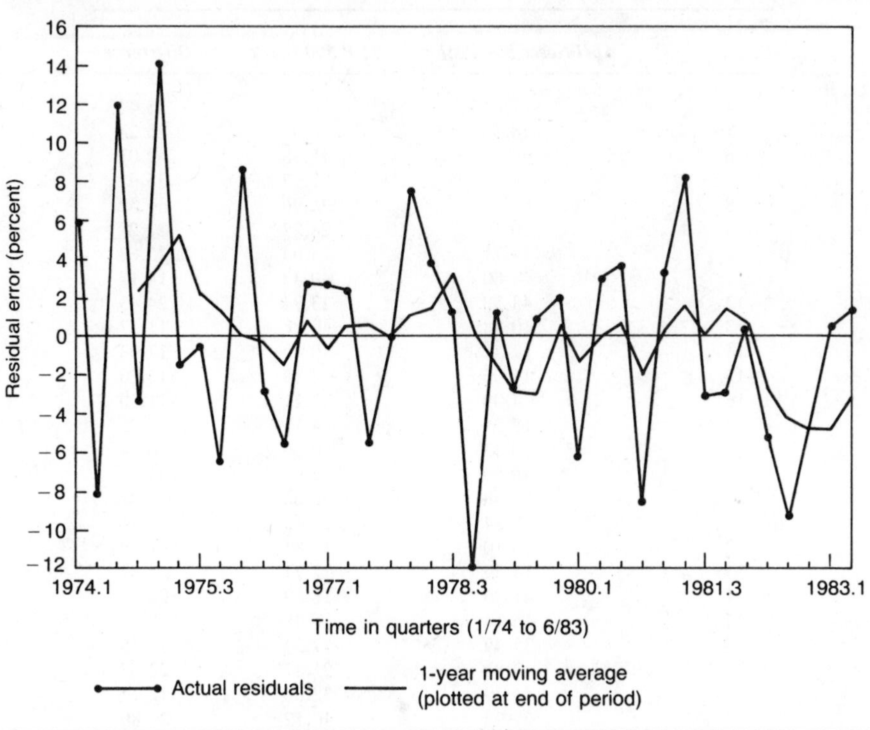

Figure 6 displays the cumulative variability of the model's results around its trend line (measured as the log-normal ratio of actual to trend) juxtaposed against that of the S&P 500. Cumulative variability was larger for the model relative to the S&P 500 than one might have inferred by looking at their respective betas. The steeper slope of the model's trend line, of course, somewhat reduces the significance of its added cumulative volatility. The coefficients of dispersion (standard error divided by the quarterly return in log-normal format) were 2.09 and 4.31. Because relative wealth uncertainties change (assuming independence over time) with the $\sqrt{n}/n$, where n is the number of quarters considered for the coefficient of dispersion, risk-averse investors should quickly prefer the more aggressive portfolio (e.g., mean difference in expected wealth for the more aggressive should be statistically superior at the .05 level by the sample law of differences within eight quarters because wealth grows faster than its uncertainty).

Performance in more protracted up *and* down markets was also attractive for the Abel/Noser portfolio. These results are recorded in Table 4.

FIGURE 4
Cumulative Value of $1 Invested for the Model Relative to S&P 500 Index

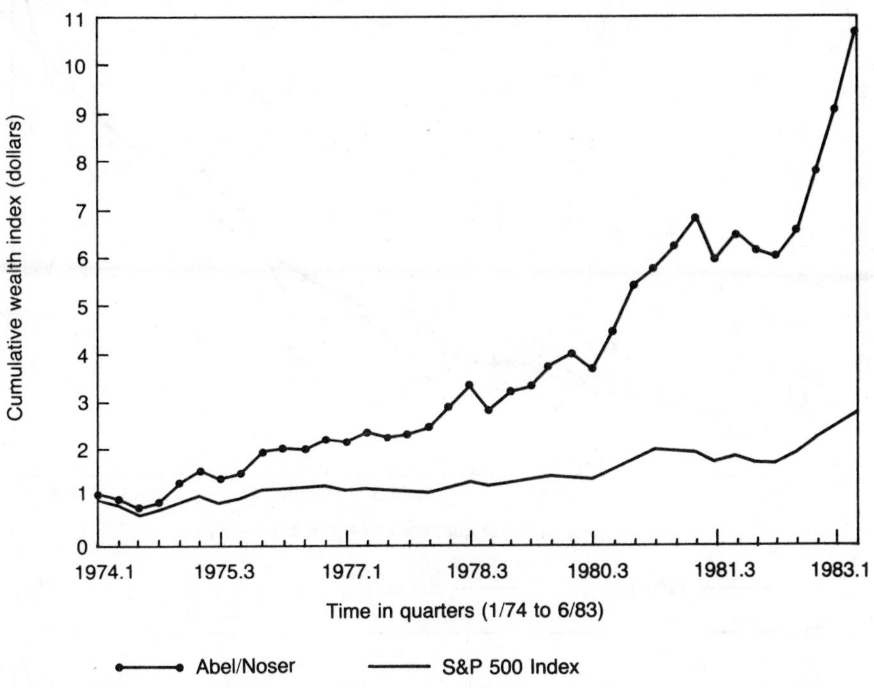

Active management, as the results of this test model demonstrate, should have a further positive benefit. It should increase the skewing of the return distribution in a very favorable way. Table 5 shows the quarterly total-return data for the model and the S&P, ranked from best to worst, along with the mean and standard deviation of the distribution. The higher dispersion of the model's output seems more attributable to "good" risks than to "bad" ones.

Downside semivariance relative to an actuarial goal of 1.5 percent per quarter (approximate) was somewhat lower for the model (34.06 percent versus the S&P's 37.37 percent). Even in the short run, an investor would have to be extraordinarily risk-averse to prefer the performance of the S&P 500.

Because an actuary looks through short-term volatility, focusing instead on the average relationships between actual portfolios and required portfolio values over five years, there is no cost penalty associated with temporary adversity. Risk focus of a pension plan should be more intermediate term. Table 6 shows a four-year compound moving average (annualized) for the model and the S&P. Over a four-year period, the model's performance was always superior. Moreover, the degree

FIGURE 5
Abel/Noser Simulation: Actual versus Trend (*cumulative value of $1 invested*)

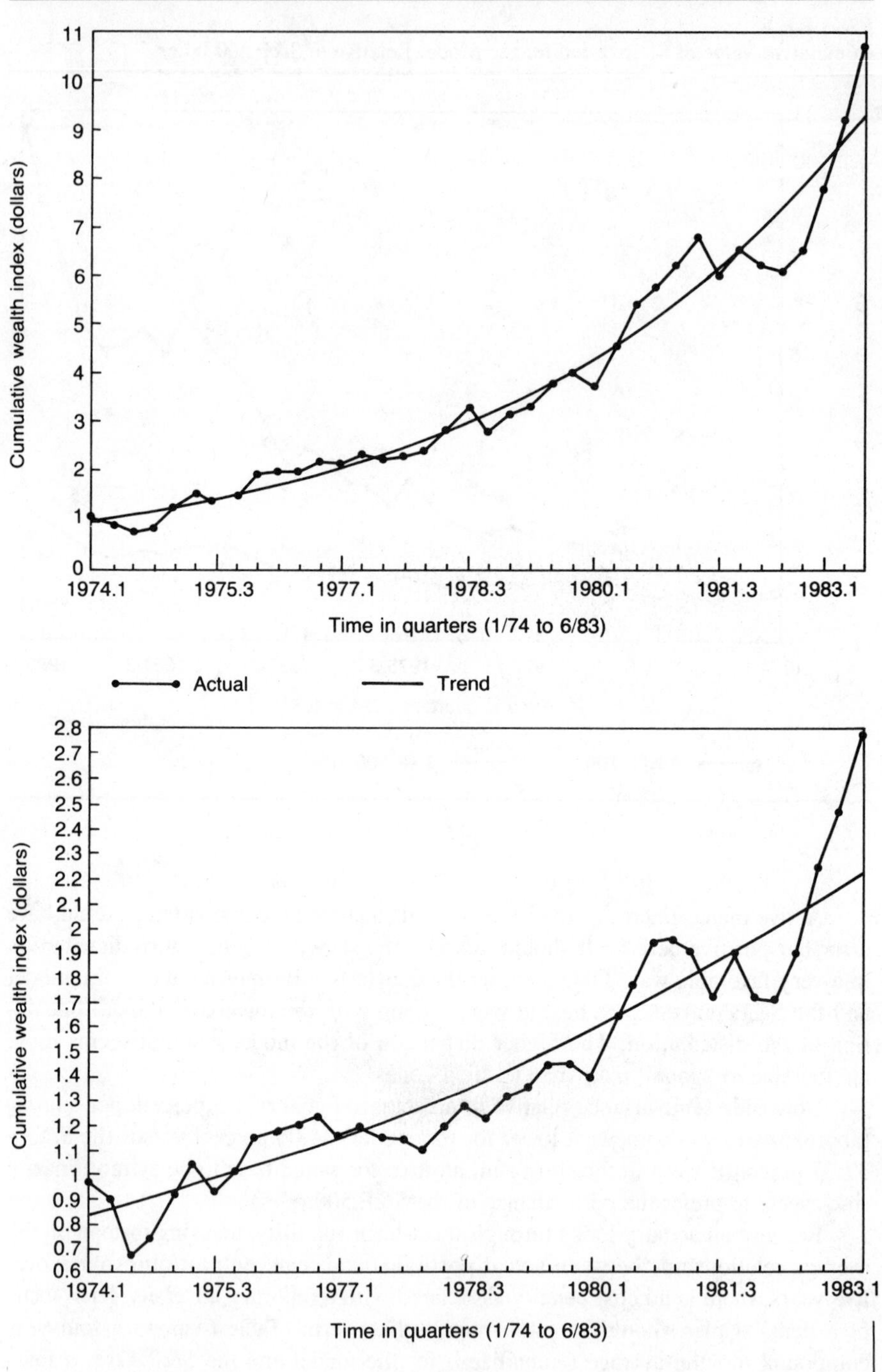

FIGURE 6
Abel/Noser Simulation: Cumulative Volatility

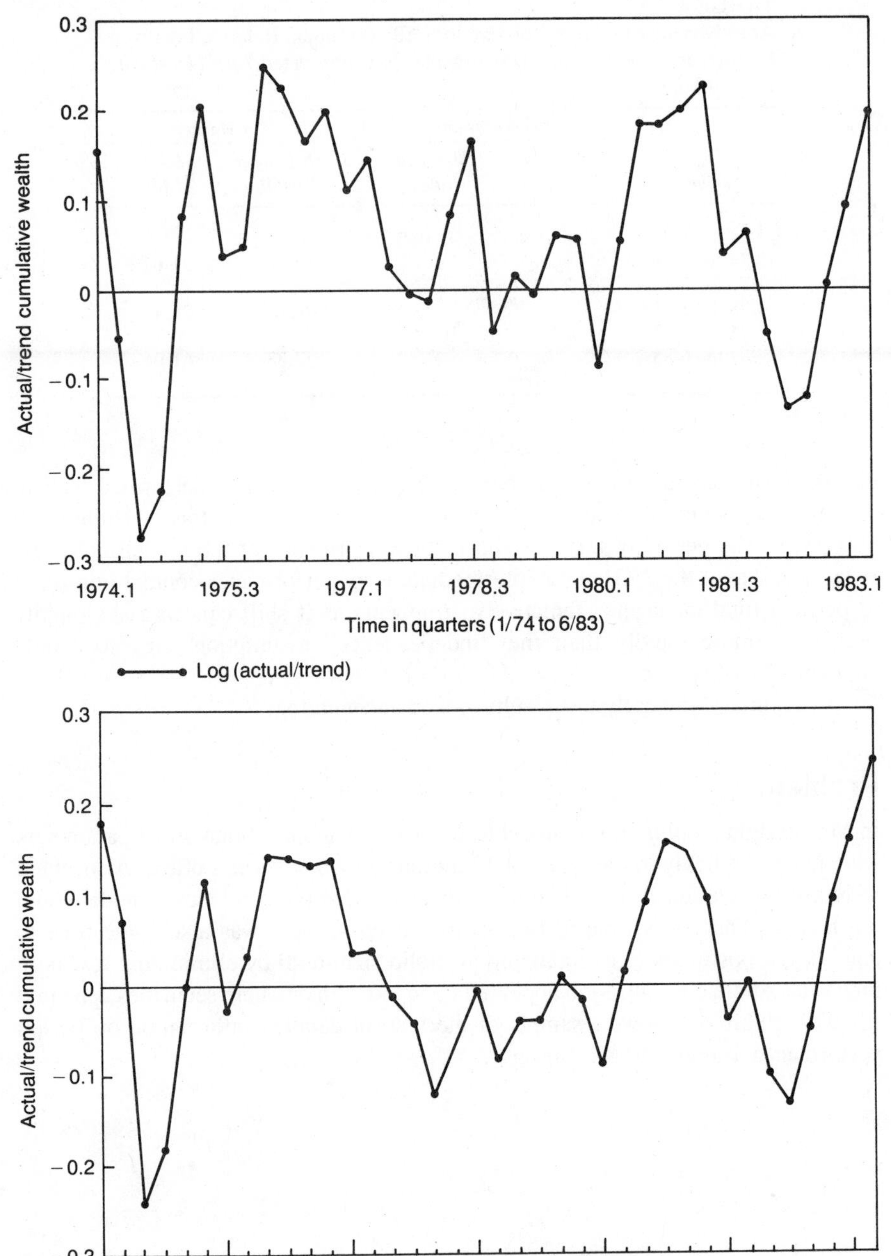

TABLE 4
Abel/Noser Simulation Relative to S&P 500 Index: Relative Portfolio Performance in Up and Down Markets (*annualized rate of return: 1/74 to 6/83*)

	Down Markets		*Up Markets*	
Period	***Abel/Noser Portfolio***	***S&P 500 Index***	***Abel/Noser Portfolio***	***S&P 500 Index***
1/74 to 9/74	−25.79%	−41.08%		
10/74 to 12/76			57.16%	31.67%
1/77 to 3/78	7.53	− 9.52		
4/78 to 3/81			36.82	21.40
4/81 to 6/82	− 2.70	−10.96		
7/82 to 6/83			77.33	61.06

of superiority appears to have stabilized. The model has also performed well in relation to an actuarial requirement of 6 percent per year, in contrast with the S&P 500. While the period of test was short, the performance of the model looks less risky than that of the S&P in the intermediate-term performance context important to pension fund managers. Tentatively, it appears as if skill cancels risks rapidly over time, more rapidly than the "independence" assumption suggests would happen.

In summary, the early test results looked encouraging.

Problem

In Mr. Straight's opinion, the model tested was too *ad hoc*. Many input parameters were reached quickly in the space of 15 minutes in Abel/Noser's office. Also, there were several relevant factors, like diversification, that the Abel/Noser model could not handle. There was time to run additional tests; there was also some time to hand-adjust portfolios (e.g., reducing portfolio size to 40 by eliminating stocks in industries where concentration appeared to be too high or where securities appeared illiquid). Exhibit 1 shows a sample of the kind of detailed information on period performance available to Mr. Straight.

TABLE 5
Abel/Noser Simulation Relative to S&P 500 Index:
Rank-Order Quarterly Performance
(*38 quarters: 1/74 to 6/83*)

	Abel/Noser Simulation	*S&P 500 Index*	*Difference*
	44.9%	22.9%	22.0%
	30.2	18.3	11.9
	22.5	15.3	7.2
	20.6	15.1	5.5
	20.6	13.5	7.1
	20.2	11.5	8.7
	17.9	11.3	6.6
	17.4	11.0	6.4
	15.8	10.0	5.8
	15.1	9.5	5.6
	13.6	9.4	4.2
	13.2	8.7	4.5
	11.3	8.6	2.7
	10.0	8.5	1.5
	9.8	7.7	2.1
	9.0	7.1	1.9
	9.0	7.0	2.0
	8.9	3.3	5.6
	8.2	3.2	5.0
	7.7	2.8	4.9
	7.2	2.5	4.7
	6.3	1.8	4.5
	5.6	1.3	4.3
	5.2	0.1	5.1
	4.1	−0.1	4.2
	3.6	−0.5	4.1
	3.1	−2.3	5.4
	0.0	−2.8	2.8
	−2.4	−2.9	0.5
	−2.7	−4.1	1.4
	−5.1	−4.9	−0.2
	−5.5	−4.9	−0.6
	−7.8	−7.3	−0.5
	−10.3	−7.4	−2.9
	−12.1	−7.5	−4.6
	−13.8	−10.3	−3.5
	−14.4	−11.0	−3.4
	−14.9	−25.2	10.3
Average	7.6	3.14	4.02
Standard deviation	12.66	9.35	4.67

TABLE 6
Abel/Noser Simulation Relative to S&P 500 Index:
(*four-year moving averages—geometric*)

End of Period	*Abel/Noser Simulation*	*S&P 500 Index*	*Difference*
16	23.17%	3.76%	19.42%
17	22.09	3.19	18.90
18	31.89	7.39	24.50
19	42.23	17.91	24.32
20	33.20	13.85	19.35
21	25.22	10.00	15.22
22	20.80	6.89	13.91
23	28.15	12.11	16.04
24	27.67	9.85	17.82
25	17.12	4.95	12.17
26	22.13	7.66	14.47
27	27.98	10.09	17.89
28	26.89	11.73	15.16
29	30.30	14.27	16.04
30	30.07	12.69	17.38
31	27.73	10.47	17.26
32	29.49	12.39	17.11
33	26.20	11.67	14.53
34	20.51	9.28	11.23
35	18.52	9.98	8.54
36	29.12	16.14	12.98
37	29.86	16.92	12.94
38	33.96	19.19	14.78
Average	27.14	10.97	16.17
Standard deviation	5.52	4.17	3.65

EXHIBIT 1

Able/Noser Simulation: Decisions and Results (*second quarter 1974*)

Name	Rank	Action Code	Cost/ Share ($)	Shares	Total Cost Including Transaction ($)	Opening Market Value ($)	% of Portfolio Value	Closing Market Value ($)	Closing Market/ Share ($)	Period Gain (%)	Cumulative Gain (%)	Closing Rank	Action Code
ASARCO	2	HO	23.09	43.30	1000.17	1087.70	2.00	860.37	19.87	−20.90	−13.98	47	S2
INSPIRATION RES	5	HO	28.53	35.00	998.64	883.75	1.63	678.30	19.38	−23.25	−32.08	119	S2
WEST POINT PEPPER	7	HO	13.63	81.80	1115.34	1104.30	2.03	1033.13	12.63	−6.44	−7.37	591	S1
McINTYRE MINES LTD	9	BO	54.54	20.40	1112.62	1101.60	2.03	635.05	31.13	−42.35	−42.92	126	S2
CASTLE & COOKE	17	HO	9.20	108.70	1000.16	894.60	1.65	745.68	6.86	−16.65	−25.44	652	S3
CENTRAL MAINE PWR	18	BO	21.08	52.90	1115.60	1104.55	2.04	634.80	12.00	−42.53	−43.10	102	HO
ESMARK INC	21	BO	15.51	71.90	1115.43	1104.38	2.04	985.03	13.70	−10.81	−11.69	120	HO
COLT IND	22	HO	5.22	191.50	999.96	1196.88	2.21	1443.91	7.54	20.64	44.40	5	HO
AMSTAR CORP	25	HO	11.74	85.10	999.61	1266.29	2.33	1127.58	13.25	−10.95	12.80	40	HO
KROGER CO	26	HO	9.47	105.60	1000.43	1214.40	2.24	996.86	9.44	−17.91	−0.36	101	HO
ZAPATA CORP	27	BO	5.39	206.70	1114.82	1103.78	2.03	721.38	3.49	−34.64	−35.29	60	HO
PHELPS DODGE	28	BO	40.40	27.60	1115.04	1104.00	2.03	969.31	35.12	−12.20	−13.07	72	HO
KAISER ALUMINUM	30	BO	11.24	99.20	1115.14	1104.10	2.03	831.30	8.38	−24.71	−25.45	659	S1
SCM CORP	32	BO	11.36	98.10	1114.66	1103.63	2.03	1018.28	10.38	−7.73	−8.65	41	HO
NBD BANCORP INC	36	HO	19.19	52.10	999.80	1074.82	1.98	901.85	17.31	−16.09	−9.80	150	HO
REYNOLDS METALS CO	38	HO	19.31	51.80	1000.32	1191.40	2.20	919.45	17.75	−22.83	−8.08	7	HO
AMERICAN MOTORS	39	BO	9.22	120.90	1114.86	1103.82	2.03	695.18	5.75	−37.02	−37.64	169	S2
ALCAN ALUMINUM LTD	42	BO	16.79	66.40	1115.27	1104.23	2.03	954.83	14.38	−13.53	−14.39	56	HO
H&R BLOCK	43	BO	12.37	90.10	1114.76	1103.73	2.03	810.90	9.00	−26.53	−27.26	473	S1
CENTRAL SOYA CO	44	BO	21.08	52.90	1115.60	1104.55	2.04	740.60	14.00	−32.95	−33.61	454	S3
AMAX INC	45	BO	29.35	38.00	1115.32	1104.28	2.03	1011.94	26.63	−8.36	−9.27	145	HO
HARSCO CORP	46	BO	6.12	182.10	1114.56	1103.53	2.03	996.09	5.47	−9.74	−10.63	284	S3
GULF OIL CORP	48	HO	23.85	41.90	999.57	958.25	1.77	832.55	19.87	−13.12	−16.71	122	HO
AVNET INC	49	HO	3.50	285.30	999.89	1069.88	1.97	892.99	3.13	−16.53	−10.69	79	HO
READING AND BATES	50	BO	7.88	141.30	1114.59	1103.55	2.03	878.89	6.22	−20.36	−21.15	58	HO
BELCO PETRO	51	BO	4.73	235.30	1114.59	1103.56	2.03	877.67	3.73	−20.47	−21.26	57	HO
KAISER STEEL	52	HO	16.03	62.40	1000.82	1115.71	2.06	1100.11	17.63	−1.40	9.92	13	HO

EXHIBIT 1 *(concluded)*

Name	Rank	Action Code	Cost/ Share ($)	Shares	Total Cost Including Transaction ($)	Opening Market Value ($)	% of Portfolio Value	Closing Market Value ($)	Closing Market/ Share ($)	Period Gain (%)	Cumulative Gain (%)	Closing Rank	Action Code
HARRIS BANCORP INC	53	BO	29.92	37.20	1113.26	1102.24	2.03	920.70	24.75	−16.47	−17.30	166	S2
TIDEWATER INC	55	BO	12.62	88.30	1114.79	1103.75	2.03	1030.46	11.67	−6.64	−7.56	243	HO
UNITED MERCHANTS	56	HO	17.04	58.70	1000.76	1174.00	2.16	1049.56	17.88	−10.60	4.88	110	HO
HECLA MINING	58	HO	12.25	81.60	999.71	1509.60	2.78	1122.00	13.75	−25.68	12.23	67	S2
ANDERSON CLAYTON	61	HO	9.90	100.90	999.73	1299.59	2.39	1148.24	11.38	−11.65	14.86	10	HO
COMINCO LTD	62	BO	31.94	34.90	1114.93	1103.89	2.03	999.19	28.63	−9.48	−10.38	27	HO
GENERAL INSTRUMENT	64	HO	4.20	238.00	999.98	1054.34	1.94	830.62	3.49	−21.22	−16.94	226	HO
WANG LABS 'B'	67	HO	1.14	876.20	1000.01	858.68	1.58	674.67	0.77	−21.43	−32.53	76	HO
MEAD CORP	68	HO	12.03	83.10	1000.46	969.78	1.79	865.90	10.42	−10.71	−13.45	50	HO
NEWPORT MINING	70	HO	32.32	30.90	998.69	919.28	1.69	814.83	26.37	−11.36	−18.41	52	HO
OCCIDENTAL PETRO	80	HO	8.33	120.00	999.90	1140.00	2.10	1185.60	9.88	4.00	18.57	9	HO
FREEPORT McMORAN	82	HO	6.37	156.90	999.94	947.68	1.75	809.60	5.16	−14.57	−19.03	12	HO
HAMMERMILL PAPER	85	HO	18.81	53.10	999.15	883.05	1.63	929.25	17.50	5.23	−7.00	8	HO
KIDDE INC	94	HO	7.63	131.00	1000.26	1113.50	2.05	909.14	6.94	−18.35	−9.11	107	HO
WITCO CHEMICAL CO	107	HO	7.41	134.90	1000.07	1110.23	2.05	1469.06	10.89	32.32	46.90	309	S1
NORTHWEST IND	112	HO	8.89	112.40	1000.15	1159.97	2.14	1061.06	9.44	−8.53	6.09	212	HO
REPUBLIC STEEL	118	HO	24.24	41.30	1001.11	1084.13	2.00	923.88	22.37	−14.78	−7.71	68	HO
FOREMOST-McKESSON	142	HO	11.74	85.10	999.61	1117.36	2.06	978.65	11.50	−12.41	−2.10	222	HO
ETHYL CORP	196	HO	6.09	164.20	1000.03	1016.40	1.87	1057.45	6.44	4.04	5.74	73	HO
CINCINNATI MIL	199	HO	4.89	204.20	1000.27	1153.73	2.13	820.88	4.02	−28.85	−17.93	313	S1
W.R.GRACE & CO	210	HO	24.62	40.60	999.73	1080.77	1.99	903.35	22.25	−16.42	−9.64	18	HO
TRAVELERS CORP	226	HO	16.91	59.10	999.82	882.95	1.63	687.33	11.63	−22.15	−31.25	285	S1
COMMUNICATIONS SAT	250	HO	19.44	51.40	999.34	867.63	1.60	771.00	15.00	−11.14	−22.85	242	HO
Total					52179.27	54267.82		46256.46					

Portfolio gain (%)	−13.80	Cash closing	539.09
S&P gain (%)	−7.50	Cash opening	0.94
Transactions costs ($)	418.08	Dividend income	538.15
Transactions costs as a percent of portfolio	0.77		

Kurtz Capital Management Co.

On May 5, 1985, Ray Kurtz, President of Kurtz Capital Management (KCM) received a phone call from an analyst reporting an "interesting" development in one of the sectors of the economy. The technology sector, stated the analyst, had begun to show signs of an impending slide. Mr. Kurtz actually had noticed this occurrence the previous day as he reviewed the latest summary analysis of technical indicators for the technology sector. The indicators for the sector as a whole had dropped two positions, from a neutral-positive to a neutral ranking. Almost half of the companies in the sector showed individual technical rankings below their fundamental rankings. Since KCM structured its portfolios with investments in several sectors in order to diversify against non-systematic risk, and technology was one of the sectors in which the company maintained positions, Mr. Kurtz had to decide what action to take, if any, in light of the change in indicators.

Most of the fundamental indicators of the individual stocks in the sector were still on the positive side of the neutral ranking, and Mr. Kurtz determined that the extent of the technical indicator decline did not warrant a "buy on bad news" strategy; his options, he believed, were to hold his positions or sell portions of them. If he believed the technical indicators and decided to sell, was now the proper time to sell? Or should he hold out a bit longer and wait for fundamental indicators to weaken as confirming evidence for a sell decision? If he did sell, how much of the portfolio holding should he trim back? If he decided to hold, what level of decline of the technical indicators would imply a definite sell signal?

This material was prepared by William P. Deuchler under the supervision of Robert F. Vandell of the Colgate Darden Graduate School of Business Administration of the University of Virginia.

Kurtz Capital Management

KCM, a relatively small investment management firm located close to New York City in a pleasant New Jersey suburb, had developed a good record by specializing in investing in small to mid-size, growth-oriented companies. Exhibit 1 illustrates the cumulative wealth index for KCM from 1977 to 1984. The wealth index indicates that if $1.00 was invested with KCM in 1977, that dollar would have grown to $5.75 by 1984. One-dollar investments over the same period in the Standard & Poor's 500 Index and the NASDAQ Industrial Index would have yielded $2.48 and $2.68, respectively.

The compound annual growth rates for this period—28.39 percent for KCM, 13.86 percent for the S&P 500, and 15.12 percent for NASDAQ Industrials—indicate KCM's superior performance. Kurtz Capital's performance is also indicated by a comparison of portfolio characteristic lines against the S&P 500 and the NASDAQ Industrial Index, as shown in Exhibits 2 and 3; the regression data are shown in Table 1.

The data in Table 1 indicate that Kurtz Capital had very good statistical performance against both the S&P 500 and the NASDAQ Industrial Index. For the NASDAQ data, an alpha of 3.4 coupled with a beta of 0.86 indicates a risk-adjusted excess return of 3.4 percent per quarter over the Index return. A beta of less than one implies that the portfolio will move with less volatility than the Index. The *t*-statistic of 14 implies a high degree of statistical significance, and the Durbin-Watson of 2.1 indicates a low probability of distortion caused by underlying trends. The R-squared statistic indicates the amount of movement in KCM portfolio returns that can be explained by the movement of the Index returns. In this case it is 89 percent, rather high, but to be expected, as the type of stocks that made up the KCM portfolio were similar in nature to the stock types found in the NASDAQ Industrial Index.

KCM based its marketing strategy on a "niche play." The firm had positioned itself as a complementary manager, designed to be used as a player on an investment team rather than as the whole team itself. The descriptive literature on KCM described the company's investment philosophy:

> The firm will focus predominantly on investments in small to mid-size seasoned companies with consistent above-average records of profitability and growth over the course of 1–3 business cycles. Particular emphasis will be placed on those

TABLE 1
Regression Data for Portfolio Characteristic Lines against S&P 500 and NASDAQ Industrial Indices

	Beta	*Alpha per Quarter*	*t-Statistics*	R^2	*Durbin-Watson*
S&P 500	1.387	2.278%	9.049	.759	1.570
NASDAQ Index	0.856	3.419%	14.998	.896	2.122

companies that have achieved this growth with relatively unleveraged, high-quality balance sheets. Our approach enables us to focus on companies with proven strong management, operating in a wide variety of industries. . . .
Further, the companies in which Kurtz Capital invests will have modest price/earnings multiples relative to most emerging growth stocks. However, they will have similar characteristics as to high profitability and growth, thereby leading to above-average appreciation. The organization will invest in soundly managed, unleveraged companies, thus minimizing a fundamental risk in investing. It will avoid a 'bet-the-bank' philosophy by employing another risk-minimization tool embodying the following concepts:

- Portfolios which are highly diversified by stocks and industries.
- Characterized by modest turnover.
- Moderate use of market timing.
- Little or no focus on unseasoned emerging growth companies or turnaround situations.

Through this philosophy, Kurtz Capital aimed to achieve superior performance with minimum risk. By using its small-capitalization, low-debt stock investment strategy, it hoped to continue to earn niche positions on pension and other asset management teams. A summary of the characteristics of KCM portfolios is presented in Exhibit 4.

Investment Procedure

KCM maintained a universe of about 150 active stocks with a supplemental list of about 40 stocks (these lists are given in Exhibits 5 and 6). The number of stocks in KCM's universe was determined as a practical matter by how many stocks the firm's two full-time analysts could effectively follow. Mr. Kurtz and one portfolio manager also devoted 30 percent and 60 percent of their time, respectively, covering the universe, to ensure complete coverage. New stocks were added to the universe through discoveries by the in-house analysts and principals, and through the use of the William O'Neil Service (WOS). WOS provided a screening service specifically for Kurtz Capital to identify promising stocks for its universe. The computer-based, screening process used a fundamental analysis of the company behind the stock that examined the degree of leverage and long-term profitability. One of the specific profitability criteria KCM requested was a five-year return-on-equity/price-to-book ratio. To pass this criterion a stock had to have a minimum five-year ROE of 16 percent and a P/BV ratio less than 4. According to Mr. Kurtz, this criterion ensured that the management could run the business profitably through one business cycle, while the ratio of ROE to P/BV was a measure of potential growth in price. In any case, companies suggested by WOS or other outside sources were subject to a full in-house analysis at KCM before the stock would be considered for addition to the universe. KCM then selected stocks to be included in specific client portfolios by using any specific client requirements and a combination of fundamental and technical analysis.

The universe was reviewed each week; the O'Neil reports were received about once every two months; and formal updates of the universe were done each quarter. KCM stocks would drop from the universe if their performance indicators showed continuing declines or if the company "grew" beyond KCM's idea of "small to mid-sized" in terms of market capitalization. Turnover of the universe averaged about 10–15 percent each year.

Fundamental Analysis

Fundamental in-house research consisted of two basic elements: spreadsheet analysis and management analysis. The spreadsheet analysis focused on the income statement and balance sheet to determine the basic economic soundness of the company and to provide a basis for forecasts. Two forecasts deemed important by KCM were based on prior five-year return on equity (ROE) and five-year growth rate. A sum-of-the-years'-digits method that weighted the four most recent quarters higher than past quarters was used to arrive at a five-year forecast. Levels of both long- and short-term debt were also analyzed to see their impact on earnings of the company. The purpose of the debt analysis was to assess the actual earning power of the company without any "artificial stimulant." Basically, KCM wanted to put themselves in the shoes of the officers of a company and make realistic judgments of its past and future performance. Table 2 contains a list of the fundamental indicators examined by KCM; these indicators are discussed in more detail in the "Sell Decision" section of this case.

In addition to the fundamental analysis, KCM also performed technical market analysis (also known as market timing). Mr. Kurtz believed that patterns of supply and demand in the market were repeatable phenomena and that technical patterns in the market anticipated fundamental changes in sectors and specific stocks. Technical indicators in the market were the result of supply and demand patterns that had their basis in the amount and dispersion of information available to the market

TABLE 2
Fundamental Indicators

Indicator	*Measures:*
Five-year sum-of-years' digits Return on equity/price to book value	Returns value
Sales % change index	Earnings proxy
Earnings stability index	Earnings volatility
Long-term growth + dividend yield/price to book value	Long-term value
Five-year sum-of-years' digits Reinvestment rate/price to future book value	Forward-looking growth potential
O'Neil data graph rating technical analysis	Earnings momentum

in general. Thus the flow of information to and through the market was important. Mr. Kurtz described three basic flows of information and their effects.

The first flow of information was to "insiders" which, as used here, does not imply persons who have foreknowledge of events that would impact the price of a stock, but those persons who would have first knowledge of events that have transpired and that may or may not influence the price of a stock. At this stage of information flow a particular stock's price and trading volume would be affected by those closest to the stock, usually employees. Given the small number of people with this information, only a relatively low level of buying or selling would take place. The next flow would be distribution of news to specialists who closely followed specific companies or sectors. The buying and selling at this stage would be by aggressive individuals or small firms willing to initiate transactions on the limited amount of information available. Finally, information would be widely circulated and the degree of confidence in the information would be high. At this point large institutions would have sufficient confidence to begin trading action and significant price and volume changes would be readily observed. This information curve is schematically illustrated in Exhibit 7.

With this information-flow model as a framework, KCM examined three general technical indicators: dollar flow, momentum, and investment sentiment. The third of these, *investment sentiment*, was a composite of various indicators such as bullish-bearish trends of market newsletters, put/call ratios, and measurement of institutional cash reserves—indicators best monitored by sources that had large (and thus statistically valid) data bases like the Merrill Lynch newsletter. Such gauges of investment sentiment helped to place specific news items about specific stocks, industries, or sectors on the information flow curve. If a particular news item was not widely reported in analyst newsletters or in the general financial press, one could assume that the information was on the low end of the curve. Should signs of insider trading accompany the announcement of the news item, it would be expected that the item would have a high probability of further impacting the stock price as the news moved along the information curve. This information-flow hypothesis was not a rigid construct of Kurtz Capital, but rather a perspective on the market that helped to explain and anticipate market moves.

As noted, one of the two other, quantitative, technical indicators used by KCM was dollar-flow analysis. Dollar flow was a measure of the total inflow and outflow of dollars for a particular stock, industry, or sector. These data, obtained through two information services (Flo/Cap and Computime), were helpful in identifying trends in stock and sector prices through the measurement of the volume of dollars along with corresponding price changes. A surge of dollar volume accompanied by a rise in the price of the stock indicated a bullish trend; a bearish trend was indicated by an increased volume with a decreasing price.

Momentum of price data, the second major quantitative indicator, was supplied by William O'Neil Service, Inc., and Quantitative Analysis Service. Momentum, a measurement of the rate of change of prices or earnings, was useful in determining the peaks and troughs of buying and selling cycles. It was also useful in determining the strength of any cycle relative to other stocks, sectors, or market history.

Moving averages were often used to develop these data, with plots of the averages giving a good visual indication of strong (steep slopes) or weak (flat slopes) momentum.

KCM compared all three general technical indicators—dollar flow, momentum, and market sentiment—to the prior 12 months of trading data to check for correlation; i.e., did the indicators accurately predict the subsequent behavior of the stock? KCM believed that, if accurate, the technical indicators would be "precursors to fundamentals," which implied that these movements in the market could be a predictive measure of eventual performance of stocks and sectors. The hypothesis of technical indicators as precursors to fundamental indicators was consistent with KCM's information-flow hypothesis; technical indicator movements caused by insider and specialist trading might precede the publication of data used in fundamental analysis. Also, technical indicator movement for one company or sector might signal a change in economic conditions moving toward a related company or sector. That change in conditions would subsequently be reflected in the fundamental performance, and hence indicators, of the related company or sector.

Overall, KCM looked upon both its technical and fundamental research as an ongoing process never to be taken in isolation or as a static condition. The weight that KCM assigned to the influence of the two types of research in investment decisions was one third technical, and two thirds fundamental. Table 3 presents a summary of the technical indicators used by KCM.

The Sell Decision

Generally the buy decision is easier for management firms to make than the sell decision. Often the criteria for selling a stock are less well defined than those for buying. One of the strengths of Kurtz Capital was the discipline with which it exercised both its buy and sell decisions—a discipline that helped to eliminate emotionally based decisions that often got other firms in trouble.

Kurtz Capital used four basic criteria for selling a particular stock held in a portfolio: (1) the stock could be overvalued, i.e., fundamental and/or technical indicators signal a discrepancy in the price versus underlying value; (2) a stock holds too large a percentage of the total portfolio value; (3) a negative change has occurred in industry/sector performance; and (4) there is a need for the portfolio to hold a larger percentage of cash or cash equivalents.

TABLE 3
Technical Indicators

Indicator	*Measures:*
Financial press	Market sentiment
Put/call ratio	Market sentiment
William O'Neil, Inc. (relative strength)	Price momentum
Flo/Cap, Inc.	Dollar flow
Quantitative Analysis Service	Price momentum
Computime	Dollar flow

To aid in the sell decision, KCM developed a summary quantification of fundamental and technical factors into an "attractiveness rating," which summarized and quantified the input of the fundamental and technical research for each stock and sector. The KCM small-capitalization stock universe attractiveness ratings are found in Exhibit 8. Each stock in the universe was labeled as positive (+), positive-neutral (+/0), neutral (0), neutral-negative (0/−), or negative (−) depending on the research indicators. The five headings represented quintiles of the universe so that the positively rated stocks held the top 20 percent of the combined research indicators. Exhibit 9 shows the breakdown of the fundamental and technical indicators and their individual attractiveness rating for each stock in the universe. The fundamental indicator (column 1) was a composite of five separate fundamental index numbers (shown in Exhibit 10). These five fundamental indices are: five-year sum-of-the-years'-digits (SOYD or SD) reinvestment rate to P/E (a sustainable growth measure, used in the Appendix only in the October 1984 report), five-year SOYD ROE/price to book value (value measure), sales percent change index (earnings proxy), earnings stability index (volatility measure), long-term growth plus dividend yield/price to book value (long-term growth), and five-year SOYD reinvestment rate/price to future book value (forward-looking value).

The first three columns in Exhibit 10 were based on historical data, with the fourth and fifth columns based on projected data. The return on equity used by KCM for the calculation in the first column of Exhibit 10 applied sum-of-the-years'-digits weightings to groupings of four quarters within a 20-quarter sample to give greater weighting. The denominator was the current price to book value ratio.

The sales percent change index in column two was used as a proxy for an earnings momentum indicator. KCM believed that sales were a more reliable indicator of future earnings than actual earnings, as the earnings line of the income statement could be manipulated more easily than the reported sales. The index was calculated as percent change in sales by quarter minus the trailing four-quarter average.

The earnings stability index, column three, was an attempt to separate pure growth from cyclical behavior. This index was from the William O'Neil Service, which assigned an index value from 1 to 100, based on the volatility of earnings relative to the historical trend of earnings growth.

The next column over holds the formula for long-term growth rate plus dividend yield divided by price to book ratio. The long-term growth rate was the analyst's estimate of a company's future five-year compound annual rate of earnings growth, based on his analysis of company prospects, using both macro- and microeconomic views. This indicator attempted to describe how good "a deal" the stock was: a small price to book ratio or a proportionately large growth rate would increase the stock's standing, according to this indicator.

The last fundamental indicator was a method of incorporating the analyst's estimate for the company's next 12 months of earnings, and its potential impact. This measure utilized a ratio of the company's five-year sum-of-the-years' digits reinvestment rate [RIR = ROE × (1 − dividend payout ratio] average (where the first year is that prospective reinvestment rate attributable to the next four quarters of earnings) divided by a forward-looking price to book value forecast four quarters ahead.

To arrive at a summary rating, each stock was sorted by the individual value of the indicator in each column from highest value to lowest. Each column was then divided into nine groups and the groups were given a rank of +4 to −4, including 0. Columns 2 through 5 of the rankings are listed on the right side of Exhibit 10. The summary fundamental indicator was then calculated by taking the weighted sum of these five columns. This indicator is listed in the first column of Exhibit 9, the attractiveness worksheet cited earlier.

The second fundamental-based indicator in Exhibit 9 is the Data-Graph column. This indicator was based on the William O'Neil Service data (a sample is shown in Exhibit 11) and served to quantify the earnings momentum of a particular company. These data, like the earnings stability data, were organized into quintiles; the rankings are shown in Exhibit 9.

The next four columns of Exhibit 9 concern technical indicators. The Relative Strength column, derived from the WOS data, was a 12-month moving average of prices, which gave an indication of relative strength of the price trend. Flo/Cap, the next column, showed data from the service that supplied KCM with a ranking of its entire universe according to capital flow in or out of specified stocks. Following Flo/Cap were the data supplied by Quantatitive Analysis Service, in time-series format; both long-term and intermediate-term data were considered in this indicator, which measured price rate of change and momentum. Monthly rankings were listed first, followed by weekly rankings. Next, from Computime, a service that supplied dollar flow data (for listed stocks) for both the stock and its industry on a 20- and 60-day basis, the specific stock ranking was listed first, followed by a combined company and industry ranking.

For each of these technical indicators, KCM performed a sorting routine similar to the process used for the fundamental indicators. Each indicator for each stock was sorted in descending order and then separated by quintiles to fit the five-group rating system of +, 0/+, 0, 0/−, and −. The weighted total for fundamental and technical indicators was arrived at by weighting the fundamental indicators at five times the weight of the technical indicators and summing across. The final ordering is shown in summary form in Exhibit 8 as the attractiveness rating.

By tracking a stock's progress across the attractiveness rating chart over time, an estimation could be made as to whether to buy more of, or sell, the stock. Two of the four sell-decision criteria used by KCM—overvalue, as gauged by a persistently low attractiveness rating, and detrimental sector change, noted by a drop of the combined stocks that constituted a sector—could be substantiated by tracking the attractiveness rating over time. The attractiveness rating was helpful in making sell decisions under the other two criteria as well. Selling a portion of the portfolio to raise cash would just as likely prompt a sale of winners as well as "dogs" in order to keep the portfolio in balance by sector. Selling under the "too-large holding" criterion was triggered when a stock's value reached approximately 4 percent of the total portfolio. Often, advance warning of this type of sell decision was signaled by a prolonged + attractiveness rating.

Mixed Signals

Mr. Kurtz picked up the latest issue of attractiveness ratings and noticed declining indicators for three stocks in the technology sector. The stocks, C3 Inc. (CEE), Tyco Laboratories (TYC), and Veeco Instruments (VEE), were rated as neutral (0), neutral-negative (0/ –), and negative, respectively, in the summary quintiles (Exhibit 8). These stocks characterized the dilemma of the technology sector as Mr. Kurtz did not recall any major drop in the fundamental ratings of these companies; as a matter of fact, all had held a neutral or neutral-positive fundamental rating last period. As Mr. Kurtz turned to the rating worksheets (Exhibit 9), the reason for the decline in the overall attractiveness ratings became apparent. Most technical indicators for the stocks were in the neutral-negative or fully negative quintiles. These low ratings were more than enough to offset the more favorable fundamental ratings. Mr. Kurtz checked the financial statements (Exhibits 12–15), then looked back at reports issued from three to seven months ago (see Appendix A) to gauge if the decline had been precipitous or slow.[1] Was the trend sufficiently pessimistic to warrant a sell signal for the stocks? Were the technical indicators precursors of future fundamentals or were they being pulled along by an irrational market streak; after all, the fundamental indicators *were* still in the acceptable range. If a sell order was issued, under which of the four sell criteria would the move be justified?

Mr. Kurtz called Glenn Sussman, a senior analyst, into his office to ask him to look over the technology situation in more detail. Both men realized that too narrow an analysis of the stocks might lead to an unwise sell or hold decision, perhaps costing thousands of dollars in missed returns. Mr. Sussman agreed to have an analysis of the situation and a preliminary recommendation to Mr. Kurtz by that afternoon.

---

[1]Appendix A reports the complete "small"-company set of rankings as of two previous dates, and additional information of interest.

EXHIBIT 1
Performance Comparisons *(total return)*

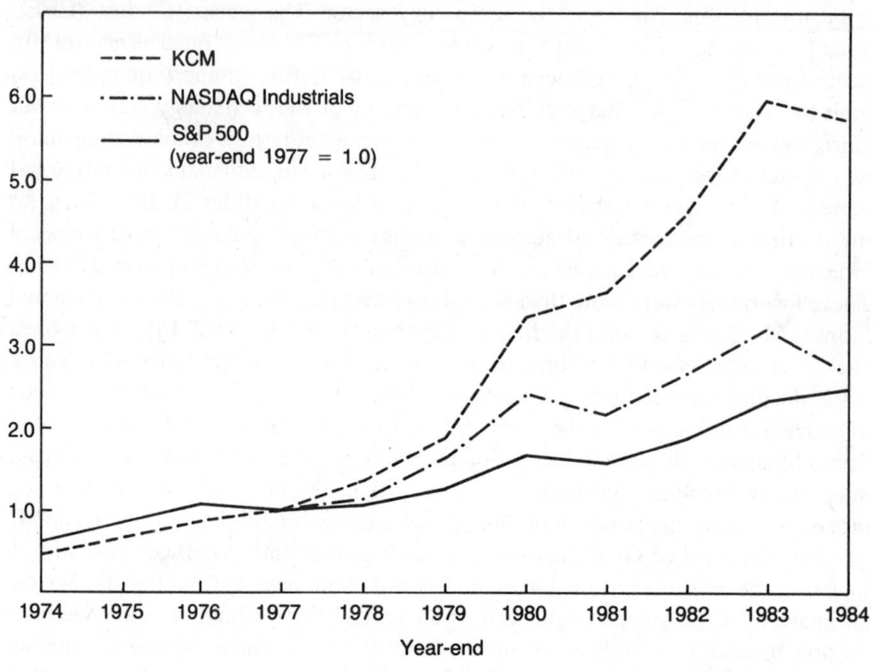

EXHIBIT 2
Portfolio Characteristic Line Relative to S&P 500 (*1978–1984; alpha = 2.3, beta = 1.4*)

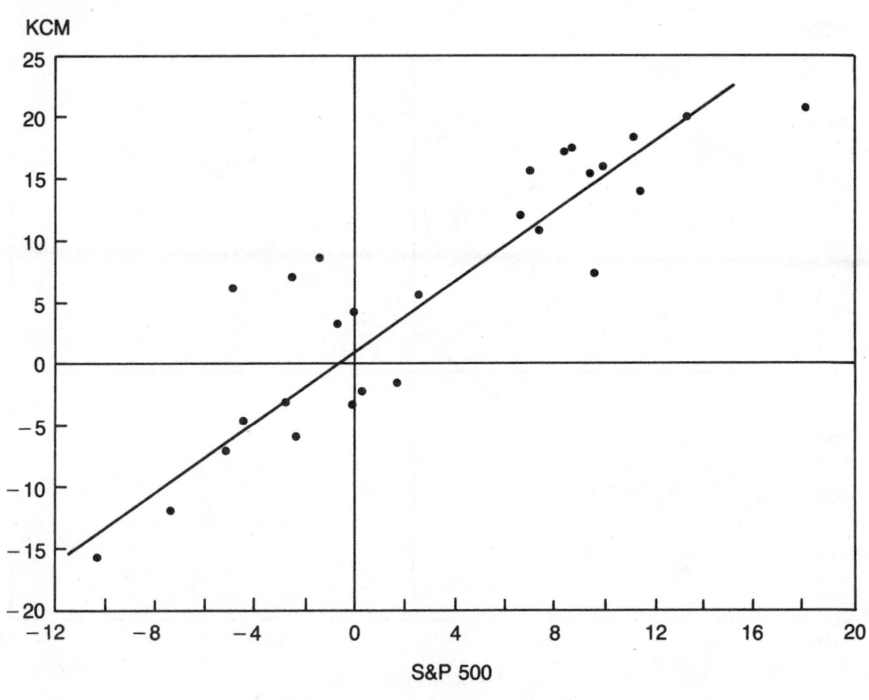

EXHIBIT 3
Portfolio Characteristic Line Relative to NASDAQ Industrials (*1978–1984; alpha = 3.4, beta = 0.86*)

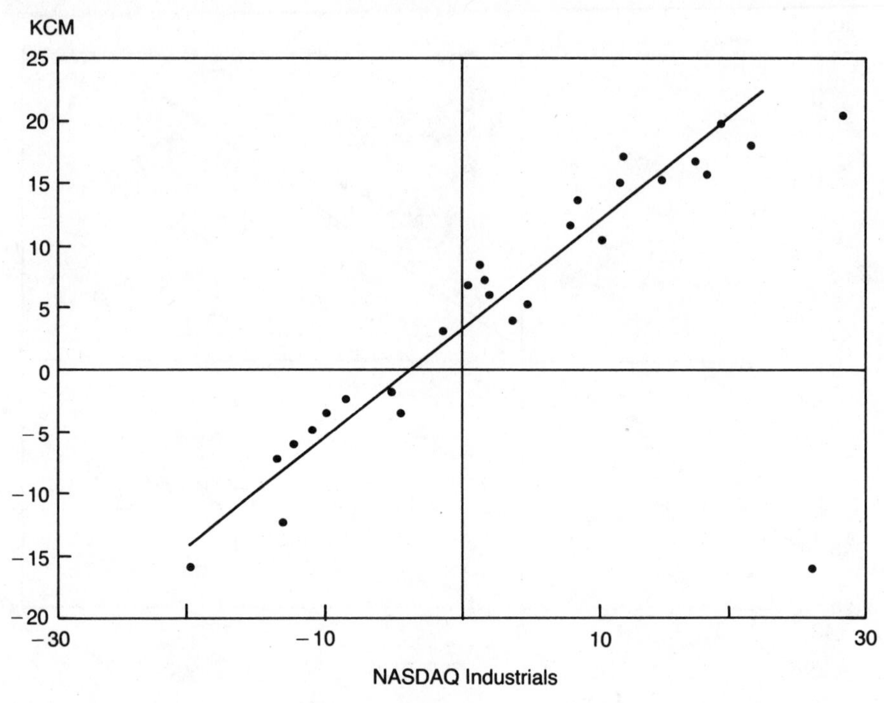

EXHIBIT 4
Financial Profile of Account (*as of May 10, 1985*)

	S&P 400	***Weighted Average of 60 Companies***	***KCM Account (Relative to S&P 400)***
Profitability/Growth Characteristics			
1. Return on average equity—5-year average (%)	13.6	23.4	1.72
2. Return on average equity—last fiscal year (%)	14.2	18.0	1.27
3. EPS 5-year compounded annual growth rate (%)	2.2	19.3	8.77
4. Projected earnings growth rate—next 4 qtrs (%)	10.8	19.1	1.77
5. Projected long-term growth rate (%)	9.0	16.8	1.86
6. Dividend payout ratio—last fiscal year (%)	41.0	19.6	0.48
7. Current dividend yield (%)	3.8	2.0	0.53
Risk Characteristics			
1. P/E ratio (based on next 12 months' earnings)	9.81	10.53	1.07
2. Price/book value ratio	1.50	2.16	1.44
3. Long-term debt/total capitalization (%)	24.6	22.0	0.90
4. Beta	1.03	1.21	1.17
Size			
Market capitalization ($ millions)	2452*	308†	0.13

* Unweighted average
† "Small Cap" component (89.1%) of equities

EXHIBIT 4 ***(concluded)***
New Horizons Fund P/E Relative to S&P 500

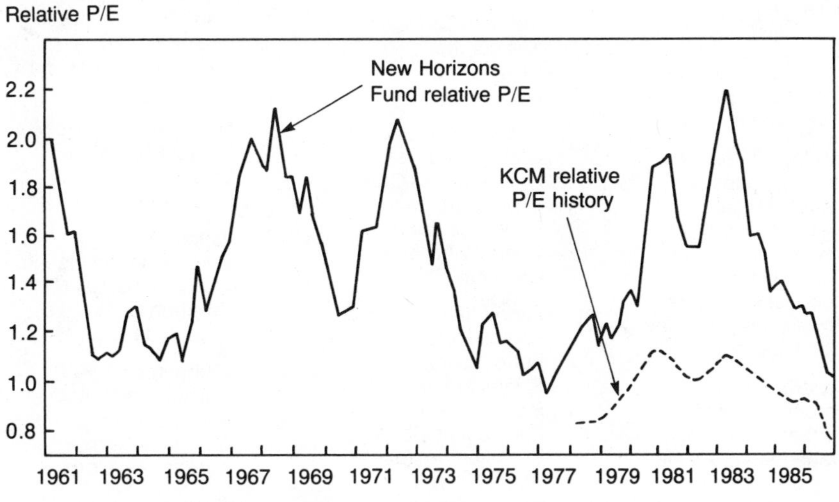

EXHIBIT 5
KCM Universe of Stocks

Acme United Corp.
AFG Industries
Agency Rent-A-Car
Air Wisconsin Svcs, Inc.
Alco Std. Corp.
American Precision
Apogee Enterprises
Aydin Corp.

Bancorp Hawaii
Bandag Inc.
Basix Corp.
Bell Industries, Inc.
Big V Supermarkets
Bindley Western
Blair John & Co.
Burlington Coat
Butler Intl. Inc.

C3, Inc.
Cintas Corp.
J. L. Clark Mfg. Co.
Colorado Natl. Bank
Computer Sciences
Coopervision
Cordura Corp.
Core Industries

Data Design Labs
Dean Foods Co.
Doyle Dane Bernbach
Dunkin' Donuts
Duplex Prods. Inc.
Dynatech Corp.

Edison Bros. Stores
A. G. Edwards, Inc.
Essex Chem. Corp.

Fab Industries, Inc.
Fairchild Industries
Federal-Mogul
First Boston Inc.
First Executive
First Union Corp.
Flexsteel Industries
Flowers Industries Inc.
John Fluke Mfg.

General Cinema
Gerber Products
Gorman Rupp Co.
Greentree Acceptance
Guilford Mills Inc.

Harper Group
Henredon Furniture
B. Hubbell Harvey
Hunt Mfg. Co.

International Aluminum
International Ctls.
Interpublic Group

Jeffrey Martin
Jostens Inc.
Jefferies Group

Kaman Corp.
Carl Karcher Enterprises
Keystone International
Kimball International
Kollmorgen Corp.
W. A. Krueger Co.

Lawter Inc.
L. D. Brinkman
Learonal
Liberty Homes Inc.
Lin Broadcasting
Liz Claiborne
Longs Drug Stores
Luria & Son
Lynden Inc.

MEI Corp.
Meredith Corp.
Midlantic Banks
Herman Miller
MTS Systems Corp.

National Convenience
Newcor Inc.
Noxell Corp.
Nucor Corp.

Oakwood Homes
Olgivy & Mather
Ohio Mattress Co.
Orbit Instruments
Oshman's Sport
Overnite Transpn.
Overseas Ship.

Paco Pharmaceutical
Pentair Corp.
Petro. Equip. Tools
Philips Industries Inc.
Piedmont Aviation
Pope Evans Robbins
Precision Castparts
Prime Motor Inns
Printronix Inc.

Quaker Chem. Corp.

Regal Beloit Corp.
Republic N.Y. Corp.
Reuter Inc.
Russ Togs Inc.
Rowan Cos. Inc.
Ryland Group Inc.

Scie. Computers
Scie. Software
SCOA Industries Inc.
Sealed Air Corp.
Serfco
Seven Oaks Interntl.
Shaklee Corp.
Shelby Williams
Shop & Go Inc.
Showboat Inc.
Sonoco Products
South. Hospitality
Sparton Corp.
L. S. Starrett Co.
Subaru of America
Supermarkets General

TBC Corp.
Team Inc.
Teleflex Inc.
Thompson Medical Inc.
Thousand Trails
Thrifty Corp.
Tokheim Corp.
Tracor Inc.
Trans Technology
Triangle Microwave
Tyco Laboratories Inc.
Tyler Corp.

United Banc. Arizona
United Stationers
Universal Foods
Universal Leaf

Varlen Corp.
Veeco Instruments Inc.
Velcro Industries N. V.
Vernitron Corp.
Vicon Industries

Walbar Inc.
Wallace Computer
Wendy's International
Windmere Corp.
Worthington Corp.

XL/Datacomp

Zero Co.

EXHIBIT 6
Supplemental Universe Listing of Large Capitalization Stocks

Abbott Laboratories
Albertson's Inc.
American Brands
American Express
Atlantic Richfield

Baker International Corp.
Bankers Trust N.Y.
Bristol-Meyers
Brown-Forman Inc.

Chesebrough Ponds
Coca-Cola Co.
Combustion Engineering
CPC International

Emerson Electric

Foster Wheeler Corp.

Gannett Co. Inc.
Gillette Co.

Halliburton Co.
Hughes Tool Co.
Hershey Foods Corp.

IBM

Johnson & Johnson

Eli Lilly & Co.

R. H. Macy
Masco Corp.
Melville Corp.
Merck & Co.
3M
J. P. Morgan & Co.

Pepsico Inc.
Phillips Petroleum

Raytheon Co.
D. S. Revco Inc.
Revlon Inc.
Rite Aid Corp.

Schlumberger, Ltd.
Standard Oil—Ohio
Super Value Stores

Tandy Corp.
Teledyne Inc.

EXHIBIT 7
Information-Flow Hypothesis

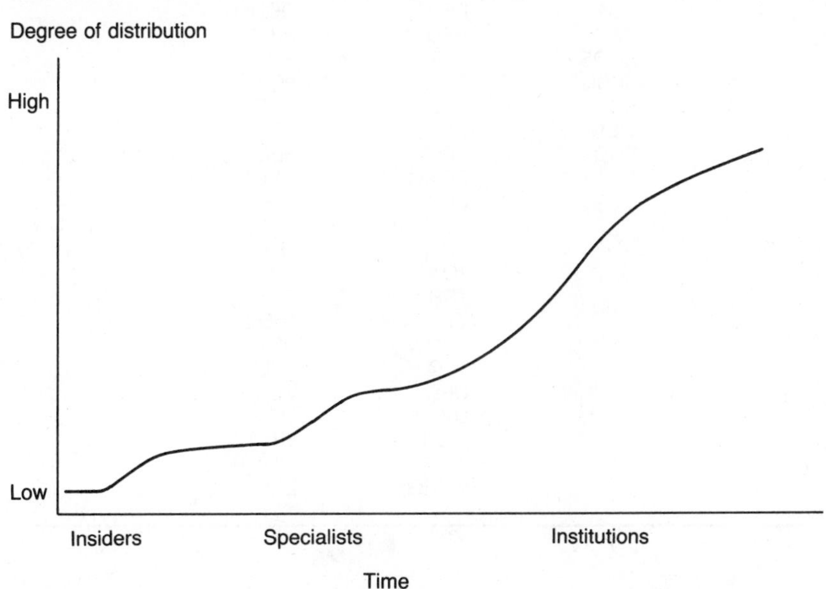

EXHIBIT 8
"Small Cap" Attractiveness Ratings (*5/3/85*)

+	0/+	0	0/–	–
ALK$^-$	ARWS	AFGN	ACU	APR
BNHI	BDG$^-$ ↑	AGNC$^+$	AYD	APOG
FUNC ↑	BINO	ASN$^+$	BI	EBS$^+$
INC	BCF$^-$	BIV	BJ	FLXS$^+$ ↓
MIDL$^-$ ↑	CTAS	CEE	BTL	KOL$^+$
FSNB ↑	COLE	CLRK$^-$	CRI	LDBC$^+$ ↓
UBAZ	EYE	CSC	DDL$^-$	MAGAF$^+$
XLDC$^+$	DF	CDU	AGE$^+$ ↓	PTCO
	DUNK	DOYL$^+$ ↓	FEN	SERF ↓
	DPX	BAS ↓	FMO$^-$	SPA
	DYTC$^-$	FEXC	FKM	TYL$^+$ ↓
	ESX	FLO	GRC	(2)
	FIT$^-$	GCN	GFD ↓	VEE ↓
	FBC$^+$	GTAC	HDON	
	GEB	HARG	IAL$^-$	
	HUBB$^-$	KRVE	JFRY	
	HUN$^-$	LRI$^-$ ↑	CARL ↓	
	IPG	LUR$^+$ ↑	KII	
	JOS	MEI	KBALB ↓	
	JEFG$^+$	MDP	LAW$^-$ ↑	
	KAMNA	MLHR	LIBAV$^-$	
	LINB ↑	MTSC	NCS$^-$	
	LIZC	NSI	NEW	
	LDG$^+$	NUE ↓	OMH ↓	
	LYND	OGIL$^+$	OMT	
	NOXLB ↑	ORBT	OVT$^+$ ↓	
	PNTA	OSHM$^-$	OSG$^+$ ↓	
	PCST	PPSI	PHL$^+$ ↓	
	RNB$^+$	PIE	PTNX	
	SOA	PER$^-$	QCHM	
	SWIX	REUT$^+$	RBC	
	SHOS	RTS	RDC	
	SBRU$^+$	RML	SCIE$^-$	
	SGL	RYL	SSFT	
	WEN	SHGO	S&P400$^+$	
	PDQ	SBO	SEE	
		SONO$^+$ ↓	QPON$^+$ ↓	
		SCX	SHC	
		TBC	TMI ↑	
		TC	TFX$^+$ ↓	
		TOK	TM	
		TRR	TRLS	
		TT	TFD ↓	
		TRMW ↓	USTR$^+$	
		TYC$^-$	VRLN$^-$	
		UPC	VLLCF	
		UVV ↓	VRN$^-$	
		WBR	VII$^+$ ↓	
		WCS	WDMR	
		WTHG$^-$	ZRO	

EXHIBIT 9
Research Universe Rating Distribution (3/21/85)

			— O'NEIL —					
		FUNDA-MENTAL	DATA-GRAPH	RELATIVE STRENGTH	FLO/ CAP	QAS	COMPU-TIME	WEIGHTED TOTAL
S&P 400		(6.6)	0		0/+ 0/+	0/+ 0/−	− −	(4.1)
ACME UNITED CORP	ACU	(1.6)↓↓	−	−	0/+		− 0/ −↑	(7.4)
AFG INDUSTRIES INC	AFGN	(1.8)	0↓	0	0/+	0/+ 0/−		0.8
AGENCY RENT-A-CAR	AGNC	(2.7)↑↑	0/+	+	0/−			2.9
AIR WIS SVCS INC	ARWS	(5.7)	0/+	+	+↑			7.7
ALASKA AIRLS INC	ALK	0.5↑↑	+	+	+	0/+↓↓	+ +	10.4
ALCO STD CORP	ASN	2.1↓↓	0	0	0/+	0/+ 0/−	0/+↑0	2.6
AMERICAN PRECISION INDS	APR	(10.1)	−	−	× +		− −	(11.5)
APOGEE ENTERPRISES INC	APOG	(0.6)↓↓	−	−	−			(11.8)
AYDIN CORP	AYD	10.6	−	−	−	0/− −	− −↓↓	7.2
BANCORP HAWAII	BNHI	10.1↓↓	0/+	+	+			14.0
BANDAG INC	BDG	0.6↑↑↑	0/+	0	0/+↓	0/+ 0/−	0/+ 0/+↑	3.8
BELL INDS INC	BI	0.9↓↓↓↓↓	0/−	−	0/− 0/−	0/−	− −/−	(7.4)
BIG V SUPERMARKETS INC	BIV	(5.4)↓↓	0↑	0/+	× +		× 0/− 0	0.6
BINDLEY WESTERN	BIND	0.6↑	0↓	0/+	+↑(2)			6.2
BLAIR JOHN & CO	BJ	3.5↓	−	−	0/−	0/− 0/↓↓	+0/−	(5.2)
BURLINGTON COAT	BCF	5.4↑	0	0	0/+			4.2
BUTLER INTL INC	BTL	(12.0)	0/+	0	0/+	0/+ −	− −	(5.4)
C 3 INC	CEE	5.9↓↓↓	−↓	−	√0/−		0/+↓0/+	(2.2)
CINTAS CORP	CTAS	(4.3)↑↑↑↑	0/+	+	0/+			6.3
CLARK J L MFG CO	CLRK	(1.2)↑↑	0/−1	0/−↑	+↑(2)	0/− −		(2.9)
COLORADO NATL BANKSHARE	COLC	0.6↓↓↓	0	0	+	0/+0/+		4.7
COMPUTER SCIENCES CORP	CSC	6.2↓↓	0/−	0/−↓0/−	0/+ −	0 0	0 0	(1.7)
COOPERVISION INC	EYE	2.2↑	0/+	0/+	√0/+↓		+ 0/+	7.4
CORDURA CORP	CDU	(3.3)↓↓↓	0/+	0/+	0/+↓	+0/−	0/−↓01 −↓	1.7
CORE INDS INC	CRI	(5.6)↑	−	0/−	0/−	0/− 0/−	0/+ 0	(6.4)
DATA DESIGN LABS	DDES	(0.4)↓↓↓	−	−↓	√ −↓	0/− 0/−		(9.2)
DEAN FOODS CO	DF	0.1↓↓↓↓	0/+	0/+↓	+	0/+ +↑	√0/+ 0/+	8.4
DOYLE DANE BERNBACH INT	DOYL	(8.8)↓	0/+↓	0/+	x +	+0/+		3.2
DUNKIN' DONUTS	DUNK	1.2	0/+	0/+	+	0/+ 0/+		8.0
DUPLEX PRODS INC	DPX	3.8↓↓	+	0/+	+		√ + +	9.0
DYNATECH CORP	DYTC	1.8↑↑	√0/+	0/+√	0/−	+0/−		4.4
EDISON BROS STORES INC	EBS	(4.5)↓↓	0/−	−	0/−	0/−0/−	− −	(10.4)
EDWARDS A G INC	AGE	1.3↑↑	0↓	0/−↓↓	0/−	0/− 0/−	−↓↓↓↓0	(4.3)
BASIX	BAS	1.1	0/−	0/−	0/+			(1.6)

EXHIBIT 9 *(continued)*

			— O'NEIL —					
		FUNDA-MENTAL	DATA-GRAPH	RELATIVE STRENGTH	FLO/CAP	QAS	COMPU-TIME	WEIGHTED TOTAL
S&P 400								
ESSEX CHEM CORP	ESX	(5.4)↓	0/+	0/↑	+	0/+ 0	+/0/+	5.0
FAB INDS INC	FIT	3.7↓↓↓↓	0	0↑	0/+		0/+ 0	3.7
FAIRCHILD INDS INC	FEN	(4.3)↑	–	0/–	0/+	o/– –	0/+↓0	(5.3)
FEDERAL-MOGUL	FMD	(4.0)↑			o/–	× 0/+	× o/– –	(9.4)
FIRST BOSTON INC	FBC	7.9	0/+	+	0/+	+ 0/–	0/+↓0↓↓	9.2
FIRST EXECUTIVE CORP	FEXC	14.5↓↓↓	0	0/–	0/–	0/– –		0.6
FIRST UNION CORP	FUNC	4.0↓	+↑↑↑	+	+	0 o/+		11.4
FLEXSTEEL INDS INC	FLXS	(0.7)↓↓↓	0/–	–↓	–	0/– –		(10.03)
FLOWERS INDS INC	FLO	(6.1)↑↑↑	0	0/+	0/+	0/– 0/–	√0/+ +	1.2
FLUKE JOHN MFG INC	FKM	(0.6)	0/+	0/–	0/–	0/– –	– –	(5.6)
GENERAL CINEMA CORP	GCN	(3.1)↑↑↑	0/+	0/+	0/–↓	0 0/–	0/– 0	(0.8)
GERBER PRODUCTS CO	GEB	(2.2)↓	0/+	0↓	+	0/+ 0↓	0/+ 0/+	4.52
GORMAN RUPP CO	GRC	(3.9)↓↓	0/–↓	0↑	× 0/+		0/– 0/+	(4.6)
GREENTREE ACCEPT CORP	GTAC	7.8↑	0/–	–↓	0/+			(0.9)
GUILFORD MLS INC	GFD	0.9↓↓↓↓	0/–	0/–↑	× 0/+	0/– 0/–	0/–↓ –↓↓	(6.2)
HARPER GROUP	HARG	0.5	0/+	0/–	o/–	0/+ –		(2.1)
HENREDON FURNITURE INDS	HDON	(1.8)↓↓	0	0/–	–	0/– –↓		(6.1)
HUBBELL HARVEY INC. B	HUBB	(1.1)	0/+	0	+	0 0	+↓0	4.4
HUNT MFG CO	HUN	0.1↑↑↑	0/+	0↓	0/+↓	0/+ 0/–	0/+ 0/+	3.6
INTERNATIONAL ALUM CORP	IAL	(2.9)↓↓↓	0/–	0/–	–	0/– 0/–	– –	(9.6)
INTERNATIONAL CTLS CORP	INC	4.4↓	+	+	√0/+		+↑0	12.3
INTERPUBLIC GROUP COS I	IPG	(7.7)↑↑	0/+	0/+	+	0/+ +	√+ +↑	5.9
JEFFE RIES GROUP	JEFG	4.6	0/+↑↑	0/+↓	√0/+			9.8
JEFFREY MARTIN INC	JFRY	4.0	–	0/–↓	× 0/+			(6.4)
JOSTENS INC	JOS	(4.0)↑	0/+↑	0/+	+	+ –↓	√0/+ 0/–↑	6.2
KAMAN CORP	KAMNA	0.0↓↓	0/+	0/+	0/+↑	0/+ 0/–		4.5
KARCHER CARL ENTR	CARL	8.8↑↑	× –↓	–	–↓↓			(8.5)
KEYSTONE INTL INC	KII	(9.2)↑	0/–	0/–	0/+	0/+ 0/–	0/– –	(6.7)
KIMBALL INTL INC	KBALB	(3.3)↓	0↓	0	0/–	0/– –↓		(5.1)
KOLLMORGEN CORP	KOL	(4.6)↓	–	–	√–	– 0/–↑	√ – 0/–	(10.8)
KRUEGER W A CO	KRUE	(6.1)↑↑↑	0	+	× +	+ 0/–		2.8
LAWTER INC	LAW	(10.00)	–	0/–	0/+	0/– 0/–↓	– 0/–	(9.4)
LD BRINKMAN	LDBC	2.0	–	–	–	0/– –		(10.5)
LEARONAL	LRI	(8.4)↑↑	0	0	√0/–	– 0/–	0/– 0/–	(2.8)

EXHIBIT 9 *(continued)*

		FUNDA-MENTAL	— O'NEIL — DATA-GRAPH	RELATIVE STRENGTH	FLO/CAP	QAS	COMPU-TIME	WEIGHTED TOTAL
S&P 400								
LIBERTY HOMES INC	LIBAV	5.5↓↓↓	–	–	NR			(9.8)
LIN BROADCASTING CORP	LINB	(0.4)↑↑	0/+↑↑	0/+↕	+	0/+ 0/–		5.8
LIZ CLAIBORNE	LIZC	(3.3)↑↑	+	+	× +			8.7
LONGS DRUG STORES INC	LDG	0.7↑↑	0/+	+	+	+ 0/+↓	+↑0/+	9.9
LURIA & SON	LUR	7.7	0/–	–	0/–		0 0↑	(2.9)
LYNDEN INC	LYND	9.5↓	0/+	0	× +			7.8
MAGNA INTERNATIONAL	MAGAF	2.7↓	–	–	–			(10.9)
MEI CORP	MEI	2.7↑↑↑	0	0/–	+	– 0/–	0/+ 0	1.0
MEREDITH CORP	MDP	(0.5)	0/+↑↑	0↓	0/+	0/– 0/–	0/– 0/–↓	(0.2)
MIDLANTIC BKS INC	MIDL	7.2↓↓↓	0/+	0/+	+↑			10.9
MILLER HERMAN INC	MLHR	(6.2)↑↑↑↑	0/+	0	0/+	0/– –↓		(1.7)
MTS SYS CORP	MTSC	(3.7)	0/+	0/+↑	0/–↓			(0.5)
NATIONAL CONVENIENCE ST	NCS	3.2↓	–	–	–	– –	– 0↑	(9.5)
NATIONAL SVC INDS INC	NSI	3.3	0/+↑	0	× 0/+	0/– 0	0 0	0.7
NEWCOR INC	NEW	(3.5)↓	–	–	0/+↑(2)		0/– 0	(6.7)
NOXELL CORP	NOXLB	(3.3)↑↑↑	0/+	0/+	+↑	0/+ 0/+↑		6.2
NUCOR CORP	NUE	1.6↑	0/+	0/–↓	+	0/+ 0/–↓↓	– –↓	0.6
OAKWOOD HOMES CORP	OMH	0.4↓↓↓↓↓	–↓	–	0/–	0/+ –	+ 0/–↓	(4.8)
OGILVY & MATHER INTL	OGIL	(7.7)↑↑	0/+	0/+	+	0/+ 0/–		2.9
OHIO MATTRESS	OMT	5.5↓	–	–	0/–↑	– –	– –	(8.6)
ORBIT INSTRUMENTS	ORBT	0.5↓	0	0/–↓	0/+			0.2
OSHMANS SPORTING GOODS	OSHM	4.5	0/–↓	–	0/+↓	0/– 0/–		(2.7)
OVERNITE TRANSN CO	OVT	0.0	0	0	0/–	0/+ –↓	–↓ –↓	(4.0)
OVERSEAS SHIPHOLDING GR	OSG	6.1↓↓↓↓	–	– e↓	0/+	0/– 0/–	0 –↓	(3.6)
PACO PHARMACEUTCAL	PPSI	3.8↓↓	0/–↓	–	0/+			2.48
PENTAIR CORP	PNTA	4.0	0	0	+	0/– +		5.4
PETROLEUM EQUIP TOOLS C	PTCO	(6.4)	–	–	–			(14.6)
PHILIPS INDS INC	PHL	(1.7)↑↑↑↑	0↓	0↓	× 0/+	0/+ –↓	0/–↓↓↓–↓↓↓	(4.3)
PIEDMONT AVIATION INC	PIE	4.4	0/+	0/–↕	0/–	0 0/–↕	+↑↑↑↑↑+	0.6
POPE EVANS ROBBINS IN	PER	8.4↕	0/–	–	0/–	0/– –	0 0	(3.0)
PRECISION CASTPARTS	PCST	(3.7)↑↑	0/+↓	+	+			(8.5)
PRIME MOTOR INNS INC	PDQ	(5.7)↑↑↑	0/+	+	+	+ +	√+ +	8.5

EXHIBIT 9 *(continued)*

		FUNDA-MENTAL	— O'NEIL — DATA-GRAPH	RELATIVE STRENGTH	FLO/CAP	QAS	COMPU-TIME	WEIGHTED TOTAL
S&P 400								
PRINTRONIX INC	PTNX	8.2↓↓	–	–	0/–			(6.7)
PUGET SOUND BANCORP	PSNB	8.3↓	0/+↑↑	+	+	0 0/+		11.6
QUAKER CHEM CORP	QCHM	(4.5)↓↓	0/–	0/–	0/–↑			(7.8)
REGAL BELOIT CORP	RBC	(11.2)	0/–	0/–↑	0/–		√0/+↑0	(7.5)
REPUBLIC N Y CORP	RNB	5.7↓↓↓	0	0/+	+		+ +	9.8
REUTER INC	REUT	3.5↓	0/+	0/–↓	√0/–			3.4
ROWAN COS INC	RDC	(0.9)↓↓↓↓	0/–	–	0/+↑		– 0/–	(5.6)
RUSS TOGS INC	RTS	6.7↓↓↓	0/+↑	0/+	0/+		–↓0/–	1.9
RUSSELL CORP	RML	5.5↑	0/–	0	√0/–	0/+ –↓	0 0/–↓	(1.4)
RYLAND GROUP INC	RYL	(6.0)↑	0	0↓	0/+	0/+ –	+ 0	(0.6)
SCIENTIFIC COMPUTERS IN	SCIE	(10.0)↑↑	–	–	0/+			(10.0)
SCIENTIFIC SOFTWARE	SSFT	3.1	0/–	–	√–			(6.8)
SCOA INDS INC	SOA	0.5	0/+	0	+	+ 0/–↓	+ 0	5.6
SEALED AIR CORP	SEE	(10.1)↑	0↓	–↓	0/+	– 0/–	0/–↓0/–	(8.2)
SERVICE FRACTURING CO	SERF	2.0↓↓↓	–	–	–			(11.2)
SEVEN OAKS INTL	QPON	1.1↑↑	0/–	–↓	0/+			(3.6)
SHAKLEE CORP	SHC	2.3↓↓↓	–	–	0/–	0/– –	0/+ +↑	(5.1)
SHELBY WILLIAMS	SWIX	(7.7)↑↑↑↑	0/+	+	+			6.9
SHOP & GO INC	SHGO	(2.2)↑↑↑↑	0/+	+	–	0/+ 0/–		0.3
SHOWBOAT INC	SBO	4.0	–	–	× +		0 0/+	(1.4)
SONOCO PRODS	SONO	(2.2)↓	0/+	0	+	0/– 0↓		2.9
SOUTHERN HOSPITALITY	SHOS	1.1	0↓	0/+	+			6.4
SPARTAN CORP	SPA	(12.8)↑	–	–	√–		– –	(17.1)
STARRETT L S CO	SCX	(7.7)↓	0/+↑↑	0/+	+		0 0/–↓	2.2
SUBARU AMER INC	SBRU	5.0	0/+	0/+	+			10.0
SUPERMARKETS GEN CORP	SGL	1.3↑↑	+	+	+	0/+ 0/–↓↓	√0 0/+	8.9
TBC CORP	TBC	2.7↓	0	0/+	0/–			1.1
TEAM INC	TMI	(10.0)	0↑	–	0/+		0/–↓0/–	(7.8)
TELEFLEX INC	TFX	4.4	0/+	0/–	–↓	0/+ –↓	– –	(3.6)
TELEX CORP	TC	(1.2)↑↑↑↑	0/+	0/+	0/+	0/+ 0/–	0/–↓↓ –↓	1.3
THOMPSON MED INC	TM	4.2	–	–	–		– 0↑	(8.1)
THOUSAND TRAILS	TRLS	3.7	0/–	–	0/–			(6.5)
THRIFTY CORP	TFD	(1.0)↑↑	0↓	0/–↓	–↓↓	0/– –	0↓0	(5.8)

EXHIBIT 9 *(concluded)*

		FUNDA-MENTAL	— O'NEIL — DATA-GRAPH	— O'NEIL — RELATIVE STRENGTH	FLO/CAP	QAS	COMPU-TIME	WEIGHTED TOTAL
S&P 400								
TOKHEIM CORP	TOK	(2.2)	0/–↓	0	+		0/– 0	(0.2)
TRACOR INC	TRR	0.5↑↑	0/+	0/+	0/+	+ 0/–	– –↓	2.0
TRANS TECHNOLOGY	TT	20↓	0	0↓	0/+		×↓↓0↓	0.8
TRIANGLE MICROWAVE	TRMW	5.7↑	0/–↓	0↓	0/+			2.3
TYCO LABS INC	TYC	(0.7)↑	0/+	–↓	0/–	0/– –	√+↑0	(2.6)
TYLER CORP	TYL	(2.9)↓	–↓	–↓	0/–	0 –	– –	(10.8)
UNITED BANCORP ARIZ	UBAZ	3.5	0/+	+	+	0/+ +		11.2
UNITED STATIONERS INC	USTR	(6.2)↓5	0	0↑	0/–			(4.48)
UNIVERSAL FOODS CORP	UFC	(2.6)	0↕	0	0/+↓		+↑↑↑↑0/–	1.2
UNIVERSAL LEAF TOB INC	UVV	10.1	↓↓	0/–↓	–↓	0 0/–↕	+ 0↓	(1.4)
VARLEN CORP	VRLN	(0.7)↓↓↓	–	–	0/–	0/– 0/–		(9.3)
VEECO INSTRS INC	VEE	(1.6)↑↑↑	–↓	–	–	– –	0/–↓↓0/–↓	(11.4)
VELCRO INDS N V	VELCF	(1.2)↑	0	–	0/–	0/– 0/–		(6.5)
VERNITRON CORP	VRN	2.2↓↓↓↓↓	–	–	0/–↑	– –	– 0/↓	(9.3)
VICON INDS INC	VII	1.2↓↓	0↑	0/–	0/–		0/–↓0/↓	(4.0)
WALBAR INC	WBR	(2.2)	0/+	0	0/+		0/– 0↑	1.4
WALLACE COMPUTER SVCS I	WCS	(2.7)↑↑↑↑	0/+	0	0/+	0 0/–	0↓0/+	1.3
WENDYS INTL INC	WEN	(3.4)↑↑↑↑	0↑	0/+	+	0/+ 0/–↓↓	√+ 0/+↓	4.6
WINDMERE CORP	WDMR	12.1	–	–	–	0/– 0/–		(5.7)
WORTHINGTON INDS INC	WTHG	(2.3)↑↑↑	0↓	0	0/–	0/+ –↓		(3.2)
XL DATACOMP	XLDC	11.2↑	NR	NR	NR			
ZERO CO	ZRO	1.7↑↑↑	0/–	0/–	0/–	– –↓	0/–↓↓0/–↓	6.5

EXHIBIT 10
"Small Cap" Research Universe Report 2 (*statistical database* B)

						Ranked Fundamental Criteria					
Company	5yr SD ROE/ (P/BV)	Sales % Chg Index	Earns Stab. Index	(LTGR +DY)/ (P/BV)	5yr SD RIR/ (P/FBV)	5yr SD ROE/ (P/BV)	Sales % Chg Index	Earns Stab. Index	(LTGR +DY)/ (P/BV)	5yr SD RIR/ (P/FBV)	Total
S&P 400	8.96			5.84	4.71	−1	0	0	−1	−4	−6.6
ACME ' 'NITED CORP	9.16	−3.50	−14.50	8.31	5.98	0	1	0	1	−3	−1.6
AFG INDUSTRIES	11.08	−22.00	−99.00	6.96	14.58	1	−3	−4	0	3	−1.8
AGENCY RENT-A-CAR	7.54	−2.75	−23.17	3.95	20.06	−2	1	−2	−3	4	−2.7
AIR WIS SVCS INC	6.79	−28.25	−17.50	6.72	8.26	−3	−4	0	0	0	−5.7
ALASKA AIRLS INC	15.98	−15.50	−71.33	5.12	15.58	4	−1	−4	−3	4	0.5
ALCO STD CORP	9.96	−16.00	−4.17	9.36	6.45	0	−2	4	2	−3	2.1
AMERICAN PRECISION	7.27	−35.25	−17.17	4.19	7.73	−3	−4	0	−3	−1	−10.1
APOGEE ENTERPRISES	9.55	−13.00	−16.33	8.21	8.87	0	−1	0	0	0	−0.6
AYDIN CORP	15.64	6.00	−23.33	12.68	13.37	4	3	−2	3	3	10.6
BANCORP HAWAII	14.11	17.75	−5.67	9.41	7.40	3	4	3	2	−1	10.1
BANDAG INC	7.06	−0.75	−4.67	3.02	12.69	−3	1	4	−4	3	0.6
BASIX CORP	9.54	−7.75	−16.33	5.80	13.77	0	0	0	−2	3	1.1
BELL INDS INC	11.09	−29.00	−13.33	12.64	6.79	1	−4	1	3	−2	0.9
BIG V SUPERMARKETS	8.27	3.50	−24.67	8.66	6.11	−2	2	−2	1	−3	−5.4
BINDLEY WESTERN IND	9.82	−0.75	−30.33	6.33	13.16	0	1	−2	−1	3	0.6
BLAIR, JOHN, & CO	9.72	29.25	−38.33	10.06	12.08	0	4	−3	2	2	3.5
BURLINGTON COAT	15.12	−18.50	−25.00	8.50	16.04	3	−2	−2	1	4	5.4
BUTLER INTL INC	6.32	2.00	−58.67	8.19	3.77	−4	2	−4	0	−4	−12.0
C3 INC	13.78	66.75	−37.33	14.75	9.67	2	4	−3	4	0	5.7
CINTAS CORP	5.86	0.00	−15.33	3.78	14.09	−4	2	0	−4	3	−4.3
CLARK, J. L., MFG CO	8.95	−19.00	−5.33	5.23	7.79	−1	−2	4	−2	−1	−1.2
COLORADO NATL BANK	12.57	−3.75	−11.33	8.17	6.33	2	1	1	0	−3	0.6
COMPUTER SCIENCES	12.80	8.75	−16.17	9.66	8.74	2	3	0	2	0	6.2
COOPERVISION	7.15	−9.00	−20.67	7.78	11.61	−3	0	−1	0	2	−2.2
CORDURA CORP	11.72	−7.75	−46.83	4.69	11.74	1	0	−3	−3	2	−3.3
CORE INDS INC	9.08	−19.25	−18.50	7.60	4.51	0	−2	0	0	−4	−5.6
DATA DESIGN LABS	9.58	−25.75	−12.00	9.63	7.80	0	−3	1	2	−1	0.4

DEAN FOODS CO	6.53	5.50	−2.67	3.37	11.14	−3	2	4	−4	2	0.1
DOYLE DANE BERNBACH	7.33	−6.50	−13.50	5.36	4.03	−3	0	1	−2	−4	−8.8
DUNKIN' DONUTS	7.27	0.50	−1.33	5.47	10.14	−3	2	4	−2	1	1.2
DUPLEX PRODS INC	9.81	−4.25	−16.00	5.51	7.06	0	1	0	−2	−2	−3.8
DUNATECH CORP	7.52	14.25	−9.67	3.63	16.84	−2	3	2	−4	4	1.8
EDISON BROS STORES	11.11	−18.75	−19.00	7.59	5.31	1	−2	0	0	−4	−4.5
EDWARDS A G INC	10.72	30.75	−20.33	5.98	9.27	1	4	−1	−1	0	1.3
ESSEX CHEM CORP	8.41	2.50	−19.67	7.86	5.11	−1	2	−1	0	−4	−5.4
FAB INDS INC	15.51	−24.25	−21.00	11.47	8.21	3	−3	−1	3	0	3.7
FAIRCHILD INDS	8.37	3.25	−69.33	15.72	1.55	−1	2	−4	4	−4	−4.3
FEDERAL-MOGUL	9.80	−23.25	−19.33	12.24	5.05	0	−3	−1	3	−4	−4.0
FIRST BOSTON INC	14.27	26.00	−55.67	11.93	12.15	3	4	−4	3	3	7.9
FIRST EXECUTIVE	20.43	103.50	−10.67	21.08	9.69	4	4	2	4	1	14.5
FIRST UNION CORP	10.68	12.00	−8.83	6.82	8.34	0	3	2	0	0	4.0
FLEXSTEEL INDS	12.46	−23.75	−15.00	8.41	7.40	2	−3	0	1	−2	−0.7
FLOWERS INDS INC	5.89	−12.50	−7.50	4.49	7.86	−4	−1	3	−3	−1	−6.1
FLUKE, JOHN, MFG	8.32	−11.50	−19.17	7.84	10.15	−1	−1	0	0	1	−0.6
GENERAL CINEMA	8.17	5.00	−14.67	3.30	13.15	−2	2	0	−4	3	−2.1
GERBER PRODUCTS	9.00	−7.75	−5.83	5.67	5.91	0	0	3	−2	−3	−2.2
GORMAN RUPP CO	8.94	−12.75	−11.67	9.32	5.24	−1	−1	1	1	−4	−3.9
GREENTREE ACCEPTANCE	19.52	5.00	−23.67	7.13	16.87	4	2	−2	0	4	7.8
GUILFORD MLS INC	14.47	−36.00	−28.67	10.35	9.22	3	−4	−2	2	0	0.9
HARPER GROUP	9.75	−11.50	−15.33	6.68	11.48	0	−1	0	−1	2	0.5
HENREDON FURNITURE	10.13	−22.50	−11.00	8.42	7.06	0	−3	1	1	−2	−1.8
HUBBELL HARVEY, B	9.48	−6.25	−6.50	6.58	6.32	0	0	3	−1	−3	−1.1
HUNT MFG CO	7.12	3.00	−3.67	5.10	9.06	−3	2	4	−2	0	0.1
INTERNATIONAL ALUM	11.80	−20.00	−23.00	11.77	5.52	1	−3	−2	3	−3	−2.9
INTERNATIONAL CTLS	13.90	−9.00	−16.50	6.74	11.15	2	0	0	0	2	4.4
INTERPUBLIC GROUP	7.32	−6.00	−13.33	4.34	7.32	−3	0	1	−3	−2	−7.7
JEFFERIES GROUP	14.68	66.75	−35.33	5.57	19.93	3	4	−3	−2	4	4.6
JEFFREY MARTIN INC	21.13	9.75	−32.50	4.56	33.20	4	3	−3	−3	4	4.0
JOSTENS INC	8.01	2.00	−2.83	3.96	7.52	−2	2	4	−3	−1	−1.0
KAMAN CORP	8.63	−6.75	−5.50	6.69	7.80	−1	0	3	−1	−1	0.0
KARCHER, CARL, ENT	14.29	−10.25	−11.33	11.02	10.49	3	0	1	3	1	8.8
KEYSTONE INTL Inc	5.59	8.50	−22.17	5.32	6.04	−4	3	−1	−2	−3	−9.2
KIMBALL INTL INC	8.17	−10.00	−15.00	6.73	8.20	−2	0	0	0	−1	−3.3
KOLLMORGEN CORP	8.62	−26.75	−17.50	13.63	4.77	−1	−4	0	3	−4	−4.6

EXHIBIT 10 *(continued)*

Company	5yr SD ROE/ (P/BV)	Sales % Chg Index	Earns Stab. Index	(LTGR +DY)/ (P/BV)	5yr SD RIR/ (P/FBV)	Ranked Fundamental Criteria: 5yr SD ROE/ (P/BV)	Sales % Chg Index	Earns Stab. Index	(LTGR +DY)/ (P/BV)	5yr SD RIR/ (P/FBV)	Total
S&P 400	8.96			5.84	4.71	−1	0	0	−1	−4	−6.6
KRUEGER, W A, CO	7.01	−12.25	−18.00	4.17	10.07	−3	−1	0	−3	1	−6.1
LAWTER INC	6.23	−15.75	−10.83	5.43	4.83	−4	−2	2	−2	−4	−10.0
L. D. BRINKMAN	14.96	−30.00	−27.50	8.50	11.03	3	−4	−2	1	2	2.0
LEARONAL	8.20	−25.25	−14.17	3.83	9.47	−2	−3	0	−4	0	−8.4
LIBERTY HOMES INC	13.80	−11.00	−15.50	14.97	7.47	2	0	0	4	−1	5.5
LIN BROADCASTING	6.47	14.75	−3.17	4.88	10.07	−4	3	4	−3	1	−0.4
LIZ CLAIBORNE	7.74	−9.50	−20.33	2.90	29.64	−2	0	−1	−4	4	−3.3
LONGS DRUG STORES	7.80	8.75	−4.00	5.55	7.52	−2	3	4	−2	−1	0.7
LURIA & SON	14.10	−5.25	−12.67	9.02	10.56	3	0	1	1	2	7.7
LYNDEN INC	22.92	13.00	−55.67	15.94	12.97	4	3	−4	4	3	9.5
MAGNA INT	13.13	−15.50	−32.67	9.89	12.09	2	−1	−3	2	2	2.7
MEI CORP	8.46	−11.75	−4.17	4.04	13.56	−1	−1	4	−3	3	2.7
MEREDITH CORP	8.24	−1.75	−6.33	5.70	9.54	−2	1	3	−2	0	−0.5
MIDLANTIC BKS INC	15.41	−1.00	−9.83	8.21	9.68	3	1	2	0	1	7.2
MILLER HERMAN INC	6.26	−23.00	−8.83	3.11	11.28	−4	−3	2	−4	2	−6.2
MTS SYS CORP	7.55	7.00	−30.50	11.56	5.32	−2	3	−2	3	−4	−3.7
NATIONAL CONVENIENCE	10.66	−17.75	−4.67	9.71	7.90	0	−2	4	1	−1	3.2
NATIONAL SVC INDS	10.00	−5.00	−4.50	6.85	7.66	0	0	4	0	−1	3.3
NEWCOR INC	9.61	−54.00	−23.00	11.19	6.93	0	−4	−2	3	−2	−3.5
NOXELL CORP	6.43	−5.00	−4.17	3.40	10.20	−4	0	4	−4	1	−3.3
NUCOR CORP	9.21	−14.50	−30.33	13.80	8.34	0	−1	−2	4	0	1.6
OAKWOOD HOMES CORP	10.51	−21.00	−9.33	8.08	9.01	0	−3	2	0	0	0.4
OGILVY & MATHER	6.69	−10.75	−8.83	3.12	7.32	−3	0	2	−4	−2	−7.7
OHIO MATTRESS CO	10.94	−9.50	−9.33	14.33	6.72	1	0	2	4	−2	5.5
ORBIT INSTRUMENT	9.97	−12.25	−29.00	9.22	11.56	0	−1	−2	1	2	0.5
OSHMAN'S SPORT	11.15	1.50	−11.67	9.23	9.08	1	2	1	1	0	4.5
OVERNITE TRANSN	10.16	−7.50	−9.67	5.64	9.54	0	0	2	−2	0	0.0
OVERSEAS SHIP	16.67	−3.00	−14.83	21.86	5.53	4	1	0	4	−3	6.1

PACO PHARMACEUTICAL	12.72	−14.50	−33.33	12.98	12.02	2	−1	−3	3	2	3.8
PENTAIR CORP	11.63	7.50	−18.83	8.66	8.81	1	3	0	1	0	4.0
PETRO EQUIP TOOLS	−0.76	25.50	−62.37	43.38	−1.11	−4	4	−4	4	−4	−6.4
PHILIPS INDS INC	8.55	−15.25	−12.00	5.89	9.41	−1	−1	1	−1	0	−1.7
PIEDMONT AVIATION	15.76	−11.25	−47.67	10.32	9.96	4	0	−3	2	1	4.4
POPE EVANS ROBBINS	29.49	10.00	−85.00	12.38	12.97	4	3	−4	3	3	8.4
PRECISION CASTPARTS	6.19	13.50	−16.50	5.37	10.34	−4	3	0	−2	1	−3.7
PRIME MOTOR INNS	5.53	−36.25	−9.17	2.77	13.82	−4	−4	2	−4	3	−5.7
PRINTRONIX INC	21.85	−13.50	−20.67	14.07	9.84	4	−1	−1	4	1	8.2
PUGET SOUND BANCORP	12.70	−0.75	−7.83	9.93	8.34	2	1	3	2	0	8.3
QUAKER CHEM CORP	8.99	−18.25	−17.83	7.89	6.66	0	−2	0	0	−3	−1.5
REGAL BELOIT CORP	8.42	−35.00	−31.17	7.86	4.71	−1	−4	−3	0	−4	−11.2
REPUBLIC N Y CORP	14.91	33.50	−19.50	8.89	8.41	3	4	−1	1	0	5.7
REUTER INC	11.08	69.25	−46.83	11.33	9.41	1	4	−3	3	0	3.5
ROWAN COS INC	13.47	81.00	−61.33	9.05	6.71	2	4	−4	1	−2	−0.9
RUSS TOGS INC	13.91	3.00	−9.33	10.67	6.79	3	2	2	2	−2	6.7
RUSSELL CPR-	11.99	−10.75	−9.50	9.37	8.41	1	0	2	2	0	5.5
RYLAND GROUP INC	8.76	−1.50	−46.83	7.09	7.26	−1	1	−3	0	−2	−6.0
SCIENTIFIC COMPUTERS	6.71	−17.75	−16.67	4.90	6.93	−3	−2	0	−3	−2	−10.0
SCIENTIFIC SOFTWARE	20.34	−82.50	−39.50	28.19	8.68	4	−4	−3	4	0	3.1
SCOA INDS INC	10.00	−12.75	−8.67	5.62	9.67	0	−1	3	−2	0	0.5
SEALED AIR CORP	6.88	−33.75	−22.83	6.68	7.12	−3	−4	−1	−1	−2	−10.1
SERVICE FRACTURING	18.91	−26.00	−65.83	13.87	8.54	4	−4	−4	4	0	2.0
SEVEN OAKS INTL	10.86	−11.00	−23.17	7.81	11.89	1	0	−2	0	2	1.1
SHAKLEE CORP	14.46	2.00	−48.00	14.47	6.05	3	2	−3	4	−3	2.3
SHELBY WILLIAMS	5.35	−9.25	−20.33	4.16	10.34	−4	0	−1	−3	1	−7.7
SHOP & GO INC	6.22	−7.25	−7.50	3.49	13.15	−4	0	3	−4	3	−2.2
SHOWBOAT INC	11.21	13.75	−9.50	9.53	5.78	1	3	2	2	−3	4.0
SONOCO PRODS	8.61	−10.00	−11.00	6.86	7.26	−1	0	1	0	−2	−2.2
SOUTHERN HOSPITALITY	12.07	−8.75	−58.17	6.70	15.84	2	0	−4	−1	4	1.1
SPARTON CORP	7.46	−24.25	−56.00	7.28	5.11	−2	−3	−4	0	−4	−12.8
STARRETT, L S, CO	8.81	−5.00	−20.67	6.27	5.45	−1	0	−1	−1	−4	−7.7
SUBARU AMER INC	11.15	−3.50	−8.33	3.70	22.88	1	1	3	−4	4	5.0
SUPERMARKETS GEN	8.26	32.75	−9.33	4.61	10.61	−2	4	2	−3	2	1.3
TBC CORP	12.64	−14.75	−21.33	6.33	12.50	2	−1	−1	−1	3	2.7
TEAM INC	5.26	−18.00	−84.83	20.54	1.39	−4	−2	−4	4	−4	−10.0
TELEFLEX INC	10.63	−6.75	−8.67	7.09	10.41	0	0	3	0	1	4.4

EXHIBIT 10 *(concluded)*

Company	5yr SD ROE/ (P/BV)	Sales % Chg Index	Earns Stab. Index	(LTGR + DY)/ (P/BV)	5yr SD RIR/ (P/FBV)	Ranked Fundamental Criteria: 5yr SD ROE/ (P/BV)	Sales % Chg Index	Earns Stab. Index	(LTGR + DY)/ (P/BV)	5yr SD RIR/ (P/FBV)	Total
S&P 400	8.96			5.84	4.71	−1	0	0	−1	−4	−6.6
TELEX CORP	9.90	−17.00	−70.50	6.89	18.33	0	−2	−4	0	4	1.2
THOMPSON MED INC	17.46	−67.25	−18.50	5.59	18.06	4	−4	0	−2	4	4.2
THOUSAND TRAILS	13.86	−23.00	−33.50	9.46	17.33	2	−3	−3	2	4	3.7
THRIFTY CORP	7.90	−0.50	−7.17	6.17	7.05	−2	2	3	−1	−2	−1.0
TOKHEIM CORP	8.97	−38.25	−16.33	7.23	8.47	0	−4	0	0	0	−2.4
TRACOR INC	7.34	−11.75	−6.00	7.46	8.53	−2	−1	3	0	0	0.5
TRANSTECHNOLOGY	13.64	−28.25	−16.50	10.11	8.33	2	−4	0	2	0	2.0
TRIANGLE MICROWAVE	12.11	43.75	−72.00	8.53	20.52	2	4	−4	1	4	5.7
TYCO LABS INC	11.50	−20.75	−22.67	7.27	9.68	1	−3	−1	0	1	−0.7
TYLER CORP	10.73	−23.00	−32.83	13.83	6.16	1	−3	−3	4	−3	−2.9
UNITED BANCORP ARIZ	9.69	28.25	−9.50	6.54	9.47	0	4	2	−1	0	3.5
UNITED STATIONERS	5.31	−22.25	−12.50	3.25	12.55	−4	−3	1	−4	3.5	−6.2
UNIVERSAL FOODS	10.70	7.50	−22.67	8.09	5.51	0	3	−1	0	−3	−2.6
UNIVERSAL LEAF	14.13	46.00	−1.00	9.98	7.40	3	4	4	2	−2	10.1
VARLEN CORP	15.60	−25.00	−15.33	8.30	7.07	3	−3	0	0	−2	−0.7
VEECO INSTRS INC	7.57	−2.95	−18.83	8.31	8.87	−2	1	0	0	0	−1.6
VELCRO INDS N V	9.45	−16.50	−5.67	2.98	10.41	0	−2	3	−4	1	−1.2
VERNITRON CORP	13.37	−5.75	−12.17	10.15	6.27	2	0	1	2	−3.5	2.2
VICON INDS INC	9.71	2.75	−30.67	12.46	7.61	0	2	−2	3	−1	1.2
WALBAR INC	8.87	−8.75	−20.00	5.55	10.91	−1	0	−1	−2	3	−2.2
WALLACE COMPUTER	6.26	−4.00	−4.50	4.09	8.86	−4	1	4	−3	0	−2.7
WENDY'S INTL INC	6.76	−16.75	−8.33	3.67	10.74	−3	−2	3	−4	2	−3.4
WINDMERE CORP	16.14	−10.25	−13.67	13.70	10.89	4	0	1	4	2	12.1
WORTHINGTON INDS	8.42	−17.25	−15.17	7.09	8.46	−1	−2	0	0	0	−2.3
XL/DATACOMP	17.92	46.00	N/A	6.93	28.24	4	4	0	0	4	11.3
ZERO CO	7.22	−3.25	−5.17	5.97	9.80	−3	1	4	−1	1	1.7

EXHIBIT 11 William O'Neil Service

86	C 3 INC	(CEE)	NYSE COMPUTER-MINI/MICRO	9,590 SHARES	6.234 FLOAT AVG % OWNED	$29,850 RESTON, VA.	INC 1968

EARNINGS SCALE PRICE = 20 × EPS

BUSINESS:
DESIGNS/ASSEMBLES/MARKETS MINICOMPUTER AND IBM PLUS COMPATIBLE COMPUTER SYSTEMS PRIMARILY SOLD TO DEPT. OF DEFENSE (ABOUT 70% OF SALES) AND NON-DEFENSE AGENCIES AND COMMERCIAL MARKET. COMPANY'S PRODUCTS ARE USED AS COMMUNICATIONS FRONT-END PROCESSORS TO LARGE MAINFRAME COMPUTERS, AS MESSAGE STORE-AND-FORWARD SYSTEMS, AS DATA SECURITY SYSTEMS, ETC. SYSTEM PRICES RANGE FROM $10,000 TO IN EXCESS OF $1 MIL. ($250,000 AVERAGE).
3 84 RECEIVED $09.3 MIL CONTRACT TO SUPPLY MINICOMPUTER SYSTEMS TO U.S. NAVY. 3 84 ATLANTIC RESEARCH CORP SOLD ITS 4% INTEREST IN COMPANY FOR $3.5 MIL.

EARNINGS DUE 5 25 85 × - DIV N A SALES 68 MIL 9.38 (011 - 60%)

LAST QTR EARNINGS RANK 87

PRICE SCALE

		1976	1977	1978	1979	1980	1981	1982	1983	1984	1985 ESTIMATE	1986 ESTIMATE
A	EARNINGS (MAR. 1)	0.04	0.07	0.16	0.26	0.35	0.86	0.98	1.05	0.47	0.50 + 8%	0.50 + 0%
N	PRETAX MARGIN, %	19.0	19.3	27.6	32.0	33.1	30.2	33.5	26.2	12.1	EARNING GROWTH RATE STABILITY RANK	
N	RET. ON EQUITY, %	30.5	29.6	42.0	42.6	38.3	26.5	24.3	20.5	7.3	1980-84 + 1%	1101 00
U	SALES & CHANGE		+ 77	+ 87	+ 44	+ 33	+ 132	+ 50	+ 29	- 2	1978-82 + 53%	1141 05
A	# DAYS INVENTORY										1976-80 + 77%	1161 09
L	EMPLOYEE % CHANGE					+ 4	+ 8	+ 79	+ 81	+ 7	INVENTORY TURNOVER N A	
W	DATAGRAPH RATING	40	51	70	68	62	62	56	49	51	DEBT % 1902-84	3% 3% 3%
E	AVG DAILY VOLUME	21600	29600	31900	31900	23700	25200	23600	23500	24000	TAX RATE 02-84	48.6% 49.7% N A
E	UP DOWN VOLUME	2.9	3.5	3.3	3.2	2.4	2.5	2.4	2.3	1.8	BACKLOG 02-84	N A N A N A
K	BLOCK TRADES	0.6	1.4	1.3	1.2	0.9	1.4	1.3	1.3	1.1	R&D N A	1.27 × 84 BK. VAL.
L	RELATIVE STRENGTH	63	77	87	70	60	70	49	23	13	ALPHA - 0.28	DIV. NONE
Y	GROUP RANK	137	54	31	41	55	60	78	32	15	BETA 1.95 (21)	DIV GR RT N A

12/84 PENN CENTRAL CORP RAISED STAKE IN COMPANY TO 10% FROM 0% HELD 7/84 AS INVESTMENT.

7/84 RCVD $73 MIL. CONTRACT TO SUPPLY U.S. GENL SVCS ADMINISTRATION WITH AUTOMATION EQUIP.

5/84 JUSTICE DEPT. SUED CO FOR $7.4 MIL. FOR ALLEGED OVERBILLING PRACTICES FOR ARMY EQUIP.

3.50 3.00 2.50 2.40 2.30 2.20 2.10 2.00 1.90 1.80 1.70 1.60 1.50 1.40 1.30 1.20 1.10 1.00 0.95 0.90 0.85 0.80 0.75 0.70 0.65 0.60 0.55 0.50 0.45 0.40 0.35 0.30 0.25 0.24 0.23 0.22 0.21 0.20 0.19

2/1 1 + 5K 2 + 2K 3 θ 88K 2 θ 158K 1 + 2K NYSE 1 θ 1K 2 θ 6K PPO PO PO 12 MO. 8 MO WPT 5/28/84 1 1K 26% RS 13

PRICE '70-80

PE '70-80'

OPTIONS NONE

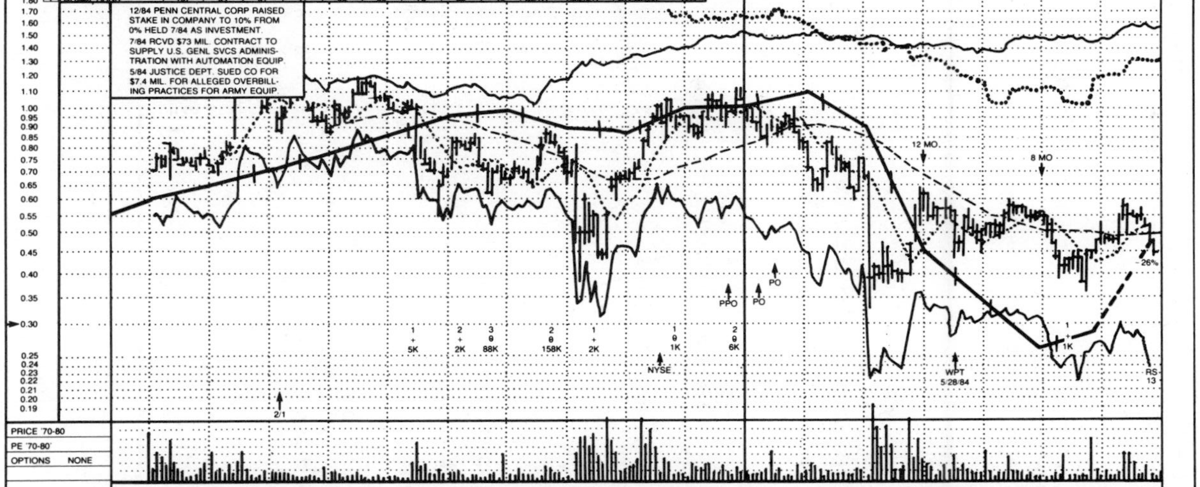

SALES (MIL $1)		10.1	10.6	11.3	13.2	13.5	12.2	10.4	17.1	22.8	16.6	16.5	12.8	15.2	15.6	18.3	19.7	
% CHANGE		+ 63%	+ 56%	+ 57%	+ 57%	+ 34%	+ 15%	- 8%	+ 30%	+ 69%	+ 36%	+ 59%	25%	33%	6%	+ 11%	+ 54%	
EARNINGS/SHR ($)		.18	.21	.23	.26	.28	.25	.13	.25	.42	.26	.22	.05	.06	.15	.13	.00	
% CHANGE		+ 38%	+ 40%	+ 44%	+ 53%	+ 58%	+ 19%	+ 43%	41%	+ 50%	+ 4%	+ 89%	80%	N A	42%	41%	+ 60%	
MARGIN AFTER TAX		15.8%	17.0%	17.7%	16.7%	17.8%	17.0%	10.6%	12.5%	15.8%	13.9%	12.1%	3.4%	2.8%	9.0%	7.1%	3.8%	
PF LOW-HIGH	N A	23-26	20-32	22-31	21-27	13-21	12-16	14-19	40-17	13-21	17-22	14-17	14-18	17-30	27-33	38-44	26-38	
FUNDS/SHARES (000)		12 245	9 333	10 829	11 835	12 879	10 768	10 887	5 369	7 364	8 381	10 691	8 598	3 158	3 129	2 180	1 80	
AS OF 12/31/84		MAR	JUN	SEP	DEC 81	MAR	JUN	SEP	DEC 82	MAR	JUN	SEP	DEC 83	MAR	JUN	SEP	DEC 81	MAR

2 MUTUAL FUNDS OWNED 180,000 (3%)	6 ADVISORS 566,300 UNDER MANAGEMENT	8 BANKS 922,052 (15%)	3 INSURANCE CO. 839,300
AMR EO 100,000N SAFCOGR 80,000	MANUFHA 475,000N BOST CO 50,000N MITCHEL 18,200N EBRSING 3,000N FROLEY 2,000 CG INV 18,100	NWST NB 11,400N IRVN TR 81,500 + MFR HAN 475,000 IEX COM 234,500 NATL WES 46,200 FCBC TX 32,500 WEL FAR 23,552 AMMA CH 17,400	PRUONTL 627,300 COLGRET 130,000 SAFECO 80,000

EXHIBIT 12

C3, Inc.
Consolidated Balance Sheets

	March 31	
	1984	**1983**
Assets		
Current assets:		
Cash and temporary investments	$ 9,541,000	$ 7,266,000
Accounts receivable	27,188,000	25,765,000
Current portion of net investment in sales-type leases	15,503,000	14,374,000
Inventories	22,446,000	13,678,000
Prepaid expenses	185,000	107,000
Total current assets	74,863,000	61,190,000
Net investment in sales-type leases, net of current portion	4,149,000	5,312,000
Property, plant and equipment, net of accumulated depreciation	10,414,000	9,214,000
Other assets	1,281,000	
	$90,707,000	$75,716,000
Liabilities and Stockholders' Equity		
Current liabilities:		
Current portion of long-term debt	$ 1,304,000	$ 196,000
Accounts payable	7,219,000	11,136,000
Other current liabilities	1,672,000	1,965,000
Income taxes payable:		
Current		3,441,000
Deferred	6,136,000	7,354,000
Total current liabilities	16,331,000	24,092,000
Long-term debt, net of current portion	1,825,000	1,676,000
Deferred income taxes	1,918,000	2,049,000
Stockholders' equity:		
Common stock, $.01 par, authorized 25,000,000 shares, issued and outstanding 9,569,902 shares, 1984, 8,413,663 shares, 1983	96,000	84,000
Capital in excess of par	39,662,000	21,216,000
Retained earnings	30,875,000	26,599,000
	70,633,000	47,899,000
	$90,707,000	$75,716,000

EXHIBIT 13

Tyco Laboratories, Inc.
Consolidated Statement of Income
Years ended May 31
(in thousands of dollars except per share data)

	1985	1984	1983	1982	1981
Revenue:					
Sales	$673,932	$650,064	$573,930	$552,160	$360,873
Gain (loss) from sale or exchange of investments and other assets	650	(1,660)	4,319	5,200	864
Equity accounting	—	—	334	358	(2,295)
Interest	1,877	1,084	3,020	5,993	7,875
Dividends	—	4,694	6,033	4,216	805
Other	2,041	(138)	(1,410)	2,254	1,420
Total	$678,500	$654,044	$586,226	$570,181	$369,542
Costs and expenses:					
Cost of sales	$525,935	$513,056	$451,958	$434,304	$267,851
Selling, general and administrative	89,142	85,288	86,697	79,695	54,250
Interest	2,797	6,883	14,898	18,935	2,729
Total	$617,874	$605,227	$553,553	$532,934	$324,830
Income before income taxes	$ 60,626	$ 48,817	$ 32,673	$ 37,247	$ 44,712
Income taxes	25,521	18,722	11,198	14,047	22,193
Net income	$ 35,105	$ 30,095	$ 21,475	$ 23,200	$ 22,519
Net income per share:					
Primary	$3.73	$3.22	$2.47	$2.56	$2.69
Fully diluted	$3.73	$2.97	$2.16	$2.22	$2.17
Common equivalent shares (in thousands)	9,420	9,360	8,700	9,080	8,380
Cash dividends per common share	$ .775	$ .70	$ .70	$ .70	$ .60

EXHIBIT 13 *(continued)*

	1985	1984
Assets		
Current assets:		
Cash	$ 5,131	$ 14,407
Investments	22,197	10,646
Receivables, less allowance for doubtful accounts of $3,970 in 1985 and $2,870 in 1984	96,020	102,101
Insurance claim receivable	9,766	—
Contracts in process	9,894	8,497
Inventories	67,076	91,836
Prepaid expenses	2,295	1,712
Total	$212,479	$229,199
Property and equipment:		
Land	$ 3,366	$ 4,759
Buildings	44,625	53,243
Machinery and equipment	133,813	137,470
Leasehold improvements	3,699	3,517
Construction in progress	3,544	2,731
Accumulated depreciation	(71,398)	(59,330)
Total	$117,649	$142,390
Cost in excess of net assets of acquired companies	$ 7,943	$ 8,155
Other assets	7,603	7,195
	$345,674	$386,939

EXHIBIT 13 *(concluded)*

	1985	1984
Liabilities and Shareholders' Equity		
Current liabilities:		
Loans payable and current maturities of long-term debt	$ 1,630	$ 1,922
Accounts payable	36,585	41,656
Accrued expenses	37,597	39,631
Contracts in process—billings in excess of costs	5,694	5,386
Income taxes	11,489	19,476
Deferred income taxes	13,274	13,432
Other	9,167	8,179
Total	$115,536	$129,682
Deferred income taxes noncurrent	$ 21,800	$ 13,923
Long-term debt:		
Loans payable	—	$ 36,000
Industrial revenue bonds and other	$ 15,798	18,702
Total	$ 15,798	$ 54,702
Deferred subordinated earn-out liability	—	4,049
Shareholders' equity:		
Preferred stock, $1 par value, authorized 2,000,000 shares; none outstanding	—	—
Common stock, $.50 par value, authorized 30,000,000 shares; outstanding 9,620,397 shares in 1985 and 10,247,311 shares in 1984, net of reacquired shares of 2,222,386 in 1985 and 1,578,286 in 1984	$ 4,810	$ 5,123
Capital in excess of par value, net of deferred compensation of $21,337 in 1985 and $22,504 in 1984	22,189	41,198
Retained earnings	165,541	138,262
	192,540	184,583
	$345,674	$386,939

EXHIBIT 14

Veeco Instruments Inc. and Subsidiaries
Consolidated Statements of Income
Years ended September 30
(dollars in thousands, except for per share amounts)

	1984	1983	1982
Net sales	$158,010	$122,132	$114,345
Cost of sales	83,895	66,630	64,683
Gross profit	74,115	55,502	49,662
Research and development expense	8,889	6,228	5,656
Selling and administrative expense	35,312	28,675	25,983
Interest expense	1,836	1,584	1,635
Other (income)/expense—net	(158)	(980)	18
	45,879	35,507	33,292
Income before taxes and minority interest	28,236	19,995	16,370
Provision for income taxes	12,214	8.860	7,355
Income before minority interest	16,022	11,135	9,015
Minority interest in net income of subsidiary	(1,447)	(1,077)	(493)
Net income	$ 14,575	$ 10,058	$ 8,522
Net income per share	$1.52	$1.05	$ .89
Dividends per share	$ .32	$ .22	$ .20

EXHIBIT 15

Veeco Instruments Inc. and Subsidiaries
Consolidated Balance Sheets
Years ended September 30
(dollars in thousands)

	1984	1983
Assets		
Current assets:		
Cash and certificates of deposit	$ 9,425	$ 14,976
Trade notes and accounts receivable, less allowance for uncollectibles—$908 and $800	39,280	27,743
Inventories	49,628	35,145
Prepaid expenses and other current assets	4,719	2,407
Total current assets	103,052	80,271
Other assets	594	560
Property, plant and equipment—at cost, less accumulated depreciation and amortization	26,982	23,349
Excess of cost of investment over net assets of businesses acquired	3,310	2,771
	$133,938	$106,951
Liabilities and Shareholders' Equity		
Current liabilities:		
Notes payable—banks	$ 3,116	$ 1,171
Trade notes and accounts payable	18,843	11,829
Accrued expenses and sundry liabilities	10,392	6,867
Federal, foreign and local income taxes	3,846	2,788
Current installment of long-term debt	1,288	1,669
Total current liabilities	37,485	24,324
Long-term debt	11,135	9,326
Deferred taxes	2,227	1,473
Other liabilities	1,464	1,037
Minority interest in subsidiary	3,171	2,758
Shareholders' equity		
Preferred stock—par value $1 per share:		
Authorized—500,000 shares		
Issued and outstanding—none		
Common stock—par value $1 per share:		
Authorized—20,000,000 shares		
Issued and outstanding—9,617,889 and 9,615,489 shares	9,618	9,615
Paid-in capital	243	227
Retained earnings	71,339	59,841
Equity adjustment from translation	(2,662)	(1,650)
Treasury stock—at cost—4,300 shares	(82)	
Total shareholders' equity	78,456	68,033
	$133,938	$106,951

Appendix A

SUPPLEMENTARY DATA

EXHIBIT A–1
"Small Cap" Attractiveness Ratings by Sector *(5/3/85)*

	+	0/+	0	0/−	−	Raw score
Consumer nondurables	0.0	36.5	38.5	23.1	1.9	9.6
Consumer durables	0.0	33.3	25.0	33.0	8.3	− 16.6
Technology	6.9	6.9	37.9	37.9	10.3	− 37.8
Basic industry	0.0	20.0	40.0	32.0	8.0	− 28.0
Transportation	12.5	25.0	25.0	37.5	0.0	12.5
Energy	0.0	0.0	0.0	60.0	40.0	− 140.0
Interest - sensitive (excluding public utilities)	20.8	16.7	16.7	33.3	12.5	0.0

EXHIBIT A–2
Worksheet *(5/3/85)*

CONSUMER NONDURABLE

ACU	0/–
AGNC	0
AGN	0
BCF	0/+
BIND	0/+
BIV	0
BJ	0/–
CARL	0/–
CDU	0
DF	0/+
DOYL	0
DPX	0/+
DUNK	0/+
EBS	–
EYE	0/+
FLO	0
GCN	0
GEB	0/+
HUN	0/+
IPG	0/+
JFRY	0/–
JOS	0/+
KRUE	0
LDG	0/+
LINB	0/+
LUR	0
MDVP	0
NEI	0
NCS	0/–
NOXLB	0/+
NSI	0
OGIL	0
OSHM	0
PDQ	0/+
PPSI	0
QPON	0/–
SBO	0
SGL	0/+
SHC	0/–
SHGO	0
SHOS	0/+
SOA	0/+
SWIX	0/+
TFD	0/–
TM	0/–
TRLS	0/–
UFC	0
USTR	0/–
UVV	0
VELCF	0/–
WCS	0
WEN	0/+

+	0/+	0	0/–	–
0	19	20	12	1
	36.5	38.5	23.1	1.9

CONSUMER DURABLE

BDG	0/+
FIT	0/+
FMO	0/–
GFD	0/–
LIZC	0/+
MAGAF	–
RML	0
RTS	0
SBRU	0/+
TBCC	0
TFX	0/–
WDMR	0/–

+	0/+	0	0/–	–
0	4	-3	4	1
	33.3	25.0	33.3	8.3

BASIC INDUSTRY

BAS	0
APR	–
CLRK	0
CRI	0/–
CTAS	0/+
ESX	0/+
GRC	0/–
HUBB	0/+
KAMNA	0/+
KII	0/–
LAW	0/–
LRI	0
MLHR	0
NEW	0/–
NUE	0
PER	0
PNTA	0/+
QCHM	0/–
RBC	0/–
SCX	0
SONO	0
TOK	0
TYL	–
VRLN	0/–
WTHG	0

+	0/+	0	0/–	–
0	5	10	8	2
	20.0	40.0	32.0	8.0

TECHNOLOGY

AYD	0/–
BI	0/–
CEE	0
CSC	0
DDL	0/–
DYTC	0/+
FEN	0/–
FKM	0/–
INC	+
KOL	–
MTSC	0
ORBT	0
PCST	0/+
PTNX	0/–
REUT	0
SCIE	0/–
SEE	0/–
SPA	–
TC	0
TRMW	0
TRR	0
TT	0
TYC	0
VEE	–
VII	0/–
VRN	0/–
WBR	0
XLDC	+
ZRO	0/–

+	0/+	0	0/–	–
2	2	11	11	3
6.9	6.9	37.9	37.9	10.3

ENERGY

PTCO	–
RDC	0/–
SERF	–
SSFT	0/–
TMI	0/–

+	0/+	0	0/–	–
0	0	0	3	2
			60.0	40.0

TRANSPORTATION

ALK	+
ARWS	0/+
BTL	0/–
HARG	0
LYND	0/+
OSG	0/–
OVT	0/–
PIE	0

+	0/+	0	0/–	–
1	2	2	3	0
12.5	25.0	25.0	37.5	

INTEREST-SENSITIVE

JEFG	0/+
AFGN	0
AGE	0/–
APOG	–
BNHI	+
COLC	0/+
FBC	0/+
FEXC	0
FLXS	–
FUNC	+
GTAC	0
HDON	0/–
IAL	0/–
KBALB	0/–
LDBC	–
LIBH	0/–
MIDL	+
OMH	0/–
OMT	0/–
PHL	0/–
PSNB	+
RNB	0/+
RYL	0
UBAZ	+

+	0/+	0	0/–	–
5	4	4	8	3
20.8	16.7	16.7	33.3	12.5

EXHIBIT A–3
"Small Cap" Universe Rankings *(10/5/84)*

+	0/+	0		0/–		–
BNHI^{-} ↑	BIND	AFGN	PCT	ARWS	LINB^{+} ↓	ACU^{+}
FBC	CTAS	ALK	PNTA	ASN	LUR ↓	BJ
FUNC	DDL	APR	PHL^{+}	APOG	MEI	DFDI
RNB^{-}	DPX	BDG	PIE	AYD	MMO	JFRY
SCIE	ESX^{-}	BTL	PRY	BI^{+}	PTCO	KII
SBRU	FEN^{-}	CEE	PNC	BIV ↓	QCHM^{-}	KOL
UBAZ^{-}	FLO ↑	CLRK^{-}	PER	BDC^{+}	RBC	OSHM^{+} ↓
	GCN	COLC^{+}	PDQ^{+} ↓	CDU^{-}	RTO?	PPSI ↓
	HUBB^{-}	CSC	REWT	EBS	RYL ↓	SBO^{+} ↓
	H&J	CRI	RML^{-}	FIT ↓	SERF	TM^{+}
	INC	DF	SSFT^{-} ↑	FMO	S&P400^{+}	
	KGC	DOYL^{-} ↑	SOA	FEXG^{+} ↓	SHC	
	KG2C	DUNK ↓	SEE	FLXS	SPA	
	LICC ↓	ACE	QPON	FKM	TBCC ↓	
	MIDL ↑	GRC^{-}	SEX	GEB^{+} ↓	TMI^{-} ↑	
	MLNR	HDON	SGL^{+} ↓	GFD	TRN	
	NCS^{+}	JAL^{-}	TXI	HVU	VEE^{+} ↓	
	NSI	JOS	TFD	IPG^{+} ↓	VRN	
	NOXLB	KARNK^{-}	TRR ↓	CARL	VII^{+} ↓	
	OMN	LRI	TYL	LAW	UDG^{-}	
	OGIL	LIBH	USTR^{+} ↓			
	OVT	LDG	UFC			
	PCST	LYND	UVV^{+} ↓			
	PSNB^{+}	MKP^{+} ↓	VRLN			
	RDC	MARS	WCS^{+}			
	SHGO	MDP ↓	WDMR			
	SONO	MTSC	ZRO			
	TRLS	NEW^{-} ↑	PTNX^{-}			
	TOK	NUE	WBR^{+}			
	TYC	OMT				
	VELCF	OSG				
	WEN^{-}					
	WTHG^{-} ↑					

+ = Near upper 6 boundary.
– = Near lower 6 boundary.

EXHIBIT A–4
Sector Attractiveness *(10/5/84)*

Rating	+	0/+	0	0/–	–
Percent in rating	4	24	36	32	4

EXHIBIT A–5

Research Universe Rating Distribution *(9/21/84)*

			— O'NEIL —					
		FUNDAMENTAL	DATAGRAPH	RELATIVE STRENGTH	FLO/CAP	QAS	COMPUTIME	WEIGHTED TOTAL
S&P 400		(9)	0		– 0/ +	0/ – 0/ +	– 0/ +	(55)
A F G INDS		0						
ACME UNITED CORP	ACU	0↑	–	–	–		– 0/ –	(13)
AIR WIS SVCS INC	ARWS	18	–	–	–			(9.5)
ALASKA AIRLS INC	ALK	3↓	0/ –	0↑	0/ –	–		(0.3)
ALCO STD CORP	ASN	7	0/ –	–	–	– 0/ – ↓	– –	(88)
AMERICAN PRECISION IND	APR	(7)	0/ +	+	0/ +		– 0	0.5
APOGEE ENTERPRISES	APOG	2	–	0/ –	0/ –			(7)
AYDIN CORP	AYD	4↓	0/ –	–	–	– 0/ –	0/0	6.5
BANCORP HAWAII	BNHI	16	0/ –	0/ + ↑	0/ +			13
BANDAG INC	BDG	(8)	0/ +	0/ +	+		0	2.2
BELL INDS INC	BI	(1)↓↓	0↓	–	√0/ – ↓(2) –			(5.0)
BIG V SUPERMARKETS INC	BIV	6↑	– ↓	– ↓	0/ – ↓↓			(8.0)
BINDLEY WESTERN	BIND	3	0/ +	+	0/ +			11.5
BLAIR JOHN & CO	BJ	(2)	0/ – ↓	–	–	– – ↑	– –	(13.2)
BURNDY CORP	BDC	(1)↓↓	–	–	0/ + ↑↑	– 0 –		(5.5)
BUTLER INTL INC	BTL	2↑	– ↓	0/ – ↓	+	– ↑ –	– 01 – ↓	(1)
C 3 INC	CEE	(1)	–	0/ –	0/ +	not rated	+ 0/ +	(0.5)
CINTAS CORP	CTAS	(5)↓↓	0/ +	+	0/ +			7.5
CLARK J L MFG CO	CLRK	(4)	0	0↓	0/ – ↓			(4)
COLO NATL BANKSHARE	COLC	8	0↑	0/ +	0/ –			4
COMPUTER SCIENCES CORP	CSC	2↓↓	0/ –	0/ –	+	– –	–	2.2
CORDURA CORP	CDU	(2)	0/ –	0/ – ↑	–	– – ↓	– 0	(11)
CORE INDS INC	CRI	1↓	0/ – ↓	0/ –	0/ – ↓	– –	0	(2.9)
DATA DESIGN LABS	DDES	8	0	0	+			10
DEAN FOODS CO	DF	(5)↑	0/ +	0/ +	+ ↑		√00/ – ↓	1
DIVERSIFOODS INC	DFDI	(3)↓↓	–	–	–			(15.5)
DOYLE DANE BERNBACH INT	DOYL	(3)	0/ + ↑↑		0/ –	0/ –		(4.5)
DUNKIN' DONUTS	DUNK	(1)↓	0/ +	0/ + ↑	0/ +			2.5
DUPLEX PRODS INC	DPX	(1)↓↓	0/ +	0/ +	+		+ 0↓	8.5
EDISON BROS STORES INC	EBS	0↓	– ↓	0/ –	0/ – ↑			(7.2)
EDWARDS A G INC	AGE	(3)↑↑	0/ +	0/ +	0/ +		+ +	4
ESSEX CHEM CORP	ESX	0	0/ +	0/ +	0/ +			5.4
FAB INDS INC	FIT	8	– ↓	0/ – ↓	–		– –	(8)
FAIRCHILD INDS INC	FEN	6	0/ +	0	0/ +			5.5

EXHIBIT A–5 *(continued)*

		— O'NEIL — FUNDA-MENTAL	DATA-GRAPH	RELATIVE STRENGTH	FLO/CAP	QAS	COMPU-TIME	WEIGHTED TOTAL
S&P 400								
FEDERAL-MOGUL	FMD	1↑	0/−↓	0/−↓	0/−	00/−	0/+0/+	(29)
FIRST BOSTON INC	FBC	8	0/+	+	0/+	0/+0/+	− +	14
FIRST EXECUTIVE CORPS	FEXC	10	−↓	−	−	− +		(5)
FIRST UNION CORP	FUNC	9	0/+	+	0/+	0/−0/+		13.5
FLEXSTEEL INDS INC	FLXS	(1)	−	−	−	− +		(10.5)
FLOWERS INDS INC	FLO	(8)	0/+	+	+		0/+0/+	6.8
FLUKE JOHN MFG INC	FKM	(6)	0↓	0/−	0/−			(9.8)
GENERAL CINEMA CORP	GCN	(1)	0/+	+	0/+		− 0	6.5
GERBER PRODUCTS CO	GEB	(2)↑↑	0/−↓↓	0/−↓	0/+		√	(5)
GORMAN RUPP CO	GRC	(6)	0/+	0/+	0/−			(4.5)
GUILFORD MLS INC	GFD	4↑	0/−	−	−	− −	− 0/−	(10.2)
HARPER GROUP	HARG	2	0/+	0/+↓	+	0+↑0−↓		10
HENREDON FURNITURE	HDON	(1)	0↓	0/−↓	+	↓		0.5
HOOVER UNVL INC	HVU	(11)	0/−	0	0/+		−	(7.3)
HUBBELL HARVEY INC B	HUBB	(1)	0/+	0/+	0/+↓			5.0
HUNT MFG CO	HUN	(6)↓↓	0/+	+	+		0/+0/+↑	8
INTL ALUM CORP	IAL	1	0/−↓↓	0/−↓	0/−		00	4.3
INTL CTLS CORP	INC	9	0/+	0/+	√0/+			6.5
INTERPUBLIC GRP COS I	IPG	(9)	0/+	× 0/−↓				(5.0)
JEFFREY MARTIN INC	JFRY	(2)	−	−	−			(15)
JOSTEMS INC	JOS	4	0/−	0	+			3.2
KAMAN CORP	KAMNA	(1)↓	0↓	0	0/−			(4.5)
KARCHER CARL ENTR	CARL	2	0/−	−↓	0/−			(9)
KEYSTONE INTL INC	KII	(9)↕	−	0/−	−	0/−0/−	− −	(15.5)
KIMBALL INTL INC	KBALB	(6)↓	0↓	+	+			5
KOLLMORGEN CORP	KOL	(2)	0/−↓	−	−	− −	− −	(14)
KRUEGER W A CO	KRUE	(6)↑	0/+	+	+	0/+0/+		8
LAWTER INC	LAW	(10)	−	0/−↓	+	0/− −		(8.5)
LEARONAL	LRI	1↑↑	−	0/−	√0/+	0		(2.3)
LIBERTY HOMES INC	LIBH	3↓	−	0/−	0/+			(0.5)
LIN BROADCASTING CORP	LINB	2↑↑↑	0/−↓↓	0/−↓↓	0/−↓	00/−		(5)
LIZ CLAIBORNE	LIZC	(2)	+	+	0/+↓			10
LONGS DRUG STORES INC	LDG	1	0/+	0	0/+	0−		3.0

EXHIBIT A–5 *(continued)*

			— O'NEIL —					
		FUNDA-MENTAL	DATA-GRAPH	RELATIVE STRENGTH	FLO/CAP	QAS	COMPU-TIME	WEIGHTED TOTAL
S&P 400								
LURIA & SON	LUR	3	0/−	−↓	−↓		0 0	(7.5)
LYNDEN INC	LYND	5	0/−	0/−	0/+			1.5
MARK PRODUCTS	MKP	3↓	0/+	0↓	0/+		0 0	4.5
MARSH SUPERMARKETS INC	MARS	(8)↓↓	0↑	0↑	0/+↑↑			(1)
MEI CORP	MEI	(6)↓	0/+↓↓	0↑	0/−↑			(5.8)
MEREDITH CORP	MOP	1↑	0/+	0/−	0/+↓↓↓(8)			2.3
MIDLANTIC BKS INC	MIDL	8↑	0/−↓	+↑	0/−			6
MILLER HERMAN INC	MLHR	(5)	0/+	+	+			7.5
MONARCH MACH TOOL CO	MMO	7	0/−	−	0/−↑			(7.3)
MTS SYS CORP	MTSC	(2)↑↑	0/+	0	0/−↓↓			(3)
NATL CONVENIENCE ST	NCS	(1)↓	0/+	+	+		+ +	11
NATIONAL SVC INDS	NSI	2	0/+	0/+↓	0/+	0/+0/+		9
NEWCOR	NEW	3↑↑	−	0/−	0/−			(3.5)
NOXELL CORP	NOXLB	(10)	0/+	+	+			6
NUCOR CORP	NUE	4	0/+	0/−	0/+			2.2
OAKWOOD HOMES CORP	OMH	(1)↓↓	0↓	+	+		0	8.5
OGILVY & MATHER INTL	OGIL	(7)	+	+	0/+	+ +		8.5
OHIO MATTRESS	OMT	(3)↑↑↑↑	0/−	0/+	+		− 0	(0.3)
OSHMANS SPORTING GOODS	OSHM	(3)↓	−	−	0/−	−		(12.5)
OVERNITE TRANSN CO	OVT	(3)	0/+	0/+	+	0/− −	+ 0/+	6.3
OVERSEAS SHIPHOLDING GR	OSG	9	−	0/−	0/+↑		0/− 0	1.7
PACO PHARMACEUTICAL	PPSI	(1)↑	0/−	−	−↓			(13.5)
PAPERCRAFT CORP	PCT	(3)	0/−	0/+	0/+↓			2
PENTAIR CORP	PNTA	3	0/+	0/+	0/−			15
PETROLEUM EQUIP TOOLS C	PTCO	10↓	−	−	√−			(8)
PHILIPS INDS INC	PHL	(2)	0/−	0/+	+		0 0	4
PIEDMONT AVIATION INC	PIE	2	0/+	0/−	0/−			(1.8)
PITTWAY CORP	PRY	0	0/+↑	0/+	0/−	0/+0/+		2.5
PNEUMO CORP	PNC	(5)↑↑↑	0/+	+	0/+		− 0/−	1.5
POPE EVANS ROBBINS IN	PER	1	0/−↓	−	√0/+			(2.5)
PRECISION CASTPARTS	PCST	(5)↓	+	+	0/+			8.5
PRIME MOTOR INNS INC	PDQ	(2)	0	0/+↓	0/+			4
PRINTRONIX INC	PTNX	6	0/−	0/−	0/−			(4)

EXHIBIT A–5 *(continued)*

			— O'NEIL —					
		FUNDA-MENTAL	DATA-GRAPH	RELATIVE STRENGTH	FLO/ CAP	QAS	COMPU-TIME	WEIGHTED TOTAL
S&P 400								
PUGET SOUND BANCORP	PSNB	8↓	0/+↑	0/+	+	0 –		12
QUAKER CHEM CORP	QCHM	(4)↓	0	0/–	–			(11)
REGAL BELOIT CORP	RBC	(10)	0↓	0/–	–			(9)
REPUBLIC N Y CORP	RNC	10↓	0	0/+	+		· 0/+	13
REUTER INC	REUT	6	0/+	0	–			(2)
ROWAN COS INC	RDC	7	–	0	0/+	0/– +	+ +	6.7
RUSS TOGS INC	RTS	8	–	–	–		– –	(10)
RUSSELL CORP	RML	4↑	–	–↓	0/–			(3.8)
RYLAND GROUP INC	RYL	(8)	0/–	0↑	0/–↓		– 0	(5.8)
SCIENTIFIC COMPUTERS IN	SCIE	3	0/+	+	+			14.5
SCIENTIFIC SOFTWARE	SSFT	12	0/–↓	–	0/–↑			(4)
SCOA INDS INC	SOA	(1)↑	0/+	0/–	0/+	0/–↑	+ 0	0.5
SEALED AIR CORP	SEE	(11)	0/+↓	0/+	0/+	0/	+0/–↓	(15)
SERVICE FRACTURING CO	SERF	8↑	0/–	–	–			(8)
SEVEN OAKS INTL	QPON	(7)↓↓	0	0	0/+			(0.5)
SHAKLEE CORP	SHC	4	–	–	–	–0/–	0	(9)
SHOP & GO INC	SHGO	(5)↓	0/+	+	+			105
SHOWBOAT INC	SBO	(1)	–	–↓	–		0/+0/–	(125)
SONOCO PRODS	SONO	(6)	0/+	0/+	+			6
SPARTON CORP	SPA	(4)	–	0/–↓	0/–		0 0	(9)
STARRETT L S CO	SCX	(0)↓	0/+	0	+		0/– –↓	2
SUBARU AMER INC	SBRU	8	0/+	+	0/+↓			14
SUPERMARKETS GEN CORP	SGL	(2)	0/+	+	0/+		0/– 0	4.2
TBC CORP	TBCC	6	0/–	0/–	–			(7)
TEAM INC	TMI	(5)	–↓	–	0/–↓			(11.5)
TEXAS INDS INC	TXI	(3)↑	0/+	0↑	0/–	– 0	+ 0/+	(1.3)
THOMPSON MED INC	TM	(4)	0/–	–	–		0/– 0/–	(13)
THOUSAND TRAILS	TRLS	(6)↑↑	0/+	+	0/+			7
THRIFTY CORP	TFD	(10)↓	0/+	0/+↓	+		0	(0.2)
TOKHEIM CORP	TOK	(1)↑	+	0/+↓	+		√ +0/+	10.5
TRACOR INC	TRR	0↓↓	0/+	0/+	× 0/+			3.2
TRINITY INDS INC	TRN	(5)↓	–	0/–	0/–↑			(6.7)
TYCO LABS INC	TYC	(2)↑↑↑	0/+↓	+	0/+	0 0↓	+ +↑	6.8

EXHIBIT A–5 *(concluded)*

			— O'NEIL —					
		FUNDA-MENTAL	DATA-GRAPH	RELATIVE STRENGTH	FLO/ CAP	QAS	COMPU-TIME	WEIGHTED TOTAL
S&P 400								
TYLER CORP	TYL	(1)↓↓	0/+	0/+	0/−	0/−0/+	− −	(25)
UNITED BANCORP ARIZ	UBAZ	12↓↓	0/+	+	0/+	0↓0↓		13
UNITED STATIONERS INC	USTR	(11)	0/+	+	0/+			4.5
UNIVERSAL FOODS CORP	UFC	(3)↓↓	0/−	0/−↑	0/+			(2.5)
UNIVERSAL LEAF TOB INC	UVV	4	0/−↓	0↓	0/+			4
VARLEN CORP	VRLN	2	0/−↓	0/−↓	0/+↓			(2)
VEECO INSTRS INC	VEE	(5)	0/+	0/−↓	0/−	0/−0/−	+ 0/−	(5.3)
VELCRO INDS N V	VELCF	(10)	+	+	+			7
VERNITRON CORP	VRN	1	0/−	−	0/−			6.5
VICON INDS INC	VII	1	0/−	0/−	−		0	(5.5)
WALBAR INC	WBR	0↑↑	0↓	0/+	0/+			4
WALLACE COMPUTER SVCS I	WCS	(6)↓	0/+	0/+	+		+ 0	4
WENDYS INTL INC	WEN	(5)↑	0/+	+	× 0/+		+ 0	5.3
WINDMERE CORP	WDMR	14	0/−	0/−↑	0/−			0
WOODS PETE CORP	WOG	4↑	−	−	−	−	−	(12)
WORTHINGTON INDS INC	WTHG	(3)	0/+	0/+↑	+	−		5.5
ZERO CO	ZRO	(5)	0/+	0	0/+			(3.0)

EXHIBIT A–6
"Small Cap" Research Universe Report 2 (*statistical database* B) *(10/4/86)*

							Ranked Fundamental Criteria					
Company	5yr SD RIR/ (P/E)	5yr SD ROE/ (P/BV)	Sales % Chg Index	Earns Stab. Index	(LTGR + DY)/ (P/BV)	5yr SD RIR/ (P/FBV)	5yr SD ROE/ (P/BV)	Sales % Chg Index	Earns Stab. Index	(LTGR + DY)/ (P/BV)	5yr SD RIR/ (P/FBV)	Total
S&P 400	0.68	9.23			6.06	2.99	−1	0	0	−2	−4	−7
ACME UNITED CORP	1.33	11.08	−7.25	−8.33	7.89	5.28	0	−3	3	0	0	0
AFG INDUSTRIES	2.40	10.62	11.25	−99.00	6.93	8.72	0	1	−4	0	3	0
AIR WIS SVCS INC	1.55	15.88	31.50	−17.50	11.76	9.08	3	4	0	3	3	13
ALASKA AIRLS INC	2.54	17.46	5.50	−72.17	7.38	11.54	3	0	−4	0	4	3
ALCO STD CORP	1.22	12.05	4.75	−3.67	10.19	4.97	1	0	4	2	0	7
AMERICAN PRECISION	0.80	6.15	55.00	−17.33	3.26	3.19	−4	4	0	−4	−3	−7
APOGEE ENTERPRISES	1.19	10.08	17.00	−14.67	7.38	5.94	0	2	0	0	0	2
AYDIN CORP	2.91	16.22	−22.25	−18.83	10.54	14.46	3	−4	−1	2	4	4
BANCORP HAWAII	1.99	19.39	17.75	−6.83	13.92	8.82	4	2	3	4	3	16
BANDAG INC	1.39	5.47	1.00	−4.33	2.78	3.16	−4	−1	4	−4	−3	−8
BELL INDS INC	1.43	10.39	−1.00	−13.67	9.69	6.14	0	−2	0	1	0	−1
BIG V SUPERMARKETS	2.04	14.87	−3.00	−17.33	12.40	8.14	3	−2	0	3	2	6
BINDLEY WESTERN IND	2.06	12.75	3.50	−31.00	7.72	11.66	2	0	−3	0	4	3
BLAIR, JOHN, & CO	1.44	9.91	10.50	−24.67	6.59	5.21	0	1	−2	−1	0	−2
BURNDY CORP	0.69	10.37	8.00	−15.30	13.01	3.09	0	0	0	3	−4	−1
BUTLER INTL INC	0.79	10.65	13.25	−15.00	10.79	3.72	0	2	0	2	−2	2
C3 INC	1.26	12.60	−15.75	−31.67	11.41	7.15	1	−4	−3	3	2	−1
CINTAS CORP	1.16	7.02	24.25	−16.00	4.21	5.26	−4	3	0	−4	0	−5
CLARK, J L, MFG CO	1.11	8.93	6.50	−4.83	5.01	3.43	−2	0	4	−3	−3	−4
COLORADO NATL BANK	1.81	16.03	6.75	−9.33	8.78	7.86	3	0	2	1	2	8
COMPUTER SCIENCES	1.37	11.60	−3.25	−16.67	9.24	7.83	1	−2	0	1	2	2
CORDURA CORP	1.75	16.41	12.25	−54.17	5.88	5.65	3	1	−4	−2	0	−2
CORE INDS INC	0.96	10.14	21.50	−13.33	7.14	3.98	0	3	0	0	−2	1
DATA DESIGN LABS	1.10	12.54	16.50	−10.17	10.51	6.25	1	2	2	2	1	6
DEAN FOODS CO	1.18	7.03	4.00	−3.67	3.77	4.00	−3	0	4	−4	−2	−5
DIVERSIFIEDFOODS INC	1.24	8.75	3.75	−15.50	7.44	4.57	−2	0	0	0	−1	−3
DOYLE DANE BERNBACH	0.72	10.29	5.50	−12.00	7.79	2.73	0	0	1	0	−4	−3

DUNKIN' DONUTS	1.32	8.49	1.25	−1.83	6.30	5.25	−2	−1	4	−2	0	−1
DUPLEX PRODS INC	1.24	11.93	8.75	−18.50	6.17	5.86	1	1	−1	−2	0	−1
EDISON BROS STORES	1.31	12.48	8.00	−17.83	7.77	4.88	1	0	−1	0	0	0
EDWARDS A G INC	1.58	13.76	−43.25	−18.67	6.43	6.63	2	−4	−1	−1	1	−3
ESSEX CHEM CORP	1.42	10.21	13.25	−18.83	7.86	4.42	0	2	−1	0	−1	0
FAB INDS INC	2.56	16.35	17.50	−21.17	10.73	9.87	3	2	−2	2	3	8
FAIRCHILD INDS	0.88	17.36	9.75	−35.50	14.95	6.83	3	1	−3	4	1	6
FEDERAL-MOGUL	1.00	10.30	13.75	−20.00	13.58	3.57	0	2	−2	4	−3	1
FIRST BOSTON INC	2.22	19.39	12.50	−79.00	15.58	9.79	4	1	−4	4	3	8
FIRST EXECUTIVE	2.57	18.96	−4.75	−12.67	29.85	15.74	4	−3	1	4	4	10
FIRST UNION CORP	1.97	13.90	24.25	−10.83	9.42	7.48	2	3	1	1	2	9
FLEXSTEEL INDS	1.46	11.56	−9.25	−17.50	8.71	5.26	1	−3	0	1	0	−1
FLOWERS INDS INC	0.85	6.66	5.00	−8.17	5.04	3.02	−4	0	3	−3	−4	−8
FLUKE, JOHN, MFG	1.04	6.36	5.50	−15.17	6.67	4.49	−4	0	0	−1	−1	−6
GENERAL CINEMA	2.32	10.20	−1.25	−8.67	3.38	8.74	0	−2	2	−4	3	−1
GERBER PRODUCTS	0.88	9.19	5.00	−6.00	6.30	3.14	−1	0	3	−1	−3	−2
GORMAN RUPP CO	0.59	8.61	−11.25	−10.17	9.09	2.53	−2	−3	2	1	−4	−6
GUILFORD KLS INC	2.90	18.81	−32.50	−31.17	11.08	11.68	4	−4	−3	3	4	4
HARPER GROUP	1.63	10.82	9.50	−17.00	6.30	7.16	0	1	0	−1	2	2
HENREDON FURNITURE	1.41	10.83	−13.00	−9.67	7.97	5.43	0	−3	2	0	0	−1
HOOVER UNVL INC	1.00	9.18	−30.30	−23.17	8.01	3.02	−1	−4	−2	0	−4	−11
HUBBELL HARVEY, B	0.91	9.53	5.75	−5.83	6.93	3.69	−1	0	3	−1	−2	−1
HUNT KFG CO	0.92	6.72	8.00	−3.50	5.05	3.35	−4	0	4	−3	−3	−6
INTERNATIONAL ALUM	1.31	13.21	−1.50	−20.00	12.39	5.39	2	−2	−2	3	0	1
INTERNATIONAL CTLS	1.70	14.99	39.25	−18.00	7.82	9.46	3	4	−1	0	3	9
INTERPUBLIC GROUP	1.03	8.64	0.00	−13.67	5.79	3.52	−2	−1	0	−3	−3	−9
JEFFREY MARTIN INC	8.65	36.69	−16.25	−26.33	5.33	52.59	4	−4	−3	−3	4	−2
JOSTENS INC	1.20	10.76	15.75	−3.00	6.47	4.21	0	2	4	−1	−1	4
KAMAN CORP	1.28	8.99	−3.25	−5.00	8.14	4.57	−2	−2	4	0	−1	−1
KARCHER, CARL, ENT	1.49	10.30	−8.25	−10.00	8.95	7.42	0	−3	2	1	2	2
KEYSTONE INTL INC	0.84	7.03	10.00	−19.00	5.99	2.86	−3	1	−1	−2	−4	−9
KIMBALL INTL INC	1.00	7.68	2.00	−13.00	6.73	3.80	−3	−1	1	−1	−2	−6
KOLLKORGEN CORP	1.01	7.68	22.25	−13.83	9.10	3.55	−3	3	0	1	−3	−2
KRUEGER, W A, CO	1.37	8.14	16.00	−17.83	5.66	3.98	−2	2	−1	−3	−2	−6
LAWTER INC	0.55	5.87	−0.25	−10.00	5.62	1.02	−4	−1	2	−3	−4	−10
LEARONAL	1.33	9.92	42.75	−13.83	4.41	5.23	0	4	0	−3	0	1
LIBERTY HOMES INC	1.63	13.93	−14.25	−16.33	13.20	7.77	2	−4	0	3	2	3

EXHIBIT A–6 ***(continued)***

Company	5yr SD RIR/ (P/E)	5yr SD ROE/ (P/BV)	Sales % Chg Index	Earns Stab. Index	(LTGR + DY)/ (P/BV)	5yr SD RIR/ (P/FBV)	Ranked Fundamental Criteria: 5yr SD ROE/ (P/BV)	Sales % Chg Index	Earns Stab. Index	(LTGR + DY)/ (P/BV)	5yr SD RIR/ (P/FBV)	Total
S&P 400	0.68	9.23			6.06	2.99	−1	0	0	−2	−4	−7
LIN BROADCASTING	1.21	9.18	10.50	−4.67	5.67	6.85	−1	1	4	−3	1	2
LIZ CLAIBORNE	3.52	8.07	34.25	−21.50	3.08	10.87	−3	4	−2	−4	3	−2
LONGS DRUG STORES	1.10	9.41	1.75	−4.17	7.02	4.22	−1	−1	4	0	−1	1
LURIA & SON	2.34	13.98	−1.75	−13.67	7.69	10.60	2	−2	0	0	3	3
LYNDEN INC	2.89	31.22	−4.75	−50.50	17.80	23.71	4	−3	−4	4	4	5
MARK PRODUCTS INC	1.40	11.74	20.75	−62.50	9.81	6.74	1	3	−4	2	1	3
MARSH SUPERMARKETS	0.44	9.18	−3.50	−35.50	9.51	3.37	−1	−2	−3	1	−3	−8
MEI CORP	1.53	7.78	−7.25	−4.00	3.67	5.24	−3	−3	4	−4	0	−6
MEREDITH CORP	1.24	9.05	9.00	−6.17	6.47	5.16	−2	1	3	−1	0	1
MIDLANTIC BKS INC	1.73	14.80	25.75	−13.33	8.45	5.60	3	3	1	1	0	
MILLER HERMAN INC	1.06	5.52	27.25	−5.67	2.92	3.34	−4	3	3	−4	−3	
MONARCH MACH TOOL	0.54	16.44	63.00	−57.67	17.36	5.79	3	4	−4	4	0	7
MTS SYS CORP	0.89	8.75	4.00	−24.00	12.08	4.41	−2	0	−2	3	−1	−2
NATIONAL CONVENIENCE	0.98	9.12	10.25	−6.83	6.00	3.87	−1	1	3	−2	−2	−1
NATIONAL SVC INDS	1.26	9.80	3.50	−3.83	6.45	4.37	0	0	4	−1	−1	2
NEWCOR INC	1.45	11.32	13.00	−24.83	10.20	6.14	1	2	−2	2	0	3
NOXELL CORP	0.86	5.36	−1.00	−4.50	3.16	2.65	−4	−2	4	−4	−4	−10
NUCOR CORP	1.71	10.38	19.00	−27.67	13.85	6.52	0	2	−3	4	1	4
OAKWOOD HOMES CORP	1.23	8.99	8.50	−9.83	6.51	5.83	−2	0	2	−1	0	−1
OGILVY & MATHER	0.88	6.71	15.00	−7.33	3.42	2.67	−4	2	3	−4	−4	−7
OHIO MATTRESS CO	0.75	7.57	−30.75	−8.67	9.96	2.81	−3	−4	2	2	−4	−7
OSHMAN'S SPORT	1.75	9.54	−8.25	−12.67	8.19	6.04	−1	−3	1	0	0	−3
OVERNITE TRANSN	1.35	9.45	3.00	−9.33	5.22	4.72	−1	0	2	−3	−1	−3
OVERSEAS SHIP	1.54	19.99	−3.75	−14.00	20.38	10.52	4	−2	0	4	3	9
PACO PHARMACEUTICAL	1.50	11.78	−20.25	−32.67	10.20	8.30	1	−4	−3	2	3	−1
PAOERCRAFT CORP	0.67	9.16	8.25	−14.17	10.47	2.81	−1	0	0	2	−4	−3
PENTAIR CORP	1.78	13.00	4.75	−19.00	8.88	6.18	2	0	−1	1	1	3
PETRO EQUIP TOOLS	−0.16	14.10	57.50	−58.00	32.43	10.84	3	4	−4	4	3	10

PHILIPS INDS INC	1.60	9.60	−12.75	−12.83	9.58	4.74	0	−3	1	1	−1	−2
PIEDMONT AVIATION	1.79	13.91	7.50	−47.50	10.69	7.84	2	0	−4	2	2	2
PITTWAY CORP	1.15	11.11	5.75	−14.00	7.39	5.40	0	0	0	0	0	0
PNEUMO CORP	1.50	8.47	−0.75	−11.50	4.67	4.86	−2	−1	1	−3	0	−5
POPE EVANS ROBBINS	3.23	23.43	−12.00	−82.33	8.34	16.26	4	−3	−4	0	4	1
PRECISION CASTPARTS	0.82	5.47	37.25	−17.67	6.25	3.80	−4	4	−1	−2	−2	−5
PRIME MOTORS INNS	1.48	9.99	0.00	−9.50	3.87	6.60	0	−1	2	−4	1	−2
PRINTRONIX INC	1.66	12.72	8.50	−24.83	14.82	8.17	2	0	−2	4	2	
PUGET SOUND BANCORP	1.94	14.50	−0.75	−8.67	12.88	6.92	3	−1	2	3	1	0
QUAKER CHEM CORP	1.29	9.56	−1.75	−15.00	8.16	4.70	−1	−2	0	0	−1	−4
REGAL BELOIT CORP	0.62	7.44	0.00	−22.67	7.75	1.91	−3	−1	−2	0	−4	−10
REPUBLIC N Y CORP	2.20	19.56	25.75	−21.17	10.91	10.09	4	3	−2	2	3	10
REUTER INC	1.47	11.62	37.50	−50.17	11.74	7.18	1	4	−4	3	2	6
ROWAN COS INC	0.77	19.02	28.75	−57.33	6.63	11.40	4	4	−4	−1	4	7
RUSS TOGS INC	1.60	17.61	−3.75	−12.33	13.29	7.31	3	−2	1	4	2	8
RUSSELL CORP	1.75	13.68	−5.75	−10.83	9.81	7.53	2	−3	1	2	2	4
RYLAND GROUP INC	1.25	9.68	−82.00	−48.83	8.11	5.36	0	−4	−4	0	0	−8
SCIENTIFIC COMPUTERS	1.38	12.25	2.25	−16.83	8.46	6.74	1	0	0	1	1	3
SCIENTIFIC SOFTWARE	1.65	18.24	20.75	−38.00	15.93	11.96	4	3	−3	4	4	12
SCOA INDS INC	2.28	9.61	2.00	−10.17	5.87	5.48	0	−1	2	−2	0	−1
SEALED AIR CORP	0.73	5.83	7.50	−17.83	5.94	2.68	−4	0	−1	−2	−4	−11
SERVICE FRACTURING	1.34	13.68	38.75	−25.67	11.95	7.37	2	4	−3	3	2	8
SEVEN OAKS INTL	1.81	10.28	−24.75	−30.33	6.63	6.82	0	−4	−3	−1	1	−7
SHAKLEE CORP	1.79	21.39	−14.75	−30.67	13.89	10.47	4	−4	−3	4	3	4
SHOP & GO INC	1.50	8.14	−2.75	−7.17	4.72	5.26	−3	−2	3	−3	0	−5
SHOWBOAT INC	1.16	11.56	−32.00	−7.67	7.48	4.77	1	−4	3	0	−1	−1
SONOCO PRODS	1.08	8.35	−12.25	−9.33	6.49	3.88	−2	−3	2	−1	−2	−6
SPARTON CORP	1.41	8.46	23.75	−46.00	6.66	4.20	−2	3	−3	−1	−1	−4
STARRETT, L S, CO	0.76	10.16	26.75	−17.17	7.76	3.66	0	3	0	0	−3	0
SUBARU AMER INC	3.95	14.30	34.25	−11.50	4.38	14.14	3	4	1	−4	4	8
SUPERMARKETS GEN	1.62	10.07	−0.50	−15.50	5.95	6.19	0	−1	0	−2	1	−2
TBC CORP	2.96	19.66	0.50	−19.00	8.11	14.76	4	−1	−1	0	4	6
TEAM INC	0.02	0.97	23.00	−76.00	20.77	0.09	−4	3	−4	4	−4	−5
TEXAS INDS INC	1.11	9.60	5.00	−33.17	9.02	4.35	0	0	−3	1	−1	−3
THOMPSON MED Inc	4.23	13.73	−25.50	−20.17	4.01	12.42	2	−4	−2	−4	4	−4
THOUSAND TRAILS	3.38	9.15	−11.75	−37.33	5.79	9.01	−1	−3	−3	−2	3	−6
THRIFTY CORP	0.80	6.52	−1.25	−7.00	5.64	2.50	−4	−2	3	−3	−4	−10

EXHIBIT A–6 *(concluded)*

							Ranked Fundamental Criteria					
Company	5yr SD RIR/ (P/E)	5yr SD ROE/ (P/BV)	Sales % Chg Index	Earns Stab. Index	(LTGR + DY)/ (P/BV)	5yr SD RIR/ (P/FBV)	5yr SD ROE/ (P/BV)	Sales % Chg Index	Earns Stab. Index	(LTGR + DY)/ (P/BV)	5yr SD RIR/ (P/FBV)	Total
S&P 400	0.68	9.23			6.06	2.99	−1	0	0	−2	−4	−7
TOKHEIM CORP	1.14	8.46	26.75	−14.83	7.08	4.05	−2	3	0	0	−2	−1
TRACOR INC	1.09	7.90	10.50	−8.17	8.23	4.70	−3	1	3	0	−1	0
TRINITY INDS INC	0.39	9.47	47.25	−65.83	6.10	3.89	−1	4	−4	−2	−2	−5
TYCO LABS INC	1.36	9.07	24.75	−25.17	5.90	4.80	−1	3	−2	−2	0	−2
TYLER Corp	1.03	8.84	13.25	−21.67	11.53	4.14	−2	2	−2	3	−2	−1
UNITED BANCORP ARIZ	2.08	13.78	30.50	−8.50	9.69	8.34	2	4	2	1	3	12
UNITED STATIONERS	0.92	4.69	8.25	−12.33	2.85	3.10	−4	0	1	−4	−4	−11
UNIVERSAL FOODS	1.16	13.17	−15.00	−17.67	9.18	4.69	2	−4	−1	1	−1	−3
UNIVERSAL LEAF	1.45	12.63	−3.50	−4.17	9.00	5.12	1	−2	4	1	0	4
VARLEN CORP	1.41	13.62	9.50	−13.83	5.81	6.37	2	1	0	−2	1	2
VEECO INSTRS INC	1.26	6.95	11.00	−16.83	7.08	4.07	−4	1	0	0	−2	−5
VELCRO INDS N V	1.17	7.60	−7.00	−5.67	2.30	3.67	−3	−3	3	−4	−3	−10
VERNITRON CORP	1.35	11.77	7.00	−11.17	6.02	6.95	1	0	1	−2	1	1
VICON INDS INC	1.36	10.22	1.00	−25.00	11.27	6.64	0	−1	−2	3	1	1
WALBAR INC	1.76	11.23	2.25	−17.67	5.97	7.26	1	0	−1	−2	2	0
WALLACE COMPUTER	1.06	7.31	3.75	−5.17	4.40	4.06	−3	0	3	−4	−2	−6
WENDY'S INTL INC	1.12	7.04	13.75	−10.17	3.74	4.01	−3	2	2	−4	−2	−5
WINDMERE CORP	3.08	19.40	25.00	−14.33	11.45	13.47	4	3	0	3	4	14
WOODS, PETE, CORP	1.24	10.70	40.75	−23.17	9.71	5.08	0	4	−2	2	0	4
WORTHINGTON INDS	0.99	8.03	18.00	−13.00	6.95	3.33	−3	2	1	0	−3	−3
ZERO CO	1.02	6.64	10.25	−4.50	5.40	3.51	−4	1	4	−3	−3	−5

EXHIBIT A–7
"Small Cap" Attractiveness Ratings (*2/8/85*)

+	0/+		0	0/–	–
ALK	AFGN	MDP	APR	ACU	SPA
BNHI	AGNC	MIDL	APOG	BI	TMI
FBC ↑	ARWS^{+}	MLHR ↑	BDG	BCF	
FEXC	ASN	MMO	BJ^{-} ↑	EBS^{+} ↓	
FUNC	AYD	MTSC	COLC	GEB ↓	
GCN^{-} ↑	BIV^{-}	NSI^{-}	CRI ↑	KOL^{+}	
HARG	BIND	NEW	DDL	LAW ↑	
LIZC^{-}	BTL^{-} ↑	NUE^{-} ↑	DF	PPSI^{-}	
PSNB^{-} ↑	CEE^{+}	OMH	DPX	PTCO	
RNB^{-}	CTAS ↑	OGIL	ESX ↑	SCIE^{+} ↓	
REUT ↑	CLRK^{-}	ORBT	FIT ↑	SSFT	
SBRU ↑	CSC ↑	OUT	FMO	SEE^{-} ↑	
TBCC^{-} ↑	EYE ↑	PNTA	FKM ↓	SERF	
TRMW^{-} ↑ ↑	COU^{-}	PHL	GRC^{+} ↓	TM ↓	
	DOYL	PER^{-} ↑	HVU^{+}	TRLS	
	DUNK^{+}	PCST ↑	IPG	USTR^{+} ↓	
	DYTC^{+}	PDQ	CARL^{-}	VRLN	
	AGE^{+}	RML	KII	VRN^{+}	
	FEN	RYL	LRI	WOG	
	FLXS^{-}	SOA ↑	LIBH^{-} ↑		
	FLO^{-}	QPON	LUR ↑		
	GTAC^{-} ↑	SWIX	MKP		
	GFD^{-} ↑	SHGO ↑	MEI		
	HDON	SGL	NCS		
	HUBB^{-}	TFX^{-} ↑	NOXLB^{+} ↓		
	HUN	TC	OMT		
	IAL	TRR	OSHM		
	INC	TYC^{-}	OSG^{+}		
	JFRY^{-}	TYL	PCT		
	JOS	UBAZ ↓	PIE^{+} ↓		
	KAMNA^{+}	UVV	PTNX^{-} ↑		
	KBALB^{-} ↑	VEE^{-} ↑	QCHM		
	KRUE	WBR	RBC		
	LINB	WCS	RDC		
	LDG	WTHG ↑	RTS ↑		
	LYND^{+}	ZRO ↑ ↑	SHC		
			SBO		
			SONO^{+}		
			SCX		
			TFD		
			TOK		
			UFC		
			VELCF		
			VII		
			WEN		
			WDMR ↑		

EXHIBIT A–8
"Small Cap" Attractiveness Ratings by Sector *(2/8/85)*

	+	0/+	0	0/−	−	Raw score
Consumer nondurables	1.9	50.0	32.7	15.4	0.0	38.4
Consumer durables	27.3	27.3	45.5	0.0	0.0	81.9
Technology	7.4	55.6	14.8	18.5	3.7	44.5
Basic industry	0.0	46.2	46.2	7.7	0.0	38.5
Transportation	25.0	50.0	25.0	0.0	0.0	100.0
Energy	0.0	0.0	28.6	57.1	14.3	−85.7
Interest-sensitive (excluding public utilities)	27.3	54.5	18.2	0.0	0.0	109.1

EXHIBIT A–9
Worksheet *(2/8/85)*

CONSUMER NONDURABLE	
ACU	0/–
AGNC	0/+
AGN	0/+
BCF	0/–
BIND	0/+
BIV	0/+
BJ	0
CARLO	
CDU	0/+
DF	0
DOYL	0/+
DPX	0
DUNK	0/+
EBS	0/–
EYE	0/+
FLO	0/+
GCN	+
GEB	0/–
HUN	0/+
IPG	0
JFRY	0/+
JOS	0/+
KRUE	0/+
LDG	0/+
LINB	0/+
LUR	0
MDVP	0/+
MEI	0
NCS	0
NOXLB	0
NSI	0/+
OGIL	0/+
OSHM	0
OCT	0
PDQ	0/+
PPSI	0/–
QPON	0/+
SBO	0
SGL	0/+
SHC	0
SHGO	0/+
SHOS	0/+
SOA	0/+
SWIX	0/+
TFD	0
TM	0/–
TRLS	0/–
UFC	0
USTR	0/–
UVV	0/+
VELCF	0
WCS	0/+
WEN	0

+	0/+	0	0/–	–
1	26	17	8	0
9	50.0	32.7	15.4	

CONSUMER DURABLE	
BDG	0
FIT	0
FMO	0
GFD	0/+
LIZC	+
RML	0/+
RTS	0
SBRU	+
TBCC	+
TFX	0/+
WDMR	0

+	0/+	0	0/–	–
3	3	5	0	0
27.3	27.3	45.5		

BASIC INDUSTRY	
APR	0
CLRK	0/+
CRI	0
CTAS	0/+
ESX	0
GRC	0
HVU	0
HUBB	0/+
KAMNA	0/+
KII	0
LAW	0/–
LRI	0
MLHR	0/+
MMO	0/+
NEW	0/+
NUE	0/+
PER	0/+
PNTA	0/+
QCHM	0
RBC	0
SCX	0
SONO	0
TOK	0
TYL	0/+
VRLN	0/–
WTHG	0/+

+	0/+	0	0/–	–
0	12	12	2	0
	46.2	46.2	7.7	

TECHNOLOGY	
AYD	0/+
BI	0/–
CEE	0/+
CSC	0/+
DDL	0
DYTC	0/+
FEN	0/+
FKM	0
INC	0/+
KOL	0/–
MTSC	0/+
ORBT	0/+
PCST	0/+
PTNX	0
REUT	+
SCIE	0/–
SEE	0/–
SPA	–
TC	0/+
TRMW	+
TRR	0/+
TYC	0/+
VEE	0/+
VII	0
VRN	0/–
WBR	0/+
ZRO	0/+

+	0/+	0	0/–	–
2	15	4	5	1
7.4	55.6	14.8	18.5	3.7

ENERGY	
MKP	0
PTCO	0/–
RDC	0
SERF	0/–
SSFT	0/–
TMI	–
WOG	0/–

+	0/+	0	0/–	–
0	0	2	4	1
		28.6	57.1	14.3

TRANSPORTATION	
ALK	+
ARWS	0/+
BTL	0/+
HARG	+
LYND	0/+
OSG	0
OVT	0/+
PIE	0

+	0/+	0	0/–	–
2	4	2	0	0
25	50	25		

INTEREST-SENSITIVE	
AFGN	0/+
AGE	0/+
APOG	0
BNHI	+
COLC	0
FBC	+
FEXC	+
FLXS	0/+
FUNC	+
GTAC	0/+
HDON	0/+
IAL	0/+
KBALB	0/+
LIBH	0
MIDL	0/+
OMH	0/+
OMT	0
PHL	0/+
PSNB	+
RNB	+
RYL	0/+
UBAZ	0/+

+	0/+	0	0/–	–
6	12	4	0	0
27.3	54.5	18.2		

EXHIBIT A–10
Research Universe Rating Distribution *(2/7/85)*

			— O'NEIL —					
		FUNDAMENTAL	DATAGRAPH	RELATIVE STRENGTH	FLO/CAP	QAS	COMPUTIME	WEIGHTED TOTAL
S&P 400								
ACME UNITED CORP	ACU	1.5↓	0/−	−	0/+		− −	(5.4)
AFG INDUSTRIES	AFGN	(4.0)↑	0/+	0/+	+	0/+ +		6.7
AGENCY RENT-A-CAR	AGNC	(7.1)	+	+	0/+			7.2
AIR WIS SVCS INC	ARWS	3.3↓↓↓	0/+	0/+	+			9.3
ALASKA AIRLS INC	ALK	.7↑↑	+	+	+	0/+ +	+ +	11.7
ALCO STD CORP	ASK	2.1↓	0/+	0	+	0/− +	0/+ 0/+	6.2
AMERICAN PRECISION INDS	APR	(11.0)	0/+	0/+	+		0 0	1.6
APOGEE ENTERPRISES INC	APOG	1.2	0/−	0/−	+			.5
AYDIN CORP	AYD	8.8	0/+	0/−	+	0/− +	− 0/−↓	4.7
BANCORP HAWAII	BKHI	13.9↑	0/+	0/+	+			13.6
BANDAG INC	BDG	(7.7)	0	0/+	+	0/+ 0↓	0/− 0/−	0.0
BELL INDS INC	BI	.9 ↓	0/−	−	0/−	− 0/+	− 0/−	(6.8)
BIG V SUPERMARKETS INC	BIV	3.9↑↑	0/−	0/+	+		0 0/−↓	3.8
BINDLEY WESTERN	BIND	.1	0/+	0/+	0/+			6.0
BLAIR JOHN & CO	BJ	6.2↓↓	0	−	0/−	− 0/+	√ − 0	(2.9)
BURLINGTON COAT	BCF	5.3↓	−	−	0/−			(7.9)
BUTLER INTL INC	BTL	(4.8)↓↓	0	+	0/+	0/+ 0/+	0/+↑ 0/+↑	4.1
C 3 INC	CEE	6.2	0	0/+	+	NOT RATED	+ +	10.0
CINTAS CORP	CTAS	(5.5)	0/+	0/+	+			5.8
CLARK J L MFG CO	CLRK	(7.3)	0/+	0	+	0/+↑ +		3.8
COLORADO NATL BANKSHARE	COLC	12.7	0/−	−	0/+	− 0/−		(.2)
COMPUTER SCIENCES CORP	CSC	5.6	0	0	0/+	0/+↑ 0↓	0/+ +	5.8
COOPERVISION INC	EYE	(7.3)↓↓↓	0/+	0/+	+		√ + +↑	6.1
CORDURA CORP	CDU	(3.9)↑↑↑	0/+	0	+	0/+ +	0/+ 0	4.4
CORE INDS INC	CRI	(2.1)	0/−	0	0/+	0/− +↑↑	0/− 0	(.8)
DATA DESIGN LABS	DDES	(3.9)↓	0/+	0	0/+			2.4
DEAN FOODS CO	DF	(2.1)↓	0/+	0	0/+	0 − 0/−↑	0/+↑ 0/+↑	1.6
DOYLE DANE BERNBACH INT	DOYL	(2.7)↑↑	0/+	0/+	+	0/− +		5.7
DUNKIN' DONUTS	DUNK	2.8↓↓	0/+	0/+	+	0/+↑ +↑		9.1
DUPLEX PRODS INC	DPX	0.0↑	0/+	0	+		− −	1.5
DYNATECH CORP	DYTC	(2.6)↑	0/+	+	+			9.0
EDISON BROS STORES INC	EBS	1.1	0/−	0/−	0/−	0/− 0/+	× 0/−↓ 0/−↓	(4.4)
EDWARDS A G INC	AGE	(2.6)↓	0/+	+	+	0/+↑ +↑	+ +	9.2

EXHIBIT A–10 *(continued)*

		FUNDA-MENTAL	— O'NEIL — DATA-GRAPH	RELATIVE STRENGTH	FLO/CAP	QAS	COMPU-TIME	WEIGHTED TOTAL
S&P 400								
ESSEX CHEM CORP	ESX	.4↑↑↑	0	0/ −	0/ +	0 0/ −	× − 0/ −	(2.2)
FAB INDS INC	FIT	8.1↑↑	0/ −	0/ −	0/ +		− 0/ +↑	1.0
FAIRCHILD INDS INC	FEN	6.6↓	0/ +	0/ +	+	0/ − 0/ −	√ + +↑	8.6
FEDERAL-MOGUL	FMO	(2.3)	0/ +	0	0/ +	0/ −↑ +	0/ − 0	1.5
FIRST BOSTON INC	FBC	6.8	0/ +	+	+	+↑0/ +	0/ +↑ +↑	12.3
FIRST EXECUTIVE CORP	FEXC	16.7	0	0/ +	+	0/ +↑ +↑		13.4
FIRST UNION CORP	FUNC	6.2	0/ +	0/ +	+	0/ + 0↓		11.4
FLEXSTEEL INDS INC	FLXS	(1.3)↑	0	0	+	0/ +↑0/ +↓		4.0
FLOWERS INDS INC	FLO	(9.4)↑	0/ +	+	+	0/ + 0/ +	√0/ + 0↕	4.0
FLUKE JOHN MFG INC	FKM	(5.0)↑	0/ +	0/ −	0/ +	0/ −↑ +	0/ + 0/ +↑	1.0
GENERAL CINEMA CORP	GCN	.6↓	+	+	+	0/ +↑ +	0/ + 0/ +↑	10.4
GERBER PRODUCTS CO	GEB	(5.0)↓↓↓	0/ −	0/ −	0/ +	0/ −↑0/ +	−↓ −↓	(5.6)
GORMAN RUPP CO	GRC	(4.6)↑	0/ +	0	+		0 0/ +	3.4
GREENTREE ACCEPT CORP	GTAC	4.9↑↑	0/ −	0	+			4.0
GUILFORD MLS INC	GFD	6.6↑	0	0/ −	+	0/ −↑ +↕↕	0/ −↑0↑	3.8
HARPER GROUP	HARG	.1↓	0/ +	+	+	+↕ +		14.0
HENREDON FURNITURE INDS	HDON	.4↑	0/ +	0	+	0/ − +		6.2
HOOVER UNVL INC	HVU	(6.6)↑↑↑	0/ +	0	+	0/ +↕ +	0↕0	2.8
HUBBELL HARVEY INC. B	HUBB	(2.3)↑	0	0/ +	0/ +	0/ + +	0/ + 0/ +	4.5
HUNT MFG CO	HUN	(2.2)↑↑	0/ +	0/ +	+		0/ + 0/ +	6.6
INTERNATIONAL ALUM CORP	IAL	(5.7)↑↑↑↑	0/ +	+	+	0/ +↑ +	0/ + 0↕	6.1
INTERNATIONAL CTLS CORP	INC	9.0	0/ +	0/ +	0/ +		×0↑0/ +↑	8.9
INTERPUBLIC GROUP COS I	IPG	(7.7)↓	0/ +	0	+	0 0/ +↕	0/ + 0↑	1.7
JEFFREY MARTIN INC	JFRY	4.6	0/ −	0	+			3.8
JOSTENS INC	JOS	(2.1)	0/ +	0/ +	+	+ 0/ +	0/ −↓0/ −	4.6
KAMAN CORP	KAMNA	(1.8)	+	0/ +	+	0/ +↑ +		9.0
KARCHER CARL ENTR	CARL	8.1↓	0	−	0/ −			(2.8)
KEYSTONE INTL INC	KII	(10.9)↓	0	0	+	0/ + 0↑ +	0/ + 0↓	.4
KIMBALL INTL INC	KBALB	(7.8)↓↓	0/ +	+	+	0/ − 0/ +↑		4.4
KOLLMORGEN CORP	KOL	(3.8)	0	−	0/ +	0/ −↑ +	− 0/ −	(3.9)
KRUEGER W A CO	KRUE	(9.3)↑↑	0/ +	+	+	+↑0/ +		6.0
LAWTER INC	LAW	(10.6)↓	−	0/ −	0/ +	− 0/ +	− 0↑	(8.4)
LEARONAL	LRI	(9.0)↓↓↓	0/ +	0/ +	+	0/ −↕ +	√0/ + 0	1.8

EXHIBIT A–10 *(continued)*

			— O'NEIL —					
		FUNDA-MENTAL	DATA-GRAPH	RELATIVE STRENGTH	FLO/CAP	QAS	COMPU-TIME	WEIGHTED TOTAL
S&P 400								
LIBERTY HOMES INC	LIBH	7.1↑↑	0/−	0/−				(3.2)
LIN BROADCASTING CORP	LINB	(1.1)↓	0/+	0/+	+	0/−↓+		6.3
LIZ CLAIBORNE	LIZC	(3.7)	+	+	+			10.5
LONGS DRUG STORES INC	LDG	(1.6)↓	0/+	0/+	+	0/+ 0↓	0 0	4.8
LURIA & SON	LUR	6.0	0/−	−	0/+		0/− 0/−	(2.1)
LYNDEN INC	LYND	7.6	0/+	0	+			9.0
MARK PRODUCTS	MKP	2.4↑	0/−	0	0/+		×0/− 0	1.7
MEI CORP	MEI	(.6)↑↑	0/+	0	0/+	0/− 0	0/− 0/−	.4
MEREDITH CORP	MDP	(1.6)	0/+	+	+	0/+↑0/+	√0/−↓0	6.0
MIDLANTIC BKS INC	MIDL	5.7	0/+	0/+	+	0/+ 0/−		8.3
MILLER HERMAN INC	MLHR	(11.1)	0/+	+	0/+	0/+ 0↕		2.3
MONARCH MACH TOOL CO	MMO	5.7	+	0	+	0/−↑+	0/+↑0↑	8.3
MTS SYS CORP	MTSC	(.4)	0/+	0/+	+			7.8
NATIONAL CONVENIENCE ST	NCS	(1.2)↓	0	0/+	+	0/− 0/+	− 0/+↑	2.5
NATIONAL SVC INDS INC	MSI	3.3	0/+	0	0/+	0/+↑0/+	0/− 0/−	3.7
NEWCOR INC	NEW	1.2↑	0/+	0	+		+ +↑	8.0
NOXELL CORP	NOXLB	(8.8)	0/+	0/+	+	0/+ 0/+↓		2.5
NUCOR CORP	NUE	1.0↑	0/+	0	+	0/− +	0↑0/−	4.0
OAKWOOD HOMES CORP	OMH	3.4↑↑↑	0/+	0	0/+		0↓ +	5.9
OGILVY & MATHER INTL	OGIL	(8.1)	0/+	+	+	+ 0/+		6.5
OHIO MATTRESS	OMT	1.1↑	0	0/−	0/+	0/− +↑	− 0/−	(.8)
ORBIT INSTRUMENTS	ORBT	2.1↑↑	0	0/+	+			6.8
OSHMANS SPORTING GOODS	OSHM	0.0↓	0/−	0/−	0/+	0/− +		(.8)
OVERNITE TRANSN CO	OVT	(6.2)↓	0/+	+	+	0/+ 0/+	0/+ 0/+	5.9
OVERSEAS SHLIPHOLDING GR	OSG	12.1	0	0/−	0/+	− 0/+↑	0/− 0/−	3.0
PACO PHARMACEUTICAL	PPSI	.6	0/−	−	−			(9.8)
PAPERCRAFT CORP	PCT	1.2↑↑	0/−	0/−	0/−	0/+ 0/+	0/+ 0/−	(1.9)
PENTAIR CORP	PNTA	3.3↑	0/	0	+	0/− 0/+		5.8
PETROLEUM EQUIP TOOLS C	PTCO	10.1↓	−	−	0/−			(6.0)
PHILIPS INDS INC	PHL	(8.3)↓	0/+	+	+	+↑ +	+ +	7.5
PIEDMONT AVIATION INC	PIE	1.5↑	0	0/−	0/+	0/+ 0/−↓	+ +	3.0
POPE EVANS ROBBINS IN	PER	10.1	0/+	−	+		0/−↓0/−	4.0
PRECISION CASTPARTS	PCST	(5.9)	0/+	+	0/+			5.6

EXHIBIT A–10 *(continued)*

		FUNDA-MENTAL	— O'NEIL — DATA-GRAPH	RELATIVE STRENGTH	FLO/CAP	QAS	COMPU-TIME	WEIGHTED TOTAL
S&P 400								
PRIME MOTOR INNS INC	PDQ	(8.4)↓	0/+	+	+		√+ +	7.1
PRINTRONIX INC	PTMX	8.1↓	0	–	0/–			(2.8)
PUGET SOUND BANCORP	PSNB	9.9	0/+	+		0/+ 0		11.0
QUAKER CHEM CORP	QCHM	(2.2)	0/–	0	+			1.1
REGAL BELOIT CORP	RBC	(11.1)	0/+	0	+		√0/+ 0↑	.8
REPUBLIC N Y CORP	RNB	11.2↓	0/+	0	+		0/+ 0/+	10.5
REUTER INC	REUT	1.3↓↓↓	+	+	+			12.5
ROWAN COS INC	RDC	7.9↑	0/–	–	0/–	– 0/–	× + 0/+↑	(1.6)
RUSS TOGS INC	RTS	10.9↑↑↑	0	0/–	0/–		× – –↓	(1.6)
RUSSELL CORP	RML	6.0↑↑	0/–	0/+	+	0/+↑ +↑	0/+ 0/–	6.6
RYLAND GROUP INC	RYL	(6.5)↓↓	+	+	0/+	0/+ +	√+ +	7.6
SCIENTIFIC COMPUTERS IN	SCIE	9.3↓↓	0/–	–	0/–			(4.3)
SCIENTIFIC SOFTWARE	SSFT	7.5	0/–	–	0/–			(5.0)
SCOA INDS INC	SOA	(.6)↓	0/+	0	+	0/– 0/+	+ 0/+	5.2
SEALED AIR CORP	SEE	(13.4)↓	0/+	0/–	–	0/– 0/–	– –	(9.6)
SERVICE FRACTURING CO	SERF	5.3	–	–	0/–			(7.9)
SEVEN OAKS INTL	QPON	(3.5)	+	0/+	+			8.6
SHAKLEE CORP	SHC	4.5↓↓	0/–	0/–	0/+	0/– 0/+	× 0/– 0↑	0.0
SHELBY WILLIAMS	SWIX	(9.9)	+	+	+			8.0
SHOP & GO INC	SHGO	(3.9)↑↑↑	0	+	+			6.4
SHOWBOAT INC	SBO	5.1↑	–	0/–	+		0/– +	2.0
SONOCO PRODS	SONO	(.6)	0/+	0	0/+	– +↑		2.8
SPARTON CORP	SPA	(10.1)↓	–	–	0/+		× –↓–	(11.5)
STARRETT L S CO	SCX	(2.2)	0/+	0	+		0/– 0/–	2.1
SUBARU AMER INC	SBRU	1.8	0/+	+	+			10.7
SUPERMARKETS GEN CORP	SGL	(1.5)↑	0/+	+	+	+ 0	+ 0/+	8.4
TBC CORP	TBC	7.2↑	0/+	0/+	+			10.9
TEAM INC	TMI	(10.0)	0	–	0/–		× – 0/–	(10.8)
TELEFLEX INC	TFX	1.1	0/+	0	0/+	0/+↑ +	0 0/–↑	4.0
TELEX CORP	TC	(7.6)↓	+	+	+	0/+ +	+ 0/+	7.8
THOMPSON MED INC	TM	2.0↑	–	–	0/–		0/–↓0/–	(8.2)
THOUSAND TRAILS	TRLS	2.0↑↑↑	0/–	–	0/–			(7.2)
THRIFTY CORP	TFD	(7.7)↑	0/+	+	+	0/+ 0/+	– 0↑	2.9

EXHIBIT A–10 *(concluded)*

			— O'NEIL —					
		FUNDA-MENTAL	DATA-GRAPH	RELATIVE STRENGTH	FLO/CAP	QAS	COMPU-TIME	WEIGHTED TOTAL
S&P 400								
TOKHEIM CORP	TOK	(1.2)↑↑	0/+	0	–		– 0	(3.5)
TRACOR	TRR	(2.2)	0/+	+	+	+↑+	+ +↑	9.9
TRIANGLE MICROWAVE	TRMW	.2↓↓↓↓↓	0/+	+	+			10.1
TYCO LABS INC	TYC	(4.5)	0/+	0/+	+	0/+↑+	– 0/+↑	3.6
TYLER CORP	TYL	(4.6)↓↓	0/+	0/+	+	0/+↑+	0/+↓0	5.4
UNITED BANCORP ARIZ	UBAZ	7.9↑	0	0/+		0/+↓0/–↓		5.2
UNITED STATIONERS INC	USTR	(9.9)↑	0/+	0/+	–			(4.0)
UNIVERSAL FOODS CORP	UFC	3.4↑	0	0/–	+		–↓↓↓↓ –↓↓	(.1)
UNIVERSAL LEAF TOB INC	UVV	7.8↓	0/+	0	0/+	+ 0— –	0/+↑↑0/+↑	7.9
VARLEN CORP	VRLN	4.3	–	–		0/–↑0/+		(6.3)
VEECO INSTRS INC	VEE	(8.4)↓	0/+	0	+	0/–↑+	+ +	3.8
VELCRO INDS N V	VELCF	(3.9)↑	0/+	0/+	0/+	0/– 0/+		2.9
VERNITRON CORP	VRN	3.9	0/–	0/–	0/–	0/–↑0/+↑	X – 0/–	(3.8)
VICON INDS INC	VII	4.4↑↑	0/–	0/–	0/+		0/–↓0/–	(1.2)
WALBAR INC	WBR	(1.5)↓	+	+	+		0/– 0/–↑	6.9
WALLACE COMPUTER SVCS I	WCS	(6.0)↓↓	+	+	+	0/+↑0/+	√0/+↑ +↑	7.8
WENDY'S INTL INC	WEN	(4.4)	0/+	0	0/+	0/– 0/+↑	√ –↓0	(.6)
WINDMERE CORP	WDMR	12.7↓	0/–	–	0/+			1.1
WOODS PETE CORP	WOG	2.4	0	–	0/–	– 0/–	0/– 0↑	(5.0)
WORTHINGTON INDS INC	WTHG	(7.8)↑	0/+	0/+	+	0/+↑+		5.1
ZERO CO	ZRO	(4.4)↑↑	0/+	0/+	+	0/+ +	0↓0↑	4.8

EXHIBIT A–11
"Small Cap" Research Universe Report 2 (*statistical database* B) (2/7/85)

Company	5yr SD ROE/ (P/BV)	Sales % Chg Index	Earns Stab. Index	(LTGR + DY)/ (P/BV)	5yr SD RIR/ (P/FBV)	Ranked Fundamental Criteria: 5yr SD ROE/ (P/BV)	Sales % Chg Index	Earns Stab. Index	(LTGR + DY)/ (P/BV)	5yr SD RIR/ (P/FBV)	Total
S&P 400	8.35			5.48	2.71	0	0	0	−1	−4	−5.5
ACME UNITED CORP	10.44	−18.50	−9.00	7.32	4.85	1	−3	2	0	0	1.5
AFG INDUSTRIES	9.18	−15.50	−99.00	5.99	7.53	0	−3	−4	0	2	−4.0
AGENCY RENT-A-CAR	6.47	1.75	−20.00	3.48	6.47	−3	1	−1	−4	1	−7.1
AIR WIS SVCS INC	10.07	−5.00	−17.33	7.45	5.75	1	0	0	1	1	3.3
ALASKA AIRLS INC	11.98	14.50	−70.83	4.93	8.00	2	3	−4	−2	3	0.7
ALCO STD CORP	8.95	−10.75	−4.17	8.29	3.40	0	−2	4	1	−2	2.1
AMERICAN PRECISION	6.07	0.75	−17.83	3.22	3.15	−3	0	0	−4	−3	−11.0
APOGEE ENTERPRISES	8.34	8.25	−16.33	5.97	4.97	0	2	0	0	0	1.2
AYDIN CORP	13.94	−4.00	−19.83	9.06	12.26	3	0	−1	2	4	8.8
BANCORP HAWAII	15.26	17.75	−6.50	9.89	7.01	3	3	3	3	2	13.9
BANDAG INC	5.66	−3.75	−5.17	2.81	3.19	−4	0	4	−4	−3	−7.7
BELL INDS INC	9.77	−35.25	−13.33	9.74	5.49	0	−4	0	3	0	0.9
BIG V SUPERMARKETS	11.52	3.50	−21.67	8.98	5.76	2	1	−2	2	1	3.9
BINDLEY WESTERN IND	10.29	9.75	−31.00	5.80	7.52	1	2	−3	−1	2	0.1
BLAIR, JOHN, & CO	12.26	13.50	−14.67	8.41	5.94	2	3	0	1	1	6.2
BURLINGTON COAT	15.87	−20.75	−25.00	8.72	12.86	3	−4	−2	2	4	5.3
BUTLER INTL INC	7.36	20.50	−14.83	7.00	2.56	−2	3	0	0	−4	−4.8
C3 INC	12.02	12.75	−36.33	10.88	6.70	2	3	−3	3	2	6.2
CINTAS CORP	6.92	0.50	−15.67	4.12	5.19	−2	0	0	−3	0	−5.5
CLARK, J L, MFG CO	7.56	−17.50	−5.33	4.48	3.04	−2	−3	3	−3	−3	−7.3
COLORADO NATL BANK	16.94	2.50	−9.67	9.53	8.28	4	1	2	2	3	12.7
COMPUTER SCIENCES	10.18	8.75	−16.17	8.10	6.86	1	2	0	1	2	5.6
COOPERVISION	6.58	−13.25	−21.17	7.93	4.03	−3	−3	−2	1	−1	−7.3
CORDURA CORP	13.86	−8.00	−52.33	4.86	4.65	3	−1	−4	−2	0	−3.9
CORE INDS INC	8.42	7.75	−16.33	6.49	2.90	0	2	0	0	−3	−2.1
DATA DESIGN LABS	6.57	−8.25	−12.00	7.79	3.56	−3	−1	1	1	−2	−3.9
DEAN FOODS CO	6.80	5.00	−2.83	3.62	3.88	−2	2	4	−4	−1	−2.1

EXHIBIT A–11 *(continued)*

						Ranked Fundamental Criteria					
Company	**5yr SD ROE/ (P/BV)**	**Sales % Chg Index**	**Earns Stab. Index**	**(LTGR +DY)/ (P/BV)**	**5yr SD RIR/ (P/FBV)**	**5yr SD ROE/ (P/BV)**	**Sales % Chg Index**	**Earns Stab. Index**	**(LTGR +DY)/ (P/BV)**	**5yr SD RIR/ (P/FBV)**	**Total**
S&P 400	8.35			5.48	2.71	0	0	0	−1	−4	−5.5
DOYLE DANE BERNBACH	8.48	2.00	−11.67	6.04	2.24	0	1	1	0	−4	−2.7
DUNKIN' DONUTS	7.66	3.00	−1.67	5.64	4.74	−1	1	4	−1	0	2.8
DUPLEX PRODS INC	11.25	−0.50	−16.83	5.65	5.57	1	0	0	−1	0	0.0
DYNATECH CORP	6.78	14.25	−9.67	3.24	6.32	−3	3	2	−4	1	−2.6
EDISON BROS STORES	12.09	−3.50	−18.67	7.39	4.57	2	0	−1	0	0	1.1
EDWARDS A G INC	10.58	13.50	−22.33	4.65	5.04	1	3	−2	−3	0	−2.6
ESSEX CHEM CORP	10.76	−14.75	−19.17	8.52	4.48	1	−3	−1	2	0	0.4
FAB INDS INC	16.11	−16.00	−20.83	10.75	9.08	4	−3	−1	3	3	8.1
FAIRCHILD INDS	16.16	−1.00	−34.67	13.58	6.33	4	0	−3	4	1	6.6
FEDERAL-MOGUL	9.07	−11.50	−19.33	11.43	3.13	0	−2	−1	3	−3	−2.3
FIRST BOSTON INC	14.53	35.25	−72.67	10.90	7.34	3	4	−4	3	2	6.8
FIRST EXECUTIVE	16.91	29.00	−12.33	16.27	13.19	4	4	1	4	4	16.7
FIRST UNION CORP	11.44	12.00	−9.67	7.22	6.21	1	3	2	0	1	6.2
FLEXSTEEL INDS	10.93	−21.25	−16.00	7.33	5.08	1	−4	0	0	0	−1.3
FLOWERS INDS INC	5.91	−8.50	−7.83	4.45	2.71	−4	−1	3	−3	−4	−9.4
FLUKE, JOHN, MFG	6.49	−8.75	−19.17	7.00	4.51	−3	−1	−1	0	0	−5.0
GENERAL CINEMA	8.13	2.25	−7.67	2.67	6.92	−1	1	3	−4	2	0.6
GERBER PRODUCTS	7.96	−7.75	−5.83	5.45	2.78	−1	−1	3	−2	−4	−5.0
GORMAN RUPP CO	8.23	−22.75	−10.83	8.58	2.49	−1	−4	1	2	−4	−4.6
GREENTREE ACCEPTANCE	15.31	−6.75	−19.67	5.76	11.72	3	−1	−1	−1	4	4.9
GUILFORD MLS INC	13.96	−4.30	28.67	8.63	8.00	3	0	−2	2	3	6.6
HARPER GROUP	9.00	9.25	−17.00	5.20	5.95	0	2	0	−2	1	0.1
HENREDON FURNITURE	9.57	−19.25	−9.83	6.88	4.74	0	−3	2	0	0	0.4
HOOVER UNVL INC	8.43	−1.25	−22.00	7.07	2.80	0	0	−2	0	−4	−6.6
HUBBELL HARVEY, B	8.27	−10.25	6.50	5.78	3.24	−1	−2	4	−1	−3	−2.3
HUNT MFG CO	6.87	−2.75	3.33	5.21	3.40	−2	0	4	−2	−2	−2.2
INTERNATIONAL ALUM	9.23	−20.00	−21.83	8.50	3.72	0	−4	−2	1	−2	−5.7
INTERNATIONAL CTLS	12.90	23.25	−17.17	6.73	8.07	3	4	0	0	3	9.0

INTERPUBLIC GROUP	7.46	−3.75	−14.33	4.83	3.05	−2	0	0	−2	−3	−7.7
JEFFREY MARTIN INC	20.59	26.00	−34.33	4.34	23.01	4	4	−3	−3	4	4.6
JOSTENS INC	8.06	9.25	−3.00	3.93	3.16	−1	2	4	−3	−3	−2.1
KAMAN CORP	7.44	−15.50	−5.50	6.43	3.79	−2	−3	3	0	−1	−1.8
KARCHER, CARL, ENT	13.52	−15.25	−10.33	8.89	9.44	3	−3	1	2	3	8.1
KEYSTONE INTL INC	6.03	10.75	−19.67	4.99	2.44	−4	2	−1	−2	−4	−10.9
KIMBALL INTL INC	6.55	−10.75	−15.17	5.65	3.30	−3	−2	0	−1	−2	−7.8
KOLLMORGEN CORP	7.03	1.75	−15.33	8.28	3.01	−2	1	0	1	−3	−3.8
KRUEGER, W A, CO	6.15	3.50	−18.33	4.12	2.99	−3	1	0	−3	−3	−9.3
LAWTER INC	5.84	−17.00	−10.83	5.53	1.00	−4	−3	1	−1	−4	−10.6
LEARONAL	7.99	−25.25	−14.17	3.42	4.23	−1	−4	0	−4	−1	−9.0
LIBERTY HOMES INC	12.08	−8.00	−15.50	11.20	6.53	2	−1	0	3	2	7.1
LIN BROADCASTING	7.04	1.00	−4.17	4.35	5.24	−2	0	4	−3	0	−1.1
LIZ CLAIBORNE	6.29	17.25	−20.33	2.38	8.56	−3	3	−1	−4	3	−3.7
LONGS DRUG STORES	7.34	4.25	−3.83	5.19	3.29	−2	1	4	−2	−2	−1.6
LURIA & SON	11.77	−5.25	−12.67	7.23	8.50	2	−1	1	0	3	6.0
LYNDEN INC	28.49	−9.50	−52.33	16.25	21.73	4	−2	−4	4	4	7.6
MARK PRODUCTS INC	10.70	37.75	−67.00	8.94	6.33	1	4	−4	2	1	2.4
MEI CORP	7.90	−7.50	−3.67	3.69	5.29	−1	−1	4	−3	0	−0.6
MEREDITH CORP	7.08	2.75	−6.33	4.79	4.01	−2	1	3	−2	−1	−1.6
MIDLANTIC BKS INC	12.47	25.75	−10.50	6.72	4.76	2	4	1	0	0	5.7
MILLER HERMAN INC	4.56	−9.50	−7.50	2.43	2.79	−4	−2	3	−4	−4	−11.1
MONARCH MACH TOOL	13.59	50.50	−61.17	13.55	4.80	3	4	−4	4	0	5.7
MTS SYS CORP	8.11	11.50	−30.50	11.20	4.12	−1	3	−3	3	−1	−0.4
NATIONAL CONVENIENCE	8.57	−13.00	−5.50	5.52	3.68	0	−2	3	−1	−2	−1.2
NATIONAL SVC INDS	10.02	−0.50	−4.17	6.95	4.32	0	0	4	0	−1	3.3
NEWCOR INC	9.29	6.50	−22.17	9.21	4.65	0	2	−2	2	0	1.2
NOXELL CORP	5.67	−3.75	−4.33	3.35	2.82	−4	0	4	−4	−4	−8.8
NUCOR CORP	8.89	−9.50	−28.83	11.72	5.62	0	−2	−2	4	0	1.0
OAKWOOD HOMES CORP	8.28	5.00	−9.33	6.32	4.34	0	2	2	0	0	3.4
OGILVY & MATHER	5.84	11.00	−7.83	2.98	2.32	−4	3	3	−4	−4	−8.1
OHIO MATTRESS CO	7.76	−3.25	−9.00	10.16	2.88	−1	0	2	3	−3	1.1
ORBIT INSTRUMENT	10.81	−12.25	−30.83	9.63	8.41	1	−2	−3	2	3	2.1
OSHMAN'S SPORT	8.27	−0.25	−12.67	7.00	5.10	−1	0	1	0	0	0.0
OVERNITE TRANSN	7.61	−14.25	−10.17	4.09	3.80	−2	−3	2	−3	−1	−6.2
OVERSEAS SHIP	18.78	−1.00	−14.50	18.87	9.85	4	0	0	4	3	12.1
PACO PHARMACEUTICAL	1.37	1.50	−32.17	14.41	9.20	−4	1	−3	4	3	0.6

EXHIBIT A–11 *(concluded)*

Company	5yr SD ROE/ (P/BV)	Sales % Chg Index	Earns Stab. Index	(LTGR +DY)/ (P/BV)	5yr SD RIR/ (P/FBV)	Ranked Fundamental Criteria: 5yr SD ROE/ (P/BV)	Sales % Chg Index	Earns Stab. Index	(LTGR +DY)/ (P/BV)	5yr SD RIR/ (P/FBV)	Total
S&P 400	8.35			5.48	2.71	0	0	0	−1	−4	−5.5
PAPERCRAFT CORP	9.48	7.25	−14.33	11.04	2.89	0	2	0	3	−3	1.2
PENTAIR CORP	12.33	0.75	−19.67	8.42	5.82	2	0	−1	1	1	3.3
PETRO EQUIP TOOLS	15.81	73.00	−58.00	36.38	11.96	3	4	−4	4	4	10.1
PHILIPS INDS INC	6.19	−6.50	−12.50	4.38	3.25	−3	−1	1	−3	−2	−8.3
PIEDMONT AVIATION	12.88	−17.50	−47.67	9.82	7.27	2	−3	−4	3	2	1.5
POPE EVANS ROBBINS	20.59	69.00	−83.67	10.21	12.45	4	4	−4	3	4	10.1
PRECISION CASTPARTS	4.92	13.50	−16.50	5.58	3.46	−4	3	0	−1	−2	−5.9
PRIME MOTOR INNS	6.30	−16.00	−9.17	3.05	4.29	−3	−3	2	−4	−1	−8.4
PRINTRONIX INC	17.42	−16.75	−20.67	10.01	10.91	4	−3	−1	3	3	8.1
PUGET SOUND BANCORP	12.16	−0.75	−7.67	10.15	5.84	2	0	3	3	1	9.9
QUAKER CHEM CORP	8.23	−4.00	−16.50	6.76	4.03	−1	0	0	0	−1	−2.2
REGAL BELOIT CORP	6.57	−11.75	−25.83	6.69	1.71	−3	−2	−2	0	−4	−11.1
REPUBLIC N Y CORP	17.73	33.50	−19.50	9.72	9.11	4	4	−1	2	3	11.2
REUTER INC	9.13	69.25	−43.50	8.98	5.58	0	4	−3	2	0	1.3
ROWAN COS INC	22.37	82.75	−59.17	7.88	13.46	4	4	−4	1	4	7.9
RUSS TOGS INC	16.27	−13.00	−11.17	11.82	6.69	4	−2	1	4	2	10.9
RUSSELL CORP	11.55	−5.25	−9.50	7.98	6.30	2	−1	2	1	1	6.0
RYLAND GROUP INC	7.02	6.75	−46.67	5.47	3.93	−2	2	−3	−1	−1	−6.5
SCIENTIFIC COMPUTERS	16.08	−7.75	−16.67	10.11	7.80	3	−1	0	3	3	9.3
SCIENTIFIC SOFTWARE	21.31	−162.75	−38.00	18.60	13.54	4	−4	−3	4	4	7.5
SCOA INDS INC	8.45	−6.50	−9.67	5.01	4.45	0	−1	2	−2	0	−0.6
SEALED AIR CORP	5.99	−38.75	−21.83	6.06	2.77	−4	−4	−2	0	−4	−13.4
SERVICE FRACTURING	15.54	−26.00	−32.67	13.57	8.09	3	−4	−3	4	3	5.3
SEVEN OAKS INTL	9.84	−23.25	−25.00	6.35	5.80	0	−4	−2	0	1	−3.5
SHAKLEE CORP	14.03	5.00	−43.00	11.11	5.68	3	2	−3	3	0	4.5
SHELBY WILLIAMS	5.54	−4.25	−15.33	4.43	3.60	−4	0	0	−3	−2	−9.9
SHOP & GO INC	6.75	−7.25	−7.50	3.89	4.43	−3	−1	3	−3	0	−3.9
SHOWBOAT INC	11.11	14.50	−9.50	8.43	4.12	1	3	2	1	−1	5.1

SONOCO PRODS	8.57	−5.50	−10.50	6.67	3.94	0	−1	1	0	−1	−0.6
SPARTON CORP	8.15	−24.25	−47.17	6.58	3.70	−1	−4	−4	0	−2	−10.1
STARRETT, L S, CO	9.10	−0.50	−18.00	6.71	3.31	0	0	0	0	−2	−2.2
SUBARU AMER INC	9.26	11.00	−10.50	3.13	8.49	0	3	1	−4	3	1.8
SUPERMARKETS GEN	7.69	23.00	−12.23	4.40	4.75	−1	3	1	−3	0	−1.5
TBC CORP	14.47	4.25	−18.33	5.97	10.91	3	1	0	0	3	7.2
TEAM INC	1.01	−13.00	−85.33	21.77	0.09	−4	−2	−4	4	−4	−10.0
TELEFLEX INC	9.47	−2.75	−9.67	5.90	5.41	0	0	2	−1	0	1.1
TELEX CORP	5.87	8.25	−70.50	5.12	6.48	−4	2	−4	−2	2	−7.6
THOMPSON MED INC	16.09	−92.00	−19.50	4.78	13.87	3	−4	−1	−2	4	2.0
THOUSAND TRAILS	12.89	−38.25	−33.67	8.17	11.34	2	−4	−3	1	4	2.0
THRIFTY CORP	5.95	−1.25	−7.67	4.69	2.40	−4	0	3	−2	−4	−7.7
TOKHEIM CORP	8.85	−12.00	−15.50	7.57	4.24	0	−2	0	1	−1	−1.2
TRACOR INC	6.47	−2.50	−6.00	6.65	3.25	−3	0	3	0	−2	−2.2
TRIANGLE MICROWAVE	9.90	53.50	−72.00	7.16	7.46	0	4	−4	0	2	0.2
TYCO LABS INC	8.95	−11.75	−25.00	5.87	4.74	0	−2	−2	−1	0	−4.5
TYLER CORP	8.08	−25.25	−30.67	10.41	3.81	−1	−4	−3	3	−1	−4.6
UNITED BANCORP ARIZ	10.89	28.25	−9.83	7.44	6.63	1	4	2	0	2	7.9
UNITED STATIONERS	5.52	−4.75	−12.67	3.06	3.76	−4	0	1	−4	−2	−9.9
UNIVERSAL FOODS	12.20	6.50	−22.00	8.72	4.97	2	2	−2	2	0	3.4
UNIVERSAL LEAF	11.40	5.50	−4.00	7.76	4.47	1	2	4	1	0	7.8
VARLEN CORP	15.69	−9.75	−14.17	6.95	7.35	3	−2	0	0	2	4.3
VEECO INSTRS INC	6.04	−13.50	−18.83	6.29	3.49	−3	−3	−1	0	−2	−8.4
VELCRO INDS N V	7.79	−6.00	−5.83	2.40	3.92	−1	−1	3	−4	−1	−3.9
VERNITRON CORP	11.33	3.75	−11.67	5.86	6.61	1	1	1	−1	2	3.9
VICON INDS INC	10.52	−5.00	−29.50	11.59	6.68	1	0	−3	4	2	4.4
WALBAR INC	8.89	15.00	−19.33	4.69	5.72	0	3	−1	−3	1	−1.5
WALLACE COMPUTER	5.93	4.50	−5.00	3.51	3.27	−4	1	4	−4	−2	−6.0
WENDY'S INTL INC	7.08	1.00	−9.00	3.83	4.02	−2	0	2	−3	−1	−4.4
WINDMERE CORP	19.36	4.25	−13.67	11.43	12.85	4	1	0	3	4	12.7
WOODS, PETE, CORP	9.84	26.25	−21.83	8.76	4.64	0	4	−2	2	0	2.4
WORTHINGTON INDS	6.89	−12.25	−15.33	5.81	2.89	−2	−2	0	−1	−3	−7.8
ZERO CO	6.15	−3.25	−5.17	5.00	3.24	−3	0	4	−2	−3	−4.4

Donald Smith & Co., Inc.

It was late May 1985 and the market had been advancing strongly for six months. Mr. Smith, president of Donald Smith & Co., Inc., an institutional money management firm, had been wrestling with the problem of how to allocate the funds he had just received from a new client. He was seriously considering increasing his typical 10 percent position in the steel industry to a "full" position of 15 percent, but he knew this move would expose him to further industry-specific risk and put added pressure on the correctness of his fundamental analysis. Although he was not worried about missing the market, he did not wish to remain in cash with these new funds very long. Many of his portfolio stocks, including the steels, were faring relatively well in the recent advance, and he still believed the fundamentals of the steel industry fit with his investment technique.

The Firm

Donald Smith & Co., Inc., was a registered investment adviser formed in 1975 as Home Portfolio Advisors, Inc. Donald G. Smith joined the firm as president after working 12 years for The Capital Guardian Trust Co. and Capital Research Co. The name and ownership of Home Portfolio Advisors were changed to their present forms in 1983. The firm consisted of two portfolio manager/analysts, one economist, and a full-time trader. Exhibit 1 gives some relevant asset information on Donald Smith & Co., Inc., and background on firm personnel.

This case was prepared by Todd J. Kelly under the supervision of Robert F. Vandell of the Colgate Darden Graduate School of Business Administration of the University of Virginia.

Management Goals and Style

Mr. Smith was what many people liked to call a "bottom-raker" or "bottom-fisher"—that is, a practitioner of an investment style that concentrated portfolio investments in deeply undervalued securities. But what determined value and which parameters were its best measures were difficult questions to answer. For Mr. Smith the answer was price-to-book ratio, the lower the better. Exhibit 2 gives a price-to-book ratio profile of Mr. Smith's portfolio history versus the S&P 400, which clearly demonstrates the bottom-raker's preference for low price/book. This graph demonstrates that, while the market in general was willing to pay approximately one and a half times book value for a given security, Mr. Smith limited his investment choices to those securities trading at a ratio of less than .80, with an average for the composite portfolio of approximately .50. This method did not mean that the firm's composite portfolio was simply a statistical, computer-generated portfolio of lowest price/book stocks. It was a carefully chosen concentration of industry representatives that, for one reason or another, had fallen on hard times and consequently out of Wall Street's favor. After his fundamental analysis, the portfolio manager's opinion was that the industry in general, and certain industry member stocks in particular, had fallen to their lowest support levels, ridding themselves of downside risk, and demonstrating considerable likelihood of eventual recovery.

Mr. Smith addressed the logic behind his investment technique in the firm's new client brochure:

Why Our Investment Philosophy Produces Superior Results

While the investment approach at Donald Smith & Co., Inc., is unique among those followed by institutional investors, it must be described initially in a phrase which has become commonplace, namely—the search for value.

Value means different things to different people. To some, a security is an attractive value if it provides a high current return with relatively little risk. To others, a good value implies a rapid growth rate for a company's earnings combined with a relatively low price/earnings ratio. A third definition relates the current price to some, much higher, projected price in the future. And, frequently, value is seen to exist merely in a price which is down from where it had been.

At our firm, value often incorporates one or more of the foregoing, but always there is another element, sharp and clear and unequivocal. It is—a substantial discount from asset value. Pure and simple, we buy stocks below book value. Not every stock. And not blindly or with some naive faith in the historical costs on a corporate balance sheet. But, without question, that group of stocks selling below book value does constitute our hunting ground.

In pursuing this approach, we frequently go against the consensus—buying when others are selling and vice-versa. We do not do so just to be contrary, however. Also, by purchasing below book value, we often acquire stocks that have high yields and are selling at low price/earnings ratios and which are well down from past highs, but these are just extra benefits. They are not the primary goals.

There are two main reasons why we do what we do. The first is our belief—our perception—that the essential pattern of the securities markets is one of cycles rather than trends. We believe that stocks tend to fluctuate around some intrinsic, central

> value, imprecise though it may be, and that it is, therefore, profitable to buy them when they are significantly below such value and to sell them when they reach or exceed it. In fact, the lower a stock goes, the more attractive it becomes. Allowing for all of that, the question must still arise: Why limit ourselves to stocks selling below book value? Why not exploit the fluctuations experienced by glamour stocks and growth stocks and stocks in general?
>
> The answer—the second reason why we utilize this approach—follows from the economic principle which says that capital tends to flow toward areas of high return and away from areas of low return. When companies earn 20 percent or more on their net worth or book value, other companies try to enter the industry. Returns of 5 percent will not attract new producers and will even cause existing investors to seek ways to get their capital out.
>
> High returns on book value are therefore self-defeating. With productive capacity rising rapidly (not just from new entrants, but also from the reinvestment of huge profits and the proceeds of stock financing), supply increases, competition intensifies, and the return on net assets starts to decline. That is why we stay away from highly profitable companies even when they sell at seemingly low price/earnings ratios. In a free economy, a high degree of profitability is difficult to sustain.
>
> Subprofitable industries, with low returns on investment (or even deficits), experience an opposite series of events. Newcomers are deterred from entering, while many producers are liquidated or merged or go bankrupt or simply shift to other products. Little capacity is added because retained earnings are small and equity financings to raise new money are rare. Under such conditions, competitive pressures start to moderate, and just the slightest pickup in demand causes product prices to firm. As the subprofitable industry begins to heal itself, the return on book value begins to rise.
>
> The significance of book value then is that, when placed alongside earnings, it permits the world to see whether a company or an industry is profitable or subprofitable. Stocks often sell at deep discounts from book value because the companies they represent are earning a below-normal return on investment. Since such returns have a natural tendency to recover—there is no need for a "story"—the stocks themselves are often descending to all-time lows just as their earnings are about to rise.

With this type of investment philosophy, the portfolio manager's challenge was to decide which stocks to buy because they represented true values, and which to leave alone because they were true dogs. He had to be able to see what other people didn't see. Consequently, research at the firm was 95 percent internally generated, and outside research for industry and company investment recommendations was not used. The majority of companies of interest were so out of favor that few analysts actively followed them. The 5 percent of the firm's research that Wall Street did supply was limited to factual information. If Donald Smith & Co., Inc., was interested in investing in a new or unfamiliar industry, Wall Street research provided an understanding of some of the key success factors for participants in the industry, such as what constituted a good product, how the particular products of each company compared with what the customer was looking for, where the industry was going for its supplies, and who were the big R&D spenders.

Internal investment research usually began with a computer sort of ascending-order price/book ratios as shown in Exhibit 3. The next step, sorting into industries, allowed the analyst to examine other stock-picking flags relative to the industry average, such as sales revenue/share and stock price/sales revenue per share. These parameters were used to provide additional insight into the relative value of the security. An industry sort is illustrated in Exhibit 4. The last two columns in the industry sort show the two-to-four-year estimated EPS and the accompanying P/E multiple if the stock price remained at its present level. These extremely low P/E multiples were another reason why Mr. Smith believed many of these securities had limited downside risk. A sensitivity analysis of the EPS projections would illustrate significant price immunity to downgrading of estimates if one assumed reasonable P/E multiples. Also shown in Exhibit 4 is the fully diluted number of shares outstanding. Another attempt to limit downside risk was by concentrating portfolio investments in larger-capitalization stocks. This approach provided liquidity to the portfolio and, assuming the assets were of acceptable quality, attempted to assure the investor of good asset protection in case of bankruptcy proceedings. It also avoided the issues of control and SEC filings if the manager decided to take a substantial position in the stock, since Donald Smith & Co., Inc., was interested in investing in companies, not owning them.

With the list narrowed to stocks in a few select industries, the analyst would begin his fundamental analysis. Company research consisted of: management interviews, annual report and 10K analysis, industry economic forecast, market-share analysis, etc. The most critical issue was how a company was positioned to take part in an industry turnaround. If a company was uniquely qualified to take better advantage of an upsurge in demand than its competitors or if the company was so undervalued that simple share maintenance in an industry upturn would allow its stock price to reflect true value better, then it was a candidate for investment.

The analysts were assisted in their short- and long-term outlooks by the firm's economist, who was responsible for the normal econometric analysis, as one would expect, but who took this work one step further. He combined econometric analysis, socioeconomic behavior trends, and common sense to attempt to isolate unique situations in the market beneficial to exploitation by the bottom-raking manager. He was, in effect, an economist/strategist.

The Portfolio

Exhibits 5 and 6 show consolidated and client-specific portfolios for Donald Smith & Co., Inc. The first item to note is the portfolio asset mix. The allocation decision depended on the availability of acceptable candidates for investment. The portfolio cash position was normally between 5 and 50 percent. "If there just aren't enough issues we like around we'll move to a cash position." A rule of thumb was to try to keep the portfolio at less than half the S&P 400 price/book ratio, which significantly narrowed the stock-picking universe. Fixed-income investments were added if the fundamentals were good, but the managers at Donald Smith & Co., Inc., believed that the most potential for superior returns was in following their equity investment strategy, and hence, their emphasis was on equities.

By most standards the portfolio size and turnover would have been considered small. The average number of securities held was 15; turnover approximated 25–30 percent annually. These attributes presented both benefits and drawbacks. The most significant benefit was simpler management. The resources needed to maintain a large, high-turnover portfolio, with an investment strategy other than pure "black box," would have required the purchase and adoption of outside research opinions and/or a significant increase in research personnel. According to Mr. Smith, "That would cause considerable internal decision-making problems. The more effective investment decisions are made when the process is limited to three people or less. That way you ensure consistency in the investment philosophy. When you start making decisions by consensus, the discipline of the strategy is threatened." The main drawback to small size was the possible lack of diversification.[1]

Mr. Smith's stylistic flare was to industry-overweight relative to the S&P 500 Index—more from necessity than by choice. The value screen used by the firm generally resulted in the majority of investment candidates being concentrated in two or three industries, which allowed substantial positive portfolio performance when only a few industries moved higher. Unfortunately, the method worked exactly the same way in the negative direction. The overweighting lowered the portfolio's correlation with the market and, in accordance with theory, subjected the portfolio to more unsystematic company-specific and industry-specific risk. A few examples may help:

Industry	*Smith Consolidated Portfolio**	*S&P 500†*
Steel	9.5%	0.5%
Utilities, Electric	10.1	5.0
Savings & Loan	10.7	2.4 (banks)

*The percent of portfolio holdings attributable to the specific industry.

†The percent of the S&P 500 Index attributable to the specific industry (values as of May 1985).

Although Mr. Smith liked to industry-overweight, there were limits. A full position in a specific industry for the portfolio would be 15 percent. This position did not occur often and had to be backed up by very favorable fundamentals. Ownership in individual companies was normally between 1–5 percent but could be as high as 7 percent. If special circumstances existed, i.e., the stock was a particularly good buy and no substitute stock was available, the firm was willing to take up to a 10 percent position in a single company. Portfolio-returns generation in the short term (one year) was expected from approximately five good movers. In the long term (3 to 5 years), the advisers expected all members to show positive returns, relative to the market.

[1]The work of William F. Sharpe concerning the behavior of risk in portfolios of differing numbers of securities could be of help here. Exhibit 7 shows the relationship between randomly selected securities and portfolio risk. It must be pointed out that this analysis pertains to a hypothetical and most unusual universe of securities with correlation of returns equal to zero and identical standard deviations. The exhibit shows that, although holding 100 or more stocks would be optimal, the most efficient reduction of unsystematic risk is achieved with about 15 stocks.

Bottom-raking could present some unique problems. The first was efficiently managing in and out of basically illiquid securities. Even with a portfolio core of large-capitalization stocks, this maneuvering could become a very real difficulty for the bottom-raker, given his chosen investment arena. Because of institutional non-interest in the firm's favored securities, the availability of large block trades was unpredictable at best. To circumvent this problem, the firm carried a full-time trader. According to Mr. Smith, "Mr. Henry is the company's window to Wall Street. The firm's size doesn't warrant a full-time trader; however, we keep one and it has proven to be the right choice time and again. By using someone full time we are better able to monitor present ownership of large blocks of stock and when they will be coming available." This approach helped to secure positions in a stock on a timely basis and kept transactions costs (both brokerage fees and market pressure cost[2]) low. It also allowed the two money managers to concentrate on analysis and decision making.

Another difficulty the investment strategy could present was client understanding and acceptance. Convincing clients that their money would earn excess returns by investing in securities many people believed wouldn't be around in five years could be difficult. Don Smith did it by educating his clients "up front." He focused on the investment philosophy in general and the specific qualitative factors he believed the market had not correctly priced into the securities. This method required more initial client contact than in most firms. Meetings with new clients after this initial period were generally semiannual. Once a client was established and familiar with the returns behavior of the investment strategy, less contact was needed and periodic updates over the phone became the norm.

A third problem was patience and discipline. An investment strategy like bottom-raking could present many situations that severely tested the conviction of the investment manager. He had to be secure in the logic of the strategy and patient enough to wait for the company or industry to turn around. In the meantime he had to be prepared for the problems and distressing news that accompanied struggling industries. A case in point was Wheeling-Pittsburgh Steel. Fitting the classic mold, Wheeling-Pittsburgh was a company Mr. Smith liked in an industry he liked. There were obviously problems with the company (otherwise he wouldn't have bought into it), but the level the stock had dropped to had, in Mr. Smith's opinion, rid it of as much downside risk as possible. Then Wheeling-Pittsburgh declared bankruptcy. Exhibit 8 gives an example of the types of opinions in the financial press and investment community that the bottom-raker must live with. For Mr. Smith, a veteran of the philosophy, this news was not cause for panic. "As far as I can remember, in my 16 years of bottom-raking, Wheeling-Pittsburgh was my first bankruptcy, and I don't think it was for real. I think it was done for leverage in their upcoming labor negotiations. The stock is still a very attractive one. Given all

---

[2]For example, "buy pressure" cost is the normal rise in security price when there is heavy buy demand relative to supply. This effect is magnified for the bottom-raker because of the low level of liquidity (day-to-day trading volume) in most of the securities in which he is interested, particularly for buying purposes.

the uncertainties, it's amazing the price has held between $7 and $8 a share. That suggests strong asset protection."

The Firm's Role in the Investment Community

Mr. Smith realized that he was filling a niche in the tax-exempt investment community and was not worried about becoming the largest fund in the business. He was providing a service to the investment community, and that service was diversification. The bulk of large institutional portfolios traded in securities with price/book ratios above the market average. Donald Smith & Co., Inc., provided the fund manager with another investment style to use in his overall asset-allocation decision. Large-fund managers liked to split their assets among different investment-style managers to diversify away style risk. The key success factor in this activity was to be sure the different managers' positive alphas did not cancel out in the diversification attempt. Because Mr. Smith saw himself providing this type of service, he was hesitant to take a large percentage of a fund. He looked for money managers with large portfolios and tried to capture a 5–10 percent share of their equity portfolio. Managing 10 percent of a client's equity funds and investing 10 percent of that fund in the steel industry gave the client a 1 percent exposure to the industry. This type of low exposure for the client in suspect industries, combined with an impressive record of success, allowed, for the most part, a good client-manager relationship.

Performance Analysis

After reviewing the investment technique that had done so well for him in the past, Mr. Smith thought some formal performance measurements might be helpful in solving his present investment dilemma. Cumulative wealth relatives, performance characteristic lines, and varying-period annualized total returns were compared to the S&P 500 over two different time periods, using two different intervals of measurement. Annual 1969–84 cumulative wealth relatives are given in Exhibit 9, and quarterly 1/80–1/85 values (all available data) are shown in Exhibit 10. Two regression models of Donald Smith portfolio "excess" returns versus S&P 500 "excess" returns were run.[3] Exhibit 11 summarizes the regression results for the annual data. (Annual returns data and cumulative values are shown in Exhibit 12.) Exhibit 13 regression results are based on quarterly data. Quarterly returns data and cumulative values are shown in Exhibit 14. Both showed lower-than-market betas, statistically significant alphas, and higher than usual residual errors. Performance in bear markets was quite attractive. Regression models had been used in the past as both performance indicators and forecasting models. For purposes of his analysis, he was primarily concerned with the models' illustration of historical risk/return performance.

---

[3]"Excess returns" equal either portfolio returns less the U.S. Treasury bill return or S&P 500 returns less the same Treasury bill rate.

The Decision

The decision still had to be made—go to a full position in the steel industry or invest the new funds somewhere else. If the steel position was advanced to 15 percent, how should it be done? Increase holdings in one of the steel companies already in the portfolio, increase holdings in all the present steel investments, or look for new steel investments? Would it matter? Although the information in the analysis was by no means perfect, it was the best Mr. Smith had developed after trying a number of ways of looking at the data, and he hoped it would help answer the key questions.

He knew the most important issues were, as always, related to risk/return. In order to increase his percentage holding in the steel industry, other industries' portfolio equity weightings would decrease accordingly. What would be the effect on diversification and risk? Would the excess returns generated by such a move be sufficient to warrant the increase in unsystematic risk, as would be evidenced by a lower R^2? Wasn't most of the downside risk in these securities already gone, given the extremely depressed nature of the stock price at the time of purchase? After all, that theory was the whole "bottom-raking" philosophy. Could anything worse occur? When would the "recovery" process begin? Was the upside potential large enough to warrant a concentrated exposure?

The steel industry's future depended on the interplay of many complex factors, and almost everyone "on The Street" was betting the results would not be favorable. But that was precisely why the stocks were such a bargain. "The Street" had been wrong before and allowed Mr. Smith to make a good living exploiting that fact. "Maybe," Mr. Smith thought, "I should check that summary steel report Richard wrote up [shown in Appendix A] one more time."

Appendix A

THE STEEL INDUSTRY

Donald Smith & Co., Inc., is currently reviewing its major investment in the steel industry and is considering increasing an already large position in the stocks of the major integrated U.S. steel producers. While this decision is somewhat dependent on individual security selection and choice, the purpose of this paper is simply to summarize our outlook for this unloved industry, rather than to analyze individual steel companies. The critical investment decision is to be right on the overall industry fundamentals since the factors influencing profitability and stock performance for steel companies tend to be homogeneous in nature.

The negatives for this industry are well known, so I will not dwell upon them. (It takes imagination, however, to come up with the positives!) The negative factors include:

1. Labor costs that are substantially higher than those of foreign steel producers and a union that has historically been considered the strongest in the country.
2. A decline in steel consumption due mainly to stagnant economic growth, material substitution, and downsizing in end markets.
3. A strong dollar coupled with record high import levels.
4. High barriers to exit (e.g., pension and raw material obligations) which have prevented the shutdown of outmoded open hearth capacity and helped lead to worldwide overcapacity.
5. Managements which do not always act in the best interest of their shareholders by making dilutive acquisitions, issuing stock below book value, making uneconomic capital expenditures, etc.
6. Weakened balance sheets as a result of large writedowns and poor earnings
7. The increasing use of mini-mill-produced specialty products.

While these negatives may appear insurmountable, there are offsetting positives:

1. A decline in oil price (which we expect) would stimulate worldwide economic growth and might slow the pace of downsizing in end markets (e.g., consumers would again favor larger cars).
2. There has been a massive shutdown in steel capacity, mainly in the U.S. and Europe. It takes about seven years to build new capacity, so if demand ever increased more than expected, a shortage situation could result.
3. The dollar may have peaked. Even if it hasn't, we believe that the recently enacted import quotas limiting foreigners' share of the domestic steel market to 18.5 percent for five years will eventually prove effective.
4. Cost cutting has been extensive, leading to reduced costs of up to 50 percent in some cases. Labor costs have declined dramatically and should continue to do so as the steel companies take a harder bargaining tack with the unions. The closing of open hearth capacity and installation of cost-reducing production methods such as continuous casting is leading to a more modern U.S. steel industry. Capital spending for the U.S. steel companies should decline, so cash flow will improve.
5. Hidden assets include: coal reserves, land, tax-loss carryforwards, LIFO reserves.
6. The U.S. steel companies are closest to the largest end markets (i.e., the U.S. customer) so transportation costs are low.
7. The stocks are at all-time absolute and relative lows. They sell at large discounts to book value and low prices relative to earnings potentials.

It is our general view that basic industry in America currently represents the most attractive value in the stock market today, using a 2–4 year time horizon. The idea that America is converting from an industrial-based to an information-based society has already been reflected in the institutional favorite stocks (e.g., health care, technology, service companies) as these stocks sell at many multiples of book value and earnings. As these industries attract competition, returns will drop. Meanwhile, those basic industry companies whose stocks sell below book value will see their returns rise as capital is withdrawn and competition abates. The steel group, the most downtrodden and unloved of all basic industry, offers the best value for our dollar.

EXHIBIT 1
Firm Asset Information and Background of Key Personnel

Total assets managed	$230,000,000
Tax-exempt assets managed:	
Total	$230,000,000
Fully discretionary	$230,000,000
Minimum separate account	$ 20,000,000
Tax-exempt clients (as of 5/1/85)	5
Types of accounts managed:	
1. Corporate	
2. Educational endowments	
3. State, local, provincial governments	

Biography of Investment Officers

Donald G. Smith (born 1941)		
Trinity College	1959–61	Economics
University of Illinois	1961–63	B.S. Accounting & Finance
U.C.L.A. Law School	1963–66	Doctor of Jurisprudence
Harvard Business School	1966–68	M.B.A.
Capital Guardian Trust Co.	1968–79	V.P. & Director
Home Insurance Company	1980–83	Chief Investment Officer
Donald Smith & Co., Inc.	1980–	President
Robert D. Leppo (born 1943)		
Stanford University	1961–65	B.A. History & Economics
Harvard Business School	1967–69	M.B.A.
Capital Research Co.	1969–77	Vice President
Private Investor	1977–83	
Donald Smith & Co., Inc.	1983–	Vice President
Richard L. Greenberg, CFA (born 1957)		
S.U.N.Y.—Binghamton	1975–79	B.A. Psychology
Wharton Business School	1979–81	M.B.A.
Home Insurance Company	1981–83	Industry Specialist
Donald Smith & Co., Inc.	1981–	Vice President
William J. Henry (born 1942)		
U.S. Merchant Marine Academy	1959–63	B.S. Nautical Science
Wharton Business School	1964–66	M.B.A.
E.I. du Pont de Nemours & Co.	1973–79	Equity Trader
Ford Foundation	1979–83	Equity Trader
Home Insurance Company	1983–84	Sr. Invest. Officer
Donald Smith & Co., Inc.	1984–	Vice President

EXHIBIT 2
Price-to-Book Value Ratio—Average Smith Portfolios versus S&P 400 Index
(*December 31, 1980, to March 31, 1984*)

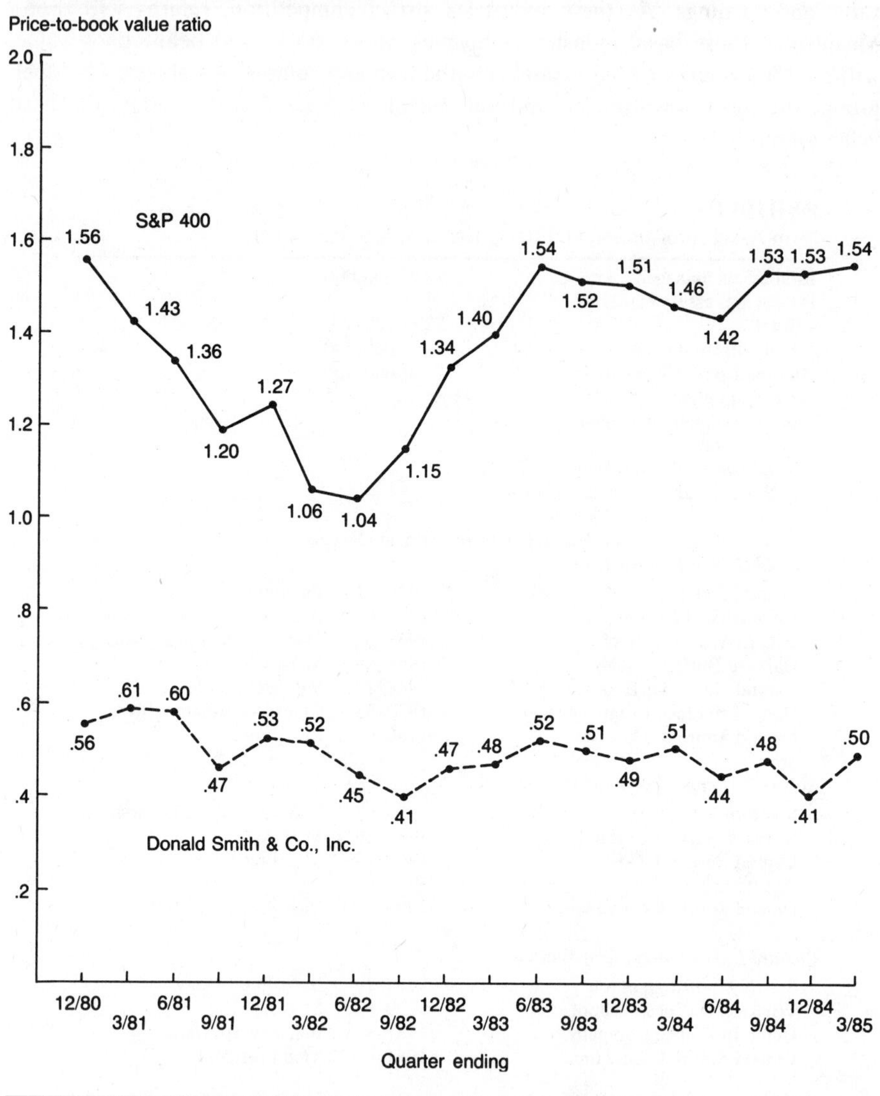

EXHIBIT 3

Characteristics of Stocks of Possible Interest *(ranked from lowest to highest price/book value)*

Description	F.D. Shs Outstg.	Price	Range	EPS:Last 12 Mo.	EPS:85 Est.	P/E Est. EPS	Yield	Book Value	Price/ Bk. Val.	Rev/ Sh.	Pr/Rev per Sh.	Est. ROE	2–4 Yrs EPS	P/E 2–4 Yrs
WHEELING-PITTSBURGH	5.1	7.50	6–36	−17.34	−3.00	−2.50	0.0	49.73	0.15	207	0.04	−6.0	10.00	0.75
KEYSTONE CONSOL.	1.9	2.75	2–7	−2.03	−4.00	−0.69	0.0	18.00	0.15	110	0.03	−22.2	2.00	1.38
PUBLIC SERVICE N.H.	55.0	3.88	3–13	2.84	2.40	1.61	0.0	18.12	0.21	10	0.39	13.2	2.00	1.94
CONSUMERS POWER	88.0	6.75	4–16	0.44	0.75	9.00	0.0	25.92	0.26	37	0.18	2.9	2.00	3.38
P. S. INDIANA	54.0	7.38	7–13	1.00	1.25	5.90	13.6	27.37	0.27	17	0.43	4.6	2.00	3.69
GLOBAL MARINE	44.0	3.38	3–10	−3.94	−1.00	−3.38	0.0	12.00	0.28	9	0.38	−8.3	1.50	2.25
LILCO	110.0	6.38	3–12	3.09	3.25	1.96	0.0	22.24	0.29	18	0.35	14.6	2.50	2.55
EVANS PRODUCTS	14.0	2.13	2–11	−4.29	−1.00	−2.13	0.0	7.00	0.30	100	0.02	−14.3	3.00	0.71
NORTHEAST SAVINGS	5.1	9.63	6–13	−0.89	2.00	4.81	0.0	31.50	0.31	77	0.13	6.3	5.00	1.93
ATLANTIC FINANCIAL	4.7	10.25	8–12	2.76	2.50	4.10	0.0	32.00	0.32	74	0.14	7.8	4.75	2.16
FIRST SAVINGS WISCONSIN	1.3	7.00	6–14	−8.47	0.25	28.00	0.0	20.35	0.34	111	0.06	1.2	6.00	1.17
TESORO	19.0	10.75	9–21	−0.49	−0.25	−43.00	3.7	30.88	0.35	163	0.07	−0.8	4.50	2.39
GLENDALE FEDERAL	21.0	10.75	7–12	2.21	3.00	3.58	0.0	30.36	0.35	59	0.18	9.9	4.50	2.39
DWG CORP.	23.0	2.13	2–4	0.24	0.70	3.04	0.0	6.00	0.35	43	0.05	11.7	1.70	1.25
PHILADELPHIA SAVING	35.0	9.13	7–12	1.76	1.75	5.21	2.2	25.49	0.36	39	0.23	6.9	3.25	2.81
WESTERN UNION	27.0	9.13	5–40	−3.95	−1.00	−9.13	0.0	24.00	0.38	42	0.22	−4.2	3.50	2.61
EASTMET	8.0	2.25	2–11	−4.60	−0.75	−3.00	0.0	5.91	0.38	25	0.09	−12.7	2.00	1.13
NORTHWESTERN STEEL & WIRE	7.5	10.25	9–26	−5.09	−2.00	−5.13	0.0	25.68	0.40	27	0.38	−7.8	5.50	1.86
WASHINGTON MUTUAL	6.7	13.38	8–14	−1.33	2.25	5.94	0.0	29.97	0.45	66	0.20	7.5	4.00	3.34
UNITED ILLUMINATING	15.0	15.25	9–24	5.37	4.75	3.21	13.1	33.80	0.45	34	0.45	14.1	5.00	3.05
FIRST FED. OF S.C.	2.6	8.63	4–10	0.91	1.50	5.75	0.0	18.90	0.46	67	0.13	7.9	3.50	2.46
KEYCON INDS.	1.9	12.00	7–12	6.19	1.00	12.00	0.0	25.95	0.46	63	0.19	3.9	4.00	3.00
PACIFIC FIRST FEDERAL	7.5	12.00	7–12	0.43	1.75	6.86	0.0	25.89	0.46	39	0.31	6.8	3.25	3.69
LANDMARK SAVINGS	1.5	14.00	3–15	2.04	2.00	7.00	0.0	29.20	0.48	93	0.15	6.8	5.75	2.43
GPU	63.0	12.50	7–13	2.06	2.00	6.25	0.0	26.05	0.48	43	0.29	7.7	3.00	4.17
BOHEMIA	4.2	10.13	8–18	−1.05	0.50	20.25	0.0	21.00	0.48	42	0.24	2.4	4.00	2.53
SUAVE SHOE	2.7	5.38	3–9	−0.96	−1.00	−5.38	0.0	11.02	0.49	35	0.15	−9.1	1.50	3.58

EXHIBIT 3 ***(concluded)***

Description	F.D. Shs Outstg.	Price	Range	EPS:Last 12 Mo.	EPS:85 Est.	P/E Est. EPS	Yield	Book Value	Price/ Bk. Val.	Rev/ Sh.	Pr/Rev per Sh.	Est. ROE	2–4 Yrs EPS	P/E 2–4 Yrs
GREAT LAKES FEDERAL	3.2	12.25	5–13	2.78	3.50	3.50	1.6	24.91	0.49	69	0.18	14.1	4.25	2.88
VALLEY FEDERAL	2.6	14.25	7–18	−4.08	2.50	5.70	0.0	28.61	0.50	108	0.13	8.7	7.00	2.04
METROPOLITAN FEDERAL	2.2	14.50	8–16	3.13	4.00	3.63	4.1	29.01	0.50	74	0.20	13.8	6.00	2.42
CALFED	21.0	19.88	11–19	2.76	4.50	4.42	2.4	38.80	0.51	98	0.20	11.6	6.50	3.06
ALGOMA STEEL (IN CAN. $)	15.0	21.75	16–31	−2.16	0.50	43.50	0.0	42.28	0.51	105	0.21	1.2	10.00	2.18
BROADVIEW FINANCIAL	4.0	4.13	3–9	−6.47	−1.00	−4.13	0.2	7.99	0.52	54	0.08	−12.5	3.25	1.27
INLAND	27.5	21.88	20–33	0.69	2.50	8.75	2.3	42.14	0.52	121	0.18	5.9	10.00	2.19
FIRST CITY BANC.	34.0	12.50	11–18	1.44	1.00	12.50	10.4	24.00	0.52	58	0.22	4.2	3.50	3.57
DOMINION TEX. (IN CAN. $)	15.0	11.00	11–20	−0.04	0.75	14.67	6.5	21.08	0.52	59	0.19	3.6	3.00	3.67
HUDSON'S BAY (IN CAN. $)	24.0	15.88	15–25	−5.40	−1.00	−15.88	3.8	30.00	0.53	201	0.08	−3.3	4.50	3.53
KAISER ALUM	49.0	14.00	12–23	0.81	1.00	14.00	0.0	26.40	0.53	53	0.26	3.8	5.25	2.67
TEXSCAN	7.5	3.50	3–17	0.06	−1.00	−3.50	0.0	6.60	0.53	12	0.29	−15.2	1.25	2.80
GEO INT'L	13.0	4.75	4–10	−1.38	−0.25	−19.00	0.0	8.94	0.53	22	0.22	−2.8	2.00	2.38
ARMCO	71.0	7.38	6–23	−4.07	−0.50	−14.75	0.0	13.68	0.54	57	0.13	−3.7	4.50	1.64
SMITH INT'L	23.0	10.75	9–21	−0.17	−0.25	−43.00	3.0	19.80	0.54	30	0.36	−1.3	3.50	3.07
UNION CARBIDE	73.0	38.25	33–65	4.34	5.00	7.65	8.9	68.00	0.56	130	0.29	7.4	13.00	2.94
L. E. MYERS	2.3	2.38	2–16	−7.84	−0.50	−4.75	0.0	4.22	0.56	78	0.03	−11.8	2.00	1.19
AMERICAN HOIST & DERRICK	7.0	9.75	7–15	−3.75	−0.25	−39.00	0.0	17.11	0.57	47	0.21	−1.5	3.50	2.79
ZAPATA	21.0	13.38	13–24	0.36	0.25	53.50	6.3	23.21	0.58	20	0.67	1.1	3.75	3.57
SOUTHWEST FOREST IND.	13.0	11.88	12–23	0.30	0.50	23.75	0.0	20.33	0.58	60	0.20	2.5	4.00	2.97
STEIGER TRACTOR	4.5	6.00	5–10	−0.81	−1.00	−6.00	0.0	10.24	0.59	27	0.22	−9.8	2.75	2.18
HANNA MINING	11.3	19.25	17–24	1.22	1.75	11.00	2.1	32.56	0.59	18	1.07	5.4	5.00	3.85
BURLINGTON	31.0	24.75	23–43	0.36	1.75	14.14	6.6	41.82	0.59	102	0.24	4.2	6.00	4.13
CENTRAL MAINE POWER	24.0	9.63	8–15	1.96	1.75	5.50	14.5	16.17	0.60	21	0.46	10.8	2.00	4.81
SALANT	3.5	5.38	4–13	−5.32	−0.50	−10.75	0.0	9.00	0.60	57	0.09	−5.6	2.00	2.69
REYNOLDS METALS	24.0	34.88	26–42	5.14	3.00	11.63	2.9	58.00	0.60	155	0.23	5.2	11.00	3.17
INSPIRATION RESOURCES	63.0	5.63	4–12	−3.34	0.50	11.25	0.0	9.35	0.60	15	0.38	5.3	1.50	3.75
FIELDCREST	4.0	26.75	26–35	1.69	1.25	21.40	7.5	44.00	0.61	143	0.19	2.8	6.75	3.96
LUKENS	5.2	14.88	10–17	1.48	1.50	9.92	2.7	24.36	0.61	80	0.19	6.2	4.50	3.31

EXHIBIT 4
Stocks of Interest Sorted by Industry *(May 1985)*

Description	F.D. Shs Outstg.	Price	Range	EPS:Last 12 Mo.	EPS:85 Est.	P/E Est. EPS	Yield	Book Value	Price/ Bk. Val.	Rev/ Sh.	Pr/Rev per Sh.	Est. ROE	2–4 Yrs EPS	P/E 2–4 Yrs
STEELS														
U.S. STEEL	140.0	28.75	22–33	1.10	3.00	9.58	3.5	35.00	0.82	136	0.21	8.6	11.00	2.61
BETHLEHEM	59.0	16.63	14–30	−3.47	0.50	33.25	2.4	20.00	0.83	91	0.18	2.5	9.50	1.75
INLAND	27.5	21.88	20–33	0.69	2.50	8.75	2.3	42.14	0.52	121	0.12	5.9	10.00	2.19
NATIONAL	23.0	26.38	24–35	−1.51	1.50	17.58	0.9	43.00	0.61	105	0.25	3.5	10.00	2.64
ARMCO	71.0	7.38	6–23	−4.07	−0.50	−14.75	0.0	13.68	0.54	57	0.13	−3.7	4.50	1.64
WHEELING-PITTSBURGH	5.1	7.50	6–36	−17.34	−3.00	−2.50	0.0	49.73	0.15	207	0.04	−6.0	10.00	0.75
LTV CORP.	107.0	9.13	9–20	−5.62	0.25	36.50	0.0	10.83	0.84	79	0.12	2.3	7.00	1.30
LUKENS	5.2	14.88	10–17	1.48	1.50	9.92	2.7	24.36	0.61	80	0.19	6.2	4.50	3.31
NORTHWESTERN STEEL & WIRE	7.5	10.25	9–26	−5.09	−2.00	−5.13	0.0	25.68	0.40	27	0.38	−7.8	5.50	1.86
KEYSTONE CONSOL.	1.9	2.75	2–7	−2.03	−4.00	−0.69	0.0	18.00	0.15	110	0.03	−22.2	2.00	1.38
KEYCON INDS.	1.9	12.00	7–12	6.19	1.00	12.00	0.0	25.95	0.46	63	0.19	3.9	4.00	3.00
ALGOMA STEEL (IN CAN. $)	15.0	21.75	16–31	−2.16	0.50	43.50	0.0	42.28	0.51	105	0.21	1.2	10.00	2.18
EASTMET	8.0	2.25	2–11	−4.60	−0.75	−3.00	0.0	5.91	0.38	25	0.09	−12.7	2.00	1.13
METALS (NON-STEEL)														
KAISER ALUM.	49.0	14.00	12–23	0.81	1.00	14.00	0.0	26.40	0.53	53	0.26	3.8	5.25	2.67
REYNOLDS METALS	24.0	34.88	26–42	5.14	3.00	11.63	2.9	58.00	0.60	155	0.23	5.2	11.00	3.17
PHELPS DODGE	31.0	20.88	13–28	−3.42	−1.00	−20.88	0.0	33.63	0.62	29	0.72	−3.0	5.00	4.18
HANNA MINING	11.3	19.25	17–24	1.22	1.75	11.00	2.1	32.56	0.59	18	1.07	5.4	5.00	3.85
MOORE McCORMACK	9.8	25.50	18–26	1.78	2.50	10.20	4.1	40.10	0.64	54	0.47	6.2	6.00	4.25
CLEVELAND CLIFFS	12.5	20.00	17–26	2.38	3.00	6.67	5.0	25.78	0.78	32	0.63	11.6	4.50	4.44
AMAX	70.0	16.25	15–28	−4.37	−0.25	−65.00	1.2	20.28	0.80	34	0.48	−1.2	5.00	3.25
INSPIRATION RESOURCES	63.0	5.63	4–12	−3.34	0.50	11.25	0.0	9.35	0.60	15	0.38	5.3	1.50	3.75
ASARCO	32.0	23.75	17–35	−2.08	0.25	95.00	0.0	26.73	0.89	41	0.58	0.9	6.00	3.96
CHEMICALS														
UNION CARBIDE	73.0	38.25	33–65	4.34	5.00	7.65	8.9	68.00	0.56	130	0.29	7.4	13.00	2.94
WILLIAMS	35.0	28.75	22–32	3.11	4.00	7.19	4.2	37.43	0.77	97	0.30	10.7	6.00	4.99
BEKER	12.0	5.38	4–9	−1.31	−1.00	−5.38	0.0	8.00	0.67	22	0.24	−12.5	2.00	2.69
OLIN	26.0	31.00	25–37	3.13	4.00	7.75	4.3	37.88	0.82	79	0.39	10.6	6.00	5.17
PAPER & CONTAINER														
SOUTHWEST FOREST IND.	13.0	11.88	12–23	0.30	0.50	23.75	0.0	20.33	0.58	60	0.20	2.5	4.00	2.97
INT'L PAPER	50.0	50.75	46–60	3.86	4.00	12.69	4.7	61.00	0.83	94	0.54	6.6	10.00	5.08
CHAMPION INT'L	100.0	23.13	17–29	2.28	2.50	9.25	1.7	25.27	0.92	69	0.34	9.9	5.00	4.63
BOISE CASCADE	29.0	40.75	32–45	4.47	5.00	8.15	4.7	48.20	0.85	132	0.31	10.4	9.00	4.50
BOHEMIA	4.2	10.13	8–16	−1.05	0.50	20.25	0.0	21.00	0.48	42	0.24	2.4	4.00	2.55
BROCKWAY INC.	9.1	22.00	14–22	1.52	1.75	12.57	6.0	26.45	0.83	121	0.18	6.6	4.50	4.89
OWENS-ILLINOIS	30.0	45.25	31–46	4.60	5.50	8.23	3.7	47.66	0.95	117	0.39	11.5	8.50	5.32
ANCHOR HOCKING	10.5	22.75	19–36	−2.38	2.00	11.38	6.5	24.30	0.94	68	0.33	8.2	5.00	4.55

EXHIBIT 4 *(continued)*

Description	F.D. Shs Outstg.	Price	Range	EPS:Last 12 Mo.	EPS:85 Est.	P/E Est. EPS	Yield	Book Value	Price/ Bk. Val.	Rev/ Sh.	Pr/Rev per Sh.	Est. ROE	2–4 Yrs EPS	P/E 2–4 Yrs
BUILDING														
KAISER CEMENT	9.0	17.00	14–26	−0.72	0.50	34.00	1.2	16.95	1.00	28	0.61	2.9	4.25	4.00
EVANS PRODUCTS	14.0	2.13	2–11	−4.29	−1.00	−2.13	0.0	7.00	0.30	100	0.02	−14.3	3.00	0.71
JIM WALTER	26.0	33.00	22–37	4.77	5.00	7.00	4.0	37.45	0.93	88	0.40	13.4	7.00	5.00
U.S. HOME	40.0	7.00	5–13	−1.28	0.25	28.00	0.0	7.38	0.95	28	0.25	3.4	1.50	4.87
LONE STAR INDS.	15.0	25.25	18–30	0.07	1.75	14.43	7.5	31.99	0.79	67	0.38	5.5	6.00	4.21
BIRD INC.	5.0	8.38	5–11	−2.19	0.75	11.17	0.0	9.00	0.93	40	0.21	8.3	2.50	3.35
IDEAL BASIC	16.0	15.00	13–26	−1.92	−0.25	−60.00	0.0	22.38	0.67	25	0.60	−1.1	4.00	3.75
TEXTILES														
J.P. STEVENS	20.0	19.00	15–24	0.76	1.25	15.20	6.3	30.84	0.62	107	0.18	4.1	4.00	4.75
BURLINGTON	31.0	24.75	23–43	0.36	1.75	14.14	6.6	41.82	0.59	102	0.24	4.2	6.00	4.13
SUAVE SHOE	2.7	5.38	3–9	−0.96	−1.00	−5.38	0.0	11.02	0.49	35	0.15	−9.1	1.50	3.58
SALANT	3.5	5.38	4–13	−5.32	−0.50	−10.75	0.0	9.00	0.60	57	0.09	−5.6	2.00	2.69
DOMINION TEX. (IN CAN. $)	15.0	11.00	11–20	−0.04	0.75	14.67	6.5	21.08	0.52	59	0.19	3.6	3.00	3.67
WOLVERINE WORLDWIDE	7.2	10.50	9–17	0.02	0.75	14.00	2.3	15.61	0.67	53	0.20	4.8	2.50	4.20
FIELDCREST	4.0	26.75	26–35	1.69	1.25	21.40	7.5	44.00	0.61	143	0.19	2.8	6.75	3.96
RIEGEL TEXTILE	4.0	20.88	18–35	0.05	1.00	20.88	8.6	33.55	0.62	107	0.20	3.0	4.00	5.22
MACHINERY														
CHICAGO PNEUMATIC	4.3	22.63	16–27	2.84	3.50	6.46	1.8	24.24	0.93	96	0.24	14.4	6.00	3.77
AMERICAN HOIST & DERRICK	7.0	9.75	7–15	−3.75	−0.25	−39.00	0.0	17.11	0.57	47	0.21	−1.5	3.50	2.79
ALLIS CHALMERS	25.0	6.88	5–18	−10.24	−3.00	−2.29	0.0	3.00	2.29	35	0.20	−100.0	2.00	3.44
BARBER-GREENE	2.3	5.50	3–13	−6.54	−1.50	−3.67	0.0	2.06	2.67	50	0.11	−72.8	2.50	2.20
PEABODY INT'L	11.3	7.75	6–14	0.42	0.50	15.50	2.6	8.84	0.88	32	0.24	5.7	2.00	3.88
STEIGER TRACTOR	4.5	6.00	5–10	−0.81	−1.00	−6.00	0.0	10.24	0.59	27	0.22	−9.8	2.75	2.18
L. E. MYERS	2.3	2.38	2–16	−7.84	−0.50	−4.75	0.0	4.22	0.56	78	0.03	−11.8	2.00	1.19
AUTOS & TIRE														
FORD	188.0	43.00	33–52	14.35	13.00	3.31	6.7	52.86	0.81	279	0.15	24.6	16.00	2.69
GOODRICH	24.0	33.00	24–37	2.20	3.25	10.15	4.7	45.20	0.73	143	0.23	7.2	6.00	5.50
FIRESTONE	42.0	20.63	15–23	1.53	2.00	10.31	3.9	28.50	0.72	95	0.22	7.0	4.50	4.56
CHRYSLER	105.0	35.63	21–38	12.85	12.00	2.97	2.8	27.22	1.31	186	0.19	44.1	12.00	2.97
GENERAL MOTORS	320.0	68.88	61–85	12.37	15.00	4.59	7.3	66.03	1.04	262	0.26	22.7	18.00	3.83
A. O. SMITH	7.6	18.75	10–21	2.55	2.50	7.50	3.2	21.65	0.87	115	0.16	11.5	5.00	3.75

ENERGY													
TESORO	19.0	10.75	9–21	−0.49	−0.25	−43.00	3.7	30.88	0.35	163	0.07	−0.8	4.50	2.39
WESTBURNE INT'L (IN U.S. $)	10.5	10.88	8–14	0.63	1.00	10.88	1.4	16.00	0.68	92	0.12	6.3	2.50	4.35
TEXACO	263.0	37.00	31–48	4.11	4.25	8.71	8.1	51.03	0.73	180	0.21	8.3	8.00	4.63
DRESSER INDS.	75.0	20.25	15–23	1.32	1.50	13.50	4.0	24.73	0.82	50	0.41	6.1	5.00	4.05
SMITH INT'L	23.0	10.75	9–21	−0.17	−0.25	−43.00	3.0	19.80	0.54	30	0.36	−1.3	3.50	3.07
VALERO ENERGY	34.0	10.38	5–24	−1.58	−1.00	−10.38	4.2	14.88	0.70	68	0.15	−6.7	2.75	3.77
READING & BATES	32.0	9.50	7–14	0.06	0.25	38.00	4.2	14.80	0.64	12	0.79	1.7	2.50	3.80
PARKER DRILLING	30.0	6.25	6–13	−2.78	−2.00	−3.13	2.6	8.50	0.74	8	0.78	−23.5	2.00	3.13
HUGHES TOOL CO.	56.0	14.38	12–21	−2.13	0.50	28.75	3.3	16.82	0.85	22	0.65	3.0	3.50	4.11
GEO INT'L	13.0	4.75	4–10	−1.38	−0.25	−19.00	0.0	8.94	0.53	22	0.22	−2.8	2.00	2.38
ENTERRA CORP.	9.0	20.25	9–21	−1.06	−0.25	−81.00	0.0	14.05	1.44	18	1.13	−1.8	2.75	7.36
WESTMORELAND COAL	8.3	17.75	15–28	0.33	1.50	11.83	2.3	20.77	0.85	71	0.25	7.2	4.00	4.44
WESTERN COMPANY	45.0	6.50	4–11	−0.73	−0.25	−26.00	0.0	7.51	0.87	13	0.50	−3.3	1.75	3.71
ZAPATA	21.0	13.38	13–24	0.36	0.25	53.50	6.3	23.21	0.58	20	0.67	1.1	3.75	3.57
GLOBAL MARINE	44.0	3.38	3–10	−3.94	−1.00	−3.38	0.0	12.00	0.28	9	0.38	−8.3	1.50	2.25
AIRLINES														
FRONTIER HOLDINGS	14.0	14.13	8–15	−2.98	−1.00	−14.13	0.0	14.00	1.01	48	0.29	−7.1	3.00	4.71
PSA	6.8	26.50	15–27	0.16	1.50	17.67	2.3	29.19	0.91	101	0.26	5.1	6.00	4.42
TWA	40.0	17.25	7–17	0.78	1.50	11.50	0.0	16.35	1.06	92	0.19	9.2	3.50	4.93
UAL	41.0	47.75	28–49	5.97	7.00	6.82	2.1	47.29	1.01	170	0.28	14.8	8.00	5.97
PAN AM	150.0	5.63	4–8	−2.66	−0.25	−22.50	0.0	2.17	2.59	25	0.23	−11.5	1.50	3.75
EASTERN	85.0	8.63	3–8	0.29	0.50	17.25	0.0	2.00	4.31	51	0.17	25.0	2.00	4.31
FOOD & BEVERAGE														
COORS	35.0	16.50	12–22	1.09	1.75	9.43	2.4	25.00	0.66	32	0.52	7.0	3.25	5.08
UNITED BRANDS	16.0	15.00	10–22	0.78	1.00	15.00	0.0	18.00	0.83	205	0.07	5.6	3.50	4.29
ALLIED SUPERMARKETS	11.4	5.13	2–6	−0.01	0.10	51.25	0.0	7.23	0.71	47	0.11	1.4	0.80	6.41
UTILITIES														
GPU	63.0	12.50	7–13	2.06	2.00	6.25	0.0	26.05	0.48	43	0.29	7.7	3.00	4.17
P. S. INDIANA	54.0	7.39	7–13	1.00	1.25	5.90	13.6	27.37	0.27	17	0.43	4.6	2.00	3.69
CONSUMERS POWER	88.0	6.75	4–16	0.44	0.75	9.00	0.0	25.92	0.26	37	0.18	2.9	2.00	3.38
LILCO	110.0	6.38	3–12	3.09	3.25	1.96	0.0	22.24	0.29	18	0.35	14.6	2.50	2.55
CINCINNATI GAS & ELEC.	45.0	14.88	9–16	2.51	2.50	5.95	14.5	20.44	0.73	32	0.46	12.2	2.50	5.95
PUBLIC SERVICE N.H.	55.0	3.88	3–13	2.84	2.40	1.61	0.0	18.12	0.21	10	0.39	13.2	2.00	1.94
CENTRAL MAINE POWER	24.0	9.63	8–15	1.96	1.75	5.50	14.5	16.17	0.60	21	0.46	10.8	2.00	4.81
PUGET SOUND P & L	48.0	14.50	9–15	1.82	2.00	7.25	12.1	16.00	0.91	14	1.04	12.5	2.75	5.27
UNITED ILLUMINATING	15.0	15.25	9–24	5.37	4.75	3.21	13.1	33.80	0.45	34	0.45	14.1	5.00	3.05
TOLEDO EDISON	34.0	17.50	13–19	3.75	3.50	5.00	14.4	23.76	0.74	16	1.09	14.7	3.50	5.00
MIDDLE SOUTH UTIL.	192.0	13.88	9–15	2.78	2.50	5.55	12.5	18.35	0.76	16	0.87	13.6	3.00	4.63
DWG CORP.	23.0	2.13	2–4	0.24	0.70	3.04	0.0	6.00	0.35	43	0.05	11.7	1.70	1.25
PHILADELPHIA ELECTRIC	170.0	15.63	9–16	2.68	2.50	6.25	14.1	17.81	0.88	18	0.87	14.0	2.80	5.58
COLUMBIA GAS	40.0	30.25	27–38	4.86	2.00	15.13	10.5	39.11	0.77	115	0.26	5.1	6.00	5.04
MONTANA POWER	24.0	23.75	16–30	2.59	3.00	7.92	8.4	27.67	0.86	15	1.58	10.8	4.25	5.59

EXHIBIT 4 *(concluded)*

Description	F.D. Shs Outstg.	Price	Range	EPS:Last 12 Mo.	EPS:85 Est.	P/E Est. EPS	Yield	Book Value	Price/ Bk. Val.	Rev/ Sh.	Pr/Rev per Sh.	Est. ROE	2–4 Yrs EPS	P/E 2–4 Yrs
SAVINGS & LOANS														
FIRST FED. OF MICHIGAN	10.0	17.25	5–16	3.27	3.00	5.75	0.0	22.57	0.76	101	0.17	13.3	5.50	3.14
FEDERAL NAT'L MORTGAGE	74.0	17.88	11–26	−1.35	1.25	14.30	0.9	17.80	1.00	123	0.15	7.0	7.75	2.31
IMPERIAL CORP. OF AMER.	14.2	8.75	5–10	0.71	1.75	5.00	0.0	13.55	0.65	57	0.15	12.9	4.00	2.19
CARTERET	8.2	11.00	6–12	1.69	2.25	4.89	0.0	16.60	0.66	66	0.17	13.6	4.00	2.75
NORTHEAST SAVINGS	5.1	9.63	6–13	−0.89	2.00	4.81	0.0	31.50	0.31	77	0.13	6.3	5.00	1.93
ATLANTIC FINANCIAL	4.7	10.25	8–12	2.76	2.50	4.10	0.0	32.00	0.32	74	0.14	7.8	4.75	2.16
CALFED	21.0	19.88	11–19	2.76	4.50	4.42	2.4	38.80	0.51	98	0.20	11.6	6.50	3.06
GLENDALE FEDERAL	21.0	10.75	7–12	2.21	3.00	3.58	0.0	30.36	0.35	59	0.18	9.9	4.50	2.39
VALLEY FEDERAL	2.6	14.25	7–18	−4.08	2.50	5.70	0.0	28.61	0.50	108	0.13	8.7	7.00	2.04
WASHINGTON MUTUAL	6.7	13.38	8–14	−1.33	2.25	5.94	0.0	29.97	0.45	66	0.20	7.5	4.00	3.34
PHILADELPHIA SAVINGS	35.0	9.13	7–12	1.76	1.75	5.21	2.2	25.49	0.36	39	0.23	6.9	3.25	2.81
AHMANSON	28.0	34.63	16–35	2.40	4.50	7.69	3.5	33.70	1.03	97	0.36	13.4	7.25	4.76
FIN. CORP. SANTA BARBARA	4.5	4.25	2–9	−4.15	0.25	17.00	0.0	0.26	16.35	69	0.06	96.2	3.00	1.42
BROADVIEW FINANCIAL	4.0	4.13	3–9	−6.47	−1.00	−4.13	0.2	7.99	0.52	54	0.08	−12.5	3.25	1.27
FIRST SAVINGS WISCONSIN	1.3	7.00	6–14	−8.47	0.25	28.00	0.0	20.35	0.34	111	0.06	1.2	6.00	1.17
GREAT LAKES FEDERAL	3.2	12.25	5–13	2.78	3.50	3.50	1.6	24.91	0.49	69	0.18	14.1	4.25	2.88
FIRST FED. OF S.C.	2.6	8.63	4–10	0.91	1.50	5.75	0.0	18.90	0.46	67	0.13	7.9	3.50	2.46
LANDMARK SAVINGS	1.5	14.00	3–15	2.04	2.00	7.00	0.0	29.20	0.48	93	0.15	6.8	5.75	2.43
METROPOLITAN FEDERAL	2.2	14.50	8–16	3.13	4.00	3.63	4.1	29.01	0.50	74	0.20	13.8	6.00	2.42
GUARANTEE FINANCIAL	6.1	7.25	5–9	0.50	1.50	4.83	0.0	10.85	0.67	46	0.16	13.8	3.00	2.42
PACIFIC FIRST FEDERAL	7.5	12.00	7–12	0.43	1.75	6.86	0.0	25.89	0.46	39	0.31	6.8	3.25	3.59
FIN. CORP. OF AMERICA	42.0	6.75	4–25	−17.40	1.00	6.75	0.0	4.53	1.49	78	0.09	22.1	4.50	1.50

BANKS														
CROCKER	21.0	26.50	16–30	−13.58	1.25	21.20	1.5	42.14	0.63	127	0.21	3.0	7.00	3.79
MARINE MIDLAND	20.0	34.50	20–35	4.35	5.50	6.27	4.6	50.66	0.68	130	0.27	10.9	8.00	4.31
CHASE MANHATTAN	38.0	57.38	35–55	9.03	10.50	5.46	6.6	91.63	0.63	260	0.22	11.5	17.00	3.38
MANUFACTURER'S HANOVER	41.0	40.13	22–42	7.25	8.00	5.02	7.9	49.82	0.81	203	0.20	16.1	11.00	3.65
BANKAMERICA	152.0	20.88	14–23	1.85	2.75	7.59	7.3	28.74	0.73	95	0.22	9.6	5.00	4.18
CHEMICAL N.Y.	49.0	41.88	23–43	6.38	6.75	6.20	5.6	46.86	0.89	120	0.35	14.4	9.00	4.65
FIRST CHICAGO	48.0	24.25	18–27	1.20	4.00	6.06	5.4	34.12	0.71	94	0.26	11.7	6.00	4.04
BANK OF BOSTON	20.0	48.75	29–49	6.24	7.50	6.50	4.8	51.54	0.95	162	0.30	14.6	11.00	4.43
FIRST WISCONSIN	8.5	28.38	16–28	3.40	4.25	6.68	4.2	34.22	0.83	69	0.41	12.4	5.50	5.16
FIRST CITY BANC.	34.0	12.50	11–18	1.44	1.00	12.50	10.4	24.00	0.52	58	0.22	4.2	3.50	3.57
NORWEST CORP.	30.0	25.13	21–34	1.64	3.50	7.18	7.2	35.66	0.70	90	0.28	9.8	6.00	4.19
INSURANCE														
CIGNA	73.0	55.25	27–56	0.44	2.50	22.10	4.7	62.79	0.88	202	0.27	4.0	9.50	5.82
MISSION INSURANCE	19.0	8.50	6–27	−16.80	−0.50	−17.00	0.0	0.71	11.97	27	0.31	−70.4	2.50	3.40
MISCELLANEOUS														
PHILLIPS NV	240.0	15.63	10–18	1.33	2.00	7.81	4.4	19.45	0.80	58	0.27	10.3	3.00	5.21
CHROMALLOY AMERICAN	19.0	10.13	9.14	−0.06	0.75	13.50	0.0	13.74	0.74	46	0.22	5.5	3.00	3.38
HUDSON'S BAY (IN CAN. $)	24.0	15.88	15–25	−5.40	−1.00	−15.88	3.8	30.00	0.53	201	0.08	−3.3	4.50	0.53
STORAGE TECHNOLOGY	37.0	2.88	2–15	−14.62	−2.00	−1.44	0.0	1.00	2.88	22	0.13	−200.0	1.50	1.90
SOO LINE	7.6	29.50	23–30	2.73	2.00	14.75	4.1	36.46	0.81	80	0.37	5.5	6.00	4.90
CONTROL DATA	39.0	32.13	24–48	1.40	2.00	16.06	2.2	43.61	0.74	129	0.25	4.6	7.00	4.59
WHITE CONSOL.	16.0	26.38	24–48	2.94	2.50	10.55	5.7	29.73	0.89	119	0.22	8.4	6.50	4.06
SEA-LAND	26.0	19.13	15–28	2.91	2.50	7.65	0.0	29.70	0.64	68	0.28	8.4	5.50	3.48
WESTERN UNION	27.0	9.13	5–40	−3.95	−1.00	−9.13	0.0	24.00	0.38	42	0.22	−4.2	3.50	2.61
WILLIAMS ELECTRONICS	8.0	4.63	2–10	−1.32	0.25	18.50	0.0	2.75	1.68	7	0.66	9.1	1.50	3.08
HEALTHDYNE	14.0	3.50	2–22	−1.13	−0.25	−14.00	0.0	4.00	0.88	10	0.35	−6.3	0.75	4.67
MURRAY OHIO	4.0	18.00	16–25	1.16	1.50	12.00	3.3	28.93	0.62	96	0.19	5.2	4.75	3.75
TEXSCAN	7.5	3.50	3–17	0.06	−1.00	−3.50	0.0	6.60	0.53	12	0.29	−15.2	1.25	2.80
BALLY MFG.	27.0	14.88	11–23	0.15	1.25	11.90	1.3	11.00	1.35	50	0.30	11.4	3.50	4.25

EXHIBIT 5

Portfolio Characteristics: Consolidation Smith Portfolio *(stocks only; May 13, 1985)*

Description	Shares	Price	Mkt. Value ($M)	% of Port.	EPS:Last 12 Mo.	EPS:85 Est.	P/E Est. EPS	Curr. Yld	Book Value	Price/ Bk. Val.	Rev/ Sh.	Pr/Rev per Sh.	Est. ROE	2–4 Yrs EPS	P/E 2–4 Yrs	Beta
FEDERAL NATIONAL MTG.	903,000	17.63	15,915	6.9	−1.35	1.25	14.10	0.9	17.80	0.99	123	0.14	7.0	7.75	2.27	1.3
FIRST FEDERAL OF MICHIGAN	859,600	17.00	14,613	6.4	3.27	3.00	5.67	0.0	22.57	0.75	101	0.17	13.3	5.50	3.09	1.0
GLENDALE FEDERAL S & L	915,000	10.88	9,951	4.3	2.21	3.00	3.63	0.0	30.36	0.36	59	0.18	9.9	4.50	2.42	1.0
FORD MOTOR CO.	230,000	42.00	9,660	4.2	14.35	13.00	3.23	6.9	52.86	0.79	279	0.15	24.6	16.00	2.63	1.1
INLAND STEEL CO.	438,000	21.88	9,581	4.2	0.69	2.50	8.75	2.3	42.14	0.52	121	0.18	5.9	10.00	2.19	0.9
LONG ISLAND LIGHTING	1,399,500	6.38	8,922	3.9	3.09	3.25	1.96	0.0	22.24	0.29	18	0.35	14.6	2.50	2.55	0.6
GENERAL PUBLIC UTILITIES	684,800	12.75	8,731	3.8	2.06	2.00	6.38	0.0	26.05	0.49	43	0.30	7.7	3.00	4.25	0.9
LTV CORP.	929,700	9.38	8,716	3.8	−5.62	0.25	37.50	0.0	10.83	0.87	79	0.12	2.3	7.00	1.34	1.5
KAISER ALUM. & CHEM CORP.	635,000	13.63	8,652	3.8	0.81	1.00	13.63	0.0	26.40	0.52	53	0.26	3.8	5.25	2.60	1.1
ALLIS CHALMERS CORP.	983,100	6.68	6,759	2.9	−10.24	−3.00	−2.29	0.0	3.00	2.29	35	0.20	−100.0	2.00	3.44	1.2
CONSUMERS POWER CO.	800,000	6.88	5,500	2.4	0.44	0.75	9.17	0.0	25.92	0.27	37	0.19	2.9	2.00	3.44	0.7
WHEELING PITTSBURGH STEEL	447,100	7.75	3,465	1.5	−17.34	−3.00	−2.58	0.0	49.73	0.16	207	0.04	−6.0	10.00	0.78	1.2
BROCKWAY INC.	92,900	22.50	2,090	0.9	1.52	1.75	12.86	5.9	26.45	0.85	121	0.19	6.6	4.50	5.00	0.8
J. P. STEVENS	92,000	18.63	1,714	0.7	0.76	1.25	14.90	6.4	30.84	0.60	107	0.17	4.1	4.00	4.66	0.9
IMPERIAL CORP. AMERICA	131,500	8.88	1,167	0.5	0.71	1.75	5.07	0.0	13.55	0.65	57	0.16	12.9	4.00	2.22	1.4
			115,436	50.2			8.16	1.1		0.52		0.16	6.4		2.37	1.0
COMMON STOCKS			115,436	50.2												
PREFERRED STOCKS			3,570	1.6												
BONDS			30,525	13.3												
CASH EQUIVALENTS			80,323	34.9												
TOTAL PORTFOLIO			229,854	100.0												

EXHIBIT 6

Portfolio Characteristics *(stocks only; representative portfolio, February 22, 1985)*

Description	Shares	Price	Mkt. Value ($M)	% of Port.	EPS:Last 12 Mo.	EPS:85 Est.	P/E Est. EPS	Curr. Yld	Book Value	Price/ Bk. Val.	Rev/ Sh.	Pr/Rev Per Sh.	Est ROE	2–4 Yrs EPS	P/E 2–4 Yrs	Beta
CONSUMERS POWER	150,000	6.13	919	9.3	1.66	0.50	12.25	0.0	27.00	0.23	37	0.17	1.9	2.00	3.06	0.7
FIRST FEDERAL OF MICHIGAN	80,000	11.13	890	9.0	2.76	3.50	3.18	0.0	22.57	0.49	101	0.11	15.5	5.50	2.02	1.0
ALLIS CHALMERS CORP.	100,000	7.38	738	7.5	−8.03	−3.00	−2.46	0.0	8.00	0.92	78	0.09	−37.5	5.00	1.43	1.2
LONG ISLAND LIGHTING	100,000	7.13	713	7.2	2.99	3.25	2.19	0.0	21.00	0.34	18	0.40	15.5	2.50	2.85	0.6
FEDERAL NATIONAL MTG.	40,000	16.88	675	6.8	−0.87	2.50	6.75	0.9	18.50	0.91	136	0.12	13.5	8.50	1.99	1.3
INLAND STEEL CO.	25,000	25.13	628	6.4	0.94	3.50	7.18	2.0	39.00	0.64	123	0.20	9.0	11.00	2.28	0.9
KAISER ALUM & CHEM CORP.	40,000	15.50	620	6.3	1.56	2.25	6.89	3.9	26.00	0.60	65	0.24	8.7	6.00	2.58	1.1
WHEELING-PITTSBURGH STEEL	40,000	15.50	620	6.3	−10.42	3.00	5.17	0.0	47.00	0.33	156	0.10	6.4	10.00	1.55	1.2
LTV	50,000	12.00	600	6.1	−5.84	2.00	6.00	0.0	13.00	0.92	75	0.16	15.4	7.00	1.71	1.5
FORD MOTOR CO.	10,000	44.13	441	4.5	15.79	14.00	3.15	5.7	55.00	0.80	279	0.16	25.5	16.00	2.76	1.1
GENERAL PUBLIC UTILITIES	33,200	12.25	407	4.1	2.05	2.25	5.44	0.0	25.00	0.49	43	0.28	9.0	3.00	4.08	0.9
GLENDALE FED S & L	30,000	11.50	345	3.5	2.19	2.75	4.18	0.0	30.36	0.38	59	0.19	9.1	4.50	2.56	1.0
			7,595	77.0			6.47	0.9		0.47		0.15	7.2		2.18	1.0
COMMON STOCKS			7,595	77.0												
CASH EQUIVALENTS			2,273	23.0												
TOTAL PORTFOLIO			9,868	100.0												

EXHIBIT 7
Analysis of Diversification (*assuming stock risks are independent*)

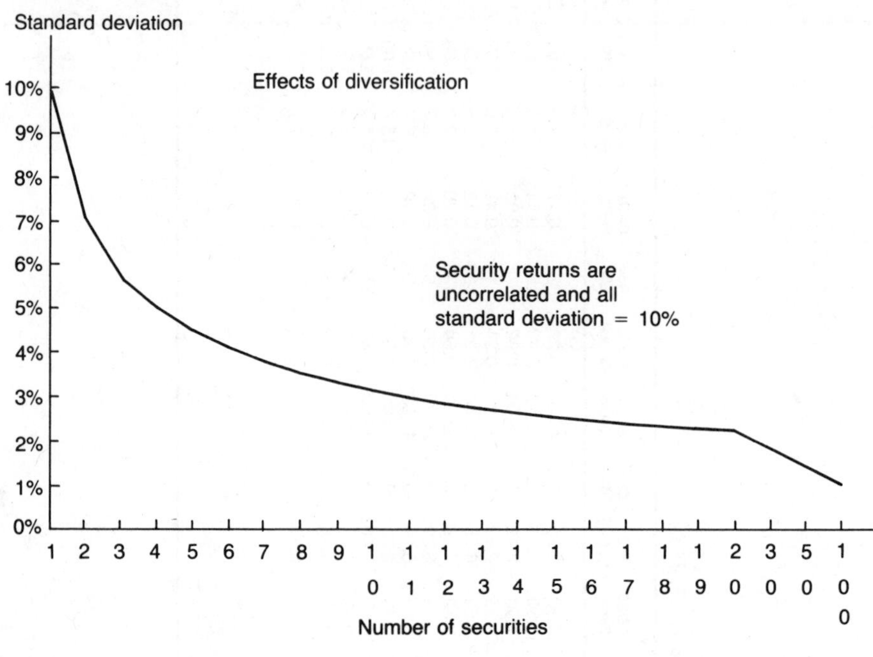

EXHIBIT 8
Commentary on Wheeling-Pittsburgh Steel from *The Wall Street Journal*

Wheeling-Pittsburgh Holders May Be Betting
They Will Like the Company's Reorganization

By Thomas F. O'Boyle

Shareholders of Wheeling-Pittsburgh Steel seem to be betting the company's Chapter 11 reorganization will prove to their liking. But they may be forgetting that bankruptcy-law proceedings rarely are kind to stockholders.

The seventh-ranked U.S. steelmaker sought court protection from its creditors April 16 after the United Steelworkers union vetoed a compromise debt restructuring plan. Unlike most Chapter 11 cases, Wheeling-Pittsburgh shares haven't lost much ground since the bankruptcy-law filing. Yesterday, the stock closed at 7¾, up ¼. In the four weeks since the petition, it has traded as high as 8⅝, the stock's low the day before the filing.

"People are betting they'll come out a strong competitor," says William Schorling, a Pittsburgh bankruptcy attorney. "Is that a smart bet? It might be, but there are certainly a lot of uncertainties out there."

In fact, those uncertainties, which include the vagaries of both steel markets and bankruptcy court proceedings, have scared off many professionals who trade in so-called

EXHIBIT 8 ***(continued)***

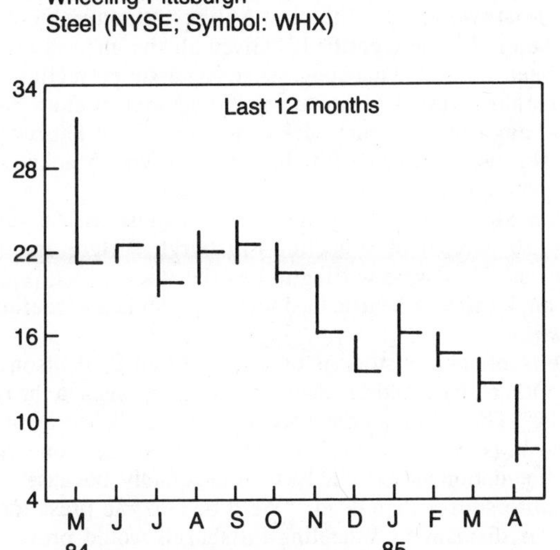

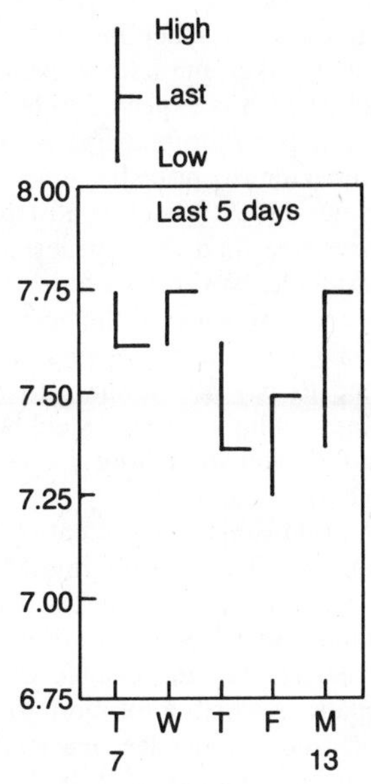

Business: Seventh-largest U.S. steelmaker.

Year ended Dec. 31, 1984:
Sales:$1.05 billion
Loss: $59 million

First quarter, March 31, 1985:
Sales: $241 million
Net loss: $26 million vs. $5 million

Average daily trading volume:
32,700 shares (April)

Common shares outstanding:
5.1 million

distressed stocks. One such money manager is Robert Torray of Torray Clark & Co., Bethesda, Md. Mr. Torray isn't touching Wheeling-Pittsburgh shares, and he's avoiding the entire steel industry as well. "I don't know what the future holds for steel," he says.

Although recently imposed U.S. restrictions on foreign steel might cause some drop in steel imports this year, steel experts note the outlook for the domestic industry is still uncertain. Even with a decline in imports, U.S. producers won't be ensured of higher prices for their product. Slowing economic growth this year could dash the industry's hopes for a recovery and sidetrack the Wheeling-Pittsburgh reorganization.

Some money managers also fear the reorganization will result in a sizable dilution of the common stock. Such dilution occurs more often than not in Chapter 11 cases. Don Parker, an analyst at Mutual Shares Corp., a New York mutual fund that occasionally invests in troubled companies, reasons that Wheeling-Pittsburgh needs and will secure substantial debt relief in its reorganization. But that won't come without a price—probably a large chunk of common stock issued to lenders and other creditors, according to Mr. Parker.

EXHIBIT 8 *(concluded)*

Investors in Wheeling-Pittsburgh maintain the quality of the company's assets gives the steelmaker and its shareholders a good chance of emerging intact from the reorganization, which is expected to last at least two years. "I think it's a very attractive stock," says one portfolio manager who asked not to be identified. "Given all the uncertainties, it's amazing the price has held between 7 and 8. That suggests strong asset protection."

Since 1979, Wheeling-Pittsburgh has invested in new plant and equipment at an even heavier rate than the Japanese. Although the company lacks some big-ticket hardware, for example, world-class finishing facilities, Wheeling-Pittsburgh is still widely acknowledged to have some of the best equipment in the world.

Only a year ago, Japan's Nisshin Steel took a long, hard look at those assets—and agreed to pay $35 a share to buy 10 percent of Wheeling-Pittsburgh. "Here are the Japanese, who are in the steel business. They were willing to buy the stock at that price. That tells you something," says John Teutsch, a Seattle businessman who is a Wheeling-Pittsburgh holder.

An additional 34 percent of the steelmaker's stock is owned by Allen E. Paulson, a Savannah, Ga., private investor. Other shareholders may benefit from such a heavy concentration of stock in two hands. "They'll be a concerted voice to speak out against dilution," says Ken Elliott of Wedbush, Noble & Cooke, a West Coast securities concern.

Analysts say the chance of a liquidation is extremely remote, chiefly because the company is worth a lot more to creditors alive than dead. "We'd be crazy to press for a liquidation," concedes one lender. A dismantled Wheeling-Pittsburgh would probably only fetch a fraction of its book value, which was $50 a share at year-end.

Even assuming that Wheeling-Pittsburgh won't be liquidated, shareholders might still be disappointed in the outcome of the Chapter 11 proceedings. There are additional uncertainties, for example, on the labor and pension fronts. The company faces some contentious bargaining to forge a new labor contract, and it has said it plans to terminate its pension plan.

That would force Uncle Sam to pick up a $200-million unfunded pension liability and make the federal government a major creditor with a huge claim. In addition, termination of the pension plan would trigger payment of $80 million in deferred pension funding.

EXHIBIT 9
Cumulative Wealth Relatives: Donald Smith's Individual Record versus Standard & Poor's 500 Index and Treasury Bills *(annually, 1968 to 1984)*

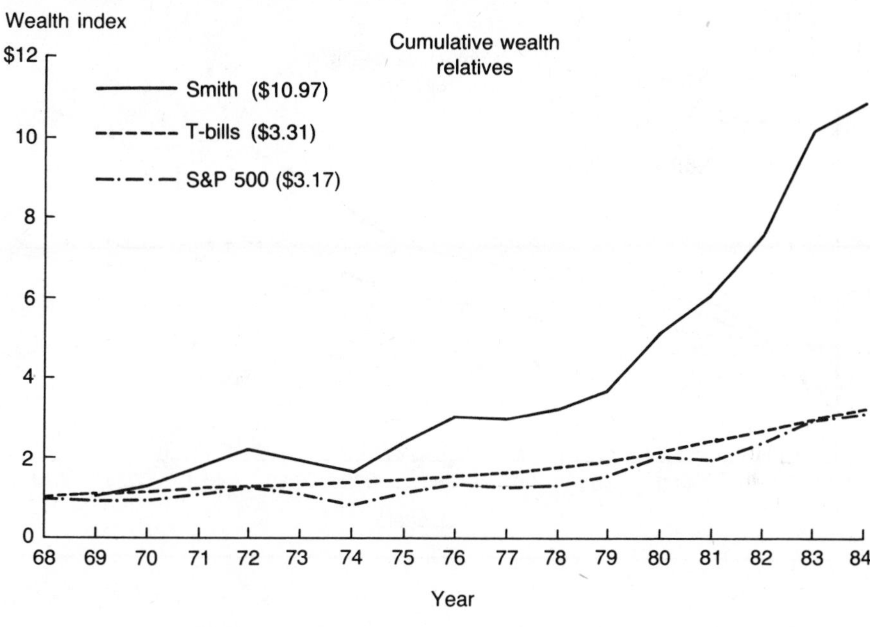

EXHIBIT 10
Cumulative Wealth Relatives: Donald Smith's Personal Record versus Standard & Poor's 500 Index and Treasury Bills *(quarterly, January 1980 to March 1985)*

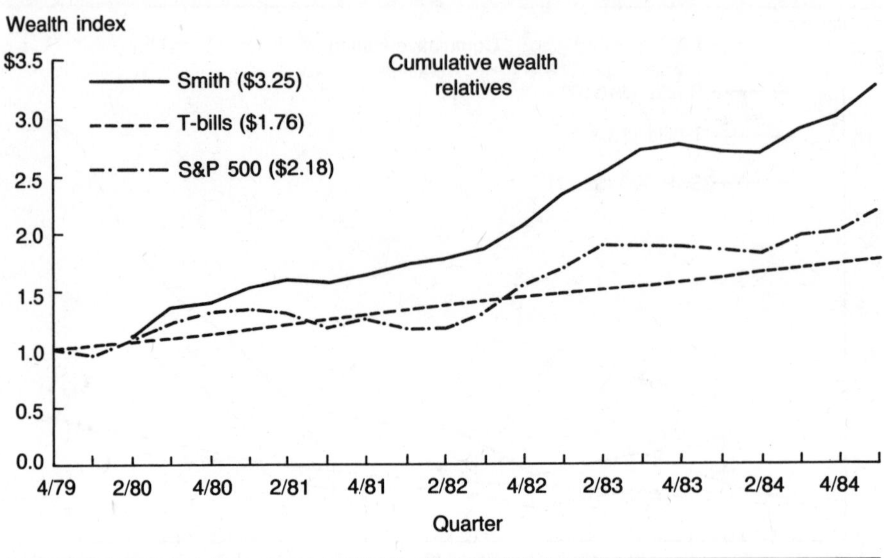

EXHIBIT 11
Performance Characteristic Regression Analysis *(annual data, 1969 to 1984)*

Dependent variable: Smith
Independent variable: S&P 500

Correlation Matrix

	Smith	**S&P 500**
Smith	1.000	
S&P 500	0.866	1.000

Coefficient Data

	Constant	**Std Error**	**t-statistic**
S&P 500	0.933	0.143	6.487
Constant	8.850	0.158	55.879

R-Squared = 0.750
Adjusted R-Squared = 0.733

Means and Standard Deviations

	Mean	**Std Dev**
Smith	9.8769	19.4911
S&P 500	1.1012	18.0987

Residual Data

Row No.	**Smith**	**Fitted**	**Residual**
1	−10.990	−5.162	−5.828
2	27.030	6.433	20.597
3	35.860	18.094	17.766
4	17.460	22.917	−5.457
5	−20.310	−11.440	−8.870
6	−21.700	−23.400	1.700
7	41.780	38.170	3.610
8	22.410	26.136	−3.726
9	−6.780	−2.905	−3.875
10	1.270	8.085	−6.815
11	3.900	16.210	−12.310
12	27.070	28.421	−1.351
13	3.920	−9.640	13.560
14	14.150	19.167	−5.017
15	25.820	21.537	4.283
16	−2.860	5.407	−8.267

Std. deviation of residuals = 10.080
Durbin-Watson: D = 1.726

EXHIBIT 12
Relative Performance Data *(annually, 1969–1984)*

Year	Total Rates of Return		Risk-Free	Total Rates of Return Risk-Free Rate		Cumulative Wealth Relative Using Total Rates of Return			Cumulative Wealth Relative Using Total Rates of Ret. Risk-Free Rate	
	Don. Smith	S&P 500	(T-Bills)	Don. Smith	S&P 500	Don. Smith	S&P 500	T-Bills	Don. Smith	S&P 500
						1	1	1	1	1
1969	−4.41	−8.44	6.58	−10.99	−15.02	0.96	0.92	1.07	0.89	0.85
1970	33.56	3.94	6.53	27.03	−2.59	1.28	0.95	1.14	1.13	0.83
1971	40.25	14.30	4.39	35.86	9.91	1.79	1.09	1.19	1.54	0.91
1972	21.30	18.92	3.84	17.46	15.08	2.17	1.29	1.23	1.80	1.05
1973	−13.38	−14.82	6.93	−20.31	−21.75	1.88	1.10	1.32	1.44	0.82
1974	−13.70	−26.57	8.00	−21.70	−34.57	1.62	0.81	1.42	1.13	0.54
1975	47.58	37.23	5.80	41.78	31.43	2.40	1.11	1.50	1.60	0.70
1976	27.49	23.61	5.08	22.41	18.53	3.05	1.37	1.58	1.95	0.84
1977	−1.66	−7.48	5.12	−6.78	−12.60	3.00	1.27	1.66	1.82	0.73
1978	8.45	6.36	7.18	1.27	−0.82	3.26	1.35	1.78	1.84	0.72
1979	14.28	18.27	10.38	3.90	7.89	3.72	1.60	1.97	1.92	0.78
1980	38.31	32.22	11.24	27.07	20.98	5.15	2.11	2.19	2.44	0.94
1981	18.63	−5.11	14.71	3.92	−19.82	6.11	2.00	2.51	2.53	0.76
1982	24.69	21.60	10.54	14.15	11.06	7.62	2.44	2.77	2.89	0.84
1983	34.64	22.42	8.82	25.82	13.60	10.26	2.98	3.02	3.63	0.96
1984	6.99	6.16	9.85	−2.86	−3.69	10.97	3.17	3.31	3.53	0.92
Average	17.69	8.91	7.81	9.88	1.10					
Std. dev.	19.24	17.79	2.93	19.49	18.10					
				Compound growth rate		16.15%	7.47%	7.77%	8.20%	−0.52%

EXHIBIT 13
Performance Characteristic Regression Analysis *(quarterly data, January 1980 to March 1985)*

Dependent variable: Smith
Independent variable: S&P 500

Correlation Matrix

	Smith	***S&P 500***
Smith	1.000	
S&P 500	0.681	1.000

Coefficient Data

	Coefficient	***Std Error***	***t-statistic***
S&P 500	.534	0.132	4.049
Constant	2.511	0.180	13.893

R-Squared = 0.463
Adjusted R-Squared = 0.435

Means and Standard Deviations

	Mean	***Std Dev***
Smith	3.2248	6.5999
S&P 500	1.2987	3.0034

Residual Data

Row No.	***Smith***	***Fitted***	***Residual***
1	−7.390	−1.707	−5.683
2	11.510	8.536	2.974
3	21.250	7.532	13.718
4	−1.260	5.876	−7.136
5	5.990	1.189	4.801
6	1.740	−0.955	2.695
7	−5.970	−5.428	−0.542
8	1.780	4.607	−2.827
9	1.450	−3.430	4.880
10	0.450	0.409	0.041
11	1.780	7.565	−5.785
12	8.280	11.590	−3.310
13	11.310	6.970	4.340
14	5.380	7.532	−2.152
15	5.960	1.144	4.816
16	−0.130	1.504	−1.634
17	−4.680	−0.135	−4.545
18	−3.120	−0.349	−2.771
19	4.950	6.471	1.521
20	1.630	2.301	−0.671
21	6.810	6.499	0.311

Std. deviation of residuals = 4.961
Durbin-Watson: D = 2.565

Forecast Data

Forecast	***S&P (Fitted)***	***S&P (Predicted)***
3.620	1.087	5.079

EXHIBIT 14
Performance Data *(quarterly, January 1980 to March 1985)*

Year	Total Rates of Return		Risk-Free	Total Rates of Return Risk-Free Rate		Cumulative Wealth Relative Using Total Rates of Return			Cumulative Wealth Relative Using Total Rates of Return Risk-Free Rate	
& Qtr.	Don. Smith	S&P 500	(T-Bills)	Don. Smith	S&P 500	Don. Smith	S&P 500	T-Bills	Don. Smith	S&P 500
						1	1	1	1	1
80.1	−4.00	−4.07	3.40	−7.40	−7.47	0.96	0.96	1.03	0.93	0.93
80.2	14.05	13.41	2.54	11.51	10.87	1.09	1.09	1.06	1.03	1.03
80.3	23.58	11.20	2.33	21.25	8.87	1.35	1.21	1.08	1.25	1.12
80.4	2.21	9.45	3.47	−1.26	5.98	1.38	1.32	1.12	1.24	1.18
81.1	9.63	1.32	3.63	6.00	−2.31	1.52	1.34	1.16	1.31	1.16
81.2	5.50	−2.31	3.75	1.75	−6.06	1.60	1.31	1.21	1.33	1.09
81.3	−2.15	−10.22	3.82	−5.97	−14.04	1.57	1.18	1.25	1.25	0.93
81.4	4.82	7.01	3.04	1.78	3.97	1.64	1.26	1.29	1.28	0.97
82.1	4.71	−7.23	3.26	1.45	−10.49	1.72	1.17	1.33	1.29	0.87
82.2	3.58	−0.62	3.12	0.46	−3.74	1.78	1.16	1.37	1.30	0.84
82.3	4.25	11.46	2.47	1.78	8.99	1.85	1.29	1.41	1.32	0.91
82.4	10.28	18.14	2.00	8.28	16.14	2.05	1.53	1.44	1.43	1.06
83.1	13.34	10.05	2.03	11.31	8.02	2.32	1.68	1.47	1.60	1.14
83.2	7.51	11.11	2.12	5.39	8.99	2.49	1.87	1.50	1.68	1.25
83.3	8.28	−0.14	2.32	5.96	−2.46	2.70	1.87	1.53	1.78	1.22
83.4	2.04	0.34	2.17	−0.13	−1.83	2.75	1.87	1.57	1.78	1.19
84.1	−2.39	−2.27	2.29	−4.68	−4.56	2.69	1.83	1.60	1.70	1.14
84.2	−0.64	−2.58	2.48	−3.12	−5.06	2.67	1.78	1.64	1.64	1.08
84.3	7.57	9.68	2.61	4.96	7.07	2.87	1.96	1.68	1.72	1.16
84.4	3.89	1.76	2.26	1.63	−0.50	2.99	1.99	1.72	1.75	1.15
85.1	8.88	9.35	2.06	6.82	7.29	3.25	2.18	1.76	1.87	1.24
Average	5.95	4.04	2.72	3.23	1.32					
Std. dev.	6.34	7.62	0.62	6.60	7.99					
				Compound growth rate		5.77%	3.77%	2.72%	3.03%	1.01%

Part VIII

Multi-Manager Portfolios

National Instrument Company Pension Fund (B)

In late 1979, Clark Wilson, the Director of Pension Programs for the National Instrument Company, was deciding upon the proposal he would present to the Pension and Retirement Committee (PRC). Mr. Wilson had just completed a lengthy review of National's pension management system, including its passive core fund for equities, and its four active equity managers. He now wanted to decide whether the core fund should be substantially reduced in size (or for that matter, increased), whether it should be revised to include smaller companies, and/or whether it should be rebalanced more frequently. He also wanted to decide to what extent National should attempt to induce its active money managers to produce less diversified portfolios, and what additional encouragement, fee arrangements, or guarantees they might need to make them feel more comfortable with these less diversified portfolios.

Background

In early 1977, National had established a new and innovative form of pension management. They had decided to divide the total fund among a number of specialized money management firms, including a fixed-income manager, an index fund manager for the core equity portfolio, four active specialized equity managers, and one additional firm that served as a consultant in the overall asset and manager

---

This case was prepared by Jay O. Light as a basis for class discussion rather than to illustrate either effective or ineffective handling of an administrative situation. Reprinted by permission of the Harvard Business School.

allocation process. The initial funds had been divided among these managers according to the "policy mix" which had been chosen as the desired normal or long-term disposition of the funds. This policy mix is shown in Exhibit 1. The bond manager was allocated 30 percent of the total fund for fixed-income securities, and 70 percent was given to the equity managers. Of this 70 percent, 28 percent (40% of 70%) was allocated to a core fund managed by an index manager, and designed to track the S&P 500 through holding a stratified sample of about 250 stocks. The remaining equity was divided equally among four specialized equity managers, each of whom therefore received 10½ percent of the total fund. Two of these managers typically followed relatively low-risk strategies, and by design were to hold portfolios with betas (volatilities) of about .75. The other two were to hold portfolios with betas of about 1.25, producing an overall equity portion beta of about 1.00. All four firms had quite distinct investment philosophies. Among other differences, one might be described primarily as an individual stock picker specializing in relatively current investment ideas or concepts, another might be described as a sector picker (big versus little stocks, growth versus yield stocks, etc.), another as a practitioner of modern portfolio theory including stock valuation models, and another as a specialist in convertibles and other hybrid equity securities.

Each of the seven firms was represented by a particular portfolio manager who had primary responsibility for National's account. In addition, these six individuals composed a group called the Investment Advisory Board (IAB), a team that provided an important link in the investment decision-making process for the pension fund. The IAB met quarterly to review the overall investment policy of the total fund, and each of its segments. Those meetings typically lasted a full day, and their location was rotated among the offices of each firm and National's home office so that each firm would host the meeting about once every two years. In each meeting, the managers reviewed the current state of the capital markets, the current policies of the fund and its individual segments, and discussed alternative recommendations to National's Pension and Retirement Committee (PRC) for the allocation of each quarter's new cash flows among themselves. In addition, the IAB was chartered to recommend major asset re-allocations for the existing funds when circumstances were unusual. Formal votes were rarely taken within the IAB, but Clark Wilson (who formally served as chairman of the IAB) reported the consensus of its deliberations back to National's PRC. The IAB also spent a good deal of time reviewing transaction costs, and discussing ways to reduce these costs. They evaluated the operations of the core fund, which was involved in trying to reduce transaction costs. Finally, they each brought up any new investment ideas that might affect their own portfolio operations in the future, or be adopted by any of the other managers.

Clark Wilson returned to National immediately after each meeting, and reported the results at the quarterly meeting of the PRC. The PRC reviewed the recommended allocation of new cash flows, and invariably had approved this allocation for the coming quarter. At one point, the IAB consensus taken as a whole had suggested a major shift in the existing asset allocation. This had also been approved by the PRC. The PRC also reviewed the investment performance of the total fund, and each of its segments, on a quarterly basis. Finally, they discussed any changes in their pension policies and procedures that might be suggested by Clark Wilson or others.

The core fund was not only designed to provide diversification, but it also served as an inventory fund to reduce transaction costs. If any of the active equity managers wanted to sell a stock that was in the S&P 500, they had to sell it to this passive fund, which paid them in cash. In addition, if they wanted to buy any stock in the core fund (a stratified sample of 250 stocks from the S&P 500), they had to buy it from the core fund up to the amount of the core fund's holdings. Over 350 of these inventory fund transactions had already taken place, saving important commission dollars for the fund.

The money management firms were compensated by an unusual fee agreement which was based on the market value of the total fund, not on the value of that portion of the fund for which each manager was currently responsible. Specifically, each firm received a current fee computed on the basis of their normal fee schedule, except that the account size was assumed to be the baseline percentages in Exhibit 1 times the current market value of the total fund, regardless of the actual value of the assets each firm was currently managing.

Risk and Return Management

As part of the overall management system, National utilized a carefully designed set of risk and return measurements. After each quarter, the actual returns of each manager were reported. Moreover, the prospective risk posture of each manager was measured and reported on the same quarterly basis. National used a "fundamental risk measurement service" marketed by a West Coast consulting firm to estimate the future beta, residual risk, and total risk for each equity segment of the fund and for the total fund. The underlying framework of this risk measurement service is described in Exhibit 8. Basically, the service assumed that betas and residual risk could be estimated for each stock and then combined into estimates for a total fund on the basis of a relatively sophisticated set of statistical measures derived from the stocks' past price fluctuations and various fundamental information characterizing each stock. The current summary risk measures for each equity segment, and the total fund, are shown in Exhibit 2.

As Exhibit 2 suggests, this particular measurement service predicted that the National equity fund would have a future beta of 1.12, and a future residual risk of 2.8 percent. If this was true, it could be shown that the residual risk would have an almost inconsequential effect upon the total risk of the portfolio. For example, assuming, as in Exhibit 2, that the future standard deviation of the market is 21.1 percent (the prediction of the risk service), then the portfolio would have had a total risk of 23.6 percent even if it had no residual risk. Including the residual risk, the total risk increased only .3 percent to 23.9 percent.

The core fund seemed to be well-positioned to fulfill its role, namely tracking the S&P 500, for its residual risk was only 1.6 percent. In contrast, the active manager portfolios had residual risks ranging from 5 to 8 percent. The betas of several segments were predicted to be higher than designed, including a beta of 1.07 for the core fund and betas of 1.12 and 1.01 for the conservative managers.[1]

Exhibit 3 displays some of the back-up information supplied by the risk measurement service to explain the portfolio risk measurements. The different active managers seemed to be positioning their portfolios differently on most of the key dimensions shown in Exhibit 3. But all of them invested, on average, in stocks smaller than the average stock in the S&P 500. In addition, even the core fund, because of its "inventory fund" transactions with other managers, had (on average) smaller stocks than the average stock in the S&P 500. Thus, National's total fund was invested in stocks considerably smaller (on average) than the S&P 500.[2] Indeed, it had approximately the same average size as a more extensive market-weighted average of 3,000 stocks compiled by the risk measurement service.

Performance Results

The performance results of National's pension management system had been gratifying to date. While 27 months was hardly a sufficient time for making conclusive judgments, all segments of the portfolio had thus far performed up to their expectations. The performance results for the most recent 12 months are shown in Exhibit 4. The performance results since inception (27 months) are shown in Exhibit 5. The actual historical betas (measured relative to the S&P 500 on the basis of the actual past returns of the funds and the S&P) and performance results for the 27 months are displayed pictorially in Exhibit 6. Over the full 27 months, the total fund had outperformed a naive 70/30 mix of the S&P 500 Index and the bond index while experiencing much less volatility. The bond manager had done consistently well relative to the Lehman/Kuhn-Loeb Bond Index, primarily because the firm had invested relatively more of their funds in short-term instruments throughout this period during which long-term bonds had declined. The core fund had tracked the S&P 500 quite well. The conservative managers had experienced less volatility than the S&P 500, while the aggressive managers had experienced more. And perhaps most importantly, all four active equity managers had outperformed the S&P 500, some by considerable amounts.

Clark Wilson regularly interpreted these results for the PRC, but with a note of caution. Compared with the market indices, they were encouraging. Compared with other yardsticks, they were also encouraging. For example, a large consulting service which regularly measured up to 4,000 pension, endowment, and other funds indicated that the average fund in this 4,000-fund sample had underperformed the market during this same period. On the other hand, a number of active equity

---

[1]In general, the two conservative managers had experienced a good deal of difficulty keeping their betas low. It turned out that only a very small number of stocks had betas below .80 (AT&T, etc.). The target for the conservative managers had therefore recently been raised to a beta of .95. Clearly, the conservative managers were still having some difficulty meeting this target, at least as regards the betas predicted by the risk measurement system.

[2]By "on average," we mean an average in the market-value-weighted sense in all these statements.

managers had done quite well during this period, including National's. In particular, small stocks had on average outperformed the S&P 500 during this period, and this might well account for some of the active managers' results, including National's, for throughout the period both manager EC-2 and EA-2 had emphasized smaller stocks. Clark Wilson continually cautioned the PRC not to automatically assume the performance records of their managers would continue. Still, he was not displeased with the results thus far.

Meetings of IAB

The Investment Advisory Board (IAB) seemed to be developing into an important deliberative investment policy group. After some initial problems, all participants seemed to approach these meetings with a cooperative, constructive spirit.

Each meeting began with a general discussion of the capital markets by the sixth firm, a consultant on investment policy and asset mix. The individual members of the IAB would then take turns challenging the views of this firm and each other. Toward the end of the session, each firm would articulate its recommendations for directing the new cash flows for the next calendar quarter. The most recent meeting provided a typical example of these recommendations. The current division of funds (at market value) is shown in Exhibit 7. Manager B, the fixed-income manager, thought equities were attractive and wanted to divide the allocation of funds among EC-1 and EC-2. Manager E, the passive equity manager, wanted to allocate the funds to fixed income. Manager EC-1 wanted to allocate the funds to himself and fixed income. Manager EC-2 wanted to allocate the funds to the passive equity portfolio. Manager EA-1 wanted to allocate the funds to EC-2 and EA-2, the best performers. Manager EA-2 wanted to allocate some of the funds equally among the active managers, but the bulk of the funds to fixed income. While there was often relatively little consensus within the IAB, they did not appear to approach these discussions in a self-interested way. Indeed, they appeared to approach them in an objective way, clearly focusing on what they thought would be in the best interest of the total fund.

As a result of the generally rising equity market, the differential performances of the fund segments, and the allocation of new funds, the actual segments were drifting away from the policy mix. In particular, the actual stock/bond mix had become 81/19 rather than the baseline 70/30 policy mix. The IAB and Clark Wilson were somewhat concerned about this trend toward a heavier equity exposure, particularly given the current investment outlook. This concern was the principal reason that several equity managers now wanted to allocate the new funds to the fixed-income manager.

Transactions Costs

The IAB also regularly reviewed the whole matter of transactions costs, including their own and those for the fund as a whole. Clark Wilson was particularly pleased with the results of the new system in controlling these costs. For the active managers as a whole, 20 percent of their trades, representing 40 percent of the dollar volume of trading, had been done with the indexed inventory fund at zero cost, yielding an immediate and sizable savings.[3] In addition, another 37 percent of the dollar volume of trading was channeled through specific brokers at National's request, for which they obtained partial rebates of the commission costs. Only 23 percent of the dollar volume of trading by the active managers actually was accomplished through normal trading. And the managers tended to watch even these costs rather closely, for they knew they would be regularly reviewed in the IAB. Clark Wilson estimated that these procedures had already saved National at least several million dollars of transaction costs. These savings, he believed, accrued directly to the fund and thus to its beneficiaries and National.

Issues Regarding the Core Fund

There were a number of issues about the core fund that concerned Clark Wilson. First, it had grown over time to be somewhat bigger than he had planned. When the active equity managers sold any stock within the S&P 500, they had to sell it to the core fund, but they only purchased stocks from the core fund if they were actually held in that fund (in the beginning, a stratified sample of only 250 of the S&P 500 stocks). Thus, there was a tendency for them to sell more to the fund than they bought from it. Because of this, the core fund had tended to grow over time. As Exhibit 7 shows, it had become $155 million, substantially larger than 28 percent of the total fund. The compensating deficit occurred in the fixed-income account, which had to finance the other purchases of the active equity managers.

Furthermore, Clark Wilson wondered if the core fund shouldn't be cut back from even its planned 28 percent of the total fund. National's active equity managers had proven themselves over more than two years now. The value added of their active trading had clearly more than covered their fees in all cases. Given these clearly favorable results of the new specialized money manager system, he wondered if the core fund might not be scaled back to a very small level, just large enough to help reduce transaction costs. Or, for that matter, he wondered if it should be eliminated altogether. Several members of the PRC were clearly very encouraged by the active managers' performance, particularly firm EA-2, and had several times wondered out loud if the funds currently managed passively in the core fund shouldn't be given instead to this firm.

The diversification of the core fund was another issue. The core manager (Manager E) had recently recommended expanding the core fund to include a stratified sample of smaller companies. Their principal concern with tracking the S&P 500 was that it, by definition, overweighted large companies. By adding small companies, the core fund could be made to simulate the average market performance of a larger universe of companies, albeit at the loss of a convenient and well-known index to use as a reference. On balance, the idea of a more diversified core fund appealed to Clark Wilson. In the meetings of the IAB, though, the idea had

[3]The total dollar volume of trading by the active equity managers (purchases and sales) was over $400 million in the 27-month period.

been vigorously opposed. The active managers believed that smaller companies were an inherently riskier and less efficient segment of the market where active management, not passive management, could and should be used.

Finally, Clark Wilson wondered if the core fund shouldn't be rebalanced more actively to track the S&P 500 more closely. In the 27 months since inception, it had not been rebalanced. The core manager believed that the fund should only be rebalanced if its residual risk exceeded 2 percent, the standard for several other index fund services available to institutional investors. Thus far, the residual risk had not exceeded 1.6 percent (see Exhibit 2). In the interests of saving unnecessary transaction costs, the core manager argued that major rebalancings should not be undertaken.

Issues Regarding the Active Equity Managers

The active equity managers presented a greater problem for Clark Wilson. He had hoped that those specialized managers would invest in very particular portfolios with a good degree of specific (residual) risk, especially because of the existence of the core fund for diversification. That was why he had been willing to accept fee schedules higher than the industry average. Unfortunately, however, the measurements of the fundamental risk service suggested that they were still investing in fairly diversified portfolios. The residual risk for these managers was shown in Exhibit 2. By comparison, surveys had shown the following typical residual risks for other managers:

Typical Residual Standard Deviation Levels

Manager Type	*σ of Residual Risk*
Index fund	0.5 to 2.5%
"Closet index fund"	3 to 4%
Typical bank pooled fund	5 to 6%
Median of a large group of pension fund segments (Becker)	5.6%
An individual stock	20 to 50%

As this information suggests, the National managers were not taking much less diversified positions than the average equity manager, despite Clark Wilson's repeated urgings to do so. At several IAB meetings, he had attempted to demonstrate how even rather large residual risk resulting from their portfolios' "bets" would be largely diversified away when viewed from the level of National's overall portfolio (see Exhibit 2, for example). While the managers did not argue with the arithmetic, they had made only somewhat modest and grudging moves toward less diversified portfolios. Indeed, the subject had been the source of the only real tension that occasionally arose in the IAB.

Clark Wilson had been considering a new requirement that all active equity managers place sizable "bets" in their portfolios, such that their portfolio residual risk would be greater than 7 percent but less than 15 percent. This would at least ensure that they were making more active bets than the typical pension fund manager, as might befit the role of a specialized manager. Such a requirement seemed particularly appropriate in light of the core fund with its diversifying effect and the demonstrated track record of the active managers. He knew, however, that this requirement would not be well received by the active managers. He knew they, unfortunately, felt quite uncomfortable with undiversified portfolios and considered them rather risky to themselves and their firms, quite apart from their risks to National. One manager had suggested, perhaps only partly in jest, that his firm would insist on a very long-term no-cut contract before accepting an undiversified role. Clark Wilson wondered how he could make the managers more comfortable with a less diversified role, including possible changes in fee schedules, contracts, or other aspects of their relationship. He wondered what would be needed to make the active managers support a requirement to raise their residual risks to the 7–15 percent range.

The Attitudes of the Money Managers

By and large, the money managers seemed to be pleased with the National system. They seemed to enjoy the IAB meetings, and their own identification with a new and innovative investment management system. They seemed to respect each other, and got along extremely well in what can be a rather competitive industry. In fact, there were almost never any signs of tension among them.

The only real signs of tension arose around the aforementioned issue of undiversified portfolios. Several of the active managers did not agree with the policy of moving toward less diversified portfolios. First, they argued, the residual risk measurements could be very misleading. They believed that their portfolios were built around, and predicated upon, investment judgments not considered by the fundamental risk measurement service in its statistical processing. Manager EC-2, in particular, believed that his portfolio had a considerably lower beta and a considerably higher residual risk than the measurement service indicated. While he had a very large number of stocks (almost 100) in his portfolio, they were all chosen for a common set of reasons. And those reasons, whether they proved successful or not, meant that he and his firm were taking considerable risks. He was neither comfortable with the risk measures of the system, nor with the idea of moving toward a more exposed position. Moreover, he resented being forced to move toward a less diversified position when the core fund would just swallow some of the stocks he sold anyway, thus exposing National to exactly the same composite portfolio. In general, several of the managers had warned Clark Wilson of placing too much reliance upon sophisticated statistical measures and not enough reliance upon the judgment of his managers. It was possible, they argued, to over-engineer a basically good system.

In general, they also might be tiring of the IAB meetings. One or two managers wondered if the time commitment of these meetings wasn't excessive. While the discussions were certainly more interesting than their regular client meetings, they wondered if anything was really getting done in these meetings. The meetings could sometimes remind them of typical investment meetings, where no consensus was reached and no decisions were made. In the long run, they wondered, would this team concept continue to prove a productive use for so much of their and Clark Wilson's time?

The PRC Meeting

Clark Wilson now had to prepare for the upcoming PRC meeting. He wanted to review for them the results of the new pension management system. He also wanted to recommend any suitable changes in the system, including but not limited to: changes in investment managers; changes in the passive core fund; changes in the role of the specialized managers, including possibly requiring less diversified positions; changes in the transaction rules; and changes in the respective roles of the IAB and PRC. He knew that, in general, he still wanted to manage the pension investment mechanism just as National's main business was managed—that is, with carefully established objectives, closely monitored performance, an emphasis on cost control and diversification, and an emphasis on obtaining above-average results.

EXHIBIT 1
The Policy Mix for National's Pension Fund

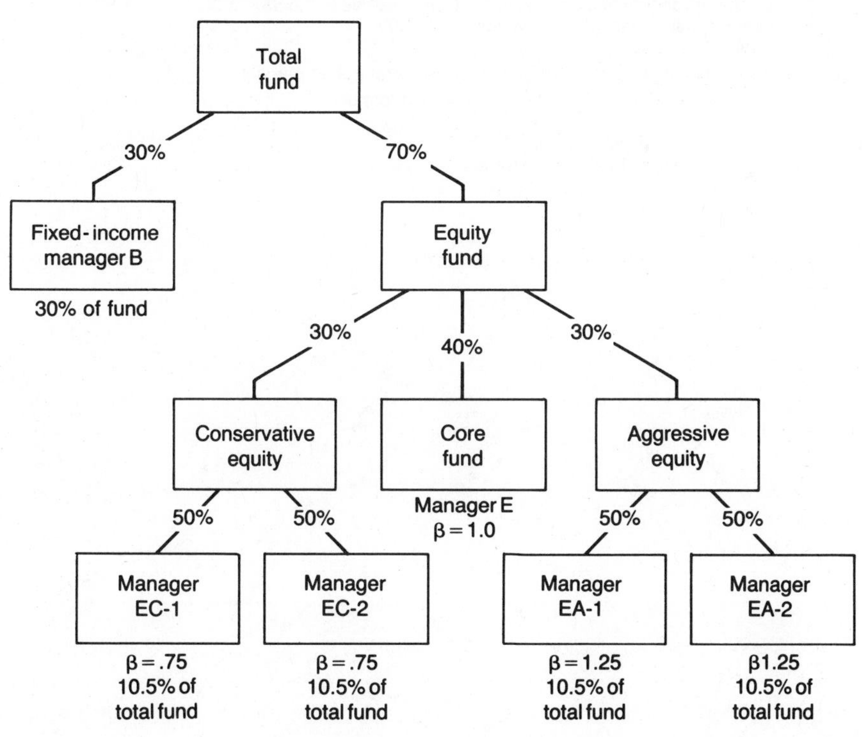

EXHIBIT 2
The Current Prediction of Future Risk for the Equity Fund

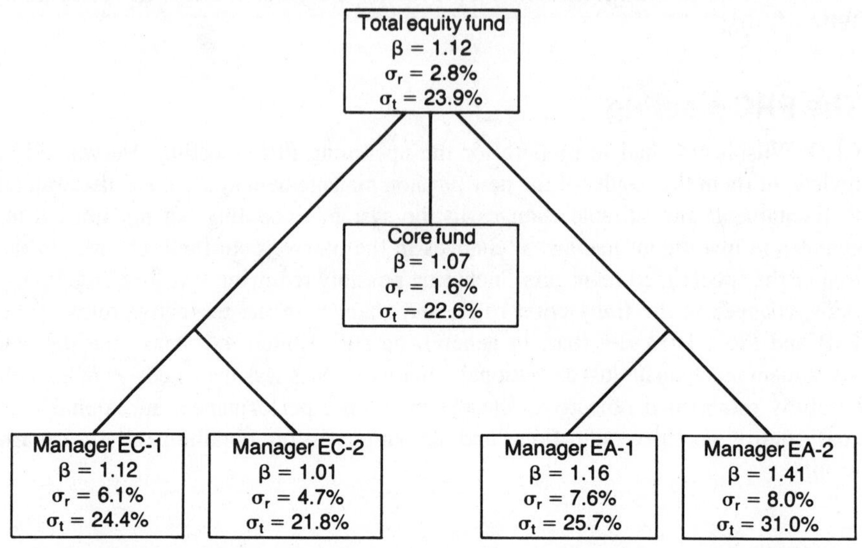

1. Definitions:
   β = Beta, the volatility of the portfolio measured relative to the S&P 500.
   σ_r = Residual risk, measured relative to the S&P 500.
   σ_t = Total risk.
2. The assumed future standard deviation for the market is 21.1 percent.
3. The total risk (σ_t) can be obtained by the following formula:

$$\underbrace{\sigma_t^2}_{\text{Total risk}} = \underbrace{\sigma_r^2}_{\text{Residual risk}} + \underbrace{\beta^2 \times (21.1)^2}_{\text{Market risk}}$$

EXHIBIT 3
Risk Indices for the Portfolio Segments

Six dimensions characterizing common stocks form the basis for analyzing the extent to which they co-vary

Characteristics of Stocks	*S&P 500*	*Index of 3,000 Stocks*	*Total National Portfolio*	*Core Fund*	*EC-1*	*EC-2*	*EA-1*	*EA-2*
Market variability	0.0	.19	.24	.15	.21	−.15	.16	1.12
Earnings variability	0.0	.30	.17	.04	.21	−.11	.36	.74
Low value, unsuccess	0.0	−.02	−.01	−.02	−.02	.05	.41	−.51
Immaturity and smallness	0.0	.62	.61	.21	.56	1.09	.87	1.18
Growth orientation	0.0	.18	.10	.09	−.13	−.17	−.03	.75
Financial risk	0.0	.11	.07	.01	.55	−.19	.39	−.04

The measure of each risk index for a portfolio is just the value-weighted average of risk index measurements for all stocks in the portfolio. For each stock, the risk index measurements are defined with respect to the cross-sectional variation of each characteristic across all stocks, and then normalized relative to the S&P 500. Thus, a risk index measurement of 0 indicates that the average stock in a portfolio is exactly comparable to the average stock in the S&P 500 on this particular characteristic. A risk index greater (lesser) than zero, indicates this portfolio on average has stocks with relatively more (less) of this characteristic compared to the S&P 500 Index—for example, earnings variability, or expected growth, or financial risk. Roughly speaking, the measurements correspond to the cross-sectional standard deviation for all stocks; thus two thirds of all stocks fall within plus or minus 1 on a given measurement. Therefore, one can think of plus or minus 1 as being extreme measurements for a portfolio relative to the S&P 500.

EXHIBIT 4
Performance Results for the Most Recent Year Ended 9/30/79

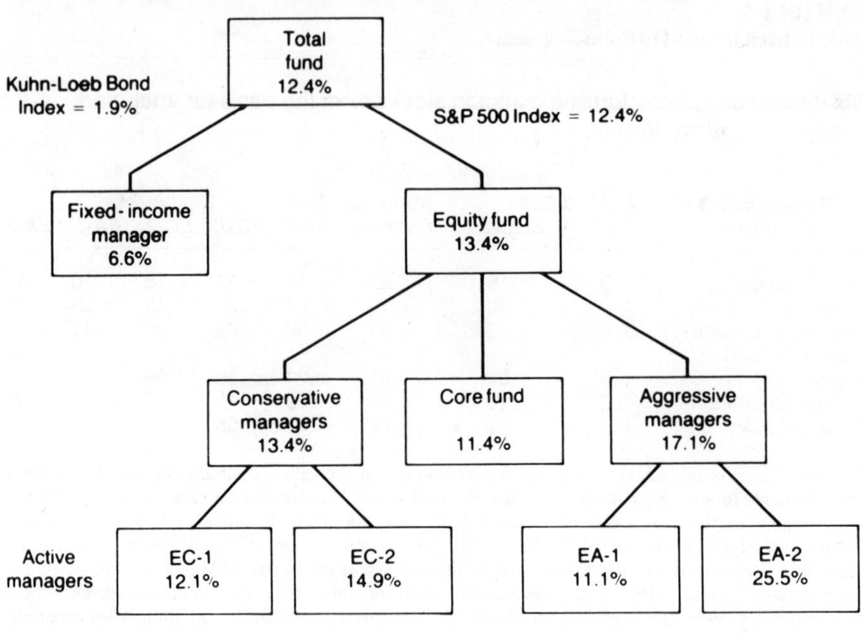

EXHIBIT 5
Performance Results Since Inception *(27 months annualized rates of return)*

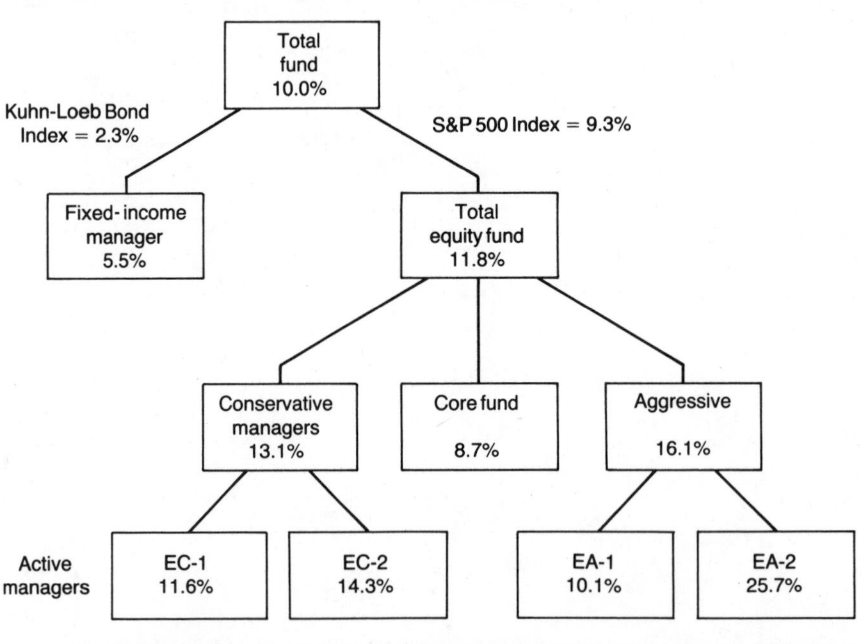

EXHIBIT 6
Actual Betas and Total Returns for All Managers Compared to Market Indices *(27 months since inception)*

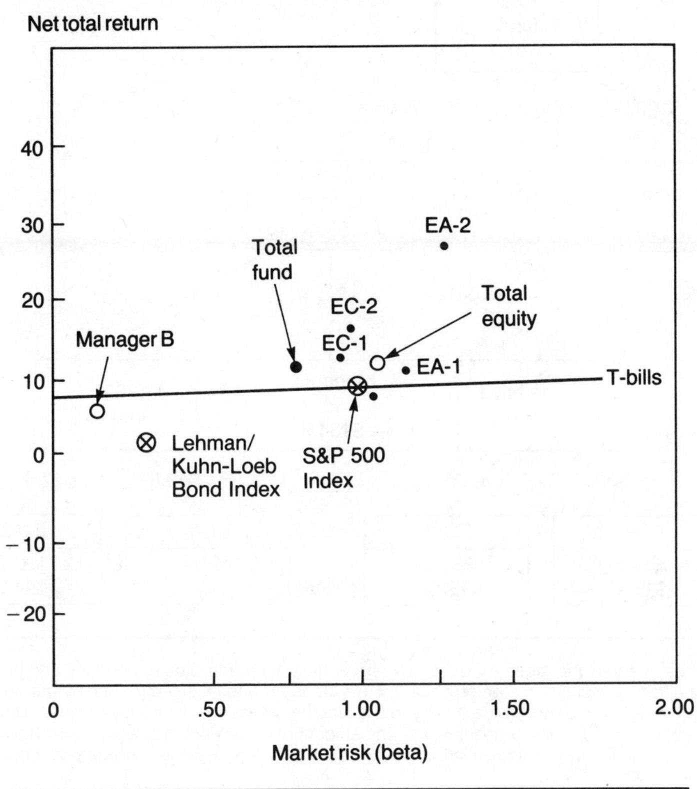

EXHIBIT 7
Current Allocation of Funds among Managers *(all $ in millions)*

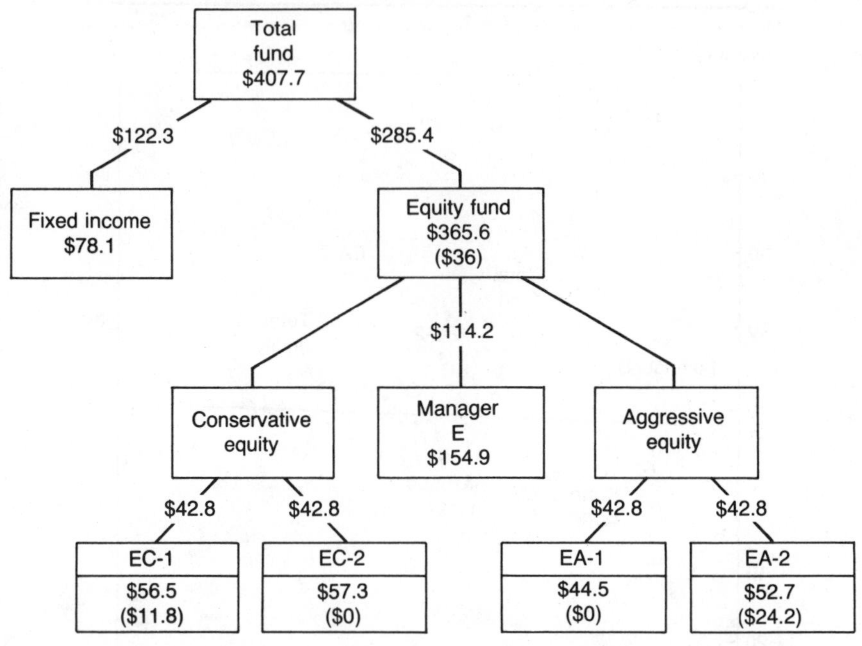

Note: For each equity manager, a closed box shows the total funds allocated to him, and (in parentheses) the cash position currently held by this manager and invested for him by the bond manager. The difference between the two figures is just the manager's net equity position. On the line above each box is the policy position, i.e., the amount of funds each manager would have been allocated under the policy mix shown in Exhibit 1, presumably the long-run average position of the fund.

EXHIBIT 8
A Brief Description of the Risk Measurement Service

The "fundamental risk measurement service" used at National furnishes estimates of non-market risk for each security and for each portfolio in the money management system.[1]

1. This is a brief, largely non-technical introduction to the system, focused primarily upon the estimation and prediction of non-market risk. More complete descriptions are available in: (1) Barr Rosenberg, "Extra-Market Components of Covariances among Security Prices," *Journal of Financial and Quantitative Analysis* 9, pp. 263–74, (2) Barr Rosenberg and Vinay Marathe, "Prediction of Investment Risk: Systematic and Residual Risk," *Proceedings of the Seminar on the Analysis of Security Prices,* University of Chicago (November 1975), and (3) Barr Rosenberg, "Security Appraisal and Unsystematic Risk," Working Paper No. 58, Research Program in Finance, University of California at Berkeley, 1977.

EXHIBIT 8 ***(continued)***

The Underlying Model

The non-market risk estimates are constructed on the basis of a multiple-factor model, which includes as factors both various fundamental accounting data and industry classifications. The multiple-factor model assumes that the uncertain future return of the *j*th stock in some particular month can be represented by:

$$\tilde{r}_j = \beta_j \cdot \tilde{r}_m + \tilde{n}_j \qquad (1)$$

Return of the *j*th stock; Sensitivity to the market; The market return; The non-market, or residual, return

and that, for our present purposes, the β_j are known or can be estimated.[2] Further, the model assumes that the non-market return can be de-composed into three components: industry returns, common factor returns, and company specific returns. That is, it assumes that the *j*th stock's uncertain future return can be expressed as:

$$\tilde{r}_j = \beta_j \cdot \tilde{r}_m + \lambda_{1j}\tilde{f}_1 + \lambda_{2j}\tilde{f}_2 + \ldots + \lambda_{kj}\tilde{f}_k + \tilde{F}_I + \tilde{e}_j \qquad (2)$$

Common factors; Return for industry *I*, to which firm *j* belongs; Specific return to stock *j*

and that we know, for each stock, the appropriate "factor loadings," λ_{1j} through λ_{kj}, and that we know the industry (*I*) to which it belongs.

The Choice of Common Factors

The power and value of this approach to forecasting portfolio risk are clearly only as good, or as bad, as the choice of factors in the multiple-factor model. If the factors have been chosen in such a way that the factor loadings are reasonably stable, and more importantly in such a way that most plausible future sources of covariance among stocks are likely to be captured by one or more of the factors, then the forecasts of future portfolio risk may be rather good, and vice-versa.

In this particular system, the industry factors (the $\tilde{F}_I$) are just the returns for 39 different industries, classified in a reasonably traditional way, e.g., apparel, chemicals, drugs and medicine, motor vehicles, insurance, etc.

In addition, there are six different common factors (the $\tilde{f}k$), each one of which is, itself, a combination of many different characteristics of a stock or of the fundamentals of the underlying company. The set of six common factors used in this risk measurement system is shown below, along with the constituent characteristics:

2. Actually, as part of the risk measurement service, the betas are estimated using the same variables described later in this exhibit.

EXHIBIT 8 *(continued)*

Common Factor 1: Market Variability
- Historical beta estimate
- Historical sigma estimate
- Historical beta squared
- Historical sigma squared
- Historical beta times sigma
- Bayesian adjustment for beta
- Share turnover, quarterly
- Share turnover, 12 months
- Share turnover, five years
- Trading volume/range of price
- Current price
- Average monthly range, 12 months
- Average monthly range, five years

Common Factor 2: Earnings Variability
- Variance of earnings
- Extraordinary items
- Variance of cash flow
- Earnings covariability with U.S. corporate earnings
- Earnings/price covariability with market E/P

Common Factor 3: Unsuccess and Low Valuation of Earnings
- Growth in earnings/share
- Recent earnings change
- Relative strength
- Negligible earnings indicator
- Book/price ratio
- Tax/earnings, five years
- Dividend cuts, five years
- Return on equity

Common Factor 4: Immaturity and Smallness
- Total assets (log)
- Market capitalization (log)
- Market capitalization
- Market share
- Net plant/gross plant
- Gross plant/total assets
- Real plant/equity
- Number of years listed on exchange
- Indicator of earnings history

Common Factor 5: Growth Orientation
- Payout last five years
- Current yield
- Yield last five years
- Indicator of zero yield
- Growth in total assets
- Variance in capital structure
- Earnings/price ratio
- Earnings/price normalized
- Earnings/price, five years

Common Factor 6: Financial Risk
- Book leverage
- Leverage at market
- Debt/assets
- Uncovered fixed charges
- Cash flow
- Liquid assets/current liabilities
- Potential dilution
- Adjustment to earnings for inflation
- Tax-adjusted monetary debt

These six common factors were presumably chosen because they were plausibly related to risk, and more importantly, to the correlations that may exist among the returns from many different stocks. In addition, these variables had earlier been used by the same risk measurement service in forecasting the betas of individual stocks, so that they were conveniently available to also estimate non-market risk.

The Estimation of the Covariance among Stocks

The next step in the development of the risk measurement system was to estimate an actual historical time series for each of the industry and common factors in the model described above. The actual historical monthly returns for each stock, and for the market

EXHIBIT 8 *(continued)*

as a whole, can be used to estimate these time series, provided that the factor loadings (λ_{kj}) are known for the past time periods.[3] Specifically, the risk measurement service estimated, for each past month, the return for each common factor (f_1 through f_k) and the return for each industry (F_I for all I). It also estimated the variance (standard deviation) of each stock's specific return (e_j), that is, the magnitude of the "random" components of return unrelated to the industry and common factors.

Given the estimated time series of industry and common factors, the service then estimated a covariance matrix for these factors. That is, it estimated:

σ_k = The variability of each of the common factors, for all $1 \leq k \leq K$

σ_I = The variability of each of the industry factors, for all industries.

ρ_{lm} = The matrix of pairwise correlations between *all* of the industry and common factors.

This covariance matrix is the heart of the risk measurement system. It attempts to quantitatively capture the way securities will co-vary with each other by modeling the industry and common factors which are responsible for this tendency to co-vary, and then estimating the actual past behavior of these factors, both their individual variability and their tendency to be correlated with each other.

The Computation of Portfolio Risk

Having estimated a covariance matrix from past data, the risk measurement system then forecasts the future risk of individual stocks. In particular, (1) given values for λ_{1j} through λ_{kj} and β_j, and (2) having estimated the variability in the market, in each of the f_k and F_I, and in e_j, the future uncertainty from all of these sources will merely combine according to the algebra of probability theory. The total future variance will merely be the combination of market-related variance, the extra-market variance stemming from the industry and common factors, and the specific variance unique to the jth security.

More importantly, for this was the initial objective, the risk measurement system then forecasts the future risk of any *portfolio* of stocks. Specifically, the portfolio's beta (β_p) will just be the weighted average of individual securities' betas.[4] The portfolio's "factor loadings," λ_{1p} through λ_{kp} will just be the weighted average of the individual securities' factor loadings. And the industry exposure will merely be the capitalization-weighted composition of the portfolio among the industries. The total variance of any portfolio will just be the sum of the market-related variance, the extra-market covariance stemming from industry and common factors, and the specific variances of all individual stocks. The risk measurement system thus quantifies a rather intuitive idea: one can take risk by betting on the market, by betting on certain common factors (e.g., "data processing" stocks, or "growth" stocks) or by betting on an individual company (e.g., Digital Equipment).

---

3. In this risk measurement system, the factor loadings (λ_{kj}) are defined to be a set of six normalized variables which denote a particular stock's attributes measured along the six common factors described above, relative to all other stocks. They are described more fully in the next part of this exhibit.

4. The weights in the weighted average will just be the fraction of the portfolio held in each security.

EXHIBIT 8 ***(concluded)***

In actual operation, the risk measurement service computes each of the many characteristics listed in the earlier table for each of several thousand stocks. Each characteristic is then normalized cross-sectionally, so that its value is a ready reference to how this stock compares to all other stocks along a particular characteristic. For example, a normalized variable of "0" for a given characteristic would mean the stock is exactly "average" (as measured by some particular average, such as the S&P 500). Two thirds of all stocks would, roughly speaking, fall between ± 1 for any particular characteristic. For each individual stock a weighted sum of the particular characteristics listed under each common factor yields the normalized value of each of the six common factors. These normalized values are just the factor loadings described in equation (2). Finally, for a portfolio, a weighted average across all stocks of each of the six normalized common factors yields a set of six normalized common factors for the portfolio (see, for example, Exhibit 3).

The set of six normalized common factors for a portfolio are an indication of the degree to which the portfolio manager is betting, knowingly or unknowingly, on the common factors. The industry composition (relative to the S&P 500, or some other index) is an indication of the degree to which the same portfolio manager is betting, knowingly or unknowingly, on industries. And, to the extent that this risk measurement system is based upon a set of industries and common factors that are likely to capture the potential future covariances among stock, the risk measurement system produces an appropriate forecast of the total future portfolio risk. In addition, it produces forecasts of the components of total risk: market-related (or systematic) risk, and non-market risk, the latter of which can be further divided into the extra-market risk (from industry and common factors), and the specific risk of betting on individual stocks.

John Sain, Ph.D.

In early July 1982, Dr. John Sain was hired to advise the pension committee of the Board of Directors of Flaunt, Ltd., a specialty retailer of casual clothing for young adults with stores throughout the upper Midwest. His initial task was threefold: (1) to appraise the performance of the five equity fund managers employed by the firm, (2) to appraise the current asset-mix distribution of funds among the five managers and suggest a better distribution, and (3) to develop an approach for deciding how new monies flowing into the fund should be allocated in the future. Since Dr. Sain hoped he would continue to advise on these and other issues in the future, he wanted to perfect a system that would enable him to generate quick and thorough analyses of pertinent problems. Toward this end, he hoped a newly acquired Apple II would prove helpful.

Since its founding in 1961, Flaunt, Ltd., had specialized in the needs of young adults. Jeans and corduroys were now prominently featured in its stores, although almost all currently fashionable clothing items were stocked. Emphasis had changed over the years with the interests of Flaunt's patrons.

Upon graduation from Ohio State, Mr. Edward Mathews purchased from an elderly uncle an Army/Navy store adjacent to the Columbus campus. He reoriented the store toward the collegians at his doorstep. Gradually, the Flaunt merchandising "mod" image was perfected. In 1964, the opening of a second store in a large new

---

This case was prepared by a Professor of the Colgate Darden Graduate School of Business Administration of the University of Virginia.

shopping center serving a relatively affluent suburb of Columbus initiated a period of rapid growth capitalizing upon the enclosed mall concept.

By 1982, Flaunt, Ltd., operated approximately 350 stores in approximately 15 states, generating a sales volume in excess of $500 million. Growth tapered off in the late 1970s as the firm's natural marketplaces became saturated. This slowdown in growth enabled the firm to strengthen its overextended financial position to a more comfortable level. Ownership remained private, although about 70 employees owned about 10 percent of the shares.

The environment in the early 1980s for specialty retail stores was a competitive one. Flaunt's unit growth had slowed, particularly in the more hard-hit communities. Consumers were much more price conscious in their purchasing habits, and margins had been squeezed accordingly. With interest rates still running at very high levels, it was hard to forecast when a recovery might begin.

Now in his mid-forties, Mr. Mathews found it increasingly difficult to sustain his interest in the business. His time was increasingly absorbed by civic, club, and other community activities. He had, in fact, begun to consider the possibility of a political career. For these and other reasons, Mr. Mathews had decided to sell Flaunt, Ltd., as soon as business conditions were more propitious and profitability recovered from a recent slump.

Flaunt, Ltd., employees now numbered almost 2,400, most of whom were not career employees. Almost 80 percent of employees moved on to some other activity within two years of their employment. For this reason the company's cost of funding pension benefits, as well as other fringes such as vacations, tended to be very low.

No pension benefits were set aside during the first three years of employment, and benefits did not become fully vested until the tenth year. Only about 300 employees had fully vested benefits in a work force that remained relatively young. There was only one employee over 50, and no one had yet retired. Past service liabilities and other unfunded benefits were nominal in amount. Annual pension costs had grown to $480,000 in 1982 (for 1981 services). Total pension assets had a market value of approximately $5.1 million. Management was assisted in its funding decisions by a well-known regional actuarial firm.

Technically, the Board of Directors was responsible for appropriate funding decisions and prudent investment policies for these pension assets. At Flaunt, the Board consisted of Mr. Mathews, Chairman; Mr. Lombardi, President and Chief Operating Officer; Mr. Aaron, Vice President for Finance; and Mr. Spawen, the firm's local banker.

In the wake of ERISA and upon the advice of counsel, the Board appointed a three-member pension fund committee and delegated to it considerable oversight responsibility. Mr. Aaron, Mr. Spawen, and the firm's treasurer, Mr. Parnell, served on this committee.

Until mid-1978, the pension funds were managed by the local bank (Century Federal) where Mr. Spawen was a senior lending officer. This circumstance proved awkward, for as best Mr. Aaron and Mr. Parnell could determine, the bank's record in managing these funds had been poor. A "Becker" survey confirmed their fears.

Over a 5-year period (ending in 1977) the bank had performed in the bottom 10 percent of both equity and debt fund managers. Further action seemed called for in the face of this record.

A consultant specializing in pension funds was hired to recommend how the funds should be deployed, and although his report was elaborate, his recommendations were simple. They included (1) changing the portfolio asset mix to 30 percent fixed income/70 percent equity from 60 percent/40 percent fixed income/equity, (2) investing the fixed-income component of the portfolio in short-term marketable securities, and (3) investing the equity funds in approximately equal amounts in five mutual funds: Decatur Income Fund, Chemical Fund, Pioneer Fund, Investment Company of America, and Rowe Price New Horizons Fund. The consultant demonstrated that the first four funds had superior earnings records over the preceding 20 years. New Horizons' record was also very strong over its life, but it had only been founded in 1960. The consultant had also argued that the management styles of these firms tended to be quite different (see Exhibit 1 for performance information on these funds).

All of these recommendations were followed, although with some modification. The asset-mix of 30 percent/70 percent was adopted. Century Federal bank was retained as the fixed-income manager and was given the freedom to manage these assets as it saw fit. The bank was encouraged to shorten the maturity considerably—which it did. The main exception to the recommendations was the way funds were allocated to the equity managers.

Mr. Aaron had called each of the five proposed equity managers to learn more about their investment styles. Perhaps because the commitment to each was to be only about $330,000 from a total portfolio of $2.4 million, only the manager of the Chemical Fund seemed particularly excited about discussing style with Mr. Aaron. The general investment style of the Chemical Fund was similar to his own, and he felt very comfortable about having them manage available funds. At the same time, Mr. Aaron gained the impression that Pioneer and New Horizons were riskier ventures.

As a result of these investigations, Mr. Aaron made, and the committee accepted, the following equity allocation recommendations:

Chemical Fund	40%
Investment Co. America	20
Decatur Income	20
Pioneer Fund	10
New Horizons	10

The decision, implemented in late 1978, proved almost perfectly timed. The equity market was very strong in 1979 and 1980. The long-term bond market, in contrast, had been very weak.

Subsequently, cash flows were reinvested in each of the five equity and the fixed-income funds as they became available. New monies were allocated to one or the other of the funds as seemed necessary to keep the asset mixes more or less in line with targets. (Century Federal had requested permission to shift a substantial part of the assets it managed into much longer fixed-income maturities in September of 1981, and this change represented the only significant shift in thinking since late 1978.)

For the first two years, 1979 and 1980, the decisions seemed above question. Results for the most recent 18 months, however, particularly for the first six months of 1982, had proved very disappointing (see Exhibit 1). Mr. Spawen had persistently warned of bad times ahead and expressed a gloomy satisfaction at seeing his worst fears realized. He was especially pessimistic about prospects in June of 1982.

Mr. Aaron found Mr. Spawen's harping on the negative disturbing. What if Mr. Spawen should prove right? When a more experienced employee was fired recently, the employee's lawyer examined a wide range of ways he might sue the company and/or its executives for damages. This lawyer had, among other things, sought and, after due process, received records on the performance of the pension fund for the 15-year period of his client's employment. For these and other reasons, Mr. Aaron decided to seek out an adviser, who he hoped would provide both good advice and leave "footprints in the snow" indicating the care with which pension decisions had been made.

Mr. Aaron first approached the firm making the recommendations in 1978. Quarterly review and advice from this firm, however, would cost $60,000, not a trivial amount given the size of the firm's portfolio.

At this point Mr. Aaron met John Sain at a church picnic. Dr. Sain had received a Ph.D. in Financial Economics from the University of Pennsylvania (Wharton) in 1981, and had been employed at Ohio State's business school for a year, teaching primarily in the investments area. Dr. Sain struck Mr. Aaron as quite practical for an economist. When further discussions with Dr. Sain continued to impress him, Mr. Aaron had asked if Dr. Sain would be interested in serving as an adviser to Flaunt's pension fund committee.

To John Sain, the opportunity to use his understanding of investment theory to a practical end and to be paid for it seemed ideal. A more experienced friend had suggested to him that $500 per day was an appropriate fee for a young faculty member just starting out. Dr. Sain had, therefore, proposed to advise Flaunt for $2,000 per quarter. He was prepared to spend more time—since there was no opportunity cost in doing so—than four days if necessary. His proposal was accepted for the balance of 1982 and would be renewed if the arrangement proved satisfactory. The initial task, as set forth at the outset of the case, had also been agreed upon.

Dr. Sain had gathered the quarterly rate-of-return data shown in Exhibit 1 for each of the mutual funds from mid-1962 forward, whichever was applicable. These data were now stored in his Apple II. He had also gathered data for the Standard & Poor's 500 Index and 90-day Treasury bills as reported in Ibbotson and Sinquefield[1] for the same period.

---

[1]R. Ibbotson and A. Sinquefield, *Stocks, Bonds, Bills, and Inflation: The Past and the Future* (Charlottesville, Va.: Financial Analysts Research Foundation, 1982).

Dr. Sain recalled from his courses at Wharton that equity performance was usually measured from data by the following formula:

$$R_{pt} - R_{ft} = \alpha_p + \beta_p (R_{mt} - R_{ft}) \tag{1}$$

where

R_{pt} = Total rate of return on a portfolio in period t.
R_{ft} = Total rate of return on the risk-free security in period t.
R_{mt} = Total rate of return on the "market portfolio" in period t.
α_p = Excess rate of return per period on the portfolio.
β_p = Systematic risk of the portfolio.
σ_p = Standard deviation of portfolio returns.

Two issues were often debated in relation to the foregoing model: (1) whether measurement should be arithmetic or logarithmic [using log $(1 + r)$ in place of r] and (2) the time periods over which measurement should be made. A little experimentation in this respect seemed in order.

Dr. Sain also recalled the two alternative systems for ranking performance, known respectively as the Treynor and the Sharpe methods.[2] Dr. Sain planned to evaluate the suitability of each of these methods and to consider whether either was really appropriate for the circumstances he now found himself facing.

Dr. Sain also had to consider appropriate mixes for the portfolio in the future. He had been taught that betas alone provided the necessary risk perspective because residual errors and covariance were random. However, these theories applied when there was no evidence of management skills on the part of the portfolio manager. Would he also have to worry about unsystematic risk (residual errors: $\sigma_{R_p} \cdot R_m$) and perhaps even covariances of errors here, he wondered?

Finally, Mr. Aaron had stressed the long-term outlook of Flaunt's pension fund portfolio. According to Flaunt's actuaries, the market value of the fund currently exceeded actuarial requirements by 21.3 percent. As this was based on an actuarial return-on-investment target of 6 percent per year, the value assessment seemed quite conservative, considering current market expectations. There would be no material cash outflow required for the fund for at least 15 years. All this led him to wonder if the relatively short-term volatility focus of existing modern portfolio theory was appropriate.

As a first step in exploring this issue, Dr. Sain decided to simulate what portfolio performance would have been from July 1, 1962, to June 30, 1982, if the equity portfolio had been invested according to existing targets and rebalanced (through cash inflows) every six months.

---

[2]For one illustrative source, see James H. Lorie and Mary T. Hamilton, *The Stock Market: Theories and Evidence* (Homewood, Ill.: Richard D. Irwin, 1973). See pages 235–41 for a short description. These models are also described in most basic investment texts.

EXHIBIT 1
Performance Record for Five Mutual Funds (*June 1962–June 1982*)

Period (Quarter/ Year)	Investment Co. of America	Pioneer Fund	Decatur Income Fund	Chemical Fund	Rowe Price New Horizons	R_m Standard & Poor's 500 Index	R_f 90-Day Treasury Bills
3/62	1.75%	5.65%	−0.21%	3.34%	5.58%	3.68%	0.71%
4/62	11.41	6.79	4.28	15.62	6.34	13.28	0.68
1/63	4.85	8.81	6.13	4.36	2.10	6.34	0.71
2/63	7.26	2.95	8.42	4.81	2.27	5.01	0.72
3/63	3.07	1.83	−0.83	6.68	1.59	4.10	0.79
4/63	5.99	0.41	−0.28	11.05	3.43	5.61	0.85
1/64	8.72	5.61	6.80	4.58	−2.31	6.06	0.87
2/64	3.35	0.21	5.22	5.23	−1.13	4.20	0.85
3/64	3.34	6.41	8.69	2.93	1.56	3.78	0.86
4/64	0.08	1.86	1.58	−2.40	3.79	1.58	0.89
1/65	8.30	7.77	4.70	6.37	11.46	2.39	0.94
2/65	−4.12	−3.86	1.81	−0.31	−7.62	−1.63	0.97
3/65	12.12	9.38	2.70	10.93	17.50	7.71	0.95
4/65	8.96	10.08	5.94	8.52	18.70	3.66	0.99
1/66	4.70	0.69	2.46	2.71	4.48	−2.73	1.11
2/66	−2.74	−1.47	−3.36	−1.44	2.93	−4.25	1.13
3/66	−11.24	−8.66	−8.09	−11.74	−4.16	−8.85	1.16
4/66	11.97	5.07	2.52	9.92	14.99	5.96	1.26
1/67	13.59	17.15	12.72	17.56	27.60	13.21	1.18
2/67	5.58	12.55	4.74	6.39	14.10	1.28	0.92
3/67	7.31	7.21	10.43	6.72	16.04	7.50	0.94
4/67	0.13	2.55	0.22	3.84	10.53	0.59	1.08
1/68	−5.84	−2.12	3.97	−9.47	−10.98	−5.72	1.17
2/68	13.96	17.75	11.45	15.55	23.66	11.24	1.32
3/68	4.57	6.24	5.31	−1.01	6.16	3.89	1.34
4/68	4.20	5.36	10.37	2.91	5.46	1.96	1.30
1/69	−2.77	−3.37	−6.43	−3.42	−8.27	−1.50	1.46
2/69	−5.64	−7.25	−7.08	−0.38	−4.37	−3.00	1.53
3/69	−2.68	−4.56	−3.99	2.15	−0.22	−3.92	1.66
4/69	0.00	−1.32	3.11	7.68	13.82	−0.31	1.77
1/70	−10.22	1.43	−6.75	−6.93	−7.58	−1.71	1.80
2/70	−9.68	−19.57	−6.47	−16.88	−28.24	−18.03	1.62
3/70	17.70	14.65	13.34	11.61	23.03	16.91	1.60
4/70	8.13	7.85	2.20	8.63	14.33	10.43	1.35
1/71	9.90	12.60	18.40	11.00	16.67	9.70	1.01
2/71	0.88	−1.19	−1.37	3.90	7.60	0.17	0.94
3/71	1.17	−2.80	2.32	0.05	10.08	−0.59	1.25
4/71	4.28	4.76	−3.52	4.53	15.14	4.66	1.11
1/72	5.93	9.34	11.95	9.82	17.09	5.74	0.81
2/72	−1.16	−1.48	−2.27	6.28	6.36	0.67	0.88
3/72	2.49	0.61	−0.25	4.17	25.48	3.91	0.94
4/72	7.88	6.34	5.30	7.49	−20.00	7.56	1.14
1/73	−9.99	−3.14	−7.20	−3.82	−26.05	−4.89	1.32
2/73	−8.86	−3.60	−12.36	−5.17	−11.19	−5.77	1.55
3/73	12.13	9.62	10.75	5.85	29.57	4.81	2.03
4/73	−9.72	−5.62	−8.06	−11.55	−18.34	−9.16	1.86
1/74	−0.33	4.62	−1.54	−1.81	−5.61	−2.82	1.78
2/74	−7.35	−12.80	−3.08	−3.44	−14.46	−7.56	2.11
3/74	−18.95	−16.45	−12.20	−29.79	−26.68	−25.16	2.12
4/74	9.63	6.92	10.15	12.25	7.51	9.38	1.76
1/75	21.38	23.36	15.41	18.66	34.80	22.94	1.43
2/75	15.56	16.03	13.58	12.76	19.37	15.37	1.30
3/75	−10.27	−7.07	−5.41	−15.38	−16.25	−10.95	1.50
4/75	6.69	4.09	4.82	6.96	7.34	8.65	1.46
1/76	16.88	22.97	20.23	11.31	14.78	14.97	1.21
2/76	4.35	4.24	5.75	0.00	−4.17	2.48	1.22
3/76	1.68	−0.29	1.55	0.12	−0.22	1.92	1.34
4/76	4.44	6.68	2.40	−2.76	−6.82	3.14	1.21

EXHIBIT 1 *(concluded)*

Period (Quarter/ Year)	Investment Co. of America	Pioneer Fund	Decatur Income Fund	Chemical Fund	Rowe Price New Horizons	R_m Standard & Poor's 500 Index	R_f 90-Day Treasury Bills
1/77	−7.15%	−1.17%	3.49%	−8.83%	−6.82%	−7.44%	1.09%
2/77	5.62	4.78	6.74	1.34	8.89	3.32	1.15
3/77	−3.18	−4.18	−4.42	−2.31	3.40	−2.82	1.30
4/77	2.58	4.40	1.00	1.88	7.50	−0.13	1.49
1/78	−2.00	−1.53	−2.36	−4.15	2.30	−4.92	1.49
2/78	13.17	9.06	5.35	13.59	17.43	8.50	1.60
3/78	9.76	11.65	6.50	7.23	10.52	8.67	1.75
4/78	−5.79	−6.55	−6.42	−4.14	−9.05	−4.93	2.18
1/79	5.27	9.41	8.43	7.07	8.89	7.07	2.33
2/79	3.10	5.83	12.84	1.98	1.53	2.72	2.45
3/79	10.00	9.94	7.89	8.04	12.71	7.55	2.39
4/79	−0.17	0.57	1.55	5.67	8.69	0.13	2.84
1/80	−6.24	−6.32	−4.29	−6.86	−9.38	−4.08	2.93
2/80	9.49	16.51	14.75	13.16	18.50	13.41	2.70
3/80	11.75	14.61	6.75	15.30	28.66	11.20	1.93
4/80	5.96	4.87	5.93	8.81	14.48	9.45	3.25
1/81	4.35	4.46	5.12	0.75	−5.68	1.32	3.36
2/81	0.54	−3.03	1.60	−1.54	−0.90	−2.31	3.62
3/81	−8.10	−11.66	−9.42	−11.82	−16.36	−10.22	3.81
4/81	4.28	8.12	8.75	10.03	8.53	7.01	3.18
1/82	−2.21	−10.16	−1.72	−8.70	−11.94	−7.23	2.72
2/82	1.82	−4.47	0.59	−1.37	−2.63	−.62	3.18

John Sain's Preliminary Report

In October 1982, Dr. John Sain presented to Flaunt, Ltd.'s Pension Fund Committee his preliminary report on the performance of the firm's five equity managers (see John Sain, Ph.D.). The purpose of this meeting was to outline the approaches that he planned to undertake in his analysis, and to begin to sense what sort of information might be considered most useful by the members of the committee and by Mr. Mathews, Flaunt's president. His report is attached as an Appendix.

Much of the meeting was spent explaining terminology. The Pension Fund Committee did not, he found, understand simple concepts such as compound total returns or standard deviations of portfolio returns, nor did they see how these statistics should affect portfolio construction. By the end of the meeting, he believed that he had hit a long foul ball.

The group tended to focus on returns. They were very impressed with the record of the Rowe Price New Horizons Fund (despite its high systematic and unsystematic volatility) and disappointed in the performance of the Chemical Fund. The five-year moving-average data tended to confirm for them that New Horizons was not very risky and Chemical was.

The committee appeared to like the graphics, although for such things as the performance characteristic line, they were concerned that using quarterly data was

---

too short a focus to be appropriate. They also liked the simulation analysis, although they wondered why Dr. Sain had not considered the fixed-income investments in his analysis. Fixed-income securities would, they thought, tend to reduce portfolio volatility.

Dr. Sain had also been influenced by some of his findings. The fact that two of the funds had higher returns and lower standard deviations than the market portfolio over the 20-year period he had used for his analysis was disconcerting. Most optimizing models, he noted, tended to assume that the market portfolio was the most efficient portfolio. Were these models still valid? Also, the Pension Fund Committee at Flaunt appeared to have a longer-term interest in performance than this approach. Five-year return data did offer a different picture of risk results. Risks seemed not to be independent over time, as modern portfolio theory tended to assume. What implications did this development have for portfolio construction?

With these problems and circumstances in mind, Dr. Sain wondered what his next analytical steps should be.

Appendix

PRELIMINARY REVIEW FLAUNT EQUITY ASSET MANAGERS

Longer-Term Performance of Equity Funds

Arithmetic Returns and Risks (20 years)

The data below reflect the average quarterly return for each of the funds for the 20-year period, July 1962 to June 1982.

Fund	*Arithmetic Mean Quarterly Return*	*Standard Deviation*	*Mean Performance Relative to S&P 500*
Investment Co. of America	2.85%	7.71%	+0.63%
Pioneer	3.09	8.20	+0.87
Decatur Income	2.86	6.95	+0.66
Chemical	2.66	8.46	+0.46
New Horizons	4.10	13.27	+1.88
S&P 500 Index	2.22	8.02	—
T-bill	1.56	0.75	−0.66

As you can see, each of the funds had an average total rate of return higher than the Standard & Poor's 500 Index total rate of return for the period.

The two defensive funds, Decatur and Investment Co. of America, had lower volatility than the index as measured by the standard deviation of the quarterly returns. Only the most aggressive fund, New Horizons, had a volatility significantly higher than the index.

Compound Returns

Compound returns are a more useful way of viewing total-return performance since they represent the rate at which capital will grow. The following table shows the compound annual rates of total return for the various funds over the 20-year period.

Compound Return Performance *(20 years)*

Fund	*Compound Return/ Quarter*	*Compound Return per Year*	*Compound Qtr. Return + 1 Std. Dev.*	*Compound Qtr. Return − 1 Std. Dev.*
Investment Co. of America	2.55%	10.60%	10.66%	−4.97%
Pioneer	2.76	11.49	11.37	−5.19
Decatur Income	2.63	10.93	9.82	−4.09
Chemical	2.29	9.47	11.54	−6.20
New Horizons	3.22	13.51	17.77	−9.53
S&P 500	1.88	7.75	10.71	−6.24
T-bill	1.55	6.38	2.29	0.81

Again, each of the funds significantly outperformed the benchmark index over this period of time. The last column is one measure of downside risk in bad markets. Only the New Horizons Fund shows substantially higher downside exposure in the short run than did the stock index.

Compound Return Performance (Most Recent Five Years)

Since the managers recommended to you only a few years ago were superior, it is not surprising that their performance was good over the long run. The most recent five-year data are a better reflection of performance potential, however, because only a short part of this history was available at the time these funds were recommended to you.

Compound Return Performance *(most recent 5 years)*

Fund	*Compound Return/ Quarter*	*Compound Return per Year*	*Compound Qtr. Return +1 Std. Dev.*	*Compound Qtr. Return −1 Std. Dev.*
Investment Co. of America	2.54%	10.56%	8.67%	−3.32%
Pioneer	2.26	9.34	10.67	−5.51
Decatur Income	2.70	11.25	9.19	−3.40
Chemical	2.35	9.73	10.24	−4.98
New Horizons	3.76	15.90	15.57	−6.85
S&P 500	1.84	7.56	8.62	−4.52
T-bill	2.54	10.57	3.32	1.78

In the most recent five years, the stock index performed below the 20-year average. Only three of the funds performed better than their 20-year average. On an absolute basis, all five funds outperformed the stock index over this time period.

Wealth Relatives

The implications of compound rate of return differentials are often underestimated. If $1 were invested in each of these funds on July 1, 1962, the wealth accumulated (including reinvestment of dividends and capital gains) would be as follows as of June 1982.

	Wealth June 1982 Resulting from Investing $1 in July 1962
Investment Co. of America	$ 7.50
Pioneer Fund	8.81
Decatur	7.97
Chemical	6.11
New Horizons	12.61
S&P 500 Index	4.45

More rapid wealth accumulation will either (1) facilitate larger distributions of benefits or (2) reduce the cost of funding specified benefits. The differences reported above are *not* trivial.

Exhibit 1 shows the details of wealth accumulation by years for all five funds over the 20-year period, assuming again $1 is invested in each in July 1962.

Period Results

Despite the generally favorable performance of the five funds over the 20 years, the performance in the short run was more erratic. Exhibit 2 reports the annual compound performance results for each of the 20 years. Not only did individual funds fail to outperform the Standard & Poor's 500 Index in a number of years, but the shortfall was occasionally startlingly large.

1982 Results: First Three Quarters

Performance in 1982 was more mixed, as indicated by the following results.

Fund Performance Analysis* *(9/30/82)*

	1st Quarter 1982	*2nd Quarter 1982*	*3rd Quarter 1982*	*9 Mos. 1982*	*Sept. 81 to Sept. 82*
Invest. Co. of America	−2.21%	1.82%	12.13%	11.65%	16.40%
Pioneer	−10.16	−4.47	12.72	−3.26	4.66
Decatur Income	−1.72	0.59	12.72	11.44	21.27
Chemical	−8.70	−1.37	10.02	5.69	13.60
New Horizons	−11.94	−2.63	12.97	−3.13	5.34
S&P 500	−7.31	0.65	11.52	2.79	9.96
Mutual Fund Index Average	−4.50	0.45	11.42	7.06	15.84
Equity Fund Average	−6.32	0.80	10.53	3.77	11.81

	Most Recent	
	5 Years	*10 Years*
Invest. Co. of America	91.72%	135.34%
Pioneer	84.12	186.83
Decatur Income	90.59	177.93
Chemical	82.01	48.00
New Horizons	147.68	51.50
S&P 500	63.48	74.30
Mutual Fund Index Average	90.86	104.98
Equity Fund Average	107.11	111.53

*Percentage change in wealth after considering reinvestment of dividends and gains.

These data suggest why diversification reduces risk. For the last 12 months, those funds specializing in smaller firms had a rough time of it. The three other funds, in contrast, outperformed the Standard & Poor's 500 Index significantly.

In looking at 10-year results, it is important to bear in mind that September 1972 was very near the peak in the growth-stock, high-p/e ratio craze. That Chemical and New Horizons funds did as well as they did in this period of dramatic declines in growth-stock p/e ratios is encouraging, although these funds underperformed the Standard & Poor's 500 Index.

In general we see that defensive funds, Decatur and Investment Co., tended to fare well in down markets, and that the more aggressive funds, New Horizons and Pioneer, did better in up markets.

The fourth quarter of 1982 should be a good one for composite equity funds.

Trend Line Analysis

Compound rates of return have one intrinsic limitation. They can be computed from two pieces of data: the opening and the closing wealth relative. The pattern of wealth growth between these dates has no impact on the calculation. Also, if one or the other of these data points is distorted by temporary conditions (cyclical high, poor market for a particular fund's strategy, etc.), the intrinsic growth rate may be misestimated.

While not perfect, a trend-line analysis may provide a more accurate picture of performance. A trend line could be fit in several ways. I chose to use the following formula:

$$\log(W_{pt}) = a + bt$$

where

W_{pt} = Wealth relative for portfolio p in time period t.

t = Time period for each of the 80 quarters measured sequentially from quarter 1 (3rd quarter 1962).

a, b = Coefficients.

Perhaps the implications of this formula are best illustrated graphically. Exhibit 3 shows the actual pattern of wealth accumulation for each of the five funds and the Standard & Poor's 500 Index. Superimposd on each chart is the fitted trend line.

The following data summarize the growth rate implied by those trend analyses:

	Annual Growth Rate
Investment Co. of America	8.87%
Pioneer	10.60
Decatur	9.86
Chemical	7.51
New Horizons	13.15
Standard & Poor's 500	6.08

Note that there are significant differences between these results and the compound annual growth data reported earlier.

Portfolio Performance Characteristic Lines

Performance characteristic lines are determined by relating periodic (quarterly) results for a fund to the general market results for the same period, using all the periods in the measuring interval (20 years). A least-squares linear regression technique was used for this purpose.

The general regression equation was:

$$R_p - R_f = \alpha_p + \beta_p (R_m - R_f)$$

The following definitions of terms may help with the interpretation of results:

Portfolio beta (β_p): A measure of systematic or nondiversifiable risk: an index of relative co-movement of portfolio results with market (S&P) results. A beta of less than 1 shows lower-than-market risks in the portfolio.

Portfolio alpha (α_p): A measure of "risk-adjusted" (quarterly) total excess returns relative to capital asset pricing model (CAPM) benchmarks.

R^2: A measure of diversification. With the possible exception of the Chemical Fund, all funds had low diversification, a sign of very active management.

Standard Error of the Regression: A measure of unsystematic risk that we hope can be reduced through diversification.

The portfolio performance characteristics of the funds are reported below:

Investment Company of America

	Coefficient	*Std. Error*	*t-Stat*
Alpha	.705	.372	1.89
Beta	.875	.045	19.30

Corrected $R^2 = .824$
Std. error regression = 3.32%

Pioneer Fund

	Coefficient	*Std. Error*	*t-Stat*
Alpha	.935	.467	2.00
Beta	.893	.056	15.69

Corrected $R^2 = .756$
Std. error regression = 4.17%

Decatur Income Fund

	Coefficient	*Std. Error*	*t-Stat*
Alpha	.849	.489	1.74
Beta	.685	.059	11.51

Corrected $R^2 = .624$
Std. error regression = 4.36%

Chemical Fund

	Coefficient	*Std. Error*	*t-Stat*
Alpha	.447	.359	1.24
Beta	.983	.043	22.46

Corrected $R^2 = .864$
Std. error regression = 3.21%

Rowe Price New Horizons

	Coefficient	*Std. Error*	*t-Stat*
Alpha	1.702	.972	1.75
Beta	1.263	.118	10.68

Corrected $R^2 = .588$
Std. error regression = 8.67%

Somewhat surprisingly, four of the five funds had portfolio betas of less than 1. The alpha is stated in quarterly terms. A measure of .6 indicates the fund had excess risk-adjusted returns of 60 basis points per quarter over the 20 years. These measures are arithmetic.

To the extent nonsystematic risks can be reduced by combining funds, the composite portfolio, these data suggest, would have provided above-average return performance for below-average risks.

Some caution is necessary in interpreting these results. The CAPM performance characteristic line tends to misstate a more realistic, yet not readily measurable, benchmark. There is a strong tendency to overstate excess risk-adjusted returns for portfolios with betas that are significantly less than 1. The reverse is done for portfolios well above 1.[1]

The five scatter diagrams shown in Exhibit 4 further indicate the results of each fund.

Upside/Downside Performance

While performance characteristic lines afford an overall view of performance, they do not distinguish between performance in good and bad markets. To get some perspective on upside potential and downside exposure, we recalculated performance for each fund in two steps: The first step looked at performance of each fund relative to the actuarial required rate of return, R_a (6 percent per year), using the following regression equation:

$$R_p - R_a = \alpha_p + \beta_p(R_m - R_a)$$

The group of observations was then subdivided into two sets depending on whether $R_m - R_a$ was positive (good market) or negative. For each subset, the regression was rerun, using the following formula:

$$R_p - R_a - \alpha_p = \beta_p(R_m - R_a - \alpha_p)$$

The use of α_p from the first regression forced the upside and downside line through the same intercept.

Results were as follows:

---

[1]Studies indicate that the empirical capital asset pricing model differs from the theoretical one. The empirical intercept is typically higher and the slope less. Performance should be related to what is empirically feasible.

	Overall Beta	R^2	*Upside Beta*	*Downside Beta*	*Alpha*
Investment Co. of America	.870	.82	.937	.807	.720
Pioneer	.884	.75	.967	.806	.952
Decatur	.679	.62	.745	.617	.883
Chemical	.978	.86	.944	1.018	.453
New Horizons	1.262	.58	1.291	1.236	1.678

Investment Co., Pioneer, and Decatur all showed (statistically significant) lower downside beta exposure. Only Chemical had higher downside exposure, but here the difference was too small to be conclusive.

In general, it is attractive to have managers that can get favorable downside performance while outperforming the market on average over a cycle.

Results of Interim Five-Year Periods

Five years is often used as a useful period for comparing the performance of a fund against the market index. Short-term volatility effects will tend to have canceled out. The following table shows the five-year quarterly moving average total returns for each fund and for the S&P Index.

Arithmetic Moving Averages of Quarterly Returns *(five-year periods)*

Five Years Ending Qtr/Year	*Invest. Co. of America*	*Pioneer*	*Decatur*	*Chemical*	*New Horizons*	*S&P 500 Index*
2/67	4.85%	4.46%	3.30%*	5.26%	6.16%	3.51%
2/68	4.36	4.52	3.67	4.68	7.31	2.78
2/69	3.32	4.17	3.23	3.21	7.18	1.85
2/70	1.81	2.36	1.69	2.18	5.61	0.35†
2/71	2.49	3.12	2.93	2.90	6.50	1.99
2/72	2.01	2.30	2.76	2.83	6.32	1.93
2/73	0.86*	1.05*†	0.73*†	2.13	2.76	1.29†
2/74	0.53*†	0.79*†	0.53*†	1.68	2.37	1.03†
2/75	3.03	3.48	2.58*	3.07	5.24	2.96
2/76	2.08	3.00	2.22	1.49*†	2.24	1.85
2/77	1.81	3.01	2.50	−0.08*†	−0.44*†	1.38†
2/78	2.76	3.38	3.21	0.24*†	2.68	1.37†
2/79	3.64	4.61	4.37	1.39*†	3.71	2.25
2/80	2.91	4.15	4.02	1.78*	3.49	2.37
2/81	3.16	3.99	3.72	2.72	5.23	2.59
2/82	2.72	2.58	2.92	2.25	4.36	2.05

*Failed to beat Standard & Poor's 500 Index.

†Failed to meet actuarial requirement.

It should be noted that each fund had at least one bad spell where it failed to beat the index. The Chemical Fund had the most difficulty in the late 1970s, when "growth" stock investing was particularly difficult. Of somewhat greater concern, three funds failed to beat the index concurrently for two back-to-back five-year periods in the early 1970s. (Results for all feasible five-year periods are shown in Exhibit 5.)

On the whole, however, this performance record is most encouraging.

Moving Geometric Averages

The table below shows the five-year geometric moving averages for each of the five funds and the Standard & Poor's 500 Index for all feasible five-year periods.

Five-Year Compound Growth Rates

Five Years Ending Qtr/Year	*Invest. Co. of America*	*Pioneer*	*Decatur*	*Chemical*	*New Horizons*	*S&P 500 Index*
2/67	20.0%	18.3%	13.5%	21.8%	25.5%	14.3%
2/68	17.7	18.5	15.0	18.9	30.3	11.0
2/69	13.0	16.6	12.8	12.4	29.4	7.1
2/70	6.2	8.1	6.0	7.3	20.3	0.5†
2/71	8.9	11.6	11.3	10.4	24.2	6.8
2/72	7.2	8.1	10.3	10.6	23.8	6.8
2/73	2.2*†	3.1*†	1.7*†	7.8	6.3	4.2†
2/74	0.9*†	1.8*†	1.0*†	5.6	3.4†	2.9†
2/75	10.4	12.7	9.0*	10.3	14.7	9.3
2/76	1.0*	10.4	7.2	3.3*†	2.0*†	4.6†
2/77	5.2	10.5	8.8	−2.8*†	−7.8*†	2.7†
2/78	9.3	12.1	11.8	−1.6*†	6.2	2.6†
2/79	13.3	17.7	17.3	3.1*†	11.9	6.3
2/80	11.2	16.4	16.1	5.8*†	12.7	8.8
2/81	12.5	16.0	15.1	10.4*	20.4	10.1
2/82	10.6	9.4	11.3	9.7	15.9	7.6

*Failed to beat the Standard & Poor's Index.
†Failed to beat actuarial requirement.

Again, these results indicate quite favorable performance for the various funds.

Diversification Prospects

Will it be easy to diversify these funds to reduce risks without hurting return prospects? One way to gain perspective on this question is to see if the funds tend to beat the market concurrently or not. We did this by cross-correlating the excess returns (relative to the market portfolio, the Standard & Poor's 500 Index) for each pair of funds, using all the quarterly data available in the 20-year study period. The results of these cross-correlations are as follows:

Correlation $R_p - R_m$ of Pairs of Funds *(all 80 quarters)*

	R^2(adj)	*Constant*	*Slope*	*SER*
Invest. Co. versus Pioneer	.274	.246	.435	2.94
Invest. Co. versus Decatur	.307	.376	.385	2.88
Invest. Co. versus Chemical	.125	.448	.400	3.23
Invest. Co. versus New Horizons	.100	.379	.130	3.28
Pioneer versus Decatur	.299	.566	.465	3.55
Pioneer versus Chemical	.017	.765	.229	4.20
Pioneer versus New Horizons	.090	.580	.152	4.04
Decatur versus Chemical	−.000	.598	.099	5.07
Decatur versus New Horizons	−.010	.590	.027	5.08
Chemical versus New Horizons	.191	.134	.161	2.87

As indicated by the R^2, the co-movement of the various funds is quite low. In particular, the growth-oriented funds, Chemical and New Horizons, tend to move out of phase with the remaining funds.

Cumulative Cyclicality

Exhibit 6 shows graphically the cumulative cyclicality of each of the five funds and of the Standard & Poor's 500 Index. These data were developed by dividing the cumulative wealth index for each fund in each period by the corresponding trend-line measure of cumulative wealth. The plots thus reflect cyclical movements around fundamental trend lines.

Although there is some coincidence of movement with the market (e.g., all funds bottom in or near period 49), there is nevertheless considerable diversity in the timing, particularly of market peaks.

Relative Cyclicality

Exhibit 7 displays the cumulative relative-wealth measures for each of the five funds. They were derived by taking the relative cyclical-wealth measures for each of the five funds (as shown on the charts in Exhibit 6) and dividing them by the relative cyclical-wealth measure for the Standard & Poor's 500 Index. The data for these graphs are summarized in Exhibit 8.

These data suggest that the timing of cyclical movements is not as coincidental as one might expect. It also suggests that beta is not necessarily a good measure of cumulative risk exposure to the cyclical movements of the various funds. All this suggests that there are good opportunities for diversification against the more adverse cumulative movements of the market index.

Portfolio Simulations

A preliminary preview of a simplified approach to determining asset mixes that are more likely to be better is provided through recreated simulations.

In this preliminary analysis, we prespecified target asset mixes for three illustrative portfolios (which were rebalanced, without cost, each quarter). We then determined the quarterly rate of return for the overall portfolio, using the actual returns in the quarter of each fund.

Results of three simulations are shown below:

Portfolio Simulation

Annual Period, Year End Qtr/Year	*S&P 500*	*.23 Invest. Co. .12 Pioneer .22 Decatur .35 Chemical .08 New Horizons (current portfolio wts.)*	*Equal Weights*	*.25 Invest. Co. .25 Pioneer .25 Decatur .15 Chemical .10 New Horizons*
2/63	+31.2%	+26.0%*	+24.4%*	+24.8%*
2/64	+21.5	+19.2	+14.6*	+15.1*
2/65	+ 6.2	+10.1	+18.6	+11.2
2/66	+ 4.0	+21.0	+24.2	+20.9
2/67	+10.7	+22.1	+27.1	+23.1
2/68	+13.4	+21.9	+25.5	+24.1
2/69	+ 1.2	− 0.4*	− 0.4*	+ 0.0*
2/70	−22.8	−17.6	−19.1	−18.8
2/71	+41.9	+41.7*	45.6	+41.9
2/72	+10.8	+17.3	20.8	+15.7
2/73	+ 0.2	− 7.3*	−10.9*	− 8.9*
2/74	− 4.5	− 7.7*	− 7.7*	− 6.6*
2/75	+ 4.0	+19.1	+22.6	+23.6
2/76	+14.0	+12.3*	+13.0*	+16.5
2/77	+ 0.5	+ 1.2*	+ 2.5	+ 5.1
2/78	+ 0.1	+ 8.5	+11.4	+ 8.6
2/79	+13.6	+15.4	+15.7	+16.7
2/80	+17.1	+19.5	+21.7	+19.6
2/81	+20.5	+24.5	+26.1	+24.3
2/82	−10.4	−10.1*	−12.2*	−10.6*
Annual compound return	7.8%	10.7%	11.5%	11.3%
Annual arithmetic average return	8.5	11.7	12.7	12.3
Arithmetic standard deviation	14.1	14.9	16.4	15.1

*Failed to beat S&P 500.

While these results show a strong tendency to outperform the Standard & Poor's 500 Index, there was nevertheless considerable variability.

The variability tends to be damped down over five-year periods as the following data indicate:

Five-Year Compound Annual Rates of Returns *(three simulations)*

Five Years Ending Quarter/Year	*Current Weights*	*Equal Weights*	*.25 Invest Co. .25 Pioneer .25 Decatur .15 Chemical .10 New Horizons*	*Standard & Poor's 500 Index*
2/67	19.6%	20.0%	18.9%	14.3%
2/68	18.8	20.2	18.8	11.0
2/69	14.6	16.9	15.5	7.1
2/70	8.1	9.8	8.4	0.5
2/71	11.6	13.4	11.6	6.8
2/72	10.7	12.2	10.6	6.8
2/73	4.8	4.8	3.9*	4.2
2/74	3.2	3.2	2.5*	2.9
2/75	12.5	12.2	12.1	9.3
2/76	6.1	6.6	7.2	4.6
2/77	3.0	3.2	5.2	2.7
2/78	6.3	7.9	8.9	2.6
2/79	11.1	12.9	13.9	6.3
2/80	11.2	12.6	13.2	8.8
2/81	13.5	15.1	14.7	10.1
2/82	10.3	9.1	10.8	7.6

*Failed to beat Standard and Poor's 500 Index.

EXHIBIT 1
Wealth Relatives of Five Mutual Funds *(by years, July 1962–June 1982)*

Year Ending June	Invest. Co. of America	Pioneer	Decatur	Chemical	New Horizons	S&P 500 Index
1963	1.27	1.26	1.20	1.31	1.17	1.31
1964	1.56	1.37	1.33	1.70	1.19	1.59
1965	1.68	1.54	1.57	1.82	1.29	1.69
1966	2.09	1.83	1.69	2.21	1.94	1.76
1967	2.49	2.32	1.88	2.68	3.11	1.95
1968	2.87	2.94	2.41	3.11	4.39	2.21
1969	2.87	2.95	2.43	3.05	4.31	2.24
1970	2.27	2.27	2.10	2.59	3.25	1.73
1971	3.20	3.12	2.84	3.63	5.73	2.45
1972	3.53	3.42	3.07	4.43	9.05	2.71
1973	3.20	3.42	2.62	4.52	5.96	2.72
1974	3.00	3.23	2.55	4.01	5.10	2.59
1975	3.73	4.13	3.23	4.23	6.46	2.70
1976	4.36	5.12	4.07	4.27	6.39	3.07
1977	4.54	5.63	4.68	3.84	6.03	3.09
1978	5.00	6.05	4.64	4.16	8.05	3.09
1979	5.61	7.31	5.56	4.67	8.95	3.52
1980	6.63	8.82	6.81	5.61	11.77	4.12
1981	7.86	10.74	8.23	6.99	16.20	4.96
1982	7.50	8.81	7.97	6.11	12.61	4.45

Note: Compound annual growth in wealth for any sales period can be computed as follows:

$$\log(1+r) = (\log W_E - \log W_B)/n$$
$$r = [\text{antilog of } \log(1+r)] - 1$$

where:
W_E = Wealth at end of period.
W_B = Wealth at beginning of period.
n = Number of years from beginning to end of period (W_B at 6/62 = 1.00).

The rank order of performance changes, depending upon the subperiod analyzed. For example, Chemical did quite well in the first 10-year period; quite poorly in the second 10-year period.

EXHIBIT 2
Annual Returns of Five Funds *(20 years)*

Period Ending Qtr./Year	Invest. Co. of America	Pioneer	Decatur	Chemical	New Horizons	S&P 500 Index
2/63	27.49%*	26.38%*	19.74%*	30.69%*	17.23%*	31.15%
2/64	22.75	8.21*	11.13*	30.37	1.49*	21.50
2/65	7.39	12.31	17.68	6.53	8.53	6.18
2/66	24.40	19.45	7.73	21.86	50.00	3.99
2/67	19.19	26.54	11.24	21.34	60.45	10.74
2/68	15.30	26.71	28.24	15.92	41.19	13.41
2/69	−0.03*	0.32*	1.06*	−1.99*	−1.79*	1.21
2/70	−21.08	−23.17*	−13.66	−14.91	−24.68*	−22.83
2/71	41.10*	37.57*	35.27*	39.83*	76.58	41.86
2/72	10.46*	9.69*	8.00*	22.06	57.84	10.75
2/73	−9.30	−0.10*	−14.57*	2.13	−34.07*	0.17
2/74	−6.52*	−5.61*	−2.83	−11.23*	−14.57*	−4.53
2/75	24.63	27.86	26.77	5.45	26.84	4.00
2/76	16.76	23.99	26.06	0.75*	−1.12	14.00
2/77	4.14	10.15	14.87	−10.05*	−5.66*	0.53
2/78	10.15	7.43	−0.70*	8.32	33.53	0.12
2/79	12.23*	20.81	21.94	12.24*	11.13*	13.63
2/80	12.73*	20.68	20.33	20.33	31.55	17.21
2/81	24.23	21.75	20.77	24.45	37.68	20.47
2/82	−4.58	−18.03*	−3.13	−12.63*	−22.16*	−10.37
Geometric mean	10.60%	11.49%	10.93%	9.47%	13.51%	7.75%
Arithmetic mean	11.58%	12.65%	11.82%	10.23%	17.50%	8.66%
Arithmetic std. dev.	14.77	15.82	13.92	16.50	30.95	14.35

*Failed to beat the Standard & Poor's 500 Index.

EXHIBIT 3
Trend Line of Wealth Accumulation *(six funds; July 1962 to June 1982, by quarters)*

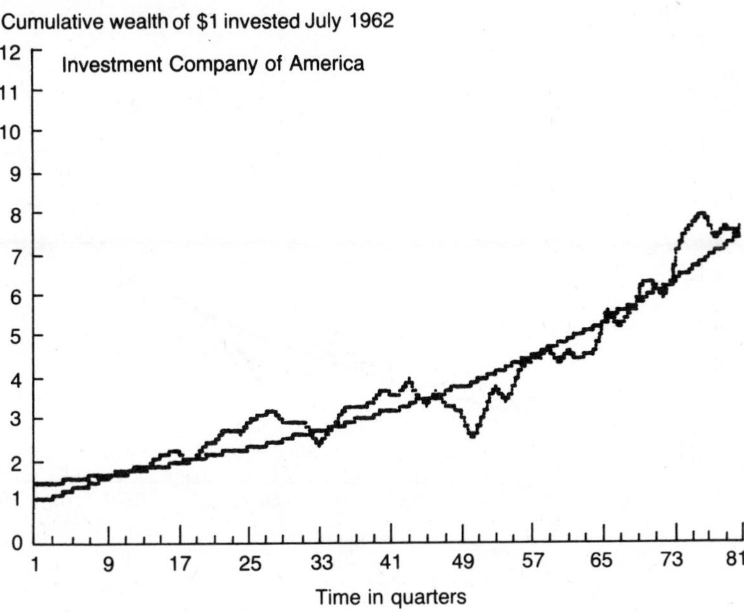

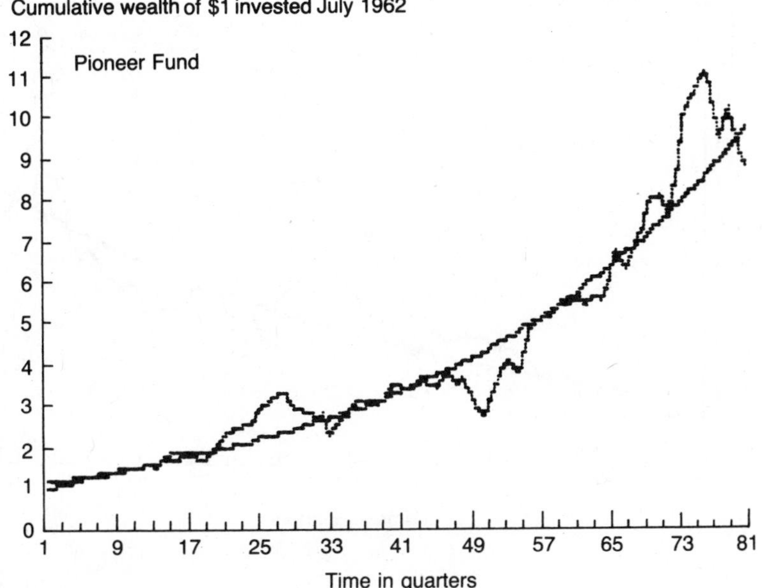

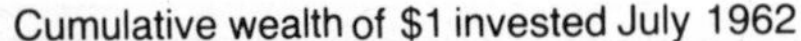

EXHIBIT 3 ***(continued)***

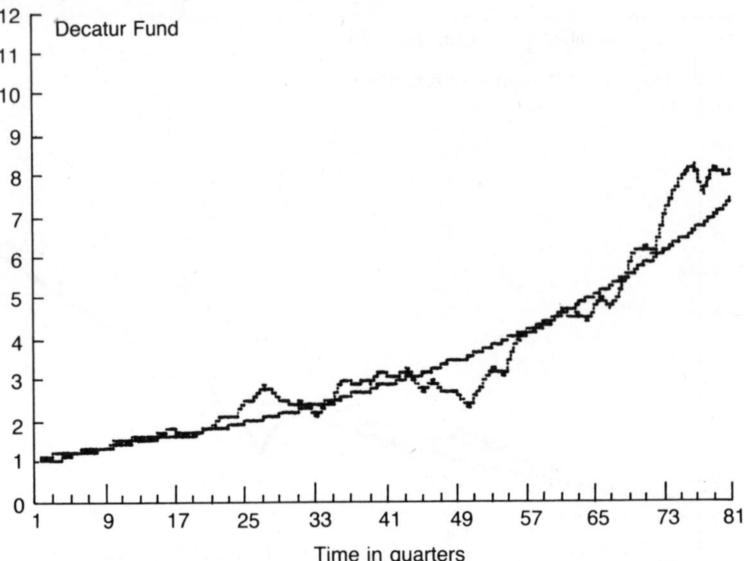

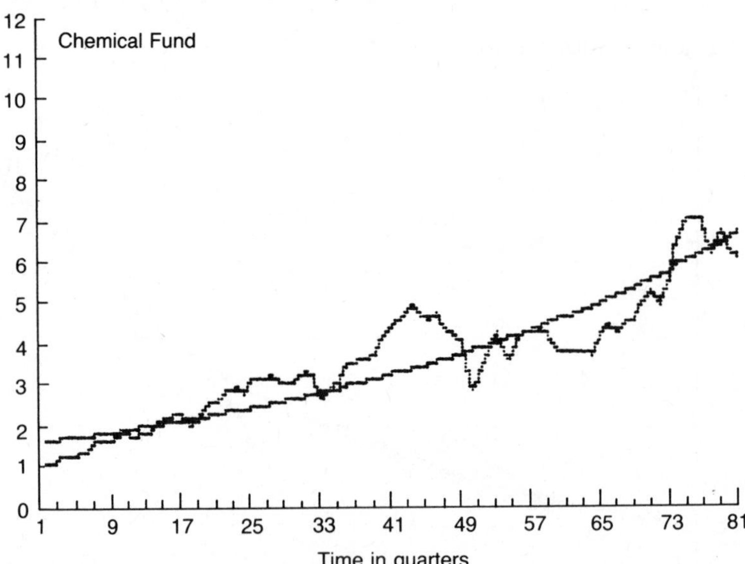

EXHIBIT 3 *(concluded)*

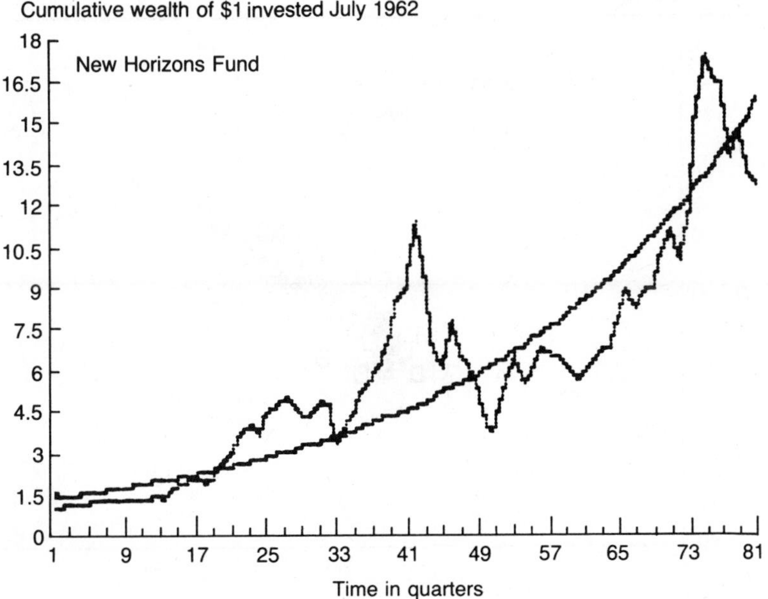

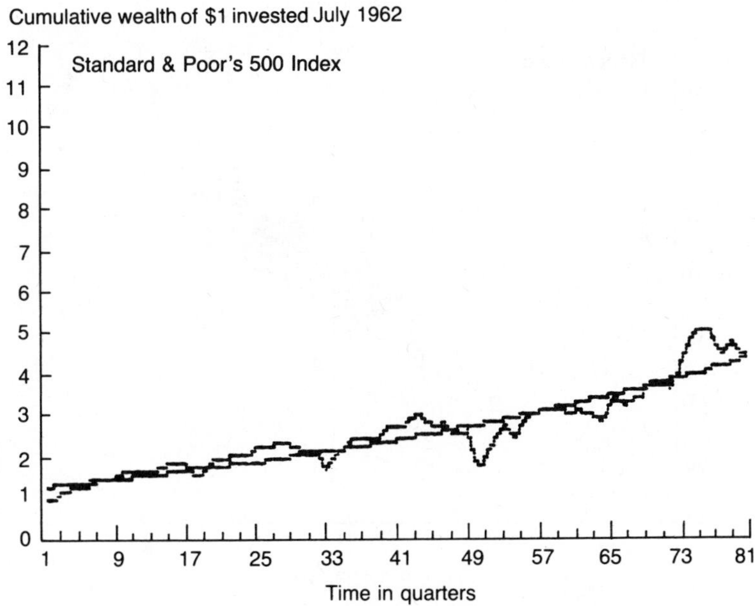

EXHIBIT 4
Performance Characteristic Charts *(five mutual funds; using quarterly data, July 1962 to June 1982)*

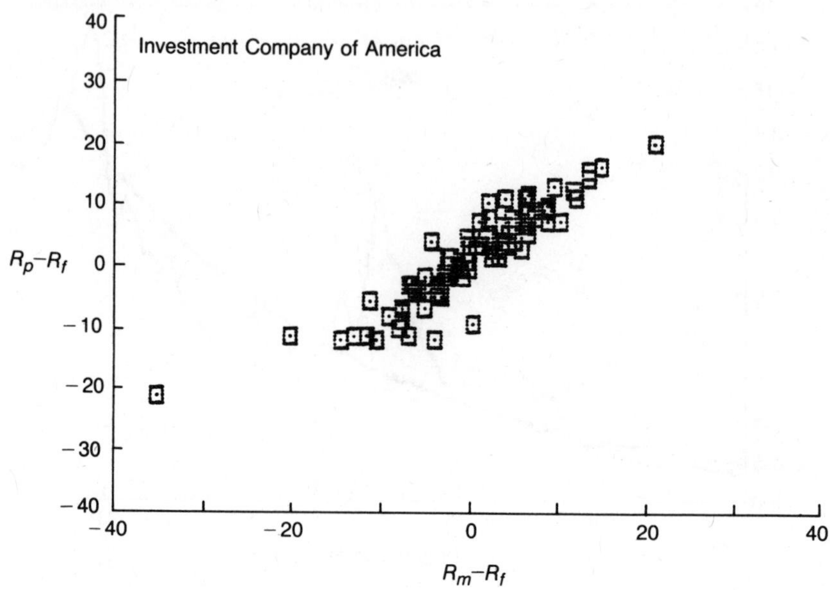

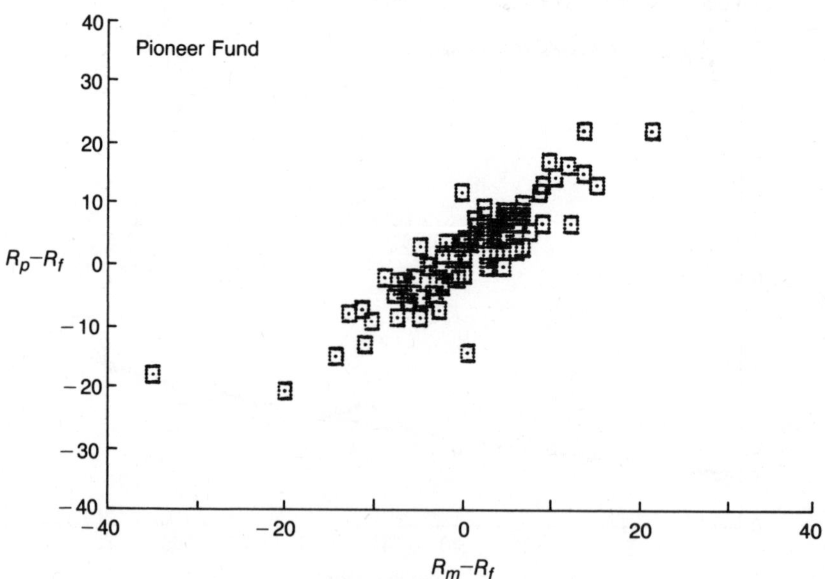

□ Denotes paired performance results for a quarter.

EXHIBIT 4 ***(continued)***

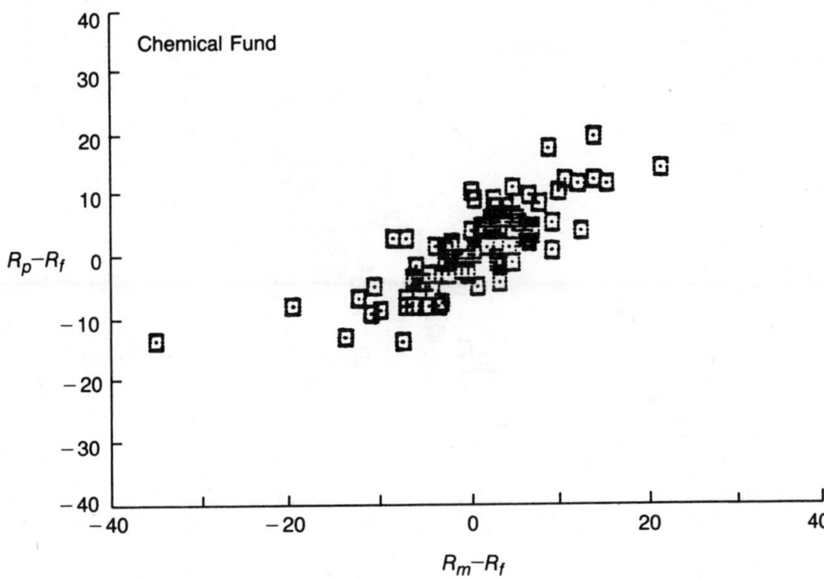

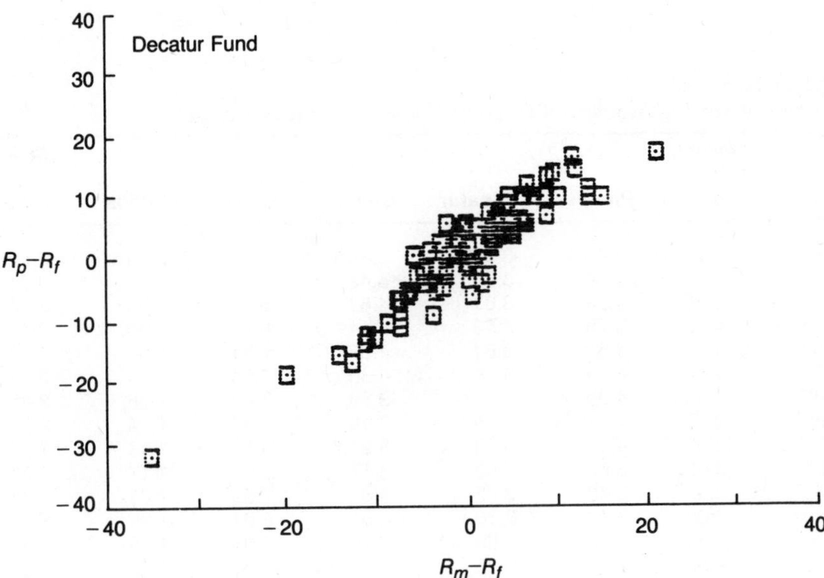

▣ Denotes paired performance results for a quarter.

EXHIBIT 4 *(concluded)*

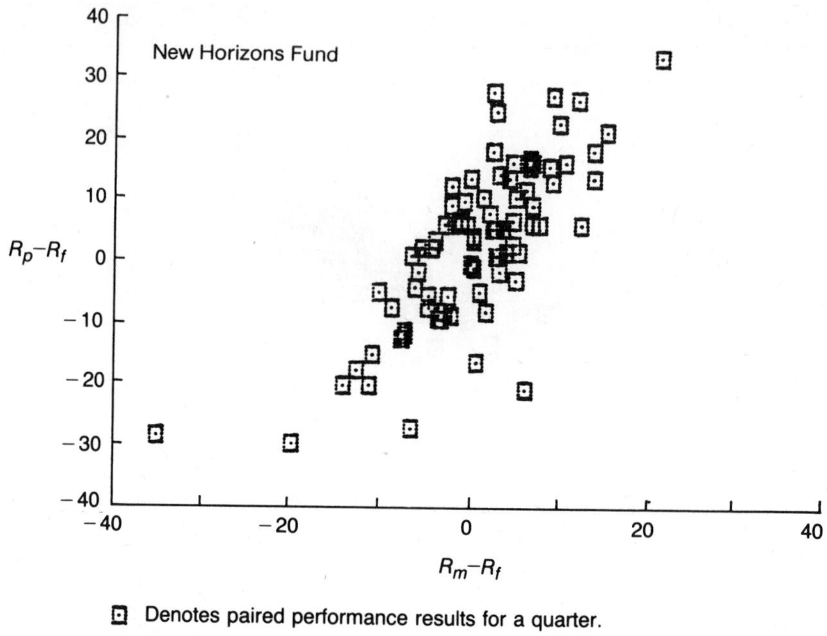

EXHIBIT 5
Arithmetic Moving Averages of Quarterly Returns *(five-year average)*

	Invest. Co. of America	Pioneer	Decatur	Chem.	New Horiz.	T-bills	S&P 500 Index
2–67	4.85%	4.46%	3.30%*	5.26%	6.16%	0.93%	3.52%
3–67	5.13	4.54	3.83	5.42	6.68	0.94	3.71
4–67	4.56	4.33	3.63	4.84	6.89	0.96	3.08
1–68	4.03	3.78	3.52	4.14	6.24	0.98	2.47
2–68	4.36	4.52	3.67	4.68	7.31	1.01	2.78
3–68	4.44	4.74	3.98	4.30	7.54	1.04	2.77
4–68	4.35	4.99	4.51	3.89	7.64	1.06	2.59
1–69	3.77	4.54	3.85	3.49	7.34	1.09	2.21
2–69	3.32	4.17	3.23	3.21	7.18	1.13	1.85
3–69	3.02	3.62	2.60	3.17	7.09	1.17	1.67
4–69	3.02	3.46	2.68	3.67	7.59	1.21	1.37
1–70	2.09	3.14	2.10	3.01	6.64	1.25	1.17
2–70	1.81	2.36	1.69	2.18	5.61	1.28	0.35
3–70	2.09	2.62	2.22	2.21	5.88	1.32	0.81
4–70	2.05	2.51	2.03	2.22	5.67	1.34	1.15
1–71	2.31	3.10	2.83	2.63	6.28	1.33	1.77
2–71	2.49	3.12	2.93	2.90	6.51	1.32	1.99
3–71	3.11	3.41	3.45	3.49	7.22	1.33	2.40
4–71	2.73	3.40	3.15	3.22	7.23	1.32	2.34

EXHIBIT 5 *(concluded)*

	Invest. Co. of America	Pioneer	Decatur	Chem.	New Horiz.	T-bills	S&P 500 Index
1–72	2.35%	3.01%	3.11%	2.83%	6.70%	1.30%	1.96%
2–72	2.01	2.30	2.76	2.83	6.32	1.30	1.93
3–72	1.77	1.97	2.23	2.70	6.79	1.30	1.75
4–72	2.16	2.16	2.48	2.88	5.26	1.30	2.10
1–73	1.95*	2.11*	1.92*	3.17	4.51	1.31	2.14
2–73	0.81*	1.05*	0.73*	2.13	2.77	1.32	1.29
3–73	1.18*	1.21*	1.00*	2.47	3.94	1.35	1.34
4–73	0.49*	0.67*	0.08*	1.75	2.75	1.38	0.78
1–74	0.61*	1.06	0.33*	1.83	2.88	1.40	0.72
2–74	0.53*	0.79*	0.53*	1.68	2.37	1.43	1.03
3–74	−0.29	0.19	0.12	0.08	1.05	1.45	−0.42
4–74	0.19	0.60	0.47	0.31	0.74	1.45	0.06
1–75	1.77	1.70	1.58	1.59	2.85	1.43	1.29
2–75	3.04	3.48	2.58*	3.07	5.24	1.41	2.96
3–75	1.64	2.40	1.64	1.72	3.27	1.41	1.57
4–75	1.56	2.21	1.77	1.64	2.92	1.42	1.48
1–76	1.91	2.73	1.86	1.65*	2.83	1.43	1.74
2–76	2.09	3.00	2.22	1.46*	2.24	1.44	1.86
3–76	2.11	3.12	2.18	1.46*	1.72*	1.44	1.98
4–76	2.12	3.22	2.48	1.10*	0.63*	1.45	1.91
1–77	1.47	2.69	2.05	0.17*	−0.57*	1.46	1.25
2–77	1.81	3.01	2.50	−0.08*	−0.44*	1.48	1.38
3–77	1.52	2.77	2.30	−0.41*	−1.55*	1.49	1.05
4–77	1.26	2.67	2.08	−0.69*	−0.17*	1.51	0.66
1–78	1.66	2.75	2.32	−0.70*	1.25	1.52	0.66
2–78	2.76	3.38	3.21	0.24*	2.68	1.52	1.37
3–78	2.64	3.48	3.00	0.30*	1.72	1.51	1.57
4–78	2.84	3.44	3.08	0.67*	2.19	1.52	1.78
1–79	3.12	3.68	3.58	1.12*	2.91	1.55	2.27
2–79	3.64	4.61	4.37	1.39*	3.71	1.57	2.25
3–79	5.09	5.93	5.38	3.28*	5.68	1.58	4.27
4–79	4.60	5.61	4.95	2.95*	5.74	1.64	3.81
1–80	3.22	4.13	3.96	1.68*	3.53	1.71	2.46
2–80	2.91	4.15	4.02	1.70*	3.49	1.78	2.36
3–80	4.01	5.24	4.63	3.23*	5.73	1.80	3.47
4–80	3.98	5.27	4.68	3.32*	6.09	1.89	3.51
1–81	3.35	4.35	3.93	2.79*	5.07	2.00	2.83
2–81	3.16	3.99	3.72	2.72	5.23	2.12	2.59
3–81	2.67	3.42	3.17	2.12	4.42	2.24	1.98
4–81	2.66	3.49	3.49	2.76	5.19	2.34	2.17
1–82	2.91	3.04	3.23	2.53	4.94	2.45	2.18
2–82	2.72	2.58	2.92	2.25	4.36	2.55	2.05

*Failed to beat Standard & Poor's 500 Index.

EXHIBIT 6
Cumulative Measures of Cyclicality around Geometric Wealth Trends
(five firms and Standard & Poor's 500 Index, 20 years)

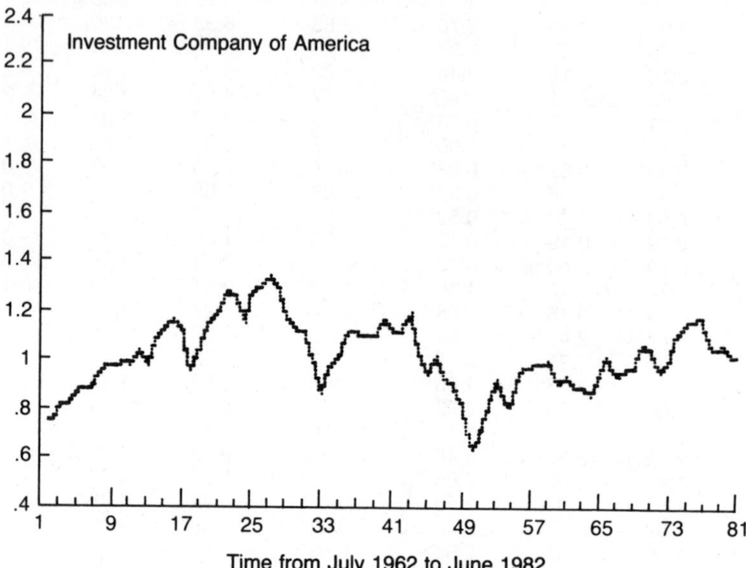

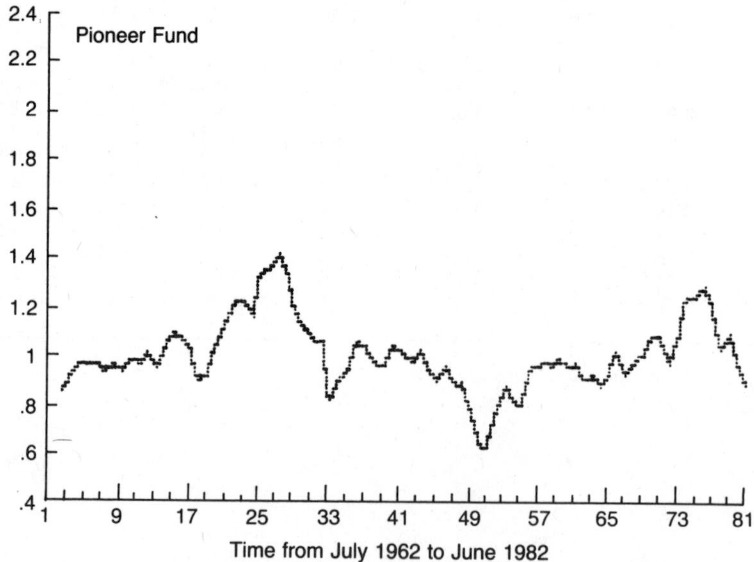

EXHIBIT 6 *(continued)*

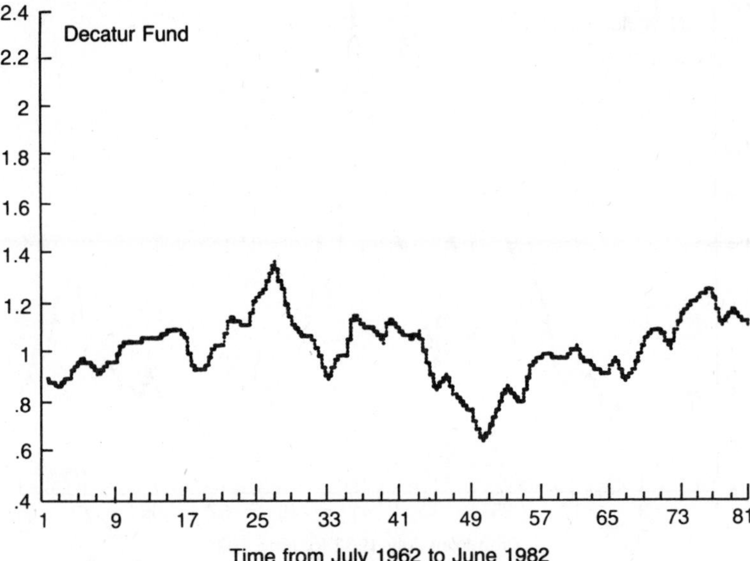
Cumulative wealth index ÷ Trend line wealth index
2.4
2.2
2
1.8
1.6
1.4
1.2
1
.8
.6
.4
Decatur Fund
1
9
17
25
33
41
49
57
65
73
81
Time from July 1962 to June 1982

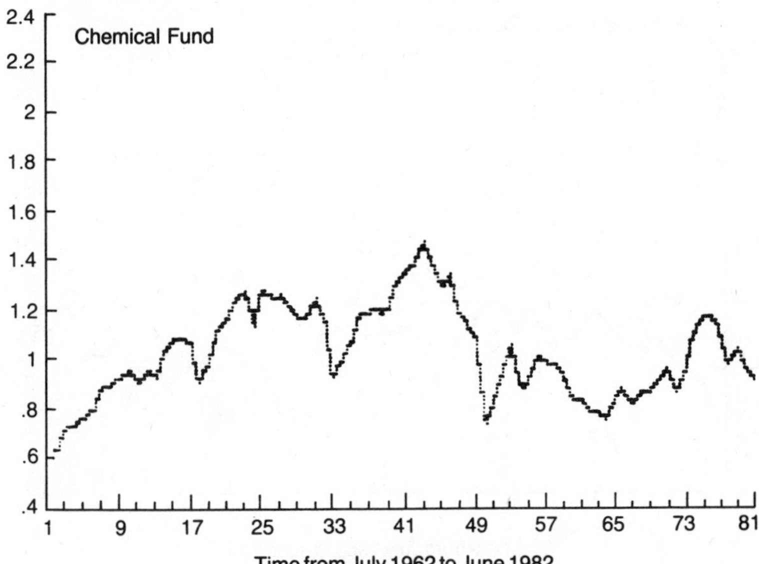
Cumulative wealth index ÷ Trend line wealth index
2.4
2.2
2
1.8
1.6
1.4
1.2
1
.8
.6
.4
Chemical Fund
1
9
17
25
33
41
49
57
65
73
81
Time from July 1962 to June 1982

EXHIBIT 6 ***(concluded)***

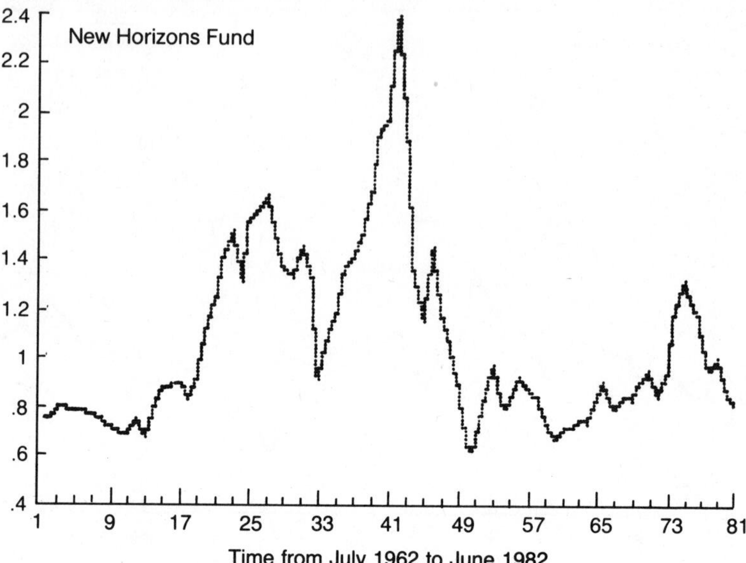
Cumulative wealth index ÷ Trend line wealth index
New Horizons Fund
2.4
2.2
2
1.8
1.6
1.4
1.2
1
.8
.6
.4
1
9
17
25
33
41
49
57
65
73
81
Time from July 1962 to June 1982

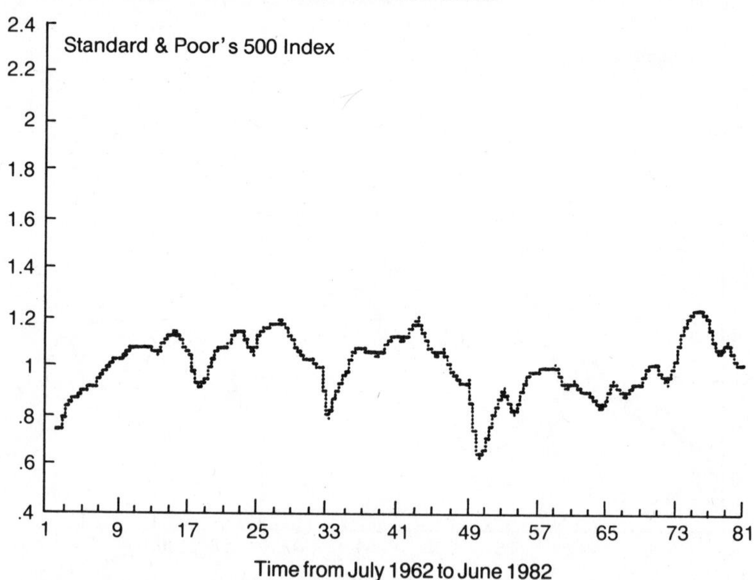
Cumulative wealth index ÷ Trend line wealth index
Standard & Poor's 500 Index
2.4
2.2
2
1.8
1.6
1.4
1.2
1
.8
.6
.4
1
9
17
25
33
41
49
57
65
73
81
Time from July 1962 to June 1982

EXHIBIT 7
Cyclical Wealth Measures Relative to the Standard & Poor's 500 Index
(five funds; July 1962 to June 1982)

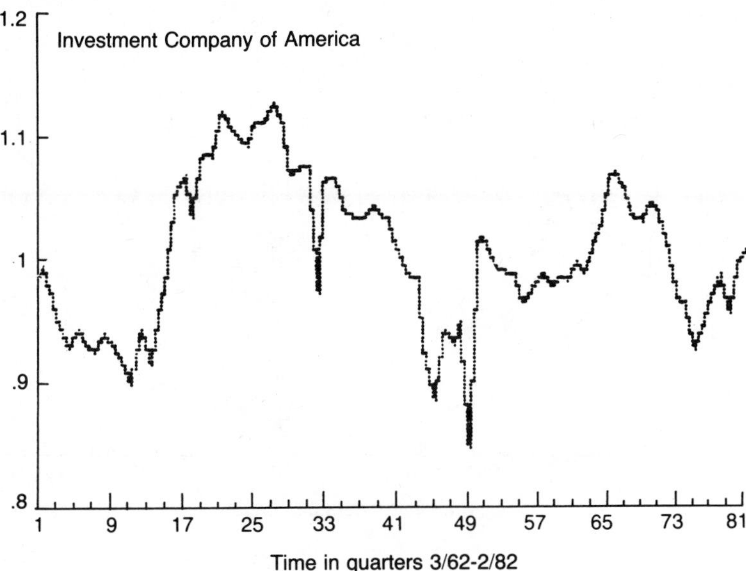

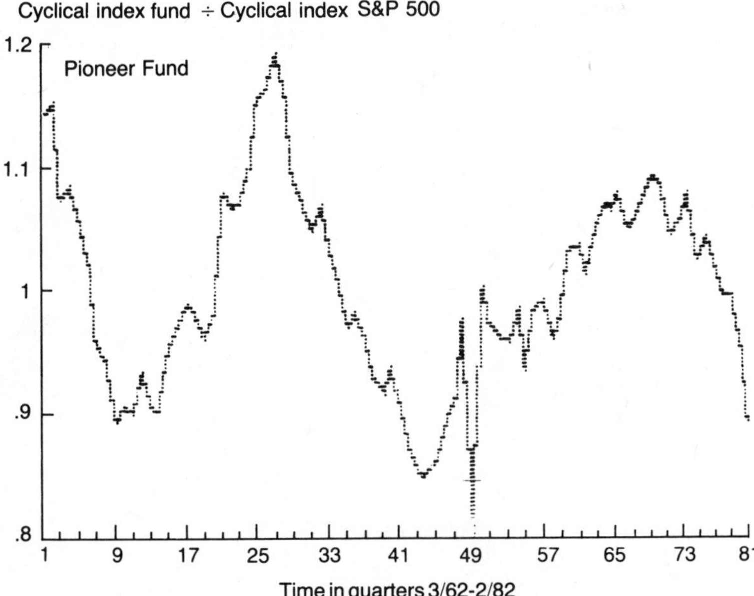

EXHIBIT 7 *(continued)*

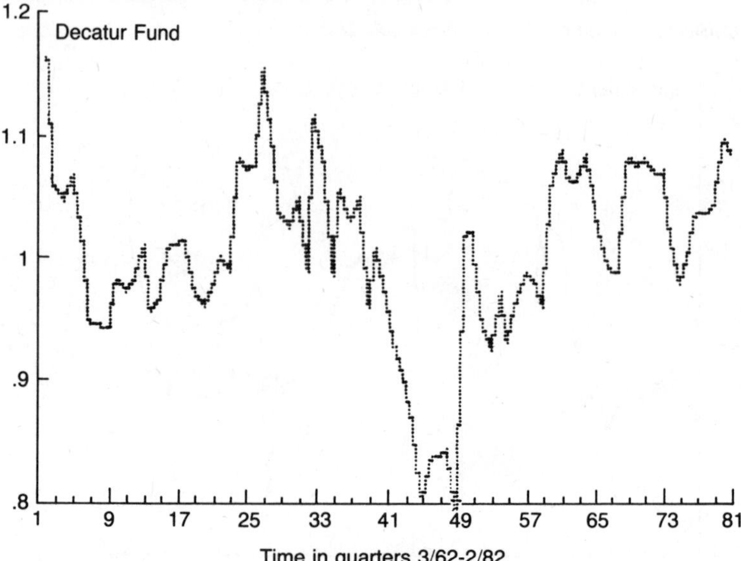

Cyclical index fund ÷ Cyclical index S&P 500

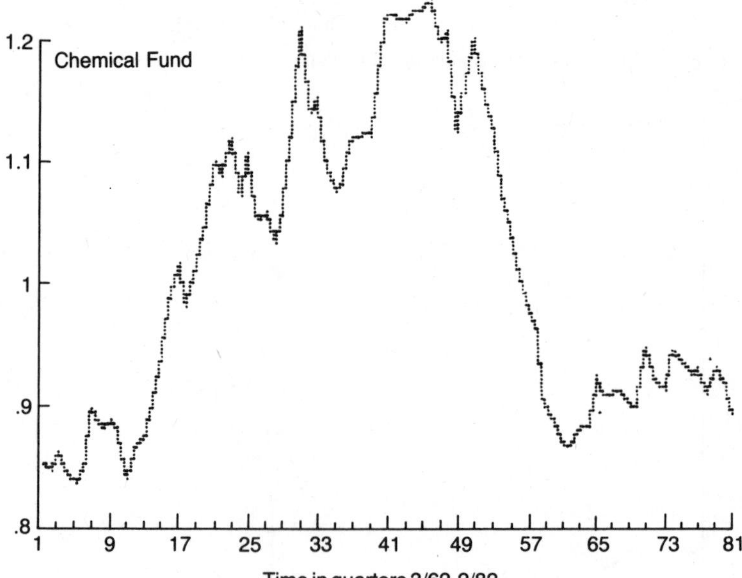

EXHIBIT 7 ***(concluded)***

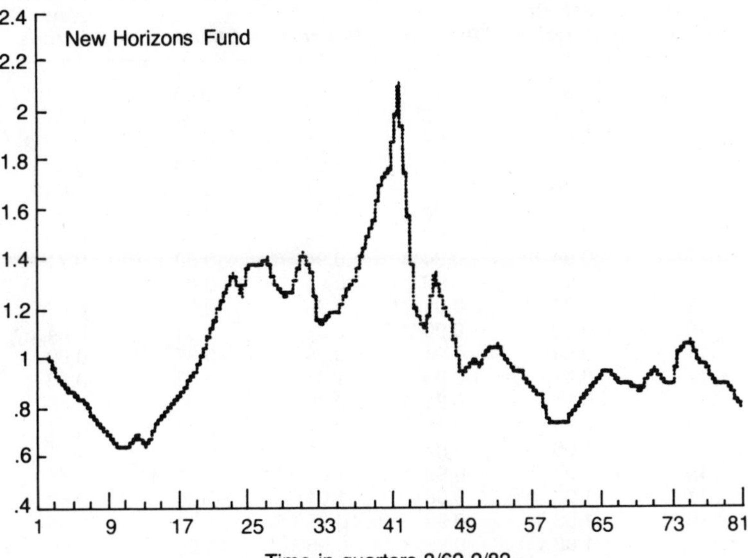

EXHIBIT 8
Cyclical Wealth Index Fund/Cyclical Wealth Index Standard & Poor's 500 *(five funds; July 1962 to June 1982, by quarters)*

Period	Invest. Co. of America	Pioneer	Decatur	Chemical	New Horizons
0	0.99	1.15	1.21	0.85	1.01
1	9.97	1.15	1.15	0.84	1.01
2	0.95	1.07	1.05	0.86	0.93
3	0.93	1.09	1.04	0.84	0.88
4	0.94	1.05	1.07	0.84	0.84
5	0.93	1.02	1.01	0.85	0.81
6	0.92	0.96	0.94	0.90	0.78
7	0.94	0.94	0.94	0.88	0.71
8	0.93	0.90	0.94	0.89	0.66
9	0.92	0.91	0.98	0.88	0.64
10	0.90	0.90	0.97	0.84	0.64
11	0.94	0.94	0.98	0.87	0.69
12	0.91	0.90	1.01	0.88	0.63
13	0.95	0.91	0.95	0.90	0.68
14	0.99	0.95	0.97	0.94	0.77
15	1.06	0.97	1.01	0.99	0.81
16	1.07	0.99	1.01	1.01	0.86
17	1.03	0.98	1.01	0.98	0.89
18	1.08	0.96	0.97	1.01	0.95
19	1.08	0.98	0.95	1.05	1.05
20	1.12	1.08	0.98	1.10	1.16
21	1.11	1.07	1.00	1.09	1.24
22	1.10	1.07	0.98	1.12	1.34
23	1.09	1.10	1.08	1.07	1.24
24	1.11	1.15	1.07	1.11	1.36
25	1.11	1.17	1.07	1.05	1.37
26	1.13	1.19	1.15	1.06	1.39
27	1.10	1.15	1.08	1.03	1.28
28	1.07	1.09	1.03	1.06	1.24
29	1.07	1.07	1.02	1.12	1.27
30	1.07	1.05	1.05	1.21	1.42
31	0.97	1.07	0.98	1.14	1.32
32	1.06	1.04	1.11	1.15	1.13
33	1.06	1.01	1.07	1.10	1.17
34	1.04	0.97	0.98	1.07	1.20
35	1.03	0.98	1.05	1.08	1.25
36	1.03	0.96	1.02	1.12	1.32
37	1.04	0.93	1.05	1.12	1.44
38	1.03	0.92	0.96	1.12	1.56
39	1.03	0.94	1.00	1.16	1.70
40	1.00	0.91	0.97	1.22	1.77

EXHIBIT 8 *(concluded)*

Period	Invest. Co. of America	Pioneer	Decatur	Chemical	New Horizons
41	0.98	0.87	0.92	1.22	2.10
42	0.98	0.85	0.89	1.21	1.54
43	0.92	0.85	0.86	1.22	1.18
44	0.89	0.86	0.79	1.23	1.09
45	0.94	0.89	0.83	1.23	1.33
46	0.93	0.92	0.84	1.20	1.18
47	0.95	0.98	0.84	1.21	1.12
48	0.85	0.92	0.78	1.13	0.92
49	1.02	1.00	1.01	1.17	0.99
50	1.01	0.97	1.01	1.20	0.95
51	0.99	0.96	0.94	1.16	1.03
52	0.99	0.96	0.92	1.13	1.05
53	0.99	0.99	0.97	1.07	0.97
54	0.96	0.93	0.93	1.05	0.94
55	0.97	0.99	0.96	1.01	0.93
56	0.99	0.99	0.98	0.98	0.85
57	0.98	0.96	0.97	0.96	0.82
58	0.98	0.98	0.95	0.90	0.73
59	0.98	1.04	1.06	0.89	0.72
60	1.00	1.04	1.08	0.87	0.75
61	0.99	1.01	1.06	0.87	0.79
62	1.01	1.05	1.06	0.88	0.83
63	1.03	1.07	1.08	0.89	0.88
64	1.07	1.06	1.04	0.93	0.94
65	1.07	1.08	1.01	0.91	0.94
66	1.05	1.05	0.98	0.92	0.89
67	1.03	1.06	0.99	0.91	0.89
68	1.03	1.08	1.08	0.90	0.96
69	1.04	1.09	1.07	0.90	0.89
70	1.04	1.08	1.08	0.95	0.95
71	1.01	1.05	1.06	0.92	0.88
72	0.96	1.06	1.07	0.92	0.91
73	0.96	1.08	1.02	0.95	1.03
74	0.93	1.02	0.97	0.94	1.06
75	0.95	1.04	1.00	0.93	0.98
76	0.97	1.02	1.03	0.93	0.97
77	0.99	1.00	1.03	0.91	0.89
78	0.95	1.00	1.04	0.94	0.89
79	1.00	0.95	1.09	0.87	0.83
80	1.01	0.89	1.08	0.83	0.79

Ellington Pension Fund

On April 12, 1978, Mr. Richard Monday, senior vice president of United Leisure Equipment, Inc., received a report from the firm's treasurer, Mr. Dunstan Baker, indicating that the pension fund portfolio of a wholly owned subsidiary, the Ellington Manufacturing Company, was in an extremely defensive position (see Exhibit 1). The report had generated several responses from members of the firm's Pension Fund Committee and the fund managers. Now, a month later, Mr. Monday was considering whether the issues raised were more or less settled or whether further action would be required.

United Leisure Equipment was a diversified manufacturing company with about half of its business in athletic equipment and apparel. Sales in 1977 had exceeded $250 million. The firm had been experiencing rapid growth (about 12 percent a year for the last 10 years), most of which had been achieved by internal means. While sales were modestly cyclical around the growth trend, earnings per share tended to flatten out during downturns. The growth had been financed internally or through borrowing. A low dividend payout had facilitated this policy. Nevertheless, the firm had to borrow heavily and was now borrowing near its debt capacity. A sale of common stock in late 1978 or early 1979 seemed to be necessary, but the current price of the company's stock, when related to projected 1978 earnings, showed a price/earnings ratio of 10.1 times, which was disappointing to

---

the managers. Every reasonable effort was being made to improve earnings for the year 1978.

The total pension fund portfolio of United Leisure exceeded $50 million. Pension fund costs were now running at 8.6 percent of payrolls and 12.8 percent of profit before taxes. The total portfolio consisted of a major fund and two smaller funds; the latter were carryovers from two acquisitions made in the late 1960s. The Ellington Pension Fund of slightly more than $5 million was the larger of these small accounts.

Shortly after ERISA was enacted, United Leisure's board of directors appointed a Pension Fund Committee of board members to oversee pension fund investment policies, evaluate performance, and recommend, if necessary, changes in fund management. Mr. Monday was chairman of this committee. The other two members were Mr. Reginald Smith, former president of Ellington Manufacturing Company and now retired, and Mr. William Sutton, a professor of finance at a nearby university.

Most of the committee's attention had been focused on the largest part of the pension portfolio, now approaching $42 million, which was managed by a nearby large Chicago bank. The historic performance of this account had been so-so relative to indices, and poor as compared with the two smaller accounts. Therefore the committee's focus on this account appeared to be fully justified.

As shown by the Becker Fund Evaluation Service (see Exhibit 2 for selected excerpts), on the other hand, the performance of the Ellington Pension Fund had been very good. There was little reason to question this evaluation. The Ellington Pension Fund was managed by the Mountaineer National Bank, a bank that had been the main bank of account for that firm prior to its acquisition by United Leisure. The account was 80 percent invested in the bank's common trust account and 20 percent invested in a pooled bond trust. While a little lopsided, this balance had not seemed inappropriate to the committee.

The quarterly report from Mountaineer National Bank in April 1978 indicated that only 15 percent of the Ellington Pension Fund was invested in common stocks, and these were quite defensive in nature. The balance was invested in short-term marketable securities.

While Mr. Monday was considering what action if any to take concerning the Ellington portfolio position, he received a sharply critical letter from committee member Mr. Sutton (see Exhibit 3). In response, after consulting further with Messrs. Russell and Smith, Mr. Monday wrote Mr. Thomas John of Mountaineer National Bank the letter shown in Exhibit 4. One of the requests in this letter was for Mr. John to outline in a meeting with the Pension Fund Committee in May how his bank planned to manage the Ellington Pension Fund in the future. Mr. John's written response is shown in Exhibit 5.

On May 22, 1978, Mr. Monday was preparing for a meeting later that morning with Mr. John and the Pension Fund Committee. Although he did not want to prejudge the bank's presentation, he wanted to consider what actions might have to be taken by the committee. The committee met infrequently, and decisions would have to be reached after the close of the presentation part of the meeting. In general,

Mr. Monday believed it was unwise to force a fund manager to pursue an investment program that would prove uncomfortable or stretch an organization's capabilities.

EXHIBIT 1
Report from Mr. Baker

April 12, 1978

To: Richard Monday

From: Dunstan Baker

As you know, a little more than $5,000,000 of the Ellington Pension Fund is managed by Mountaineer National Bank of Wheeling, West Virginia.

The bank has invested this money in units of Common Trust Fund B (bonds) and Common Trust Fund C (common stock), on a ratio of about 20–80.

However, as the attached report from the trustee shows, 85 percent of the common stock fund is invested in cash equivalents. Of the remaining 15 percent, a little less than half is in gold stocks.

When they say they are being defensive, that's an understatement.

Needless to say, the results have been good relative to the market indices.

Enclosure

cc: William Russell (President)
Reginald Smith (Pension Fund Committee)
William Sutton (Pension Fund Committee)

MOUNTAINEER NATIONAL BANK

Wheeling, West Virginia

TRUST DIVISION

April 7, 1978

TO OUR RETIREMENT FUND CUSTOMERS:

Summary

During the 1st quarter of 1978, blue chip common stocks extended the 18-month decline begun in September 1976. The Dow Jones Average of 30 industrial stocks dropped 7.5 percent, while the more broadly based Standard & Poor's 500 Stock Index declined 4.5 percent (after accounting for dividends received during the quarter). Also, bond prices fell as interest rates rose; so the total return (interest earned minus the capital loss) for the average high-quality bond during the period was a modest .3 percent.

EXHIBIT 1 ***(continued)***

The U.S. business cycle seems to be nearing a peak, evidenced by rising interest rates and a flattening of the leading indicators of future economic activity. Unfortunately, the Federal Government's options to maintain economic growth are limited in light of the continued very large budget deficit.

The Carter Administration has addressed itself to the unemployment problem, more so than to fighting inflation, by stimulating economic growth. While good in the short run, this policy has resulted in increased demand in the U.S. for foreign imports—especially oil; and our trade deficit has worsened, causing a decline in purchasing power of the dollar relative to most leading foreign currencies.

We believe that the primary depressants on stock prices are their continued low income returns relative to bonds and investor concern for the long-term profitability of our industrial plant. In light of these considerations, we have maintained a defensive position relative to both bonds and common stocks.

Common Stock Fund

During the 1st quarter of 1978 the COMMON STOCK FUND (Common Trust Fund C) rose 1.5 percent, in contrast to a decline of 4.5 percent for the Standard & Poor's 500. This relatively good showing reflects the very defensive nature of investments presently held by the FUND, with 85 percent now in short-term cash reserves and only 15 percent in common stocks.

	Common Stock Fund Unit Value
December 31, 1977	$20.63
January 31, 1978	20.67
February 28, 1978	20.66
March 31, 1978	20.98

Assets as of March 31, 1978

		Market Value
Cash Reserves (85%)		
$ 8,240,000	U.S. Treasury bills due 4/4–27/78 @ 6.10%–6.20%	$ 8,240,000
$72,252,800	Commercial paper due 4/4–5/15/78 @ 6.40%–6.63%	72,252,800
	Cash uninvested	76,800
	Total	$80,569,600
Common Stocks (15%)		
48,800	shares Allied Chemical	$ 1,951,340
160,000	shares Dr Pepper	2,380,800
48,000	shares Dome Mines	3,244,800
96,000	shares Homestake Mining	3,299,200
58,000	shares Koppers Corp.	1,417,600
64,000	shares Texas Oil and Gas	1,929,600
	Total	$14,253,340
	Total market value	$94,829,940

EXHIBIT 1 ***(concluded)***

Fixed Income Fund

In the 1st quarter long-term interest rates continued to move higher, placing further downward pressure on bond prices. On a total-return basis, the Salomon Brothers Long Term Bond Index increased 0.3 percent. The Fixed Income Fund (Common Trust Fund B) rose 1.5 percent during the same period. As in the Common Stock Fund, the assets remain quite defensively invested with 100 percent of the portfolio in cash reserves.

	Fixed Income Fund Unit Value
December 31, 1977	$15.08
January 31, 1978	15.15
February 2, 1978	15.22
March 31, 1978	15.31

Assets as of March 31, 1978

Cash Reserve (100%)		
$ 1,580,000	U.S. Treasury bills due 4/27/78 @ 6.05%–6.20%	$ 1,572,000
$50,886,000	Commercial paper due 4/5–5/15/78 @ 6.45%–6.55%	50,660,000
$ 4,230,000	Repurchase agreements due 4/7–17/78 @ 6.70%	4,230,000
$ 4,000,000	Certificate of deposit due 9/7/78 @ 7.14%	4,000,000
	Cash uninvested	24,000
	Total market value	$60,486,000

Outlook

We continue to maintain a cautious attitude toward both bonds and equities, despite lower prices. This is a time to preserve capital, not only in an absolute sense, but also to be able to take advantage of major buying opportunities which may develop later this year.

TRUST DEPARTMENT

EXHIBIT 2
Becker Fund Evaluation Report (Excerpts)

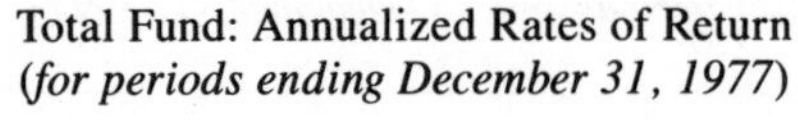
Total Fund: Annualized Rates of Return
(for periods ending December 31, 1977)

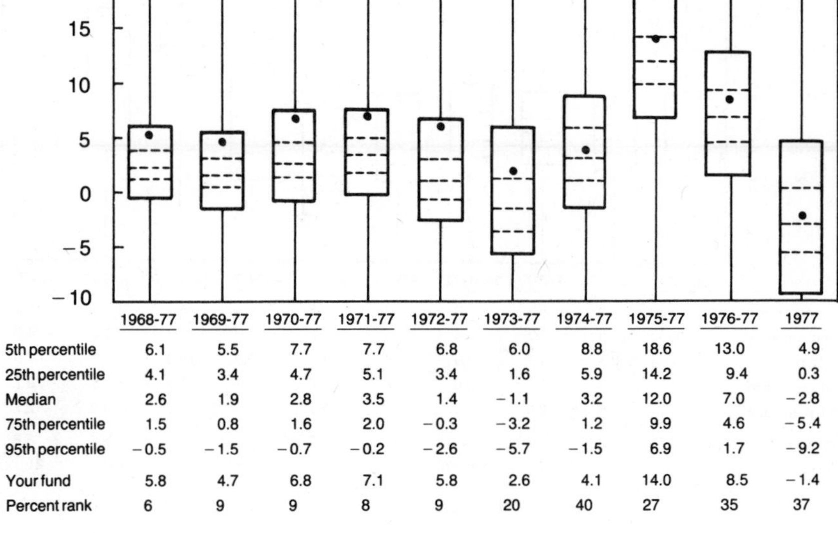

	1968-77	1969-77	1970-77	1971-77	1972-77	1973-77	1974-77	1975-77	1976-77	1977
5th percentile	6.1	5.5	7.7	7.7	6.8	6.0	8.8	18.6	13.0	4.9
25th percentile	4.1	3.4	4.7	5.1	3.4	1.6	5.9	14.2	9.4	0.3
Median	2.6	1.9	2.8	3.5	1.4	−1.1	3.2	12.0	7.0	−2.8
75th percentile	1.5	0.8	1.6	2.0	−0.3	−3.2	1.2	9.9	4.6	−5.4
95th percentile	−0.5	−1.5	−0.7	−0.2	−2.6	−5.7	−1.5	6.9	1.7	−9.2
Your fund	5.8	4.7	6.8	7.1	5.8	2.6	4.1	14.0	8.5	−1.4
Percent rank	6	9	9	8	9	20	40	27	35	37

Total Fund: Rates of Return
(for years ending December 31)

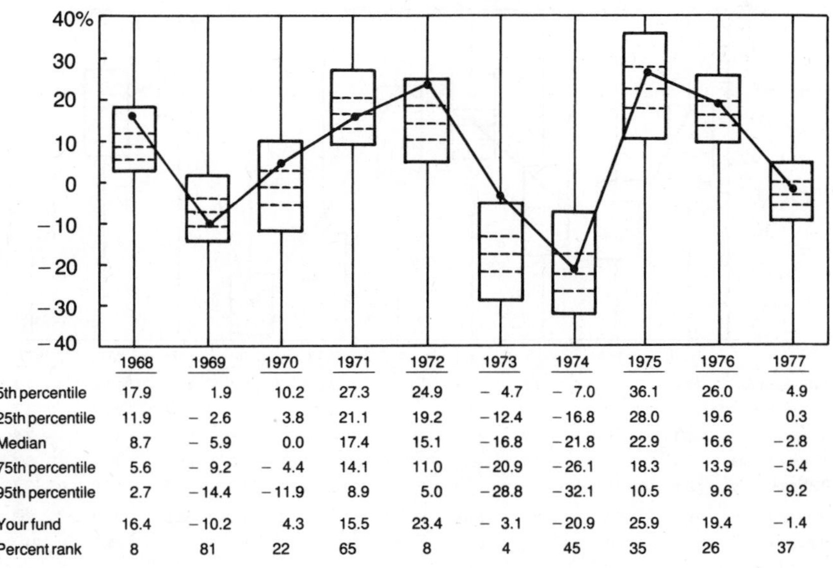

	1968	1969	1970	1971	1972	1973	1974	1975	1976	1977
5th percentile	17.9	1.9	10.2	27.3	24.9	− 4.7	− 7.0	36.1	26.0	4.9
25th percentile	11.9	− 2.6	3.8	21.1	19.2	−12.4	−16.8	28.0	19.6	0.3
Median	8.7	− 5.9	0.0	17.4	15.1	−16.8	−21.8	22.9	16.6	−2.8
75th percentile	5.6	− 9.2	− 4.4	14.1	11.0	−20.9	−26.1	18.3	13.9	−5.4
95th percentile	2.7	−14.4	−11.9	8.9	5.0	−28.8	−32.1	10.5	9.6	−9.2
Your fund	16.4	−10.2	4.3	15.5	23.4	− 3.1	−20.9	25.9	19.4	−1.4
Percent rank	8	81	22	65	8	4	45	35	26	37

EXHIBIT 2 *(continued)*

Equities: Annualized Rates of Return
(for periods ending December 31, 1977)

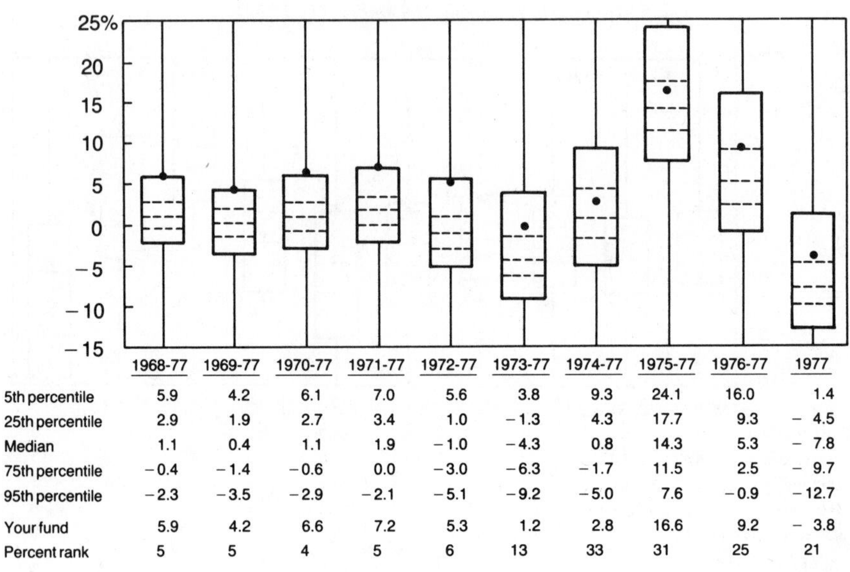

	1968-77	1969-77	1970-77	1971-77	1972-77	1973-77	1974-77	1975-77	1976-77	1977
5th percentile	5.9	4.2	6.1	7.0	5.6	3.8	9.3	24.1	16.0	1.4
25th percentile	2.9	1.9	2.7	3.4	1.0	−1.3	4.3	17.7	9.3	− 4.5
Median	1.1	0.4	1.1	1.9	−1.0	−4.3	0.8	14.3	5.3	− 7.8
75th percentile	−0.4	−1.4	−0.6	0.0	−3.0	−6.3	−1.7	11.5	2.5	− 9.7
95th percentile	−2.3	−3.5	−2.9	−2.1	−5.1	−9.2	−5.0	7.6	−0.9	−12.7
Your fund	5.9	4.2	6.6	7.2	5.3	1.2	2.8	16.6	9.2	− 3.8
Percent rank	5	5	4	5	6	13	33	31	25	21

Equities: Rates of Return
(for years ending December 31)

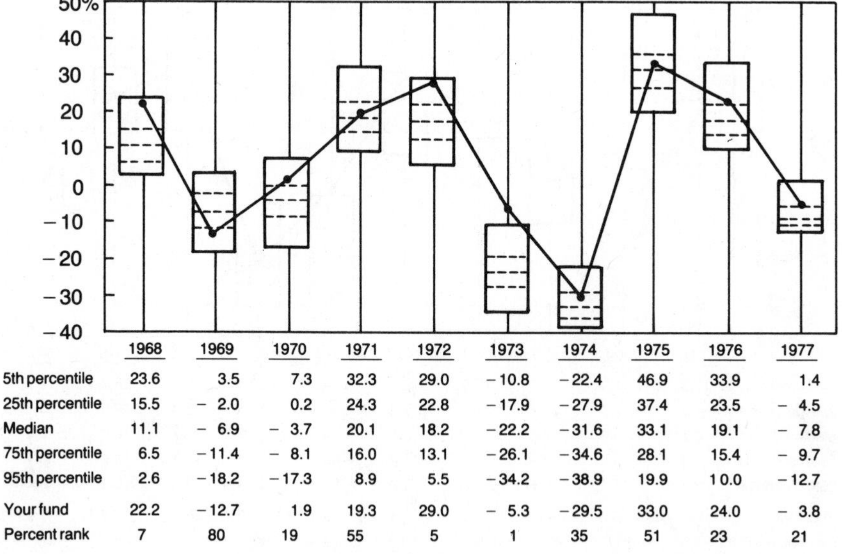

	1968	1969	1970	1971	1972	1973	1974	1975	1976	1977
5th percentile	23.6	3.5	7.3	32.3	29.0	−10.8	−22.4	46.9	33.9	1.4
25th percentile	15.5	− 2.0	0.2	24.3	22.8	−17.9	−27.9	37.4	23.5	− 4.5
Median	11.1	− 6.9	− 3.7	20.1	18.2	−22.2	−31.6	33.1	19.1	− 7.8
75th percentile	6.5	−11.4	− 8.1	16.0	13.1	−26.1	−34.6	28.1	15.4	− 9.7
95th percentile	2.6	−18.2	−17.3	8.9	5.5	−34.2	−38.9	19.9	10.0	−12.7
Your fund	22.2	−12.7	1.9	19.3	29.0	− 5.3	−29.5	33.0	24.0	− 3.8
Percent rank	7	80	19	55	5	1	35	51	23	21

EXHIBIT 2 *(concluded)*

Bonds: Annualized Rates of Return
(for periods ending December 31, 1977)

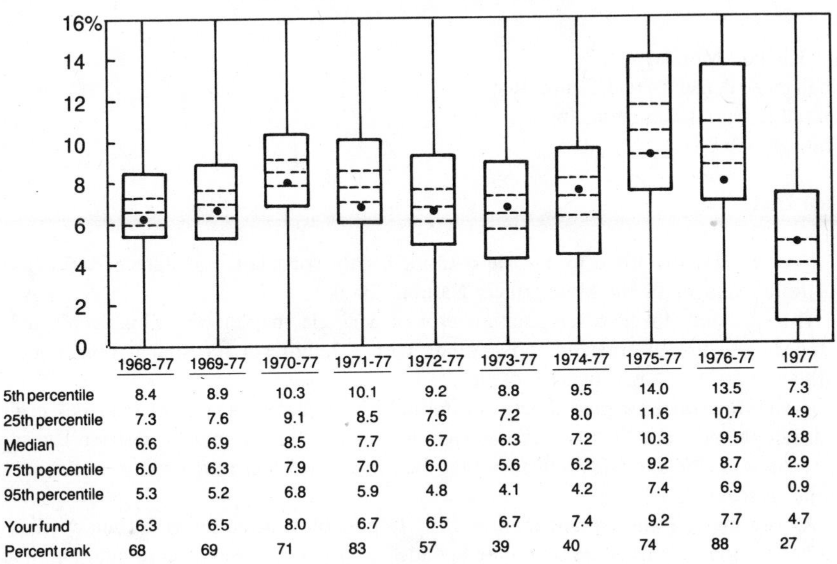

	1968-77	1969-77	1970-77	1971-77	1972-77	1973-77	1974-77	1975-77	1976-77	1977
5th percentile	8.4	8.9	10.3	10.1	9.2	8.8	9.5	14.0	13.5	7.3
25th percentile	7.3	7.6	9.1	8.5	7.6	7.2	8.0	11.6	10.7	4.9
Median	6.6	6.9	8.5	7.7	6.7	6.3	7.2	10.3	9.5	3.8
75th percentile	6.0	6.3	7.9	7.0	6.0	5.6	6.2	9.2	8.7	2.9
95th percentile	5.3	5.2	6.8	5.9	4.8	4.1	4.2	7.4	6.9	0.9
Your fund	6.3	6.5	8.0	6.7	6.5	6.7	7.4	9.2	7.7	4.7
Percent rank	68	69	71	83	57	39	40	74	88	27

Bonds: Rates of Return
(for years ending December 31)

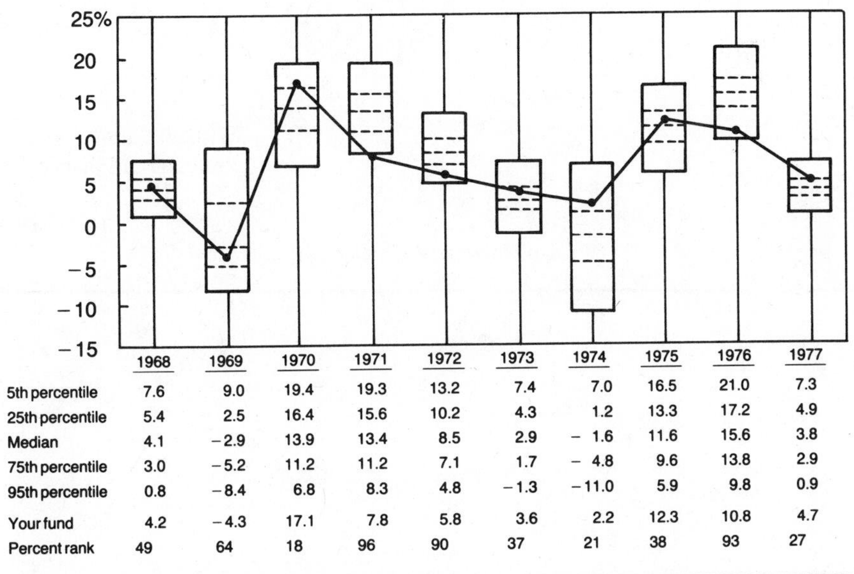

	1968	1969	1970	1971	1972	1973	1974	1975	1976	1977
5th percentile	7.6	9.0	19.4	19.3	13.2	7.4	7.0	16.5	21.0	7.3
25th percentile	5.4	2.5	16.4	15.6	10.2	4.3	1.2	13.3	17.2	4.9
Median	4.1	−2.9	13.9	13.4	8.5	2.9	− 1.6	11.6	15.6	3.8
75th percentile	3.0	−5.2	11.2	11.2	7.1	1.7	− 4.8	9.6	13.8	2.9
95th percentile	0.8	−8.4	6.8	8.3	4.8	−1.3	−11.0	5.9	9.8	0.9
Your fund	4.2	−4.3	17.1	7.8	5.8	3.6	2.2	12.3	10.8	4.7
Percent rank	49	64	18	96	90	37	21	38	93	27

EXHIBIT 3
Letter from Mr. Sutton

April 13, 1978

Mr. Richard Monday
Chairman, Pension Fund Committee
United Leisure Equipment, Inc.
Chicago, Illinois

Dear Dick:

I am greatly disturbed by the short-term, highly speculative posture of the pension portfolio managed by the Mountaineer National Bank.

There is only token diversification around a single market bet. This seems to me inappropriate use of trusted funds—funds with a long-term investment objective and with an interest in diversification of risk.

Even if the trustee expected very substantial further declines in bond and stock prices, and thought the odds of this scenario were very high, this extreme a position leaves us very exposed. We know from history that the times when these events have occurred are in the clear minority.

As you know, I am perhaps more willing to give the trustee room to time cyclically, but believe that this freedom should be bounded by prudence—say, a minimum/maximum equity range of 50/80%.

I am well aware that Mountaineer has a very creditable investment record and that their defensive position has helped us over the last fifteen months. Nevertheless, the bank has exceeded the bounds of long-term prudence in taking such a pronounced short-term speculative position.

Sincerely,

William Sutton
Professor of Finance

WS/tg

Chicago University, Chicago, Illinois

EXHIBIT 4
Letter to Mr. John

UNITED LEISURE EQUIPMENT, INC.

Chicago, Illinois

April 28, 1978

Mr. Thomas John
Vice President & Trust Officer
Mountaineer National Bank
Wheeling, West Virginia

Dear Tom:

As you may know, there is a Pension Fund Committee of United's Board of Directors. I am the Chairman of that committee and the other two members are Reginald Smith and William Sutton.

The committee has been giving considerable thought to the kind of prudent investment program our trustees should undertake for the pension funds. We have concluded that, due to the long-range character of pension obligations, the investment horizon should be long rather than short.

We are concerned about the prospects for continued inflation over the long term. Thus, we believe a substantial portion of the pension funds should be invested in equities. To the degree that it is appropriate (and possible) to consistently time the market, we believe the equity ratio should be adjusted within a relatively narrow band of perhaps 50 percent when the market appears overbought and 80 percent when the market appears to be oversold.

Despite our concerns about inflation, that is not the only factor which affects long-term investment results, and consequently we do believe that the balance of the funds should be invested in fixed-income securities with the maturities depending upon the yield curve. In other words, at times it might be appropriate for the fixed-income portion to be invested entirely in cash equivalents and, at other times, it might be appropriate to invest them in longer-term bonds.

For these reasons, we are quite concerned about the investment policy of the Mountaineer National Bank Trust Department. To say that it is defensive is an understatement. We are well aware that Mountaineer has a very creditable investment record and that its defensive position has helped the pension funds over the last 15 months. However, there is only token diversification around a single market bet. This seems to us inappropriate for pension funds—funds with a long-term investment objective and with an interest in diversification of risk.

Even if the trustee expects very substantial further decline in bond and stock prices, and believes the odds of this scenario are very high, this extreme position leaves the pension funds very exposed. We know from history that the times when these events have occurred are in the clear minority.

EXHIBIT 4 *(concluded)*

Letter to Mr. John
Page 2

Consequently, we would like to have an opportunity to meet with you and discuss this further. We believe we should give consideration to having you manage the Ellington Pension Fund as a separate account, rather than invest it in the bank's common trust funds. This would seem an appropriate time to make such a change, since the common trust funds are in a highly liquid position and nothing need be sold if such a change were made.

Therefore, we would like you to develop a program for investing these funds on a separate account basis and tell us what you propose to do.

Will you please give me some dates when it would be convenient for you to get together with us in late May?

Sincerely,

Mr. Richard Monday
Chairman, Pension
Fund Committee

RM/ca

EXHIBIT 5
Letter from Mr. John

MOUNTAINEER NATIONAL BANK

Wheeling, West Virginia

TRUST DIVISION

May 15, 1978

Mr. Richard Monday
Chairman, Pension Fund Committee
United Leisure Equipment, Inc.
Chicago, Illinois

Dear Dick:

We welcome this opportunity to set forth our proposed investment program for the Ellington Manufacturing Company's pension trust.

EXHIBIT 5 ***(concluded)***

Letter from Mr. John
Page 2

For the foreseeable future the company expects contributions to the Fund to exceed payments to retirees. Therefore, the requirement for portfolio liquidity is minimal. The overall objective of the Fund is to provide qualified employees with fixed dollar benefits at retirement. Therefore, investments should be made which have the potential of providing a superior long-term total return. For planning purposes, an investment horizon of at least five to ten years is appropriate.

Common stocks should comprise 50 to 55 percent of the total portfolio, except when stock prices are judged to be unusually attractive. During these times of extreme undervaluation, the equity ratio may rise to around 80 percent. Common stock investments should be restricted to high-quality companies which have demonstrated in the past and have the potential in the future for above-average earnings and dividend growth. The equity portfolio should be diversified with 25 to 50 different stocks, representing at least ten different industry groups. Sales of common stocks should be made based primarily upon changes in the fundamental outlook for a company's earnings and dividend growth. A judgment that the stock price is temporarily overvalued is not an appropriate reason to sell the stock.

That portion of the portfolio not invested in common stocks should be invested in high-quality fixed-income securities. The minimum quality criteria for any single investment would be "A"; however, the overall portfolio should maintain an average rating of at least "AA". In managing the bond portfolio, consideration should be given to anticipating changes in interest rates in maximizing total return. The average maturity of the bond portfolio could range from a few days to many years.

In implementing the above strategy designed to achieve Ellington's pension fund objectives, we plan to utilize our commingled bond fund and to invest the equity portion in individual common stocks.

Please let me know if the objectives and strategy as outlined above meet with your approval.

Sincerely,

Thomas John
Vice President and
Trust Officer

TJ/cf

Part IX

Alternative Investment Vehicles

Batterymarch Financial Management Corporation International Index Fund

In May of 1977, Mr. Evan Schulman, senior vice president of the Batterymarch Financial Management Corporation, was reviewing arguments relating to a proposal for an internationally diversified common-stock portfolio service for the firm's current and prospective clients. This new service would involve investing in an indexed portfolio of common stocks made up from each of the ten largest companies from each of six industrialized countries plus ten gold stocks. The international-index concept was a logical extension of Batterymarch's increasingly popular index-matching service, a service that strove to invest in a portfolio similar in performance to the Standard and Poor's 500 Index. However, problems of cost and risk would have to be resolved before the new international-index portfolio service could be successfully marketed.

The Batterymarch Operation

Batterymarch was founded by Mr. Dean LeBaron in October 1969. He and three of the five original portfolio managers had previously worked at Keystone Financial Management. Mr. Schulman had been director of computer research at Keystone before joining Batterymarch in 1975. By May 1977, the staff had grown to 18, half of them professional. Brief biographies of the professional staff are given in Exhibit 1.

This case was prepared by Alan E. Riffer under the supervision of Professor Robert F. Vandell of the Colgate Darden Graduate School of Business Administration of the University of Virginia.

Mr. LeBaron had stated in *Business Week,* October 11, 1976, "My idea of the future investment management organization is a few senior people and one big machine." This concept had guided his firm's structure and strategy since its inception. A somewhat mechanistic approach was used to seek out and take advantage of market imperfections. The underlying philosophy was stated in one of the firm's brochures as follows:

> While we agree that in the *aggregate* the market cannot be "beaten," since all investment managers *are* the market, we do believe that there are imperfections in the system which can be exploited. Since about 60 percent of trading volume is accounted for by institutions, their behavior tends to be the dominant market influence, particularly in so-called "institutional favorites." Due to the enormous quantity of capital involved, an overwhelming amount of analysis and decision making is concentrated in the 30 percent of the stocks which account for about 85 percent of the value of publicly held corporations. Further, institutions tend to be conformist in their thinking and concentrate their holdings and changes on an even smaller subgroup at any moment in time. Pricing in the remainder of the stock market *tends,* therefore, to be much less efficient. The stocks of the small- to medium-sized companies are followed much less closely, by many fewer analysts, and are owned by the institutional investors only infrequently. In addition, stocks of the out-of-favor larger companies tend to develop information and pricing lags similar to the smaller companies. It is within these sectors that we, at Batterymarch, concentrate our efforts.

Batterymarch had developed efficient methods for identifying potentially attractive stocks in its actively managed portfolios. This case, however, concerns expanding a side of the business that was "unmanaged" in the sense that portfolios were predesigned (indexed) and held constant (relative to the design) over time. No effort was spent on "picking securities" in the unmanaged portfolios. Unmanaged funds, while a widely used term, was not entirely descriptive of Batterymarch's approach; it had evolved carefully designed and controlled procedures to implement its index funds efficiently and effectively.

Batterymarch Index Matching

Batterymarch had begun its research on index matching in 1973. The managers had continued to believe that their techniques of active management provided the opportunity for superior performance, but they realized that the slow and painstaking search required to find unrecognized value meant that this approach could only be pursued with relatively small amounts of money. The problems of liquidity and market impact prevented the solicitation of large accounts.

Alternatively, for those investors desiring equity exposure for large sums of money, Mr. LeBaron believed that the only practical route was through investing in large, actively traded, efficiently priced stocks. Batterymarch's strategy for these clients was to match, as nearly as possible, the performance of the market as a whole while investing large sums in these efficiently priced stocks. The S&P 500 Index was selected as the appropriate market indicator to be *replicated*. Some analysts argued that investors should aim for superior results rather than merely accepting average market performance. However, many studies[1] had shown that the average risk-adjusted return on professionally managed money had underperformed the S&P 500, generally by the amounts spent on research and transaction costs. Mr. LeBaron believed that a fund that could reduce management and transaction costs to the minimum would consequently outperform the average results achieved by most other managed funds.

Of the three major financial management firms offering index-matching services, all three chose the S&P 500 as the target index. First, the S&P 500 was a value-weighted index, whereas the Dow Jones Average was an equally weighted average of its 30 component stocks, and the Value Line Index was a *geometrically* weighted average of the prices of its 1,400 component stocks. Second, the S&P 500 was commonly used as a benchmark to measure the performance of portfolio managers.

The three financial institutions used different methods of constructing their portfolios from the S&P, however. Wells Fargo Bank bought every one of the 500 stocks in the index (except about 20 that failed to pass a "prudence" test) in proportion to their weight in the index. American National Bank divided the 500 stocks into groups based on risk level, industry, and capitalization. A random sample was selected from each group, and a portfolio of about 250 stocks was assembled. Both Wells Fargo and American National Bank constructed a portfolio of pooled funds to match the indices. They believed that the more sizable the pool, the greater was the assurance that portfolio performance would actually match the performance of the S&P 500 Index.

Batterymarch used yet a different approach. Each client's funds were kept separate. Batterymarch estimated that it would cost at least $150,000 in legal fees to establish a commingled fund, and that there were no commensurate gains. Stocks were purchased in proportion to their weight in the S&P 500. To reduce costs, round lots were purchased and held. If all 500 stocks were purchased, the minimum fund size would have had to be about $100 million, since the smallest stock represented .001 percent of the S&P Index and traded for $10. Reducing the number of stocks held in Batterymarch's "index" reduced the minimum portfolio size for a client and the costs of acquiring and maintaining the indexed portfolio, but it also reduced the tracking ability of the portfolio.

A portfolio of the largest 250 stocks in the S&P 500 Index was chosen as the best balance between cost and tracking ability. The minimum portfolio size thus became $4 million. However, management costs became truly insignificant at $10 million. Performance of the Batterymarch indexed portfolio was expected to be within ± 2 percentage points of the actual S&P 500 total annual return with 98 percent probability.

Batterymarch sold index matching as the passive portion of an active/passive investment strategy, as a low-cost market-timing vehicle, or simply as a parking

---

[1]See, for example, Jensen, "The Performance of Mutual Funds in the Period 1945–1964," *Journal of Finance*, May 1968, pp. 389–416.

place where one could secure low-cost equity exposure with an historically better-than-average performance while searching for strategies that might have a reasonable chance of outperforming the S&P 500. Clients with very large portfolios might require sizable indexed portfolios as one element in their total risk/return strategy.

Cost reduction was a central feature of Batterymarch's index management. Indexing reduced the frequency of transactions. Most of the portfolio remained unchanged. Batterymarch had only to invest (or divest) fund inflows (outflows) from clients and dividends received (net of management fees), and occasionally adapt the portfolio to changes made by Standard & Poor in the composition of its 500 Index. From the beginning, every effort was made to minimize transaction and holding costs. In May 1975, fixed commission rates were eliminated for stock market transactions. Batterymarch's response was to minimize the difficulty and expense of executing transactions. Transactions for the various client funds were pooled into one set of purchase (or sale) requirements each month and put out to brokers for bids. At the beginning of 1977, Batterymarch opened its order book through the use of an accessible computer, making its transaction needs available to all brokers with tie-in facilities. These efforts were effective. One major client reported that transaction costs for Batterymarch's index funds averaged 4 cents per share, while the costs incurred by their other six fund managers ranged from 12 to 15 cents per share.

Batterymarch estimated that annual costs for management of a $100 million portfolio would have been $1.8 million under conventional management, yet were only $145,000 under index matching. As a result, performance net of cost tended to look comparatively favorable.

Batterymarch acquired its first index-matching account in December 1974. In September 1976 it had seven accounts with $224 million of assets, and in May 1977, twelve accounts and $500 million in assets. As this facet of its operation grew, Batterymarch looked for ways to offer similar services of potential interest to its clients.

Fund managers within the United States tended to look at the New York Stock Exchange as the universe of stocks from which they could choose the most attractive securities. A number of sizable international firms, however, were not listed on any American exchange. To Mr. LeBaron, an international fund might appeal to fund managers as a part of their portfolios. In the instance of several clients or potential clients, even a 5 percent piece of a total portfolio would mean tens of millions of dollars to manage.

An international portfolio might also appeal to fund managers as a diversification. The capital markets in several leading countries tended to be out of synchronization. The risks of a bear market in one market might be offset by the benefits of a bull market in another. Academic arguments supported the idea that risk reduction could be achieved by international investment. The underlying concept was that a portfolio became more efficient in terms of risk/return as the variety of stocks from which the portfolio was composed increased. The effect of diversification was more pronounced as the risk interrelationships of the securities were reduced. If underlying economic forces affected international securities (or groups of securities) in different ways, the argument of risk reduction was reinforced.

Batterymarch recognized that no security market was perfectly efficient. However, just as the American market was dominated by a relatively small number of relatively efficient stocks, the security markets of the other industrial nations were dominated by large-company, relatively efficient stocks as well. They decided to base their international portfolio on the most efficient markets outside the United States. Somewhat arbitrarily, they focused on the stocks of the six largest of the industrial nations and on gold-mining stocks as a seventh category.[2]

An analysis of the covariance of these markets with the New York Stock Exchange (as represented by the S&P 500) is shown in Exhibit 2, along with certain other information about the international markets. The six markets chosen for investment were Australia, France, West Germany, Japan, Switzerland, and the United Kingdom.

The international-portfolio strategy was to be implemented by investing in the ten largest companies in each of six country markets and in stocks from the gold industry. Each market would be weighted by its share of the total capitalization of the seven groups. Within each country, investments would be made in the ten companies in proportion to their individual capitalizations. The technique was self-correcting, both for fluctuations of a stock within its domestic market and for re-evaluations of one currency versus the others. Exhibit 3 lists the 67 stocks and their shares of a hypothetical portfolio constructed in October 1976.

To test the strategy, Batterymarch created a simulation of the results from investing in this portfolio for the period from 1971 through 1975. A correlation matrix of "converted" foreign-market price changes is shown in Exhibit 4. During that period, significant currency fluctuations occurred in each of the six national currencies relative to the dollar. Exhibit 5 shows the effects of these currency fluctuations on funds invested in these markets by U.S. residents. Exhibit 6 restates the correlation matrix of market changes, ignoring the currency fluctuations. These results were then compared with the performance of the foreign markets, the U.S. market, and their simulation, both including and excluding the current fluctuations. Exhibit 7 presents the results: The net effect of the strategy was both to increase the return and to reduce the risk of holding a portfolio during this period. Exhibits 8 and 9 show the data upon which the calculations were based.

Mr. Schulman intended to attract clients by using the past simulated results and by using the appeal of the strategy as an additional kind of diversification. The cost of implementing this strategy, however, was a major concern. Putnam International Fund offered an internationally diversified fund to non-U.S. residents with an annual charge of approximately 3 percent of assets. Batterymarch expected to reduce these costs significantly by using techniques similar to those they used in

---

[2]Gold stocks were frequently mentioned as a hedge against inflation. The movement of the prices of gold stocks was often somewhat out of phase with NYSE firms. Gold stocks were listed on diverse international exchanges.

their American index-matching service, but the costs might still remain higher than was true for the domestic index fund.

Another concern facing Mr. Schulman was risk. The passage of ERISA by the U.S. Congress in 1974 focused attention on the issues of risk and prudency. However, while some obstacles to investing overseas existed because of ERISA, the legislative intent was quite clearly to accommodate such investments, as stated in the U.S. Congress Conference Committee Report on ERISA (p. 704):

> It is recognized that investments in securities of foreign companies and governments have been and may well continue to be in the best interests of plan participants in appropriate circumstances and with proper safeguards, and that the physical transfer of securities back and forth overseas may involve unduly high cost and impose unreasonable limitations on the investment of plan funds in such securities. The basic objective of the requirement that the indicia of ownership remain within the jurisdiction of a United States District Court is to preclude frustration of adequate fiduciary supervision and remedies for breach of trust. However, the risk of misappropriation of plan assets or their removal beyond the effective process of an American court is minimal where the assets are under the management or control of a bank, trust company, or similar institution which is subject to adequate regulation and examination by State or Federal supervisory agencies. Such an institution would be responsive to legal process and to the traditional principles of fiduciary responsibility under trust law. Accordingly, it is contemplated that the Secretary of Labor will, as a general rule, grant an exemption to such institutions meeting standards that would assure the safety of plan assets. It is further contemplated that the Secretary will issue temporary regulations authorizing institutions with a history of investing pension funds in foreign securities as a matter of policy to continue to do so pending formal action on an application for exemption.

Transferring foreign securities to the United States was expensive, but requesting exemptions for each of the many foreign security transactions would be both onerous and expensive. The dilemma seemed to prevent utilization of the foreign diversification strategy. However, the Labor Department had published draft ERISA rules for comment in the *Federal Register*. One of these rules allowed a U.S. trustee to hold foreign securities abroad. With final issuance of this rule, Batterymarch could proceed with the solicitation of clients for its strategy. It was in anticipation of this event that Mr. Schulman was reviewing the opportunities and drawbacks of the strategy.

One of Mr. Schulman's perplexing concerns was how to market the service. The potential clients would all be guided by the "prudent man" constraints. Was his simulation representative? Were there any unforeseeable risks? Moreover, the index as presently constructed was value-weighted. Was this type of construction of an index most appropriate for the clients that would now be sought?

Note: A bibliography of articles read by Mr. Schulman is attached as Exhibit 10.

EXHIBIT 1
Professional Staff

Dean LeBaron, president, had been vice president and manager of Keystone Custodian Growth Fund (K-2) before founding Batterymarch in 1969. He had been director of research at Keystone and at F. S. Moseley and Company, a NYSE member. He was a graduate of Harvard College and Harvard Business School (Baker Scholar) and was a chartered financial analyst.

Alexis L. Belash, senior vice president, came to Batterymarch in 1973 from the Boston electronics firm of Teradyne, Inc., where he inaugurated and ran the customer-training program for computer-operated electronic test systems. He majored in analytic philosophy at Cornell and went on to do graduate work at Oxford University, where he concentrated on logic and philosophy of science. His computer and analytical skills were used in securities market research and in the development of new portfolio management techniques.

John T. Bennett, Jr., senior vice president, had been executive vice president of the Putnam Management Company and senior vice president and director of the Putnam Advisory Company prior to joining Batterymarch in 1975. He had been a member of Putnam's Investment Policy Committee; most recently he had been director of the bond department and responsible for supervision of equity research and market analysis. Before joining Putnam, he had been with Anchor Corporation and Danforth Associates. He received his initial training in security analysis with The Old Colony Trust Company. He was a graduate of Harvard College and Harvard Business School.

John Wagstaff Callahan, senior vice president, had been a vice president of Thorndike, Doran, Paine & Lewis, a subsidiary of Wellington Management Company, where he was responsible for the management of profit-sharing, pension, and college endowment plans, as well as individual portfolios. Previously, he had been regional corporate vice president of the Citizens & Southern National Bank of Georgia. He was a graduate of Harvard College, where he majored in economics.

Kingsley Durant, treasurer since 1969, had worked in property management at Meredith & Grew as the manager of Technology Square in Cambridge and was the managing trustee of the Batterymarch Trust. He was a graduate of Stanford University.

Jeremy Grantham, senior vice president, had been a financial analyst at Keystone and worked with Dean LeBaron on the Keystone Custodian Growth Fund. Before joining Keystone, he was a consultant with Cresap, McCormick and Paget and an economist with Royal Dutch Shell. He was a graduate of Sheffield University (U.K.) and Harvard Business School. He had been with Batterymarch since 1969.

Richard Mayo, senior vice president, was an analyst for the Growth Fund at Keystone prior to joining Batterymarch in 1970. Previously he had worked in the money management and trust departments at the First Union National Bank in Charlotte, North Carolina. He was a graduate of the University of Virginia and the University of Virginia Graduate Business School.

Evan Schulman, senior vice president, had been director of computer research at Keystone Custodian Funds, supervising projects on security classification systems and transaction cost control before coming to Batterymarch in 1975. He was also a member of the Investment Policy Committee. Prior to his association with Keystone, he worked in portfolio management, securities research, and computer research at the Royal Trust Company (Montreal). He was a graduate of the University of Toronto and did graduate

EXHIBIT 1 ***(concluded)***

work at the University of Chicago. He had lectured at the University of Western Ontario and Babson College.

Alan J. Strassman, senior vice president, had been president and chief investment officer of Bernstein-Macaulay, Inc., prior to joining Batterymarch in 1974. Previously he had been a vice president and director of Putnam Management Company, serving as a senior portfolio manager, member of the investment policy committee, and director of corporate planning and development. He was a graduate of Princeton and Harvard Business School.

EXHIBIT 2
Analysis of Leading International Markets

Markets	Covariance with the U.S. Market	Market Capitalization* (billion dollars)	Percentage of: World Markets*	Percentage of: Non-U.S. Markets*	Batterymarch International Portfolio
Australia	.60	$ 24	1.8%	4.8%	6.6%
France	.46	31	2.4	6.2	8.5
West Germany	.41	51	3.9	10.3	14.1
Japan	.38	155	11.9	31.2	42.8
Switzerland	.58	21	1.6	4.2	5.8
United Kingdom	.51	70	5.4	14.1	19.3
Gold	.10	10	0.8	2.1	2.9
			27.8%	72.9%	100.0%

*Source: *Capital International Perspective,* July 1976.

EXHIBIT 3
International Equity Diversification: Sample Portfolio (*October 1976*)

Country	Percent	Industry Code	Security
Japan	5.00	1	Toyota Motor
Japan	5.00	14	Nippon Steel
Japan	4.18	5	Matsushita El Ind.
United Kingdom	4.10	6	Shell T & T
United Kingdom	4.10	6	British Pete
Japan	3.90	1	Nissan Motors
Japan	3.62	13	Sony
United Kingdom	3.42	4	Imperial Chemical Ind
Japan	3.35	5	Hitachi
Japan	3.35	17	Tokyo Elect Pwr
Japan	3.07	2	Sumitomo Bank
Japan	2.79	2	Sanwa Bank
Japan	2.79	2	Mitsubishi Bank
West Germany	2.35	5	Siemens
West Germany	2.24	1	Daimler Benz
France	1.66	15	Michelin
France	1.61	6	Aquitaine SNPA
United Kingdom	1.57	16	BAT Industries
Gold	1.57	8	West Driefontein
Australia	1.56	14	Broken Hill
West Germany	1.49	4	BASF
West Germany	1.46	4	Bayer
West Germany	1.46	2	Deutsche Bank
West Germany	1.39	4	Hoechst
United Kingdom	1.37	5	General Elect UK
United Kingdom	1.37	7	Unilever
West Germany	1.24	17	RWE
Gold	1.19	8	Western Holdings
France	1.17	3	St.-Gobaim P-A-M
United Kingdom	1.16	11	Marks & Spencer
West Germany	0.96	17	VEBA
West Germany	0.96	2	Dresdner Bank
United Kingdom	0.96	16	Imperial Group
France	0.93	4	Air Liquide
United Kingdom	0.89	9	Beecham Group
United Kingdom	0.89	2	Barclays Bank
Switzerland	0.88	7	Nestlé
West Germany	0.85	14	Thyssen Huette
Gold	0.84	8	President Brand
France	0.83	12	Pechiney-Ucine
Australia	0.80	12	Conzinco Rio Tinto
Switzerland	0.79	2	Schweiz Bankverin-SB
France	0.78	10	Dassault Breguet
France	0.78	9	L'Oreal
France	0.78	11	Carrefour
France	0.78	6	Francaise-Petroles
Switzerland	0.73	2	Schweiz Bankgesell U
Switzerland	0.72	9	Hoffman Laroche
Australia	0.70	12	MIM Holdings
France	0.68	13	Moulinex
Gold	0.67	8	Free State Geduld
Gold	0.67	8	Western Deep Levels
Australia	0.57	7	CSR
Gold	0.54	8	Blyvooruitzicht

EXHIBIT 3 *(concluded)*

Country	Percent	Industry Code	Security
Australia	0.53	12	Hamersley
Switzerland	0.53	2	Schweiz Kreditanstal
Gold	0.52	8	President Steyn
Switzerland	0.50	4	Ciba-Geigy
Australia	0.42	11	Myer Emporium
Australia	0.38	12	Bougainville Copper
Australia	0.36	12	Western Mining
Australia	0.34	2	Bank New South Wales
Australia	0.32	12	Comalco
Switzerland	0.30	9	Sandoz
Switzerland	0.23	10	Oerlikon-Buhrle
Switzerland	0.17	12	Aluminum Suisse
Switzerland	0.15	5	Brown Boveri

Industry codes:

1. Automobiles
2. Banking
3. Building components
4. Chemicals
5. Electrical and electronics
6. Energy
7. Food and household products
8. Gold mines
9. Health and personal care
10. Machinery and engineering
11. Merchandising
12. Metals and mining
13. Radio, TV, and appliances
14. Steel
15. Tires and rubber
16. Tobacco
17. Utilities

EXHIBIT 4
Foreign Markets' Price-Change Correlation Matrix (*currency adjusted*)

Amount ($ billions)	Percent of World	U.S.	Japan	West Germany	France	U.K.	Australia	Switzerland
$808	61.9 U.S.	1.00						
155	11.9 Japan	.38	1.00					
51	3.8 W. Ger.	.41	.51	1.00				
31	2.1 France	.46	.30	.61	1.00			
70	5.4 U.K.	.51	.32	.41	.61	1.00		
24	1.8 Australia	.60	.29	.36	.46	.46	1.00	
21	1.6 Switz.	.58	.46	.68	.73	.59	.48	1.00
10	0.8 Gold	.10	.09	.23	.22	−.04	.14	.33
$1,170	89.6%							
Batterymarch sample as percent of total national market		80%	13%	40%	20%	30%	30%	75%
Beta (relative to national market)		.99	1.04	1.03	1.04	.94	1.10	.98
Standard error		.90%	2.97%	1.05%	1.25%	2.26%	2.16%	1.42%
Correlation with national index		.99	.91	.98	.98	.97	.97	.97

EXHIBIT 5
Foreign Markets' Currency-Exchange Benefits to U.S. Residents

	1971	*1972*	*1973*	*1974*	*1975*	*Average*
Australia	6.9	4.2	19.2	−12.2	−4.0	2.3
France	5.5	1.7	4.9	9.8	−.5	4.2
West Germany	11.2	2.2	18.6	12.3	−8.2	6.8
Japan	13.6	4.3	7.5	−6.9	−1.5	3.2
Switzerland	10.4	4.0	16.0	28.1	−3.1	10.6
U.K.	6.7	−8.2	−8.2	1.0	1.0	−3.4
Simulation	3.4	−1.9	6.5	2.1	−6.7	.6*

*Reweighting due to moves in the underlying equity portfolio added another 1.2 percent to the 5-year compound return of the simulated portfolio. The total exchange gain was thus an average of 1.8 percent per year over the 5 years.

EXHIBIT 6
Foreign Markets' Price-Change Matrix (*currency* ***unadjusted***)

Amount ($ billions)	*Percent of World*	*U.S.*	*Japan*	*West Germany*	*France*	*U.K.*	*Austra-lia*	*Switzer-land*
$ 808	61.9 U.S.	1.00						
155	11.9 Japan	.35	1.00					
51	3.8 W. Ger.	.37	.41	1.00				
31	2.4 France	.42	.21	.58	1.00			
70	5.4 U.K.	.52	.26	.33	.54	1.00		
24	1.8 Australia	.58	.29	.37	.42	.52	1.00	
21	1.6 Switz.	.59	.39	.58	.68	.53	.59	1.00
10	0.8 Gold	.10	.09	.07	.17	−.09	.10	.23
$1,170	89.6%							

EXHIBIT 7
Results of Strategy

Annual Returns: Percentage Change
(adjusted for currency fluctuation)

	1971	1972	1973	1974	1975	Avg.
Foreign markets*	29	27	−16	−24	33	7
Simulation	20	22	−13	−22	32	6
U.S. market†	11	16	−17	−30	32	0

Simulation versus U.S. market
Alpha = 2.37 ± 1.76 annualized
Beta = .67 ± .10
R^2 = .38

Annual Returns: Percentage Change
*(**not** adjusted for currency fluctuation)*

	1971	1972	1973	1974	1975	Avg.
Foreign markets*	19	29	−21	−24	45	6
Simulation	9	23	−16	−26	45	4
U.S. market†	11	16	−17	−30	32	0

Simulation versus U.S. market
Alpha = 1.37 ± 1.61 annualized
Beta = .63 ± .09
R^2 = .40

*Data Source: *Capital International Perspective*, monthly issues, 1970–76.
†S&P 500.

EXHIBIT 8
Monthly Market Returns by Countries (*1970 to 1977*)*

Year	Jan.	Feb.	Mar.	Apr.	May	June	July	Aug.	Sep.	Oct.	Nov.	Dec.
Australia												
1970	−6.3	−2.4	−0.7	13.0	−8.6	14.5	1.4	0.9	2.2	−12.6	−3.4	−1.0
1971	−4.6	−3.2	9.0	−6.9	−5.3	−0.7	−7.6	−8.0	−13.5	−1.0	−3.0	21.0
1972	−6.4	12.8	1.6	−5.4	4.0	3.2	−9.1	−0.3	−3.8	5.2	4.0	−5.1
1973	8.4	−13.8	−0.8	−5.8	8.7	−1.8	2.1	−13.3	−4.1	3.4	−9.3	−0.1
1974	18.0	10.2	−7.9	−2.8	−14.9	−4.8	−16.4	1.1	−22.4	28.1	2.3	−1.9
1975	16.6	−1.1	−2.0	0.1	14.1	−2.5	−1.2	−1.0	4.4	−1.6	7.3	1.8
1976	−1.8	2.3	1.8	5.2	2.8	−0.4	10.9	−1.8	−8.1	−6.5	−2.8	8.0
1977	1.6	−5.3	6.5	−2.2	2.1	−3.7	−10.7	−3.3	−3.2	3.1	−5.2	4.8
England												
1970	−3.3	−6.9	2.7	−10.7	−5.0	3.8	4.5	1.0	3.4	0.3	−7.2	5.9
1971	−1.8	−1.5	6.2	12.2	5.0	1.8	5.6	−4.3	−2.6	−3.8	−2.9	2.6
1972	3.5	4.2	−7.2	0.6	2.4	−0.9	6.6	0.9	−10.5	3.8	3.7	0.9
1973	−5.1	−0.8	0.6	0.9	0.1	−2.0	−2.3	−6.3	0.8	1.9	−9.0	−2.0
1974	5.6	4.8	−15.7	3.1	−9.7	−9.3	−7.4	−13.2	−11.0	1.0	−15.9	0.3
1975	52.7	22.9	−10.7	16.3	10.1	−5.9	−3.5	14.5	0	3.9	1.8	4.2
1976	6.4	−1.9	2.1	6.3	−3.5	−0.7	−4.0	−5.5	−1.7	−3.2	7.3	15.3
1977	6.4	2.1	−2.1	7.7	0.5	3.4	−3.6	8.1	4.3	−4.1	−3.0	−1.8

EXHIBIT 8 ***(concluded)***

Year	Jan.	Feb.	Mar.	Apr.	May	June	July	Aug.	Sep.	Oct.	Nov.	Dec.
France												
1970	1.7	−2.5	−1.4	−7.3	−2.2	−1.5	6.1	−1.0	−3.3	1.2	0.3	2.3
1971	4.9	−0.9	−1.6	−1.4	7.9	−1.2	4.0	−8.1	−8.3	−5.8	6.5	−1.0
1972	3.8	4.3	7.7	0.3	3.0	−7.1	6.4	2.3	−0.2	−1.6	−7.3	−1.8
1973	4.7	1.3	5.5	6.3	−0.1	−2.3	−6.5	−4.1	1.1	4.0	−12.5	−1.3
1974	7.8	−1.9	−8.4	−3.2	−5.6	−7.9	−1.2	−9.4	−16.9	10.4	−1.2	1.4
1975	22.7	−4.4	10.2	9.0	−5.1	−9.5	8.6	−1.7	−4.4	1.1	7.9	−2.7
1976	5.1	3.8	−3.4	−4.2	−1.2	0.1	−5.5	−0.7	−6.6	−6.0	−4.4	13.1
1977	−2.2	−4.1	−9.9	−3.6	6.7	7.3	−2.7	8.6	0.8	2.1	−6.3	−5.0
West Germany												
1970	−5.2	−3.2	1.9	−5.4	−7.4	−5.9	5.6	−1.1	−1.4	−1.8	−3.0	−3.3
1971	14.9	4.8	0.3	−8.4	2.4	−2.3	3.6	−5.1	−4.0	−8.7	2.1	8.7
1972	4.1	6.7	4.7	−3.3	1.6	−3.0	7.0	−2.7	−3.9	−0.9	1.4	−1.6
1973	4.9	−3.3	5.0	−6.2	−8.6	−3.3	−4.3	0	−1.8	7.7	−12.3	−1.2
1974	7.2	−7.4	1.1	5.7	−3.6	−2.4	−0.8	0.7	−5.7	3.4	2.3	0.3
1975	8.0	10.8	−0.1	2.0	−7.9	−1.0	10.1	−4.7	−1.9	9.8	6.2	0.9
1976	2.5	2.1	0.9	−6.5	−0.2	0.5	−2.2	−1.2	1.4	−7.4	5.0	0.5
1977	0.6	−2.3	3.0	6.9	−1.5	−3.8	0.1	0.2	1.3	2.3	0.4	−2.1
Japan												
1970	−7.2	0.7	2.2	−12.9	−5.4	−3.1	4.1	6.9	0.2	2.9	−7.4	−1.0
1971	8.8	4.8	16.8	8.8	−3.9	14.2	0.2	−16.3	1.0	−7.0	7.1	7.6
1972	3.9	12.1	4.9	7.9	9.3	1.4	4.3	0.2	1.6	1.7	13.0	9.7
1973	−2.2	−4.1	0.3	−6.9	1.5	2.5	2.2	−3.6	−5.0	−1.9	−12.0	−10.4
1974	11.3	−0.5	−2.4	−1.2	0.2	−2.5	−9.1	−9.7	0.6	−9.8	7.5	−0.6
1975	3.0	14.7	6.8	−1.0	−0.9	7.0	−8.1	−4.2	−7.0	9.6	4.4	−0.6
1976	5.1	1.3	0.3	0.5	4.0	4.8	−1.9	0.7	−0.7	−0.9	−3.2	23.2
1977	−5.1	2.1	−5.4	−0.8	1.5	−0.6	−2.0	3.2	−0.5	−4.4	−2.7	−3.5
Switzerland												
1970	−2.0	−1.8	−0.9	−9.7	−3.2	0.1	7.3	4.0	−3.4	−0.8	−3.2	2.7
1971	8.2	0.7	3.6	3.9	−2.1	4.9	3.1	−0.3	−5.3	−5.5	8.9	1.2
1972	6.6	4.0	0.7	0.4	6.5	−9.4	7.5	4.5	0	−2.1	−5.8	4.2
1973	−0.0	−5.0	−0.9	−4.7	1.0	−3.0	−8.8	−2.9	6.4	3.8	−11.4	−2.5
1974	5.4	−8.1	0.9	−5.0	−11.4	−2.0	−0.6	−14.9	−9.0	7.1	−4.4	−6.0
1975	21.4	4.3	2.4	6.1	−2.8	−3.9	3.2	−5.5	−4.9	8.5	8.1	1.4
1976	4.0	−3.5	−0.2	−1.4	−2.2	3.0	−0.4	3.3	−0.7	−2.4	2.0	7.8
1977	2.7	−1.1	−0.2	2.2	−4.3	1.3	−0.4	3.3	3.3	−0.7	−0.1	−0.5
Gold												
1970						1.7	2.9	7.0	−2.9	5.9	8.0	−4.5
1971	1.4	10.2	−0.4	−2.2	−4.9	−3.2	9.8	−18.5	−1.0	−8.0	15.4	−9.1
1972	19.0	2.7	0.2	−1.4	24.5	3.5	7.9	−7.6	−6.3	−4.6	0.4	5.3
1973	3.5	13.9	7.3	6.5	14.6	22.6	−7.0	−7.7	−0.1	−7.2	10.0	23.1
1974	23.6	10.3	31.0	−13.6	−11.3	−2.6	21.2	−11.4	−20.7	22.1	−1.3	−8.4
1975	−3.5	18.7	3.5	−13.3	9.5	0.4	−4.5	−11.1	−18.2	0.6	−17.7	8.0
1976	−9.7	−1.6	−14.9	8.1	−5.4	−11.6	−15.8	−24.0	13.5	13.1	12.5	−6.7
1977	−4.9	22.2	−8.9	−7.7	1.0	1.0	5.2	4.8	21.7	−11.2	8.1	0.6

*Price change only: No currency adjustment

Opening weights:

Australia	9.1%	Japan	14.7%
England	45.3	Switzerland	4.7
France	8.7	Gold	4.6
West Germany	13.0		

EXHIBIT 9
Monthly Gains and Losses as a Result of Currency Revaluation (*1971–1977; none in 1970*)

Year	Jan.	Feb.	Mar.	Apr.	May	June	July	Aug.	Sep.	Oct.	Nov.	Dec.
Australia												
1971							1.1	1.9	0.4	0	0	3.4
1972										0	0	4.2
1973	0	13.2	−0.3	0.4	−0.1	0	0.3	−0.2	5.0	−0.2	0.3	0.1
1974	−0.3	0.3	−0.3	0.1	−0.1	0	0.1	0	−12.0	0	0	0
1975	2.4	1.9	0	−1.7	0.1	−1.4	−0.5	−3.0	−1.7	1.0	−0.8	−0.3
1976	0.3	0.1	−0.9	−0.9	−0.9	0.6	0.6	0.2	−0.6	−0.9	−17.4	7.4
1977	−0.2	0.9	0.7	0.1	0	0.8	0.8	−1.5	0	2.0	0	1.2
England												
1971							1.1	1.9	0.8	0.4	0	2.3
1972	1.5	0.4	0.4	−0.2	0.3	−6.2	−0.2	−0.1	−1.1	−3.7	0.9	−0.3
1973	1.4	4.3	−0.2	0.4	3.0	0.6	−3.3	−1.6	−1.7	0.8	−3.5	−1.0
1974	−2.6	1.8	4.1	1.3	−1.5	−0.6	−0.2	−2.5	0.7	0	−0.4	1.1
1975	1.2	2.0	−0.7	−2.3	−1.8	−5.5	−1.6	−1.8	−3.3	1.5	−2.7	0.3
1976	0.3	−0.1	−5.5	−3.8	−4.5	1.3	0.1	−0.5	−6.2	−3.9	3.1	3.2
1977	0.7	−0.2	0.6	0	−0.1	0.1	1.0	0.3	0.2	4.9	−0.9	4.9
France												
1971								3.3	−1.5	−0.3	0.3	3.7
1972	2.1	1.0	4.1	−0.3	0.1	2.6	0.4	−1.9	−1.5	−2.9	−0.5	−1.3
1973	2.0	11.0	−0.1	−0.8	4.5	5.7	−1.5	−4.2	1.3	−0.2	−7.4	−4.2
1974	−6.1	8.0	0.9	−2.0	−0.4	1.2	2.9	−2.6	1.7	0.9	1.4	4.2
1975	2.9	3.8	−1.2	1.8	2.4	0	−7.5	−0.4	−3.4	4.3	−2.3	−0.3
1976	−0.1	−0.1	−3.9	0.2	−1.4	−0.3	−3.6	0.2	−0.3	−1.6	0.2	0.6
1977	−0.2	−0.3	0.4	0.1	0.3	0.6	0.9	−0.7	0	1.4	−0.5	3.5
West Germany												
1971							5.2	1.9	2.4	−0.6	0.8	1.1
1972	2.0	0.7	0.5	−0.2	0.3	0.5	−0.7	−0.5	−0.4	−0.1	0.3	−0.2
1973	1.5	11.0	0.3	0	3.9	12.7	3.0	−4.5	2.0	−1.2	−6.7	−3.1
1974	−2.3	3.6	5.9	3.0	−2.9	−1.4	−1.2	−2.9	0.5	2.8	4.2	2.9
1975	2.8	2.4	−2.5	−1.5	1.4	−0.4	−8.5	−0.3	−2.9	4.2	−2.9	0.3
1976	1.0	1.3	1.1	0	−2.2	0.7	1.1	0.9	3.4	1.5	0	1.8
1977	−2.5	1.0	0.3	1.3	0.1	0.8	2.1	−1.5	0.4	2.6	1.2	5.7
Japan												
1971								6.4	0.6	1.7	0.4	4.0
1972	1.7	1.8	0.2	−0.4	−0.1	1.2	0	0	0	0	0.3	−0.5
1973	0.1	14.3	−0.8	0	0.2	0.1	0.5	−0.8	−0.1	0	−5.2	0
1974	−6.4	4.0	4.5	−1.6	−0.7	−0.9	−4.8	−1.5	2.0	−1.0	0	−0.2
1975	0.9	3.9	−2.0	0.1	0.3	−1.9	−0.2	−0.3	−1.6	0.5	−0.5	−0.6
1976	0.4	0.5	0.9	0.1	−0.2	1.1	1.1	1.6	0.5	−2.3	−0.8	1.2
1977	1.6	2.0	1.9	0.1	0	4.1	0.1	−0.4	1.5	5.4	2.1	2.0
Switzerland												
1971					5.8			2.7	0.6	0.8	0.9	0.9
1972	1.2	0	1.0	−0.7	0.5	2.6	−0.7	−0.1	−0.6	0.1	0.6	0.1
1973	4.0	14.8	−2.5	0	4.4	5.8	2.5	−5.6	0.3	−2.3	−3.4	−1.5
1974	−1.3	5.4	3.8	3.3	−2.0	−0.8	0.8	−1.1	2.2	2.6	5.9	6.7
1975	1.6	4.1	−5.3	−0.8	2.0	0.1	−7.6	0.9	−2.3	4.8	−2.2	2.3
1976	0.8	1.5	1.1	0.9	2.8	−1.1	−0.1	−0.1	1.0	0.6	−0.2	−0.3
1977	−2.7	−1.5	0.5	0.8	0.8	1.7	2.4	0.3	2.4	4.7	3.2	7.9

EXHIBIT 10
Bibliography of Mr. Evan Schulman, Senior Vice President

Bergstrom, Gary L., "A New Route to Higher Returns and Lower Risks," *Journal of Portfolio Management,* Fall 1975, pp. 30–38.

Cohn, Richard A., and John J. Pringle, "Imperfections in International Financial Markets: Implications for Risk Premia and the Cost of Capital to Firms," *Journal of Finance,* March 1973, pp. 59–66.

EEC, "The Development of a European Capital Market" (Brussels: European Economic Community, 1966).

Fama, E., "Tomorrow on the New York Stock Exchange," *Journal of Business,* July 1965, pp. 285–99.

Grubel, H. G., *"Forward Exchange, Speculation and the International Flow of Capital* (Palo Alto: Stanford University Press, 1966).

Grubel, H. G., "Internationally Diversified Portfolios: Welfare Gains and Capital Flows," *American Economic Review,* December 1968, pp. 1299–1314.

Grubel, H. G., and K. Fadner, "The Interdependence of International Equity Markets," *Journal of Finance,* March 1971, pp. 89–94.

IMF, "Annual Report on Exchange Restrictions," *International Monetary Fund,* 1972.

King, B. F., "Market and Industry Factors in Stock Price Behavior," *Journal of Business,* January 1966, pp. 139–90.

Lessard, Donald R., "International Diversification," *Financial Analysts Journal,* January/February 1976, pp. 32–38.

Lessard, Donald R., "International Portfolio Diversification: A Multivariate Analysis for a Group of Latin American Countries," *Journal of Finance,* June 1973, pp. 619–33.

Levy, H., and M. Sarnat, "International Diversification of Investment Portfolios," *American Economic Review,* September 1970, pp. 668–75.

Lintner, John, "Security Prices, Risk, and Maximal Gains from Diversification," *Journal of Finance,* December 1965, pp. 587–615.

Markowitz, H., *Portfolio Selection, Efficient Diversification of Investments* (New York: Wiley, 1959).

Modigliani, F.; G. A. Pogue; M. S. Scholes; and B. H. Solnik, "Efficiency of European Capital Markets and Comparison with the American Market," *Proceedings of the 1st International Congress on Stock Exchanges* (Milan: 1972).

OECD, "Capital Market Study," Committee for Invisible Transactions, OECD publication, August 1967.

OECD, "The Business and Industry Advisory Committee Report on Capital Markets and Capital Movement" (Brussels: March 1969).

OECD, "Code of Liberalization of Capital Movements" (Paris: 1970).

Pogue, Gerald A., and Bruno H. Solnik, "The Market Model Applied to European Common Stocks: Some Empirical Results," MIT Working Paper, Sloan School of Management, MIT, May 1973.

Solnik, B. H., "The Behavior of European Stock Prices," MIT Working Paper, Sloan School of Management, MIT, January 1972.

Solnik, B. H., *European Capital Markets* (Lexington, Mass.: Lexington Books, 1973).

Templeman, D., "Liberalization of Portfolio Investment and the Development of Securities Markets in the OECD," *Journal of World Trade Law,* 1972.

Theil, H., and C. T. Leenders, "Tomorrow on the Amsterdam Stock Exchange," *Journal of Business,* July 1965, pp. 277–84.

Tidewater Railways, Inc.

Carolyn Kline, the treasurer of Tidewater Railways, Inc., and chairman of the Pension Advisory Committee, had just returned to her office, following the Pension Advisory Committee's regular meeting. Ms. Kline had expected a constructive discussion during the meeting concerning her proposal to invest between 5 and 10 percent of the plan's assets in a commingled equity real estate fund. What she had not anticipated was the strong negative reaction of George Williams and other committee members to the presentations by the real estate departments of the Prudential and the Equitable insurance companies, sponsors of the two largest commingled equity real estate funds in the United States.

Tidewater Railways was one of the more important railroads connecting coal fields in the Appalachian Mountains with major port facilities in the Southeast. Unlike many railroads, Tidewater had a long record of relatively stable earnings, which had risen sharply in the last three years as world demand for alternative fuel sources grew in response to the rapid increase in oil prices. Return on equity, which had averaged 11.6 percent over the last decade, had risen to 16.2 percent in 1980. Long-term debt amounted to 22.3 percent of capital structure, and significant cash flows seemed likely to supply most of the sizable investments planned for modernized port and railroad facilities. In fact, only the firm's low price/earnings ratio—recently 5.2—marred a record that management considered quite attractive.

This case was prepared by Robert F. Vandell, Charles C. Abbott Professor of Business Administration, of the Colgate Darden Graduate School of Business Administration of the University of Virginia.

Ms. Kline had been with Tidewater Industries for just nine months, having been hired to replace Mr. Williams, who had retired as the treasurer of Tidewater Industries shortly after Ms. Kline was hired. Before taking this job, she had been a vice president in a large commercial bank, where she had worked for the eight years since receiving her MBA. The proposal to invest in a commingled real estate fund had been the first major pension fund policy change she had recommended.

In order to retain Mr. Williams's counsel after his retirement and to show their respect for his judgment, the directors had asked him to remain on the Pension Advisory Committee. Mr. Williams, during his long career, had become known for his very conservative outlook, which stemmed from his having observed his own family's fortune dissolve. Ms. Kline learned that his father's bank had failed during the Great Depression of the 1930s, largely as a result of failed real estate loans. Mr. Williams's normally conservative attitudes thus became intensified when anything concerning real estate was being considered. A few years back, the liquidation of an REIT—and the subsequent loss of some pension fund assets invested in it by one of the equity managers—had only reinforced his conservatism.

Tidewater's Pension Fund

Mr. Williams had guided the pension fund since it was established in the 1950s, and had followed the Advisory Committee's policy of maintaining a debt/equity ratio of 50/50 for investments. The committee's policy, written by Mr. Williams, required that the portfolio be rebalanced to a 50/50 mix whenever the market value of investments in either long-term debt or equity exceeded 55 percent of total assets at the end of a quarter. Rebalancing was sometimes accomplished by the placement of new pension contributions, but with increasing frequency, had recently required the shifting of existing equity investments into fixed-income securities.

By policy design, the fixed-income portfolio was largely composed of long-term quality corporate or government bonds. Mr. Williams believed that bonds—given the times and circumstances in which they were purchased—provided an attractive low-risk long-term investment, if held to maturity. He tended to pay little attention to the ups and downs of prices in the bond market, until ERISA forced the actuary and the accountants to consider market values of financial assets in determining funding adequacy (1974). The fixed-income securities, managed by a local bank, had a market value as of December 31, 1980, of only 72.3 percent of their purchase cost, largely as the result of steeply rising interest rates. The ratio of market value to book cost would have been lower had it not been for recent, fairly sizable investments.

The equity portion of the portfolio was managed by two conservative managers. The record of both these managers had been quite good during the tough markets of 1969 to 1977, but more recently each had been underperforming, according to such conventional yardsticks as the Standard & Poor's 500 Index. Their portfolios had tended to be overweighted with large smokestack firms, producing, for example, chemicals, papers, and steels, international oils, and other basic industrials. Overall, the market value of the pension fund at the end of 1980 was below actuarial requirements.

Over the past six years, the poor performance of the bond market and the policy of limiting equity holdings had led to the investment of almost all new pension contributions in long-term debt to maintain the required balance, despite the significantly more attractive returns available in the equity markets. Over this period the annualized rate of return on corporate bonds was 4.34 percent, compared to 17.53 percent for equities (see Exhibit 1 for a 15-year record of security returns).

Ms. Kline had noted that the annual cost of funding the pension liability had been rising relative to total payroll and to profits before pension costs, interest, and taxes. This trend was likely to continue. Benefits were determined based on the average salary for the last three years of employment before retirement, and in response to rapid inflation, the firm had increased salaries at a faster rate in recent years. The company was also under considerable pressure to tie all benefits, both past and future, to some index such as the CPI. Some older retired employees, it had been found, were unable to maintain reasonable standards of living because their fixed incomes were insufficient to counter rising costs.

Over the past 15 years, the annualized return on equities, according to a recent study, was 6.72 percent, or just short of the increase in the CPI of 6.87 percent, while the return on long-term corporate debt was 3.19 percent. If a similar pattern of returns were earned in the future, Ms. Kline feared that the cost to the company of funding the pension liability could rise sharply.

Pension assets currently represented 35 percent of the firm's equity and were expected to rise to 50 percent by the mid-1980s. With the help of an actuary, Ms. Kline estimated that, if the real return on the portfolio averaged in the 2 to 3 percent range, portfolio funding costs as a percentage of payroll would tend to stabilize. If a 5 to 6 percent real return were earned, funding costs would tend to decrease and the company could consider improving benefits. But, if no real return was obtained, then pension costs could double their current levels even if there were no indexing of benefits.

Upon review of the status of the pension fund, Ms. Kline concluded that both the mix and the management of the portfolio were overly conservative. She was worried about how to achieve change without seeming to cast aspersions on the plan of Mr. Williams, who commanded considerable respect among Tidewater's top management and directors, and whose cronies were other members of the Pension Advisory Committee.

Ms. Kline had learned about the potential attractiveness of investing pension fund assets in real estate equities through reading the Focus section of *Pensions & Investment Age* (February 16, 1981). (See the Appendix.) This series of articles dealing with equity real estate investment suggested that such investments could offer above-average yields, better protection against inflation, and a more stable rate of return. Ms. Kline reasoned that, if real estate was considered to be a part of the pension fund's debt portfolio for asset-mix determination purposes, real estate could improve the portfolio's performance. Real estate should produce returns more like those of the equity portfolio. She had shortly thereafter invited Prudential and Equitable to make presentations to the Pension Advisory Committee.

Real Estate as Pension Investments

A decade ago, other pension funds had held loans secured by mortgages on real estate in their investment portfolios, but only a few had invested directly in real estate equities and then only in very limited amounts. In 1970, seeing a potential change in the attitude of pension fund managers toward real estate investments, The Prudential Insurance Company founded PRISA, the first commingled real estate investment fund in the United States, with a $5 million investment from its own pension plan. At the end of 1980, 16 major funds had been established, having a combined total of $6.1 billion in assets, an increase of over 75 percent from the $3.5 billion held at the end of 1979. Interest had grown to the point where the major commingled funds would not always take proffered investments from new clients.

While U.S. pension funds were just beginning to invest in real estate, their European counterparts had long favored such investments. Most European managers invested about 15 to 20 percent of available assets in real estate, and some individual funds went as high as 35 percent. Some of the recent interest in real estate as an investment by U.S. firms could be traced to the increase in the amount of prime U.S. real estate being acquired by foreign pension funds.

A recent change in the tax code permitted qualified pension and profit-sharing plans to invest in the equities of debt-financed real estate without incurring the "unrelated business" tax on the income. While some situations caused the income to be taxable, a careful manager could now invest in single-property leveraged real estate and maintain the special tax status of the fund. Commingled funds met these tax tests, which made real estate investments even more attractive.

Assessing equity real estate as a potential investment was difficult because of the dearth of information on performance. Ms. Kline found most long-term information on performance reflected opinions, not hard evidence. The PRISA record might well be the best data available.

Objectives of Real Estate Investment

Ms. Kline had defined three main objectives of investing in a real estate fund:

1. Greater diversification of the pension fund portfolio.
2. Improvement in the stability of portfolio income and assets.
3. Inflation protection of both principal and income.

Ms. Kline elected to consider first those commingled funds managed by large and well-respected companies. The advisory committee might later consider direct investment by the pension plan in single properties or in closed-end funds. A commingled fund offered an opportunity for greater diversification and more professional management of properties held than would be possible if the pension plan tried to manage the assets in-house. She believed that including a diversified portfolio of real estate would serve to improve the short-term portfolio cash yield and provide long-term capital appreciation, without exposure to higher risk.

PRISA and Equitable managed the two largest commingled equity real estate funds, and both had long track records. It was largely for these reasons that Ms. Kline had asked these two firms to make presentations to Tidewater's Pension Advisory Committee.

PRISA and Equitable Fund #8

In their separate presentations to the Pension Advisory Committee, Prudential and Equitable representatives stressed the long experience of their firms in the real estate field, the size of their organizations, and the geographic diversity of their field representatives, all of which enabled them to locate superior properties. They also emphasized their experience in managing properties.

Neither firm purchased speculative properties. Rather, they predominantly invested in equity real estate that was largely leased at the time of purchase. Purchases were conservatively financed, and though some properties were mortgaged, the size of the mortgages was low compared to the market value of the properties.

Both firms looked for properties where lease revenues could be increased as property values rose with inflation. In the case of shopping centers, overrides based on sales volume also provided a measure of protection against inflation.

They both sought properties primarily in areas of the country where development was at a fast pace. While they recognized that over-building occasionally occurred, the types of properties they usually invested in had proven not to be subject to this kind of disruption.

Exhibit 2 presents the performance record of PRISA and Equitable Fund #8 for the years data were available. Exhibit 3 gives information on the types of properties acquired and their location.

Committee Members' Comments

During and after the meeting with the insurance companies' representatives, a variety of questions had been asked and objections raised to an investment in real estate. Henry Alston, a retired bank president and member of both the Board of Directors and the Pension Advisory Committee, who had asked several questions about the potential investments, was first concerned about the illiquidity both of real estate in general and of the commingled fund in particular. He commented, "What would happen if a number of investors want out at the same time? We could be forced, under the fund rules, to ride through an unattractive investment period because the fund manager is unable or unwilling to liquidate properties fast enough to settle claims. A crash like in 1932, or even an expansion to other areas of the country of the deflation in real estate values now seen in some California markets, could quickly lead to a major liquidity crunch for the funds.

"Another thing I'm not really comfortable with—the type of real estate they invest in. Take shopping centers for an example: remember how busy the Washington Square Shopping Center was just a few years ago? Look at it today: first they lost Robert Hall, then Grants, and then the new mall opened across town. Remember their old slogan, 'A mile of shopping convenience'—well, it's more like a ghost town now. The industry is changing, too: just look at how busy that new Best Store is. Customers used to buy retail, but now the game is discount or wholesale. Also don't forget TV! Why, Tidewater Cable Company has been telling us that they plan to offer a two-day cable alternative shortly, and when they do, you will be able to sit at home and do your shopping. Home computers will also facilitate this event. A lot of things are happening all over the country and could cause real estate to be a very risky investment."

Louis Ducros, a local businessman and investor, was concerned about the lack of a local promoter or investor in these deals. " A good real estate deal is somewhat speculative—you need an investor who is high-risk/high-reward-driven to make it work. Real estate is best left to tax shelters, where the depreciation and high leverage can be used to their best advantage. The main problem I see with this alternative is it seems that everyone is playing a 'me too' game with real estate. With so many groups bidding against each other for a limited number of good properties, it is no surprise that prices are going up and possibly quality is going down. Speaking of quality, Prudential and Equitable purchase real estate for their own central insurance accounts. What assurances do we have the properties in the commingled accounts aren't inferior to those held in their own accounts?"

George Williams spoke just before the meeting was to end. "I tell you I don't like the idea at all. It sounds to me like you count a gain just because some property assessor says it is so. Well, those guys have the same integrity as used-car salesmen, in my opinion.

"Before we jump into this thing blind, we need to think about the markets we're in. Granted, they have not performed as well as we would have liked during the last couple years; rising inflation rates have always tended to adversely affect stock and bond prices in the short run. Things are looking better now: the Bureau of Labor Statistics recently released figures showing that the annual rate of inflation was 8.5 percent for the first five months of 1981, which represents a significant drop from the 12.5 percent in 1980. Yield to maturity on Moody's AA-rated industrial bonds was 14.3 percent as of July 1, 1981. The expected long-term rate of return on equities is about 18–19 percent, according to several sources. Both types of securities, in short, have a healthy allowance for future inflation rates built into current prices, so that attractive inflation-adjusted returns are likely without the high risk of real estate.

"I'm very concerned that we have to purchase units in these equity real estate programs at assessed values. These values may bear no relation to their true worth. In my opinion these values are overinflated," continued Mr. Williams.

"I'm against the idea at this time. However, if we do go ahead and make an investment, the funds should come from our equity allocation, not our debt allocation. Real estate is a highly speculative type of investment, as we would quickly learn if assessed values were ever put to a true market test during a depression."

The Issue

Ms. Kline was somewhat startled by the reaction of the Pension Fund Advisory Committee to real estate investments. She believed, however, that real estate was still a wise hedge against inflation, and thought the issue should be pursued further. Toward this end, she began reviewing the material she had collected on PRISA and Equitable Fund #8. (Exhibits 4 through 11 give the detailed information about these funds that was available to the Advisory Committee.)

While this review was under way, PRISA reported a first quarter return (not annualized) of 3.4 percent.

EXHIBIT 1
Representative Returns: Certain Key Indicators (*1966–1980*)

Year	Common Stocks (S&P 500 Index)	Long-Term Bonds (Salomon Bros Index)	Short-Term Money Market (3-Mo. T-Bills)	Consumer Price Index
1966	−10.06%	0.20%	4.76%	3.35%
1967	23.98	−4.95	4.21	3.04
1968	11.06	2.57	5.21	4.72
1969	−8.50	−8.09	6.58	6.11
1970	4.01	18.37	6.53	5.49
1971	14.31	11.01	4.39	3.36
1972	18.98	7.26	3.84	3.41
1973	−14.66	1.14	6.93	8.80
1974	−26.47	−3.06	8.00	12.20
1975	37.20	14.64	5.80	7.01
1976	23.84	18.65	5.08	4.81
1977	−7.18	1.71	5.12	6.77
1978	6.56	−0.07	7.18	9.03
1979	18.44	−4.18	10.38	13.31
1980	32.42	−2.62	11.24	12.40

EXHIBIT 2
Performance Record: PRISA and Equitable Fund #8 (*stated as percent of market value*)

	PRISA*				
Year	**Income Net of Management Fee**	**Appreciation**	**Total Return**	**Calendar Year Total Returns**	**Equitable Fund #8 Total Returns**
1970	1.4%†	-0-	1.4%†	—	
1971	−5.0	0.2%	5.2	5.3%	
1972	5.3	1.1	6.4	5.9	
1973	6.6	2.3	8.9	9.2	‡
1974	7.6	1.1	8.7	8.8	10.2%
1975	7.2	1.4	8.6	8.3	7.6
1976	7.4	0.7	8.1	8.5	10.2
1977	7.5	2.5	10.0	10.7	11.3
1978	8.7	5.2	13.9	19.5	13.9
1979	9.2	18.2	27.4	23.9	14.8
1980	8.5	14.8	23.3	22.0	12.5

*Year ended September 30.
†Two months only.
‡Initial investment August 20, 1973; partial year 1973 not available.

EXHIBIT 3
Types of Properties Acquired by PRISA and Equitable Fund #8

	September 30, 1980 Prudential	**December 31, 1980 Equitable**
Number of Properties	284	192
Total appraised value	$1,953.0 million	$1,058.9 million
Outstanding mortgages	22.8	174.3
Other assets	384.0	—
Net assets	2,381.6	903.1
Distribution of Property Values by Usage		
Industrial	12.7%	15.8%
Office	38.7	23.7
Retail	47.3	50.2
Hotel	—	7.9
R&D/Land/Agriculture	1.3	2.4
Distribution of Property Values by Location		
South	48.0%	36.8%
Central	18.9	23.5
West	21.9	12.6
Mid-Atlantic	11.2	13.4
Northeast		13.7
Distribution of Property Values by Age		
Under 5 years	n.a.	24.8%
5–10 years	n.a.	46.6
10–20 years	n.a.	27.1
Over 20 years	n.a.	1.5

Note: n.a. = Not available.

EXHIBIT 4
Prudential's Real Estate Investment Department

Investment Objective and Policy

The objective of PRISA is to obtain an attractive rate of current income from the property investments which offer prospects of long-term growth, in order to enhance the resources of participating pension plans to provide benefit payments. To fulfill that objective, Prudential invests PRISA funds primarily in the purchase of income-producing real property, including office and industrial buildings, shopping centers, other retail stores, apartments, hotels, and motels. Suitable diversification is maintained as to type of property and location. Particular attention is given to properties which are located in growth areas, may be leased on a basis permitting suitable rent revisions, and are considered to have good appreciation potential.

PRISA may, in some cases, hold the land under a building, as well as a leasehold mortgage loan on the building. Other assets which may be held in PRISA include undeveloped land, interests in agricultural property, and other forms of property, and common stocks or other interests in companies which acquire, develop, manage, or otherwise deal with real estate.

Prudential will continuously review the relative values of individual PRISA properties held, in the light of opportunities available elsewhere, and will sell any property for which such action seems advisable.

PRISA funds awaiting permanent investment will be placed primarily in short-term investments, such as commercial paper, certificates of deposit, and Treasury bills.

In recognition of the long period of time required to identify, evaluate, negotiate and acquire properties, and in order to limit the proportion of PRISA assets in short-term investments, Prudential has established procedures under which payments to PRISA by contract-holders are generally limited in amount and agreed upon well in advance. However, there may be times when additional payments to PRISA may be accepted which have not been scheduled in advance, such as when more than the expected volume of properties can be acquired for PRISA.

The decentralized organizational structure of Prudential's Real Estate Investment Department gives Prudential an advantage over most other institutional real estate investors, in buying, managing and selling properties. Because of Prudential's large number of regional offices, it is quickly able to recognize and act on attractive real estate opportunities. Unlike most institutional investors, who use correspondent systems, Prudential deals directly with regional and national real estate developers, brokers, and owners.

Virtually all investments originate and are negotiated and processed at the regional office level. Our regional real estate professionals are well known to local developers, bankers, and others in the financial community. They are familiar with the effects of economic trends on real estate at the local level, and can move quickly when an attractive potential acquisition becomes available. In fact, many of the properties PRISA has acquired first came to Prudential's attention when it was directly contacted by the owners at local offices. Such opportunities may have been missed entirely under a totally centralized operation. Our presence in local markets and accessibility to prospective buyers has also helped to maximize proceeds on properties sold.

Home Office: Newark, New Jersey

EXHIBIT 4 ***(concluded)***

Local Real Estate Investment Offices (unless otherwise indicated):

Eastern Division	*Southern Division*	*Western Division*	*Canadian*
Boston, MA	Atlanta, GA	Bakersfield, CA	Toronto, Ontario*
Newark, NJ*	Blytheville, AR	Fresno, CA	Montreal, Quebec
New York, NY	Coral Gables, FL	Los Angeles, CA*	Darmouth, Nova Scotia
Philadelphia, PA	Dallas, TX	Newport Beach, CA	Calgary, Alberta
Pittsburgh, PA	Greenville, MS	Pasco, WA	Winnipeg, Manitoba
Stamford, CT	Houston, TX*	Phoenix, AZ	
Washington, DC	Little Rock, AR	Pleasanton, CA	
	Memphis, TN	Sacramento, CA	
Midwest Division	Monroe, LA	San Francisco, CA	
Chicago, IL*	New Orleans, LA	Seattle, WA	
Cincinnati, OH	Oklahoma City, OK	Sunnyvale, CA	
Cleveland, OH	Orlando, FL	Van Nuys, CA†	
Creve Coeur, MO		Visalie, CA	
Dublin, OH		Westlake, CA	
Denver, CO		Woodland Hills, CA†	
Indianapolis, IN			
Kearney, NE			
Louisville, KY			
Minneapolis, MN			
Overland Park, KS			
Southfield, MI			
Springfield, IL			

*Divisional Home Office.
†Mortgage Loan Service Office.

EXHIBIT 5
Objectives of Equitable Fund #8

Equitable's Real Estate Account

Investment Objective

The investment objective of the Real Estate Account is to achieve a stable rate of return over an extended time horizon with the potential for growth of rental income and appreciation of property value. The performance objectives of the Account are to attain time-weighted rates of return which are: (1) above the average for comparable equity real estate funds; (2) greater than a portfolio of high-quality bonds; and (3) greater than a portfolio of high-quality mortgages.

Portfolio Investment Policy

The investment policy of the Real Estate Account emphasizes the acquisition and long-term ownership of high-grade, income-producing, commercial real property located in

EXHIBIT 5 *(continued)*

strong markets. The portfolio is diversified by property usage and location. We look for property holdings that enjoy excellent rental markets and continuous resale potential.

To provide a relatively nonvolatile income component to the overall return of the Account, we stress high occupancy levels. The major components of the Account include retail properties, office and industrial buildings, hotels and specialized properties such as research and development and medical buildings. Properties are leased under arrangements that protect against inflation and take advantage of rising property demand. Such mechanisms include net leases or gross leases that require the tenant to pay increases in operating expenses, indexing, short-term leases, and participation in the retail components' sales.

Diversification

The Real Estate Account is diversified by property usage and geographic location. The Account includes the following types of property:

Industrial properties, both single- and multi-tenant warehouses, are selected principally on the strength of the industrial markets and local economy, location in attractive, well-planned industrial parks and versatility for a variety of tenants.

Office buildings situated in proven and prominent urban locations or in well-positioned suburban areas. The Account seeks modern, efficiently designed, attractive office buildings with adequate parking facilities and convenient transportation.

Retail properties, primarily regional shopping centers which are anchored by well-established national or regional department store chains. Some of the important considerations in selecting a retail property for inclusion in the portfolio are demographic trends, sound locations, growth potential, and effective management.

Hotels located in commercial and resort areas which serve the overall market. A major consideration concerning hotel investment is management capability.

Other specialized properties, such as research and development facilities and medical office buildings, are selected based on marketability, location, and the potential for above-average yields.

The Organization

Equitable's real estate organization, one of the largest in the nation, includes over 544 full-time professionals. Through a network of 36 offices strategically located throughout the country, full national coverage is provided. Moreover, our decentralized office system insures that our professionals are totally familiar with local market conditions and that they maintain close contact with prominent real estate developers. These offices generate investment proposals for both mortgages and equity ownership.

The Field Operations Sector handles all facets of real estate transactions from appraisal through negotiation. In addition, it provides specialized local personnel for property management, construction, property expansion and leasing.

The Real Estate Production and Management Sector, located in the New York Home Office, consists of five key areas which work in conjunction with field offices:

The Joint Venture Coordination and Sales Department utilizes its business, financial, accounting and tax experience to evaluate and work with all aspects of complex joint ventures. The Department is also responsible for all activities related to the sale of Equitable-owned properties.

EXHIBIT 5 *(continued)*

The Property Information Department provides accounting and financial support for the Realty Operation Area.

The Property Management and Development Department is responsible for managing and developing all real estate owned by Equitable.

The Construction and Design Department supervises construction and/or expansion of all properties on which construction plans have been made. It also analyzes the construction and design of prospective purchases.

The Equity Acquisition and Portfolio Management Department reviews proposals for property purchases and works directly on complex major transactions. The department develops acquisition strategy and portfolio policies for the Real Estate Account.

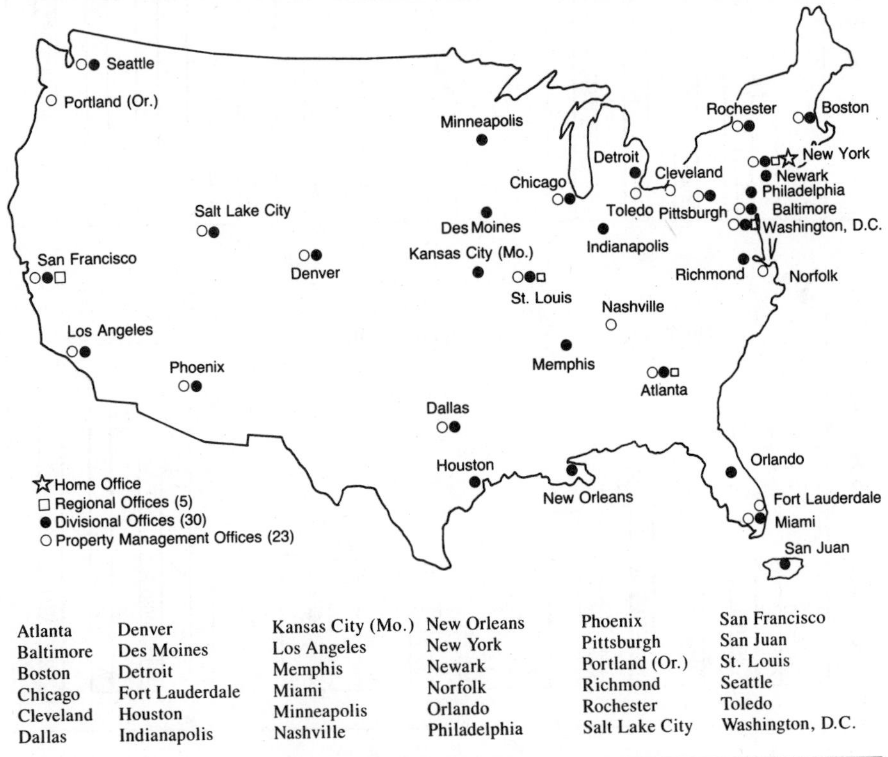

Atlanta	Denver	Kansas City (Mo.)	New Orleans	Phoenix	San Francisco
Baltimore	Des Moines	Los Angeles	New York	Pittsburgh	San Juan
Boston	Detroit	Memphis	Newark	Portland (Or.)	St. Louis
Chicago	Fort Lauderdale	Miami	Norfolk	Richmond	Seattle
Cleveland	Houston	Minneapolis	Orlando	Rochester	Toledo
Dallas	Indianapolis	Nashville	Philadelphia	Salt Lake City	Washington, D.C.

EXHIBIT 6
1980 Performance of Equitable Fund #8

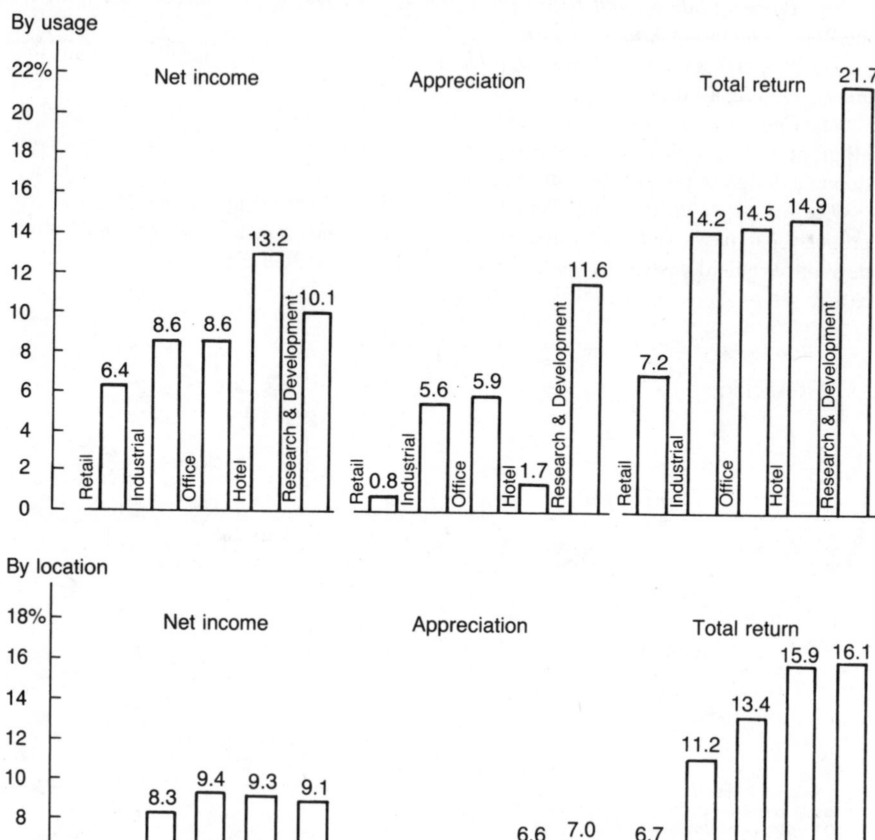

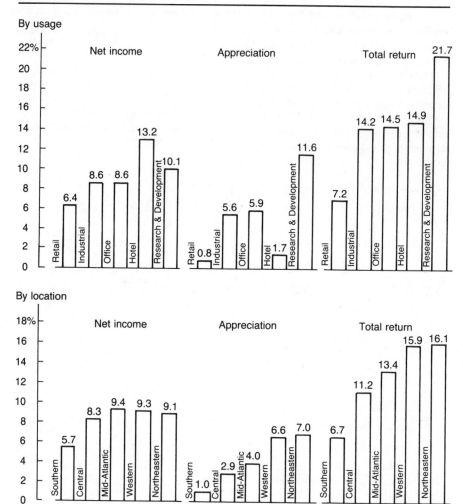

EXHIBIT 7
PRISA Investments, 1980

In the year covered by this report, the total investment in PRISA property acquisitions amounted to $481.1 million, which included $440.7 million in cash disbursements and $40.4 million in encumbrance assumptions. Disbursements for improvements on properties previously acquired were $17.6 million (including $0.9 million for disbursements cn properties sold during the year).

In addition, two mortgage loans in the amount of $1.7 million were paid in full during the fiscal year.

EXHIBIT 7 *(continued)*

Properties purchased during the year are described below.

Offices

Office building in Atlanta, Georgia, *Property 388*
Office building in Chicago, Illinois, *Property 395*
Office building complex in Park Ridge (Chicago), Illinois, *Property 397*
Office building complex with a parking garage in Newport Beach, California, *Property 399*
Office building complex in Renton (Seattle), Washington, *Property 402*
Office building in Long Beach (Los Angeles), California, *Property 405*
Office retail building in Birmingham (Detroit), Michigan, *Property 412*
Office building in Washington, D.C., *Property 414*
Office building in Des Plaines (Chicago), Illinois, *Property 429*
Office building complex in Park Ridge (Chicago), Illinois, *Property 430*
Office building complex in Houston, Texas, *Property 448*
Office research building in Gaithersburg (Washington, D.C.), Maryland, *Property 456*
Office building in Dallas, Texas, *Property 471*
Office building in Oklahoma City, Oklahoma, *Property 482*

Commercial

Community shopping center in New Orleans, Louisiana, *Property 375*
Regional shopping center in Orlando, Florida, *Property 403*
Neighborhood shopping center in Chatham Township (Morris County), New Jersey, *Property 409*
Community shopping center in Gardner (Worcester County), Massachusetts, *Property 418*
Six neighborhood shopping centers in Sun City (Phoenix), Arizona, *Properties 423–428*
Regional shopping center in Plantation (Fort Lauderdale), Florida, *Property 443*
Regional shopping center in Houston, Texas, *Property 445*

Industrial

Three warehouse buildings in Troy (Detroit), Michigan, *Property 385*
Warehouse building in Aurora (Denver), Colorado, *Property 386*
Warehouse building in Woburn (Boston), Massachusetts, *Property 394*
Warehouse building in Glendale (Los Angeles), California, *Property 398*
Office/warehouse building in St. Paul, Minnesota, *Property 401*
Warehouse building in Industry (Los Angeles), California, *Property 406*
Eight industrial/warehouse buildings in Bensalem (Philadelphia), Pennsylvania, *Property 410*
Warehouse building in Providence, Rhode Island, *Property 411*
Two industrial buildings in Burbank (Los Angeles), California, *Property 415*
Office/warehouse building in Eden Prairie (Minneapolis), Minnesota, *Property 421*
Two office/warehouse buildings in Kent (Seattle), Washington, *Property 433*
Office/warehouse building in Dallas, Texas, *Property 436*
Office/warehouse building in Eden Prairie (Minneapolis), Minnesota, *Property 438*
Warehouse building in Orlando, Florida, *Property 439*
Office/warehouse building in Omaha, Nebraska, *Property 446*
Five office/warehouse buildings in King County (Seattle), Washington, *Property 454*
Warehouse building in Detroit, Michigan, *Property 457*
Warehouse building in Madison Heights (Detroit), Michigan, *Property 462*
Warehouse building in Madison Heights (Detroit), Michigan, *Property 463*
Warehouse building in Madison Heights (Detroit), Michigan, *Property 464*
Warehouse building in Carrollton (Dallas), Texas, *Property 469*
Warehouse building in Grand Prairie (Dallas), Texas, *Property 470*
Warehouse building in Carrollton (Dallas), Texas, *Property 472*
Warehouse building in Madison Heights (Detroit), Michigan, *Property 473*
Warehouse building in Jackson, Mississippi, *Property 474*

Agricultural

Farm in Lonoke County, Arkansas, *Property 432*

EXHIBIT 7 *(concluded)*

The following table shows the distribution of PRISA's purchases during the year by class of property and geographical area, based on property values as of September 30, 1980. The number of properties in each category is shown in parentheses.

Class	*West*	*South*	*Mid-West*	*East*	*Total*
Offices	(3) 12.7%	(4) 4.2%	(5) 14.7%	(2) 7.1%	(14) 38.7%
Commercial	(6) 5.8	(4) 39.4	— —	(2) 2.1	(12) 47.3
Industrial	(5) 3.4	(6) 3.1	(11) 4.2	(3) 2.0	(25) 12.7
Agricultural	— —	(1) 1.3	— —	— —	(1) 1.3
Total	(14) 21.9%	(15) 48.0%	(16) 18.9%	(7) 11.2%	(52) 100.0%

PRISA Properties Sold October 1, 1979, to September 30, 1980

Property Identification Number	*Description*	*Date Purchased*	*Cost*
274	Retail store	August 1974	$ 88,800
53 (partial)	Office	August 1972	385,253
127	Warehouse	November 1972	468,653
55	Warehouse	December 1972	457,150
85	Office	December 1972	287,070
45	Apartment complex	August 1972	20,421,170
170	Warehouse	December 1974	2,290.915
32	Department store	June 1972	7,302,210
220	Office	October 1974	13,775,995
Total			$45,477,216

Property Identification Number	*Date Sold*	*Gross Sale Price*	*Net Proceeds*	*Last Appraised Value Before Sale*
274	October 1979	$ 90,000	$ 83,919	$ 79,000
53 (partial)	October 1979	475,000	474,510	390,000
127	October 1979	700,000	660,347	600,000
55	November 1979	450,220	424,330	402,000
85	December 1979	185,000	174,417	160,000
45	January 1980	34,585,000	34,009,703	32,000,000
170	February 1980	2,734,971	2,727,064	2,430,000
32	April 1980	6,500,000	6,477,250	5,956,000
220	August 1980	14,900,110	14,882,415	13,800,000
Total		$60,620,301	$59,913,955	$55,817,000

EXHIBIT 8
Summary of 1980 Real Estate Investments of Equitable Fund #8

In selecting a property, we weigh:

- The location of the property.
- The potential income stream.
- The relationship of cost and income.
- The prospects for increasing rental income and capital appreciation.
- The resale marketability.
- Architectural and other physical attributes.

We also consider the risks involved and the probability and potential impact of changes in the local economy.

Wholly-Owned Property Acquisitions

Property Number	*Description*
173	Multi-tenant 14-story office building located in the center of the state capital's central business district; Raleigh, N.C.
174	Three one-story industrial buildings with on-site parking for 143 cars, 29 truck doors and 1 rail door; Fort Worth, Tex.
175	Single-tenant industrial plant and warehouse with on-site parking facilities; Livonia, Mich.
176	Two multi-tenant industrial buildings within Northgate Business Park, with 8 rail doors and 28 truck doors combined and parking facilities; Dallas, Tex.
177	Industrial park with 15 single-story buildings; Nashville, Tenn.
178	The Des Peres Shopping Center; St. Louis County, Mo.
179	The Crossroads Shopping Center; Olathe, Kans.
180	Research & development one-story industrial building; San Jose, Cal.
181	Two one-story multi-tenant office buildings; Dallas, Tex.
182	Multi-tenant one-story industrial building; Dallas, Tex.
183	Two single-tenant one-story industrial buildings; Dallas, Tex.
184	Four multi-tenant one-story industrial buildings; Dallas, Tex.
185	Multi-tenant 32-story office building and annex garage with combined parking for 1,389 cars; Miami, Fla.
186	Anchorage Business Park consists of 14 multi-tenant industrial buildings combining offices and warehouses, with paved on-site parking for 665 cars; Anchorage, Ak.
187	Anchorage Distribution Center, two multi-tenant industrial buildings with 63 truck doors, 21 rail doors and on-site parking for 425 cars; Anchorage, Ak.
188	Two one-story multi-tenant industrial buildings with paved on-site parking for 88 cars; San Francisco, Cal.
189	Single-tenant industrial building with paved on-site parking for 31 cars; Rock Island, Il.
190	Marriott Hotel with 760 guest rooms, restaurants and lounges, swimming pool, racquetball court, grand ballroom, meeting rooms and exhibit hall, located in the city's central business district. Parking for 630 cars; Atlanta, Ga.
191	Marriott's Rancho Las Palmas hotel with 348 guest rooms, 3 restaurants, banquet and meeting rooms, 2 swimming pools and spas, use of golf course, 25 tennis courts and clubhouse and parking for 900 cars; Rancho Mirage, Cal.
192	Three multi-tenant warehouses with paved parking for 116 cars and 49 truck doors; Marietta, Ga.
193	Three multi-tenant warehouses with paved parking for 169 cars, 39 truck doors and available rail; Chamblee, Ga.

EXHIBIT 8 *(continued)*

Property Number	*Description*
194	Single-tenant industrial building with paved parking for 92 cars in the Woodlands Business Center; Grand Prairie, Tex.
195	One Boston Place, a 41-story office building located in the city's financial district; Boston, Mass.
196	Multi-tenant one-story industrial building; Houston, Tex.

Joint Ventures, Construction Loans, and Mortgages Receivable

Property Number	*Description*
JV5	Hammond Square Mall is an enclosed, split-level shopping mall; Hammond, La.
JV6	Marriott Motor Inn consists of a 3-, 4- and 10-story structure containing 301 motel rooms, an 800-seat ballroom, 7 meeting rooms, two 200-seat restaurants and parking for 564 cars; Harrisburg, Pa.
JV7	A six-story office building plus a penthouse and two-level basement with enclosed garage parking for 338 cars is under construction; Alexandria. Va.
JV8	The St. Regis Sheraton Hotel, located in the heart of midtown, contains 441 guest units, 11 meeting rooms and 2 penthouse banquet rooms; under renovation; New York, N.Y.
JV9	The Royal Palace Hotel in Disney World will have 826 guest rooms in the combination of a 27-story highrise as well as midrise and lowrise facilities, ballrooms, meeting rooms, a 300-seat dining facility, a 125-person specialty restaurant, a 200-seat cocktail lounge, a rooftop restaurant and lounge seating 200 and 175 people, respectively, swimming pools, tennis courts and health club, and parking for 950–1,050 cars; Lake Buena Vista, Fla.
CL7	A 204-room luxury hotel is to be owned upon completion under a joint venture; Village of Coconut Grove, Miami, Fla.
CL8	A 427-room luxury Four Seasons Hotel is to be owned under a joint venture upon completion; Dallas, Tex.
CL9	A 27-story office building with a two-level retail galleria and a garage complex is to be acquired upon completion and leasing under a joint venture; San Diego, Cal.
CL10	Convertible second mortgage on a multi-level open-air collection of high-fashion boutiques and restaurants; Village of Coconut Grove, Miami, Fla.
CL11	Convertible second mortgage on an 11-story multi-tenant office building; Village of Coconut Grove, Miami, Fla.
CL12	A two-building suburban office complex will be acquired upon completion; St. Louis County, Mo.
CL13	A one-story industrial building is to be purchased upon completion; Plymouth, Minn.
CL14	A 300-room Sheraton Hotel is to be owned upon completion under a joint venture; Dallas, Tex.

Property Sales

All properties in the Account are purchased for long-term ownership. However, a property may become a candidate for sale if it does not continue to meet existing investment criteria.

EXHIBIT 8 *(concluded)*

1980 Property Sales

Property Number	*Description Location*	*Year Purchased*	*Date Sold*	*Last Appraised Value*	*Net Proceeds*
129	Leased fee interest Gaithersburg, Md.	1978	February 1980	$120,000	$121,449

EXHIBIT 9
PRISA, Statement of Operations, 1980

	Year Ended September 30	
	1980	***1979***
Investment Income:		
Revenue from properties	$177,256,417	$137,117,047
Net income from partnerships	26,103,410	20,196,844
Interest from mortgage loans	2,426,903	2,320,370
Interest from short-term investments	17,068,631	4,391,894
	222,855,361	164,026,155
Expenses:		
Real estate expenses and taxes	73,348,497	56,391,447
Interest on encumbrances	18,782,892	15,529,452
Provision for uncollectible amounts	580,966	143,814
	92,712,355	72,064,713
Net Income from Investments	130,143,006	91,961,442
Management Fee	17,781,509	12,034,041
Net Income	$112,361,497	$ 79,927,401
Realized and Unrealized Gain on Investments:		
Proceeds from property sales	$ 60,622,760	$ 8,024,042
Less: Cost of properties sold	45,483,695	7,179,404
Realization of prior period's appreciation on investments sold	11,446,274	735,935
	3,692,791	108,703
Increase for the year in unrealized appreciation of investments held at end of year	189,152,588	157,782,501
Realized and Unrealized Gain on Investments	$192,845,379	$157,891,204

EXHIBIT 10
Equitable Fund #8, Statement of Operations and Changes in Net Assets

	Year Ended December 31	
	1980	**1979**
From Investment Activities:		
Investment Income		
Rental income	$ 142,355,252	$ 96,416,842
Income from partnership operations and interest from related construction loan	7,983,032	749,021
Interest from mortgage and construction loans	3,216,527	1,558,576
Interest from direct placement debt security	5,986,732	—
Interest from short-term debt securities	8,698,648	3,480,062
Other	91,097	104,907
Total	168,331,288	102,309,408
Expenses		
Real estate taxes	16,111,213	12,981,013
Real estate operating expenses	41,907,085	29,178,467
Investment management fees	10,824,231	5,448,912
Interest on mortgages payable	15,617,410	9,495,208
Total	84,459,939	57,103,600
Net Investment Income	83,871,349	45,205,808
Realized and Unrealized Gain (Loss) on Investments:		
Realized gain (loss) from real estate transactions		
Net proceeds from sales	82,391	790,341
Cost of investments sold	121,648	567,637
Net realized gain (loss)	(39,257)	222,704
Unrealized appreciation of investments		
January 1	49,032,298	18,267,034
December 31	93,465,497	49,032,298
Unrealized appreciation	44,433,199	30,765,264
Net Realized and Unrealized Gain on Investments	44,393,942	30,987,968
Increase in net assets attributable to investment activities	128,265,291	76,193,776
From Client Transactions:		
Allocations	399,840,802	464,391,308
Withdrawals	(6,963,687)	(15,284,638)
Administrative fees	(340,662)	(123,739)
Increase in net assets attributable to client transactions	392,536,453	448,982,931
Increase in Net Assets	520,801,744	525,176,707
Net Assets—January 1	903,091,239	377,914,532
Net Assets—December 31	$1,423,892,983	$903,091,239
Separate Account Unit Value	$2,168.36	$1,927.56
Separate Account Units Outstanding	656,676	468,516

EXHIBIT 11
Appraisal Procedures: Prudential and Equitable

Prudential

Valuation Procedures

Properties are shown at market value in accordance with the terms of PRISA contracts. These values are based upon appraisal reports prepared by independent real estate appraisers (members of the American Institute of Real Estate Appraisers) shortly after acquisition of the property and no less frequently than annually thereafter. The property valuations are reviewed quarterly by Prudential's management and adjusted if there has been a significant change in circumstances related to the property since the most recent independent appraisal.

The purpose of an appraisal is to estimate the fair market value of a property as of a specific date. Fair market value has been defined by the courts as the highest price in terms of money which a property will bring if exposed to the open market, allowing a reasonable time to find a purchaser who buys with knowledge of all the uses to which it is adapted and for which it is capable of being used. This estimate of fair market value generally is a correlation of three approaches, all of which require the exercise of subjective judgment. The three approaches are: (1) current cost of reproducing a property less deterioration and functional and economic obsolescence; (2) capitalization of the property's net earning power; and (3) value indicated by recent sales of comparable properties in the market. In the reconciliation of these three approaches, the one most heavily relied upon is the one generally recognized for the type of property in the market.

Net partnership interests in properties are valued at PRISA's equity in net assets as reflected by the partnerships' financial statements (such partnerships, in each of which PRISA has a 50% interest, had total assets of $564,221,420 and $437,161,729 and total liabilities of $64,909,133 and $67,828,547 at September 30, 1980 and September 30, 1979, respectively) with properties valued as described in the preceding paragraphs.

Fees

On a quarterly basis, Prudential charged a management fee of one fourth of the current annual rate. The current annual rate is 1¼ percent of net assets less 1 percent of short-term investments and cash included in net assets, before any increases or reductions in participation on the respective report date.

Equitable

Valuation of Investments

The appraised values of real estate investments are determined in accordance with the following procedures for the purpose of calculating separate account unit values and do not necessarily represent the prices at which the real estate investments would sell since market prices of real estate investments are determined by negotiation between a willing buyer and seller. However, it is management's opinion that the aforementioned appraised values are reasonable approximations of the market prices. Substantially all of the real estate investments are being held for long-term appreciation and income production.

Appraisals of real estate investments have been prepared in accordance with guidelines published by the New York Insurance Department (Department) and conform to Equitable's Summary of Operations for group separate accounts, which has been ap-

EXHIBIT 11 *(continued)*

proved by the Department. Some of the procedures used in estimating appraised values involve subjective judgment.

Investments allocated to the Account by Equitable do not have a readily available market, and the ability of a Client to withdraw funds from the Account depends on the availability of cash for such withdrawals. Such cash would normally arise from net investment income, new contributions allocated to the Account and the sales of properties in the normal course of business.

Real Estate Properties

The initial valuation of real property allocated to the Account is based on a full appraisal report prepared by Equitable's staff appraiser or by an independent real estate appraiser engaged by Equitable for this purpose. Subsequent values are determined quarterly from certificates of value prepared by Equitable's staff appraisers on the basis of all applicable information called for by the Department's guidelines. Full appraisal reports are also prepared annually by Equitable's staff appraisers on certain selected properties.

Since appraisals take into consideration the effect of actual depreciation on properties, management believes that a better financial statement presentation is achieved if the unrealized increase (decrease) in appraised value of real estate properties is not affected by the deduction of historical cost depreciation from net investment income. The financial statements have therefore been presented to exclude the historical cost depreciation as a deduction from net investment income. Such presentation does not affect the appraisal value, net assets or unit value of the Account, but does result in an increase in net investment income and a decrease (increase) in the amount reported as unrealized increase (decrease) in appraised value of real properties. The amount of historical cost depreciation (computed on a straight-line basis over useful lives ranging from 25--50 years) approximated $19.1 million and $11.8 million for 1980 and 1979, respectively.

Mortgages payable are stated at the principal amount of obligations outstanding. The difference between the present value of mortgage obligations, discounted at current interest rates, and the actual obligations due is considered to be related to the property being appraised and therefore is included in determining the appraised value of the property. Real estate at an appraised value of $775.7 million is encumbered by mortgages. Aggregate annual payments of mortgage principal at interest rates ranging from 5.0% to 10.625% are as follows:

Year Ending December 31	*Remaining Mortgage Principal ($000)*
1981	$ 40,208
1982	5,359
1983	5,771
1984	6,212
1985	11,108
1986–1990	47,288
1991–1995	50,727
1996–2000	47,326
Thereafter	6,162
	$220,161

EXHIBIT 11 ***(continued)***

Construction Loans and Related Purchase Contracts

The fair value of the construction loans held in the Account, on properties committed to be purchased for the Account upon completion (subject to certain contractual conditions), has been determined on the basis of estimated mortgage interest rates on December 31, 1980, of loans of comparable quality and maturity, adjusted to recognize (1) the present value of the loans, discounted to reflect the difference between the estimated current market interest rate, assuming for the purpose of this calculation that such difference will remain constant for the duration of the loans, (2) the present principal amount of the loans outstanding, (3) amounts and disbursement dates for future advances, and (4) other factors.

The fair value of the contracts to purchase properties securing the construction loans represents the difference between the contractual purchase price and the appraised value of the properties (assuming completion) and other factors.

Real Estate Partnership Equities and Related Construction Loan

Net partnership equities in properties are valued at the Account's equity in the net assets of the partnerships in accordance with the valuation procedures described under Real Estate Properties. Partnerships' construction loan and related contracts for equity participations are valued in accordance with the valuation procedures described under Construction Loans and Related Purchase Contracts. As of December 31, 1980, the value of the construction loan outstanding and related contract for equity participation was $57.3 million.

Mortgages Receivable

The fair value of the mortgages receivable held in the Account has been determined (1) on the basis of estimated mortgage interest rates on December 31, 1980, of loans of comparable quality and maturity, and (2) by recognizing the value of options to enter into joint ventures contained in certain mortgage instruments.

Direct Placement Security and Related Real Estate Acquisition

The fair value of the direct placement debt security of Marriott Corporation has been determined on the assumption that such security will be held to maturity and on the basis of interest yields on December 31, 1980, of publicly traded debt securities of comparable quality and maturity, adjusted to recognize any difference in interest rates applicable to direct placement investments and other factors. This valuation procedure was authorized by the Investment Committee of Equitable's Board of Directors and reviewed by the New York State Insurance Department. Such fair value does not necessarily represent the value at which this security could be sold.

As of December 31, 1980, $53.5 million of the original $80.5 million principal balance has been repaid. Equitable is contractually obligated to purchase the remaining property for $27 million during 1981. With the proceeds from this purchase, Marriott is obligated to repay the debt security due Equitable.

Fees

Investment management fees are based on the prior month-end net asset value (as defined) of each Client's aggregate interest in Equitable's separate accounts and are determined monthly at the annual rates shown below:

EXHIBIT 11 *(concluded)*

Aggregate Interest	*Annual Rate*
First $10 million	0.25 of 1%
Next $15 million	0.20 of 1%
Next $25 million	0.15 of 1%
Excess over $50 million	0.125 of 1%

There is an additional annual charge of 0.75 of 1 percent of the Account's net assets.

Administrative fees charged to Clients may also be paid from the Account.

Appendix*

EXHIBIT A–1

Bargain Prices for Real Estate Draw Stanford

LOS ANGELES—High interest rates have forced some developers to put equity real estate they won on the market at discount prices, say two investors from different sides of the financial street.

Rodney Adams, director of finance at Stanford University and James Muzzy, president of Pacific Investment Management Co., said in separate interviews that the high interest rates have perked their interest in real estate.

Stanford has set aside $40 million for possible investment in real estate, and PIMCO is sponsoring a closed end real estate fund that will be soon available for subscription.

"High interest rates mean that people who have a lot of borrowed money hurt, and when they hurt they sometimes decide they would like to avoid that by disposing of properties quite often at an attractive price," said Mr. Adams.

A few hundred miles south of Mr. Adams, in Newport Beach, Ca., Mr. Muzzy agreed, saying:

"High interest rates are providing an opportunity. What has happened is that interest rates that have gone sky high are forcing a lot of the developers that have held equity real estate to put it on the market, and it has provided an avenue of opportunity for the pension funds and cash buyers."

Also, he said, a number of companies are finding tax advantages in selling off their home offices or other buildings, and then getting the use of them back through a lease-back arrangement.

"They do this because of the tax advantage for them as a corporation. The rent is an expense item," he said.

But it takes a discerning investor to take advantage of some of the opportunities resulting from high interest rates, said Mr. Adams.

*All articles in this appendix are reprinted, with permission, from *Pensions & Investment Age*, February 16, 1981. © Crain Communications, Inc., 1981.

EXHIBIT A–1 ***(continued)***

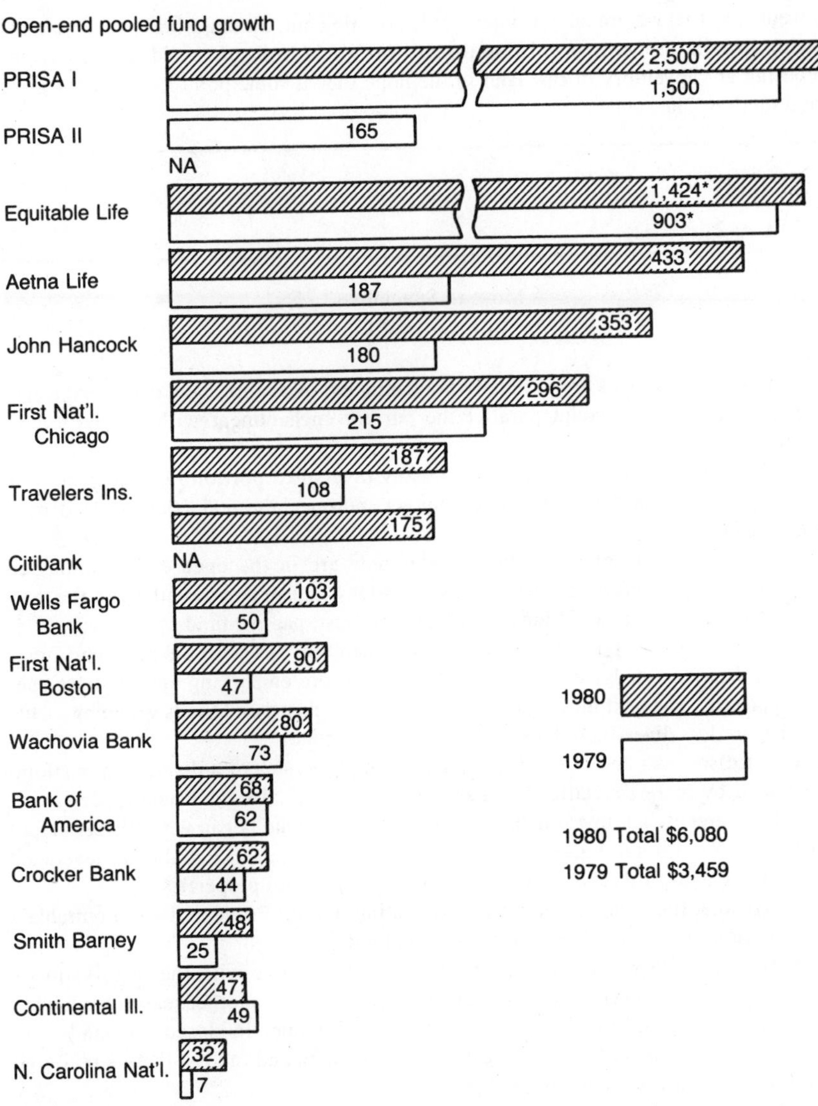

"It means that you have to be willing to accept something that maybe doesn't look that good on paper right at the moment because it might have suffered losses, and the losses might have come because of high debt service obligations," added Mr. Adams.

He said Stanford would be interested in ones where its economic worth could be shown on a fundamental basis.

EXHIBIT A–1 *(concluded)*

"I would say that we probably wouldn't rule anything out, although we would probably look with disdain on more speculative things. We would probably avoid things like the warehousing and inventory of raw land in the hope that at some point a city might grow in that direction," he said.

EXHIBIT A–2

A Move to Specialists?
By Clare Minick

NEW YORK—Fund sponsors are gradually branching out into more specialized real estate managers, a move which could parallel the current enchantment with special equity managers.

While the idea of setting up a core or broadly diversified portfolio supplemented by equity specialists seems firmly implanted among sponsors, the real estate equivalent is just beginning to crop up.

For instance the bulk of real estate monies now are in the open end commingled funds—PRISA I alone has $2.5 billion in assets. Many industry observers liken the very large open end funds to 'index' funds or, at the very least, passive funds.

The tendency among sponsors has been to get their feet wet with the open end funds raising both their knowledge and comfort quotients before embarking upon a more specialized approach. The next move typically has been the closed end funds which by virtue of their size are less diversified than the large open end funds.

McGraw-Edison was one of the first funds to adopt the idea of a diversified portfolio complemented by more specialized managers (*IA*, Sept. 23, 1980). Richard McGahan, director of retirement plan investments, explained that the fund began with PRISA before committing $5.5 million to LaSalle Partners and Coldwell Banker. LaSalle has leveraged properties and Coldwell Banker invests in some developmental properties.

A Pennsylvania fund which has been participating in both Prudential and Equitable's commingled funds has now added two closed end funds.

While conceding that, "you can correlate what we've done with the (equity) index fund idea," the fund's pension executive added that, "There's another reason for having both open and closed end funds—you can't put enough money in closed end funds." In his opinion, "most pension funds are starting off with open end funds—there's really no difference between them and an index."

At Conoco, William Smith, coordinator of pension investments, said the $580 million fund has $25 million with John Hancock, $20 million with Travelers, and another $8 million separately managed by First National Bank of Dallas.

"You have big, broad exposure with the insurance companies," said Mr. Smith. "First National Bank of Dallas has a special niche—they concentrate on the Southwest." Conoco has taken a similar approach with equities. It retains four special equity managers in conjunction with Morgan Guaranty for broad market exposure, according to Mr. Smith.

A gradual approach to real estate is the current posture at InterNorth, which has a $230 million fund.

"We're in a large pooled fund with an insurance company (Equitable)," explained Jon

EXHIBIT A–2 ***(concluded)***

Minks, investment specialist. "We hired another fund (First National Bank of Boston) but we won't do more for several years. We want to be well diversified, we just don't want to take risk," he said.

The fund has $14.6 million, or 6.3% of its assets, invested in real estate.

One Midwest sponsor maintained that open end funds cannot be likened to index funds simply because there is no broad market index for real estate like there is for equities.

He did, however, endorse the idea of the large open end funds being core, or broadly diversified portfolios.

The fund now has money invested in commingled funds at Aetna Life Insurance and Prudential.

This sponsor, though, is making plans for the future. At some point he would like to make real estate investments in about 10 cities around the country that are noted for growth. Working in tandem either with brokers in those cities or with an adviser, he plans to make direct investments.

"Commingled funds are not the cheapest way to do it," said the pension executive. "You get more bang for your buck if you do it yourself. But in the meantime we are taking our bets with specialized funds," he concluded.

A large Midwestern fund admitted to being "laggards in real estate." The fund has less than 1% of its assets in real estate.

However, should the fund decide on real estate, "we'd probably go the commingled route," said a company spokesman.

As for the specialized real estate manager approach, the pension executive said "It seems like a natural evolution if you've been in real estate for a while. But equities have been very good. If we look at real estate it will probably be as a replacement for fixed income. People are bailing out of bonds—it's probably going into real estate."

Consolidated Foods Corp. has about 10% of its $100 million pension fund invested in real estate through PRISA, according to Martha Binzel, senior treasury analyst.

While the company has discussed broadening its real estate portfolio, Ms. Binzel said nothing had been concluded. "We may diversify by region or property type but it's early to say," she said.

John Lillard, president of JMB Institutional Realty sees the large open end fund as essentially passive.

"But pension funds will get more involved with the decision-making process," he predicted. He foresees "specialist real estate firms cropping up." Sponsors may begin to hire firms with either a geographic or property-type specialty, he said.

The head of American Agricultural Investment Co., William Cotter, sees the current move to specialized real estate managers as "right on."

He contends, however, that pension funds cannot have broadly diversified portfolios—even through the large open end funds—if they don't have a portion in agricultural land.

"How can you really be diversified if you don't own farmland? Forty percent of all real estate in this country is farmland . . ." he stated.

As for the popularity of open end funds by sponsors, Mr. Cotter noted, "It's the herd instinct. It's always warmer in the center of the herd."

Switching metaphors, he added, "Ninety five percent of the people sit back watching to see if the guy who ate the oyster dies. If he smacks his lips, another 5% move in . . ."

Mr. Cotter predicts that money will move to developmental deals because of the "shortage of institutional quality deals."

EXHIBIT A–3

Real Estate Market Still Offers Acceptable Returns
By Gary Barth

Many U.S. pension funds have expressed concern that their entry into the real estate investment market will come at a time when the demand for quality income-producing property has pushed yields down to levels which make them unattractive when compared with those investment alternatives with which the funds are intimately familiar.

This concern is generally unjustified in today's real property marketplace. While first-year, cash-on-cash yields are often 6% or less on the best properties (witness the Pan Am building sale in New York), the near to intermediate term upside potential from these same properties can be substantial. In fact, first-year yields can often be academic for a property whose well-below-market-rent leases are expiring within the first few years of ownership in a strong market for that property's space.

Most institutional investors in the real property marketplace today use discounted cash flow studies as they analyze investment opportunities. The benchmark yield, most often called the internal rate of return (I.R.R.), is a measure of the expected benefits from the property's ownership over a presumed holding period, for example 10 or 15 years.

Obviously, the assumptions made by the purchaser with respect to rental and capital growth make this yield calculation fraught with potential pitfalls. Nevertheless, experienced practitioners can and do make projections upon which valid investment decisions may be based.

We are presently involved in transactions for quality real estate for which analysis indicates an expected I.R.R. of 14% to 16% over a 10-year holding period, using relatively conservative assumptions.

Risk-reward considerations indicate the relative attractiveness of these investments for their inclusion in a balanced portfolio, especially in light of the quality property's ability (with a proper leasing structure of few or no long-term, fixed-rent leases) to respond to further inflationary pressures. These same 14% to 16% yields attained by projecting moderate inflationary growth could easily become 18% to 20% if inflation were to become more pervasive.

With the relative demise of the long-term, fixed-interest rate mortgage, real estate development financing will take on an entirely new dimension. Institutions and, increasingly, pension funds, will find opportunities in the development of new properties.

If properly structured, yields in this area should surpass those mentioned above. There is no gain-saying the fact that real property development is a riskier venture than the acquisition of proven "bricks and mortar." Nevertheless, deals can be structured which minimize, or even eliminate, construction risk on the part of the fund and leave the fund with a return commensurate with the leasing risk it is willing to take.

Many U.S. real estate developers will become manufacturers of real estate investments for pension funds as did many of the British developers during the decade of the 1970s.

Most U.S. developers are not yet ready to accept the fact that the decade of the 80s will find them giving up increasing shares of the equity pie to their institutional funders and, in some cases, becoming merchant builders.

We have for some years now been representing U.K. pension funds who have "graduated" from investing in existing property to the development of their own investments in Great Britain.

EXHIBIT A–3 ***(concluded)***

Now some of these same funds, having invested in U.S. property for five years or so, are now embarking upon developments through their U.S. advisers. In this way, they are balancing their U.S. portfolios with higher yielding, albeit more risky, investments. It is up to their adviser to properly quantify the added yield expectation against the risk actually being taken by the fund.

For example, we are now negotiating on behalf of a foreign pension trust the forward funding of a 200,000 square foot office building in an excellent location within a major U.S. city.

The developer has bought the land and will construct the property in accordance with plans and specifications approved by my firm as the fund's adviser. The developer has the financial muscle to guarantee completion of the project so that the fund has no construction risk—an important consideration.

Interestingly, the fund is also providing the construction financing, again guaranteed by the developer's (a public corporation) net worth.

Upon completion of the project, the fund will acquire the property according to a predetermined formula, which should provide it with a minimum first year cash-on-cash yield of 9.25%. Successful completion of the project and leasing should also provide the developer with a fair profit for his efforts.

Once U.S. pension funds have had the chance to study and understand the real estate investment marketplace, they will agree that opportunities indeed exist which provide attractive investment alternatives to traditional modes of investment for their portfolios.

With assistance from their real property advisers, these funds will be able to quantify the risks entailed in various types of property investment and will make appropriate and prudent investment decisions in the decade of the 80s.

EXHIBIT A–4

Pitfalls in Real Estate Investing

SAN FRANCISCO—Real estate markets are relatively inefficient, and therefore the chances for exposure to loss are greater than in the comparatively efficient corporate securities markets, according to Stephen E. Roulac, president of Questor Associates.

Mr. Roulac, speaking at the Callan Investments Institute, said that information and analysis are at a premium in the real estate markets, and that the markets present pitfalls for the unwary.

Nevertheless, increased yields are likely on a selective basis for those plan sponsors who understand real estate investing and use appropriate real estate portfolio structures, selection and management techniques.

At present, he said, it is unclear that there has been good investment performance, overall, in real estate investment, and performance is unlikely under current management arrangements.

Mr. Roulac said that those seeking maximum returns in real estate should bear in mind that the economics of investing in real estate are different from the economics of investing in corporate securities.

EXHIBIT A–4 *(concluded)*

Current fixed-rate compensation schemes discourage a resource-intensive and return-maximizing acquisition process, he said.

Mr. Roulac said that the primary attribute of a successful real estate management operation is an emphasis on strategy, "employing a decision hierarchy of policy, portfolio, specific investment.

"Acquisition and evaluation roles will be separated and the personnel and their skills will be more diverse than that of securities portfolio advisors.

"Presently," he said, "too few firms are appropriately structured to achieve superior performance.

"Portfolio compensation and diversification are more important than individual building selection."

Both managers and plan sponsors, he said, have miscalculated by electing approaches that are inconsistent with the strategies and styles employed in corporate securities.

Some institutions that favor modern portfolio theory approaches to their stock investments have elected real estate styles at the opposite end of the spectrum, he said.

This inconsistency of approach compromises the prospects for successful real estate involvement, but more seriously, may threaten the primary stock and bond market position, Mr. Roulac said.

EXHIBIT A–5

Sponsors Eye 14% Realty Return

SOUTHPORT, CT.—Sponsors have modest expectations about rates of return from real estate investments.

Sponsors believe that a total return (discounted internal rate) of 14% represents an appropriate investment goal, assuming an 8% inflation rate.

That was one conclusion drawn from a survey of Fortune 300 companies (industrial) by a real estate management firm here, E. P. Wilbur & Co. Inc. The survey is the initial stage of a larger survey of Fortune 1000 companies which attempts to probe sponsors' psyches on real estate.

"While much has been written about sponsors' interest in real estate, there's been little said about detailed investment strategy," explained C. Wheaton Vaughan, executive vp. "You have to be guided by what sponsors want and expect from their investments."

Commenting on the 14% return goal (71% answered this way), Packer Wilbur, president, said, "We would agree that returns on institutional quality real estate with appreciation and cash returns should exceed 14%—a range of 14% to 18% is realistic."

Mr. Vaughan added, "Our experience over the last five years has been in the 16% to 22% range." But he cautioned, "There are no guarantees that will continue."

The firm manages $125 million in real estate for individual clients. Mr. Vaughan explained that his figures were adjusted for leverage and assume a non-taxable client.

EXHIBIT A–5 *(continued)*

"With an 8% inflation rate, a 6% real return is about what I would expect from equities," Mr. Vaughan added. "This suggests that pension funds may be putting their real estate expectations in the equity range."

Sponsors forecasted an inflation rate of 8% to 10% over the next 10 years. Eighty-eight percent predicted that range, with a 99% response ratio. Furthermore they believe that inflation mandates portfolio diversification into less traditional investments. Sixty-five percent said this.

Not only do the sponsors believe that real estate offers features unavailable from other investment media, they are betting on long-term capital appreciation. Eighty-four percent answered this way, with a 97% response ratio.

Along the same vein, 88% believe that real estate will protect against erosion in portfolio values due to inflation.

The survey also asked sponsors how low a cash yield they would be willing to accept if yield must be sacrificed (ultimately) to achieve a superior rate of return.

On average they said 6.5%, with very low variance on the response, said Mr. Vaughan.

"I think 6.5% is realistic" noted Mr. Wilbur. "Six percent to 11% is realistic depending on the assets bought. Also bear in mind that most funds prefer unleveraged properties."

Mr. Vaughan added "10% yields on a free and clear basis are not as readily available as they were. But 6.5% is still well below what is attainable, generally a 8.5% to 9% range. On a leveraged basis it would be about 6% to 7%."

But Mr. Wilbur pointed out that yields on properties depend on a number of variables including property type. For instance, he said that "demand for shopping centers and warehouses has been softer, so yields are a bit higher. As a result there's an opportunity for increasing cash flows."

Sponsors also indicated in the survey that they are willing to accept lower liquidity in real estate to gain the benefits. Ninety-two percent answered this way with a 98% response ratio.

While saying it's critical for sponsors to take this point of view, Mr. Vaughan noted that "liquidity in real estate doesn't only mean market liquidity.

"You have to look at the economic structure inherent in the real estate market. For instance it takes time and money to find, negotiate, close, and manage a property. It doesn't make economic sense to buy it if you're going to sell in a year or two."

Fifty percent of the sponsors had 0% to 5% of their assets in real estate, with another 40% in the 5% to 10% range. The other 10% had 10% to 20% of assets in real estate. Seventy-seven percent indicated they intended to move up one notch, from 5% to 10% etc.

The sponsors gave a curious answer to a question asking whether they expected superior total returns from real estate compared with other investments. Sixty-seven percent (92% response ratio) said they did not expect superior results.

While the answer seems somewhat puzzling, it may suggest that sponsors are looking to real estate for its unique characteristics and to add diversification.

For instance, 84% (95% response ratio) said real estate will provide improved cash flows over time in contrast to fixed income. Further 88% said that real estate reduces portfolio volatility.

"The idea that stocks are automatically indexed to inflation is not necessarily holding

EXHIBIT A–5 *(concluded)*

true," noted Mr. Vaughan. "When inflation is high the stock market does not always rise—sponsors are looking for a hedge."

While sponsors are obviously interested in real estate, 74% (97% response ratio) indicated that they are not as knowledgeable about it as they would like to be.

As for Wilbur & Co., the firm intends to tap the pension market.

"We think the funds will want an independent pension-oriented manager staffed by a small team of professionals," said Mr. Vaughan.

Like his counterparts on the equity side, Mr. Vaughan believes that a small firm can move decisively, giving it an edge over the giant companies.

The firm has set up a group trust for potential clients. "We think this (group trust) has greater appeal than, for example, a limited partnership arrangement," noted Mr. Vaughan. "In effect the fiduciary responsibility is transferred from the pension fund to the investment manager."

EXHIBIT A–6

Real Estate Growth Projected

By James A. Ulmer, III

Pension fund investments in real estate, which have been moderately underweighted in the past to the exclusion of true real estate equities, will increase dramatically in the next 15 years.

The level of pension funds' investment in real estate equities over this time should rise from the current $5 billion to a substantial $350 billion by 1995 with the bulk of this asset growth in leveraged or unleveraged real estate equities.

While investment in commercial mortgages will increase more slowly, the combined growth should bring total real estate-related investments by pension funds up to a market weighting over the next 10 to 15 years.

The next few years will also be a period of considerable innovation as the traditional, passive buy and hold strategy of the commingled funds is supplanted by bond-substitute participating mortgage funds and equity-substitute ventures taking more aggressive management or development risks. New criteria will also be needed by fund sponsors in the way real estate managers are evaluated.

The fact that real estate will be the fastest growing area of pension fund investment in the 1980s should be neither surprising nor disturbing to fund sponsors. Real estate has been a major institutional investment for decades. The traditional form of investment, however, has been the long-term, self-amortizing, fixed-rate commercial mortgage.

While only a few tax-exempt investors have participated directly in this field—notably Teacher's Investment and Annuity, several of the state and municipal retirement systems, and certain union funds—considerable participation has been achieved through the pension funds' share of mortgages managed in the general accounts of insurance companies. At the end of 1979, these holdings amounted to:

EXHIBIT A–6 *(continued)*

Funds	*Mortg.*	*Real Estate Equities $ billions*	*% of Pension Assets*
Private funds	$ 3	2	2%
Public funds	5	2	4
Life companies*	30	1	22
Total	38	5	8

*Pension fund reserves share of total life company assets.

The next 15 years will see great growth in all kinds of pension fund assets and a particularly high growth rate in the real estate area. It should be recognized, though, that the overall economy will be in a period of high nominal growth during this period as well, and the share of pension fund assets or fund real estate assets should not increase as a proportion of the total economy to an extent which would produce a "crowding out" phenomenon in terms of product. This is illustrated below.

Projected Growth of Real Estate Assets Held by Pension Funds

	1979	*1985*	*1990*	*1995*
Commercial & multi-family real estate[1]	$1,023	$2,019	$3,559	$6,271
Financial & real estate assets[2]	$11,113	$20,786	$35,025	$59,020
Real estate percentage	9.2%	9.7%	10.2%	10.6%
Pension fund assets[3]	$555	$1,191	$2,258	$4,280
Share in real estate & mortgages	7.7%	9.0%	10.0%	10.6%
All pension fund real estate assets	$43	$107	$226	$454
Less mortgages[4]	38	57	80	112
Real estate equities in pension funds	5	50	146	342
Fund holdings as % of all real estate				
Including mortgages	4.2	5.3	6.4	7.2
Equity only	0.8	2.5	4.1	5.5

[1]12% growth rate, versus 11% nominal GNP growth.
[2]Federal Reserve flow of funds outstanding 11% growth rate.
[3]ICF, Inc. estimate for Dept. of Labor.
[4]7% growth rate from 1979 base.

The decade of the 70s was characterized by the growth of somewhat commodity-oriented commingled funds, largely devoted to the free-and-clear acquisition and holding of whole interests in major commercial properties. The first half of the 1980s, in contrast, is likely to be a time of considerable innovation, as new managers, products, and relationships evolve among plan sponsors, fund managers, and real estate professionals.

Several examples will suffice to identify these trends. The Koger Co. will sell clients of Endowment Management and Research up to a 50% interest in the company, which is engaged in owning and operating suburban office parks throughout the south; Lomas and

EXHIBIT A–6 *(concluded)*

Nettleton, the largest mortgage banker, is organizing a REIT which will make participating mortgages on new apartment developments to be constructed and managed by various real estate developers; several clients of a leading pension fund consultant committed to purchase an interest in a package of troubled properties being acquired from a major commercial bank by a leading real estate turnaround specialist.

These new ventures, and a variety of others in the works, have several characteristics which may tend to outmode the more passive policies of the traditional commingled fund. Bond-substitute real estate investments will take on more mortgage characteristics with a current coupon supplemented by a share of future gains. This has the advantage of leaving a property's depreciation in the hands of a taxable entity, where it has value, and of leaving the management of the property in the more innovative hands of the real estate professionals.

In using real estate as an equity substitute, client sponsors will be taking more fundamental risk in the expectation that this risk-taking will be rewarded. Development joint ventures, specialty properties, such as hotels, and investment in portfolios of properties requiring physical or management rehabilitation will be undertaken.

Real estate developers should be able to work easily in this environment. Developers have always given up the bulk of ownership to financial sources; rarely has a developer retained more than 15% of cash flow and 50% of depreciation and appreciation. The development of large-scale pools of capital may well work to the advantage of the quality real estate company, which will be in great demand as a partner-sponsor.

All of this increases the challenges facing a fund sponsor interested in diversifying into real estate.

While there are no 10 Commandments, the following criteria should help a sponsor determine the likelihood of success of an investment in a new venture:

- Does the manager understand the real estate business as a real estate professional?
- Is he able to present the investment program in terms a trustee can understand, and does he recognize the pension fund's objectives for the real estate segment of its portfolio?
- How experienced is the manager in the type of property or activity being considered by the fund?
- What conflicts of interest exist, bearing in mind that intelligently handled conflicts allow involvement with real estate professionals who are doing things, rather than simply talking about them?
- Are the fees in line with common industry practice, but are they high enough to ensure that the manager is able to attract and retain first-class talent in an entrepreneurially-oriented business?
- If the manager of a fund participates in the success of a project or fund, is the participation arrangement such that the interests of the manager and fund beneficiary are as closely allied as possible?

EXHIBIT A–7

Foreign Competition to Affect U.S. Real Estate

By Henri Alster

With the question of the unrelated business income tax issue being recently settled through Congressional action yet another obstacle was removed, enabling U.S. pension funds to acquire commercial properties on a less restrictive basis.

These domestic funds, however, are not alone at the starting gate.

The European pension funds, especially the Dutch and British, have been quietly but steadily acquiring prime U.S. commercial properties over the past few years.

Prompted by a dwindling supply of such properties in their own countries and spurred on by favorable market conditions here, their rate of acquisition has shown considerable growth. It is from them that their U.S. counterpart stands to discover a few surprising facts concerning this specialized type of investment.

Emulation of European investment patterns will have far-reaching consequences for the real estate industry as a whole.

Recent trends, such as the declining enchantment with shopping centers and the subtle shift of interest to office buildings as the better investment choice in real estate are happening for certain clear reasons.

Problems of leakage caused by long-term leasing to major tenants, often without escalation clauses, have become a financial burden to owners thanks to double digit inflation. The ever-increasing operating costs to the landlord are passed onto the smaller tenants who renew their leases more frequently.

There is, however, a limit to this cozy practice, and the limit is what the market will bear. It does not bear much when these smaller tenants, especially vulnerable to the ravages of "stagflation," watch their sales drop and costs continue to soar. Aside from overage clauses, which frequently carry offsets and other excuses to an appreciable degree, there is little in today's standard major tenant lease which provides adjustment to inflation, forcing the landlord and smaller tenants to pick up the extra costs.

This aberration is due to the unusual clout major tenants have as it is their agreement to lease that constitutes the cornerstone of shopping center development, enabling the developer to obtain mortgage financing from the lending institutions. This situation ceases to apply, however, because the tight money markets have now transferred the "clout" to where it naturally belongs, namely to the property's financier.

Having had to contend with high inflation in the past and having witnessed these trends in their own countries, investors in Europe have thus developed the strategy of devising a lease structure which seeks to provide the owner with certain built-in hedges against inflation—and then some. A European investor will therefore favor a lease which also provides index clauses and expense pass-through features, such as is increasingly typical in office buildings.

Another lease-related consideration, which attempts to do something about inflation but which contains a very important inherent trap, is the much-touted Consumer Price Index (CPI) clause. This clause, which allows rents to increase at a steady rate, merely helps to smooth out but does not create appreciation. It is sadly not the panacea with which investors ought to rest content, because if the market will not bear the increase, the rents will simply revert back to market level upon renewal.

EXHIBIT A–7 ***(continued)***

Land scarcity situations, a condition of which Europeans are very sensitive and Americans are, understandably, less so. It is an essential viewpoint of Europeans and one which enables them to look beyond initial low yields in favor of long-term appreciation.

This type of situation is epitomized by the case of Park Avenue in New York, where no more building can take place in the midtown district due to restrictive zoning laws. Such factors as its history, corporate tenancy and its attractive appearance all help to create its undeniable "snob appeal," which thus stimulates interest. It also stimulates prospective and present tenants to gladly pay in excess of $60 per square foot for the signal privilege of bearing what is deemed the "proper" address.

Rentals bear no relationship to construction costs because one can't build another structure on the 'Avenue.' It is thus the overriding consideration of being able to enter into a "monopoly" situation which creates enticement for the investor.

Conversely, to own and develop property in a location such as Houston, where space can be provided according to demand, has less appeal. While the facility may be easily filled, assuring the developer of low risks, the abundance of land and the ability to duplicate similar facilities ad infinitum tend to limit rental appreciation to inflation of construction costs.

Thus, an office building in the more exclusive part of town, the regional mall which is the only such property for miles around, and the warehouses located in and around major distribution centers, all enjoy a very unique and favored position in the European investor's eyes.

A special word about warehouses in relation to land scarcity considerations—since warehouses are strictly functional investments to the exclusion of such factors as aesthetics or snob appeal, land scarcity can only be created by actual considerations and not artificially induced ones. Their value rests on true scarcity situations where, in essence, there is no more land upon which to build in the specific area where such services are desired. Prime example: the New York/New Jersey harbor warehousing facilities.

Thus, historically and psychologically, European investors differ significantly in their approach to real estate investment in that they tend to place emphasis on two paramount considerations: land scarcity and appreciation.

This is in contrast to the traditional U.S. approach which treats real estate much as a financial instrument.

Alas, by favoring higher initial yields offered by long-term credit leases, a conservative investor agrees to forego any appreciation on his investment and may, in fact, have set himself up for serious inflationary losses.

Because of the disappearance of long-term fixed rate mortgages, the industry will experience increased institutionalization, as developers are now unable to mortgage out and will therefore become increasingly dependent on wealthy and liquid partners or purchasers for their projects.

Contract development—under which experienced property operators develop projects on behalf of institutional owners for an incentive fee on a free and clear basis—will emerge as a common way of life.

The ascendency of domestic pension funds as the most substantial landlords in North America will become pervasive. Tax shelter syndication will be stifled by the disappearance of ultra-high leverage. As occurred in the stock market, there will be greater concentration of ownership in fewer hands which will favor the more established development contracting firms and wipe out the marginal operators.

EXHIBIT A–7 *(concluded)*

It may result in larger average project sizes, greater uniformity, and less speculative recklessness. Over the years, professional sophistication will result in greater availability of trade information, a more formally organized industry and less fluctuation in real estate values.

Properties with existing straight interest mortgages will be exorbitant. Free and clear investors will enjoy greater respect, better prices, and the advantages associated with funding power.

EXHIBIT A–8

Strategic Issues in Realty

By John McMahan

The long anticipated, often delayed move of U.S. pension funds into real estate equities appears finally to be under way. A recent survey by Greenwich Research Associates indicated that 22% of pension funds responding reported they were currently investing in real estate equities, more than double the percentage in 1976. Among plans with assets in excess of $500 million, the percentage was even higher—54% compared to 35% in 1976. Reflecting this changing attitude, the commitment of pension fund portfolios to real estate equities has increased from approximately $1 billion in 1976 to over $5 billion today.

The plan manager considering real estate is faced with a variety of concerns including: What proportion of the total portfolio should be in real estate? What is the minimum size of real estate portfolio to achieve diversification? Should leverage be used in building the real estate portfolio? What are the risks associated with various stages of the development process? When should properties be sold out of the portfolio? These and other strategic planning issues are addressed in this and two subsequent articles.

Once a fund has decided to invest in real estate, the first concern is the amount of the total portfolio to be devoted to this new capital market.

One approach is to make some "range of investment" assumptions based on common sense and historical experience of other institutions.

On the lower side of the range, it would appear that any new capital market should comprise at least 10% of the total portfolio in order to justify the management time necessary to understand the nature of the asset and to monitor its performance successfully over a reasonable period of time.

In establishing the upper end of the range, we can look to the experience of institutions which have been investing in real estate for many years and have, presumably, a better understanding of the performance of the asset.

British pension funds, as of 1979, had approximately 20% of their assets in real estate. Several of the larger Dutch pension funds have reportedly invested as much as 30% to 35% of their assets in real estate. If mortgages are included, U.S. life insurance companies had approximately 31% of their assets in real estate as of the end of 1979.

EXHIBIT A–8 *(continued)*

This approach would suggest that a reasonable range for real estate investment in a pension fund portfolio is 10% to 30%, with initial consideration toward the lower end of the range and increasing over time, depending upon the experience of the fund and its overall investment objectives.

It is necessary at this point to consider the problems of non-systematic risk diversification inherent in real estate. There are several areas of concern.

Geographical Diversification: Individual assets should not be unduly concentrated in a single geographical area where the portfolio would be exposed to substantial loss as a result of a natural disaster, a major deterioration in the local economy, or an adverse regulatory environment. While a portion of physical damage from natural disaster can be recovered through insurance proceeds, this takes time and may reduce portfolio earnings for a period.

In some situations insurance may be available only at prohibitive costs, or it may not be available at all. Also, a major natural disaster may have an adverse effect on the local economy.

It is also necessary to diversify geographically in order to reduce substantial risk from a weakened or disrupted local economy. Since commercial real estate depends upon employment (office, industrial) and individual earnings (retail, hotel) it is essential that the portfolio not be unduly concentrated in a single local economy. This is particularly true if the local economy is highly dependent upon one firm or industry.

A final reason to diversify geographically is portfolio exposure created by variations in state and local regulatory laws and procedures. Since land use is largely regulated at the local level, it's possible to have wide differences among jurisdictions which may affect market value of the assets. It is also possible that state courts may interpret laws affecting real estate in a different manner.

Product Diversification: Also essential is diversification of a real estate portfolio based on the type of real estate asset, such as offices, industrial properties, and shopping centers. A high degree of concentration in any one product type could expose the portfolio to deterioration in value as a result of changes in the national economy, lifestyle preferences, or governmental policy.

As an example, the anticipated shift in national emphasis from consumption to savings in the 1980s may reduce the demand for shopping centers and increase the demand for office and industrial facilities. A portfolio with an excessive concentration of shopping centers will no doubt be under greater pressure than one that is well diversified.

Lease Diversification: The current yield, and in some cases the appreciation potential, of a real estate portfolio is defined in large measure by the leases that have been or will be executed. It is necessary, therefore, to diversify leases based on credit and terms in order to avoid exposing the portfolio to undue risk.

A good "mix" of tenants is important in order to provide both deflationary and inflationary protection. Strong national credit tenants provide a sound base for the portfolio and assure a continuing income stream during periods of recession.

Strong credit tenants, however, can generally avoid or mitigate landlord attempts to "pass through" increases in costs through consumer price index clauses, percentage of sales, and other arrangements. They also tend to "lock in" their operating advantages for relatively long periods of time (10 to 20 years).

Smaller, local tenants have less leverage in negotiating leases and generally will accept inflationary pass-throughs and shorter lease terms. The income stream generated

EXHIBIT A–8 *(continued)*

by this portion of the portfolio provides "upside" protection in an inflationary environment.

Establishing desirable diversification goals and achieving them are two quite different things. The pension fund manager buying into an existing, well-diversified pooled fund does not have a problem. The difficulty arises in connection with a new pooled fund or a separately managed account.

The problem is created because real estate, unlike securities, requires a certain "threshold" of investment funds in order to acquire individual assets. As an example, the minimum amount of funds (non-leveraged) required to acquire good quality, investment-grade properties in most urban areas today is $2 million for an industrial building, $3.5 million for an office building, and $5 million for a shopping center.

Since the goal has generally been to purchase a 100% interest in the property, the investor is faced with the issue of determining at what stage in its development the portfolio is diversified. Some pension funds, however, are now negotiating a less than 100% position through joint venture and similar arrangements. While it is difficult to resolve this matter with great precision, it is possible to establish some rough guidelines through common sense reasoning.

For simplicity, let's assume that, as a result of an evaluation of the overall economy and the objectives of the pension fund, it is decided to diversify a real estate portfolio with the product mix presented in Table 1.

Let's further assume that the average current yield on each investment is 8.5% and a "substantial loss" for the portfolio would be to forego the current yield for the total portfolio for a maximum of one year as a result of a loss in the income-generating ability of a single asset.

It is also necessary to make an assumption regarding the maximum loss that could reasonably be expected from any one asset. Since it is generally possible to ensure against most natural disasters, the most likely risk is from a loss of market value.

During the 1973–75 recession, one of the worst for real estate, troubled investment-grade properties sold under "fire sale" conditions at discounts of between 20% and 30%. For purposes of this analysis, however, let's assume that a "worst case" scenario would involve a market loss of 50% of asset value.

Table 2 illustrates the nature of the risk exposure for the hypothetical portfolio under these assumptions. With the purchase of the first property, the portfolio is exposed to a possible loss of 50% of value. This is reduced with each successive purchase until, with the purchase of the sixth property, the loss of value associated with a single property is 8.3%, which is roughly equivalent to the average yield on the total portfolio. This would

TABLE 1
Product Mix

	% of Portfolio	*Minimum Investment $ millions*	*Weighted Average*
Industrial	10%	2.0	.20
Office	50	3.5	1.75
Shopping center	40	5.0	2.00
Total	100%	10.5	$3.95

EXHIBIT A–8 *(concluded)*

indicate that a real estate portfolio reaches a "critical mass" of diversification when it contains approximately six properties. We will subsequently refer to this as the "core" portfolio.

TABLE 2
Minimum Property Holding for Active Diversification

No. of Properties	*Average Investment*	*Portfolio Investment ($ millions)*	*Maximum Loss Exposure*	*% of Total Portfolio*
1	$4.0	$4.0	$2.0	50.0
2	4.0	8.0	2.0	25.0
3	4.0	12.0	2.0	16.0
4	4.0	16.0	2.0	12.5
5	4.0	20.0	2.0	10.0
6	4.0	24.0	2.0	8.3

Source: John McMahan Associates.

EXHIBIT A–9

Funds Hit the $6 Billion Mark

By Linda Sojacy

NEW YORK—Open-end commingled real estate funds of banks and insurance companies continued to lure pension and profit-sharing assets last year, bringing in about $1.8 billion in net contributions from existing and new clients.

The funds attracted so much attention by the tax exempt sponsors that the market value of the assets of the 16 largest funds hit about $6.1 billion for the end of 1980, versus about $3.5 billion for the end of 1979, a whopping 75.7% increase.

Spokesmen for the various funds indicated the investment strategies of the funds were in line with past philosophies, concentrating investments in office-type facilities, shopping centers and industrial projects.

In fact, Prudential's PRISA I account, the country's largest commingled real estate fund, with market value of assets at $2.5 billion, purchased 67 properties in its 1980 fiscal year, with the majority of them—40—in industrial/warehouse situations.

Most funds continued to focus on existing properties, acquiring 100% equity ownership. Property development is still a stranger to most of the funds, although at least two real estate commingled funds, those at Wachovia Bank & Trust and North Carolina National Bank & Trust, have definitely favored property development.

Via the commingled funds, pension sponsors virtually have their assets in every corner of the U.S. The real estate investments of the commingled funds last year appear to be almost equally divided among the South, West, East and Midwest, with the West having a slight edge over the other regions.

EXHIBIT A–9 *(continued)*

Following is a description of the various funds and some of their investments for the last year.

Aetna's net new money into its commingled real estate separate account was $160 million during 1980. The total market value of the assets was $433 million at the end of 1980, compared with $187 million at the end of 1979. Net investment income was $22 million, the credited appreciation was $19.4 million, mortgages payable was $42 million, and the balance of the difference between the 1979 market value figure and the 1980 figure was in miscellaneous.

The year's purchases were highlighted by the acquisition of a package of five shopping centers in the Midwest. The total market value of the centers was slightly over $80 million. The fund's cash investment was $51 million. The remainder was leveraged. Another purchase was two hotels in the Southeast.

Bank of America's net new money into its real estate fund last year was about $4 million. The total market value of the fund was $68 million at the end of 1980, compared with $62 million for the prior year. Net investment income was $4 million, plus $1.4 million in appreciation.

During 1980, the real estate fund bought an office building in Cherry Hill, N.J. for $2 million. The deal was equity ownership. The fund also made substantial capital improvements in several buildings. Two of the most significant were a rejuvenation of a Seattle shopping center and capital improvements on a large warehouse distribution center in Fort Worth.

Richard Clark, vp, explained the total increase in net assets last year was $9.2 million, bringing the net asset figure to $58 million (excluding debt). The increase, he said, was comprised of the net investment income, appreciation, and net new money coming into the fund. He also said a $3.2 million loan and other liabilities were paid off in 1980.

Citibank started its real estate equity fund in January 1980. At year end the fund had $175 million in assets, and six properties. Money into the fund was $130 million.

The fund's major investment last year, according to vp Kenneth Simpson, was in two existing high rise office buildings in Century City, Ca. The fund's investment was $50 million, out of a total investment of $140 million. R & B Development Co., Los Angeles, put up some money, and the remainder was third-party debt.

Continental Illinois National Bank and Trust Co. of Chicago has not been accepting money from new clients in the past year for its Real Estate Fund No. 1, and has not been marketing it during that time. It did, however, receive $700,000 from existing clients in 1980, and received $4 million in net investment income.

Larry Ginnegaw, marketing manager for trust investment services, explained "We're evaluating all the approaches pension funds are now taking to real estate, and all of the capabilities we have and we're trying to determine what structure to use."

At the end of 1980, the fund's market value of assets was $47 million, compared with $49 million for 1979. No properties were added in 1980.

Crocker Bank had $11 million in net new money flow into its real estate equity fund last year. Total market value of the assets was about $62 million, versus $44 million for 1979. Investment income was $4 million.

During last year, the fund entered into a purchase agreement for a shopping center in the Seattle area. It committed a total of $11 million subject to the completion of construction.

EXHIBIT A–9 ***(continued)***

Another investment was $6 million for an office building in Dallas which was also a purchase agreement. Both of these investments were equity ownership.

Arthur De Boer, senior vp, explained last year Crocker set up separate account transactions for individual larger pension funds. Market value of assets totaled $27 million. Equity positions in real estate will be taken through different vehicles, such as joint ventures development programs and convertible mortgages.

Equitable Life's Separate Account No. 8 attracted $393 million in net new contributions last year, plus $95 million in investment income.

Net assets at the end of 1980 were $1.424 billion versus $903 million at the end of 1979.

During last year, the account acquired 29 properties. Of those, five were joint ventures with a developer, and 24 were 100% owned by the fund. The majority, 15, were in industrial properties. Fifteen were also in the Sun Belt.

The two largest acquisitions, according to account executive Don Conover, were $52 million for the AmeriFirst office building in Miami, and $68 million for the One Boston Place office building in Boston. Both are 100% owned by the fund.

First National Bank of Boston's market value of its pooled real estate fund at the end of 1980 was $99 million, compared with $47 million the prior year.

Of the $52 million increase, $45 million was from net new money into the fund, and the majority of the balance was from reinvestment income.

One of the fund's major investments last year was a joint venture with a developer in a suburban office park in Connecticut—two existing buildings, a third building which was subsequently completed, and a fourth building to be completed in late 1981. The fund has 70% equity interest, while the developer has 30%. The fund's total commitment to that project will be about $15 million, purchasing the buildings as they're completed.

Another major investment was a $12.5 million commitment in a suburban office building in Massachusetts, to be completed in March.

The First National Bank of Chicago's real estate fund had a total market value of assets of $295 million at the end of last year, compared with $215 million for 1979. Net new contributions into the fund were $42 million; net investment income was $20 million. The fund also had a $16 million net gain from realized and unrealized appreciation.

Last year, it funded about $9 million each to two multi-tenant office buildings in the form of first mortgages; one building was in the Denver metropolitan area, and one was in the Chicago vicinity. Kurt Freundlich, head of the acquisitions division and vp, FNB-Chicago, said the final price on the properties will be higher. They will be owned by the fund within a year.

"We don't typically make mortgage loans as an investment," Mr. Freundlich said. "We do them as short-term steps to full ownership."

John Hancock Mutual Life Insurance Co. had $153 million in net new contributions funneled into its ERA equity real estate account last year.

Year-end assets were $353 million against $180 million at the end of 1979. Investment income was $20 million.

Two of the largest investments were equity ownership in a warehouse complex in Ohio for about $22 million, and an office building complex in Texas, with an investment of just under $23 million.

The fund made between 18 and 20 purchases last year, with the concentration in industrial properties.

EXHIBIT A–9 ***(continued)***

Richard Troy, vp, group pension department, said the "outstanding commitments for properties to be taken down in 1981 have changed a little, with more concentration in office buildings."

North Carolina National Bank's real estate fund brought in approximately $24 million in net new money last year. Total market value of assets was about $32 million, versus $7 million at the 1979 year-end.

Several investments were made last year, including an initial $2 million to acquire land to develop an 80 acre business park in Charlotte, N.C. The fund has sold 11 of those acres.

Two of the projects planned for the remaining acreage are the construction of a 100,000 square foot office distribution facility, and 160,000 square feet of pure office space.

The fund expects to have $50 million invested in that business park over the next five years, according to Floyd Boyce, vp, manager of the real estate investment area.

In addition to other investments, the fund acquired 53 acres in Raleigh, N.C. for a business park, with an expected completion cost of $25 million to $30 million in the next five years.

The fund also sold 59 acres of property in an industrial park in Charlotte it has owned since 1974. The price per acre was in excess of $20,000.

The bank also manages separate real estate accounts for individual pension funds who do not want real estate investments on a commingled basis. In 1980, it started a $25 million office park for one account, and also committed $9 million for two office buildings to be built in Raleigh participating with a developer.

Prudential's PRISA I had $577 million in net new money for 1980; the fund did not accept any money in December.

Total market value of assets at the end of 1980 was $2.5 billion, compared with $1.5 billion for the end of 1979.

Income from investments for fiscal 1980 (ended Sept. 30) was $112 million, after management fees.

PRISA I acquired complete equity ownership in 67 properties across the country in its 1980 fiscal year, with the bulk of them—40—in industrial/warehouse type facilities.

Among the acquisitions was an agricultural property in Arkansas, the fund's second such investment in its 10 year existence.

PRISA II, a non-diversified equity real estate portfolio, became operational in July 1980, according to Bob Dunphy, Prudential vp.

PRISA II took in $75 million in July, and has acquired only one property so far—the Hyatt on Union Square in San Francisco. In December, the fund took in another $75 million for the purpose of acquiring six shopping centers in partnership with May Centers. The centers are in four states. Mr. Dunphy said they would be acquired in the first quarter. Market value of PRISA II's assets was $165 million.

Smith Barney Real Estate Corp. had $15 million in net new money flow into its real estate fund. Market value at year end was $48 million, compared with $25 million the prior year.

Investments last year included $7 million for a 225,000 square foot shopping center in the Philadelphia area, and $9 million for a 525 unit apartment complex in Laurel, Md. Stephen Treadway, vp, explained the shopping center acquisition was about 50% cash, 50% debt; the apartment complex was $4 million cash, and the remainder mortgage debt.

EXHIBIT A–9 *(concluded)*

Travelers received $80 million in its Separate Account R during the last year. Of that, 80% was directed into property ownerships, and 20% was for real estate debt with equity features. In July, 1980, Travelers separated the fund into an equity fund and a debt fund and gave its clients the option of putting money into either fund or a mixture of both.

The market value of the assets in Separate Account R at the end of 1980 was $187 million versus $108 million for the end of 1979. Net investment income was $12.5 million.

Tom Keating, vp, said major investments last year included $6.5 million for an office warehouse in Fullerton, Ca., and $5 million for an office warehouse in Elk Grove, Il.

During 1980, property investments ranged from $2.5 million to $5 million. However, Mr. Keating said "at the tail end of 1980, we increased the maximum size to $20 million because of the growth of the fund. For current acquisitions, we're looking for $5 million to $20 million."

Wachovia Bank & Trust Co. received $5 million in net new money into its real estate fund last year. Total market value of the assets was $89 million, compared with $73 million the prior year. Income plus appreciation totaled $11 million.

The fund earmarked most of the money coming into it for its ongoing development programs, which are primarily industrial and industrial office-type parks.

During 1980, investments included an initial investment of $4 million in an industrial park property in Houston, a three- to five-year development program.

Another investment was $4 million for the development of a San Diego industrial office park. The first of three phases has been completed. Robert Smedley, vp, said the fund's activities in 1980 "were all involved in development areas. The acquisition of existing properties was not as attractive as the development of properties."

Wells Fargo's real estate equity fund received $40 million in net new money last year. The assets totaled $103 million, versus $59 million for 1979. Investment income of $4 million was held in liquid assets.

Last year, the fund put $15 million into office buildings in Texas, California, and Arizona, all equity ownership; $15 million in industrial buildings in the same states, and $10 million in shopping centers in those same states, plus other Western states. All were equity ownership.

Thomas Richardson, vp, said forward commitments accounted for 80% of the investments made last year, whereby the fund made a forward commitment to buy the properties which will be developed for it. He said the fund was more into forward commitments last year than it was in the past, and he planned to continue to emphasize them.

Part X

Pension Topics

Brookmere, Inc.

Brookmere, Inc., was a rapidly growing, privately owned firm of medium size. Sales and profits from internal growth and diversification were doubling about every eight years, and several cash acquisitions of moderate scope had assisted in this growth. Return on book equity was above average, even though the firm had a modest long-term debt-to-equity ratio. Brookmere had established relatively protected positions in its various markets, and the continued need for its type of products seemed relatively secure, even encouraging. The business was somewhat cyclical, but much less so than for most manufacturing firms.

In January 1977, Dr. George Wayword, an economist at a well-known private research institute and one of Brookmere's directors, was named to the firm's pension committee. By training and experience, Dr. Wayword had some familiarity with portfolio management theory and practice. He knew little, however, about managing pension fund portfolios. He knew, on the one hand, that certain prudent-man requirements for investing pension fund portfolios would set some upper limit as to how risky the portfolio should be. On the other hand, it seemed likely that the company's cost for funding this pension plan would be minimized if the portfolio earned a relatively high rate of return. Dr. Wayword, however, was not sure how fluctuations in the value of the portfolio might affect the pension-funding costs of the firm. As the first step in performing his new responsibilities, he decided to investigate how pension funding worked at Brookmere. From the review, he hoped

---

This case was prepared by a professor of the Colgate Darden Graduate School of Business Administration of the University of Virginia as a basis for class discussion.

to learn more about the income/risk considerations involved in managing the portfolio—in setting its objectives and evaluating its performance.

Brookmere's pension plan was designed to be competitive—that is, sufficient to attract the best-qualified people for the variety of skilled positions the company required. Key people were offered other inducements that were probably more important than the pension plan in winning and holding their loyalty.

The rationale underlying Brookmere's present pension fund plan and management's attitude toward it had been explained to Dr. Wayword by Mr. Lloyd Phignumb, financial vice president of the firm, as follows:

> As you know, from 1948 to 1974, we had a final-average pay plan which was only minimally integrated with social security. Originally, it was intended to supplement what was considered to be a meager social security benefit so that employees could live out their retired lives in some measure of dignity. However, since then, Congress has seen fit to improve social security benefits materially, and [the employees] have more than kept pace with inflation. In the early 1970s, it became obvious to us that, as social security benefits continued to improve, the average employee would ultimately be able to retire with a greater after-tax combined benefit than his pre-retirement after-tax take-home pay.
>
> Considering all the priorities (current salary levels, adequate medical insurance, life insurance, etc.) relating to compensation, that situation didn't seem to make a whole lot of sense, since it skewed the compensation program too much toward the older or retired employee rather than toward the younger people whom we might desire to attract and keep. Moreover, the future cost implications were staggering, assuming continued inflation.
>
> Therefore, we converted to a career-average plan designed to integrate fully with social security. Personally, I think this balanced the equities. For many years, social security provided a benefit of about 30 percent of pre-tax final pay, but over time the ratio had crept up above 35 and was heading for 40 percent. The new law, which [then President] Carter just signed, is intended eventually to bring that ratio down to 33 percent and hold it there. However, I have my doubts that it will really stay there, given the voting record of Congress.
>
> When we changed the plan in 1974, the changes, for most employees, particularly long-service employees, were on balance quite positive. For example, an employee with 35–40 years service now earns a larger pension than one with 20 years of service. Also, we added survivors' benefits and vesting. Vesting, of course, was later mandated by ERISA.
>
> For these reasons, I don't believe we will improve plan benefits in the foreseeable future. If we ever do, the improvement is likely to be prospective, rather than retroactive. Moreover, other types of fringe benefits such as more life insurance or a long-term disability income plan seem to me to represent a higher priority need.
>
> If we acquire a company that does not have a pension plan and we decide to put one in, our wisest decision would be to give no credit for past service. That would avoid the problem of, in effect, paying a lot more for the acquisition than the seller obtained. Putting in the Brookmere pension plan (without crediting past service) results in an increase in the prospective operating cost by a factor of perhaps 5 percent of payroll. In a situation where [acquired companies'] payrolls are 40 percent of total revenues, the impact is a 2 percent immediate reduction in the margin. If the perceived benefit of [our adding] a pension plan and better management can't overcome that hurdle [the reduction in our margin], we probably ought not to do the

acquisition anyway. And, of course, we don't really have to put in as good a plan as the Brookmere plan with its 1.3/2.3 percent schedule. Perhaps a flat .75 percent would be good enough in many cases.

Pension costs tended to run 7 percent to 9 percent of total annual payroll, above and beyond social security costs. Pension costs also amounted to approximately 10 percent of profits before pension fund costs and taxes. Each year an actuary determined the pension plan's minimum funding requirement by using certain prespecified formulas. Management could fund more than this minimum without deferring the tax-deductibility of the pension payments into a future year, and tended to do so on a moderate scale. Some "pre-funding" seemed desirable to management to keep the accumulated fund level from becoming inadequate, either because of poor portfolio results or because of actuarial errors (perhaps at a point when the firm might be suffering a profit or financial squeeze). Partly as a result of the pre-funding policy, Brookmere's pension costs were not rising materially as a percentage of payroll or of profits, unlike the circumstances of many other firms.

Even so, Mr. Phignumb expressed concern about the actuarial assumptions. As he noted in a 1972 memorandum to the firm's president, "Unfortunately, we cannot have much confidence in the estimates of the adequacy of size of the pension fund and of the annual funding, since these estimates are derived from an unrealistically low assumption of the future rate of increase in salary levels, offset more or less by an unrealistically low assumption of turnover and of the earning rate on the pension funds." Since 1972, poor performance of the security markets in general had raised further questions about the assumed equality between pension fund earnings and payments. Dr. Wayword recalled seeing estimated returns (total compound rates of return including appreciation or depreciation) for the last 10 years: a quality corporate bond index returned 6.7 percent per year, whereas a broad-based stock index had returned 5.4 percent. Inflation, in contrast, had averaged 6.0 percent over the same time span.

Brookmere's Pension Plan

This pension plan was designed to supplement social security retirement benefits, for which the company and each employee both contributed 5.85 percent of the employee's salary up to the wage base (of $16,500 during 1977). The wage base was scheduled to increase in the future as shown in Exhibit 1.

From time to time, the company's plan had been amended in a way that affected the determination of benefits retroactively. Such an action could create a prior-service liability, which then had to be funded in subsequent years.

Every employee 25 years of age or older who had one year of service was covered by the plan.[1] Each year, beginning with 1974, an employee accrued a benefit equal to 1.3 percent of his or her W-2 earnings up to the social security wage base, plus 2.3 percent of W-2 earnings in excess of this wage base. Upon retirement the dollar amount of these annual accrued benefits due an employee

[1]One exception was a new, small division that operated on such thin margins that a pension program was not at the moment feasible.

were totaled, and the total constituted the annual benefits that this individual would receive during retirement. Although the normal retirement age was 65, there were provisions for both early and late retirement. An employee's benefits became fully vested after 10 years of service, credited after age 22, and certain survivor benefits existed as well. Benefits had also accrued prior to 1974, but on a different basis. The company bore the entire cost necessary to fund these benefits.

An employee who worked for 30 years in the firm and accrued a benefit of 1.67 percent of his average annual salary would receive a retirement payment equal to 50 percent of his average salary per year before considering social security benefits. During a period of rapid inflation, these retirement benefits might come to look inadequate. Social security benefits, which were adjusted upward from time to time by Congress and which would not be taxable, would influence the adequacy of an employee's retirement income, but in unpredictable ways. The real value of the company's payments to retired employees decreased under inflationary conditions. If the plan were amended retroactively as a result of these erosive effects, a large prior-service obligation could be created. The company's plan had undergone certain retroactive changes, but management at Brookmere was not concerned about the prior-service liability, even after a decade of rapid inflation.

The pension portfolio itself was valued in three ways. The first and most obvious way was to total the "market value" of the securities in the portfolio. Since almost all of the securities in the Brookmere pension fund portfolio were actively traded, the market value could be assessed accurately. A second method totaled the cost value of the securities in the portfolio. This "book value" method did not consider unrealized gains and losses of portfolio securities, but did consider reinvested income and realized gains or losses. The third method "adjusted" the market value so that, when "performance" of the fund exceeded the 6 percent actuarial assumption, the excess (up to 20 percent) was put into an adjustment account that could be drawn upon when "performance" was less than the actuarial assumption. However, the adjustment account was not permitted to be negative. Thus, in a series of low-performance years, the actual market value was used to calculate the funding requirement. These valuation procedures played a role in determining the company's minimum funding obligation each year.

Determination of Annual Minimum Normal Cost

Legally, Brookmere had several options for computing the annual minimum funding requirement. However, since 1948 when the first pension plan was adopted, the firm had determined the pension cost using the "entry-age normal cost" method. This method had two advantages: it tended to prorate more costs to early years and thus reduced the danger of underfunding, and it tended to produce more stable costs as a percentage of payroll. Dr. Wayword did not plan to investigate other methods of computing obligations since management strongly preferred this more conservative funding approach. Dr. Wayword wondered, however, what implications this method might have in determining portfolio management objectives.

The actual determination of minimum funding requirements was somewhat complicated. First of all, there were two types of funding costs—normal and prior service. Normal costs were more straightforward than prior-service, which could be affected by three types of events. In effect, normal costs represented the percentage of compensation that had to be contributed to the pension fund to provide the retirement benefits accrued each year by present employees. Normal costs were computed as follows, using a highly sophisticated computer program developed by the company's actuaries:

1. For each employee, the company maintained records indicating (*a*) date of birth, (*b*) date of hire, (*c*) sex, and (*d*) current (W-2) earnings. These data were then sorted into more than 80 age/sex groups—one for each of the 40 groups for men and women between 25 and 65 years of age, plus additional ones for employees over 65 but not yet retired.
2. The earnings for each of these groups were then computed for each of the remaining service years up to age 65. (Only the current year was considered for those over 65.) Earnings were assumed to increase at what management considered to be a conservative rate of 5 percent per year. The schedule also assumed certain termination rates based on historical experience and a realistic mortality schedule, so that the total wages expected to be paid to existing employees grew by less than 5 percent. These data were used to determine total payroll costs to be paid for existing employees for each of the next 40 years.
3. The stream of present and future wage payments was then discounted to present value at the assumed rate of return of 6 percent per year for the portfolio. This present value estimate became the denominator for the normal-cost calculation.
4. The actuary next computed the amount of the annual accrual of pension payment "rights," based on the forecasted average salaries, for each wage group. In this calculation, the social security wage base was considered to increase 3 percent per year (a seemingly conservative estimate). These rights were accumulated to the retirement age to determine the prospective incremental annual retirement benefits. Allowance was made for vesting rights of employees and death benefits for individuals dying before retirement age. Retirement payments (or other benefits) were then scheduled for each age/sex group according to mortality tables. The payment of benefits for each group was then totaled by year.
5. The stream of benefit payments was then discounted at the assumed rate of return on the portfolio (6 percent) to determine the present value of the benefits to be earned.
6. The normal-cost percentage was determined by dividing item 5 by item 3. This percentage was then applied to the current annual payroll of employees covered by the pension plan to determine the normal cost.

Dr. Wayword could see that the normal-cost estimates were based on some judgments in addition to the usual actuarial data that did not seem to relate closely to recent economic conditions. Brookmere's management did not, he knew, determine these judgments; rather, the actuary did. If management insisted that the rate of salary increase be changed upward, the actuary would insist on a change in the assumed earnings rate on the portfolio; however, the net effect would be inconsequential.

As Dr. Wayword viewed it, the actuary's normal-cost estimates were also based on a commonly assumed long-term rate of inflation—about 2 to 3 percent. The actuary seemed to be assuming a 2–3 percent real merit increase or "productivity" gain in salaries. One study reported productivity gains of 2.7 percent over the long run in Brookmere's major industry. The real rate of return on the portfolio would consequently be assumed to be about 3 to 4 percent.

Dr. Wayword knew that the annual compound rate of inflation as measured by the cost of living index had averaged 2.2 percent from 1926 to 1976. It had, of course, been more substantial in recent years, and the short-term expectational estimates were running 5 to 6 percent per year.

The salary-increase assumption did not seem to be material as long as the plan was not amended. If, for example, salaries increased 10 percent this year, and the normal cost was computed on the old basis, the normal-cost percentage would increase only slightly. The present value of both salaries and benefits would increase, but the ratio would only change to the extent that a higher fraction of future salaries exceeded the social security base. The changing social security wage base—enacted and potential—would provide an offset. The dollar level of contribution would, of course, increase with an increase in total qualified earnings.

The real problem with inflation, as Dr. Wayword saw it, was that the benefits might have to be revised upward, even though management did not expect to do this. Benefits, in effect, were tied to the average salary, which for long-term employees would be the salary they had received 10 to 20 years ago (salary weights considered). If inflation continued, the step down from active salary status to retirement income status would be more substantial than expected. The benefits would erode further as retirement continued, if inflation remained high. Adjustments in social security benefits might be made to counteract inflation, but predicting these changes complicated the process of estimating the adequacy of the pension fund benefits even more.

Dr. Wayword knew that there was a trend toward fixing benefits not to the average salary during employment, but rather to the average salary in the last five years of employment. Brookmere's management believed such plans would result in very high future benefits and pension costs and believed its "career-average" plan was more feasible financially, given the tendency of Congress to improve social security benefits over time. Under a "final-average pay plan," the salary-increase assumption would be much more critical in determining the ultimate adequacy of funding than for the "career-average" plan.

The other side of the coin was, of course, the assumed rate of return on the portfolio, but further investigation would be necessary in order to analyze this factor.

Determination of Annual Minimum Prior-Service Cost

Prior-service costs arose in three ways:

1. Whenever a pension plan was introduced or extended to a new group of employees so that benefits were credited for past service, an unfunded "past-service" liability arose. Historic earnings of current employees were separated into the age/sex group classifications, and formula benefits were calculated. These benefits were then projected to determine annual retirement payments at various future dates. The cash obligations were then discounted to determine their present value. The present value represented the unfunded past-service obligation, which had to be amortized over a 40-year or less period.

Almost all of Brookmere's present employees were now covered by its pension plan; the exception was a small recent acquisition. While the pension and past-service costs of adding a pension plan for this new acquisition would be material to its profit picture (especially given its older work force), the overall effect on Brookmere would not be great. Management was still sorting out this acquisition and selling off parts of it, and felt, therefore, that instituting a pension program now would be premature. Pension costs had now been recognized, as already noted, as a factor to consider in evaluating any new acquisition.

2. If the pension fund were amended in such a way as to increase retroactively the amount of benefits accrued by employees, a "prior-service" liability would be created. (The amendments might only or also affect the future normal cost.) The present value of the incremental historic benefits would have to be determined, and this prior-service liability would be amortized over 30 years at the most.

The existing plan was probably adequate for a moderate inflationary environment—that is, one in which only moderate changes seemed likely. As noted, however, the high level of recent inflation made the adequacy of the present plan questionable.

3. If a net loss resulted from failure to achieve actuarial assumptions, this actuarial loss increased the normal cost including past- and prior-service costs. Although a net loss could theoretically arise as a result of the failure of any assumption (e.g., lower employee-termination rates, greater longevity for Brookmere's retired employees, and so on), in practice these assumptions were determined with appropriate actuarial conservatism. Errors, if any, were not likely to be material. The major exception was the assumed rate of return on the portfolio. Lower returns could significantly affect normal costs in any given year.

In practice, Brookmere funded slightly more than the minimum requirement. Past- and prior-service costs were being written off over 30 years, beginning in 1974. No significant losses had been experienced as yet.

Recent Changes

The pension reform act (ERISA) had created some further options and problems for pension fund management. First, not only losses (market value relative to actuarial value) but also gains had to be written off. Those using the entry-age normal-cost method with frozen initial liability for prior-service costs had an optional way of calculating current funding requirements as described below and as illustrated in Exhibit 2.

The present value of all retirement benefits was first computed for present employees (including past as well as future service), for retired employees, and for terminated employees with vested benefits. From this total, two items were deducted: (1) the adjusted market value of the assets and (2) the unfunded past-service liability. For the most recent year, the adjusted market value of the assets equaled the market value of the assets (determined for the year as of January 1, 1976) plus the funding commitment for the prior year, which was not paid into the fund until March 15th. (A third adjustment will be discussed later.) The unfunded past-service liability represented that part of past- and prior-service obligations that had not yet been funded (unamortized). The "present value of future normal-cost payments," as the figure resulting from this calculation was called, differed somewhat from the definition previously given.

The present value of future-covered compensation was calculated (as shown in Exhibit 2). The normal-cost percentage was determined by multiplying the normal-cost payments by the annual-covered compensation.

Prior-service costs were being amortized at the current rate of $690,000 per year, with 28 years remaining on January 1, 1976. The total recommended annual contribution was the sum of normal costs plus the amortization of prior-service expenses. Exhibit 2 shows how these costs were calculated for each of Brookmere's five divisions, and how the proposed pension-fund contribution compared with minimum contributions required under ERISA. Exhibit 2 was prepared by the actuary during 1976, and the board of directors appropriated the funds in its December meeting for payment the following March. The board generally followed the recommended contribution plan.

Dr. Wayword first observed that, at the current rate, past-service liabilities would decline as a percentage of covered payroll whenever payrolls increased. Other factors being equal, then, pension contributions should decline as a percentage of covered payroll in the future. If inflation necessitated a retroactive adjustment to benefits, the effect on normal costs might be more severe than on past-service costs, both relative to current levels.

The method of calculating the portfolio market value could affect the adequacy of the minimum funding requirement more seriously than possible problems with retroactive adjustments. Dr. Wayword recalled that market conditions were fairly normal as of January 1, 1976. If, instead, the market had been depressed so that values were, say, 30 percent below normal on that date, he estimated the effect on pension contribution requirements would be (in thousands):

Present value of future retirement benefits	$ 42,508
Less adjusted market value (70% of actual)	12,444
Less unfunded past-service liability	8,426
Equals present value of future normal-cost payments	21,638
Divided by present value of future compensation	320,350
Equals normal-cost percentage	6.75%

Times annual-covered compensation	22,647
Normal cost	1,530
Less normal cost previously calculated	1,153
Increase in annual cost	$ 377

This cost increase seemed to him potentially significant, and one which could occur in a bad year. Of course, if the market value subsequently recovered, the cost would return to normal. Dr. Wayword wondered if some measures were required to protect market values of the pension fund portfolio from undue variation.

Dr. Wayword's calculations omitted one factor of importance that was mentioned before: If the market value of the fund exceeded the "adjusted" value of the fund, the adjusted value could be used within limits in determining normal costs. This factor had been explained to Dr. Wayword as follows:

> In those years in which the "performance" of the fund exceeds 6 percent, the balance (up to a maximum of 20 percent cumulatively) goes into an adjustment account, which, in a sense, is a contingency reserve. Then, if the market goes down, the adjustment account cushions the impact on normal cost of the decline in value. Nevertheless, volatility in portfolio values introduces volatility into the funding requirement. Our adjustment-account mechanism evens the fluctuations out to some degree but not entirely.
>
> If the adjustment account was at its maximum, only 80 percent of market value would be used to determine normal cost. At the beginning of 1977, the actual adjustment account of Brookmere was such that only 92 percent of the market value would be used in the cost calculation.
>
> If the total earnings (income and net gains) on the pension fund during 1977 failed to meet the 6 percent target, then the reserve would be adjusted down by the dollar amount of the shortfall. The revised reserve amount, when divided by the market value of the portfolio, would determine the percentage that could be subtracted from the market value to determine the market value adjustment for 1978.
>
> A series of 10 back-to-back down years would materially increase the normal cost. But if that occurred, it would probably be accompanied by general price-level deflation and, while it would be appropriate to reduce the actuarial interest rate assumption, it would probably also be appropriate to reduce the assumed annual compensation increase.
>
> Other techniques exist, which we don't use, that could be used to reduce volatility further. For example, we could obtain from the actuaries a schedule showing the anticipated pension payments for those who have already retired for every year out into the future. We could then design a bond portfolio with the right mix of yield and maturity to match those benefit payments. Let's assume that the portfolio produced an average yield to maturity of 8 percent. Then, for the retired lives, we could use an actuarial interest rate assumption of 8 percent, and theoretically the bread should come out even with the gravy. Over time, there might be a fluctuation in the market value of the bond portfolio, but so long as we held the portfolio intact and it was, in effect, segregated to pay the pensions of those who have already retired, we could ignore those fluctuations in value in so far as that piece of computation was concerned.

The company could also ask its actuaries to "adjust market value so that the peaks and valleys of the stock market were offset through a valuation reserve within a greater range, say 80 to 120 percent, rather than the current 80 to 100 percent range." The adjustment would result in a negative adjustment account in some years; although this method was less conservative, the actuaries believed it would be acceptable by the Internal Revenue Service.

To gain some further perspective on adjusting market value, Dr. Wayword gathered the data shown in Exhibits 3 and 4 about the total nominal rate-of-return variability of the Standard & Poor's 500 Index and quality bond index.[2] Exhibits 5 and 6 show the same data adjusted for inflation.

On the other hand, if the portfolio performed well in real terms, this adjustment would tend to protect against any changes in benefits necessitated by inflation. If the portfolio values tended to increase at a real rate of 3 to 4 percent per year, the future nominal values of the pension portfolio assets would tend to offset the resulting revised present value of future retirement benefits, and the nominal-cost percentage would remain about the same. Superior performance would reduce this cost.

Although Brookmere was a privately owned firm, many of the key employees owned stock in the company. Buy-and-sell prices were determined by a formula. If future earnings per share were higher as a result of better control of pension costs, the repurchase value of the securities would increase. At the moment, 1000 shares—a relatively small holding—had a repurchase value of approximately $50,000. Dr. Wayword guessed that, for many employees, these stock holdings constituted an important part of their wealth.

Dr. Wayword wondered how all these factors influenced the income and risk objectives that must be established for managing the pension fund. To gain some perspective, he reviewed the actuarial recommendations for three of Brookmere's divisions as prepared by the actuaries for the year 1972 (see Exhibit 7). He realized that the 1972 data were not comparable to 1976 data, however, since each division had grown in employees during that time, ERISA had brought many more employees into the plan, the plan had been revised, and actuarial assumptions had been changed.

Prudent Man

As a final checkpoint, Dr. Wayword recalled the prudent man responsibilities. He had recently read the following brief description of these responsibilities in *The Financial Reality of Pension Funding under ERISA*[3]:

FIDUCIARY RESPONSIBILITY

ERISA mandates "fiduciary responsibility" for any pension plan trustee, for investment managers of pension assets, and for any other persons who may have responsibility and authority in the management of a plan or in controlling, allocating, and

[2]Taken from R. Ibbotson and A. Sinquefield, *Stocks, Bonds, Bills, and Inflation: The Past (1926–1977) and the Future (1977–2000)* (Charlottesville, Va.: Financial Analysts Research Foundation, 1977).

[3]Jack L. Treynor, Patrick J. Regan, and William W. Priest, Jr., *The Financial Reality of Pension Funding under ERISA* (Homewood, Ill.: Dow Jones-Irwin, 1976).

disposing of the plan's assets. Fiduciaries, so defined, must discharge their duties solely in the interests of the participants in given plans. They are made liable for asset losses resulting from violation of the "prudent man" rule, which requires them to "discharge their duties with the care, skill, prudence, and diligence which a prudent man acting in a like capacity would use under conditions prevailing at the time." More specifically, a fiduciary is prohibited from such transactions as dealing with the plan for his or her own account or selling anything to, buying anything from, receiving a gift from, or lending money from plan assets to a "party-in-interest" under a plan (i.e., the plan-sponsoring employer, plan participants, the unions involved, or persons providing services to the plan) or investing more than 10 percent of plan assets in the employer's securities or real property (present investments over 10 percent must be divested by 1984).

The act requires diversification of the investments of the plan, geographically, by industry and by type of vehicle, so that the risk of loss will be minimized, except when selling fund assets in order to diversify would itself result in substantial loss and would clearly not be prudent at the time.

ERISA empowers participants and beneficiaries—or their unions, or the U.S. Department of Labor acting on their behalf—to sue fiduciaries for "fiduciary irresponsibility" on such charges as pursuing inappropriate investment policies or making imprudent investment decisions, or persuading professional investment managers placed in charge of some part of plan assets to do either. A fiduciary may also be held liable for losses caused by other fiduciaries if the fiduciary concealed their acts or was negligent in not seriously trying to stop their breach of responsibility.

ERISA specifically voids provisions in pension plans or in trust agreements that relieve fiduciaries of personal liability for losses resulting from their acts or from their failure to act appropriately.

A Final Comment

While Dr. Wayword was gathering this information, Mr. Phignumb made the following comments about pension fund management in general:

> Dealing with equity investments is, of course, a different matter from dealing with bonds. That's because equity investments do not have the same "certainty" of return that bonds have. Nevertheless, even though we recognize that the company will have to put up the difference if the total returns on equity investments don't match the actuarial assumptions, equity investments are appropriate for a pension fund if properly managed. The problem is how do you ensure proper management? A pension fund is a long-term thing, and yet portfolio managers, even the best of them, have a horizon of only a few months or a few years at best. In today's market climate, an awful lot of very good common stocks look low relative to historic price/earnings ratios and yields. Therefore, it makes sense to put a large chunk of the portfolio in quality common stocks with the view to leaving them there and not trading in and out of them with every blip on the S&P 500.
>
> Another consideration is the type of stocks that ought to be bought for a pension fund. The argument can be made that "growth" stocks are best if the objective is to obtain appreciation in the portfolio which will ultimately reduce the company's normal cost. Historically, however, we have seen that such stocks carried a significant premium. Why is this so? Some observers believe that part of this premium is due to the fact that wealthy people are not so much interested in dividends as they are in capital gains. Thus, just as they might buy a tax-exempt bond, they buy low-

yield "growth" stocks. However, a pension fund does not pay any tax. Therefore, just as it would be inappropriate for a pension fund to invest in tax-exempt bonds, perhaps it is inappropriate for a pension fund to buy low-yield equities with the hope of getting a bigger return through appreciation. In the final analysis, the question is, if taxes were not at all involved, would a high-quality growth stock give a larger total return over time than a high-quality, proven, dividend-paying stock. That might be an academic study all in itself. Note, I am not comparing such issues as Bethlehem Steel to IBM. Rather, I am comparing, perhaps, stocks such as IBM with such perceived growth stocks as Avon Products and Disney.

On the other hand, perhaps one ought to select a mix of stocks and direct the trustee accordingly, rather than let the trustee have full discretion.

All of which reminds me of an anecdote concerning Mega Corporation and the bank trustees it selected to manage its pension fund when it was set up in 1950. MC wanted the funds invested 50 percent in bonds and 50 percent in equities, but the bank thought the ratio ought to be 90 percent bonds/10 percent equities, so it asked MC to give it a letter directing it to use the 50/50 ratio. In 1967, the people at MC got a call from the bank requesting a meeting to discuss the allocation of the fund assets. At that time, the bank pointed out that it felt the ratio should be 90 percent equities/10 percent bonds. The MC people thought it ought to remain 50/50. Therefore, the bank asked MC to furnish it with a new letter (since the old one was dated 17 years earlier), so that they would have a recently dated instruction directing them what to do. I guess the moral of the story is that if MC had each year asked the bank for its recommendations and then done the exact opposite, it would have had the most "prudent" investment policy, at least in hindsight.

EXHIBIT 1
Social Security Taxes *(original schedule)**

Year	Taxable Wage	Tax Rate	Maximum Tax
1978	$17,700	6.05%	$1,070.85
1979	18,900	6.05	1,143.45
1980	20,400	6.05	1,234.20
1981	21,900	6.30	1,379.70
1982	23,400	6.30	1,474.20
1983	24,900	6.30	1,568.70
1984	26,400	6.30	1,663.20
1985	27,900	6.30	1,757.70
1986	29,400	6.45	1,896.30
1987	31,200	6.45	2,012.40

*Note: On December 20, 1977, a new Social Security schedule became law:

Year	Taxable Wage	Tax Rate	Maximum Tax
1977	$16,500	5.85%	$ 965
1978	17,700	6.05	1,071
1979	22,900	6.13	1,404
1980	25,900	6.13	1,588
1981	29,700	6.65	1,975
1982	31,800	6.70	2,131
1983	33,900	6.70	2,271
1984	36,000	6.70	2,412
1985	38,100	7.05	2,686
1986	42,200	7.15	2,874
1987	42,600	7.15	3,046

EXHIBIT 2

Pension Plan (*summary of valuation results as of January 1, 1976*)

	Division 1	Division 2	Division 3*	Division 4	Division 5	Total
A. Present value of future retirement benefits						
1. Nonretired employees	$ 18,655,700	$ 7,160,900	$ 6,185,200	$ 3,026,400	$ 1,178,100	$ 38,206,300
2. Retired employees	3,355,400	1,221,600	1,155,500	436,700	—	6,169,200
3. Terminated employees with vested benefits	32,000	71,500	25,000	4,000	—	132,500
4. Total	22,043,100	8,454,000	7,365,700	3,467,100	1,178,100	42,508,000
B. Adjusted market value of assets	10,288,361	2,759,953	3,327,519	1,301,468	99,840	17,777,141
C. Unfunded past service liability	3,622,900	2,467,700	1,654,100	522,300	159,300	8,426,300
D. Present value of future normal-cost payments (A – B – C)	8,131,800	3,226,300	2,384,100	1,643,300	919,000	16,304,600
E. Present value of future covered compensation	159,567,700	57,646,700	59,603,800	26,943,100	16,587,500	320,349,800
F. Normal cost percentage (D ÷ E)	5.10%	5.60%	4.00%	6.10%	5.54%	5.09%
G. Annual covered compensation	$ 11,215,800	$ 4,183,800	$ 4,307,600	$ 1,785,200	$ 1,056,300	$ 22,646,700
H. Normal cost (F × G)	572,000	234,300	172,300	108,900	58,500	1,162,700
I. Recommended annual contribution						
1. Normal cost plus 28-year amortization of item C (including interest to end of year)	876,600	432,400	306,000	154,400	73,900	1,843,300
2. Recommended contribution as percent of pay covered compensation	7.8%	10.3%	7.1%	8.7%	7.0%	8.1%
J. ERISA minimum contribution (normal cost plus 40-year amortization of item C plus interest from beginning of year)	$ 847,100	$ 412,400	$ 292,600	$ 150,100	72,600	$ 1,775,800

*Pension separately funded.

EXHIBIT 3

Average Annual Total Compound Rate of Return on Corporate Bonds (*in nominal terms; for various investment periods*)

Year Beginning	Duration of Investment 1 Year	2 Years	3 Years	4 Years	5 Years	8 Years	10 Years	15 Years	20 Years	25 Years
1926	7.37%	7.41%	5.87%	5.20%	5.75%	5.95%	7.08%	6.24%	5.52%	4.76%
1927	7.44	5.12	4.50	5.36	3.87	6.73	7.02	5.93	5.24	4.35
1928	2.84	3.06	4.67	2.99	4.52	6.73	6.54	5.60	4.73	4.19
1929	3.27	5.60	3.06	4.94	6.00	7.51	6.88	5.61	4.80	4.22
1930	7.98	2.95	5.51	6.71	8.09	7.43	6.95	5.70	4.81	4.30
1931	−1.85	4.29	6.28	8.12	8.42	7.20	6.49	5.44	4.51	4.00
1932	10.82	10.61	11.67	11.15	10.25	7.97	6.97	5.69	4.47	3.79
1933	10.38	12.10	11.26	10.11	8.60	7.04	6.15	4.81	4.11	3.70
1934	13.84	11.71	10.02	8.16	7.75	6.09	5.40	4.40	3.77	3.20
1935	9.61	8.17	6.33	6.28	5.81	4.72	4.53	3.73	3.37	2.63
1936	6.74	4.73	5.19	4.88	4.54	3.88	3.99	3.24	2.92	2.61
1937	2.75	4.43	4.27	4.05	3.78	3.63	3.24	2.60	2.23	2.53
1938	6.13	5.04	4.49	4.04	3.75	3.80	2.96	2.66	2.52	2.74
1939	3.97	3.68	3.36	3.17	3.10	3.25	2.77	2.48	2.10	2.58
1940	3.39	3.06	2.90	2.88	3.25	2.45	2.70	2.57	1.85	2.61
1941	2.73	2.66	2.72	3.21	3.39	2.54	2.58	2.38	2.12	2.46
1942	2.60	2.72	3.38	3.55	3.18	2.61	2.02	1.71	2.22	2.36
1943	2.83	3.78	3.87	3.33	2.17	2.55	2.11	2.11	2.48	2.04
1944	4.73	4.40	3.50	2.01	2.43	1.85	2.17	1.76	2.45	2.03
1945	4.08	2.90	1.12	1.87	2.15	1.70	2.23	1.38	2.45	1.50
1946	1.72	−0.33	1.14	1.67	1.77	1.62	1.87	1.70	2.23	2.03
1947	−2.34	0.85	1.66	1.78	0.86	2.07	0.99	1.91	2.15	2.38
1948	4.14	3.73	3.19	1.68	2.05	2.43	2.07	2.59	2.01	2.77
1949	3.31	2.72	0.87	1.53	1.90	1.02	1.43	2.45	1.93	2.65
1950	2.12	−0.32	0.94	1.55	2.31	1.66	1.00	2.55	1.34	2.39

1951	−2.69%	0.37%	1.37%	2.36%	1.98%	1.11%	1.67%	2.38%	2.09%	2.86%
1952	3.52	3.47	4.10	3.18	1.10	1.33	2.43	2.58	2.77	3.68
1953	3.41	4.39	3.07	0.50	2.09	2.00	2.86	2.00	2.95	
1954	5.39	2.91	−0.44	1.77	0.95	2.17	2.74	1.94	2.83	
1955	0.48	−3.24	0.59	−0.11	−0.28	2.48	2.68	1.02	2.40	
1956	−6.81	0.65	−0.31	−0.48	1.36	2.70	2.58	2.13	3.08	
1957	8.71	3.10	1.72	3.15	3.77	4.21	3.33	3.30	4.34	
1958	−2.22	−1.60	1.84	2.54	3.62	3.07	1.95	3.23		
1959	−0.97	3.94	4.23	5.14	4.54	3.38	2.44	3.47		
1960	9.07	6.93	7.26	5.97	5.73	3.18	1.68	3.32		
1961	4.82	6.37	4.96	4.91	3.81	2.07	2.51	3.66		
1962	7.95	5.03	4.94	3.56	2.88	0.40	3.10	4.52		
1963	2.19	3.48	2.14	1.65	0.29	1.57	3.04			
1964	4.77	2.12	1.47	−0.17	0.37	2.63	2.93			
1965	−0.46	−0.13	−1.76	−0.70	−2.22	2.93	2.13			
1966	0.20	−2.41	−0.78	−2.65	1.22	3.13	3.59			
1967	−4.95	−1.26	−3.59	1.48	3.33	2.71	5.35			
1968	2.57	−2.91	3.72	5.50	5.84	5.14				
1969	−8.09	4.30	6.49	6.68	5.55	7.07				
1970	18.37	14.64	12.12	9.26	6.67					
1971	11.01	9.12	6.39	3.95	6.02					
1972	7.26	4.15	1.68	4.78	7.41					
1973	1.14	−0.99	3.97	7.45						
1974	−3.06	5.42	9.65							
1975	14.64	16.63								
1976	18.65									

EXHIBIT 4

Average Annual Total Compound Rate of Return on Common Stocks (*in nominal terms; for various investment periods*)

Year Beginning	Duration of Investment									
	1 Year	2 Years	3 Years	4 Years	5 Years	8 Years	10 Years	15 Years	20 Years	25 Years
1926	11.62%	23.89%	30.13%	19.18%	8.67%	2.45%	5.86%	4.04%	7.13%	7.68%
1927	37.49	40.52	21.82	7.95	−5.11	0.88	7.81	2.44	6.10	8.14
1928	43.61	14.68	−0.41	−13.51	−12.46	1.77	0.02	1.53	4.71	7.49
1929	−8.42	−17.07	−26.96	−22.66	−11.24	0.90	−0.89	0.64	3.11	5.90
1930	−24.90	−34.77	−26.89	−11.93	−9.92	−3.34	−0.05	2.46	4.45	8.09
1931	−43.34	−27.88	−7.12	−5.73	3.12	3.63	1.80	6.62	7.43	10.54
1932	−8.19	18.91	11.69	19.77	22.47	11.20	6.43	10.12	11.72	13.37
1933	53.99	23.20	30.87	28.08	14.28	10.95	9.34	11.15	13.15	13.24
1934	−1.44	20.65	24.91	6.08	10.67	3.53	7.17	8.39	10.68	12.92
1935	47.67	40.64	8.71	13.93	10.90	6.13	9.27	9.74	13.13	13.49
1936	33.92	−6.72	4.49	3.24	0.49	4.05	8.42	8.91	12.48	11.76
1937	−35.03	−7.71	−5.33	−6.46	−7.51	2.60	4.41	8.36	11.20	11.52
1938	31.12	14.27	5.61	1.02	4.61	12.57	9.62	12.78	12.98	13.04
1939	−0.41	−5.21	−7.38	−1.11	3.77	7.69	7.25	10.69	13.48	12.75
1940	−9.78	−10.69	−1.35	4.84	7.67	8.49	9.17	13.88	14.15	13.45
1941	−11.59	3.15	10.23	12.54	16.95	10.63	13.38	16.78	14.76	14.45
1942	20.34	23.10	21.96	25.43	17.87	14.79	17.28	18.24	16.85	14.63
1943	25.90	22.79	27.18	17.26	14.85	16.10	17.09	15.91	15.25	14.68
1944	19.75	27.83	14.52	12.24	10.86	15.87	14.31	16.91	15.11	14.10
1945	36.44	12.00	9.86	8.75	10.68	15.71	17.12	16.39	14.95	12.88
1946	−8.07	−1.42	0.83	5.04	9.91	11.16	16.69	14.04	13.84	11.66
1947	5.71	5.60	9.82	14.92	16.70	18.43	18.43	16.52	13.71	12.64
1948	5.50	11.95	18.18	19.61	19.36	21.72	16.44	15.38	14.63	13.17
1949	18.79	25.08	24.72	23.10	17.86	21.87	20.06	16.56	14.92	12.22
1950	31.71	27.81	24.57	17.62	23.91	17.58	19.36	16.40	13.43	10.08

1951	24.02%	21.17%	13.27%	22.04%	23.89%	18.84%	16.16%	15.18%	12.10%	10.26%
1952	18.37	8.26	21.39	23.85	20.18	17.33	16.43	12.73	11.64	10.26
1953	−0.99	22.94	25.73	20.64	13.58	14.95	13.44	13.09	11.67	
1954	52.62	41.71	28.85	17.54	22.30	18.57	15.80	13.96	10.85	
1955	31.56	18.40	7.73	15.71	14.95	11.19	12.82	10.14	6.87	
1956	6.56	−2.50	10.87	11.14	8.92	10.23	11.06	8.43	7.10	
1957	−10.78	13.10	12.70	9.52	12.78	11.47	9.17	8.94	7.90	
1958	43.36	26.69	17.26	19.60	13.30	14.74	12.85	11.05		
1959	11.95	6.06	12.59	6.83	9.84	8.21	10.00	7.27		
1960	0.47	12.92	5.18	9.33	10.73	9.63	7.81	4.31		
1961	26.89	7.63	12.46	13.45	13.25	11.01	8.18	6.49		
1962	−8.73	5.88	9.69	10.66	5.71	6.57	7.06	6.32		
1963	22.80	19.60	17.16	9.67	12.39	8.32	9.93			
1964	16.48	14.44	5.61	9.93	10.15	7.36	6.00			
1965	12.45	0.57	7.83	8.63	4.06	7.64	1.24			
1966	−10.06	5.60	7.39	3.17	3.33	3.99	3.27			
1967	23.98	17.35	8.00	6.99	8.42	1.43	6.65			
1968	11.06	0.81	1.76	4.83	7.52	2.70				
1969	−8.50	−2.45	2.84	6.66	2.01	4.11				
1970	4.01	9.04	12.25	4.81	−2.35					
1971	14.31	16.63	5.09	−3.88	3.20					
1972	18.98	0.77	−9.28	0.66	4.86					
1973	−14.66	−20.79	−4.87	1.61						
1974	−26.48	0.44	7.69							
1975	37.20	30.36								
1976	23.84									

EXHIBIT 5

Average Annual Total Compound Rate of Return on Common Stocks (*in real terms; for various investment periods*)

	Duration of Investment											
Year Beginning	1 Year	2 Years	3 Years	4 Years	5 Years	6 Years	8 Years	10 Years	15 Years	20 Years	25 Years	30 Years
1926	13.25%	25.95%	32.02%	20.45%	10.96%	.91%	6.54%	8.67%	5.75%	7.07%	6.23%	8.73%
1927	40.08	42.55	22.96	10.40	−1.40	−.75	4.43	10.37	3.66	5.03	6.37	8.41
1928	45.07	15.20	1.98	−9.68	−7.35	.76	4.74	1.90	1.73	3.11	5.63	6.69
1929	−8.52	−14.50	−22.88	−17.17	−6.32	−5.85	3.54	1.15	.78	1.40	4.00	6.59
1930	−20.09	−29.19	−19.87	−5.78	−5.30	1.47	−1.18	2.10	2.25	2.77	6.17	7.25
1931	−37.25	−19.76	−.45	−1.20	6.43	10.37	5.50	3.24	5.80	5.08	8.29	8.02
1932	2.60	25.40	14.95	21.46	23.55	10.43	11.87	5.83	7.25	8.41	10.49	10.56
1933	53.25	21.66	28.48	29.43	12.06	15.57	9.95	6.59	6.85	9.14	9.74	10.09
1934	−3.42	17.63	22.35	3.63	9.23	7.70	1.44	4.20	4.04	6.75	9.37	9.22
1935	43.28	37.70	6.09	12.65	10.06	6.30	3.12	6.25	5.61	9.25	9.95	9.86
1936	32.34	−8.71	3.97	3.05	.14	−3.45	1.09	5.49	4.63	8.76	8.34	8.90
1937	−37.02	−7.85	−5.20	−6.60	−9.35	−6.36	−.42	−.06	3.79	7.44	8.13	7.39
1938	34.82	16.32	6.50	−.71	1.37	4.58	9.37	4.43	8.18	9.15	9.69	9.73
1939	.35	−5.34	−10.34	−5.61	−.60	2.19	2.00	1.53	5.94	9.14	9.21	8.86
1940	−10.70	−15.24	−7.50	−.84	2.55	7.16	1.54	3.44	8.97	9.93	9.82	8.31
1941	−19.55	−5.86	2.70	−5.81	11.14	4.56	3.33	6.95	11.80	10.50	10.75	8.66
1942	10.14	16.03	16.45	20.49	10.19	7.84	8.73	11.05	13.70	13.00	11.09	9.82
1943	22.22	19.73	24.14	10.20	7.39	6.58	10.42	11.71	11.89	11.88	11.49	9.98
1944	17.30	25.11	6.46	3.97	3.71	6.40	9.84	9.36	12.96	11.81	10.86	8.36
1945	33.43	1.42	−.13	−.56	4.34	7.47	9.85	12.33	12.50	11.71	9.50	6.26
1946	−22.91	−13.60	−8.49	−1.89	2.92	5.18	5.74	12.13	10.28	10.65	8.18	6.12
1947	−3.16	−.29	6.33	10.64	11.92	12.81	15.24	15.50	13.96	11.32	9.75	7.65
1948	2.67	11.42	15.65	16.04	16.31	13.11	19.69	14.22	13.42	12.54	10.51	
1949	20.91	22.75	20.89	20.00	15.32	20.93	19.83	17.90	14.65	12.87	9.32	
1950	24.62	20.88	19.69	13.97	20.94	22.57	14.93	16.82	14.28	10.83	6.65	

1951	17.23%	17.29%	10.62%	20.03%	22.18%	18.85%	16.71%	14.16%	13.35%	9.53%	6.77%
1952	17.35	7.45	20.99	23.44	19.20	13.01	15.83	14.99	11.12	9.22	6.81
1953	−1.62	22.84	25.53	19.66	12.16	16.52	13.39	12.00	11.31	9.11	
1954	53.37	41.81	27.74	15.90	20.53	18.76	16.96	14.32	11.87	7.87	
1955	31.11	16.57	5.57	13.48	12.84	10.41	9.44	11.09	7.65	3.53	
1956	3.63	−5.27	8.14	8.69	6.67	9.71	8.33	9.19	5.62	3.24	
1957	−13.40	10.48	10.42	7.44	10.93	7.16	9.76	7.29	6.08	3.92	
1958	40.95	24.68	15.45	18.02	11.82	13.28	13.13	10.88	8.11		
1959	10.30	4.50	11.23	5.54	8.43	9.52	6.51	7.70	3.95		
1960	−1.00	11.71	3.79	7.96	9.36	9.52	7.67	5.14	.37		
1961	26.04	6.59	11.13	12.12	11.75	7.18	8.60	5.09	2.12		
1962	−9.86	4.35	7.83	8.45	3.76	6.36	3.56	3.73	1.68		
1963	20.81	17.94	15.34	7.48	9.93	9.28	4.72	6.30			
1964	15.14	12.70	3.38	7.38	7.11	3.30	3.57	1.78			
1965	10.31	−2.06	4.91	5.20	1.08	.65	−.79	−3.85			
1966	−13.03	2.31	3.54	−1.11	−1.17	.70	−4.29	−2.38			
1967	20.35	12.91	3.22	2.03	3.70	5.51	−3.52	.66			
1968	6.07	−4.41	−3.43	−.09	2.78	−1.79	−2.21				
1969	−13.84	−7.85	−2.07	1.97	−3.29	−9.44					
1970	−1.45	4.41	7.85	−.47	−8.53	−3.23					
1971	10.63	12.84	−.13	−10.23	−3.57	−.25					
1972	15.09	−5.07	−16.26	−6.84	−2.29						
1973	−21.77	−28.58	−13.17	−6.21							
1974	−34.79	−8.52	−.37								
1975	28.33	23.16									
1976	18.20										

EXHIBIT 6
Average Annual Total Compound Rate of Return on Corporate Bonds (*in real terms; for various investment horizons*)

	Duration of Investment										
Year Beginning	**1 Year**	**2 Years**	**3 Years**	**4 Years**	**5 Years**	**6 Years**	**8 Years**	**10 Years**	**15 Years**	**20 Years**	**25 Years**
1926	8.96%	9.30%	7.43%	6.32%	7.96%	8.04%	10.05%	9.83%	7.90%	5.39%	3.30%
1927	9.63	6.67	5.44	7.71	7.84	10.27	10.36	9.47	6.81	4.12	2.59
1928	3.80	3.42	7.08	7.40	10.41	10.29	9.95	8.42	5.71	3.07	2.32
1929	3.04	8.76	8.63	12.13	11.64	11.63	10.18	8.97	5.42	2.95	2.28
1930	14.80	11.54	15.33	13.91	13.43	12.22	9.71	9.11	5.39	3.05	2.39
1931	8.37	15.60	13.61	13.09	11.73	10.65	9.02	7.87	4.54	2.15	1.83
1932	23.30	16.32	14.71	12.58	11.12	9.10	8.51	6.38	2.91	1.32	1.10
1933	9.73	10.64	9.22	8.26	6.47	6.91	6.03	3.43	.74	.39	.19
1934	11.54	8.96	7.78	5.86	6.35	6.03	3.93	2.45	.20	.06	−.06
1935	6.44	5.93	3.79	5.10	4.95	4.53	1.71	1.59	−.19	−.20	−.59
1936	5.45	2.49	4.66	4.60	4.15	2.31	.87	1.13	−.84	−.50	−.55
1937	−.39	4.26	4.31	3.83	1.69	.33	.52	−1.58	−1.75	−1.26	−.60
1938	9.12	6.75	5.27	2.21	.48	.34	.79	−2.02	−1.56	−.97	−.33
1939	4.42	3.41	.01	−1.58	−1.33	−.69	−2.22	−2.74	−1.95	−1.60	−.66
1940	2.40	−2.13	−3.50	−2.72	−1.69	−1.12	−4.09	−2.68	−1.86	−1.93	−.69
1941	−6.44	−6.31	−4.37	−2.68	−1.80	−4.30	−4.22	−3.25	−2.01	−1.70	−.89
1942	−6.18	−3.31	−1.40	−.61	−3.54	−4.74	−2.82	−3.43	−2.22	−1.17	−.74
1943	−.36	1.10	1.32	−2.86	−4.45	−3.52	−2.47	−2.55	−1.45	−.53	−.81
1944	2.57	2.17	−3.68	−5.45	−4.14	−2.65	−3.45	−2.26	1.69	−.49	−.88
1945	1.77	−6.67	−7.98	−5.75	−3.66	−3.63	−3.45	−1.95	−2.02	−.44	−1.55
1946	−14.39	−12.50	−8.12	−4.97	−4.68	−5.27	−3.34	−2.11	−1.66	−1.63	−1.16
1947	−10.56	−4.82	−1.60	−2.08	−3.32	−2.35	−.73	−1.55	−.37	−.03	−.26
1948	1.29	3.21	.92	−1.43	−.64	−.08	.68	.08	.81	.08	.33
1949	5.17	.74	−2.32	−1.11	−.35	.67	−.72	−.44	.76	−.05	−.01
1950	−3.51	−5.86	−3.12	−1.68	−.21	−.15	−.68	−1.19	.65	−1.01	−.80

1951	-8.16%	-2.93%	-1.06%	.63%	.53%	-1.21%	-.74%	-.12%	.73%	-.25%	-.38%
1952	2.61	2.70	3.75	2.83	.24	1.11	.02	1.14	1.10	.52	.45
1953	2.77	4.32	2.89	-.34	.80	.01	.60	1.54	.38	.58	
1954	5.90	2.96	-1.35	.32	-.55	-.85	.76	1.31	.05	.07	
1955	.10	-4.79	-1.48	-2.10	-2.16	-.61	.85	1.09	-1.28	-.95	
1956	-9.44	-2.26	-2.81	-2.72	-.76	.04	.90	.83	-.59	-.61	
1957	5.50	.68	-.37	1.54	2.05	2.80	2.61	1.52	-.61	.51	
1958	-3.91	-3.18	.25	1.21	2.88	1.98	1.62	.16	.50		
1959	-2.43	2.40	2.97	3.88	3.10	3.25	1.73	.35	.27		
1960	7.47	5.78	6.07	4.67	4.44	3.27	1.01	-.84	-.54		
1961	4.12	5.38	3.74	3.70	2.45	1.51	-.15	-.41	-.56		
1962	6.65	3.55	3.55	2.04	.99	-.53	-2.43	-.10	-.00		
1963	.54	2.03	.55	-.37	-1.90	-1.93	-1.81	-.54			
1964	3.54	.55	-.68	-2.51	-2.40	-4.34	-.99	-1.15			
1965	-2.35	-2.72	-4.44	-3.85	-5.85	-3.05	-.97	-2.94			
1966	-3.08	-5.46	-4.34	-6.70	-3.19	-1.50	-1.58	-2.03			
1967	-7.79	-4.97	-7.88	-3.22	-1.17	-.38	-3.00	-.50			
1968	-2.06	-7.93	-1.64	.55	1.18	-.25	-1.15				
1969	-13.45	-1.43	1.44	2.01	.12	-2.33	.65				
1970	12.25	9.81	7.75	3.84	.06	1.21					
1971	7.42	5.56	1.18	-2.78	-.87	1.36					
1972	3.73	-1.81	-5.96	-2.84	-.18						
1973	-7.06	-10.46	-4.93	-.69							
1974	-13.73	-3.85	1.54								
1975	7.17	10.16									
1976	13.24										

EXHIBIT 7

Retirement Plan for Regular Full-Time Employees (*actuarial analysis as of January 1, 1972*)

	Division A	Division D	Division B
1. Present value of retirement benefits*			
a. Retired employees	$ 1,826,600	$ 151,500	$ 702,000
b. Active employees age 65 nearest birthday	205,700	—	43,600
and over	205,700	—	43,600
c. Active employees under age 65	9,950,300	1,510,500	3,873,700
d. Total	11,982,600	1,662,000	4,619,300
2. Adjusted assets as of 1/1/72 applicable to previous years	7,775,324	943,975	1,847,757
3. Unfunded value of future retirement benefits (1 − 2)	4,207,300	718,000	2,771,500
4. Present value of future total earnings (below age 65 nearest birthday)	69,324,300	12,314,300	25,186,900
5. Accrual rate (3 + 4)	6.07%	5.83%	11.00%
6. Normal cost percent for normal entry age	5.04%	4.85%	4.85%
7. Current annual payroll (below age 65 nearest birthday)	$ 5,681,700	$ 917,200	$ 2,174,200
8. Normal cost	286,300	44,500	105,400
9. Supplementary cost percent (5 − 6)	1.03%	.98%	6.15%
10. Supplementary cost liability (4 × 9)	$ 714,000	$ 120,700	$ 1,549,000
11. Payment for supplementary cost liability†	293,200	33,600	233,200
12. Total contribution required (8 + lesser of 10 or 11)	579,500	78,100	338,600

*Valued on the basis of the 1965 Projected Annuity Mortality Table at 4 percent interest, and moderate provisions for turnover and salary increases, but no provision for administrative expense.

†Represents 1/10th of the supplementary cost liability as of 1/1/72, plus 1/10th of the payments toward past-service liability in prior years.

Gifford Manufacturing Company Pension Fund

In late March 1979, Wilma Todd, Assistant Treasurer of the Gifford Manufacturing Company, was preparing for a combined meeting in early April of the Pension Advisory Committee (of which she was chairperson) and the five fund managers of Gifford's $106 million pension fund. Heretofore, the Pension Advisory Committee had met separately with each of the fund managers twice a year to discuss performance and prospects of each of the separately managed funds. Recently, two new meetings had been scheduled to discuss the collective fund management problems with all interested parties attending. The April 1979 meeting was the first of these meetings.

Gifford Manufacturing Company, with sales in excess of $500 million, was a broad-based manufacturer of industrial machinery and products. Sales growth over the last decade had averaged 12 percent per year, but some of this growth reflected the high prevailing rate of inflation. Profits had grown by 15 percent per annum over the same time span. Over this decade, the firm's dividend payout ratio was reduced from 50 to 30 percent in order to strengthen internal financing capability and dividends had grown slower than profits. Increasing uncertainty had slowed management's expansion plans in the last five years. As a result, Gifford had developed, what seemed to management, a strong financial position at the end of 1978: long-term debt was 24 percent of total long-term capital, and the firm had $41 million in excess liquid assets relative to its equity base of $382 million. Despite these achievements, the Gifford common stock was currently selling at a

---

price/earnings ratio of 5.2x, providing investors with a dividend yield of 5.8 percent. Management was quite concerned by this below-average market reception for their stock.

Given the industrial character of its product lines, Gifford's sales were subject to cyclical fluctuation, as were its profits. Management had been striving, with some success, to reduce this profit volatility. Profit volatility had also been reflected in higher-than-average market volatility for its stock. Gifford's stock tended to have a beta of about 1.25, according to one service.

Ms. Todd had joined Gifford upon completion of an MBA program at a leading business school in 1975. For two years she worked as a business analyst in the controller's office primarily concerned, as a central staff advisor, with the analysis of capital expenditure opportunities in various plant facilities of Gifford. She then spent a year with a newly formed central planning group working primarily on acquisition opportunities. (No acquisitions were made in this period, nor had there been any since a rather disastrous one in 1966). Her analytical work, nevertheless, received high praise.

In November 1978, Ms. Todd was assigned to the treasurer's staff with primary responsibilities for overseeing pension fund investments and for managing Gifford's growing liquid asset portfolio. Prior to this, the treasurer had supervised pension fund activities, devoting perhaps two days per month toward this end. The fact that the pension fund had grown to a significant sum had, along with ERISA, made it seem more important for management to increase the attention paid to it. Ms. Todd was to spend about half her time on this activity. She also chaired a Pension Advisory Committee consisting of the financial vice president, the treasurer, and two outside directors (one of whom had considerable investment experience). In January, Ms. Todd's salary had grown to twice the starting level and she was anxious to continue to perform impressively at her new task.

At the time of her appointment, the administration of Trusted pension funds had been relatively loose. The total portfolio was divided into five approximately equal parts, each of which had been assigned to a fund manager using a somewhat different investment style. Four of the fund managers had managed their piece of the portfolio for over five years. The fifth—an index fund manager—had received a substantial part of new fund commitments for the previous three years until his funds under management, all invested in equities, approximated 20 percent of the total portfolio.

The shift into indexing had been accompanied by a change in instructions to the four active portfolio managers. Five years previously, they had been instructed to keep on average 65 percent of their funds invested in equities. However, they had the latitude to change this mix from 50 to 80 percent depending upon the market outlook. All four had run relatively fully diversified portfolios with 60 or more equity securities invested in each portfolio. It was not atypical for the total portfolio to include 170 different securities.

In 1976, management had undertaken two studies that affected subsequent planning. A total portfolio analysis suggested that there might be too much diversification in the total portfolio, although each manager was managing the portfolio quite differently. As a result of this study, management had decided to put up to 20 percent of the portfolio into an index fund. At the same time, the four active managers were asked to reduce the number of common stocks to 30 or less by 1979. As of December 31, 1978, each had achieved this objective, and altogether, after considering overlaps, there were now only 80 different common stocks in the actively managed part of the portfolio.

Concurrently, an asset-mix study had been undertaken using an elaborate simulation model developed by a consultant. At the end of this study, management concluded that, on average, 70 percent of the portfolio should be invested in common stocks. The fact that the Gifford pension fund was, as of that time, comfortably overfunded influenced this decision on the appropriate income/risk trade-off. Since 20 percent of the fund was to be invested in an equity index fund, the remainder of the actively managed funds should on average be invested 62.5 percent in equities to achieve an overall target of 70 percent. The four active fund managers were so instructed. They were, however, given the latitude to change this asset mix between 45 and 80 percent depending upon the market outlook.

As noted, each of the five fund managers followed different equity management approaches. Manager A—the index manager—attempted to match the performance of the Standard & Poor's 500 Index as closely as possible. Manager B invested exclusively in growth stocks. Manger C concentrated in identifying high-yield, undervalued securities. Funds B and C were primarily invested in large capitalization firms. Manager D, in contrast, concentrated on stocks with capitalizations of less than $800 million, using various screening devices to identify undervalued securities. Manager E also identified undervalued securities, but used a modern portfolio theory approach to achieve this end.

Each of the managers used a somewhat different approach to managing the fixed-income part of the portfolio. Manager B shifted from long to short maturities depending on the interest rate outlook, but was otherwise quite passive. Manager C used yield spreads to identify which sector of the market was most attractive and tended to concentrate the portfolio in the most promising sector. Manager D tended to invest more passively in longer maturity, lower quality (A-rating type) issues for maximum yield. Manager E followed a similar approach to C but was an active swapper, and had the highest turnover among these managers.

In Ms. Todd's opinion, the management record of the four active managers was quite good. All four fixed-income portfolios, for example, showed small positive alphas over the last five years relative to the Salomon Brothers Index. Three of the four managers also had positive alphas for the equity part of the portfolio. The record of Manager D was particularly good in this regard over the last five years. The exception, Manager B, had done well relative to published data on other growth funds. However, growth funds as a group had not performed well in this five-year period. In composite, the actively managed equity funds had outperformed the Standard & Poor's Index, showing a positive alpha of .5 percent per annum.

Despite good management of the subparts of the portfolio, overall performance was not as good. As one measure of performance, Ms. Todd used a 30/70 percent weighted monthly average of fixed income and equities as measured by the Salomon

Brothers Bond Index and the Standard & Poor's 500 Index for total returns as a standard of performance. By this measure, the overall portfolio had an alpha that was barely positive, a beta of 1.15 and a residual error of 5 percent per year. The reason for this so-so performance seemed to lie in the cyclical timing decisions of the active managers. All four of the managers would have performed better if they had kept a constant asset mix throughout this five-year period.

Ms. Todd also noticed that the asset mix decisions were in part self-canceling. On December 31, 1978, for example, the asset mixes of the four active managers were, respectively, 70, 56, 60, and 76 percent. If one was right in this portfolio positioning, the benefits could be lost by the mispositioning of another fund. It was on this problem of cyclical timing that Ms. Todd had decided to focus attention in the April meeting of fund managers.

A part of Ms. Todd's time since November had been spent on familiarizing herself with the growing literature on modern portfolio theory. In particular, she had been intrigued by some recent writings on multiple fund management. Parts of one paper by Barr Rosenberg in particular seemed appropriate to coordinate the market timing decisions of the various managers. She had summarized the relevant subparts of this paper (see Appendix A) and distributed copies to each of the fund managers. The paper was to be the centerpiece for discussion at the forthcoming meeting.

Her cover letter suggested several questions for discussion: Should the managers of the actively managed funds be encouraged to cyclically time the debt/equity asset mix of their portfolios? If so, within what limits? Should the efforts be coordinated? If so, how—without reducing individual fund management responsibility? How could a system like Rosenberg's be made operational? How should it be controlled and monitored?

Ms. Todd was somewhat fearful of the result. First of all, two of the active managers were not overly sympathetic to the concepts of modern portfolio theory. Secondly, these managers all did market time their portfolio's asset-mix changes for better or worse and would probably resist any restrictions on doing so. Thirdly, she was uncertain what implications might arise from any efforts to coordinate this market timing activity in terms of the performance that would follow, of the ability to hold managers responsible for performance over which they had limited control, and of her responsibilities under ERISA.

She also noted that Rosenberg's paper presumed certain policies in existence that did not exist in the case of Gifford. For example, there had been no effort made to prescribe beta targets for the equity portfolios run by each manager. As shown in Exhibit 1, the portfolios had different equity betas.

Also, the Rosenberg paper was primarily focused on the management of multi-equity portfolios. Nothing was said in the paper about the suitability of the approach to managers responsible for management of both debt and equity funds. The paper appeared to assume that changes would be made by adjusting equity portfolio betas, not the asset mix. She wondered if the two were the same.

Above all, Ms. Todd wanted to run a constructive, problem solving-oriented meeting leading to firm conclusions—or at least a plan for a further analysis—

reached by the end of the four hour meeting. She recognized that she had made considerable progress up the management ladder at Gifford, and she wanted to continue to impress management. At the same time she recognized that, except for one director, she would be the least experienced investment person at the meeting. Unlike previous meetings (dominated by the reports and plans of fund managers), she would have to take a leading role in channeling discussions. With this in mind, she began to consider what she could realistically achieve in the meeting and how these results might best be brought about.

EXHIBIT 1
Portfolio Equity Betas, Four Fund Managers

	Equity Portfolio Betas	
Fund Manager	*Five-Year Least Squares Fit 1974–1978*	*Weighted-Average Stock Betas 12/31/78*
B	1.15	1.14
C	.94	.97
D	1.26	1.31
E	1.03	1.05

Appendix A

SUMMARY OF IDEAS[1]

The optimal beta for the entire portfolio at any point in time is the sum of the normal beta and a differential beta. The normal beta is a policy beta that best describes the risk/reward trade-off decision of a manager over the long run. The differential beta indicates how the portfolio beta should be shifted to reflect particular market outlooks.

Each of the fund managers would contribute to the process of determining the differential beta. The process starts by each forecasting the total rate of return for the market portfolio (presumably the Standard & Poor's 500 Index) over some appropriate short-term planning horizon. The manager's "market alpha" is then determined by subtracting the long-term expected rate of return on the market portfolio from the short-term return estimate. The market alpha (either positive or negative) is equivalent to a short-term forecast of excess positive or negative market portfolio returns. To implement this internally, we at Gifford would have to establish

[1]Barr Rosenberg, "Institutional Investment with Multiple Managers," Working Paper Number 65, Research Program in Finance, University of California, Berkeley Section 2, pp. 14–21.

an appropriate planning horizon (not discussed in paper) and a long-term market rate of return for equities.

The market alphas (α_i) for the various fund managers will differ in quality. The next step is to scale the alpha estimates to reflect their information content to reflect the comparative skill of each forecaster. To do this, previous forecasts would be correlated against related ex post results. The information content of each manager's forecasts would be reflected by the correlation coefficient, ρ_i. The product of the correlation and coefficient and the market alpha, $\rho_i \alpha_i$, for a particular manager represents the excess return that can be expected on average as the result of his cyclical timing activities.

The various managers may, to some extent, draw upon similar sources of evidence or use similar techniques in developing their "market alpha" forecasts so that their forecasts of market outlook tend to be similar. The covariance of the forecasts can be measured by the cross-correlation coefficient, π_{ij}, for each pair of managers. When this correlation coefficient is high, there is considerable redundancy of information content in the market forecast of the two fund managers. This redundancy should be eliminated. The particular method of adjusting the information coefficients for forecast redundancy is somewhat complicated but is set forth in the paper.[2] Briefly, redundancy factors for each manager, called "dependence adjustment factors, (b_i)," are developed. These factors consider the manager's forecasting skill measured after eliminating redundancy.

The aggregate skills of all the managers can be determined by summing the products of $b_i \alpha_i$.

If, according to this measure, managers collectively exhibit forecasting skill in terms of their ability to predict future market portfolio returns, then fund sponsors should be willing to increase the normal target betas for their portfolio. In the absence of forecasting skill, the normal beta is determined by trading off expected portfolio return performance against the variance of that performance for alternative beta targets. Forecasting skill reduces the expected variance of ex post portfolio performance relative to the forecast, as well as increasing the expected average portfolio returns. Both permit more aggressive use of funds without additional risk.

Each manager may be seeking to achieve results in a somewhat different way. The individual normal betas of the managers may consequently differ from the overall portfolio target beta. The weighted average of the individual portfolios' normal betas should aggregate to the decided overall normal beta. The paper did not suggest how this was to be achieved, except by suggesting "setting the normal beta for each manager to be the typical value for the manager's universe."

The appropriate beta for each manager at any given moment in time can be computed as follows:

$$B_j = NB_j + NB_E \frac{(\ 1\ )}{W_j} \frac{(b_j \alpha_j)}{E}$$

---

[2] $b_j = \frac{1}{\rho_j} (\pi^{j1}\rho_1 + \pi\, \rho_2^{j2} + \ldots + \pi^{jJ} \rho i), j = 1, \ldots, J$

where:

B_j = appropriate portfolio beta for manager j at a specific point in time.

NB_j = normal portfolio beta for manager j over the long run.

NB_E = normal overall portfolio beta over the long run.

W_j = fraction of the portfolio managed by manager j.

b_j = the dependence adjustment factor for manager j.

α_j = short-term excess rate of return on the market portfolio anticipated by manager j.

E = the normal forecast for excess portfolio reward as represented by the differential between the forecasted long-term rate of return on the market portfolio and the equivalent Treasury bill return forecast.